W9-DIS-303

Real Essays

with Readings

Writing for Success in College, Work, and Everyday Life

FOURTH EDITION

Real Essays

with Readings

Writing for Success in College, Work, and Everyday Life

Susan Anker

Bedford / St. Martin's

Boston ◆ New York

For Bedford/St. Martin's

Executive Editor for Developmental Studies: Alexis Walker
Senior Developmental Editor: Martha Bustin
Senior Production Editor: Deborah Baker
Senior Production Supervisor: Dennis J. Conroy
Senior Marketing Manager: Christina Shea
Editorial Assistant: Mallory Moore
Copyeditor: Lisa Wehrle
Indexer: Mary White
Photo Researcher: Naomi Kornhauser
Permissions Manager: Kalina K. Ingham
Senior Art Director: Anna Palchik
Text Design: Claire Seng-Niemoeller
Cover Design: Marine Miller
Cover Photo: College students with school bags running up steps of university © Exactostock/
   SuperStock.
Composition: Graphic World Inc.
Printing and Binding: RR Donnelley and Sons

President: Joan E. Feinberg
Editorial Director: Denise B. Wydra
Editor in Chief: Karen S. Henry
Director of Marketing: Karen R. Soeltz
Director of Production: Susan W. Brown
Associate Director, Editorial Production: Elise S. Kaiser
Managing Editor: Elizabeth M. Schaaf

Library of Congress Control Number: 2011927769

For information, write: Bedford/St. Martin's, 75 Arlington Street, Boston, MA 02116
   (617-399-4000)

ISBN: 978-0-312-64808-4 (Student edition)
ISBN: 978-0-312-56663-0 (Instructor's Annotated edition)

Acknowledgments

Dave Barry. "The Ugly Truth about Beauty." Originally titled "Beauty and the Beast." From
   the *Miami Herald*, February 1, 1998. Copyright © 1998 Dave Barry. Reprinted by
   permission of Dave Barry.
Amy L. Beck. "Struggling for Perfection." First published in Harvard *Crimson*, March 19, 1998.
   Used by permission.
*Acknowledgments and copyrights are continued at the back of the book on pages 843–45, which
constitute an extension of the copyright page. It is a violation of the law to reproduce these selections by
any means whatsoever without the written permission of the copyright holder.*

Contents

Thematic Contents

Preface for Instructors

The first aim of *Real Essays with Readings* has always been to communicate to students that good writing skills are both *essential* and *achievable*. When they have this perspective, students can start fresh, reframing the writing course for themselves not as an irrelevant hoop to jump or stumble through, but as a central gateway—a potentially life-changing opportunity, worthy of their best efforts. In large and small ways, this book is designed to help students prepare for their futures. It connects the writing class to their other courses, to their real lives, and to the expectations of the larger world.

Real Essays underscores this powerful message in its initial part, "College Thinking, Reading, and Writing"; in its practical advice on writing different kinds of essays; and in its step-by-step grammar sections, which build confidence and proficiency by focusing first on the most serious errors. An abundance of readable student and professional selections further encourages students to see the big picture, giving them a context for what they are learning. Profiles of Success and new "I Write" testimonials provide inspirational portraits of students and former students, now in the workplace, who reflect on the varied, important ways they use writing in their work.

Real Essays shares this practical, real-world approach with its companion texts—*Real Writing: Paragraphs and Essays for College, Work, and Everyday Life* and *Real Skills: Sentences and Paragraphs for College, Work, and Everyday Life*. All three books put writing in a real-world context and link writing skills to students' own goals in and beyond college. Maintaining this strong connection to the real world, the fourth edition of *Real Essays* introduces strategies for campus and community involvement—for example, in the first chapter, "Succeeding in College: What You Need to Know," and in the new Writing about Connections assignments in Part 2. Because critical reading and thinking skills are so vital to success in the real world, this edition also offers expanded coverage of them. These skills are introduced early and reinforced often through exercises, discussion questions, and prompts.

Features

Successful and popular features of earlier editions of *Real Essays* have been carried over to this edition, with revisions based on suggestions from many insightful instructors and students.

Motivates Students with a Real-World Emphasis

- **Profiles of Success** showcase former students, now employed in a range of professions, who provide vivid examples of why writing skills are important on the job to help students connect writing with their own long-term goals. Each person featured reflects on the practical value of critical thinking and composing abilities developed in college and provides a sample of his or her workplace writing.

PROFILE OF SUCCESS

Argument in the Real World

Background   I had what is, unfortunately, a typical kind of life for many poor, urban youth who are caught up in gangs, drugs, and violence. My brother was murdered in a crossfire, and I lived with my mother with no father around. I was an athlete and got away with not doing much in school. I had my first kid at age fifteen and in that same year almost shot a rival who had disrespected me. I didn't, mainly because I remembered my coach, who'd warned me not to leave my son fatherless. This coach, Ed Powell, had a saying I still repeat often: "He who fails to plan, plans to fail." I was lucky to have Powell and a few other adults reach out to me, help me turn around, and get me on the track of education and a better life.

A few years ago, I got together a group of my friends, all college-educated African American men with families and steady jobs. We talked about how many young black men have no positive role models and decided that we wanted to help them the way we had been helped. From that meeting came Diamond Educators, a nonprofit organization that starts working with kids in third grade by teaching them how to behave, speak, and "play the game" in a way that will lead to success in life. Teens who are in the program

Shawn Brown
Founder, Diamond
Educators

- **Numerous models of student and professional writing** address topics such as parenting, adults' and veterans' perspectives on returning to college, stereotypes, peer pressure, and the importance of getting involved on campus and in the community. After each reading, engaging comprehension questions and assignment prompts provide opportunities for students to develop their critical thinking, reading, and writing skills.

- **The "Advice from Those Who Have Been There" section in the first chapter** features advice from students who share their thoughts on effective use of campus resources, time management skills, and the importance of setting short- and long-term goals.

ADVICE

**From Those
Who Have
Been There**

Michael Dalkas, Georgia
Perimeter College

Janice Diamond, Holmes
Community College

Danita Edwards, Holmes
Community College

You might be wondering: Why do I have to take this course, anyway? The answer is that most, if not all, of your college courses will require some writing, and the better you write, the better you will do. Being able to write well will also help you get a good job and express yourself in your everyday life.

The advice on pages 4–9 comes directly from our experience. We promise it will help you.

outside sources, such as articles and books. For example, a high school teacher might assign a topic such as "Write about a time you felt peer pressure to do something you didn't want to do," but an assignment in a college course in human development might ask you to go beyond your own experience: "How does the pressure to fit in affect adolescent behavior?" When we refer to outside sources in our papers, we have to *document* our sources. (See Chapter 4.)

Writing

College writing involves new kinds of writing and new ways of writing. Here

"We have to know how to
narrow broad topics."

Presents Essay Writing in Manageable Increments

- **Four Basics boxes** guide students to focus first on the most important elements of writing. For example, "Four Basics of Good Writing" stresses audience, purpose, thesis, and support, and each chapter in Part 2, "Writing Different Kinds of Essays," begins with the four key points to remember about the particular type of writing being discussed (narration, illustration, description, and so on).

Four Basics of Good Writing

1. It considers the needs and knowledge of the audience.
2. It fulfills the writer's purpose.
3. It includes a clear, definite point.
4. It provides support that explains or proves the main point.

- **Step-by-step Writing Guides** make the writing process manageable and tailor it to the particular type of writing being done. These detailed, end-of-chapter checklists summarize and focus on key elements of each type of writing, including research papers.

- **A strong, process-oriented organization** guides students first through the interconnected steps of the writing process, with chapters 4 through 9 on understanding audience and purpose, finding and exploring a topic, writing a thesis statement, supporting a point, drafting, and revising. From this foundation, nine carefully sequenced chapters build students' confidence with a progression of chapters on common college assignments, from writing narrative and description essays (chapters 10 and 11) to analytical cause and effect essays and persuasive arguments (chapters 17 and 18).

- **Chapter 19, "Writing under Pressure,"** helps students tackle essay exams and timed writing. The chapter provides practical, concise coverage on how to review actively, read and analyze test questions, and write a thesis statement when taking an essay exam.

- **Two easy-to-follow chapters on writing research essays** break down the process into manageable steps. Chapter 20 shows students how to find and evaluate sources, in preparation for writing a research essay. Chapter 21 continues with a clear look at writing the essay, avoiding plagiarism, integrating quotations, and citing sources.

Covers Grammar and Editing Clearly and Concisely

- **Part 4, "The Four Most Serious Errors," begins with a review of the basic sentence** and includes grammar terminology that students need to know.

- **The remaining Part 4 chapters** focus on four key grammatical problems—fragments, run-ons, errors in subject-verb agreement, and errors in using verbs—that, if avoided, can make a big difference in the success of a piece of writing. Detailed coverage of each of these topics includes clear explanations, editing tips, and extra practices. Later chapters build on this foundation, presenting the rules of grammar, punctuation, and mechanics, all supported by connected-discourse exercises.

- **Cross-references to *Exercise Central*** provide additional opportunities for skill practice. Marginal references throughout the editing section direct students to *Exercise Central*, a free online database offered by Bedford/St. Martin's that includes 9,000 grammar and writing exercises, and offers immediate feedback and a gradebook for instructors.

- **Summary flowcharts and Editing Review Tests** reinforce grammar instruction. Graphic summary flowcharts at the end of each Part 4 chapter and ten cumulative Editing Review Tests cement grammar coverage.

New to This Edition

This edition includes carefully developed new features to help students become better readers and writers in college and beyond.

More Help with Critical Thinking and Critical Reading

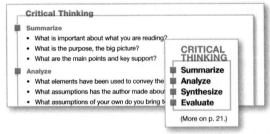

- **New to this edition, Chapter 2, "Thinking Critically: Developing Your Power of Mind,"** teaches students what critical thinking is, why it is important, and how to apply it to college, work, and beyond. The chapter covers the basics of critical thinking and introduces key critical-thinking skills—summary, analysis, synthesis, and evaluation. These skills are actively applied throughout the book, with particular opportunities for critical thinking indicated with a marginal icon.

- **Also new to this edition, Chapter 3, "Reading Critically: Developing Your Understanding,"** thoroughly and clearly presents critical reading as an essential college skill, and one that can be improved with practice. To help critical reading become second nature, the four-step process presented in the new chapter—Preview, Read, Pause to think, and Review—appears consistently throughout *Real Essays* as an integral part of writing instruction.

- **Twenty-nine new readings, including nineteen new essays by students,** comprise nearly half of the book's sixty-five readings and provide an abundance of fresh, thought-provoking material for discussion and writing. Among the memorable new selections are Daniel Flanagan's "The Choice to Do It Over Again," Anna Puiia's "What Is Hip?," Rui Dai's "A Whiff of Memory," Michael Gates Gill's "How I Learned to Be a Barista," and Howard White's "The Power of Hello." Readings are accompanied by apparatus for critical thinking and critical reading, as well as for the development of college-level writing skills.

- **New opportunities for reading and analyzing visuals.** Carefully selected images drawn from current events and the world of contemporary photography support the development of visual literacy and form the basis of engaging journal prompts and "Responding to a Visual" assignments. Photo-based assignments now also appear in Part 1, on the writing process. To practice thesis formation, for example, students are asked to interpret ambiguous images and to make a convincing case for their interpretation, using observed details and other supporting points.

New "Community Connections" Theme

- **"Writing about Connections"** assignments in the Part 2 essay chapters are built around profiles of students who have become involved in their college or local communities and who explain how these connections have kept them in school and boosted their academic performance, along with their self-esteem. Called "Community Connections," these boxed profiles (appearing within the assignments) suggest to students that many interesting activities are going on in their communities that they may not have thought to explore. These real-life accounts convey a sense of the range of things there are to do—and write about—in the community and encourage the kind of networking and résumé building that can be so important to students later, when job hunting.

- **New student readings on the benefits of community involvement** enliven Part 1—for example, Islam Elshami's "Why Join the Club?" and Deshon Briggs's "Be the Change in Your Life."

More Student Presence Throughout, and More Visuals

- **New "I Write" series** includes eight full-page portraits of students who were asked, "*What do you write in your college, work, or everyday life?*" Their answers offer an interesting cross-section of the many practical applications of the skills taught in *Real Essays* and encourage students to ask themselves: "*What do I write? What will I write?*"

- **Many new examples of student writing** function as helpful models and as jumping-off points for discussion. In addition to new pieces of student work in Parts 1 and 2, nine new selections by students have been added to Part 8, Readings for Writers, each accompanied by brief biographical headnotes about the student author.

- **A new series of photographs illustrating the rhetorical modes** appears early in the chapters in Part 2. These striking images—in boxes entitled "Seeing Narration," "Seeing Description," and so on—invite students to connect the different types of writing they are doing with ways of approaching a topic (and ways of thinking) used in the real world by photographers and photojournalists.

Student and Instructor Resources: You Get More Choices with *Real Essays*, Fourth Edition

Real Essays does not stop with a book. Online and in print, you will find both free and affordable premium resources to help students get even more out of the book and your course. You will also find convenient instructor resources, such as downloadable instructor's manuals, additional exercises, and PowerPoint slides. For information on ordering and to get ISBNs for packaging these resources with your students' books, see page xxvii. You can also contact your Bedford/St. Martin's sales representative, e-mail sales support (**sales_support@bfwpub.com**), or visit **bedfordstmartins.com/realessays/catalog**.

In the descriptions of resources below, the book icon 📖 indicates a print ancillary. The computer icon 🖥 and CD icon 💿 indicate media options.

Student Resources

- 🖥 *Student site for Real Essays* at **bedfordstmartins.com/ realessays** provides students with supplemental exercises from *Exercise Central*, helpful guidelines on avoiding plagiarism and doing research, annotated model essays, advice on writing for the workplace, graphic organizers and peer-review forms for all modes of writing covered in the book, and links to other useful resources from Bedford/St. Martin's.

■ ⬛ *Exercise Central 3.0* **at bedfordstmartins.com/ exercisecentral** is the largest database of editing exercises on the Internet—and it is completely **free**. This comprehensive resource contains over 9,000 exercises that offer immediate feedback; the program also recommends personalized study plans and provides tutorials for common problems. Best of all, students' work reports to a gradebook, allowing instructors to track students' progress quickly and easily.

Get More Resources with an Access Package

■ ⬛ *WritingClass for Real Essays with Readings* provides students with a dynamic, interactive online course space preloaded with book-specific exercises, diagnostics, video tutorials, writing and commenting tools, and more. *WritingClass* helps students stay focused and lets instructors see how they are progressing. To learn more about *WritingClass*, visit **yourwritingclass.com**. ISBN: 978-1-4576-1548-1

■ ⬛ *Re:Writing Plus,* **now with** *VideoCentral,* gathers all our premium digital content for the writing class into one online collection. This impressive resource includes innovative and interactive help with writing a paragraph; tutorials and practices that show how writing works in students' real-world experience; *VideoCentral,* with over 140 brief videos for the writing classroom; the first-ever peer-review game, *Peer Factor*; *i-cite: visualizing sources*; plus hundreds of models of writing and hundreds of readings. *Re:Writing Plus* can be purchased separately or packaged with *Real Essays with Readings* at a significant discount. ISBN: 978-0-312-48849-9

■ 📖 **Quick Reference Card.** Students can prop this handy three-panel card up next to their computers for easy reference while they are writing and researching. It gives students, in concise form, the Four Basics of Good Writing; the structure of paragraphs and essays; a checklist for effective writing; the Four Most Serious Errors; tips for writing on the computer; and advice on evaluating sources, avoiding plagiarism, and documenting sources using MLA style. **Free** when packaged with the print text.

■ 💿 *Exercise Central to Go: Writing and Grammar Practices for Basic Writers* **CD-ROM** provides hundreds of practice items to help students build their writing and editing skills. No Internet connection is necessary. **Free** when packaged with the print text. ISBN: 978-0-312-44652-9

- 📖 *The Bedford/St. Martin's ESL Workbook* includes a broad range of exercises covering grammatical issues for multilingual students of varying language skills and backgrounds. Answers are at the back. **Free** when packaged with the print text. ISBN: 978-0-312-54034-0

- 💿 The *Make-a-Paragraph Kit* is a fun, interactive CD-ROM that teaches students about paragraph development. It also contains exercises to help students build their own paragraphs, audiovisual tutorials on four of the most common errors for basic writers, and the content from the *Exercise Central to Go* CD. **Free** when packaged with the print text. ISBN: 978-0-312-45332-9

- 📖 The *Bedford/St. Martin's Planner* includes everything that students need to plan and use their time effectively, with advice on preparing schedules and to-do lists plus blank schedules and calendars (monthly and weekly). The planner fits easily into a backpack or purse, so students can take it anywhere. **Free** when packaged with the print text. ISBN: 978-0-312-5744-5

E-Book Options

- 🖥 *Real Essays with Readings* e-Book. Available for the first time as a value-priced e-Book, available either as a *CourseSmart* e-Book or in formats for use with computers, tablets, and e-readers—visit **bedfordstmartins/ebooks** for more information.

Instructor Resources

- 📖 The Instructor's Annotated Edition of *Real Essays with Readings* gives practical page-by-page advice on teaching with *Real Essays with Readings,* Fourth Edition, and answers to exercises. It includes discussion prompts, strategies for teaching ESL students, ideas for additional classroom activities, suggestions for using other print and media resources, and cross-references useful to teachers at all levels of experience. ISBN: 978-0-312-56663-0.

- 📖 🖥 *Practical Suggestions for Teaching Real Essays with Readings,* Fourth Edition, provides helpful information and advice on teaching developmental writing. It includes sample syllabi, reading levels scores, tips on building students' critical-thinking skills, resources for teaching non-native speakers and speakers of non-standard dialects, ideas for assessing students' writing and progress, and up-to-date suggestions for using technology in the writing classroom and lab. A new chapter, "Facilitating Cooperative Learning," suggests specific activities for using the cooperative, group-oriented approach to foster students' positive interdependence and personal accountability as well as improved writing skills. Available in print: ISBN: 978-0-312-56664-7. Or, to download, see **bedfordstmartins .com/realessays/catalog.**

- *Additional Resources for Teaching Real Essays with Readings,* **Fourth Edition**. This collection of resources supplements the instructional materials in the text with a variety of extra exercises and tests, transparency masters, essay planning forms, and other reproducibles for classroom use. ISBN: 978-0-312-56657-9.

- *Bedford Coursepacks* allow you to plug *Real Essays with Readings* content into your own course-management system. For details, visit **bedfordstmartins.com/coursepacks.**

- *Testing Tool Kit: Writing and Grammar Test Bank* **CD-ROM** allows instructors to create secure, customized tests and quizzes from a pool of nearly 2,000 questions covering 47 topics. It also includes 10 prebuilt diagnostic tests. ISBN: 978-0-312-43032-0

- *Teaching Developmental Writing: Background Readings,* **Third Edition,** is edited by Susan Naomi Bernstein, former co-chair of the Conference on Basic Writing. This professional resource offers essays on topics of interest to basic writing instructors, along with editorial apparatus pointing out practical applications for the classroom. ISBN: 978-0-312-43283-6

Ordering Information

To order any ancillary or ancillary package for *Real Essays with Readings,* Fourth Edition, contact your local Bedford/St. Martin's sales representative: E-mail **sales_support@bfwpub.com** or visit our Web site at **bedfordstmartins.com**.

To order your students' copies of *Real Essays with Readings* with the following package options, use these ISBNs:

Quick Reference Card	978-1-4576-1404-0
From Practice to Mastery	978-1-4576-1402-6
Bedford/St. Martin's ESL Workbook	978-1-4576-1400-2
Bedford/St. Martin's Planner	978-1-4576-1399-9
Exercise Central to Go CD-ROM	978-1-4576-1401-9
Make-a-Paragraph Kit CD-ROM	978-1-4576-1403-3
Bedford/St. Martin's Writing Journal	978-1-4576-1407-1
WritingClass access card ($5)	978-1-4576-1406-4
Re:Writing Plus access card ($5)	978-1-4576-1405-7

Acknowledgments

This edition of *Real Essays with Readings* is a collaboration among many fine teachers and students across the country, as well as the staff at Bedford/St. Martin's. I am grateful to all of these people.

Reviewers

I would like to thank the following people for helping to shape ideas for this edition. Their dedication, creativity, and insight have improved *Real Essays with Readings*, Fourth Edition, immeasurably.

Liz Ann Báez Aguilar, San Antonio College

Marty Brooks, John Tyler Community College

Karen A. Cahill, Southeastern Community College

Anthony D. Cavaluzzi, SUNY/Adirondack

Sandra Chumchal, Blinn College

Terri Decker-Kilmartin, Middlesex Community College

Joseph A. Domino, Palm Beach State College

Christopher Ervin, Western Kentucky University

Kelley Evans, Brunswick Community College

Tarasa Gardner, Moberly Area Community College

P. Gregory Gibson, Henderson State University

Deborah E. Goddin, Thomas Nelson Community College

Jeffrey A. Gonzalez, College of the Redwoods

Valerie A. Gray, Harrisburg Area Community College

Susan Guzman-Trevino, Temple College

Kelli Hallsten, Lake Superior College

Michael Held, Richard J. Daley College

Lindsay Penelope Illich, Temple College

Deirdre Kane, Middlesex Community College

Mary Jo M. Keiter, Harrisburg Area Community College

Carole D. LaBonte, Quinsigamond Community College

Liz Langemak, Bethany College

Linda G. Matthews, South Suburban College

Albert Mento, Middlesex Community College

Christine Sandoval, San Jacinto Community College

Debra L. Sharp, Doane College

John Stevens, Temple College

Debra Thomas, Harrisburg Area Community College

Monalinda Verlengia, College of the Desert

Mary Waguespack, Loyola University

Jim Wilkins-Luton, Clark College

Karen P. Woodring, Harrisburg Area Community College

I also want to acknowledge the invaluable help provided by reviewers of earlier editions. The ideas and suggestions generously provided by these reviewers have improved *Real Essays with Readings* and continue to do so:

Kathryn Barker, Ivy Tech Community College; E. Mairing Barney, Roosevelt University, Truman College; Monica Benton, Georgia Perimeter College–Decatur; Leslie Brown, Georgia Perimeter College; Gloria Burke, Terra State Community College and Lourdes College; James Andrew Clovis, West Virginia University at Parkersburg; Kathleen Collins, SUNY Ulster Community College; Steven Dalager, Lake Superior College; Seth Dugan, Mercy College; Mike Eskew, Chaffey Community College; Roy Freedman, The Citadel and South Wesleyan University; Nicole Grasse, Richard J. Daley College; Kirsi Halonen, Lake Superior College; Rochelle Harden, Parkland College; Judy Harris, Tomball College; Julie Jackson, Gavilan College; Francine Jamin, Montgomery College, Takoma Park/Silver Spring; Billy P. Jones, Miami Dade College, Kendall; Therese Jones, Lewis University; Mandy Kallus, Kingwood College; J. Damon Kapke, Lake Superior College; Craig Kleinman, City College of San Francisco; Mimi Leonard, Wytheville Community College; Ray Lightburn, Broward Community College; James McKeown, McLennan Community College; Dawn Mizwinski-Wesley, Lackawanna College; Mona Sue Moistner, Ivy Tech Community College; Lisa Oldaker Palmer, Quinsigamond Community College; Barbara Pescar, Cuyamaca College; Dr. Nicolette Rose, Georgia Perimeter College; Jennifer Rossino, Passaic County Community College; Norman Stephens, Cerro Coso Community College; Stephanie Stiles, Dominican College; Ann Stotts, Gateway Tech College; Amy Jo Swing, Lake Superior College; Jennifer Thompson, Richard J. Daley College and Moraine Valley Community College; Carole Thurston, Northern Virginia Community College; and Rhonda Wallace, Cuyahoga Community College.

One other person who continues to inspire and influence me is Wick Sloane at Bunker Hill Community College. If you want to know why, read some of his "Devil's Workshop" columns at insidehighereducation.com.

Students

Many current and former students have helped shape each edition of *Real Essays*. I am very grateful to the following students for their assistance: Michael Dalkas, Georgia Perimeter College; Janice Diamond and Danita Edwards, Holmes Community College; Irma Karpaviciute, Quinsigamond Community College; Daniel Madrid, East Los Angeles College; Rose Martinez, Passaic County Community College; and Lia Uenohara, Bunker Hill Community College.

The nine former students who are included as "Profiles of Success" are terrific role models for current students, and their examples of workplace writing show students real-world applications of writing principles. The profiles of success are Monique Rizer, Juan Gonzalez, Alex Espinoza, Patty Maloney, Rebeka Mazzone, Gary Knoblock, Garth Vaz, Jolanda Jones, and Shawn Brown.

Many student writers generously agreed to share their work: Joseph Ameur, John Around Him, Florence Bagley, Deshon Briggs, Jordan Brown, Rui Dai, Islam Elshami, Roberta Fair, Daniel Flanagan, Shannon Grady, Michael Jernigan, Dylan Marcos, Luz Medina, Heaven Morrison, Donnie Ney, Jennifer Orlando, Tam Nguyen, Anna Puiia, Liliana Ramirez, Beth Trimmer, Katie Whitehead, Kevin Willey, Meagan Willey, and Carson Williams. Thanks to these students and the many others who submitted their work.

Contributors

"It takes a village," as the saying goes, to make a book, and happily for me, my village was filled with talented, hardworking, reliable people who have made valuable contributions. In addition to the reviewers and students already mentioned, the following people made tangible contributions to this edition of *Real Essays with Readings*. Jessica Carroll contributed exercises that are lively, relevant, test worthy, and set in connected discourse. Candace Rardon created head notes for the authors of the readings, always with an interesting personal observation from the author. Jeffrey Ousborne contributed insightful and probing apparatus for readings. Lisa Wehrle ably copyedited this edition. The exciting new look of the book's interior was devised by designer Claire Seng-Niemoeller. Art researcher Naomi Kornhauser was a tremendous resource when it came to locating artists and photographers, getting permission to reprint images, and suggesting images for key spots. Patricia Lee photographed the captivating portraits of students for the new part openers. Kalina Ingham and Kristy Cassidy undertook and successfully completed the large and crucial task of securing text permissions. Many thanks to you all.

Bedford/St. Martin's

As always, I am deeply indebted to the many at Bedford/St. Martin's who collaborate with me. To continue the "village" analogy, I have benefited immensely from being a part of this community for so long. With each successive project, I am more grateful and appreciative, and with each I vow to rein in the kudos. So to all of you, please know that the words don't match the appreciation.

Alexis Walker, executive editor for Developmental Studies, has a hand in all of my books, particularly this one, since she was my editor for the previous edition. Mallory Moore, editorial assistant, coordinated many complex elements of the book's formation and helped in myriad ways. Throughout the production of this book, Deborah Baker, senior production editor, has been her exceptionally helpful self—always professional, detailed, creative, and expert as a communicator and coordinator. Many thanks to Deb for all she does. Our dynamic cover was designed by Marine Bouvier Miller. Overseeing and contributing to all aspects of design was Anna Palchik, senior art director. And the informative, memorable brochure was created by Pelle Cass.

Christina Shea, senior marketing manager, is a great advocate for all of my books, as was her predecessor, Casey Carroll. Christina forges new ground. Jim Camp, senior specialist, Developmental Studies and College Success, travels widely and absorbs much, all of which we put to good use. Dennis Adams and his team of humanities specialists continue to impress me with their wit and wisdom. And the sales managers and representatives are smart, on-task, and a joy to work with.

The New Media group continues to develop some of the most useful teaching tools available. Many thanks especially to Harriet Wald, executive editor, and Marissa Zanetti, New Media editor.

Every revision of every book is shaped by executives and long-time friends in the Boston office: Joan Feinberg, president; Denise Wydra, editorial director; Karen Henry, editor in chief; Karen Soeltz, director of marketing; and Jane Helms, associate director of marketing. I value them all more than they could know.

Finally, the biggest shaper and contributor of this edition of *Real Essays with Readings* is Martha Bustin, another long-time, valued friend. I am honestly amazed by her constant thoughtfulness and intelligence about book ideas and all else. Martha's Zen-like patience smoothes all roughness, and our work is the best of yin and yang. Thank you for everything, Martha.

As always, I thank my steady life companion and husband, Jim Anker, my main villager.

—Susan Anker

Real Support for Instructors and Students

GOALS AND LEARNING OUTCOMES	SUPPORT IN *REAL ESSAYS*	SUPPORT IN STUDENT ANCILLARIES	SUPPORT IN INSTRUCTOR ANCILLARIES
Students will connect the writing class with their goals in other courses and the larger world.	■ Chapter 1: Strategies for college success ■ Part 2: "Profiles of Success" ■ Part 4: "Why Is It Important?" feature ■ Part 8: Student writing with biographical notes and photos	■ **Quick Reference Card:** Portable guide to the basics of writing, editing, using sources, and more—for easy use in classes and workplace ■ *The Bedford/St. Martin's Planner* ■ *WritingClass:* Online course space with helpful materials and activities	■ **Instructor's Annotated Edition:** Marginal notes suggest activities and discussion topics to help students see the context and relevance of what they are learning ■ *Practical Suggestions:* Chapters 4 and 5
Students will write well-developed, organized paragraphs and essays.	■ Part 1: Thorough writing process coverage ■ Part 2: Coverage of rhetorical strategies, with detailed writing checklists; a focus on the "Four Basics" of each type of writing; and a special emphasis on main point, support, and organization ■ Parts 2 and 8: Models of different kinds of essays by students and professional writers	■ **Quick Reference Card:** Portable advice on understanding the structure of paragraphs and essays and a checklist for writing effective paragraphs and essays ■ *Student Site for Real Essays:* Additional model readings and writing advice (**bedfordstmartins.com/ realessays**) ■ *Make-a-Paragraph Kit CD-ROM:* Paragraph development advice and exercises ■ *Exercise Central to Go CD-ROM:* Writing exercises (with more available at **bedfordstmartins.com/ exercisecentral**) ■ *Re:Writing:* Additional writing support at **bedfordstmartins .com/rewriting** ■ *WritingClass:* Online course space with writing materials and activities	■ **Instructor's Annotated Edition:** Marginal notes suggest activities and questions for use in teaching development, organization, and support ■ *Practical Suggestions:* Chapters on helping students develop critical thinking skills (Chapter 6), implementing a group approach to improve students' paragraphs and essays (Chapter 7), and using writing portfolios (Chapter 12) ■ *Additional Resources:* Reproducible planning forms for writing ■ *Testing Tool Kit CD-ROM:* Tests on topic sentences, thesis statements, support, organization, and more ■ *Re:Writing:* Additional instructional support at **bedfordstmartins .com/rewriting**
Students will develop critical thinking skills.	■ Chapter 2: Step-by-step critical reading advice ■ Parts 1, 2, and 8: Critical thinking components—summary, analysis, synthesis, and evaluation—are reinforced with questions	■ *Student Site for Real Essays:* Reading quizzes and additional critical thinking advice (**bedfordstmartins .com/realessays**) ■ *WritingClass:* Online course space with critical thinking activities	■ **Instructor's Annotated Edition:** Marginal tips for critical thinking prompts and activities ■ *Practical Suggestions:* Chapter 6

GOALS AND LEARNING OUTCOMES	SUPPORT IN *REAL ESSAYS*	SUPPORT IN STUDENT ANCILLARIES	SUPPORT IN INSTRUCTOR ANCILLARIES
Students will read closely and critically.	■ Chapter 3: Coverage of the critical reading process ■ Part 1, 2, and 8: Integrated coverage of the critical reading process, with reinforcement throughout the book on the need, when reading critically, to preview, read, pause, and review	■ *Student Site for Real Essays:* Reading comprehension and critical reading quizzes (**bedfordstmartins.com/ realessays**) ■ *WritingClass:* Online course space with critical reading activities	■ **Instructor's Annotated Edition:** Marginal tips for improving students' critical reading abilities and using the critical reading prompts throughout the book ■ *Practical Suggestions:* Get help with integrating critical thinking and reading into the course
Students will build grammar and editing skills.	■ Parts 4 through 7: Thorough grammar coverage and many opportunities for practice, with a focus on the "Four Most Serious Errors" (Part 4) ■ Editing Review Tests: Ten tests following Part 7	■ **Quick Reference Card:** Portable advice on avoiding the "Four Most Serious Errors" and editing for grammatical correctness ■ *Student Site for Real Essays:* More grammar exercises, with instant scoring and feedback (**bedfordstmartins.com/ realessays**) ■ *Make-a-Paragraph Kit* CD-ROM: Tutorials on finding and fixing the "Four Most Serious Errors" ■ *Exercise Central to Go* CD-ROM: Editing exercises (with more available at **bedfordstmartins.com/ exercisecentral**) ■ *WritingClass:* Online course space with grammar and editing activities	■ **Instructor's Annotated Edition:** Marginal suggestions to help students learn or review grammar ■ *Additional Resources:* Reproducible exercises and transparencies for modeling correction of the "Four Most Serious Errors" ■ *Student Site for Real Essays:* Downloadable answer key for all exercises in the text ■ *Testing Tool Kit* CD-ROM: Test items on every grammar topic ■ *Re:Writing:* Additional instructional support at **bedfordstmartins.com/ rewriting**
Students will build research skills.	■ Chapter 20: Finding and evaluating sources for research papers ■ Chapter 21: Guidance on writing research papers; includes a sample student paper	■ **Quick Reference Card:** Portable research and documentation advice on evaluating sources, using MLA style, and avoiding plagiarism ■ *Re:Writing:* Research and documentation advice at **bedfordstmartins.com/ rewriting** ■ *WritingClass:* Online course space with research activities	■ **Instructor's Annotated Edition:** Marginal notes on helping students explore and become comfortable with the research process ■ *Additional Resources:* Reproducible research exercises and other handouts

A note to students from Susan Anker

For the last twenty years or so, I have traveled the country talking to students about their goals and, more important, about the challenges they face on the way to achieving those goals. Students always tell me that they want good jobs and that they need a college degree to get those jobs. I designed *Real Essays* with those goals in mind — strengthening the writing, reading, and editing skills needed for success in college, at work, and in everyday life. Here is something else: Good jobs require not only a college degree but also a college education: knowing not only how to read and write but how to think critically and learn effectively. So that is what I stress here, too. It is worth facing the challenges. All my best wishes to you, in this course and in all your future endeavors.

"I write multiple drafts of my college essays."

—*Mary Carmen G., student*

Part 1

College Thinking, Reading, and Writing

YOU KNOW THIS

You already use the skills necessary for college success.

- You have responsibilities that you must manage.
- You have an interest in going to college.
- You schedule competing demands.

write What do you know about being a successful student? What do you want to know about how to succeed in college?

Succeeding in College

What You Need to Know

If you are reading this chapter, you have probably just started a college writing course, and you might not know what to expect. What kind of writing will you have to do? What do you need to know to pass this course? What will the teacher expect?

In the first section of this chapter, students who have completed their first year of college supply answers to these and other common questions. These students were in your exact spot, so they are in a good position to tell you what you need to know.

In the second section of this chapter, you will learn four strategies that will be critical to your success in all your college courses—how to identify your goals, how to manage your time, how to use the resources available to you, and how to find and use your learning style. Paying attention to the students' advice and the four success strategies is definitely worth your time.

IDEA JOURNAL
Write about some good advice (or some bad advice) you have gotten in the past.

TEACHING TIP
This chapter gives students a preview of what they can expect in your course, in later writing courses, and in other college courses. Much of it comes from interviews with students who have taken at least one developmental writing course, freshman composition, and other college courses.

. . . .

PRACTICE **Describing Your Educational Experiences**

Write about your school experiences so far, such as how you would describe yourself as a student, what school activities you have been interested in, whether you changed schools, and so on. Include points that may help your instructor understand what you have done so far and what you hope to learn in this course.

. . . .

ADVICE
From Those Who Have Been There

Michael Dalkas, Georgia Perimeter College

Janice Diamond, Holmes Community College

Danita Edwards, Holmes Community College

You might be wondering: Why do I have to take this course, anyway? The answer is that most, if not all, of your college courses will require some writing, and the better you write, the better you will do. Being able to write well will also help you get a good job and express yourself in your everyday life.

The advice on pages 4–9 comes directly from our experience. We promise it will help you.

Writing

College writing involves new kinds of writing and new ways of writing. Here are some of the things we had to get used to.

TEACHING TIP Assure students that the five-paragraph essay is a useful building block to writing longer pieces, and give them a preview of the length of the average paper they will write in your course.

"Essays are not always just five paragraphs."

Many of us learned to write essays with five paragraphs (introduction, three body paragraphs, and conclusion). That is a great way to learn how to write a basic essay, but in college courses, you will hardly ever be assigned a "five-paragraph essay." Your teachers might give you a target length, but the final length will depend on what you need to develop your ideas.

"We do not do as much personal writing."

TEACHING TIP Walk students through narrowing the topic "religion and culture."

Some writing assignments let us write mainly about personal experiences, but others ask us to use material from outside sources, such as articles and books. For example, a high school teacher might assign a topic such as "Write about a time you felt peer pressure to do something you didn't want to do," but an assignment in a college course in human development might ask you to go beyond your own experience: "How does the pressure to fit in affect adolescent behavior?" When we refer to outside sources in our papers, we have to *document* our sources. (See Chapter 4.)

"We have to know how to narrow broad topics."

We might get a broad assignment like "Write a short essay on religion and culture." We would have to use some of the techniques we learned in our writing courses to come up with something manageable — for example, an Eagle Scout's request to restore the previously removed words "to God" to his badge so that it read "For Service to God and Country." (For help narrowing a topic, see pp. 65–69.)

"We have less time to write longer pieces and less step-by-step instruction in class."

Your instructors may not spend much in-class time helping you write the papers they assign. Your chance to learn how to write is now, in your writing class, so pay close attention to your instructor's comments on your

Irma Karpaviciute,
Quinsigamond
Community College

Daniel Madrid, East
Los Angeles College

Rose Martinez, Passaic
County Community
College

Lia Uenohara, Bunker
Hill Community College

writing. Also, use writing tutors if they are available.

"We have to *revise* our work."

All instructors expect us to really "dig into" our ideas. It is almost impossible to do this kind of in-depth work in a first draft, so learn how to revise. One of the best ways we have found is to read our writing aloud and then ask,

- Can I recognize the main point?
- Do I give good details to back up my point?
- What makes my ideas interesting to me?
- Do I think my reader will be interested, too?

"We have to use formal English."

In college, our instructors — all of them — expect us to use formal, academic English — the same kind that is used in newspapers, television newscasts, and radio reporting.

Using formal English in college is not "selling out" or compromising who you are. It is an opportunity to practice a language that will help you succeed at school, at work, and in all areas of your life.

"In our writing courses, we did not spend much in-class time on grammar."

Our writing teachers would often just point out our errors and refer us to parts of a textbook, to a writing center, to a writing tutor, or to a computer lab for help. A lot of what you learn about grammar will be up to you.

"Instructors take off points for grammar errors."

In some of our writing classes, we had a chance to correct errors before we received a final grade. This is not the case, though, in other college classes. That means you have to get it right before you hand in your paper, so be sure to proofread carefully.

"Be careful about using the wrong word."

When your teacher points out a word in your paper that you have used incorrectly, make a note of it, and check for the same error in your next paper. Also, be sure to reread your paper after using your computer's spell checker.

Reading and Thinking

You also have to read and think well to succeed in college. Luckily, most college writing courses offer help here, too. Here is what you should be prepared for.

"We read a lot."

Nearly all the reading we do is assigned as homework. A lot of in-class time is spent discussing what we have read. When we have not done the reading, we cannot participate in

RESOURCES
For advice on how to get students to do the reading, see *Practical Suggestions for Teaching Real Essays,* Chapter 9.

class — a bad thing, since we are usually graded on our class participation.

"We read all kinds of things."

We read a lot — textbook chapters, stories, newspaper and magazine articles, secondary sources about a research topic — and we have to know how to discuss and write about all of it.

"We had to learn how to think, read, and write critically."

Your writing course will give you good practice doing this, so take advantage of it.

"We are expected to remember what we read."

Highlighting as you read will help, and so will taking notes on the following.

- What makes the piece interesting to you?
- What does it teach you, and how does it relate to your experiences?
- What bothers you, confuses you, or excites you?

Chapters 2, 3, and 4 will give you some tools to become critical thinkers, readers, and writers.

"We often talk about how one reading or concept relates to another."

If one reading reminds you of another, make a note, and bring it up in your next class. Your teacher will be impressed, and you will have had the satisfaction of connecting ideas.

Instructor Expectations

College instructors have definite expectations of us. Basically, being successful is *your* responsibility. That means the following things.

Do treat your course as seriously as you would treat a job.

Your boss does not *give* you money — you *earn* it, through hard work and professional behavior. Likewise, your instructor does not *give* you a grade. You *earn* the grade you get. Think of your course work as a job that can lead to bigger and better things — if you work hard and perform well.

Proofreading Tips

1. Read your paper line by line, looking carefully at every word.
2. Read your paper out loud, reading every word carefully.
3. Pause at every comma, and come to a full stop at the end of every sentence.
4. Ask someone else to read your paper, looking only for errors, not for overall meaning.
5. If your computer has a speech tool, use it to read your paper back to you.
6. Check for the Four Most Serious Errors (Chapters 22–26 in this book).

Do get to class on time, and stay until your instructor dismisses you.

Again, going to class is like going to a job — you have to come and go on the boss's schedule, not your own.

Do come to class prepared.

You have to do your homework or expect to fail. Even if you have never regularly done homework before and have managed to pass, you will not pass in college. You will also have points taken off for late homework.

Do make a friend.

Students often sit in the same places for each class. Exchange names, phone numbers, and e-mail addresses with at least one student who sits near you. That way, if you miss a class, you can find out from that person what you missed. You might also want to study with that person.

Do let your instructor know if you have to miss a class, and make sure to contact him or her about work missed.

Be a good communicator. Instructors can help you make up what you have missed — but only if you have made a connection and communicate in a clear, respectful way.

Do read the syllabus carefully and hang onto it for the entire semester.

Your instructor will expect you to know what the homework is and when assignments are due: Your syllabus will tell you. Always bring your syllabus to class, in case your instructor announces updates or reminders.

Do pay close attention to the instructor's comments on your work.

Good instructors spend a lot of time commenting on your work. When you get your papers back, do not focus on the grade alone. If you do not carefully read the comments, you will miss a lot of the value in your courses. Also, each instructor has different priorities, and you can get better grades on your work for the course when you know those priorities.

Do get to know your instructor.

Communication is important. If you get a low grade or do not understand something, either ask in class, via e-mail, or visit your instructor during office hours. It is up to you to take steps to clear up anything you do not understand.

Do ask questions to make sure you understand assignments.

Your instructor may assume that you know things you do not, so expectations and assignments may not be as clearly spelled out as they were in previous classes. Do not be afraid to ask questions. If something is not clear to you, chances are it is not clear to at least some of your classmates.

Do participate in class: Ask questions, answer questions, and make comments.

Do not be afraid of making a stupid comment or giving the wrong answer. That is part of how you learn. Plus, many instructors grade on participation.

TEACHING TIP This is a good time to add your own expectations to the list that the students give. You might also ask students to write their description of a good instructor.

TEACHING TIP As a follow-up, refer your students to the syllabus often, so they know it is an important document.

Do listen and take notes.

When the instructor is talking, listen carefully, but do not try to write down every word that he or she says. To figure out what you should make a note of, look at the instructor. Important points are often signaled with an arm or a hand gesture, a note on the board, or a change in the tone of your instructor's voice.

Do sit near the front of the class.

Sitting near the front is important for a number of different reasons.

- The instructor can see you. Sitting in front also signals that you are motivated.

- You can see the instructor, the board, and any visual aids used in class.

- You are less likely to be distracted.

Don't sit in the back of the room, text message, or fall asleep.

These behaviors will create a bad impression, waste your time, and waste your money. If you do not want to be there, stay home.

Don't fall behind with your courses because it is really hard to catch up.

If you are tired when you get home, take a short break, but force yourself

---

What to Listen for While Taking Notes

1. **What is your instructor talking about?** (Listen for introductions like *today we're going to discuss. . . .*)

2. **What points does the instructor want me to know about that topic?** (Listen for words and phrases like *there are five different reasons,* and for transitions between points, like *also, it's important, another thing, remember, then.*)

3. **What is the most important thing about each point?** (Listen for words and phrases like *key, critical, this is important because, most important, primary, main.*) If you think one idea relates to another, make a note of it. Making these kinds of connections is what your teacher calls *synthesis.*

4. **What is the instructor's wrap-up?** (Listen for words and phrases that signal a conclusion like *therefore, so, in essence, in conclusion, finally, as you can see, so that's why, so we need to understand, so the point is. . . .*) Teachers often restate their major points toward the end. If you do not understand or have missed something, toward the end of class is the time to ask questions.

to do your homework and study. You have to be mature about your college responsibilities.

Don't make excuses for not having your homework or assignment.

Explain that you do not have it, and tell the instructor when the work will be completed. Then make sure it is done by the date you have promised. (If your instructor does not accept late work, it is not a bad idea to complete the assignment anyway and submit it. It might not count toward your grade, but your instructor will respect your effort — and the writing practice will not hurt.)

Don't leave big assignments until the last minute.

If you do, either you will not be able to finish, or you will do a bad job and get a bad grade.

The Big Picture

Keep your eye on all you have to learn and all you have to offer.

"Understand how you learn best."

People learn in different ways. To find out what your learning style is and how to use it effectively in college, take the Learning Styles Test at **bedfordstmartins.com/realessays**.

"Your college writing courses are important."

We have said it before, and we mean it: Do not make the mistake of taking your writing courses lightly. You have to pass them to graduate, and what you learn there will affect how well you do in your other courses. Remember, you are in charge of your success. Do not fail yourself.

"You need to really *think,* not just repeat others' ideas."

Your experience makes you unique, and your ideas reflect that. Let other people know who you are — in class discussions and in what you write.

"Have confidence in yourself."

If you try hard enough, you *will* learn. Even though you will have to work hard, remember that what you do will help you in your other courses and in your life.

For more advice from college students, visit www.cerritos.edu/ lcp/firstyear.html.

Four Strategies for Success

The strategies for success that follow here apply to your college courses, your work, and your everyday life. They are

- Identify your goals.
- Manage your time.
- Use all the campus resources available to you.
- Connect to the college.

Paying careful attention to each of these strategies can make a big difference in your daily life and long-term success.

Identify Your Goals

You may already know what kind of degree you want to pursue in college and what type of job you want. With these long-term goals in mind, you also have shorter-term goals—steps that help you get where you want to go. For example, to pass this course, you will need to develop your writing skills. Although this course is new to you, you have probably written in previous courses. You might not have thought much about your writing, but it will help you become a better writer if you have some specific writing goals in mind. Start by looking at the course syllabus, which may list goals.

Writing Goals

ACTIVITY: Think about the writing you have done in previous courses. What kinds of writing did you do? What kinds of grades did you get? When you are given an assignment, how do you begin? What problems do you think you have with writing?

Now list at least four writing goals—skills you want to learn, practice, or improve in this course. Be as specific as possible. For example, "Learn to write better" is too general to help you focus on what you need to do. Throughout the course, refer to this list of skills and abilities.

1. _____

2. _____

3. _____

4. _____

Degree Goals

Whether or not you have decided what you want to major in, you should still ask yourself some questions now.

- What courses will I need to take for the major(s) I might be interested in?
- What are the required core courses that every student must take to graduate?
- When could I take these courses?

Course requirements for each major are listed in the college bulletin and on the college Web site. Also, sit down with your academic adviser to plan a sequence of courses. If you are like most students, you are juggling a lot of important priorities, and having a plan to reach your goals will help you achieve them. Write your tentative plans in the spaces provided.

I want to major in _____.

Courses I will need for that major (If you do not know your major yet, list the courses required for all students.)

_____

_____

_____

_____

_____

_____

_____

_____

Number of courses I can take next term _____

Courses I should take if they fit into my schedule (Remember, certain courses have other courses as prerequisites.)

_____

_____

Manage Your Time

We all have too much to do to remember everything. Most successful students use a planner of some sort—a calendar or notebook that lists what they need to do and when.

Some Web sites (such as **calendar.google.com** or **myfreecalendar.com**) offer calendars as free downloads, either to use on a computer or to print out. Your e-mail program and cell phone may also feature calendars. Two examples follow: a course calendar and a general calendar.

Make a Course Calendar

A course calendar plots all the work you need to do for a course. Following is an example of a monthly calendar kept for an English course.

College Writing, Tuesday/Thursday, 8:30–10:00 a.m.
Professor Murphy
Office hours: T/Th, 11:00–12:30, and by appointment

		1	2	3	4	5
		8:30–10:00: Class. Draft due, illustration essay.	12:00: Study for test on fragments and run-ons (Chs. 23–24).	8:30–10:00: Class. Test, Chs. 23–24.		Work on revising illustration essay.
6	7	8	9	10	11	12
		8:30–10:00: Class.	11:30: Appt. at writing center.	8:30–10:00: Class. Final illustration essay due.		
13	14	15	16	17	18	19
	Study for test on subject-verb agreement (Chs. 25–26).	8:30–10:00: Class. Test, Chs. 25–26. 11:00: Appt. with Prof. Murphy.		8:30–10:00: Class. Start description essay.		
20	21	22	23	24	25	26
		8:30–10:00: Class. Draft due, description essay.		8:30–10:00: Class.		Work on revising description essay.
27	28	29	30	31		
	Study for test on past-tense verbs (Ch. 26).	8:30–10:00: Class. Test, past-tense verbs.		8:30–10:00: Class. Final description essay due.		

Make a General Calendar

A course calendar helps you manage time for course work, but you should also keep track of other commitments you have. Be sure to leave some unscheduled time for unexpected events. If you do not want to make separate calendars, make one master calendar with all of your college, work, and everyday life commitments, and refer to it daily.

Following is part of the calendar you just saw, with additional appointments, commitments, and tasks filled in. The student who made this calendar is taking two courses, working, and caring for a two-year-old daughter, Lottie.

20	21	22	23	24	25	26
12:00–6:00: Work. 7:00: Mom, dinner. 9:00: Description draft.	8:00–4:00: Work. 5:00: Pick up Lottie, day care. 8:00–9:30: Study for math test.	8:30–10:00: Class. Draft due, description essay. 12:00–6:00: Work. 7:00–10:00: Math. Test, Chs. 5–6.	8:00–4:00: Work. 12:00: Study with Genie. 4:30: Doctor. 5:30: Pick up Lottie. 8:00: Math homework.	8:30–10:00: Class. 11:00: Food shopping. 12:00–6:00: Work. 7:00–10:00: Math.	8:00–4:00: Work. 5:00: Pick up Lottie, get present for birthday party.	Work on revising description essay. Clean, do laundry. 6:00: Lottie to party.

Use All the Campus Resources Available to You

Some students do not know how many campus resources are available to them for free. For example, here is a list of student resources most colleges offer.

- Writing Center and writing tutors
- Financial Aid Office
- Employment Office
- Office of Student Affairs (with many programs)
- Counseling Office
- Mini-courses or seminars on a wide variety of topics, such as taking notes, studying for tests, and writing a résumé
- Ride-sharing and babysitting exchange boards
- Academic advising
- Library services, including assistance for specific reference searches of print and online databases

This example of a college Web page shows the wide range of services and support available to students. If you do not have a computer, use a library or lab computer to visit your college's home page and click on the "Student Services" or "Current Students" links.

Note the many services listed in the box on the left-hand side of the Web page. To get detailed information about each service listed, click on the individual item. You can read about the resources offered, find office locations (and hours), and get details on how to schedule office visits and appointments.

- -

ACTIVITY 1 Find Your Resources

Go to your college's Web site and find the page that lists student services. After locating each of the resources listed below (column 1), fill in the chart with the information you gather.

RESOURCE	LOCATION	HOW IT CAN HELP ME (BE SPECIFIC)
CAREER SERVICES		
ACADEMIC ASSISTANCE		
ADVISING		
FINANCIAL AID		
HEALTH SERVICES		

- -

Connect to the College

Often, students do not know much about their college community beyond their classes and a few student services. Colleges offer students a rich array of ways to learn and grow: activities, events, clubs, and organizations that bring students together and enrich their lives. If you commute to the college, getting involved and connecting to the campus community is important. Why?

The most successful students feel connected to their college, and they are much less likely to drop out. They know there are people who can help them when they have trouble, and they make good connections for the present and for the future. Involved students also develop their interests and experiences. Many successful students believe that if they had not connected to the college in some way beyond taking classes, they would not have stayed. Consider what one Bergen Community College student wrote for the February 2010 edition of the campus newspaper, *The Torch*.

Islam Elshami

Why Join the Club?

1   Bergen Community College (BCC) offers a variety of clubs and organizations for students to join on a weekly basis. Each club suits each student's desires; whether it is by helping others or learning about and exploring new cultures. Some of these clubs and organizations allow students to promote awareness for something they feel passionate about, such as a culture, a subject, an activity, a sport, a religion, or a tradition.

2   Clubs offer students a wide range of opportunities and benefit members in ways such as meeting new people and gaining experience, whether it is generally for life or by adding it to a résumé or application. Not only do clubs help socially, but they also help educationally and assist students in subjects that they are taking on campus. Everyone should join at least one club in a semester to experience something new and enriching to look forward to every week. You get the opportunity to hold a position in a club where you can make a difference in your school.

3   There are clubs about cultures and religions such as the African Student Union, the Christian Club, the Desi Club, the Korean Club, the Muslim Student Association, the Polish Culture Club, the Russian Club, and many more. There are activity clubs such as the Chess Club, the Dance Club, and the Theatre Club. Some of the clubs are also helpful for the community as well as for the college, such as the Environmental Club and the Community Service Club.

4   Professor Rachel Wieland, adviser to the Environmental Club, elaborates on the tasks that this club is most successful in. "When we talk about the green initiative on campus, we are no longer speaking of the environmental club; they are a subset of the green initiatives. In the past, Semester Green has enormously expanded on campus. I advise the Environmental Club, but I also co-run the Green Team, and I am also a co-sustainability officer. If students want to be involved, the best way to jump in is to simply look at what options are available on campus, to join, and go for it. Green is not a side dish anymore at BCC. It is the main event. BCC is positioning itself to be the leading sustainability community college in New Jersey. That leaves a huge amount of room for students to get involved and make a difference," says Professor Wieland.

5   Students should be encouraged to participate in clubs around their own schools to experience the feel of being able to make a difference in any way possible. Not only does it help within the school, but also helps the students themselves by teaching them leadership skills. It is always a good time to brush off the stress that has been building up from exams and assignments and get started on something you can enjoy doing.

• •

ACTIVITY 2   Read to Understand

Throughout this book (and throughout your college experience) you will practice reading to understand meaning. Although you know how to read, you need to learn how to analyze and understand what you read, a key college skill. As a start, answer the following questions about "Why Join the Club?"

1.   What is Elshami's purpose in writing the article for the student newspaper?

To persuade students to join a club on campus.
_____

2.   Underline the reasons she gives to persuade her readers.

3.   Do you agree with her position? Why or why not? _____
_____
_____

4.   If you were responding to Elshami, what would you say? If you do not agree with her points, what would you say to persuade her of your position?
_____
_____

• •

ACTIVITY 3   Find the Clubs

Go to your college Web site again, and find "Student Life" or "Student Activities." Click there to find a list of student clubs and organizations. Find out about two clubs or organizations at your college that you might be interested in, and fill in the following chart.

CLUB NAME	DESCRIPTION	LOCATION, MEETING TIMES, ADVISER

. . . .

WRITING ASSIGNMENTS

1.   Choose one of the student services you found on your college's Web site, and make an appointment to interview someone who works there. Pick up handouts or brochures. Then, write about the service, describing what you found out in your interview, and how the service helps students.

TEACHING TIP
These assignments can be done in small groups, and in addition to the writing students do, you can have them do mini-presentations to the rest of the class.

2.   Looking back at your degree goals, describe what they are and how you will reach them. You are writing a college plan for yourself that you can use. You might consult your adviser either before or after writing this plan.

3.   Write down something you are interested in, either academically, professionally, or personally. Then, go to the college Web site and choose a club or organization that matches your interest and go to a meeting of the club or talk to a student who is involved in it. Ask what the club does and pick up information about upcoming or past events. Write about what you found out.

> **reflect** Using what you have learned from this chapter, revise your responses to the "write" questions on page 3.

Thinking Critically

Developing Your Power of Mind

Understand What Critical Thinking Is

Critical thinking is actively using the power of your mind to question what you see, hear, read, and write. We all think critically in our lives when we assess situations. For example, consider the following situation.

....

PRACTICE 1 **Analyzing a Situation**

You walk into a party and see two men yelling and swearing at each other with a group of others crowded around them. The men are in each other's faces, and they are angry.

1. What is going on? <u>Two people are having a public argument.</u>

2. What elements of the situation do you notice to assess how bad the situation is? <u>Answers will vary but could include who the men are, how loudly they are yelling, whether their fists are clenched, if the veins on their necks are standing out, what the crowd is doing, what the men are saying.</u>

3. What do you think will happen? <u>The men might have a physical fight.</u>

DISCUSSION
Go over the situation and student responses in class.

4. What in your experience helps you predict what is going to happen?

I have seen other arguments get violent, have seen crowds make the

situation worse.

5. How will you act, and why? *Answers will vary but could include leaving*

the party, joining the crowd, asking someone what is going on.

Assumptions and Biases

We all have ideas that are shaped by our experience or by ideas or opinions we have been exposed to. **Assumptions** are ideas or opinions we have and do not usually question because we take them for granted: We assume they are true. Some of those assumptions are reliable about some situations and people. However, critical thinking requires that you question assumptions that underlie ideas, both your own and those of others. **Biases** are beliefs or points of view that may blind you to the truth of any situation because they cause you to fit what you see, hear, or read into a belief you already have. As you develop your critical thinking skills, practice questioning assumptions and looking for biases, in yourself and in others. When you can see situations and ideas without assumptions or bias, you can see reality and act more effectively.

Purposeful questioning is the foundation of critical thinking. In a situation such as the one you just read about, your responses to the questions may have been influenced by assumptions and biases that you did not know you had. As you practice thinking critically, be alert to assumptions and biases, both in yourself and in others.

You have assessed many situations in your life, so you already have experience with critical thinking. Using critical thinking may help you avoid danger, as in the situation described above. When you apply the same kind of questioning to college and work, you improve your chances of success. The rest of this chapter will give you tools to develop the power of your mind—the most powerful life tool you have.

Critical Thinking: Key College Skills

RESOURCES
For more on teaching critical thinking, see Chapter 6 in *Practical Suggestions for Teaching Real Essays.*

In college, critical thinking begins with focusing on what you are doing. Whether you are listening to your instructor, reading, writing, taking a test, or doing an assignment, first take the time to clear your mind of distractions and focus purposefully on what you are doing. When you are reading, take a breath and tell yourself, "*Focus.*" Then, ask yourself the following questions.

Critical Thinking

Summarize
- What is important about what you are reading?
- What is the purpose, the big picture?
- What are the main points and key support?

Analyze
- What elements have been used to convey the main point?
- What assumptions has the author made about his or her audience?
- What assumptions of your own do you bring to the work?

Synthesize
- What does the text mean, and what in your experience leads you to think it means this?
- How have experiences and sources been used to support the main point?

Evaluate
- Based on your application of summary, analysis, and synthesis, what do you think about the material you have read?
- Is the work successful? Does it achieve its purpose?
- Does the author show any biases? If so, does showing biases make the piece more or less effective?

This box represents the key college skills you will need in every course: summary, analysis, synthesis, and evaluation. These skills help you demonstrate your deep understanding of course content. The next sections will explain these skills in more detail so that you can use them effectively. The skills reflect the questions you were asked about in assessing the situation of the angry men. To show how the same skills can be applied to writing assignments, read the excerpt on page 22 from an introductory psychology textbook.

Summary

A **summary** is a condensed version (the big picture) of a situation, a piece of writing, a lecture, a meeting, an event, a visual image. A summary should include the main point of what you are summarizing, along with key supporting points. You have used summary when you have told someone what a movie was about. In reading and writing, a summary gives the main points and key support in brief form in your own words. Think of a summary as making a long story short.

CRITICAL
THINKING
■ **Summarize**
■ Analyze
■ Synthesize
■ Evaluate

TEACHING TIP
A good writing assignment (or a good discussion topic) is to ask students to discuss their daily hassles and the behaviors or physical symptoms that result from them. They can also discuss the validity of the gender differences identified in the passage.

Daily Hassles
That's Not What I Ordered!

What made you feel "stressed out" in the last week? Chances are it was not a major life event. Instead, it was probably some unexpected but minor annoyance, such as splotching ketchup on your new white T-shirt, misplacing your keys, or discovering that you've been standing in the wrong line.

Stress researcher **Richard Lazarus** and his colleagues suspected that such ordinary irritations in daily life might be an important source of stress. To explore this idea, they developed a scale measuring **daily hassles**—everyday occurrences that annoy and upset people (DeLongis & others, 1982; Kanner & others, 1981). The *Daily Hassles Scale* measures the occurrence of everyday annoyances, such as losing something, getting stuck in traffic, and even being inconvenienced by lousy weather.

Are there gender differences in the frequency of daily hassles? One study measured the daily hassles experienced by married couples (Almeida & Kessler, 1998). The women experienced both more daily hassles and higher levels of psychological stress than their husbands did. For men, the most common sources of daily stress were financial and job-related problems. For women, family demands and interpersonal conflict were the most frequent causes of stress. However, when women *do* experience a stressful day in the workplace, the stress is more likely to spill over into their interactions with their husbands and other family members (Schulz & others, 2004). Men, on the other hand, are more likely to simply withdraw.

How important are daily hassles in producing stress? The frequency of daily hassles is linked to both psychological distress and physical symptoms, such as headaches and backaches (Bottos & Dewey, 2004; DeLongis & others, 1988). In fact, the number of daily hassles people experience is a better predictor of physical illness and symptoms than is the number of major life events experienced (Burks & Martin, 1985).

Why do daily hassles take such a toll? One explanation is that such minor stressors are *cumulative* (Repetti, 1993). Each hassle may be relatively unimportant in itself, but after a day filled with minor hassles, the effects add up. People feel drained, grumpy, and stressed out. Daily hassles also contribute to the stress produced by major life events. Any major life change, whether positive or negative, can create a ripple effect, generating a host of new daily hassles (Maybery & others, 2007; Pillow & others, 1996).

Here is a summary of "Daily Hassles." The main point is double-underlined; the supporting points are underlined.

Hockenbury and Hockenbury tell us that <u><u>daily hassles often cause more stress than major problems do.</u></u> According to studies, <u>men and women report different kinds of daily stress and react to stress differently, though</u> both experience <u>psychological and physical symptoms.</u> Some research shows that <u>daily hassles produce stress because their effects are cumulative</u>—that is, they add up over time to create major stress.

CRITICAL THINKING
■ **Summarize**
■ **Analyze**
▪ Synthesize
▪ Evaluate

Analysis

An **analysis** breaks down the points or parts of something and considers how they work together to make an impression or convey a main point. When you tell someone about a movie, you might describe how the music, lighting, camera angles, and acting worked to create suspense or humor.

Here is an analysis of "Daily Hassles." The writer's main point is double-underlined, and the support points are underlined.

> We have all read about stress, but Hockenbury and Hockenbury have something new and interesting to say about it: It is not the big life crises but the million petty hassles we face every day that get to us. They mention a number of different studies on hassles and their effects on us. Two of these studies explore gender differences, and they conclude that men and women report different kinds of daily hassles and respond to them differently.
>
> These studies seem to involve only married men and women, however, which raises areas for further exploration. Do *all* men and women really experience and respond to hassles differently? For example, would unmarried male and female students be affected in the same ways that married men and women are? In a future paper, I would like to examine the kinds of daily hassles my college friends—both male and female—react to and what symptoms those hassles produce. The subject of hassles and how we react to them seems particularly relevant to students, whose lives are full of stress.

[The writer discusses one major point in "Daily Hassles" and two other studies included in the piece. She then poses questions that the article raises for her.]

Synthesis

CRITICAL
THINKING
■ **Summarize**
■ **Analyze**
■ **Synthesize**
■ Evaluate

A **synthesis** pulls together information from other experiences or sources to make a new point. Continuing with the movie example, you might relate the effect the movie had on you to an experience you have had or to something you have read about.

Here is a synthesis of "Daily Hassles." The writer wanted to understand the hassles that people experience and the effects that they cause, so she incorporated additional information from published research and her own experience. The various sources the writer pulls together are underlined.

> In *Discovering Psychology,* Hockenbury and Hockenbury present evidence that males and females react to different sources of stress and respond differently to them. The studies they use as evidence discuss only married couples, however, and they provide few details about the

First source

actual kinds and symptoms of stress. Several other studies, as well as original research done among unmarried college students, provide some additional insights into these questions.

Second source

The Mayo Clinic's Web site, produced by the staff at the Mayo Clinic, suggests that there are two main types of stress: acute stress, which is a response to specific and isolated situations (such as a car accident, a performance, or an exam) and chronic stress, which is longer term and cumulative. Acute, short-term stress can be good for people, prompting them to act. Chronic stress, however, tends to have negative effects, both physical and psychological. Daily hassles can produce either or both types of stress. Physical symptoms include headaches, back pain, stomach upset, and sleep problems. Psychological symptoms include anxiety, anger, depression, and burnout. The site offers numerous articles on stress and stress management, including a stress assessment test.

Third source

The Web site *Diabetes at Work* gives a list of the "Top 10 Daily Hassles," among them the illness of a family member, home repairs, loss of work, and crime. It includes the same symptoms of stress that the Mayo Clinic site does, such as shortness of breath, forgetfulness, reduced concentration, trouble making decisions, and irritability. Neither the *Diabetes at Work* Web site nor the Mayo Clinic site distinguishes between male and female stress sources or symptoms.

Fourth source

To these sources, I added interviews with eight friends—four men and four women—who all reported these top five daily hassles: worries about money, transportation problems, waiting in lines, unfair bosses, and automated phone systems that take forever and never get you an answer.

The only significant difference in the kind of hassles reported by the men and women I talked to was that several women (but not men) mentioned worries about physical safety (for example, while traveling home from school at night). When I asked my friends to report how they dealt with their stress, they seemed to confirm the Hockenburys' claim that women's stress spills over into the family and men tend to withdraw. Two men reported no psychological symptoms of stress, whereas the remaining six people (four women and two men) emphasized both psychological and physical symptoms.

These sources suggest that there might be some gender differences in the hassles that people experience and the symptoms that result from these hassles, but they might not be as major as the Hockenburys' passage led me to expect. Most of the stresses mentioned seem to be caused by having to do too much in too little time. Perhaps this is a comment on the quality of modern life, which affects both men and women equally.

New point

Works Cited

Hockenbury, Don H., and Sandra E. Hockenbury. *Discovering Psychology.* 5th ed. New York: Worth, 2010. 543. Print.

Mayo Clinic Staff. "Stress Symptoms: Effects on Your Body, Feelings, and Behavior." *Mayo Clinic.* The Mayo Clinic, 20 Feb. 2009. Web. 13 Oct. 2010.

"Top 10 Daily Hassles." *Diabetes at Work.* United States Dept. of Health and Human Services, 27 May 2007. Web. 10 Oct. 2010.

Evaluation

An **evaluation** is your *thoughtful* judgment about something based on what you have discovered through your summary, analysis, and synthesis. To evaluate something effectively, you have to carefully apply the Critical Thinking questions on page 21, which you will use again and again in this book, your other courses, your work, and your everyday life. To use the movie example again, if you tell the person why you liked (or hated) the movie, and why, you are evaluating it.

Here is an evaluation of "Daily Hassles."

CRITICAL THINKING
■ Summarize
■ Analyze
■ Synthesize
■ Evaluate

Hockenbury and Hockenbury present important information and raise some interesting questions about how daily hassles affect our lives. In a few paragraphs, they present a great deal of information on the subject of daily hassles—what they are, who developed the scale of daily hassles, how men and women differ in their reactions to daily hassles, and how the stress of daily hassles negatively affects people. They provide numerous credible references to support their points. Other sources—such as the Mayo Clinic's Web site, the Web site *Diabetes at Work,* and a gender-based poll I conducted—provide more details about some aspects of daily hassles and raise questions about the extent to which women and men are differently affected by them. However, the Hockenburys present a good overview of the subject in a short piece of writing. I think the authors do a great job of pulling together good information for students.

....

PRACTICE 2   Summarizing, Analyzing, Synthesizing, Evaluating

Choose one of the following items (1–4) to write about. You may want to refer to the Critical Thinking box on page 21 as you write.

1.   **Summary:** Summarize the plot of a movie or television program in one paragraph.

2.   **Analysis:** Read a letter to the editor in a newspaper or a blog posting on a particular issue. Whether you agree or disagree with the writer, write a paragraph analyzing the points he or she presents.

3.   **Synthesis:** Read three letters to the editor or three blog postings on the same subject. In one paragraph, state your position on the subject according to your reading of the letters or blog postings, and explain the range of opinions on the subject.

4.   **Evaluation:** Consider your performance in a recent activity, such as a sport, an exam, a party, or a task at work, and write a paragraph evaluating how well you performed in the situation.

....

In the next chapter, you will learn how to apply critical thinking skills when you read and write.

---

reflect Reread your response to the "write" prompt on page 19 and revise it to include what you have learned in this chapter.

Reading Critically

Developing Your Understanding

In college, you will read a variety of materials — course syllabi, handouts, assignments, textbooks, articles, essays, Web sites, and more. While you will read these materials in slightly different ways, they all require you to be able to read critically.

IDEA JOURNAL
What do you read regularly? Have you ever finished reading something and realized that you have not really remembered it? If so, why do you think you had trouble absorbing this material?

Understand What Critical Reading Is

Critical reading is paying close attention as you read and asking yourself questions about the author's purpose, his or her main point, the support he or she gives, and how good that support is. It also means that you do not just accept everything you read, but instead consider why the author arranges the points in a certain way, whether you agree or disagree, what you think, and why. It is detecting the writer's assumptions and biases (and your own), and being able to apply your critical thinking skills to summarize, analyze, synthesize, and evaluate what you read.

Critical reading is reading actively, not just passively looking at the words on the page or screen. It requires that you get involved with what you read to deeply understand it. To develop critical reading skills, you need to engage in an active reading process.

The Critical Reading Process

In this section, the steps and practices guide you through the process of reading actively and critically. The four basic steps are shown below. As always, start by focusing your mind on what you are doing. As you work through this book, the four steps of the critical reading process will be identified with the letters PRPR (**2PR**).

2PR   The Critical Reading Process

- **P**review the reading.

- **R**ead the piece, double underlining the thesis statement, underlining the major support, and circling the transitions. Consider the quality of the support.

- **P**ause to think during reading. Take notes and ask questions about what you are reading. Talk to the author.

- **R**eview the reading, your guiding question, your marginal notes, and your questions.

CRITICAL
READING
- Preview
- Read
- Pause
- Review

2PR   Preview the Reading

Before reading any piece of writing, skim or preview the whole thing, using the following steps.

Read the Title, Head Note, and Introductory Paragraphs

The title of a chapter, an article, or any other document usually gives you some idea of what the topic is. Some documents are introduced by head notes, which summarize or provide background about the selection. If there is a head note, read it. Whether or not there is a head note, writers often introduce their topic and main point in the first few paragraphs, so read those, and note what you think the main point might be.

Read Headings, Key Words, and Definitions

Textbooks and magazine articles often include headings to help readers follow the author's ideas. These headings (such as "Preview the Reading" above) tell you what the important subjects of the writing are.

Any terms in **boldface** type are especially important. In textbooks, writers often use boldface for key words that are important to the topic. Read the definitions of key words as you preview the writing.

Look for Summaries, Checklists, and Chapter Reviews

Many textbooks (such as this one) include features that summarize or list main points. Review summaries, checklists, or chapter reviews to make sure you have understood the main points.

Read the Conclusion

Writers usually review their main point in their concluding paragraphs. Read the conclusion, and compare it with the note you made after you read the introduction and thought about what the main idea might be.

Ask a Guiding Question

As the final step in your preview of a reading, ask yourself a **guiding question**—a question you think the reading might answer. Sometimes, you can turn the title into a guiding question. For example, read the title of this chapter, and write a possible guiding question. As you read, try to answer your guiding question. Having a guiding question gives you a purpose for reading and helps keep you focused.

2PR   Read the Piece: Find the Main Point and the Support

CRITICAL
READING
■ **Preview**
■ **Read**
■ Pause
■ Review

After previewing, begin reading carefully for meaning, trying especially to identify a writer's main point and the support for that point.

Main Point and Purpose

The **main point** of a reading is the central idea the author wants to communicate. The main point is related to the writer's **purpose**, which can be to explain, to demonstrate, to persuade, or to entertain. Writers often introduce their main point early, so read the first few paragraphs with special care. After reading the first paragraph (or more, depending on the length of the reading selection), stop and write down—in your own words—what you think the main idea is. If the writer has stated the main point in a single sentence, double-underline it.

For more on main points, see Chapter 6.

For online exercises on main points, visit *Exercise Central* at bedfordstmartins .com/realessays.

· ·

PRACTICE 1   Finding the Main Point

Read each of the following paragraphs. Then, write the main point in your own words in the spaces provided.

TEAMWORK Practice 1 works well as a group activity.

1. Neighbors who are too friendly can be seen just about anywhere. I mean that both ways. They exist in every neighborhood I have ever lived in and seem to appear everywhere I go. For some strange reason these people become extremely attached to my family and stop in as many as eight to ten times a day. No matter how tired I appear to be, nothing short of opening the door and suggesting they leave will make them go home at night. (I once told an unusually friendly neighbor that his house was on fire, in an attempt to make him leave, and he still took ten minutes to say goodbye.) What is truly interesting about these people is their strong desire to cook for us even though they have developed no culinary skill whatsoever. (This has always proved particularly disconcerting since they stay to watch us eat every bite as they continually ask if the food "tastes good.")

— From Jonathan R. Gould Jr., "The People Next Door"

MAIN POINT: *Answers will vary. Possible answer: Over-friendly neighbors*

plague the author.

2. When we see people chewing gum, we might think it gives an impression of immaturity or unprofessionalism. We all remember teachers in elementary school forbidding gum-chewing, though we never knew why. But new research indicates that chewing gum can actually improve certain kinds of thinking and memory. Subjects in a study conducted by Andrew Scholey in England showed that people who chewed gum during challenging mental tasks performed significantly better than subjects who did not chew gum doing the same tasks. Scholey speculated that the chewing increased heart rate, and therefore increased oxygen flowing to the brain while lowering stress and anxiety. Still, it is not a good idea to chew gum during a job interview as the negative impression of chewing is widespread.

MAIN POINT: *Answers will vary. Possible answer: Chewing gum improves*

mental functioning.

3. In communities around the United States, people are "time bank-ing," giving their individual skills in return for another's, and build-ing a sense of community in the process. For example, one person might not have a driver's license or a car but needs transportation to a regular appointment. That same person is a good baker, and so offers to make cakes, pies, or cookies in return for transportation to her appointment. Individuals offer up their skills and get what they need in return, when they need it. Time banking in some large cities is funded by AmeriCorps because the groups are large and need a central administration. People involved in time banking are highly satisfied with the practice because it is local, it saves money, and it connects people who might not otherwise meet, strengthening com-munity ties. It also reminds individuals that they have something to contribute as they offer up their skills to their neighbors.

MAIN POINT: *Answers will vary. Possible answer: Time banking, wherein people swap skills and services, has a number of benefits.*

4. Class attendance and participation are essential since we do many in-class writings and much group work, which are part of a student's grade in the course. If you must miss a class and know this in advance, please contact me so that we can discuss work and assign-ments that you will miss. For excused absences—student illness, a death in the family, an accident, and religious holidays—you must arrange to make up work missed, and that work must be submitted within a week. Other absences will be considered unexcused absences unless discussed with me. Any student who has more than three unexcused absences will be asked to drop the course.

—From a syllabus for a writing course

MAIN POINT: *Answers will vary. Possible answer: Students must attend class, do the work assigned, and follow procedures for absences.*

TEACHING TIP
Ask students to anno-tate the main points in your course syllabus.

Support and Logical Fallacies

For more on support, see Chapter 7.

Support is the collection of details that shows, explains, or proves the main point.

The author might use statistics, facts, definitions, and scientific results for support. Or he or she might use memories, stories, comparisons, quotations from experts, and personal observations. All of it could be good support, but do not assume that: Ask questions about what the writer has used for support. The facts might be incorrect, the memories hazy, the experts questionable, the personal observations biased. When you are reading for college, ask yourself: What information is the author including to help me understand or agree with the main point? Is the support (evidence) valid and convincing?

. . . .

For online exercises on support, visit *Exercise Central* at bedfordstmartins .com/realessays.

PRACTICE 2   Identifying Support

Go back to Practice 1 (p. 29) and underline the support for the main ideas of each of the passages in the practice.

. . . .

TEACHING TIP
Ask students if they can identify the main idea and support in the textbook example on page 22 or in any of the essays in Part 8, Readings for Writers.

As you read, look for examples of faulty reasoning, which we are exposed to frequently. Certain kinds of errors in reasoning are so common that they have their own name: **logical fallacies**. Here are some of the most common examples of faulty reasoning.

Either/Or Extremes.   Assuming that there are only two extreme choices with nothing in between.

> **EXAMPLE:**   My country, love it or leave it.
>
> [**Faulty reasoning:** Should people really either applaud everything a government does or move to a different country?]

Bad Analogy.   Comparing items or circumstances that are not alike enough to make a meaningful comparison.

> **EXAMPLE:**   A human fetus should have the same rights as a human adult.
>
> [**Faulty reasoning:** While some specific rights may be shared by a fetus and an adult, saying they should have all the same rights does not make sense because they are different in many ways. Should a fetus be able to vote, for example?]

Circular Reasoning.　Supporting a position by restating part of it.

EXAMPLE:　　I deserve a raise because I need to make more money.

[**Faulty reasoning:** While this may be true, it will not persuade your boss. You need to offer reasons why you are worth more than you are being paid.]

"Everyone Knows."　Appealing to people's general desire to be like the majority by supporting a statement with a claim that all or most other people believe something. A common occurrence of this is when a child says to a parent, "Everybody else's parents are letting them do *X*." (For a good example of this kind of influence, see "In Praise of Peer Pressure" on p. 290.) This kind of faulty reasoning is also called "the bandwagon effect."

EXAMPLE:　　Everyone knows that all politicians are liars.

[**Faulty reasoning:** While some research studies might measure people's perceptions about how truthful politicians are, it is not likely that any study would reveal that all people believe that all politicians lie all the time.]

Mistaken Causes or Effects.　Assuming that one thing caused another simply because it occurred beforehand.

EXAMPLE:　　The opening of the new liquor superwarehouse caused old Mr. Jones to close up his shop.

[**Faulty reasoning:** Mr. Jones might have closed for a variety of reasons. Your assumption is not evidence of his real reason for closing.]

Overgeneralization.　Making a broad statement that is not supported by enough evidence.

EXAMPLE:　　Having grown up with three brothers, I know firsthand that boys are more violent than girls.

[**Faulty reasoning:** A sample of one family is not enough to assume that all boys act in a particular way.]

Oversimplification.　Making something seem simple when it is not simple.

EXAMPLE:　　If more parking spaces were available on campus, most students would come to class.

[**Faulty reasoning:** Students miss class for many reasons, so saying parking is the problem is too simple.]

Slippery Slope.   Saying that something will create a chain reaction, even though there is no evidence that this will happen.

> **EXAMPLE:**   Using marijuana will lead to heroin addiction.

[**Faulty reasoning:** There is no overall evidence that one leads all the way to another. To make such a claim, proof of each step of the chain reaction must be given.]

"This, so That."   Pairing ideas or events that are not logically connected.

> **EXAMPLE:**   I trust my doctor, so I ask him for advice about my finances.

[**Faulty reasoning:** The fact that a medical adviser is trustworthy has no bearing on the doctor's financial reliability. This kind of faulty reasoning is also called a *non sequitur* (literally, "it does not follow").]

· ·

PRACTICE 3   Identifying Faulty Reasoning

Read the sentences below, and identify which kind of faulty reasoning each represents. In the space provided, explain why it is an example of faulty reasoning.

1.   If medical costs continue to rise, no one will be able to afford health care.

Slippery slope. While many people may not be able to afford health care,

others will.

2.   Colleges should either lower their tuitions or give all students scholarships.

Either/or extremes. There may be good options between the two extremes.

_____

3.   We can blame McDonald's for the increase in obesity in this country.

Oversimplification. McDonald's is not solely responsible.

_____

4.   Most college students are binge drinkers.

Overgeneralization. While we hear about binge drinking in college, not all

college students are binge drinkers.

5. If college were free, students would graduate within four years.

Oversimplification. This might be true for students whose only obstacle is

financial, but there are many reasons students don't graduate in four

years.

2PR Pause to Think

Critical reading requires you to actively think as you read, and taking notes and asking questions is a part of this process. As you pause to think about what you are reading, use check marks and other symbols and jot notes to yourself, so you can understand what you have read when you finish it (rather than having just looked at the words without thinking about their meaning and purpose). Here are some ways to take notes as you read.

- Note the main idea by highlighting it or writing it in the margin.
- Note the major support points by underlining them.
- Note ideas you do not understand with a question mark (?).
- Note ideas you agree with by placing a check mark next to them (✓).
- Note ideas that you do not agree with or that surprise you with an **X** or **!**.
- Note examples of an author's or expert's bias and how they seem biased.
- Pause to consider your reactions to parts of the reading and how a part or sentence relates to the main point.

2PR Review and Respond

Often, your instructor will ask you to answer questions about a reading or to write about it. To respond thoughtfully, review the reading, look at your notes, and use your critical thinking skills. The Critical Thinking guide on page 36 will help you.

A Critical Reader at Work

Read the Deborah Tannen piece on page 36. The notes in the margins show how one student, Tom, applied the process of critical reading to an essay assigned in a writing course.

Critical Thinking and Reading

Summarize

- What is the author's purpose?
- What is the author's main point?
- What information does the author give to support the main point?

Analyze

- Is the support logical?
- Does it help you understand the main point, or are you left with questions and doubts?
- Does the author make assumptions about either the subject or the reader? Have you made assumptions as you read?

Synthesize

- How does this reading relate or connect to your experience or knowledge?
- How does it relate to what you have learned in other courses?
- What new ideas has reading the piece given you?

Evaluate

- Does the author seem biased? Are you reading with a biased point of view?
- Has the author achieved his or her purpose? Why or why not?

Deborah Tannen

It Begins at the Beginning

Deborah Tannen is a professor of linguistics at Georgetown University in Washington, D.C. Linguistics — the study of human language — reveals much about people and their culture. Part of Tannen's research in linguistics has focused on differences in how women and men use language and how those differences affect communication. The following excerpt, adapted from her book *You Just Don't Understand* (1990), describes how girls' and boys' language and communication patterns differ from an early age.

GUIDING QUESTION
How do boys and girls differ in their play and the language they use in their play?

Main point

1   Even if they grow up in the same neighborhood, on the same block, or in the same house, girls and boys grow up in different worlds of words. Others talk to them differently and expect and accept different ways of

talking from them. [Most important,] children learn how to talk, how to have conversations, not only from their parents, but from their peers. . . . Although they often play together, boys and girls spend most of their time playing in same-sex groups. And, although some of the activities they play at are similar, their favorite games are different, and their ways of using language in their games are separated by a world of difference.

2   Boys tend to play outside, in large groups that are hierarchically structured. Their groups have a leader who tells others what to do and how to do it, and resists doing what other boys propose. It is by giving orders and making them stick that high status is negotiated. Another way boys achieve status is to take center stage by telling jokes, and by side-tracking or challenging the stories and jokes of others. Boys' games have winners and losers and elaborate systems of rules, and the players frequently boast their skill and argue about who is best at what.

3   Girls, on the other hand, play in small groups or in pairs; the center of a girl's social life is a best friend. . . . In their most frequent games, such as jump rope and hopscotch, everyone gets a turn. Many of their activities (such as playing house) do not have winners or losers. Though some girls are certainly more skilled than others, girls are expected not to boast about it, or show that they think they are better than the others. Girls don't give orders; they express their preferences as suggestions, and suggestions are likely to be accepted. Anything else is put down as bossy. They don't grab center stage—they don't want it—so they don't challenge each other directly. And much of the time, they simply sit together and talk. Girls are not accustomed to jockeying for status in an obvious way; they are more concerned that they be liked.

She will have to prove this point.

Signals important purpose

What about computers?

Examples (boys' play)

! But don't boys & girls play together—at least sometimes?

More examples (girls' play)

Does Tannen think these differences affect how adult men and women work together?

Reading Visual Images

Images play a huge role in our lives today, and it is important to think critically about images just as you would about what you read or hear. Whether the image is a Web site, a photograph or illustration, a graphic, or an advertisement, you need to be able to "read" it. You can apply the same critical reading skills of summary, analysis, synthesis, and evaluation to read a visual. Look carefully at (focus on) the advertisement for running shoes on page 38. Then, consider how to read a visual using the critical thinking skills you have learned.

Summarize

CRITICAL
THINKING
■ **Summarize**
■ Analyze
■ Synthesize
■ Evaluate

To summarize a visual image, ask yourself what the big picture is: What is going on? What is important (the main point) and the main impression? What is the purpose? How is it achieved (the support)? To answer those questions, consider some strategies used in visuals.

Dominant Elements

In English and many other languages, people read printed material from left to right and top to bottom, and visuals are designed to also use this pattern. Think of a **Z pattern** where a viewer's eye goes first to the top left (the start of the Z) and ends with the bottom right (the end of the Z). Artists, illustrators, and advertisers most often use this pattern of setting up an image, with the most important object in the top left area and the second most important object in the bottom right area. Often, the main point of an image or advertisement can be determined by looking at those two places.

Figures and Objects

The person who creates an image has a purpose (main point) and uses visual details to achieve (or support) that purpose. In a photograph or painting, details about the figures and objects help create the impression the artist wants to convey. Look closely at the images and ask yourself: Are the figures from a certain period in history? What kind of clothes are they wearing? What are the expressions on their faces? How would I describe their attitude? What does the body language suggest? What important details about the figures does the creator of the image want me to focus on?

· ·

PRACTICE 4   **Summarizing a Visual Image**

Focus on the advertisement on page 38 and answer the following questions.

1. What is the big picture? What is going on? _Answers will vary but should indicate that the big picture is of a man running through water and away from stress and frustration._

2. What is in the top left area of the advertisement? _The words "stress" and "frustration."_

3. What is in the bottom right part of the advertisement? _The sentence "running cleanses the mind and body" and the name "Asics."_

4.   What is the purpose of the advertisement? *To sell Asics running shoes*

5.   What details do you notice about the man in the ad? Include as many as you can. *Answers will vary: young, muscular, eyes closed, dressed in running clothes, looks calm, sideburns, dark skin.*

6.   What separates the two parts of the man? What does it suggest? *Stream of water, cleansing, refreshing, health, calm.*

7.   What details do you notice about the words on the left? What impression do they create? *Negative, smudged black speckles. Chaos, lack of control, anxiety, stress.*

8.   What are the words on the right? How do they look different from the ones on the left? *"Sound mind sound body." Clear, different type, all in a line, under control.*

TEACHING TIP Go over the practice answers in class. Prompt students to notice the detaails in the analysis questions.

CRITICAL THINKING

■ **Summarize**
■ **Analyze**
■ Synthesize
■ Evaluate

Analyze

To analyze a visual image, focus on the parts of it (figures, objects, type) and ask yourself how they contribute to the message or main impression. Consider the background, and use of light and dark, as well as the arrangement of elements, and their colors, contrast, textures, and sizes. As you look closely at the details, ask yourself what assumptions are being made about the beliefs of the person or group who created the image.

PRACTICE 5   Analyzing a Visual Image

Focus on the advertisement on page 38 and answer the following questions. Be as detailed as possible in your answers.

1.   What color is the background? What impression do the different colors suggest? *Gray on left, white on right; darkness and light.*

2.   Why are the words on the left blurred and crooked? *To create a sense of confusion and lack of balance.*

3. Why do the words on the right give a different impression?
They are in a straight line and all the same type, creating a sense of
order and balance.

4. How are the words on the bottom right the same as or different
from the words higher on the page? *They are smaller, but more like the*
words on the right, and they are on the right.

5. Both of the runner's arms lead your eye to type. Why? *The purpose*
of the ad is expressed in the words.

6. Does the creator of this image make any assumptions about the
subject or the viewers? As you analyze the image, are you making
assumptions about the subject, image, or any of the details?
Answers will vary.

Synthesize

To synthesize a visual image, ask yourself what it means, what the message
is, considering your summary and analysis. Link it to what else you know
from experience and observation.

CRITICAL
THINKING
■ Summarize
■ Analyze
■ Synthesize
■ Evaluate

PRACTICE 6   Synthesizing a Visual Image

Focus on the advertisement on page 38 and answer the following questions.

1. What mood does the image create? *Positive, healthy, calm.*

2. What beliefs does it express? *Physical health is related to mental health,*
and being athletic and fit is good.

3. What assumptions does it make about viewers? *Everyone wants to be*
fit, calm, and stress-free.

4. What is the message of the advertisement? *Answers will vary. Wearing*
Asics gets rid of stress and helps your body and mind.

5. How does this message relate to what you already know or have
heard or experienced? *Answers will vary.*

CRITICAL
THINKING
■ Summarize
■ Analyze
■ Synthesize
■ Evaluate

Evaluate

To evaluate an image, ask yourself how effective it is in achieving its purpose and conveying its main point or message. What do you think of the image, using your summary, analysis, and synthesis skills? Consider any biases or assumptions that may be working in the image.

You can read any visual image using the questions and tools you have just practiced: paintings, photographs, illustrations, Web sites, CD covers, and advertisements. As you read and write about visual images, use the following Critical Thinking box to help you.

Critical Thinking and Visual Images

Summarize

- What is the purpose of the person who created the image?
- What is the big picture? What is going on?
- What elements are in dominant positions (the Z pattern)?
- If there are figures, what are they doing? What details tell you something about them?

Analyze

- How are the figures and objects arranged in relation to each other and to the whole image?
- What do you notice about the use of color, texture, light, and type?
- What assumptions does the creator of the image make about the viewers' beliefs or attitudes?

Synthesize

- What is the mood or overall impression the image creates?
- What is the intended message of the image?
- How does the image relate to what you know or have experienced?

Evaluate

- Has the artist/creator achieved his or her purpose?
- How effectively does the image convey its message to you?
- Does the image indicate any bias in the creator's point of view? How?

PRACTICE 7   Evaluating a Visual Image

Focus on the Asics advertisement on page 38 and answer the following questions.

1. What do you think about the advertisement? *Answers will vary.*

_____

2. Does the creator of the advertisement seem to have any biases? Why or why not? *The purpose of the ad is to sell a product, so the creator favors that product over others. He or she may also assume that everyone knows that running is good for the body and mind. However, running is not good for some people.*

3. Is the image a good visual? Why? *Yes, because it is effectively arranged, it gets a viewer's attention, and its parts all contribute to the overall message.*

4. Is the advertisement effective, given its purpose? *Yes, it links a positive image to a particular product.*

Reading Real-World Documents

Applying critical reading skills to real-world documents may be even more important than applying them to college reading. Careless reading in your everyday life can cause minor problems such as a ruined recipe, but also more serious consequences such as getting yourself into major debt. The following are just some of the documents you need to read critically: loan applications, car or apartment leases, credit card applications and statements, job applications, bank forms, any legal forms, employment contracts, phone contracts, and so on. For example, if you do not read your phone contract and bill carefully, you might end up like the person who got a $5,000 phone bill for downloading material using his phone. He thought the download time was free, but it was not.

PRACTICE 8   Reading a Real-World Document

Read the credit card statement and the student's annotations on page 44. What did she notice as she read her statement carefully? What questions does she have? *A duplicate charge, an overcharge, a late charge. What happens if she pays the minimum? What are the details of the late and finance charges?*

AnyBank Card

Statement
Nov. 10–Dec. 13, 2011

SEND PAYMENTS TO:
Box 54321
Anycity

NAME: Josephine Student   **ACCOUNT #:** 54-32-1

Payment Information

New Balance:	$436.97
Minimum Payment Due:	$20.00
Payment Due Date:	1/3/12

Wow! This is a lot lower than my balance. But maybe I'll pay interest this way?

Late Payment Warning: If we do not receive your minimum payment by the date listed above, you may have to pay a late fee of $35.00.

Minimum Payment Warning: If you make only the minimum payment each period, you will pay more interest and it will take you longer to pay off your balance. For example:

If you make no additional charges using this card and each month you pay. . .	You will pay off the balance shown on this statement in about. . .	And you will end up paying an estimated total of. . .
Only the minimum payment	2 years	$519.00
$75	7 months	$458.00 (Savings = $61.00)

So I save money by paying more each month—sounds good to me.

Activity Since Last Statement

Trans	Posted	Description	Amount
11/18		Payment – THANK YOU	−152.43
11/11	11/11	Campus Cafe	12.14
11/20	11/20	Bradley's Hardware	8.00
11/20	11/20	Bradley's Hardware	8.00
11/24	11/24	SuperFoods	320.59
12/11	12/11	Howard's Department Store	53.24

Two charges for the curtain rod I bought? Must be a mistake!

No way! Hope I kept my receipt. Call bank and report error.

Cash Advances: $0.00   **Total Standard Purchases: $401.97**

Account Summary

Previous Balance	$152.43	Credit Limit	$2,000.00
Payments/Credits	$152.43	Available Credit	$1563.03
Purchases	$401.97		
Fees Charged	$35.00 (late fee*)		
Interest Charged	$0.00		
New Balance	**$436.97**		

Owe a late charge for not paying by due date?

Interest Charge Calculation

Your Annual Percentage Rate (APR) is the annual interest rate on your account.

Balance Type	APR	Balance Subject to Interest Rate	Interest
Purchases	15.99%	0.00	$0.00
Cash Advances	21.99%	0.00	$0.00

*See the reverse of this statement for an explanation of how finance charges and late charges are calculated.

I read the back and I still don't understand these charges. Better ask customer service.

Questions? Call Customer Service at 1-800-555-4321

As you read and write in college, always remember the essential Critical Thinking skills: summarize, analyze, synthesize, evaluate. Refer to the questions on page 21 and make them your own. Use these questions as you read other selections, both in this book and in other courses, and in your everyday life as well.

PRACTICE 9   Reading Real-World Documents

Read critically any document such as the ones listed below and highlight the parts of the document that contain important information that could easily be overlooked without critical reading. Note what you think makes this information easy to miss. Then, share what you have found with the rest of the class.

- Credit card applications and statements
- Job applications and reviews
- Health insurance statements and forms
- Loan and mortgage applications
- Apartment leases
- Bank statements
- Phone contracts and statements
- Tax forms
- Legal forms and documents

WRITING ASSIGNMENTS

1. Find two photographs or advertisements that have captions and bring the images to class with the caption or advertising text removed or blocked out. Exchange images with another student, and, using the Critical Thinking and Visual Images box (p. 42), write captions or advertising text for the images. Compare your captions with the actual ones.

2. Bring in one or two images to show members of the small group you will be working with. The group should choose one image and then discuss it, applying the critical thinking skills you have learned (summarize, analyze, synthesize, evaluate). As you discuss the image, take notes. Then, ask questions about any of the notes before writing a paragraph about the image for each of the four critical thinking skills.

3. Find an article in a newspaper or magazine that has one or two illustrations. Write a paragraph in which you apply your critical thinking skills to the reading and discuss how the image is used as support or illustration.

TEACHING TIP Instead of having students do Assignment 1, bring in a collection of captionless images and break students into small groups to write captions.

NOTE You can find photos, advertisements, paintings, or other images online using any search engine.

TEACHING TIP Ask the students to present their analysis orally. All group members should stand at the front of class (with the image) to help with the presentation. Other class members should ask questions about the critical analysis.

4.   Analyze the following image, applying the questions in the Critical Thinking and Visual Images box (p. 42). Then, compare your interpretation of the photo with those written by other students.

reflect   Read your answer to the "write" prompt on page 27, and revise it to include what you have learned about reading critically.

Writing Basics

Audience, Purpose, and Process

Most college courses require writing. So do most jobs, which may surprise you. Good communication skills, including good writing, will help you achieve success in life.

Four elements are key to good writing. Keep them in mind throughout the writing process.

IDEA JOURNAL
Think of something you do well and how you got to be good at it.

Four Basics of Good Writing

1 It considers the needs and knowledge of the audience.

2 It fulfills the writer's purpose.

3 It includes a clear, definite point.

4 It provides support that explains or proves the main point.

This chapter discusses audience and purpose first because they are essential to effective writing. Purpose determines what a writer's main point is, and audience determines how the writer makes that point.

The chapter shows you how to structure your writing to meet the four basics of good writing, outlines the steps of the writing process, and asks you to apply the critical thinking skills you have learned. It also explains the criteria your instructor may use to grade your writing.

For more on making a point, see Chapter 6. For more on supporting a point, see Chapter 7.

Understand Audience and Purpose

Audience

DISCUSSION You might want to have a class discussion about whether text-messaging shorthand has affected students' college writing. This is also a good opportunity to note why different Englishes are used for different contexts and why learning "academic, formal English" is important for certain contexts.

Your **audience** is the person or people who will read what you write. Whenever you write, always have at least one real person in mind as a reader. Think about what that person already knows and what he or she will need to know to understand your main idea. In most cases, assume that readers will know only what you write about your topic and main point.

Your writing may be very different for two different audiences. Read the following two examples, which describe the same situation but are written for different audiences. Notice both the tone and the content of each paragraph.

> **SITUATION:** Maggie writes a description of her first class at college for two different audiences: (A) her writing instructor and (B) her best friend.

A.

DISCUSSION For an excellent article about how Facebook has influenced students' sense of audience, read "The Facebook Mirror" by Lisa Lebduska (www.insidehighered.com/views/2011/06/10/essay_on_the_negative_impact_of_facebook_on_student_writing) and discuss with your students.

My first class in college was Math 098, and I was terrified as I walked in. I had not been in school for nine years, and math had always been my worst subject. I was scared about college in general, and now math had to be my first class! I chose a desk off to the left side by the windows, near the back. Other students were coming in, but no one sat near me. I took the book and some paper and a pencil out of my backpack, arranging them neatly on the desk. Then I looked around: Everyone looked younger and more confident than I was. My heart sank, and I stared out the window, wondering why I was there. A few minutes later, the professor, a youngish woman, walked in, smiling, put her book on her desk, and asked, "So, how many of you are a little nervous about this class?"

B.

Math class this morning. What am I doing? I'm 2 old 2 dumb u no? Am I nuts? Help!
xo M

....

PRACTICE 1   Understanding Audience

Answer the following questions about Maggie's two accounts of her first class in college.

1. What are two ways the accounts differ from each other? *Answers will vary, but A is more formal, more detailed.*

2. How do her two audiences affect what Maggie writes (the content) and how she writes (the tone)? _Maggie writes with full sentences and lots of detail for her instructor, and her tone is serious. For her friend, she is informal and does not say much. Her tone is lighter, and she asks for help._

3. How do you think the instructor and the friend would have reacted if the instructor received account B and the friend account A? _Answers will vary._

TEACHING TIP
Bring in or have students find a letter to the editor from a newspaper or magazine. As a class, discuss the letter writer's original audience, and then ask how the letter might have to be changed for various other audiences. Choose one of these, and have students form small groups to revise the letter with this audience in mind.

As you think about your audience, consider what the person knows about you and what type of content and tone the person expects. Think about the person's point of view. For example, how might Maggie's writing to her friend (B) be different if she knew that her friend thought that going to college was a bad idea?

Purpose

The **purpose** of a piece of writing is the reason for writing it. In college, your purpose for writing often will be to show something; to summarize, analyze, synthesize, or evaluate something; or to make a convincing argument. In college writing, you want to demonstrate that you understand the content of the course.

PRACTICE 2   Understanding Purpose

Reread Maggie's two accounts of her first day of class and answer the following questions. _Answers will vary but should be similar to those supplied._

1. What is Maggie's purpose in writing for her instructor? _To demonstrate her writing skills by describing her first college class_

2. What is her purpose in writing to her friend? _To check in and share her impressions_

Understanding your purpose for writing is key to writing successfully. In college, to understand your purpose, be sure to read assignments and exam questions critically, highlighting words that tell you what your

TEACHING TIP
Using your syllabus, discuss with the class the purpose of some of the assignments.

instructor wants to see in your writing. If you do not understand, ask your instructor or a classmate for help. Success in college (and in other areas of life) requires you to keep your mind active, to use the critical thinking and reading skills covered in Chapters 2 and 3 of this book, and to refer often to the Critical Thinking (p. 21) and Critical Reading Process (p. 28) boxes.

Understand Paragraph and Essay Forms

Throughout college and beyond, you will write paragraphs and essays. Each of these has a basic structure.

Paragraph Structure

A **paragraph** is a group of sentences that work together to make a point. A good paragraph has three necessary parts — the topic sentence, the body, and the concluding sentence. Each part serves a specific purpose.

PARAGRAPH PART	PURPOSE OF THE PARAGRAPH PART
1. The **topic sentence**	states the **main point.** The topic sentence is often either the first or last sentence of a paragraph.
2. The **body**	supports (shows, explains, or proves) the main point. It usually contains three to six **support sentences,** which present facts and details that develop the main point.
3. The **concluding sentence**	reminds readers of the main point and often makes an observation.

Read the paragraph that follows. The parts are labeled.

Topic sentence —

Body made up of support sentences —

Some ways to do good for our world do not require much time, effort, or money. My favorite way is to use click-and-give Web sites, where just going to the site triggers donations to it from another source (not you). Every night before I go to bed, I go to one or more of these sites. The fastest site that I click on every night is the *Animal Rescue Site* (**www.theanimalrescuesite.com**). Each click gives food to rescued animals. Another of my favorite Web sites is *Free Rice* (**www.freerice.com**)

where I play vocabulary or grammar games. With each correct answer, grains of rice are donated to hungry people. One site with lots of choices of click-and-give options is the *NonProfits* (**www.thenonprofits.com**). It lists hundreds of causes and sites, grouped under "Hunger and Poverty," "Health, Education, Misc.," and "Environment and Animals." Because I work, have a family, and take two classes, I do not have much extra time or money. Going to these Web sites allows me to feel as if I am contributing and making a small difference, and that feels good.

Concluding sentence

Essay Structure

Essays vary in length. A short essay may consist of four or five paragraphs, totaling three hundred to six hundred words. A long essay is six paragraphs or more, depending on what the essay needs to accomplish—persuading someone to do something, using research to make a point, explaining a complex concept, or explaining an idea or experience.

An essay has three necessary parts—an introduction, a body, and a conclusion.

TEACHING TIP
Have students interview a second- or third-year student in their major to find out the kind of writing that person does for his or her classes.

ESSAY PART	PURPOSE OF THE ESSAY PART
1. The **introduction**	states the **main point,** or **thesis,** generally in a single strong statement. The introduction may be a single paragraph or multiple paragraphs.
2. The **body**	supports (shows, explains, or proves) the main point. The body of an essay generally has at least three **support paragraphs.** Each support paragraph begins with a **topic sentence** that supports the thesis statement and continues with facts and details that develop the main point.
3. The **conclusion**	reminds readers of the main point. It may summarize and reinforce the support in the body paragraphs, or it may make an observation based on that support. Whether it is a single paragraph or more, the conclusion should relate back to the main point of the essay.

The parts of an essay correspond to the parts of a paragraph. The **thesis** of an essay is like the **topic sentence** of a paragraph. The **support paragraphs** in the body of an essay are like the **support sentences** of a paragraph. And the **conclusion** of an essay is like the **concluding sentence** of a paragraph.

RELATIONSHIP BETWEEN PARAGRAPHS AND ESSAYS

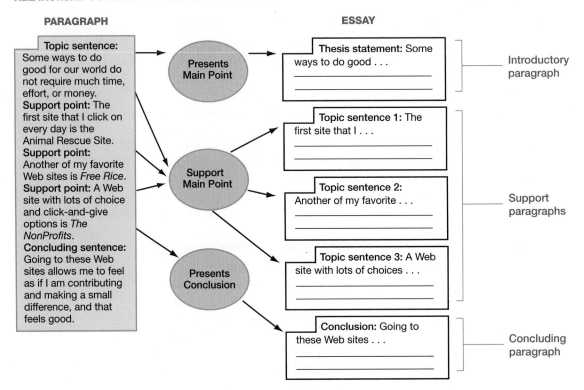

Read the following essay, in which the parts are underlined and labeled. It is about the same topic as the paragraph on pages 50–51, but because it is an essay, it presents more details.

Thesis statement ————— Introductory paragraph —————

Some ways to do good for our world do not require much time, effort, or money. My favorite way is to use click-and-give Web sites, where just going to the site triggers donations to it from another source (not you). Anyone can help out in any cause they are interested in by just one quick click. Every night before I go to bed, I go to one or more of the sites. I have particular favorites, but there are hundreds to choose from.

The first site that I click on every day is the *Animal Rescue Site* (**www.theanimalrescuesite.com**). Each click gives food to rescued animals. The Web site provides information about the sponsors of the site and where the donations go. It also has information about the site's projects and the animals who are rescued, a photo contest, and fun online games that you can play to trigger more donations. My favorite is Bubble Burst. People can become involved in "challenges." Most nights I have time only to click to give, which is why I go to this site every single night.

> Support paragraph 1

Another of my favorite Web sites is *Free Rice* (**www.freerice.com**) where I play vocabulary or grammar games. With each correct answer, grains of rice are donated to hungry people. The games are offered at increasingly difficult levels, and for each correct answer, you are told how many grains of rice you have given. A cool wooden bowl fills up with the grains as you play. When I go to this Web site, I feel as if I am doing good, having fun, and learning useful words.

> Support paragraph 2
>
> Body

One site with lots of click-and-give options is the *NonProfits* (**www.thenonprofits.com**). It lists hundreds of causes and sites, grouped under "Hunger and Poverty," "Health, Education, Misc.," and "Environment and Animals." Under "Hunger and Poverty," I go to the site named "One Click One Meal." This site says that one person dies every three seconds of starvation. A quick click will fund "One More Meal," with a donation to the World Food Programme. You can click on "WorldFoodProgramme" and read about the program, about nutrition, and about other related information. Twenty other sites help stop hunger and poverty, and many others are available in categories such as health, education, environment, and animals. Exploring the many choices, I find that each one I click on gives me so much information as well as the opportunity to help others.

> Support paragraph 3

Because I work, have a family, and take two classes, I do not have much extra time or money. Still, I know there are many problems in the world, and I would like to help in some way. Going to these Web sites allows me to feel as if I am contributing and making a small difference, and that feels good. So try it: Click and give.

> Concluding paragraph
>
> Concluding sentence

Understand the Writing Process

TEACHING TIP
Ask students to de-
scribe a process
related to their col-
lege experiences,
such as applying for
admission or financial
aid, registering for
classes, or purchas-
ing textbooks.

The **writing process** consists of four basic stages—generating ideas, planning and drafting, revising, and editing.

Whenever you are first learning to do something—playing a sport, driving a car, riding a bicycle—the steps seem complicated. However, after you practice them, the individual steps seem to blend together, and you just do them. The same thing will happen as you practice the steps in the writing process.

The flowchart on this page and the next shows the four basic stages of the writing process and the steps within each stage. The first is generating ideas and making connections among ideas. What is an idea? Ideas are what

---

The Writing Process

Generate Ideas

CONSIDER: What is my purpose in writing? Given this purpose, what interests me? What connections can I make among ideas? Who will read what I am writing? What do they need to know?

- Find and explore your topic (Chapter 5).
- Make your point (Chapter 6).
- Support your point (Chapter 7).

Plan and Draft

CONSIDER: How can I organize and present my ideas effectively for my readers?

- Arrange your ideas, and make an outline (Chapter 8).
- Write a draft, including an introduction that will interest your readers, a strong conclusion, and a title (Chapter 8).

Revise

CONSIDER: How can I make my draft clearer or more convincing to my readers?

- Look for ideas that do not fit (Chapter 9).
- Look for ideas that could use more detailed support (Chapter 9).
- Connect ideas with transitional words and sentences (Chapter 9).

Edit

CONSIDER: What errors could confuse my readers and weaken my point?

- Find and correct errors in grammar (Chapters 22–33).
- Look for errors in word use (Chapters 34–35) and punctuation and capitalization (Chapters 36–40).

---

is in and on your mind—your thoughts about matters big and small, important and unimportant; about yourself, others; about whatever you see, hear, read, remember, think about, and wonder about. Everyone has ideas.

The remaining chapters in Part 1 cover the first three stages—generating ideas, planning and drafting, and revising. Editing is detailed later in the book. You will practice each stage, see how another student works through the stages, and write your own essay using the writing process.

Before moving on to those chapters, read the following section on understanding grading criteria and writing about readings.

PRACTICE 3 Exploring What an Idea Is

Write for two minutes on each of the following questions.

1. Memory: What do you remember?

2. Observation: What do you see? What have you seen?

3. Wondering: What do you wonder about?

4. Reaction: What makes you happy? Mad? Feel like laughing? Feel safe? Anxious?

TEACHING TIP
Show students the short video on ideas at www.youtube.com/watch?v=8s7CPgRD4mA and then ask them what they think an idea is.

Understand Grading Criteria

Many instructors use a **rubric,** which is a list of the categories on which your writing is graded. If your instructor uses a rubric, it may be included in your course syllabus, and you should refer to it each time you write. A sample rubric follows on page 56, showing you some of the categories you may be graded on. Rubrics often differ from one instructor to another, so this example will give you an idea of some of the kinds of elements you might be graded on. The importance of each element in determining the final grade will also vary by instructor. The elements listed in the rubric will be covered in Chapters 5 through 9.

TEACHING TIP If you have not used a rubric before, you might want to use this one. For more on rubrics and student learning outcomes, see *Practical Suggestions for Teaching Real Essays.*

Sample Essay Rubric

ELEMENT	GRADING CRITERIA
Relevance or appropriateness	• Did the student follow the directions in writing the essay? • Are the topic, length, and so on appropriate?
Introduction	• Does the introduction give the reader a preview of the subject? • Does it include a clear and definite thesis?
Thesis	• Does the thesis clearly state a main point and use a complete sentence?
Support	• Is there enough support for the thesis statement? • Is the support presented in paragraph form with topic sentences that relate to the thesis statement?
Organization	• Is the structure logical? • Are transitions (both transitional words and transitional sentences) used to help move the reader from one idea to the next?
Conclusion	• Does the conclusion remind the reader of the main point? • Does it make an observation based on the information the writer has presented in the essay?
Coherence	• Does the essay stay on topic throughout?
Grammar	• Is the essay free of grammatical errors, especially the four most serious errors? • Are all words correctly spelled? • Are all punctuation and mechanics correct?
Timeliness	• Was the essay submitted on time?
Other:	

Sample Student Essays

The following examples and analyses of each example will help you understand how rubrics may be used to evaluate student essays. For a key to the
correction symbols used, see the chart at the back of this book.

> **TOPIC:** As we mature, our hobbies, activities, and interests are likely to
> change. In an essay of no more than five hundred words, describe how
> your interests have changed as you have gotten older.

STUDENT ESSAY 1

I had many interests over the years. I use to play T-ball but I moved on (tense)
to playing real Baseball. I played baseball for more than ten years finaly I (lc) (sp)
became a pitcher for my High School varsity squad. The one interest that (lc) (fs)
I can think of that I use to have that I don't do anymore is riding bicycles. (tense) (awk)
My friends and I cruised all over our neighborhood on our bicycles (diction)
looking for trouble to get into all the time and once even running from (con t) (unity)
the cops, who caught my friend Jimmy, the leader of our so called gang. (-)
When I got in high school, though I got another interest that took all my (diction) (,)
time and money, my car was my new love. I got it when I was 17, and I put (cs)
everything I had into it. I loved it almost as much as my girlfriend Kate. As (coord)
you can see, by my senior year, my main interests were playing baseball for
my school team and taking care of my sweet car. (diction)

Student essay 1 likely will not pass, for the following reasons.

- It is a single paragraph. The assignment called for an essay.
- There is a thesis (double-underlined above), but it is too general. A
  more compelling thesis would explain how (and perhaps why) the
  writer's interests changed.
- There is no real conclusion. The paragraph simply stops.
- The writer gives examples of interests but few supporting details.

- It does not have a clear pattern of organization, and the writer strays from the point occasionally (see "unity" on p. 57).

- The sentence structure is unvaried and contains few transitions. The paragraph has a number of grammar and spelling errors (marked on p. 57), and the language (or *diction*) is too informal for an essay.

STUDENT ESSAY 2

Everybody is interested in some kind of activity, whether playing piano or skiing. People's interests change sometimes over the years as (ref) (,) they change too. This trend is certainly true for me. I have had many interests over the years, and they have certainly changed.

As a child, I played T-ball, and eventually moved on to playing real baseball. I played baseball for more than ten years; finally, I became a (lc) (sub) pitcher for my High School varsity squad, and I played during my junior and senior years. I am looking forward to pitching in the college ranks. (trans) The one favorite interest I used to have that I don't anymore is riding (diction) bicycles. My friends and I cruised all over our neighborhood on our (diction) (,) (unity) bicycles looking for trouble to get into all the time and once even running from the cops, who caught my friend Jimmy, who was the leader of our (−) (ref) so called gang. I eventually outgrew this interest, as it was replaced by my (,) interest in a new more exciting vehicle.

When I got in high school, though I got another interest that took all (cs) (tense?) my time and money, my car was my new love. It is a Nissan 300 ZX, and (combine) (diction) it is black with a black interior. It had 16" rims and a sweet body kit. I got (coord) it when I was 17 and I put everything I had into it and I loved it almost as much as my girlfriend Kate.

As you can see, by my senior year, my main interests were playing baseball and taking care of the car. I once spent all my time riding my bicycle but I've outgrown that. The one interest that has lasted throughout my life is my love for baseball.

Student essay 2 is better for the following reasons.

- It has a clear thesis, introduction, body, and conclusion.
- The body paragraphs are generally cohesive, and the essay shows a chronological (time order) development.
- It has fewer errors in grammar and punctuation than the first essay has.

The following areas still need improvement.

- The thesis (double-underlined on p. 58) could be more specific. Again, a more compelling thesis would explain how (and perhaps why) the writer's interests changed.
- The writing still strays off-topic and still needs more transitions.
- The language is too informal in spots.
- Most of all, the essay needs more supporting details.

STUDENT ESSAY 3

While some of our personal interests last a lifetime, many fade or appear at different times during our lives. Some people play sports early on that they cannot play later in life, and some people adopt new interests and activities as adults that they would never have enjoyed when young. This trend is certainly true for me. I have had many interests over the years, and as I have gotten older, they have changed. As I have grown, I have lost my interest in riding bicycles, gained a love for cars, and undergone some changes in the way I play baseball, the one sport I have always enjoyed.

My earliest interest was one that I outgrew during junior high school: riding bicycles with my friends. As a child, my bicycle gave me my independence. My friends and I rode all over our neighborhood, looking →

for trouble and once even tangling with the police. As I got older, this activity faded, and a new one emerged, featuring a new type of vehicle.

Working on my car is my new interest. The car is a Nissan 300 ZX, and it is black with a black interior and sixteen-inch rims. I got it when I was seventeen, and, for the past two years, I have put all my time and money into it. My friends joked that I loved it almost as much as I loved my girlfriend Kate. It offers me the same sense of freedom as the bicycle, and I feel the same pride in having it.

My one love that has remained throughout my life is baseball, but even that interest has changed as I have matured. As a child, I played T-ball and loved it. I moved on to real baseball and played second base and shortstop in little league. After ten years of hard work, I became a pitcher for my high school varsity squad, and pitched in the starting rotation for both my junior and senior years. I look forward to pitching in college and beginning a new stage in my baseball "career."

My interests have changed as I have matured, but in many ways, they remain the same. My first interest, riding my bicycle, grew into my love for my car, reflecting my growing maturity. My one lifetime interest, baseball, has evolved as well. One day, I may play another position or even another sport. However, like my love for speed, my love for competition will always define my special interests.

Student essay 3 is clear, effective, and well supported. All the essential elements are present.

- The thesis is specific and clearly sets up the rest of the essay.
- The writer has described the interests in a clear chronological order, and he uses transitions effectively.
- Descriptions of the interests are detailed. They use more varied and exciting language and sentence structure than the previous essays.
- The writing stays on topic throughout and answers the essay question thoughtfully and thoroughly.

Writing about Readings

In college, you will do a lot of writing about what you have read: in papers, tests, exams, and reports. As you begin to write, always focus on your audience and purpose as you develop your main points and support paragraphs. Your instructors want to see how well you understand a concept, so they want full explanations of anything you say even though they may know all about it. When other students are your audience, they may not know the subject well, so they need plenty of detail, too. The past two chapters have given you tools to think and read critically. Use these same skills when you write about something you have read.

RESOURCES
For advice about using writing portfolios, including how to structure and evaluate them, see *Practical Suggestions for Teaching Real Essays,* Chapter 12.

Documenting Sources

When you write about readings, particularly when you are writing a synthesis or an evaluation, you may want to refer directly to sources other than the reading itself. For example, in the synthesis on page 23 the writer cites two sources within the text and also in a Works Cited list.

College writers must follow specific rules to document every work they have referred to or quoted from. The writer of the synthesis example uses the Modern Language Association's (MLA) documentation style, which is used in most English courses. Other courses may use other styles, such as that of the American Psychological Association (APA). The MLA style of documentation is presented in Chapter 21. Use that chapter to learn how to quote from another source and how to cite other sources both within and at the end of your paper.

WRITING ASSIGNMENTS

1. Reread Deborah Tannen's essay, "It Begins at the Beginning" on page 36. Summarize this for someone who has not read it.

2. Read an article in the college newspaper, the local paper, a magazine, or a blog. Write a paragraph or two analyzing the points that the author of the article makes.

3. Find a topic on the Web site **procon.org**, and read at least one pro and one con position on the issue. Then, write a synthesis of the positions, bringing in your own experience as well. Make a final observation about the issue.

4. Read a review of a movie or television show and write an evaluation of the review, considering how it presented the material and whether the reviewer showed biases or made assumptions about either the subject or the review's audience.

TEACHING TIP
Have students write about the whole robot series of images by Marrku Lahdesmaki (www.marrkuphoto .com).

5. Examine the photograph below. Write a brief analysis essay expressing what the image says or means to you. What impression does it create? Support the main point of your essay with details you observe in the image. (See the Critical Thinking and Visual Images box on p. 42.)

As you write in response to assignments, you may want to review the "Writing about Readings" checklist that follows.

CHECKLIST

Writing about Readings

FOCUS

☐ Carefully read the writing assignment.

ASK

☐ Does the assignment include any words that indicate the type of writing required (*summarize, analyze, describe, give examples of, compare,* and so on)?

☐ Is the writing supposed to be in response to the reading alone, or are you expected to bring in other sources and points of view?

☐ Are you supposed to quote from the reading to support your point?

☐ Does the assignment ask you to evaluate the reading?

WRITE

☐ Apply your critical reading skills to the reading, and write a response to the reading that fulfills the requirements of the writing assignment.

reflect Reread your response to the "write" prompt on page 47, and revise it based on what you have learned in this chapter about audience and purpose.

5

Finding and Exploring Your Topic

Choosing Something to Write About

Understand What a Good Topic Is

IDEA JOURNAL Read the "You Know This" box above, and write about a current topic of interest to you.

A **topic** is what, who, or where you are writing about. A **good topic** for an essay is one that interests you and that you can get involved in.

Any topic that you choose to write about should pass the following test.

QUESTIONS FOR FINDING A GOOD TOPIC

- Does this topic interest me?

- Can I find out more about it?

- Can I get involved with this topic? Is it relevant to my life in some way?

- Does it fit the assignment, focusing on a subject neither too broad nor too narrow to treat in the assigned length?

Choose one of the following broad topics or one of your own, and focus on one specific aspect of it that you think would make a good topic for a short essay.

My goals

Pet peeves

Personal responsibility

Taking risks

Relationships

Something I am good at

Something I am proud of

Something I am interested in or enjoy doing

Family roles

Reality TV

Popular music

Significant places

· ·

PRACTICE 1   Finding a Good Topic

Ask the Questions for Finding a Good Topic (p. 64) about the topic you have chosen. If you answer "no" to any of the questions, look for another topic, or modify the one you chose.

MY TOPIC: *Answers will vary.* _____

Keeping in mind the general topic you have chosen, read the rest of this chapter, and complete all of the practice activities. When you finish, you will have found a good topic to write about and explored ideas related to that topic.

· ·

Narrow Your Topic

To **narrow** a topic is to focus on the smaller parts of a general topic until you find a more limited topic or an angle that is interesting and specific. In real life, you narrow topics all the time: You talk with friends about a particular song rather than music, about a particular person rather than the human race, or about a class you are taking rather than about every class the college offers.

In college writing, you often need to do the same thing. A professor may give you a broad topic like "religion and culture," "cheating in our society," or "goals in life." These topics are too general to write about in a short essay, so you need to know how to narrow them.

Ask Yourself Questions

Shannon Grady was assigned the broad essay topic "religion and culture." What follows shows how she narrowed her topic. Shannon shares how she *thought* about the broad topic and the questions she asked to make it manageable.

First, I think about the words that are important. Here, that's <u>religion</u> and <u>culture</u>.

Then, I ask questions. (At first, the questions are all over the place, and I want to quit. But I tell myself I can't stop until I have something that might work, or else I'll be too frustrated to come back to it later.)

- <u>What religion—mine?</u> I don't go to church too often. But my grandmother's very religious. She came to this country from Ireland, and she always talks about her church back there. Plus, she goes to church here every single morning.
- <u>Whose culture—mine? This country's? Another country's? Now or in the past?</u> My grandmother loves to talk about her life in "the old country," and she has great stories.
- <u>What kind of culture—like art? Politics?</u> Well, Gran and all of her friends love storytelling, dancing, singing, and she's always playing Irish music. I never asked why everyone from Ireland seems to know how to sing, dance, play music, and tell great stories. But lots of the stories and songs are really sad—why?
- <u>Serious religion? Or things like Christmas music? Maybe both?</u> Talk with Gran. Ask her about the church in Ireland, and here.

Then, I review what I have so far. I've got two big topics to put together somehow:

- The Catholic church in Ireland (Gran's version)
- The Irish tradition of music, dance, storytelling, singing

The paper is supposed to be five pages long. How about:

- <u>My grandmother's religion?</u> No, this isn't really the topic.
- <u>The role of Catholicism in Ireland?</u> Too big.
- <u>Church and culture in small-town Ireland: One woman's story?</u> OK, try this as a start. I can talk to Gran about her town, her church, why the church was important, and how it relates to all the song, dance, music, storytelling. Maybe a separate paragraph for each?

Finally, I ask myself the questions for a good topic:

1. <u>Does the topic interest me?</u> Yes, I love my grandmother, and I can find out stuff I don't know about her!
2. <u>Can I find out more?</u> Yes.
3. <u>Can I get involved with this topic?</u> Yes. <u>Is it relevant to my life in some way?</u> Yes.
4. <u>Does it fit the assignment?</u> Yes, I think so—enough to say but narrowed topic.

Map Your Ideas

Use circles and lines to help visually break a general topic into more specific ones. Start in the center of a blank piece of paper, and write your topic. In the example below, the topic is "cheating." Circle your topic, and ask yourself some questions about it, such as "What do I know about it?" or "What's important about it?" Write your ideas around the topic, drawing lines from

For online mapping tools, see **www.bubbl.us** and **www.rev2.org/2007/06/04/9**.

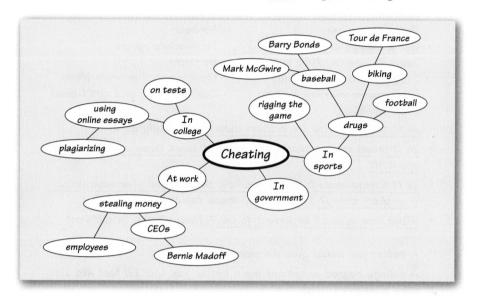

your topic to the ideas and then circling them. Keep adding ideas, connecting them with the lines and circles. This technique is called **mapping** or **clustering**. After mapping, look at each cluster of ideas, and consider using one of the narrower topics. In the example above, the student, Paul Desmots, started with the general topic of "cheating," but ended up writing about steroid use in sports and focused on recent examples in baseball.

List Narrower Topics

A student, Roberta Fair, was assigned a short essay on the general topic "personal goals." First, she listed specific personal goals.

PERSONAL GOALS
Get a better job
Get a college degree
Learn to use my time better
Stay patient with my kids
Don't argue with my mother

Stop smoking
No deadbeat guys
Be nicer
Clean my house more often
Don't buy things I don't need

Then, she asked herself some questions to help her choose one of the narrower topics on her list.

- Which of the narrowed topics is the most important to me? They're all important, but some of them aren't as important to me as others, so I'll cross those out.
  PERSONAL GOALS

Get a better job	~~No beer~~
Get a college degree	~~No deadbeat guys~~
Learn to use my time better	~~Be nicer~~
Stay patient with my kids	~~Clean my house more often~~
~~Don't argue with my mother~~	Don't buy things I don't need
Stop smoking	

- Is it the right size for a short essay? Not really sure.

- Is it broad enough that I can make at least three or four points about it? I think so.

- Is it narrow enough that I can "dig deeply" and give good details in a short essay? I think all of these topics are.

- Which one is most important to you? They all are, in different ways.

  A better job would give me more money.

  A college degree would get me a better job, and I'd feel like I'd done something important.

  To get a college degree, I have to learn to use my time better.

  Maybe I'd be more patient with my kids if I had a better job and more money.

  Stop smoking. Right now I'm not ready.

  If I had a degree, a better job, and more money, I could buy things I want and not feel guilty.

Looking them all over again, though, I think the college degree would get me other things that are important—like a better job, more money, maybe more patience with my kids. I'm going to go with that.

Roberta then chose "Getting a college degree" as her narrowed topic.

TOPIC	NARROWED TOPIC
A personal goal	Getting a college degree

. . . .

PRACTICE 2   Narrowing a Topic

Use one of the three methods on pages 65–68 to narrow your topic. Then, write your narrowed topic below.

NARROWED TOPIC: *Answers will vary.* _____

. . . .

Explore Your Topic

Explore a topic to get ideas you can use in your writing. **Prewriting techniques** are ways to come up with ideas at any point during the writing process—to find a topic, to get ideas for what you want to say about the topic, and to support your ideas.

QUESTIONS FOR EXPLORING A TOPIC

- What interests me about this topic?
- Why do I care about it?
- What do I know or want to know?
- What do I want to say?

Use prewriting techniques to find the answers.

Use Prewriting Techniques

You can explore your narrowed topic using one or more of several prewriting techniques, three of which (questioning, clustering, and listing) you have seen used on pages 65–68. Writers do not necessarily use all of these. Instead, they choose the techniques that work best for them after considering their assignment, their purpose for writing, and their audience.

- Freewrite
- List and brainstorm
- Ask a reporter's questions
- Discuss
- Cluster and map
- Use the Internet
- Keep a journal

While exploring ideas, just think; do not judge. You can decide later whether your ideas are good or not. At this point, your goal is to get as many ideas as possible. Write down all the possibilities.

The following sections detail techniques for exploring ideas and show how Roberta Fair used each one of them to get ideas about her topic, "Getting a college degree."

Freewrite

Freewriting is like having a conversation with yourself on paper. To freewrite, just start writing everything you can think of about your topic. Write nonstop for at least five minutes. Do not go back and cross anything out or worry about using correct grammar or spelling; just write.

> I don't know, I don't think about goals more than just handling every day—I don't have time. The kids, my job, laundry, food, school, it's a lot. So I just get by day by day but I know that won't get me or my kids anywhere. I really do wish I could get a better job that was more interesting and I wish I could make more money and get my kids better stuff and live in a better place and not be worried all the time about money and our apartment and all that. I really do need to get that degree cause I know we'd have a better chance then. I know I need to finish college.

List and Brainstorm

List all the ideas about your topic that come to your mind. Write as fast as you can for five minutes without stopping.

> So hard to find time to study
> Good in the long run
> Lots of advantages
> Better job
> Better place to live
> More money
> More opportunities
> A big achievement—no one in my family's ever gotten a degree
> But they don't give me support either

Ask a Reporter's Questions

Ask yourself questions to start getting ideas. The following reporter's questions—Who? What? Where? When? and How?—give you different angles on a narrowed topic, but you can also use other kinds of questions that come to you as you explore your narrowed topic.

Who? Me, a single mother and student

What? Getting a college degree

Where? Stetson Community College

When? Taking classes off and on now, want a degree in next couple of years

Why? Because I want more out of life for my kids and me

How? Working like a dog to finish school

Discuss

When you discuss ideas with someone else, you get more ideas and also feedback on them from the other person.

Team up with another person. If you both have writing assignments, first discuss one person's topic and then the other's. Ask questions about anything that seems unclear, and let the writer know what sounds interesting. Give thoughtful answers, and keep an open mind. It is a good idea to take notes when your partner comments on your ideas.

Roberta: I guess my personal goal is getting a college degree.

Maria: Why?

Roberta: Well, I think it would help me.

Maria: How?

Roberta: You know, I have a lousy job, no money, the kids, stuff like that.

Maria: Yeah, so how will a college degree help?

Roberta: I know I could get a better job that paid more, so I wouldn't have to work so much. I could spend more time with the kids, and we could live in a better place, you know.

Maria: So do it. What's the problem?

Roberta: Doing it. Time, money. But I know it's worth it, juggling everything for a while, till I get the degree.

Cluster and Map

You saw an example of clustering, also called mapping, on page 67. Here is Roberta's cluster.

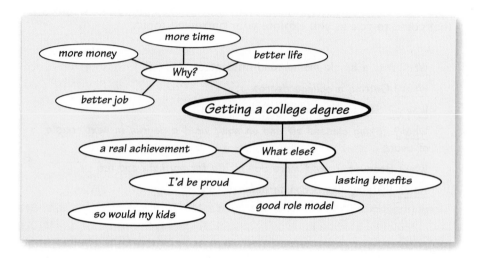

Use the Internet

Go to a search engine such as Google, and type in key words related to your topic, being as specific as possible. The search will probably yield a

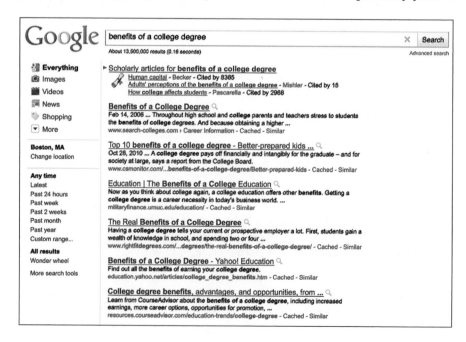

lot of results that can give you more ideas about your topic. For example, Roberta entered *benefits of a college degree* into Google and found several useful links.

Keep a Journal

Another good way to explore ideas and topics for writing is to keep a journal. Set aside a few minutes a day, or decide on some other regular schedule to write in your journal. Your journal will be a great source of ideas when you need to find something to write about.

You can use a journal in many ways:

- To record and explore your personal thoughts and feelings

- To comment on things that happen either in the neighborhood, at work, at your college, in the news, and so on

- To examine situations you do not understand (as you write, you may figure them out)

By the time Roberta had used all of the prewriting techniques, she had decided that her narrowed topic (getting a college degree) was a good one and had also generated some ideas to discuss in her essay.

ROBERTA'S JOURNAL ENTRY

> I've been taking courses at the college for a couple of years but not really knowing whether I'd ever finish or not. It's so hard, and I'm so tired all the time that I sometimes think it would be easier (and cheaper!) to stop or to go one semester and not another, but then it's so easy to get out of the habit. I need to decide whether getting a degree is worth all of the effort it will take, and I'm starting to think it is. I don't want to live like this forever. I want a better life.

PRACTICE 3   Prewriting

Choose *two* prewriting techniques, and use them to explore your narrowed topic. Keep your readers in mind as you explore your topic. Find ideas that will be effective for both your purpose and your readers' understanding.

TEACHING TIP
This is a good time to start talking with students about finding and bookmarking promising Web sites, evaluating Web sources, and avoiding plagiarism. For more on evaluating Web sources, see pages 347–50. For more on avoiding plagiarism, see pages 356–61 and bedfordstmartins .com/rewritingbasics.

TEACHING TIP
Give guidelines for what the physical journal should be: a notebook, loose-leaf paper, computer files, something of students' own choice, and so on.

TEACHING TIP
Some students will need to complete more than two prewriting activities to fully explore a topic.

Write Your Own Topic

At this point, you should have a narrowed topic (Practice 2) and some ideas about it (Practice 3). Use the checklist that follows to evaluate your topic and to understand the process of narrowing and exploring a general topic.

CHECKLIST

Finding a Good Topic

FOCUS

☐ Read the assignment carefully and consider your audience and purpose.

ASK

☐ Is the topic too big for a short essay, if that is the assignment?

☐ If it is too big, what are some more limited parts of the topic?

☐ Once I have a narrowed topic, does it pass the "Questions for Exploring a Topic" on page 69?

☐ Do I or my audience have any assumptions or biases relating to my topic that I should be aware of? If so, what are they?

☐ What can I say about my topic? What ideas do I have about my topic?

WRITE

☐ Use a prewriting technique to explore ideas about your narrowed topic.

---

reflect How can you find something to write about? Look back at your response to the "write" prompt on page 64 and explore as a possible topic one of the items you wrote about.

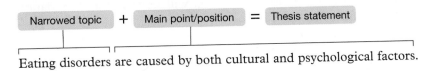
Making a Point

Writing Your Thesis Statement

Understand What a Good Thesis Statement Is

The **thesis statement** of an essay states the main point you want to get across about your topic. It is your position on whatever you are writing about.

Narrowed topic + Main point/position = Thesis statement

Eating disorders are caused by both cultural and psychological factors.

A strong thesis statement has several basic features.

BASICS OF A GOOD THESIS STATEMENT

- It focuses on a single main point or position about the topic.
- It is neither too broad nor too narrow.
- It is specific.
- It is something that you can show, explain, or prove.
- It is a forceful statement written in confident, firm language.

WEAK THESIS STATEMENT   I think college is good, and there are lots of them.

The weak statement does not follow the basics of a good thesis statement: It focuses on two points, not one; it is very broad; the word *good* is not specific; and the words *I think* are not forceful or confident.

GOOD THESIS STATEMENT	A college degree brings many potential benefits such as better jobs, more career choices, and higher salaries.

This statement has all the basics of a good thesis statement.

LANGUAGE NOTE: In some cultures, people avoid making direct points. It is considered impolite to be too direct and self-assertive. In the United States, however, writers are expected to make clear, direct points. Readers want to know early on what point the writer will make in the essay, the paragraph, or any nonfiction text.

A good thesis statement is essential to most good essays. Early in your writing process, you may develop a *draft thesis* (or *working thesis*), a first-try version of the sentence that will state your main point. You can revise it into a final thesis statement later in the writing process.

Practice Developing a Good Thesis Statement

The explanations and practices in this section are organized according to the basics of a good thesis statement (p. 75). This section will help you develop effective thesis statements that will serve as firm foundations for the essays you write.

Write a Thesis That Focuses on a Single Main Point

Your thesis should focus on only one main point. If you try to address more than one main point in an essay, you will probably not be able to give adequate support for all the points. Also, you risk splitting your focus.

THESIS STATEMENT WITH TWO MAIN POINTS

In the next decade, <u>many high schools will have a drastic shortage of teachers,</u> and <u>high school teachers should have to take competency tests.</u>

The two points are underlined. The writer would need to explain why there will be a shortage of teachers and also why teachers should take competency tests. These are both meaty points, and any writer would have trouble supporting them equally in a single essay.

REVISED

In the next decade, many schools will have a drastic shortage of high school teachers.

or

High school teachers should have to take competency tests.

THESIS STATEMENT WITH TWO MAIN POINTS

College students should be protected from taking on too much credit-card debt, and they should be allowed to stay on their parents' health insurance policies after graduation.

REVISED

New laws and educational programs are needed to protect college students from taking on too much credit-card debt.

or

College students should be allowed to stay on their parents' health insurance policies after graduation.

Although a good thesis statement focuses on a single main point, it may include more than one idea if these ideas directly relate to the main point and are closely related.

A good thesis may or may not include other information that the essay will include. If you know the points or examples that you will make to support your thesis, you can include them. For example, see how the following revised thesis statements include some points (shown in *italics*) that support the writer's thesis.

Internships offer excellent learning opportunities—*seeing how people dress and act in offices, finding out the kinds of jobs the business has, and meeting people who are good future connections for you.*

The job market for students is tight, but there are things you can do to help get a job in your field, such as *asking for an informational interview, finding a mentor, or getting an internship.*

Write a Thesis That Is Neither Too Broad Nor Too Narrow

Your thesis should fit the size of the essay assignment. A thesis that is too broad is impossible to support fully in a short essay: There is just too much to cover well. A thesis that is too narrow does not give you enough to write a whole essay on.

TOO BROAD   Family is an essential part of life.

[Both *family* and *life* are broad concepts, and the thesis would be impossible to explain in a short essay.]

REVISED   Time spent with my children is a welcome balance to time spent at work.

TOO BROAD   The Industrial Revolution was important in this country.

[The Industrial Revolution is too broad to cover in an essay.]

TEAMWORK
In small groups, have students identify the thesis statements in two or three of the readings at the back of the book, and then discuss how well those statements meet the criteria for good thesis statements.

REVISED   During the Industrial Revolution, women workers in the textile industry played an important role in Lowell, Massachusetts.

A thesis that is too narrow leaves the writer with little to show, explain, or prove. It can also make the reader think, "So what?"

TOO NARROW   My family members all have the same middle name.

[Once the writer says what the middle name is, there is not much more to say, *unless* there is an interesting family story explaining why everyone has it.]

REVISED   An interesting event from long ago explains why my family members all have the same middle name.

TOO NARROW   I tweeted this morning.

REVISED   Tweeting connects me to other people and their ideas.

Write a Thesis That Is Specific

A good thesis statement gives readers specific information so that they know exactly what the writer's main point is.

GENERAL   Writing is important for my job.

[Why is writing important for your job, and what kind of job do you have?]

SPECIFIC   Although my primary job, as a nurse, is to care for others, I have found that my ability to write clearly is essential.

[This thesis tells us that the job is nursing and suggests that the essay will discuss the types of writing a nurse does.]

One good way to be specific is to let your readers know what you will be discussing in your essay. In this way, your thesis prepares your reader for what is to come.

MORE SPECIFIC As a nurse, my ability to write clearly is essential in documents such as patient reports, status notes to nurses on other shifts, and e-mails to other hospital staff.

[This thesis tells the reader specific kinds of writing the essay will discuss.]

Write a Thesis That You Can Show, Explain, or Prove

If a thesis is so obvious that it does not need support or if it states a known fact, you will not be able to say much about it.

OBVIOUS Most teenagers drive.

Guns can kill people.

REVISED The high accident rates among new teen drivers could be reduced with better and more extended driver training.

Accidental handgun deaths could be prevented through three sensible measures.

FACT A growing number of American children are overweight.

Each year, more companies outsource jobs to foreign workers.

REVISED We must, as a nation, act to reduce obesity in our children.

As more companies export jobs to foreign countries, we will see numerous negative effects.

Write a Thesis That Is Forceful and Confident

A strong thesis statement should be forceful and definite. Avoid writing a thesis statement that begins, "In this essay I will show. . . ." Do not say you will make a point. Just make it.

WEAK In this essay, I will prove that high school dropouts have a difficult time in life.

FORCEFUL High school dropouts can expect to face surprising hardships in life.

Also, some words and phrases—such as "maybe" and "I think"—can indicate you lack confidence in your main point. Avoid them.

WEAK I think you have to be careful when buying a used car.

FORCEFUL Before you buy a used car, inform yourself about the basics so that you do not spend more than you need to.

Note that the revised thesis statements in this chapter take a clear stand on issues and express a particular point of view. Starting with a topic that you care about can help. For more advice on choosing a topic, see Chapter 5.

WEAK	Maybe it is time to evaluate our monthly spending.
FORCEFUL	Our monthly spending needs close scrutiny.

The practices that follow will help you write a good thesis statement. The first practice helps you develop a thesis statement from a narrowed topic. The rest focus on the basics of a good thesis statement (p. 75).

. . . .

PRACTICE 1   Developing a Thesis Statement from a Narrowed Topic

For each item, write a thesis statement from the narrowed topic. (Use a separate piece of paper for your answers if there is not enough room on the lines below.)

EXAMPLE

GENERAL TOPIC	NARROWED TOPIC	THESIS
Foreign languages	Learning a foreign language	Learning a foreign language has many benefits.

For practice identifying thesis statements, visit *Exercise Central* at bedfordstmartins .com/realessays. resources.

RESOURCES To gauge students' understanding of thesis statements and other writing and grammar issues, use the *Testing Tool Kit* CD available with this book.

GENERAL TOPIC	NARROWED TOPIC	THESIS
1. A memory	My first date	*Answers will vary.*
2. Music	My favorite kind of music	_____
3. Friendship	My best friend	_____
4. Owning a car	Costs of owning a car	_____
5. Reality TV	(A show that you watch)	_____

. . . .

PRACTICE 2   Writing Thesis Statements That Focus on a Single Main Point

Rewrite the following thesis statements so that they focus on just one of the points made. You can add information to make the statements more specific.

EXAMPLE: Juggling college and other responsibilities can be challenging, and rising college costs are putting higher education out of reach for many.

Juggling college and other responsibilities can be challenging.

1. Planning for college financial aid should begin long before a student's first year of college, and prospective students should also consider how attending college will affect their family life.

    Answers will vary.

2. My first job taught me the importance of cooperation, and I also learned how to manage my time effectively.

3. For several reasons, I will never own my own business, but I do have what it takes to be a top athlete.

4. Organizations can reduce absenteeism by telling workers about several measures to prevent colds and flu, and they can increase morale by including employees on committees that explore workplace issues.

5. Given recent violent incidents, Riverside Mall needs to increase security, and the mall should also do a better job of plowing its parking lots in the winter.

· ·

PRACTICE 3   Writing Thesis Statements That Are Neither Too Broad Nor Too Narrow

Read the following thesis statements, and decide whether they are too broad, too narrow, or the right size for a short essay. For statements that are too broad, write "B" in the space to the left; for statements that are too narrow, write "N"; and for statements that are the right size, write "OK."

EXAMPLE: __N__   My dog will be ten years old next month.

__B__   1. Hinduism is a fascinating religion.

__B__   2. I love food.

__OK__   3. Being a vegetarian offers a wide range of healthy food choices.

__B__   4. There are many vegetarians in this country.

__N__   5. Another gourmet coffee shop opened last week, the third one on a single block.

....

PRACTICE 4   Writing Thesis Statements That Are Specific

Rewrite each of the following thesis statements by adding at least two specific details.

> **EXAMPLE:** Electronic devices in high schools can be a huge problem.
>
> *Cell phones that ring during a high school class disrupt students'*
>
> *concentration and learning.*

1.   I have many useful skills.

Answers will vary.

2.   Studying with a partner can be helpful.

_____

3.   I have always had trouble writing.

_____

4.   Children have more allergies now than in the past.

_____

5.   After I received my first paycheck, I had many feelings.

_____

....

PRACTICE 5   Writing Thesis Statements That You Can Show, Explain, or Prove

Each of the following items is either obvious or a fact and therefore difficult to write about. Rewrite each sentence so that it would give you something to write in an essay.

> **EXAMPLE:** I have lived in this neighborhood for fourteen years. [Fact]
>
> *In the fourteen years I have lived in this town, I have learned a lot*
>
> *about small towns.*

1.   Many teenagers experiment with drugs.

Answers will vary.

2.   Every year my college fees go up.

_____

3.   I make $8.00 an hour.

_____

4.   I have just finished my first college course.

_____

5.   Public transportation makes it easier to get to work.

_____

. . . .

PRACTICE 6   **Writing Forceful Thesis Statements**

Rewrite the weak thesis statements that follow to make them more forceful.

> **EXAMPLE:** In my opinion, students who are involved with the community learn many important lessons.
>
> *Students who are involved with the community learn many important*
>
> *lessons.*

1.   I will explain some examples of history repeating itself.

Answers will vary.

2.   This college could have better parking facilities.

_____

3.   Given that I have improved my job performance and shown a lot of initiative, I am pretty sure I will get a raise this year.

_____

4.   It would be a good idea to warn young people about the possible dangers of prescription drug abuse.

_____

5.   In this paper, I will describe three reasons why going to college has been a challenge for me.

_____

....

PRACTICE 7   Revising Thesis Statements

In the spaces provided below, revise each of the possible thesis statements that you wrote in Practice 1, improving them according to the basics of a good thesis statement (p. 75). Again, think of a statement that you would be interested in writing about. You may want to add more information to your thesis statements to make them more specific and forceful, but short, punchy thesis statements also can be very powerful.

> **POSSIBLE THESIS:** When the sun is shining, people's moods improve.

> **REVISED THESIS:** Bright sunshine dramatically improves people's moods.

1.   *Answers will vary depending on the answers in Practice 1.* _____

2.   _____

3.   _____

4.   _____

5.   _____

....

Write Your Own Thesis Statement

A thesis statement does not have to come at the beginning or end of the first paragraph. Experienced writers may not get to the thesis for a few paragraphs, or they may imply their main point rather than state it in a single sentence. In most college writing, however, you will need to have a clearly identifiable thesis statement, and it should be either the first or last sentence of your first paragraph. Your instructor may have a preference for putting the thesis statement as the first or last sentence in the first paragraph; if not, you can choose. In the following two paragraphs, one has the thesis statement first, and one has it last.

THESIS FIRST

   Bright sunshine dramatically improves people's moods because of its effects on our brains. Most people know this from experience because they tend to feel better during the long, sunny days of summer. In the shorter, darker days of winter, people usually feel more tired and less energetic. Until quite recently, people assumed that this was a psychological reaction, often tied, at least in the United States, with childhood memories of the long, happy, carefree days of summer when schools were not in session. But recently we have learned that feeling better in summer is not just in our heads.

THESIS LAST

Do your moods vary during the different seasons? For many of us, the short, dark days of winter are difficult: We feel tired, and we lack energy. Most of us want to sleep more and eat hearty, hot meals. In the bright, sunny days of summer, though, we come alive. Until quite recently, people assumed that this was a psychological reaction, often tied, at least in the United States, with childhood memories of the long, happy, carefree days of summer when schools were not in session. But recently we have learned that feeling better in summer is not just in our heads. Bright sunshine dramatically improves people's moods because of its effects on our brains.

What will both essays go on to describe? *How*

sunshine affects the brain.

Remember, the thesis statement you write first is a *draft thesis*: You can modify it as often as you like while you write your essay.

Before selecting a writing assignment, read how student Takeesha Ellis developed a thesis statement from her narrowed topic. Before writing her thesis, Takeesha did some freewriting about it.

General topic   Popular Culture
Narrowed topic   Interest in Vampires

freewriting: Our teacher said popular culture is the ideas that become popular at a specific time and that we should write about something that's popular now and I thought of vampires. There are all kinds of things about vampires now, like <u>True Blood</u> and <u>Twilight</u> and books and comics and movies. I don't know why but vampires are cool now. Because they live forever and are superhuman and have control over everything? Also, vampire guys are hot. I know <u>Dracula</u> was an old movie but I wonder why vampires are all of a sudden everywhere. Why now? What does it say about us? Because they're not like us, or are they? Is it about love, power, control, never having to die or get old?

Next, Takeesha decided on a point she might make about why we like vampires.

Point: Vampires are popular because they have things everyone wants but normal humans can't have.

She then wrote a draft thesis statement.

Draft thesis statement: We love vampires because they represent things we value and things we cannot have.

Finally, Takeesha revised her draft thesis statement to make it more specific.

Revised thesis statement: People are fascinated with vampires as creatures that have both human frailties, which we can all relate to, and superhuman powers, which we wish we had.

As you write your essay, you will probably tinker with your thesis statement along the way, but the process that Takeesha followed should get you off to a good start.

WRITING ASSIGNMENTS

1. Write a thesis statement using the narrowed topic and ideas you developed in Chapter 5 or one of the following topics (which will need to be narrowed).

Friendship	Fashion or style	A good cause
Drug use	Video games	A waste of time
Popular music	YouTube	A cultural icon
Exercise	Going "green"	Reality TV

2. Using the skills you learned in Chapter 3 about reading visual images, write a thesis statement about what point you think the following photograph is making.

Before writing, read the checklist that follows.

CHECKLIST

Writing a Thesis Statement

FOCUS

☐ Read your narrowed topic.

☐ Decide what you think is important about it. You may want to use a pre-writing technique.

☐ Consider your audience and purpose.

ASK

☐ What is your position or your point about your topic?

☐ Why is it important to you?

☐ Do you have assumptions or biases? Does your audience?

☐ What do you want to show, explain, or prove?

☐ Can you think of additional ideas to support it?

☐ Is your position a single point?

☐ Is it a complete sentence?

WRITE

☐ Write a draft thesis statement, and make sure that it follows the basics of a good thesis statement (p. 75).

☐ Revise your draft statement according to the basics of a good thesis statement, and try to make it more specific and confident.

---

reflect Look back at your response to the "write" prompt on page 75. Revise your answer about thesis statements based on what you have learned.

Supporting Your Point

Finding Details, Examples, and Facts

Understand What Support for a Thesis Is

Support consists of the evidence, examples, or facts that show, explain, or prove your main point, or thesis, so you need to keep that main point in focus. **Primary support points** are the major support for your thesis. **Supporting details** (or secondary support points) are specifics that explain your primary support points.

Without support, you *state* the main point, but you do not *make* the main point. Consider the following statements:

> I did not break the bowl.
>
> I do not deserve an F on this paper.
>
> My neighborhood needs more markets.

These statements may be true, but without support they are not convincing. Perhaps you have received the comment "You need to support (or develop) your ideas" on your papers. This chapter will show you how to do so.

Writers sometimes confuse repetition with support. Restating the same idea several times using different words is not support; it is just repetition of an idea that does not help you support your thesis.

REPETITION, NOT SUPPORT	I do not deserve an F on this paper. It is not a failing paper. It should get a better grade.
SUPPORT	I do not deserve an F on this paper. It not only follows the assignment, but I was careful to apply the criteria for grading that was handed out. It has a thesis and support. Even though it has many grammar errors, the paper meets other criteria and should have received a better grade.

See Chapter 6 for advice on developing thesis statements.

As you develop support for your thesis, make sure that each point has the following basic features.

BASICS OF GOOD SUPPORT

TEACHING TIP
Emphasize that an opinion alone will not convince readers. If students use an opinion, they should support it with factual evidence.

- **It relates to your main point, or thesis.** The purpose of support is to show, explain, or prove your main point, so the support you use must relate directly to that main point.

- **It considers your readers.** Aim your support at the people who will read your writing. Supply information that will convince or inform them.

- **It is detailed and specific.** Give readers enough detail, particularly through examples, so that they can see what you mean.

- **It helps you achieve your purpose for writing.** Remember your reason for writing.

- **It is logical.** One point follows another and does not have logical fallacies (see Chapter 3).

Practice Supporting a Thesis Statement

A short essay usually has between three and five primary points that support the thesis statement. Longer pieces of writing require more support. Each primary support point becomes the topic sentence of its own paragraph. Each paragraph presents details that support that topic sentence.

The following sections detail the steps in supporting a thesis statement.

Prewrite to Find Support

For more practice with support, visit *Exercise Central* at bedfordstmartins .com/realessays.

Reread your thesis and imagine your readers asking, "What do you mean?" To answer this question and generate support for your thesis, try using one or more of the prewriting techniques discussed in Chapter 5.

⋯⋯⋯⋯⋯⋯⋯⋯⋯⋯⋯⋯⋯⋯⋯⋯⋯⋯⋯⋯⋯⋯⋯⋯⋯⋯⋯⋯⋯⋯⋯⋯⋯⋯⋯⋯⋯⋯

PRACTICE 1   Prewriting to Find Support

Choose one of the following sentences or one of your own, and write for five minutes using one prewriting technique. You will need a good supply of ideas from which to choose support points for your thesis. Try to find at least a dozen different ideas. *Answers will vary.*

TEAMWORK
Practice 1 works well in pairs or small groups if you have students choose listing or discussing as their prewriting technique.

SUGGESTED THESIS STATEMENTS

1.   Everyone in my family _____ .

2.   Although people want to "eat healthy" _____ .

3.   One way my city (or town) has improved is _____ .

4.   I have done some _____ things in my life, but the one I am

     most _____ of is _____ .

5.   Today, bullying is _____ .

NOTE: Imagine your reader asking, "What do you mean?"

RESOURCES
To gauge students' understanding of support and other writing and grammar issues, use the *Testing Tool Kit* CD available with this book.

⋯⋯⋯⋯⋯⋯⋯⋯⋯⋯⋯⋯⋯⋯⋯⋯⋯⋯⋯⋯⋯⋯⋯⋯⋯⋯⋯⋯⋯⋯⋯⋯⋯⋯⋯⋯⋯⋯

Drop Unrelated Ideas

After prewriting, remind yourself of your main point. Then, review your prewriting carefully, and drop any ideas that are not directly related to your main point. If new ideas occur to you, write them down.

⋯⋯⋯⋯⋯⋯⋯⋯⋯⋯⋯⋯⋯⋯⋯⋯⋯⋯⋯⋯⋯⋯⋯⋯⋯⋯⋯⋯⋯⋯⋯⋯⋯⋯⋯⋯⋯⋯

PRACTICE 2   Dropping Unrelated Ideas

Each thesis statement below is followed by a list of possible support points. Cross out the unrelated ideas in each list. Be ready to explain your choices.

1.   **THESIS STATEMENT:** Written communication in the workplace must be worded precisely and formatted clearly.

     POSSIBLE SUPPORT POINTS

     use bulleted lists for important short points

     ~~once I wrote a ridiculous memo to my boss but never sent it~~

     try to keep communication to a single page; people are busy

TEACHING TIP
Remind students that a point may be interesting or true, but that doesn't necessarily mean it belongs in the essay. The point must support the thesis statement.

include the date

~~get it done by the end of the day~~

read it over before sending

~~hate to put things in writing~~

~~takes too much time~~

make a copy

~~getting forty e-mails in a day is too many~~

2. **THESIS STATEMENT:** Texting while driving should be against the law.

POSSIBLE SUPPORT POINTS

people have to look away from the road

minds not on driving

younger drivers, who text most, lose control easily

texts come in all the time

statistics show how dangerous it is (get the numbers)

~~worse than talking on a cell phone~~

with cell phone, at least driver can watch the road at all times

~~people develop problems with their thumbs when they text too much~~

~~not fair to drivers who aren't texting~~

unsafe for all (find examples of accidents caused by texting)

3. **THESIS STATEMENT:** I know from experience that sometimes the customer is wrong.

POSSIBLE SUPPORT POINTS

work at supermarket

customers often misread sale flyer

they choose something like the item on sale but not it

~~get mad and sometimes get nasty~~

~~why do people bring screaming kids to the supermarket?~~

~~they don't have any right to be rude but they are~~

~~want to argue but I can't~~

customers steal food like eating the grapes sold by the pound

~~sometimes they eat a whole box of cookies and bring up the empty box~~

~~then the kids are always grabbing at the candy and whining, sometimes they just rip the candy open or put it in their mouths~~

customers misread the signs like ones that say "save $1.50" and think the item is on sale for $1.50

~~should get a different job~~

Select the Best Support Points

After dropping unrelated ideas, review the ones that remain, and select the ones that will be clearest and most convincing to your readers. As noted earlier, short essays usually have three to five primary support points. They will become the topic sentences for your support paragraphs.

PRACTICE 3   Selecting the Best Support Points

For each item, circle the three points you would use to support the thesis statement. Be ready to explain your answers.

1. THESIS STATEMENT: A college degree should not be the only factor in hiring decisions.

POSSIBLE SUPPORT POINTS

job experience

motivation and enthusiasm

friends who work at the company

appearance

persistence in applying

recommendations

good transportation

artistic talents

TEACHING TIP
Encourage students to get in the habit of asking themselves the kinds of basic questions their readers will ask: "Such as?" "In what way?" "For example?" If a student's support points answer those questions, his or her readers should understand the main point.

2. **THESIS STATEMENT:** Because people have a variety of learning styles, it helps to tailor your studying methods to your particular style.

POSSIBLE SUPPORT POINTS

learn by doing

not interested in learning anything new

learn by seeing

do not bring their books to class

disrupt the class

learn by working with others

get bored

bad learners

gifted students

Add Supporting Details

Once you have chosen your primary support points, you will need to add details to explain or demonstrate each of those points. These supporting details can be examples, facts, or evidence. As the following examples show, a supporting detail is always more specific than a primary support point.

THESIS STATEMENT	More research is needed on how to treat autism, a serious disorder affecting behavior, communication, and social interaction.
PRIMARY SUPPORT POINT	The disorder affects many people, their families, and communities.
SUPPORTING DETAILS	Autism is now diagnosed in about 1 in every 110 children.
	This rate is much higher than it was thirty years ago (was 1 in 2000).
	Parents and school staffs struggle to know how best to help autistic children.

PRIMARY SUPPORT POINT Some people go online to buy risky treatments that are not science based.

SUPPORTING DETAILS pressurized oxygen chambers

drug and vitamin supplements

special diets and nutrition consultations

blood transfusions

PRIMARY SUPPORT POINT More research has already started to have some good effects.

SUPPORTING DETAILS Funding has increased 15 percent a year between 2000 and 2010, with hundreds more scientists now studying autism.

Many of the treatments advertised online have now been scientifically proven not to work.

Children can now be diagnosed as young as one to two years old, when behavior therapy has a better success rate.

- -

PRACTICE 4 Adding Supporting Details

For each primary support point, again imagine your readers asking, "What do you mean?" Add specific details to answer that question.

THESIS STATEMENT The food industry intentionally produces foods that humans are likely to overeat, indirectly causing the country's obesity epidemic.

PRIMARY SUPPORT POINT Humans are born with a strong drive to eat sugar, salt, and fat, the primary components of junk food.

SUPPORTING DETAIL Sugar, salt, and fat stimulate our brains to want more, even though doing so may not be good for us.

TEAMWORK
Have students work in pairs to read their thesis statements and share possible supporting details. Together, partners can select the three best points. Suggest that they refer to the Basics of Good Support (p. 90) when generating and selecting support points.

In the space indicated, write the points you chose in Practice 3, item 1 (p. 93), as the best support. In the space to the right, add three details that would show, explain, or prove each primary support point.

THESIS STATEMENT: A college degree should not be the only factor in hiring decisions. *Answers will vary.*

PRIMARY SUPPORT POINT	SUPPORTING DETAILS
_____	_____
	_____
	_____

PRIMARY SUPPORT POINT	SUPPORTING DETAILS
_____	_____
	_____
	_____

PRIMARY SUPPORT POINT	SUPPORTING DETAILS
_____	_____
	_____
	_____

Review Support

When you have developed support for your main point, along with supporting details, use your critical thinking and reading skills to evaluate it. Does the support make assumptions? Does it reveal a bias in your point of view? Go back to Chapter 3 and remind yourself of the common logical fallacies described on pages 32–34. It is important to review your support in this way because errors in reasoning make it difficult to make your main point effectively. Avoiding logical fallacies and questioning assumptions and biases makes your own writing stronger. Critical thinking also helps you avoid "falling for" advertisements or documents with false claims.

Write Topic Sentences for Your Support Points

Your primary support points will form the topic sentences of the paragraphs that support your thesis statement. Each topic sentence should clearly relate to and show, explain, or prove your thesis.

THESIS STATEMENT	Playing a team sport taught me more than how to play the game.
TOPIC SENTENCE (paragraph 1)	I learned the importance of hard practice.
TOPIC SENTENCE (paragraph 2)	I also realized that, to succeed, I had to work with other people.
TOPIC SENTENCE (paragraph 3)	Most important, I learned to be responsible to others.

Once you develop topic sentences to support your thesis, back up your topic sentences with supporting details.

. . . .

PRACTICE 5   Writing Topic Sentences and Supporting Details

Using the support points you generated in Practice 4, write topic sentences that support the thesis statement. In the space under each topic sentence, list the details you selected. When you have completed this practice, you will have developed support for an essay.

THESIS STATEMENT: A college degree should not be the only factor in hiring decisions. *Answers will vary.*

TOPIC SENTENCE (primary support point 1): _____

_____

    SUPPORTING DETAILS: _____

_____

_____

TOPIC SENTENCE (primary support point 2): _____

_____

SUPPORTING DETAILS: _____

_____

_____

TOPIC SENTENCE (primary support point 3): _____

_____

SUPPORTING DETAILS: _____

_____

_____

Write Your Own Support

Before selecting a writing assignment, read how a student, Carson Williams, developed support for his thesis.

> **THESIS STATEMENT:** *Although my girlfriend and I are in love, we have some very different ideas about what a "good" relationship is.*

   1. To generate ideas that might work as support, Carson used a prewriting technique: listing and brainstorming.

LISTING AND BRAINSTORMING

> She always wants to talk
> Asks me how I feel, what I think, what I'm thinking about
> Gets mad if I don't answer or thinks I'm mad about something
> ~~Talks during movies and annoys me~~
> ~~Puts makeup on in the car~~
> Always wants to be affectionate, holding hands, kissing
> Wants me to tell her I love her all the time
> Wants to hear she's pretty
> Gets jealous if I'm looking at another girl even though I'm not interested
> ~~Always asks me if she looks fat and gets mad whatever I say~~
> ~~Even when we're out she talks on her cell forever~~
> Wants to talk about our "relationship" but I don't have anything to say, it's fine

Talks about her girlfriends and their relationships
Not wild about cars
Loves cats and tiny dogs
If I just don't feel like talking, she imagines I'm in a bad mood or mad
Hates TV sports
Wants me to go shopping with her
Doesn't like me going out with the guys

2. Next, Carson read his list and crossed out some things that seemed unrelated to his main point. (See the crossed-out items in the preceding list.)

3. He then reviewed the remaining ideas and noticed that they fell into three categories—differences about communication, differences about showing affection, and differences about how to spend time.

He grouped the ideas under these category labels and saw that the labels could serve as primary support points for his thesis. These support points could be turned into topic sentences of paragraphs backing his thesis, while the ideas under the labels could serve as supporting details for those topic sentences.

PRIMARY SUPPORT: Differences in communication styles

SUPPORTING DETAILS

She always wants to talk
Asks me how I feel, what I think, what I'm thinking about
Gets mad if I don't answer or thinks I'm mad about something
Wants to talk about our "relationship" but I don't have anything to say, it's fine
If I just don't feel like talking, she imagines I'm in a bad mood or mad

PRIMARY SUPPORT: Differences about showing affection

SUPPORTING DETAILS

Always wants to be affectionate, holding hands, kissing
Wants me to tell her I love her all the time
Wants to hear she's pretty
Gets jealous if I'm looking at another girl even though I'm not interested
→

> **PRIMARY SUPPORT:** *Differences about how to spend time*
>
> **SUPPORTING DETAILS**
>
> *Not wild about cars*
> *Hates TV sports*
> *Wants me to go shopping with her*
> *Doesn't like me going out with the guys*

4. Finally, Carson wrote topic sentences for his primary support points.

TOPIC SENTENCES FOR PRIMARY SUPPORT

> *One big difference is in our expectations about communication.*
> *Another difference is in how we show affection.*
> *Another difference is in our views of how we think a couple in a "good" relationship should spend time.*

....

WRITING ASSIGNMENTS

1. Develop primary support points and supporting details for the thesis you wrote in Chapter 6 or for one of the following thesis statements.

    William Lowe Bryan said, "Education is one of the few things a person is willing to pay for and not get."

    Elderly people in this country are not shown enough respect.

    Few people know how to really listen.

    Some movies have made me cry from happiness.

    When I think of a book that really made me look at things in new ways and learn, I think of _____.

2. Look at the photographs on pages 101–02. Write a brief statement describing what you see as the meaning of these images, or the theme that connects them. Then, turn that statement into a thesis. Finally, write a brief essay in which you support your thesis with details and other evidence drawn from the photos. (You might want to consider the questions in the checklist on page 42.)

Photographer
Jason Baker
documents
New England's
vacant
buildings.

Before writing, read the following checklist.

CHECKLIST

Supporting Your Thesis

FOCUS

☐ Reread your thesis.

☐ Think about the people who will read your writing.

☐ Think about your purpose for writing.

ASK

☐ What support can you include that will show, explain, or prove what you mean?

☐ What do your readers need to know or understand to be convinced?

☐ What examples come to mind?

☐ What have you experienced yourself?

☐ What information can you find on the Internet, in a print source, or from people you meet and interview?

☐ What details could you use to strengthen the support?

WRITE

☐ Use a prewriting technique to find as many support points as you can.

☐ Drop ideas that are not directly related to your main thesis.

☐ Select the best primary support.

☐ Add supporting details.

☐ Review and evaluate your support.

☐ Write topic sentences for your primary support points.

☐ Make sure that all of your support points have the basics of good support (p. 90).

For examples of pre-writing techniques, see pages 69–72.

---

reflect Read your response to the "write" prompt on page 89 and change it to describe the process of supporting your point.

8

YOU KNOW THIS

You often rehearse in advance.

- Your sports team plays preseason games.
- You practice what you are going to say to someone.

write What do you know about writing a draft?

Writing a Draft

Putting Your Ideas Together

Understand What a Draft Is

IDEA JOURNAL
Write about practicing something important before you do the thing itself.

A **draft** is the first whole version of your ideas in writing. Do the best job you can in writing a draft, but remember that you will have a chance to make changes later.

For more on thesis statements, see Chapter 6. For more on support, see Chapter 7.

BASICS OF A GOOD DRAFT

- It has a thesis statement that presents the main point.
- It has a logical organization of ideas.
- It has primary support points that are stated in topic sentences that develop or explain the thesis statement.
- It has supporting details that develop or explain each topic sentence.
- It follows standard essay form (introduction, body paragraphs, conclusion) and uses complete sentences.
- The introduction captures the readers' interest and lets them know what the essay is about.
- The conclusion reinforces the main point and makes an observation.

Arrange Your Ideas

Once you have generated ideas, you need to arrange them in a logical **order**. Three common ways of ordering your ideas are **chronological order** (by the time sequence in which events happened), **spatial order** (by the physical arrangement of objects or features), and **order of importance** (by the significance of the ideas or reasons).

Chronological Order

Use **chronological order** (time order) to arrange points according to when they happened. Time order works well when you are telling the story of an event or explaining how to do something. Usually, you go in sequence from what happened first to what happened last; in some cases, though, you can work back from what happened last to what happened first.

EXAMPLE USING CHRONOLOGICAL (TIME) ORDER

The cause of the fire that destroyed the apartment building was human carelessness. The couple in apartment 2F had planned a romantic dinner to celebrate the woman's raise at work. They lit candles all over the apartment and then shared a bottle of wine and ate a delicious meal. After dinner, they decided to go out to a club to continue the celebration. Unfortunately, they forgot to blow out all of the candles, and one of them was too close to a window curtain, which caught fire. The fire spread quickly throughout the apartment and then spread to others. By the time another resident smelled smoke, the fire was uncontrollable. The building was destroyed. Fortunately, rescuers were able to save everyone who was in the building. But all of the tenants lost their homes and most of their possessions. Human carelessness caused much human misery.

How does the writer use chronological order to arrange information?

The writer orders events from first to last.

TEAMWORK
Have students break into pairs or small groups. Assign each pair or group one of the three sample paragraphs on pages 105–106 to rewrite using a different type of organization. After about 10 minutes, ask each group which order they tried and how the story changed with a new organization.

Spatial Order

Use **spatial order** to arrange ideas so that your readers see your topic as you do. Space order works well when you are writing about what someone or something looks like. You can move from top to bottom, bottom to top, near to far, far to near, left to right, right to left, back to front, or front to back.

EXAMPLE USING SPATIAL (SPACE) ORDER

I stood watching in horror while all-powerful flames destroyed an entire building, including my apartment and everything I owned. The first few floors looked normal, except that firefighters were racing into the front entry. A couple of floors up, windows were breaking and gray, foul-smelling smoke was billowing out. I could see shadows of the firefighters moving in and out of the apartments. My eyes were drawn to the top two floors, where flames of orange and white leapt from the windows. A dog with brown and white spots barked furiously from the rooftop until it was rescued. Until you have actually witnessed a severe fire, you cannot imagine how powerful it is and how powerless you feel in its presence.

What type of spatial order does the writer use?

bottom to top

Order of Importance

Use **order of importance** to arrange points according to their significance, interest, or surprise value. Save the most important point for last to end with a strong point.

EXAMPLE USING ORDER OF IMPORTANCE

Fires caused by human carelessness often have disastrous effects on people's lives. In a recent incident, when an apartment building was completely destroyed by a fire, the owner and tenants had no homes to return to. They also lost all of their possessions: furniture, clothing, and irreplaceable treasured personal items. Worse than that, however, was that the owner and many of the tenants had no insurance to help them find new housing and replace their possessions. Many had to depend completely on relatives, friends, and a fund that was started for them by neighbors. The most disastrous effect of the fire, however, was that many tenants lost their beloved pets. While firefighters bravely rescued all the people, they were not able to save all the animals. Carelessness has no place around fire, which has the power to destroy.

What is this writer's most important point about the effects of fires?

Fires can cause loss of life.

As you arrange your ideas, consider what your purpose for writing is and what kind of organization would work best to make your main point. Some examples follow in the chart.

PURPOSE	ORGANIZATION
To describe an experience To explain how something works To explain how to do something	Chronological
To help your reader visualize whatever you are describing as you see it To create an impression using your senses — taste, touch, sight, smell, sound To re-create a scene	Spatial
To persuade or convince someone To make a case for or against something	Importance

Make a Plan

When you have decided how to order your ideas, make a written plan — an **outline** — starting with your thesis statement. Then, state each of your primary support points as a topic sentence for one of the body paragraphs of the essay. Add supporting details to develop or explain the topic sentence. Your plan should also include a possible main point for the concluding paragraph. Although your outline serves as a good guide, it can be changed as you draft your essay.

Some people find it useful to write full sentences as they plan so that their outline is a more complete guide for the essay.

Also, there is no one right order for any essay. Use the order that will help you make your main point most effectively.

OUTLINE FOR A SHORT ESSAY: The example that follows uses "standard" or "formal" outline format, in which numbers and letters distinguish between primary support points and secondary supporting details. Some instructors require this format. If you are making an outline for yourself, you might choose to write a less formal outline, simply indenting secondary supporting details under the primary support rather than using numbers and letters.

For a diagram of the relationship between paragraphs and essays, see page 52.

TEACHING TIP
If students have difficulty outlining their essays, encourage them to try a visual approach — writing their outline as a cluster diagram or as a flowchart.

Thesis statement

   I. Topic sentence (primary support point 1)
      A. Supporting detail
      B. Supporting detail (and so on)

For more advice on primary support and supporting details, see Chapter 7.

II. Topic sentence (primary support point 2)
   A. Supporting detail
   B. Supporting detail (and so on)
III. Topic sentence (primary support point 3)
   A. Supporting detail
   B. Supporting detail (and so on)

Concluding paragraph

....

PRACTICE 1   Outlining an Essay

Outline the essay that follows. First, double-underline the thesis statement and the main point in the concluding paragraph. Underline each topic sentence, and put a check mark next to each supporting detail.

We all know people who seem to fall in love over and over. They love being in love. But others have different patterns. Some people seem to fall in love once and stay there. Others avoid long-term commitment. Until now, we had no way to figure out why some people were steady lovers and others not. <u>Some researchers now believe that the amount and type of certain hormones in a person's brain may determine a person's patterns of love.</u>

<u>Using mice as subjects, the researchers found that when two particular hormones (oxytocin and vasopressin) exist in the pleasure centers of the brain, they produce individuals with a pattern of long-lasting love.</u> Male mice with these hormones in their pleasure centers were faithful ✓ to their partners. They stayed with their female mouse partners through pregnancy and the raising of offspring. ✓

<u>In contrast, when those same hormones existed outside of the pleasure center, the male mice sought constant sources of new love.</u> They did not have steady partners and did not stay around when a female mouse ✓ became pregnant. The mice with hormones in this location were the ones who ran from commitment. ✓

Unfortunately, the research did not deal with the most common love pattern: individuals involved in relationships that last for some time but not for life. In this pattern, people have a serious relationships broken   ✓ off when one person wants a commitment and the other does not. Perhaps this research will come next, as it is in these relationships where much of the pain of love exists. ✓

Though these behaviors may be built into the brain, scientists are working on ways to modify the effects. They hope to find a balance so that love patterns can be modified. One humorous researcher suggested that before we select our mates, we should ask them to have a brain scan to determine whether they are likely to stay or go.

Practice Writing a Draft

The explanations and practices in this section will prepare you to write a good draft essay.

See Chapter 7 for advice on support. For a diagram showing the parts of an essay, see page 52, and for a complete draft of an essay, see page 119.

Draft the Body of the Essay

Use your plan for your essay as you begin to write your draft. The plan should include your thesis statement, the primary support points for your thesis, and supporting details for your primary support points.

First, draft complete paragraphs that support your thesis. Each should contain a topic sentence (usually the first sentence in the paragraph) that presents a primary support point as well as supporting details. At this point, draft the body of your essay; you will write the introduction and conclusion later. In general, essays have at least three body paragraphs, and they may have many more, depending on your assignment and purpose.

If you are having trouble with a word or sentence as you draft, make a note to come back to it and then keep going.

TEACHING TIP
Suggest to students that a draft is similar to a dress rehearsal before a play or a scrimmage before a big game. In addition, require students to turn in their drafts with their final papers.

PRACTICE 2   Writing Topic Sentences

Writing topic sentences for primary support points is a good way to start drafting the body of an essay. Convert each of the following primary support points into a topic sentence that supports the thesis. You can make up details if you want.

THESIS STATEMENT: Being a good customer service representative in a retail store requires several important skills.

I. Being pleasant and polite [Primary support point 1]
   A. Smiling, saying hello [Supporting detail]
   B. Looking at person [Supporting detail]

TOPIC SENTENCE I: *Answers will vary.* _____

II. Listening carefully [Primary support point 2]
   A. Making notes [Supporting detail]
   B. Asking questions [Supporting detail]

TOPIC SENTENCE II: _____

III. Figuring out how to solve the problem [Primary support point 3]
   A. Calling the right people [Supporting detail]
   B. Filling out paperwork [Supporting detail]

TOPIC SENTENCE III: _____

Write an Introduction

The introduction to your essay should capture your readers' interest and present the main point. Think of your introductory paragraph as a challenge. Ask yourself: How can I get my readers to want to continue reading?

BASICS OF A GOOD INTRODUCTION

- It should catch readers' attention.
- It should present the essay's thesis statement (narrowed topic + main point).
- It should give readers an idea of what the essay will cover.

The thesis statement is often either the first or the last sentence in the introductory paragraph, though you may find essays in which it is elsewhere.

Here are examples of common kinds of introductions that spark readers' interest.

Start with a Surprising Fact or Idea

ESL Remind non-native speakers that it is a convention of academic English to present the main point in the first paragraph, stated explicitly.

Surprises capture people's attention. The more unexpected and surprising something is, the more likely people are to take notice of it and read on.

I was saved from sin when I was going on thirteen. But not really saved. It happened like this. There was a big revival at my Auntie Reed's church. Every night for weeks there had been much preaching, singing, praying, and shouting, and some very hardened sinners had been brought to Christ, and the membership of the church had grown by leaps and bounds. Then just before the revival ended, they held a special meeting for children, "to bring the young lambs into the fold." My aunt spoke of it for days ahead. That night I was escorted to the front row and placed on the mourners' bench with all the other young sinners, who had not yet been brought to Jesus.

> —Langston Hughes, "Salvation"
> (See pp. 691–93 for the full essay.)

Open with a Quotation

A good short quotation can definitely get people interested. It must lead naturally into your main point, however, and not just be stuck there. If you start with a quotation, make sure that you tell the reader who the speaker or writer is (unless it is a general quote, like the proverb in the following excerpt).

"Grow where you are planted" is an old proverb that is a metaphor for living. Although I had heard it before, it took me many years to understand and appreciate its meaning. If I had listened to that proverb earlier, I would have saved myself and others many painful experiences.

> —Teresa Fiori, "Appreciate What You Have"

TEACHING TIP
Have students write introductions using two of the techniques. Have volunteers read them aloud and discuss how they caatch attention.

Give an Example or Tell a Story

Opening an essay with a brief story or illustration often draws readers in.

Brian Head saw only one way out. On the final day of his life, during economics class, the fifteen-year-old stood up and pointed a semi-automatic handgun at himself. Before he pulled the trigger, he said his last words: "I can't take this anymore."

> —Kathleen Vail, "Words That Wound"
> (See pp. 706–09 for the full essay.)

Offer a Strong Opinion

The stronger the opinion, the more likely it is that people will pay attention.

Sex sells. This truth is a boon for marketing gurus and the pornography industry but a rather unfortunate situation for women. Every issue of *Playboy,* every lewd poster, and even the Victoria's Secret catalog transform real women into ornaments, valued exclusively for their outward appearance. These publications are responsible for defining what is sexy and reinforce the belief that aesthetic appeal is a woman's highest virtue.

> —Amy L. Beck, "Struggling for Perfection"
> (See pp. 807–10 for the full essay.)

Ask a Question

A question needs an answer. If you start your introduction with a question, you engage your readers by inviting them to answer it.

> If you're a man, at some point a woman will ask you how she looks. "How do I look?" she'll ask.
>
> You must be careful how you answer this question. The best technique is to form an honest yet sensitive opinion, then collapse on the floor with some kind of fatal seizure. Trust me, this is the easiest way out. Because you will never come up with the right answer.
>
> —Dave Barry, "The Ugly Truth about Beauty"
> (See pp. 787–89 for the full essay.)

PRACTICE 3   Identifying Strong Introductions

TEAMWORK Practice 3 works well in pairs or small groups.

Find a strong introduction in a newspaper, a magazine, a catalog, an advertisement — anything written. Explain, in writing, why you think it is a strong introduction. *Answers will vary.*

PRACTICE 4   Selling Your Main Point

TEAMWORK Practice 4 works well in pairs or small groups. Students should be prepared to explain their choices to the rest of the class.

As you know from watching and reading advertisements, a good writer can make just about anything sound interesting. For each of the following topics, write an introductory statement using the technique indicated. Make the statement punchy and intriguing enough to motivate your readers to stay with you as you explain or defend it.

1.   **TOPIC:** Mandatory drug testing in the workplace

   TECHNIQUE: Ask a question.

   Answers will vary.
   _____

2.   **TOPIC:** Teenage suicide

   TECHNIQUE: Present a surprising fact or idea (you can make one up for this exercise).

   _____

3.   **TOPIC:** Free access to music on the Internet

   TECHNIQUE: Give a strong opinion.

   _____

4.   TOPIC: The quality of television shows

TECHNIQUE: Use a quotation (you can make up a good one for this exercise).

_____

5.   TOPIC: Blind dates

TECHNIQUE: Give an example or tell a brief story (you can just sum it up).

_____

Write a Conclusion

Your conclusion should have energy and match the force of your thesis statement; it is your last chance to drive home your main point. Fading out with a weak conclusion is like slowing down at the end of a race. In fact, you should give yourself a last push at the end because people usually remember best what they see, hear, or read last. A good conclusion creates a sense of completion: It not only brings readers back to where they started but also shows them how far they have come.

BASICS OF A GOOD CONCLUSION

- It should refer to your main point.
- It should briefly summarize the support you have developed.
- It should make a final observation.

A good way to end an essay is to refer back to something in the introduction.

- If you used a quotation, use another one—by the same person or by another person on the same topic. Or refer back to the quotation in the introduction, and make an observation.
- If you stated a surprising fact or idea, go back to it and comment on it, using what you have written in the body of the essay.
- If you asked a question, ask it again, and answer it based on what you have said in your essay.
- If you started a story, finish it.
- Remind your reader of your original point, perhaps repeating key words that you used in your introduction.

Look again at three of the introductions you read earlier, each shown here with its conclusion.

OPEN WITH A QUOTATION

INTRODUCTION A: "Grow where you are planted" is an old proverb that is a metaphor for living. Although I had heard it before, it took me many years to understand and appreciate its meaning. If I had listened to that proverb earlier, I would have saved myself and others many painful experiences.

CONCLUSION A: Finally, I have learned to grow where I am planted, to appreciate the good things in my life rather than look for the bad and be angry. I have learned to take advantage of the many opportunities I have for personal and professional growth, right here and now. And I have vowed to help others around me grow also. My life is much richer now that I follow that old wisdom, and I will pass its lesson on to my children.

—Teresa Fiori, "Appreciate What You Have"

START WITH A STRONG OPINION OR POSITION

INTRODUCTION B: Sex sells. This truth is a boon for marketing gurus and the pornography industry but a rather unfortunate situation for women. Every issue of *Playboy*, every lewd poster, and even the Victoria's Secret catalog transform real women into ornaments, valued exclusively for their outward appearance. These publications are responsible for defining what is sexy and reinforce the belief that aesthetic appeal is a woman's highest virtue.

CONCLUSION B: Women are up against a long history of devaluation and oppression, and, unfortunately, the feminist movements have been only partially successful in purging those legacies. Sexually charged images of women in the media are not the only cause of this continuing problem, but they certainly play a central role.

—Amy L. Beck, "Struggling for Perfection"

ASK A QUESTION

INTRODUCTION C: If you're a man, at some point a woman will ask you how she looks. "How do I look?" she'll ask.

You must be careful how you answer this question. The best technique is to form an honest yet sensitive opinion, then collapse on the floor with some kind of fatal seizure. Trust me, this is the easiest way out. You will never come up with the right answer.

CONCLUSION C: To go back to my main point: If you're a man, and a woman asks you how she looks, you're in big trouble. Obviously, you can't say she looks bad. But you also can't say that she looks great, because she'll think you're lying, because she has spent countless hours, with the help of the multibillion-dollar beauty industry, obsessing about the differences between herself and Cindy Crawford. Also, she suspects that you're not qualified to judge anybody's appearance. This is because you have shaving cream in your hair.

—Dave Barry, "The Ugly Truth about Beauty"

PRACTICE 5   Analyzing Conclusions

After reading the paired introductions and conclusions above, indicate the techniques used in each conclusion to refer back to its introduction.

A.   Technique used to link introduction and conclusion: *Reference back to a quotation*

B.   Technique used to link introduction and conclusion: *Restatement of main idea*

C.   Technique used to link introduction and conclusion: *Repetition of key words and restatement of main idea*

PRACTICE 6   Identifying Good Introductions and Conclusions

In a newspaper, magazine, or any other written material, find a piece of writing that has both a strong introduction and a strong conclusion. Answer the following questions about the introduction and conclusion.

1.   What method of introduction is used? *Answers will vary.*

2.   What does the conclusion do? Does it restate the main idea? Sum up the points made in the piece? Make an observation? _____

3.   How are the introduction and the conclusion linked? _____

PRACTICE 7   Writing a Conclusion

Read the following introductory paragraphs, and write a possible conclusion for each one. Your conclusions can be brief, but they should each include the basics of a good conclusion (p. 113) and consist of several sentences.

TEAMWORK
Collect the examples students bring in, separate the introductions from the conclusions, and then scramble them. In a later class, have students work in small groups to match introductions and conclusions.

TEAMWORK Have students share their own drafts in small groups, exchanging comments and suggestions with group members. Students can use the checklist on page 121 as a prompt for discussing their drafts.

1. **INTRODUCTION:** When it comes to long-term love relationships, I very much believe Anton Chekhov's statement, "Any idiot can face a crisis; it's the day-to-day living that wears you out." When faced with a crisis, couples often pull together. A crisis is a slap in the face that reminds you of who and what is important in your life. It is the routine necessities of living that can erode a relationship as couples argue over who does the laundry, who does the cleaning, or cooking, or bill paying. The constant skirmishes over day-to-day living can do more serious damage over the long term than a crisis.

    CONCLUSION: *Answers will vary.*
    _____
    _____

2. **INTRODUCTION:** Why do so many people feel that they must be available at all times and in all places? Until recently, the only way you could reach someone was by telephone or by mail. Now if you do not have a smartphone for texting, Facebook and Twitter accounts, and call waiting, people trying to reach you get annoyed. I resent the loss of privacy. I do not want to be available twenty-four hours a day.

    CONCLUSION: *Answers will vary.*
    _____
    _____

Title Your Essay

Even if your title is the *last* part of the essay you write, it is the *first* thing that readers read. Use your title to get your readers' attention and to tell them what your essay is about. Use concrete, specific words to name the topic of your essay.

BASICS OF A GOOD ESSAY TITLE

- It makes readers want to read the essay.
- It does not repeat the wording in your thesis statement.
- It may hint at the main point but does not necessarily state it outright.

One way to find a good title is to consider the type of essay you are writing. If you are writing an argument (as you will in Chapter 18), state your position in your title. If you are telling your readers how to do something (as you will in Chapter 13), try using the term *steps* or *how to* in the title. This way, your readers will know immediately both what you are writing about and how you will present it. For example, "Five Steps to Financial Independence" may be a more inviting and more accurate title for a process analysis essay than "Financial Independence."

> **LANGUAGE NOTE:** A title is centered on the line above the first line of a paragraph or essay. The first letter of most words in a title should be capitalized. (See p. 665 for more details.)

PRACTICE 8   Writing a Title

Read the following introductory paragraphs, and write a possible title for the essay each one begins. The first one is done as an example. Be prepared to explain why you worded each title as you did.

EXAMPLE: The origin of this species of rant was a toothbrush—a new toothbrush that came with an instructional DVD. The user of this advanced piece of dental equipment had been brushing his teeth lo these many years without any educational aids at all. But now he was the proud owner of an IntelliCleanSystem equipped with packets of paste to be downloaded into the toothbrush's hard drive.

POSSIBLE TITLE: *Making Life Better through Technology*

1. Many students plagiarize because they do not understand that information from Web sites must be acknowledged.

POSSIBLE TITLE: *Answers will vary.*

2. Your sweetheart or your pet. Who would you choose to dump if one had to go? Most current pet owners said they would hold on to their spouse or significant other (84 percent), but a sizable 14 percent picked their pet, according to an *AP-Petside.com* poll. — Leanne Italie, "AP-Petside Poll: Pet or Paramour? Many Say Pet," Associated Press, 25 Jan. 2011.

POSSIBLE TITLE: _____

3. Is a girl named Gloria apt to be better-looking than one named Bertha? Are criminals more likely to be dark than blond? Can you tell a good deal about someone's personality from hearing his voice briefly over the phone? Can a person's nationality be pretty accurately guessed from her photograph? Does the fact that someone wears glasses imply that he is intelligent?

The answer to all these questions is obviously "no."

Yet, from all the evidence at hand, most of us believe these things.

POSSIBLE TITLE: _____

Write Your Own Draft

Before writing your own draft, read Deshon Briggs's outline and draft.

DESHON'S OUTLINE

> **THESIS STATEMENT (part of introductory paragraph):** I learned that I can be the change in my life.
> I.   **Primary support 1 (paragraph 1):** One day, my English teacher wrote, "You are the change in your life" on the board.
>   Supporting details:
>   A.   Said that we should explore this statement by writing about it for an assignment due in four weeks
>   B.   No idea what to do, figured I had plenty of time to think about it
> II. **Primary support 2 (paragraph 2):** I took my son to play basketball at a park near us and he gave me grief when I threw my Coke can off to the side.
>   Supporting details:
>   A.   He got a bag from the car and picked up my can.
>   B.   Started picking up other cans and bottles, and I helped
>   C.   Guy I know came by with his kids, and they started collecting the stuff too
> III. **Primary support 3 (paragraph 3):** We went to local freecycle.org and posted that we wanted a big trash can for bottles and cans
>   A.   Had a bunch of offers, and other guys said they'd help with clean-up
>   B.   Got the idea to use bottle and can deposit money for a new basketball net
> IV. **Primary support 4 (paragraph 4):**
>   A.   Local paper called to do a story on the clean-up
>   B.   Got our pictures in the paper with story
>
> **POSSIBLE POINT FOR CONCLUSION** (part of concluding paragraph): Court is clean, we bought a bench, my son and I were the change in our lives.

DESHON'S DRAFT

One day, my teacher wrote "You are the change in your life" on the board. She said that statement related to our going to college and making our lives better. She gave us a writing assignment: to explore the statement that was due in four weeks. I did not really know what she was talking about but figured I had plenty of time to think about it. I learned that I really can be the change in my life.

I took my son to play basketball at the park near us, and he gave me grief when I threw my Coke can off to the side. He got a bag from my car and picked up my can. He started picking up others, and I helped. A guy I know came by with his kids, and we all started picking up cans and bottles. There were a lot.

I had the idea to go to the local freecycle.org and posted that we wanted a big trash can for bottles and cans for the park. I had a bunch of offers and other guys said they would help with clean-up. We set up a schedule. My son and I got the idea of returning the bottles and cans for the deposit money that we could use to get a new basketball net. We did that.

After a few weeks, the local paper called me and wanted to interview my son and me about the stuff we had done at the basketball court. We got our pictures in the paper, and we got some more people interested and some people made donations. Now we have enough money to get a bench. The court looks great, we met a lot of other people, and people gave us a lot of respect. It was great. And this is my paper for my English class, how my son and I were the change in our lives, starting with just picking up a Coke can.

Introductory paragraph

Thesis statement

Primary support 2

Primary support 3

Concluding paragraph

Point for conclusion

WRITING ASSIGNMENTS

1. Write an outline and a draft using one of the following thesis statements.

With the advent of so many new technologies, teenagers no longer do much traditional dating.

Although cartoons are typically intended to entertain, they may also have important messages.

The most important skills a college student should have are

_____ .

My professor does not understand that _____

_____ .

Living with roommates requires _____

_____ .

2.   Look at the images below of a sculpture by Andy Goldsworthy.
Write two or three sentences analyzing what you think is the meaning of this work. Then turn those sentences into an argument and
develop a thesis statement. Finally, using that thesis statement,
write a draft of an essay that analyzes the work.

Before writing, read the following checklist.

CHECKLIST

Writing a Draft Essay

FOCUS

☐ Review your support.

ASK

☐ Is your thesis clear?

☐ Are there topic sentences for each body paragraph?

☐ Do you have supporting details for each topic sentence?

☐ Is your support arranged in a logical order?

☐ What introductory technique will get your readers' attention and make your point stand out?

☐ How can you use the conclusion for one last chance to make your point?

☐ How can you link your conclusion to your introduction? What is the strongest or most interesting part of the introduction that you might refer back to in your conclusion?

☐ Will your title make readers want to read your essay?

WRITE

☐ Write a draft essay.

reflect Read your response to the "write" prompt on page 104 and revise it based on what you have learned about the process of drafting an essay.

Revising Your Draft

Improving Your Essay

Understand What Revision Is

Revising is rewriting your drafts to make your ideas clearer, stronger, and more convincing. When revising, you might add, cut, move, or change whole sentences or paragraphs.

Editing is correcting problems with grammar, style, usage, and punctuation. While editing, you usually add, cut, or change words and phrases instead of whole sentences or paragraphs.

Revising (covered in this chapter) and editing (covered in Chapters 22–40) are two different ways to improve a paper. Most writers find it difficult to do both at once. It is easier to look first at the ideas in your essay (revising) and then to look at the individual words and sentences (editing).

No one gets everything right in a draft—even professional writers need to revise. The tips below will help you with the revision process.

TIPS FOR REVISING

- Take a break from your draft—set it aside for a few hours or a whole day.

- Read your draft aloud, and listen to what you have written.

- Imagine yourself as one of your readers.

- Get feedback from a friend, a classmate, or a colleague (see the next section of this chapter).

- Get help from a tutor at your college writing center or lab.

You may need to read your draft several times before deciding what changes would improve it. Remember to consider your audience (your readers) and your purpose (your reason for writing it).

For more on audience and purpose, see Chapter 4.

Understand What Peer Review Is

Peer review is the exchange of feedback on a piece of writing from your fellow students, colleagues, or friends. Getting comments from a peer is a good way to begin revising your essay.

Other people can look at your work and see things that you might not—parts that are good as well as parts that need more explanation or evidence. The best reviewers are honest about what could be better but also sensitive to the writer's feelings. In addition, they are specific. Reviewers who say a paper is "great" without offering further comment do not help writers improve their work.

RESOURCES
Consider using *Comment*, a Web-based peer-review tool available with this book. Peer-review guides for all Part 2 chapters are available online at bedfordstmartins .com/realessays.

BASICS OF USEFUL FEEDBACK

- It is given in a positive way.
- It is specific.
- It offers suggestions.
- It may be given orally or in writing.

To get useful feedback, find a partner and exchange papers. Each partner should read the other's paper and jot down a few comments. The first time someone comments on what you have written, you may feel a little embarrassed, but you will feel better about the process once you see how your writing benefits from the comments.

Peer reviewers should consider the following as they read.

Questions for Peer Reviewers

1. What is the main point?
2. After reading the introductory paragraph, do you have an idea of what the essay will cover, and why?
3. How could the introduction be more interesting?
4. Is there enough support for the main point? Where might the writer add support?
5. Are there confusing places where you have to reread something to understand it? How might the writer make the points, the organization, or the flow of ideas clearer or smoother?

TEAMWORK
To model peer review, bring in a short paragraph or essay, and have students work with a partner to answer the eight questions for peer reviewers. Then, discuss the answers as a class. If possible, invite a writing center peer tutor to class to help facilitate discussion.

---

6. Does the writer have assumptions or biases that weaken the writing? What are they?
7. How could the conclusion be more forceful?
8. What do you most like about the essay? Where could it be better? What would you do if it were your essay?
9. What other comments or suggestions do you have?
10. How do you think the audience for the writing will respond to the thesis, and its support?

Practice Revising for Unity

Unity in writing means that all the points are related to your main point: They *unite* to support your main point.

Sometimes writers drift away from their main point, as the writer of the following paragraph did with the underlined sentences. The diagram after the paragraph shows where readers might get confused.

> Online dating services have many benefits, but users should be aware of the possible negatives as well. One benefit of online dating services is that people do not have to cruise bars to meet people. The Web sites offer subscribers potential matches, and the first contact is via e-mail. Contact via e-mail or text allows users to get to know each other a little before meeting. Sometimes a couple of exchanges can reveal that meeting is not necessary, so not only do users get to avoid cruising, they save time by eliminating bad matches. The services also try to match compatible people by comparing profiles, so the likelihood of having something in common is greater than in a random encounter. With all the online dating services available, people can choose ones that appeal to people with specific interests and preferences. A good place to meet is a cheap restaurant. Most people like Italian food or burgers, so those types of places are safe. Also, online dating services offer many choices of screened possible dates, more than anyone could meet in a bar in months. On the negative side, online dating services can be expensive, and there are no guarantees of a good match. Also, although the companies do minor screening, nothing prevents a person from lying. People often lie about their age, weight, and appearance. Arranging a date through a dating service can put

more pressure on people than meeting in a natural way because people sometimes have unreasonably high expectations. Online dating services can be successful, but people should be realistic about what to expect.

TOPIC SENTENCE: Online dating services have many benefits, but users should also be aware of possible negatives.

SUPPORT POINT 1: One benefit of online dating services is that people do not have to cruise bars to meet people.

SUPPORT POINT 2: Contact via e-mail or text allows users to get to know each other a little before meeting.

DETOUR

OFF MAIN POINT: A good place to meet is a cheap restaurant. Most people like Italian food or burgers, so those types of places are safe.

SUPPORT POINT 3: The services also try to match compatible people by comparing profiles, so the likelihood of having something in common is greater than in a random encounter.

SUPPORT POINT 4: Also, online dating services offer many choices of screened possible dates, more than anyone could meet in a bar in months.

SUPPORT POINTS 5, 6: On the negative side, online dating services can be expensive, and there are no guarantees of a good match. Also, although the companies do minor screening, nothing prevents a person from lying.

SUPPORT POINT 7: Arranging a date through a dating service can put more pressure on people than meeting in a natural way because people sometimes have unreasonably high expectations.

CONCLUDING SENTENCE: Online dating services can be very successful, but people should be realistic about what to expect from computerized matches.

PRACTICE 1   Evaluating Unity

Read the following two paragraphs, and underline any detours from the main point. In the lines provided at the end of paragraph 2, indicate which paragraph is more unified and explain why.

1. Identity theft is becoming common in this country, but people can take several precautions to protect themselves. One way is to buy an inexpensive paper shredder and shred documents that contain your Social Security number or personal financial information. Shredded documents do not take up as much room in the trash, either. Another precaution is to avoid mailing change-of-address postcards. Thieves can intercept these and use them to get mail sent to your old address. Half the time people never keep these cards, so they just waste the postage. It would be better to notify people of your address change by phone or e-mail. When I moved, I sent postcards that had a misprint, so they were not good anyway. A third way is to avoid ever giving out your Social Security number. Even these precautions do not guarantee that your identity will not be stolen, but they will help prevent what is a time-consuming and expensive problem to set right.

2. Many new markets have appeared to meet the needs of pet owners who treat their pets as if they were precious children. The most thriving market is clothing, especially items that allow owners and their dogs to dress alike. This clothing includes cruisewear, formal-wear, and jeweled loungewear. Another big market is made up of hotels all over the world that advertise themselves as pet-friendly. These hotels provide doggie or cat beds, on-site grooming, and pet care professionals. The rooms are uniquely decorated and provide special meals prepared and served to meet the needs of each "guest." Each guest also is treated to an individualized exercise

For more practice in achieving unity in writing, visit *Exercise Central* at bedfordstmartins .com/realessays.

program. These new markets do not cater to the conservative spender: They appeal to those pet owners who seem willing to spend any amount of money on luxuries for their pets.

MORE UNIFIED PARAGRAPH: <u>Paragraph 2</u>

REASONS THAT THIS PARAGRAPH IS MORE UNIFIED THAN THE OTHER: <u>Answers will vary, but students should note that all of the support in the second paragraph clearly relates to the main point.</u>

TEACHING TIP
Choose a student to read these essays aloud to the class, and ask the rest of the class to stop the reader as soon as the essay detours from the main point.

PRACTICE 2   Revising for Unity

Each of the following essays includes sentences that are off the main point. Underline those sentences. The main point in each essay is in boldface type.

1.   Find four off-the-point sentences.

   Oprah Winfrey is one of the most influential people of our times, but that does not mean that life is easy for her. As a child in rural Mississippi, she was dirt-poor and sexually abused. Somehow, she managed to climb out of that existence and become successful. But because she is now a superstar, every aspect of her life is under the media spotlight, and she is frequently criticized for everything from her weight to her attempts to help people spiritually.

   Oprah's roller-coaster weight profile is always news. Every supermarket tabloid, every week, seems to have some new information about Oprah and her weight. <u>I can relate to how humiliating that must be. She looked like a balloon in an old picture I saw recently, even fatter than my Aunt Greta.</u>

   Oprah is also criticized for her wealth, estimated to be $2.7 billion in 2010. <u>She has a fabulous estate in Montecito, California, but does not spend all of her time there.</u> Oprah is generous with her money, giving large amounts to charities and people in need. For example, she started a school for girls in South Africa. Despite her good work, the media is always ready to portray her as too rich, even though many businesspeople are also very wealthy and do not give as much to worthy causes.

Oprah has even been criticized for her book club, although her recommendations prompted many people to become regular readers. When she recommended *The Corrections* by Jonathan Franzen, he said he did not want to be one of her choices because she sometimes recommended books he thought were not literary enough. He is a real snob in my mind, and my friends think so, too. When it was revealed that another author she recommended, James Frey, had made up some information in his memoir, some people said Oprah should have known. If the publisher did not know, how would Oprah?

Oprah Winfrey, despite her wealth and fame, does not have an easy life. Her critics feel free to cut her down at every turn. Instead, why not celebrate her personal and professional achievements? She deserves respect, not ridicule.

2.   Find four off-the-point sentences.

A recent survey of the places students prefer to study revealed some strange results. We would expect the usual answers, such as a library, bedroom, desk, and kitchen, and the survey respondents did in fact name such areas. But some people prefer less traditional places.

One unusual place cited was a church. The respondent said it was a great spot to study when services were not taking place because it was always quiet and not crowded. Some churches are locked during the day because of vandalism. Other churches have had big problems with theft.

Another unusual study area was the locker room during a football game. A problem is that the person would miss the game. Except for half-time, the large area was empty. The person who studied there claimed that there was a high energy level in the locker room that, combined with the quiet, helped him concentrate. I wonder what the smell was like, though.

The most surprising preference for a place to study was the bleachers by the pool of a gym. The light was good, said the student, she loved the smell of chlorine, and the sound of water was soothing.

The results may seem strange—a church, a locker room, and a pool—but they do share some characteristics: quiet, relative solitude, and no interruptions, other than half-time. Perhaps we should all think about new places that might help us study.

Practice Revising for Support and Detail

For more on primary
support points and
supporting details,
see Chapter 7.

Support is the evidence, examples, or facts that show, explain, or prove your main point. **Primary support points** are the major ideas developed in the paragraphs that make up the body of your essay. **Supporting details** are the specifics that explain your primary support to your readers.

When you read your draft essay, ask yourself: Do you provide enough information for your reader to understand the main point? Do you present enough evidence to convince your reader of that point? Look for places where you could add more support and detail, and examine your writing for obvious biases or errors in logic (see pp. 32–34).

Read the two paragraphs that follow, and note the support the writer added to the second one. Notice that she did not simply add to the paragraph; she also deleted some words and rearranged others to make the story clearer to readers. The additions are underlined; the deletions are crossed out.

> This morning I learned that my local police respond quickly and thoroughly to 911 calls. I meant to dial 411 for directory assistance, but by mistake I dialed 911. I hung up after only one ring because I realized what I had done. A few seconds after I hung up, the phone rang, and it was the police dispatcher. She said that she had received a 911 call from my number and was checking. I explained what happened, and she said she had to send a cruiser over anyway. Within a minute, the cruiser pulled in, and I explained what happened. I apologized and felt stupid, but I thanked him. I am glad to know that if I ever need to call 911, the police will be there.

REVISED TO ADD SUPPORT AND DETAIL

> This morning I <u>tested the 911 emergency system and found that it worked perfectly. Unfortunately, the test was a mistake.</u> ~~learned that my local police respond quickly and thoroughly to 911 calls.~~ I meant to dial 411 for directory assistance, but <u>without thinking</u> ~~by mistake~~ I dialed 911. I <u>frantically pushed the disconnect button</u> ~~hung up~~ after only one ring because I realized <u>my error.</u> ~~what I had done.~~ <u>As I reached for the phone to dial 411,</u> ~~A few seconds after I hung up,~~ <u>it rang like an alarm.</u> ~~the phone rang, and it was the police dispatcher.~~ <u>The police dispatcher crisply announced</u> ~~She said~~ that she had received a 911 call from my number and was checking. I <u>laughed weakly and</u> explained what happened, <u>hoping she would see the humor or at least the innocent human</u>

error. Instead, the crispness of her voice became brittle as ~~and~~ she said she had to send a cruiser over anyway. I went to meet my fate. Within a minute, the cruiser pulled in, and a police officer swaggered toward me. I explained what had happened, apologized, and thanked him humbly. I felt guilty of stupidity, at the least. ~~and felt very stupid, but I thanked him.~~ We learn from our mistakes, and in this case I am glad to know that if I ever need to call 911, the police will be there.

TEACHING TIP
Try reading these or other examples out loud, removing any transitional words and phrases. Then discuss how the lack of transitions makes it difficult for the reader to connect ideas in logical order. Also ask how the paragraph is organized — by time, space, or importance.

PRACTICE 3   Evaluating Support

In the two paragraphs that follow, the main points are in bold. Underline the primary support points, and put a check mark by each supporting detail. Then, in the lines provided at the end of paragraph 2, indicate which paragraph provides better support and explain why.

1. **Women tend to learn the art of fly fishing more easily than men.** <u>For one thing, they have more patience, which is key to successful fishing.</u> It may take many hours of silent, solitary fishing to catch a single fish. ✓ Even long hours may net no fish, and men tend to be more eager for results. ✓ This eagerness can make them more careless. ✓ <u>Women also tend to be more sensitive to subtle movements.</u> This trait helps both in the casting motion and in the reeling in of a fish. <u>Women are more likely to take breaks than men,</u> <u>who continue even when they are frustrated or tired.</u> <u>Women may also spend money on the appropriate attire for fishing, gear that is waterproof and warm.</u> <u>Finally, women are more receptive to fishing advice than are men.</u> These feminine traits make a big difference in fly fishing.

2. **Because they are susceptible to certain safety problems, people over the age of seventy-five should be required by law to take a driving test every year.** Some people believe that such a law would represent age discrimination because many people are great drivers until they are in their nineties. But government

statistics indicate that people over seventy-five have more accidents than younger drivers do. <u>One common failing of older drivers is impaired peripheral vision.</u> This vision problem makes it difficult ✓ for them to see cars on either side or at an intersection. <u>Another common problem is a longer response time.</u> Although older drivers may know to stop, it takes them much longer to move their foot ✓ from the gas pedal to the brake than it does younger drivers. This lengthened response time is the most common cause of accidents ✓ among older drivers. <u>The most dangerous failing among older drivers is a loss of memory.</u> Consider this common scenario: The driver starts to back out of a parking space after checking to see that there ✓ is nothing behind him. He then notices that his sunglasses have ✓ fallen on the floor. He retrieves them and puts his foot back on the ✓ gas pedal without remembering that he needs to look again. Because he is still in reverse, the car moves quickly and hits the ✓ person or car now behind him. Although it may inconvenience older drivers to take annual driving tests, it will help prevent injuries and save lives.

PARAGRAPH WITH BETTER SUPPORT: *Paragraph 2*

REASONS THAT THIS PARAGRAPH'S SUPPORT IS BETTER: *Answers will vary,*
but students might note that paragraph 2 provides supporting details for
each primary support point, while paragraph 1 introduces certain points
without backing them at all.

RESOURCES To gauge students' understanding of revision issues, including support and coherence, use the *Testing Tool Kit* CD available with this book.

For more practice in revising for support, visit *Exercise Central* at bedfordstmartins .com/realessays.

· ·

PRACTICE 4 Revising for Support

Read the following essay, and write in the space provided at least one additional support point or detail for each body paragraph and for the conclusion. Indicate where the added material should go in the paragraph by writing in a caret (^).

Anyone who has owned a dog knows that there is a special bond between dogs and humans. Even without speech, dogs seem to understand humans' words and emotions. Dogs have been beloved family pets for a very long time, but they are also being used effectively in new educational, workplace, and therapeutic settings.

Answers will vary.

Dog rescue organizations often bring dogs into schools to talk about the dogs' resilience and responsiveness to good care. For example, Greyhound Rescue, an organization that saves dogs from death after they are too old to race or when a track is being closed, is active in schools. Students meet the dogs and learn about caring for them and ways to help them. After visits, some students become volunteers at the organization.

Dogs work hard, too. They are sometimes brought into hotels to check for bedbugs, to airports for security checks, and to hospitals and nursing homes for patient therapy. There are also programs where chronically ill children are visited weekly by the same dog. The dogs seem to sense the children's pain or weakness, and their visits give the children something to look forward to. The dogs have the same effect on nursing home residents.

Dogs are also brought into prisons to be trained by prisoners. Sometimes inmates train these dogs as seeing-eye dogs for blind people. Other times prisoners ready abandoned puppies for adoption. Many violent prisoners have been successful trainers. The sad part is that they cannot keep the dogs they have trained.

Answers will vary.

It is said that dogs are man's best friend. They are trusting companions who love unconditionally. They are able to communicate and help where words sometimes do not.

· ·

Practice Revising for Coherence

Coherence in writing means that all the support connects to form a whole that makes sense. In other words, even when the support is arranged in a logical order, it still needs "glue" to connect the various points.

A piece of writing that lacks coherence sounds choppy, and is hard for the reader to follow. Revising an essay for coherence helps readers see how one point leads to another. The best way to improve coherence is to add transitions.

Transitions are words, phrases, and sentences that connect ideas so that writing moves smoothly from one point to another. Transitions can connect sentences and ideas within a paragraph and also connect one paragraph to another. The box on page 135 lists some, but not all, of the most common transitions and their purpose.

The following essay shows how transitions link ideas within sentences and paragraphs and connect one paragraph to the next. It also shows another technique for achieving coherence: repeating key words and ideas related to the main point. The transitions and key words in this piece are underlined.

I thought I would never make it to work today. I had an important meeting, and it seemed as if everything was conspiring against me. The conspiracy started before I even woke up.

I had set my alarm clock, but it did not go off, and therefore I did not wake up on time. When I did wake up, I was already late, not just by a few minutes but by an hour and a half. To save time, I brushed my teeth while I showered. Also, I figured out what I was going to wear. Finally, I

Common Transitional Words and Phrases

INDICATE SPACE RELATION

above	below	near	to the right
across	beside	next to	to the side
at the bottom	beyond	opposite	under
at the top	farther	over	where
behind	inside	to the left	

INDICATE TIME ORDER

after	eventually	meanwhile	soon
as	finally	next	then
at last	first	now	when
before	last	second	while
during	later	since	

INDICATE IMPORTANCE

above all	in fact	more important	most
best	in particular	most important	worst
especially			

SIGNAL EXAMPLES

for example	for instance	for one thing	one reason

SIGNAL ADDITIONS

additionally	and	as well as	in addition
also	another	furthermore	moreover

SIGNAL CONTRAST

although	in contrast	nevertheless	still
but	instead	on the other hand	yet
however			

SIGNAL CAUSE OR CONSEQUENCE

as a result	finally	so	therefore
because			

hopped out of the shower ready to get dressed. <u>But the conspiracy continued.</u>

<u>The next act of the conspiracy</u> concerned my only clean shirt, which was missing two buttons right in front. <u>After finding a sweater that would go over it,</u> I ran to the bus stop.

<u>When I got to the stop,</u> I discovered that the buses were running late. <u>When one finally came,</u> it was one of the old, slow ones, and it made stops about every ten feet. <u>In addition,</u> the heat was blasting, and I was sweating but could not take off my sweater because my shirt was gaping open. Now I was sweating, and perspiration was running down my scalp and neck. <u>At least,</u> I thought, I will dry off by the time the bus gets to my work.

<u>In fact,</u> I did dry off a little, but the conspiracy did not end there. <u>When</u> I <u>finally</u> got to work, the elevator was out of service, <u>so</u> I had to walk up ten flights of stairs. I was drenched, late, and inappropriately dressed. <u>By the time I got to my desk,</u> I knew that the hardest part of the day was behind me.

....

PRACTICE 5 Adding Transitional Words

TEAMWORK Practice 5 works well as a collaborative exercise. Have pairs of students try to find at least two transitional words to fill each blank and then discuss which word seems more appropriate and why.

Read the following paragraphs. In each blank, add a transition that would smoothly connect the ideas. In each case, there is more than one right answer. *Answers will vary. Suggested answers follow.*

> **EXAMPLE:** Many workers belong to labor unions that exist to protect worker rights. *However,* until the 1930s, unions did not exist. In the 1930s, Congress passed laws that paved the way for unions. *After that,* workers had the right to organize, bargain, and strike. *Today,* unions remain a powerful force in American politics.

1. The modern-day vending machine is based on an invention by a Greek scientist named Hero, who lived in the first century C.E. The machine that he invented required that the user insert a coin. *When After* the coin fell, it hit a lever. *Then* out came the desired product—a cup of holy water.

2. _When_ Jackie Robinson joined the Brooklyn Dodgers in 1947, he became the first African American to play major league baseball in the twentieth century. _Because_ he was the first, he was faced with what was called "breaking the color line" and received many death threats. _After_ a few seasons of playing well, he spoke out against discrimination against African Americans. _During_ his career, he played in six World Series and won the National League Most Valuable Player award in 1949.

3. Alcohol affects women more quickly than men. Their bodies interact with the alcohol in different ways. Women have more fat tissue, _and_ men have more muscle tissue, which has more water than fat tissue. _When_ men drink alcohol, it is diluted by the water in muscle. _But, However, In contrast,_ when women drink, the alcohol is more concentrated. _Therefore, As a result,_ women get drunk sooner.

· ·

PRACTICE 6 Adding Transitional Sentences

Read the following essay. Then, write a transitional sentence that would link each paragraph to the one following it. You may add your transitional sentence at the end of a paragraph, at the beginning of the next paragraph, or in both places.

For more practice in achieving coherence in writing, visit *Exercise Central* at bedfordstmartins .com/realessays.

Many teenagers today do not date in the traditional sense — one boy and one girl going on dates or "going steady." Instead, they go out in groups rather than as couples. This new pattern gives many parents a sense that their sons and daughters are safe from premature sex and sexually transmitted diseases.

Answers will vary.

Although teenagers do not pair off romantically, they are getting plenty of sex, just not with people they care about. They care about their friends and do not want to risk ruining friendships, so they "hook up" with strangers they meet while out at night or online. "Hooking up" means having sex with someone, and many teens hook up only with people they have no other contact with, preferably from different schools or towns.

_____

_____

Although teenagers often think that sex without emotional involvement will avoid heartbreak and breakups, many teens, both girls and boys, admit that it is difficult not to develop feelings for someone they are physically intimate with. If one person begins to feel an attachment while the other does not, a distancing occurs: That hurts. It is a breakup of a different sort.

_____

_____

Teenagers have always experimented with ways to do things differently than their parents did. Trying new ways to do things is an important stage in teenagers' development. Experimentation is normal and sometimes produces better ways of doing things. According to most teens, however, the "hook-up" is not the answer to heartbreak: It is just another road to it. Perhaps teenagers are destined to experience some pain as they try out what "love" means.

· ·

PRACTICE 7   Adding Transitions

The following essay has no transitions. Read it carefully, and add transitions both within and between the paragraphs. There is no one correct answer.
Answers will vary. Possible answers shown.

Skydiving is the most thrilling activity I can ever imagine. I was scared, euphoric, and proud during my one skydive. I would encourage anyone to have the experience of a lifetime.

<u>First</u> I was scared as I looked down out of the plane, ready to jump. The ground was barely visible. My instructor gave the ready sign, assuring me that he would be guiding me all the way. I closed my eyes, and we jumped out of the plane together. It felt as if we were dropping very fast. I opened my eyes and saw that, <u>in fact,</u> we were. I panicked a

little, fearing that the parachute would not open or that my instructor would activate it too late, and we would be killed.

I was _also_ euphoric. My instructor opened the chute, and we just glided silently through the air. It was like flying. It was peaceful and almost religious. I had never felt this way and knew that this was an important experience.

We landed, and I was proud of myself. It had taken a lot of courage to jump and to trust my life to another individual, my instructor. I had done it and done it well. I had benefited from the experience, mentally and spiritually. It was so thrilling and wonderful I probably will not do it again for fear that the second time would be an anticlimax. Do it!

Revise Your Own Essay

Before selecting a writing assignment, reread Deshon Briggs's draft in Chapter 8 (p. 119). Then, read his revised essay below. His revisions are highlighted in green.

DESHON'S REVISION

On the first day of my English class last spring, my teacher wrote "You are the change in your life" on the board. She said that ~~statement related to our going to college and making our lives better.~~ we had already taken a step toward change by coming to college to improve our lives. She said that we would be revisiting the theme of "people connecting to their communities" in our assignments and discussions and that we should be alert to ways that people are making a difference. She also gave us a writing assignment to explore ~~the statement that was due in four weeks.~~ and find ways that we could make the statement true in our own lives. The paper would not be due for four weeks, but we should start taking action now. I did not really know what she was talking about but figured I had plenty of time to think about it. In those four weeks, though, I learned that I really can be the change in my life.

Added detail

Details

Transition

Revised Thesis

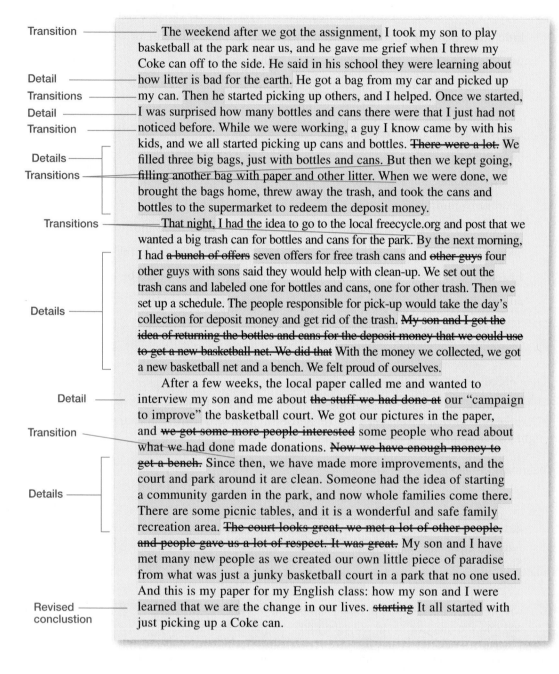

Transition —

Detail —
Transitions —
Detail —
Transition —

Details —
Transitions —

Transitions —

Details —

Detail —

Transition —

Details —

Revised conclusion —

The weekend after we got the assignment, I took my son to play basketball at the park near us, and he gave me grief when I threw my Coke can off to the side. He said in his school they were learning about how litter is bad for the earth. He got a bag from my car and picked up my can. Then he started picking up others, and I helped. Once we started, I was surprised how many bottles and cans there were that I just had not noticed before. While we were working, a guy I know came by with his kids, and we all started picking up cans and bottles. ~~There were a lot.~~ We filled three big bags, just with bottles and cans. But then we kept going, filling another bag with paper and other litter. When we were done, we brought the bags home, threw away the trash, and took the cans and bottles to the supermarket to redeem the deposit money.

That night, I had the idea to go to the local freecycle.org and post that we wanted a big trash can for bottles and cans for the park. By the next morning, I had ~~a bunch of offers~~ seven offers for free trash cans and ~~other guys~~ four other guys with sons said they would help with clean-up. We set out the trash cans and labeled one for bottles and cans, one for other trash. Then we set up a schedule. The people responsible for pick-up would take the day's collection for deposit money and get rid of the trash. ~~My son and I got the idea of returning the bottles and cans for the deposit money that we could use to get a new basketball net. We did that~~ With the money we collected, we got a new basketball net and a bench. We felt proud of ourselves.

After a few weeks, the local paper called me and wanted to interview my son and me about ~~the stuff we had done at~~ our "campaign to improve" the basketball court. We got our pictures in the paper, and ~~we got some more people interested~~ some people who read about what we had done made donations. ~~Now we have enough money to get a bench.~~ Since then, we have made more improvements, and the court and park around it are clean. Someone had the idea of starting a community garden in the park, and now whole families come there. There are some picnic tables, and it is a wonderful and safe family recreation area. ~~The court looks great, we met a lot of other people, and people gave us a lot of respect. It was great.~~ My son and I have met many new people as we created our own little piece of paradise from what was just a junky basketball court in a park that no one used. And this is my paper for my English class: how my son and I were learned that we are the change in our lives. ~~starting~~ It all started with just picking up a Coke can.

REVISING ASSIGNMENTS

1. Revise an essay using the draft you developed in Chapter 8. Before revising, read the following checklist.

2. Look back over the photographs in this chapter on pages 129 and 133, and below. Select one and write a draft essay in which you respond to the photo and summarize what it says to you. Revise what you have written using the techniques in the checklist below.

TEACHING TIP
Make revision concrete by challenging students to find at least one place in their drafts where detail can be added and at least one.place where a transition can be added.

Skydiver over the Burning Man festival in Nevada's Black Rock Desert.

CHECKLIST

Revising Your Essay

FOCUS

☐ After a break, reread your draft with a fresh perspective.

ASK

☐ What is your point or position? Does your thesis statement clearly state your main point?

☐ Does your essay have the following?

— An introductory paragraph

— Three or more body paragraphs

— A topic sentence for each paragraph that supports the main point

— A forceful concluding paragraph that reminds readers of the main point and makes an observation

☐ Does your essay have unity?

— Do all of the support points relate directly to the main point?

— Do all of the supporting details in each body paragraph relate to the paragraph's topic sentence?

— Have you avoided drifting away from the main point?

☐ Do you have enough support?

— Taken together, do the topic sentences of each paragraph give enough support or evidence for the main point?

— Do individual paragraphs support their topic sentences?

— Would more detail strengthen your support?

☐ Is your essay coherent?

— Have you used transitional words to link ideas?

— Have you used transitional sentences to link paragraphs?

REVISE

☐ Revise your draft, making any improvements you can. Be sure to look for bias or errors in reasoning.

reflect What did you look for as you revised your draft? What did you find? Describe your writing process from start to finish.

Part 2

Writing Different Kinds of Essays

Narration

Writing That Tells Stories

Understand What Narration Is

Narration is writing that tells a story of an event or experience.

Four Basics of Good Narration

1 It reveals something of importance to your reader (**main point**).

2 It includes all the major events of the story (**primary support**).

3 It uses details to bring the story to life for your audience (**secondary support**).

4 It presents the events in a clear order, usually according to when they happened.

In the following passage, each number corresponds to one of the Four Basics of Good Narration.

1 Thanksgiving is a time of repeating old traditions, such as gathering with family and friends and eating special foods like turkey, cranberry relish, and pumpkin pie. Every year, my family and I go to my older sister's and brother-in-law's house, and we enjoy the whole traditional experience. But it was there that I also learned how unexpected new traditions can enter the mix and make a holiday even more meaningful.

Ibrahim Siddo and tea-making equipment.

Attayo go denjo bon (The tea is on the fire), A go ga zarga (It is boiling), A go ga zarga (It is boiling). — From a song by Nigerian rap group Lakal Kaney (Zarma for "peace of mind")

2 My sister's son Jacob had spent a semester in Niger, a desert country in central Africa. There he made a good friend, Ibrahim, who had moved to the United States to study science and engineering. My sister and brother-in-law invited Ibrahim to Thanksgiving every year, so gradually we all came to know this warm and friendly person.

He would ask questions about Thanksgiving traditions, which were new and unfamiliar to him. We would ask questions about his country, which was unfamiliar to us. **3** In response he would often say, "Well, where I am from, whenever we gather, we drink a strong, sweet, green tea called atai." It was as though, to him, this tea seemed strangely missing from the party.

2 One year he brought with him everything necessary to make the tea in the traditional way of his country: **3** two small metal pots with lids; tea leaves; sugar; special small glasses, like shot glasses; a tiny wire grill; and charcoal. He made the tea on my sister's back porch, though the weather was drizzly and cold. The process was complicated, and involved boiling the tea a long time, then pouring it from high up, to cool it. Patience is a necessary ingredient.

2 When the tea was finally ready, we all hesitatingly took sips from the little glasses, expecting to try it, set it aside, and think "that will be that." **3** But the tea was so pleasingly tasty—smoky and sweet—and so strikingly different that this custom quickly became an essential and beloved Thanksgiving tradition. **2** Now Ibrahim carefully makes this tea every year and serves it at the end of the big meal, and the holiday would not seem right otherwise.

1 I give thanks to Ibrahim for enlarging my world and proving that, when it comes to excellent customs, there is plenty of room at the table for one more.

Telling stories is one important way in which we communicate with one another. Whether they are serious or humorous, stories provide information and examples that can show, explain, or prove a point.

Common types of narratives include stories of discovery, escape, journey, rescue, revenge, love, growth in self-knowledge, and transition to maturity. In other words, stories often involve people dealing with change. In stories we figure out ways through trials and tragedies, large and small. We learn how to define or achieve success. We overcome obstacles and break through cultural and personal limitations. And we wrestle with large forces and events beyond our control, often with the help of others.

SEEING NARRATION

write   What is the story here?

DISCUSSION
People affected by the Gulf oil spill tell their story at a news conference in Washington, D.C., showing jars of oil and water. Ask students what "props" they would use to help tell their stories.

You can use narration in many practical situations. Consider the following examples.

COLLEGE   In a U.S. history course, you trace, in your own words, the specific sequence of events that led the United States to enter World War II.

WORK   A customer becomes angry with you and lodges a complaint with your boss. You recount — in writing — what happened.

EVERYDAY LIFE   Your wallet is stolen, and you file a written account with the police reporting exactly what happened.

DISCUSSION
As a class, generate other uses of narration in these areas.

For an example of an actual narration written for work, see page 155. The piece was written by the journalist who is profiled in the box on page 154.

Main Point in Narration

Whenever you write a narration, have a **purpose** in mind, whether that purpose is to explain what happened, to prove something, or simply to entertain someone. If you do not know the purpose of your narration, your readers will not know it either.

Also consider who your audience is and what they know and do not know. Finally, be clear on your **main point**—what is important about the narration. Generally, college instructors will want your main point to indicate what is important to you about a story. For clarity, state the main point in the first paragraph, and remind readers of it at the end of your narration.

Take another look at the passage under the Four Basics of Good Narration (p. 145).

> . . . I also learned how unexpected new traditions can . . . make a holiday even more meaningful.

This statement emphasizes the event's importance to the writer.

In writing a narrative, make sure your topic sentence (for paragraphs) and thesis statement (for essays) communicate your general topic and the main point you are making about the topic.

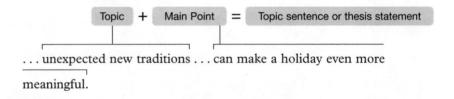

> Topic + Main Point = Topic sentence or thesis statement

. . . unexpected new traditions . . . can make a holiday even more meaningful.

PRACTICE 1   Determining the Main Point

Look back at your response to the "write" prompt on page 145. What is your main point? What is important or significant about the incident you are narrating?

Support in Narration

To **support** your main point, you will present and explain the major events in the story and describe relevant details. As you write a narration, you will have decisions to make—what to include, what to leave out, and what perspective you will take on events. Your **point of view** determines how you will present the major events and details of the story and how you will support your main point.

Point of View

In a narration, the events you include and the way you describe them create a story that is based on your point of view. For example, two people who witness or participate in the same series of events may give different accounts because they perceive what happened differently.

The stories that Gloria and Mason tell in the following two paragraphs reflect their different points of view regarding the same experience.

GLORIA'S STORY

This morning, Mason and I set out for what was supposed to be a great day at the beach, but Mason's stubborn behavior ruined everything. First, he took the longest route, so we hit traffic that we would have avoided by going the short route. Then, we got lost. When I suggested that we stop and ask for directions, Mason refused. After another hour of driving, we passed an intersection that we'd crossed earlier. I again suggested that we stop and ask for directions, but Mason wasn't buying it. So we drove some more. Finally, we were about to run out of gas, so we pulled into a gas station. While Mason was filling the tank, I asked the attendant for directions. If we hadn't needed gas, we'd still be driving around looking for that beach!

MASON'S STORY

This morning, Gloria and I set out for what was supposed to be a great day at the beach, but Gloria wanted to pick a fight. First, she insisted I was going the wrong way, it was going to take us longer, and we'd hit more traffic. Then, she decided we were lost. I knew where we were going, but Gloria kept on nagging me to stop and ask for directions. When we were almost there, I decided to get gas, and she had to ask the attendant for directions. I don't know what was going on with her, but she was really on my case.

When you write a narration, describe events in a way that will tell the story you want to tell to your audience.

Major Events and Details

The **major events** of a story are your primary support in narration, and they will usually become the topic sentences for the body paragraphs in your essay. Ask yourself what the major events are and what makes them important. To help your readers experience the events as you did, give supporting details that bring the experience to life.

ESL Ask students to describe any events they see differently from their classmates or coworkers because of language or cultural differences.

RESOURCES To gauge students' understanding of main point, support, and other writing and grammar issues, use the *Testing Tool Kit* CD available with this book.

For more on
supporting a point,
see Chapter 7.

For example, one student stated the main point of an event in the following thesis: *The theft of my wallet this morning showed me how easy it is for criminals to deceive unsuspecting victims.*

For more on listing,
see page 70.

The student then did some listing to come up with the major events and details about those events.

MAJOR EVENTS (primary support)	SUPPORTING DETAILS (secondary support)
Woman bumped into me	Light bump, but she dropped her folder of papers, and they scattered
I bent down to help her collect the papers.	Wind was blowing, so I had to work fast
A man stopped and asked if he could help.	I didn't get a good look at him because I was trying to get the papers, but he stood close to me and hung around for a minute just watching us. Then, he just left without saying anything.
Woman thanked me, and I said no problem	She had her head down and walked off fast.
When I went to get coffee, I realized the wallet was gone.	I broke into a sweat at the café and had that horrible panicked feeling.
I realized that the man and woman were working together.	Looking back on the details, it was clear how carefully they had planned the theft.

Dialogue

For more on using
quotation marks, see
Chapter 38.

As you tell the story, you might want to include direct speech or **dialogue,** the words that you or other people said. If you report exactly what was said, use quotation marks.

> The woman said, "Oh, I'm so sorry! I'll never be able to get these papers before they blow away, and my boss will have a fit."

Using direct speech can bring a narration alive.

Organization in Narration

For more on
chronological order,
see page 105.

Because narration tells a story of "what happened," it often uses **chronological (time) order**. Start at the beginning of the story, and describe the events in the sequence in which they occurred.

Time transitions (words and phrases like *next* and *meanwhile*) are important in narration because they make the order of events clear to readers. Writers of narration use these common transitions not only within a paragraph — to move from one detail about the event to the next — but also between paragraphs to move from one major event to the next.

For more on transitions, see pages 134–35.

Common Time Transitions

after	eventually	meanwhile	soon
as	finally	next	still
at last	first	now	then
before	last	second	when
during	later	since	while

Read and Analyze Narration

Before writing your narration essay, read the following three examples of narration—from college, the workplace, and everyday life—and answer the questions that accompany them.

For more examples of narration, see Chapter 41.

Narration in College

A student wrote the following essay for a college writing course. The assignment was "Write an essay describing an important decision in your life."

For each of the following three essays, review the Four Basics of Good Narration (p. 145) and practice your critical reading process by doing the following.

2PR   The Critical Reading Process

Preview the reading, including the guiding question.

Read the piece, double-underlining the <u><u>thesis statement</u></u>, underlining the <u>major support</u>, and circling the transitions. Consider the quality of the support.

Pause to think during reading. Take notes and ask questions about what you are reading: Talk to the author.

Review the reading, your guiding question, your marginal notes and questions, and your answers to the Pause prompts.

TEACHING TIP The questions following the three readings can be done either in writing or as class discussions.

TEAMWORK Have students work through the first essay together to apply the critical reading process and answer the questions after the essay.

Jordan Brown

A Return to Education

GUIDING QUESTION
How does Jordan feel about his return to college?

VOCABULARY
The following words are *italicized* in the essay: *anticipation*, *stamina*. If you do not know their meanings, look them up in a dictionary or online.

CRITICAL READING
■ Preview
■ Read
■ Pause
■ Review

PAUSE: Why did Brown join the army? Was it a good decision for him?

1   For me, college has been an experience marked by *anticipation*, fear, and pride. I sometimes find myself still surprised that I am really here. The journey to get here has been a long one, but if I can put my fears behind me, I believe I will be able to accomplish something that I can really be proud of.

2   Being able to go to college is something that I have been anticipating for many years. Since I left high school and the California Bay Area behind, I have been on the go in one way or another. After graduation, I felt that I wasn't ready for the commitments or responsibilities of college. Instead, I enlisted in the army. The army provided me with the maturity and self-discipline that I desperately needed in my life; however, being in the army also provided me with very little time or money to go to college, so I put it off until "a later date."

3   After the army, I sought a higher-paying job, first becoming a truck driver. This job provided me with money but no time. Now I work for the railroad, and with my apprenticeship behind me, I have some free time for the first time in my life.

PAUSE: How does Brown's first sentence here relate to the first paragraph? What questions does he have?

4   What I have been anticipating for years is finally here. I now have the time and money for college, but do I have the ability? It has been eleven years since I last sat in a classroom. This made me question myself: Can I do this? Will I succeed? Will I fail? Am I even capable of learning in a classroom environment? Although I had these questions, I knew that the only way to face my fears was to attack them head-on. I reminded myself that the only thing I could do is try.

PAUSE: Why was Brown nervous?

5   When I first walked into Front Range Community College, I was nervous. I couldn't help but notice how young everyone looked. I got to my study skills class, sat down, and looked around. I felt out of place. Most of the people in the class looked as if they had just graduated from high school. When we did our introductions, however, I learned that one of the women sitting across the room had graduated from high school eleven years ago. I started to feel a little younger.

6   When I got to my philosophy class, I watched the other students come in and noticed that not everyone looked like a kid. This class looked very much like an American melting pot, with students of many ages and cultures. As we went around the room introducing ourselves, I felt very much more confident about my decision to try college. Many students were even older than I was. A woman sitting near me, who looked about my mom's age, said she was in college because all of her kids were in college now. She told us that she wanted a college education and a better job. An older gentleman across the room said that he was a business executive from Germany. His job had become boring, and he was looking for something more challenging. By the end of the introductions, I was convinced that this "college thing" might just work.

PAUSE: How do the other students help Brown feel better?

7   Since I have gone back to school, there has been a lot of pride surrounding me. My parents can't stop talking about me and how proud they are. My family and friends are excited for me and congratulate me on my decision. I am also proud of myself for making the tough decision to go back to school. I know that when I get my degree, I will have something to be truly proud of.

PAUSE: How does Brown's first sentence here relate back to his thesis statement?

8   I still have fears and uncertainties. But I also have positive anticipation and hope. Now, I know that I am on the right course. I know that as long as I have *stamina* and determination, nothing can stop me from achieving my dream of getting my degree in mechanical engineering.

PAUSE: How does Brown tie his conclusion to his introduction?

1. **Summarize.** Briefly summarize Brown's essay, including his **main point** and **purpose** and the **major events** in his story. What is his point of view?

2. **Analyze.** Does Brown's **support** all relate to his main point? Is it logically organized? Does he give you enough details? How do the topic sentences relate specifically to the thesis statement? Did the title give you an idea of what the essay would be about?

3. **Synthesize.** How does Brown's experience relate to your own or to other things you have thought about, read, or heard?

4. **Evaluate.** Does Brown achieve his purpose? Does his essay have the **Four Basics of Good Narration** (see p. 145)? What do *you* think of his essay, and why?

CRITICAL THINKING
■ Summarize
■ Analyze
■ Synthesize
■ Evaluate

(More on p. 21.)

Narration at Work

The following profile shows how a journalist uses narration in her work. (Notice that the "Background" section is narration too.)

Narration in the Real World

Monique Rizer
Journalist and
Development
Associate

Background   I was the oldest of six children, and before my mother married my stepfather, she was on welfare. She homeschooled me for five years until I begged her to let me go to a public high school. There I made friends with some people who expected to go to college, and I realized I wanted to go, too. I started at Green River Community College, but just then my parents' financial situation got really bad, and the eight of us had to move to a trailer. I stopped going to school and floundered for a while, until I met my future husband, who was going to a community college and encouraged me to go back. I enrolled at Highline Community College, and several months later I became pregnant with my first son. I was determined to stay in college, so I completed one year at Highline. That summer, I had my son, got married, and found loans to transfer to Pacific Lutheran University. While there, I received a Gates Millennium Scholarship, which made continuing college possible.

Although I moved a few times, I graduated from college and went on to graduate school. After I finished graduate school, I had another son. Later, my husband was called to active duty and deployed to Iraq for fifteen months. Although he was wounded, he returned home safely.

Colleges / Degrees   B.A., Gonzaga University; M.S., Syracuse University

Employer   National Military Family Association

Writing at work   I have done many types of writing. I rewrote marketing material while working at an accounting firm, and when my husband was in Iraq, I wrote a newsletter for families of soldiers with advice on finding resources and keeping up morale and with news of what was going on with the soldiers in Iraq.

I had to find my own resources for military families, which was not easy. I had to write well, speak well, and be persistent. You have to communicate effectively to get what you need in life, and words give you the power to fight.

How Monique uses narration   Much of the writing I do involves telling people's stories so that readers can understand them and their unique problems.

RESOURCES For a discussion of how to use the profiles in Part 2, see *Practical Suggestions for Teaching Real Essays with Readings*.

Monique Rizer's Narration

The following is an excerpt from an article, published in the *Chronicle of Higher Education*, that Rizer wrote in her profession as a journalist.

GUIDING QUESTION
How has being a parent and student affected Rizer's decisions?

VOCABULARY
The following words are *italicized* in the excerpt: *fidgeted, postpartum, intangible*. If you do not know their meanings, look them up in a dictionary or online.

When Students Are Parents

Crammed behind my desk, I *fidgeted* and shifted my eyes to observe the other students in the room. I tried not to look the way I felt—like I didn't belong there with them. I couldn't help noticing that all the other women were wearing shorts, sandals, flirty summer dresses: appropriate clothes for a warm September day. I tugged at the baggy clothes hiding my *postpartum* weight. I thought of my six-week-old son and hoped I'd make it home to nurse him at the scheduled time. The thought of him reminded me that however odd I felt, I was going to stay in college this time.

It was the summer of 1998. I was a twenty-year-old new mother and wife, and it was my first day of class, though not my first day of college. I'd begun my long journey through higher education three years before, but my plans to attend full time after high school graduation were put on hold when financial difficulties forced my family of eight to move. I then found a local community college and felt prepared to start again, but instead the registration papers sat abandoned in my car, where I practically lived since home was a 32-foot trailer filled with seven other people. In the summer of 1996, I packed my bags and left to live on my own; I enrolled again the next spring and had my son in July 1998. I knew I had to stay in school and go full time. I wanted more for my son and myself, even though I wasn't sure what exactly "more" was at the time.

Focusing on my son helped me to persist in college during difficult times, and there were many. I did not have time to socialize with other students because when I was not in class, I had to rush to take care of the details of life as a mother. Grocery shopping, cooking, arranging for child care, taking my son to the doctor when he was sick, seemed to take every minute. I was exhausted every day, and finding the time and mental energy to study and do homework often seemed an overwhelming challenge. But I stuck with it, determined to finish, to do what my mother had not done. When she had me at nineteen, she quit college and never returned.

What helped me finish college, even after my marriage and the birth of my second son, was meeting other students who were also parents. I realized other people were in my situation, too, and probably felt just as stretched. As I met other mothers, we offered to baby-sit for each other or to get together with our children so that they could play, and we could study. All of us

PAUSE: Have you felt out of place in college or other places?

PAUSE: How do you think Rizer found the strength to go back to school after dropping out?

PAUSE: How was being a student parent both difficult and helpful?

wanted more for our children than we had had, and that kept us going.

My commitment to finish college has paid off. Now, I have a bachelor's in journalism from Gonzaga University and a master's in information management from Syracuse University. During my years in school, my son kept me focused and ignited my ambition to be a better student. In my experience, there is no better motivation to finish college and to appreciate the full experience than a child whose future depends on your decisions. I had to continue to use my education to give him a better life and to set an example for him to follow.

I feel a tremendous sense of accomplishment: I've learned so many *intangible* lessons about myself; I've decided that I want to help other young parents achieve their educational goals; and I see a better future for my boys (I have two now). And I keep telling my mom that she doesn't have to live vicariously through me: She can return to college any time she wants. Being a student and a parent is challenging, but nothing is more rewarding than providing a bright future for your children.

PAUSE: Do you have enough information to understand how Rizer got through college?

1. Briefly summarize Rizer's essay, including her **main point** and **purpose** and the **major events** in her story. *Answers will vary.*

2. Carefully examine the **Four Basics of Good Narration** (p. 145) and determine specifically whether Rizer's workplace writing is a good narration. Make notes to support your opinion. _____

3. What is your reaction to Rizer's essay? What would you say to her or ask her if you had the chance? _____

Narration in Everyday Life

The following address was originally broadcast on National Public Radio.

Howard White

The Power of Hello

GUIDING QUESTION
What is the power of hello in White's experience?

VOCABULARY
The following words are *italicized* in the essay: *gazillion, acknowledged, guidepost, foundation, humble*. If you do not know their meanings, look them up in a dictionary or online.

1   I work at a company where there are about a *gazillion* employees. I do not say that I know them all by name, but I know my fair share of them. I think that almost all of them know me. I would say that's the reason I've been able to go wherever it is I've made it to in this world. It is all based on one simple principle: I believe every single person deserves to be *acknowledged*, however small or simple the greeting.

2   When I was about 10 years old, I was walking down the street with my mother. She stopped to speak to Mr. Lee. I was busy trying to bulls-eye the "O" in the stop sign with a rock. I knew I could see Mr. Lee any old time around the neighborhood, so I did not pay any attention to him. After we passed Mr. Lee, my mother stopped me and said something that has stuck with me from that day until now. She said, "You let that be the last time you ever walk by somebody and not open up your mouth to speak, because even a dog can wag its tail when it passes you on the street." That phrase sounds simple, but it has been a *guidepost* for me and the *foundation* of who I am.

3   When you write an essay like this, you look in the mirror and see who you are and what makes up your character. I realized mine was cemented that day when I was ten years old. Even then, I started to see that when I spoke to someone, they spoke back. And that felt good.

4   It is not just something I believe in; it's become a way of life. I believe that all people deserve to feel someone acknowledge their presence, no

PAUSE: Why does White tell this story?

PAUSE: What does the first sentence mean?

PAUSE: Where does White echo his thesis?

CRITICAL
READING
■ Preview
■ Read
■ Pause
■ Review

matter how *humble* they may be or even how important. At work, I always used to say hello to the founder of the company and ask him how our business was doing. But I was also speaking to the people in the café and the people who cleaned the buildings, and asked how their children were doing. I remembered after a few years of passing by the founder, I had the courage to ask him for a meeting. We had a great talk. At a certain point, I asked him how far he thought I could in go in his company. He said, "If you want to, you can get all the way to this seat."

5   I have become vice president, but that has not changed the way I approach people. I still follow my mother's advice. I speak to everyone I see, no matter where I am. I have learned that speaking to people creates a pathway into their world, and it lets them come into mine, too.

6   The day you speak to someone who has his head held down and when he lifts it up and smiles, you realize how powerful it is just to open your mouth and say, "Hello."

PAUSE: Why do you think the founder feels this way about White?

PAUSE: How has what White learned helped him?

1. Briefly summarize White's essay. *Answers will vary.*

2. What is the author's purpose? *To convey an important life lesson.*

3. What did you learn from reading White's essay? *Answers will vary.*

TEACHING TIP
Have students do this in pairs, and have each pair ask the questions of the class. Or, have two pairs swap questions and answer the other pair's questions and discuss.

4. Does White's story reflect the Four Basics of Narration (p. 145)? *A reader may be curious for even more events and details.*

5. Write three questions that you would ask if you were writing a quiz on White's essay (and be able to answer your own questions). *Answers will vary.*

6. Of the three essays in this chapter, which do you think is the best narration, and why? Which did you like the best? Which made you think? *Answers will vary.*

Write a Narration Essay

In this section, you will write your own narration essay based on one of the following assignments. Use the following tools to help you.

1. Review the Four Basics of Good Narration (p. 145).
2. Use Narration at a glance as a basic organizer.
3. Use the Writing Guide: Narration checklist as you write and revise (pp. 163–64).

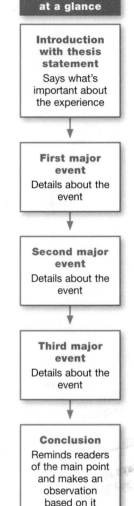

ASSIGNMENT 1   Writing about College, Work, and Everyday Life

Write a narration essay on *one* of the following topics or on a topic of your own choice.

COLLEGE
- Write about your first experiences of college, as Jordan Brown and Monique Rizer did.
- Explain what led you to start college.
- Summarize an interesting story you learned in one of your other classes, such as psychology or history.

WORK
- Tell the story of something positive you did at work (some achievement).
- Explain what you learned from getting or doing your first job.
- Describe an incident that shows your boss as _____ _____ (supportive/unsupportive, fair/unfair, clueless/sharp, realistic/unrealistic, honest/dishonest).

EVERYDAY LIFE
- Recount a time when you took a risk.
- Recount the most embarrassing, rewarding, happy, or otherwise memorable moment in your life.
- Write about a time when you were proud or ashamed of your behavior.

. . . .

ASSIGNMENT 2 Writing about an Image

Choose one of the images on this page or the next. Write a narration essay about what has happened (or is happening) in the picture. Be as creative as you like, but be sure to apply what you know about reading a visual (Chapter 3), and follow the Four Basics of Good Narration (p. 145).

A.

B.

ASSIGNMENT 3   Writing to Solve a Problem

PROBLEM: Your school is mounting an antibullying campaign, and a committee consisting of the dean of student life, five faculty members, and five students has been formed to study the issue and make recommendations. You are part of that committee. As a first step, the committee has agreed that it needs to consider the various types of bullying that people experience and to involve as many students as possible. All committee members will write about bullying that they have experienced, participated in, or witnessed, describing the event in detail. The committee will select five of the essays to post online as examples, and posters displayed around campus will invite other students to submit their experiences.

ASSIGNMENT: Write an essay about bullying from your own experience. Consider the purpose and audience, and use what you have learned about good narration.

. . . .

ASSIGNMENT 4 Writing about Connections

Read the account of Aurelius Taylor before doing the assignment that follows.

COMMUNITY CONNECTIONS

Aurelius Taylor,
Owens Community College
President, student government

Aurelius "Chris" Taylor grew up in poverty, the son of drug-addicted parents. He started at Owens Community College after graduating from high school, but he dropped out because he believed he was not smart enough and did not belong. He then made some poor choices and started selling drugs. After a few years and the birth of a child, he realized he had to be a good role model for his son. So he began again at Owens.

While working in his job on the cafeteria food line, Chris was always friendly and talked with lots of students and faculty. His life motto is "Smile." A few people encouraged him to join student government, but he was not comfortable at first because he "wasn't used to being around smart people who got good grades." He stayed with it, though, and was soon elected student government president.

Chris's English teacher, Kay Blue, taught him how to improve his writing skills, which he uses now as student government president, especially in the marketing of the organization and events such as Health Week, Spring Fling, Fall Fest, and the comedy show. His role in student government also has helped him learn important marketing, business, and people skills. He gets lots of respect on campus. He has also been a tutor in the Summer Bridge Program, where he is a role model for other urban students. He shows them "how to get their lives to be about college." He tells them it will not be easy, things will get bad at some point during the first year, and they will want to drop out, but he helps them make the commitment to education. He tells people that because of his involvement in student government, he is now an honor student. As he says, "Change is not easy, but it's worth every stressful moment."

ASSIGNMENT: Choose one of the following and write a narration essay. Work either on your own or with a partner.

- Interview someone in student government about how he or she became involved and what impact the involvement has had.
- Describe a bad choice you made and how it affected you and others.
- Write about a community you are a part of.
- Write about "life being about college."

ASSIGNMENT 5   Writing about Readings

The assignments that follow ask you to read at least two different examples of narration and draw from them to write your own essay.

- Read Jordan Brown's (p. 152) and Monique Rizer's (p. 155) essays in this chapter and Daniel Flanagan's essay, "The Choice to Do It Over Again" (p. 206). All are about education, especially the experience of returning to school after an absence. Drawing from these essays, write an essay about your experience of starting or returning to school.
- Read Langston Hughes's essay, "Salvation" (p. 691), and review Jordan Brown's and Monique Rizer's essays in this chapter. These three narratives include the experience of wanting to fit in, but with different outcomes. Write an essay about a time you felt pressured to fit in, the ways you responded, and the outcome. Draw from the readings to relate your experience to that of the other writers.

TEAMWORK
Have students, in pairs or small groups, share their plans for their narrative. Classmates can evaluate the order of the plan and suggest other supporting details.

For advice on summarizing, analyzing, synthesizing, and evaluating, see pages 21–25.

Use the steps in the Writing Guide that follows to help you prewrite, draft, revise, and edit your narration. Check off each step as you complete it.

WRITING GUIDE: NARRATION

STEPS IN NARRATION	HOW TO DO THE STEPS
☐ Focus.	• Think about your audience and what is important about your story.
☐ Explore your topic. See Chapter 5.	• Narrow your topic. • Prewrite, recalling what happened. Why is the story important?
☐ Write a thesis statement. Topic + Main Point = Thesis See Chapter 6.	• Say what is important about the story — how it affected you or others. →

STEPS IN NARRATION	HOW TO DO THE STEPS
☐ **Support your thesis.** See Chapter 7.	• Recall the major events. • Provide background information that your readers will need. • Describe the events with specific details.
☐ **Write a draft.** See Chapter 8.	• Arrange the events chronologically. • Consider using one of the introductory techniques in Chapter 8, and include your thesis statement in your introduction. • Write topic sentences for each major event. • Write a paragraph for each event giving details about them.
☐ **Revise your draft.** See Chapter 9.	• Get feedback using the peer-review guide for narration at **bedfordstmartins.com/realessays**. • Read to make sure that all events and details show, explain, or prove what is important about the story. • Add important events or details that occur to you. • Add time transitions. • Improve your introduction, thesis, and conclusion.
☐ **Edit your revised draft.** See Parts 4 through 7.	• Correct errors in grammar, spelling, word use, and punctuation.
☐ **Evaluate your writing.**	• Does it have the Four Basics of Good Narration (p. 145)? • Is this the best I can do?

reflect Reread your response to the "write" prompt on p. 145 and revise what you wrote to include what you have learned about narration. Adjust your statement of a main point, point of view, supporting details, dialogue, organization, and transitions as needed.

Illustration

Writing That Shows Examples

Understand What Illustration Is

Illustration is writing that uses examples to show, explain, or prove a point.

Four Basics of Good Illustration

1 It has a point.

2 It gives specific examples to show, explain, or prove the point.

3 It gives details to support the examples.

4 It uses enough examples to get the point across to the reader.

In the following paragraph, each number corresponds to one of the Four Basics of Good Illustration.

What is the strongest predictor of your health? 1 It may not be your income or age but rather your literacy. 2 People with low literacy skills have four times greater annual health costs than those with high skills. Why is literacy so important? 3 Most Americans read at an eighth- or ninth-grade level, and 20 percent read at just a fifth-grade level or below. However, most health-care materials are written above the tenth-grade level. 3 As many as half of all patients fail to take medications as directed, often because they don't understand the instructions. 2 Americans can improve their

4 Enough examples given to back the writer's main point

4 Enough examples given to back the writer's main point

health literacy by asking their doctor or pharmacist **3** three questions: (1) "What is my main problem?" (2) "What do I need to do?" and (3) "Why is it important to do this?" If you're still confused, don't hesitate to ask your doctor, nurse, or pharmacist to go over the information again.

—"Literacy and Health," *Parade,* 18 January, 2004

SEEING ILLUSTRATION

TEACHING TIP
Photographer Susan Barnett studies how "people reveal a part of themselves" through their T-shirts. Ask students for other examples.

write   What do these examples illustrate?

Whenever we explain something, we use examples to show what we mean. Here are some ways you might use illustration.

COLLEGE   In a criminal justice course, you discuss and give examples of the most common criminal violations.

WORK   Your written self-evaluation for work includes specific and measurable examples of how well (or poorly) you performed.

EVERYDAY LIFE   You take your car to a mechanic and give him or her examples that show how the car is not running properly.

Main Point in Illustration

Look at the opening sentences in the paragraph with the colored shading (p. 165).

What is the strongest predictor of your health? It may not be your income or age but rather your literacy.

In this case, the topic—the strongest predictor of your health—is in the opening sentence, which is followed by a surprising **main point**: that literacy might be a predictor of health. Because the point is surprising, the reader will be interested in reading on to find out how it could be true. The writer demonstrates the main point by giving examples.

For more on thesis statements, see Chapter 6.

Often, a thesis statement in illustration includes the topic and your main point.

For online exercises on main point and support, visit *Exercise Central* at bedfordstmartins .com/realessays.

Topic + Main point = Thesis statement

Getting involved in college activities has many benefits, including some you might not expect.

Support in Illustration

In illustration, the **examples** show or prove your stated main point.

A student who had written the thesis *Homeschooling is beneficial to both the child and the parent* focused her prewriting on finding examples of benefits of homeschooling. Here are some examples from her brainstorming.

individualized to child	parent and child have control
parent and child together	more flexibility
at child's own pace	considers child's learning style
one-on-one	education is part of regular life

WRITER AT WORK

JUAN GONZALEZ: Examples show people what you mean.

(See Juan Gonzalez's **PROFILE OF SUCCESS** on page 171.)

An illustration essay usually uses several examples as **support points**. The writer of the prewriting on homeschooling selected "individualized to child" as one support point and asked herself, "What do I mean? How? In what ways?" to find supporting details.

She also chose "parent and child have control" as another major example that would support the thesis. She then asked herself, "How do they have more control?" and listed potential supporting details.

control over materials used (what books, what computer programs, what approach)

control over time of instruction (what hours of the day, based on child's natural rhythms, vacations—not tied to a school's calendar)

Organization in Illustration

For more on order
of importance, see
pages 106–07.

Illustration often uses **order of importance** to organize several examples, saving the most vivid, convincing example for last.

Transitions are important in illustration because they signal to readers that you are moving from one example to another. Use transitions to move between sentences within a paragraph and also to move between paragraphs.

Common Transitions in Illustration

also	finally	for instance	in addition
another	for example	for one thing	one example . . .
			another example

Read and Analyze Illustration

Before writing an illustration essay, read the following three examples of illustration—from college, the workplace, and everyday life—and answer the questions that accompany them.

TEAMWORK
Have students work
through the first essay
together to apply the
critical reading pro-
cess and answer the
questions after the
essay.

For each of the following three essays, review the Four Basics of Good Illustration (p. 165) and practice your critical reading process by doing the following.

2PR   The Critical Reading Process

■ **P**review the reading, including the guiding question.

■ **R**ead the piece, double-underlining the thesis statement, underlining the major support, and circling the transitions. Consider the quality of the support.

■ **P**ause to think during reading. Take notes and ask questions about what you are reading: Talk to the author.

■ **R**eview the reading, your guiding question, your marginal notes and questions, and your answers to the Pause prompts.

Illustration in College

For more examples
of illustration, see
Chapter 42.

The following is part of a report that Luz Medina wrote when she served as a student representative to the Division of Student Affairs at her college. Her job was to survey some other students and present a list of suggestions for new services that would help students.

GUIDING QUESTION
What does Luz Medina learn from her interviews?

To: Vice President, Student Affairs

Fr: Luz Medina

Re: Suggestions for student services

1   To complete this report, I interviewed twenty-five students, asking them the following questions: (1) Do you know about the student services that are available on this campus? (2) What service or organization would help your college experience and why? (3) Would you be willing to help set up this program? I have attached the complete responses to these questions, but here I will summarize what I found. <u>The responses were both surprising and well worth considering in the future.</u>

2   To my surprise, <u>most of the students I interviewed were not aware of the many programs that are already available to them.</u> For example, several of the students said that they did not know what to do if they were thinking about dropping out. I told them about our Succeeding Together program and gave them the Web site that lists the people and services that are designed just for these situations. I encouraged them to go to these sites for help, telling them that the college works hard to help keep students from dropping out.

3   Another area in which we have many services that students do not know about is in preparing for a job search. Most students knew that there is an office of career planning, but they thought it just posted job announcements. They did not know about great programs like the Virtual Job Fair or the many mini-seminars on interviewing, making a good first impression, or one-on-one counseling to match students with employers. They also did not know about the program that gives very specific career counseling that matches student interests with careers and then helps students plan what courses will best help them get started in the career.

4   <u>There were many other services students did not know about.</u> Although they are listed online and we offer an orientation, I think we, as a committee, should figure out how to more successfully let students know what resources they have on this campus.

5   The students offered some good suggestions for new services. One is that we devise an instant-messaging system for communication with advisers. Students said that often they have to wait to see their advisers when

TEACHING TIP
Have students find out what services are available on your campus.

CRITICAL READING
■ Preview
■ Read
■ Pause
■ Review

PAUSE: How is the first sentence linked to the thesis statement?

PAUSE: What is Medina's purpose? Who is her audience?

PAUSE: What examples does Medina give of her topic sentence?

they have a question that would take only a minute to ask and answer. One student compared it to standing in a long line to buy a package of gum: It doesn't seem worth the wait.

PAUSE: How are paragraphs 6 and 7 related to paragraph 5?

6   Two other good suggestions regard the problems students often have with transportation and child care. Students suggested that there be a college-sponsored online bulletin board that students can go to to find rides at various times. Students looking for transportation could find other students with cars who would be willing to give students rides for a small fee. The students also suggested a similar child-care bulletin board that might help parents connect to baby-sit for each other.

7   A final suggestion that two students made was to have professors record their lectures so that they could be downloaded for students who had to miss a class. Students said that they could already get the homework assignments for a missed class, but they had no way to get the lecture material.

PAUSE: How does Medina tie paragraph 8 to the introductory paragraph?

8   Students were surprised that the college already has so many resources, and they gave serious and thoughtful suggestions for new and needed services. I am sorry to report that only five of the twenty-five students said that they would be willing to help set up a new service, but at least those few are willing. Interviewing other students was an interesting project for me, making me think about the importance of student-affairs programs and giving me experience gathering and analyzing information.

CRITICAL THINKING
- Summarize
- Analyze
- Synthesize
- Evaluate

(More on p. 21.)

1. **Summarize.** Briefly summarize Medina's essay (which is itself a summary), including her **main point** and purpose and the major **examples** she gives. What is her point of view?

2. **Analyze.** Do Medina's examples all relate to her thesis statement? How do her topic sentences state what the paragraph will be about? What word does she repeat to link the thesis and support?

3. **Synthesize.** What is Medina's conclusion? What do you know about student services at your college? Ask three other students the same question and include them in your response.

4. **Evaluate.** Does Medina achieve her purpose? Does her essay have the **Four Basics of Good Illustration** (see p. 165)? What effect did her essay have on you, and why?

Illustration at Work

The following profile shows how a university vice president uses illustration at work.

PROFILE OF SUCCESS

Illustration in the Real World

Background   I grew up in Amarillo, Texas, in a family of ten children. For most of my life, going to college never even occurred to me. I was a marginal student, on the slow track in school. I expected to either join the military or to work with the Rock Island Railroad, as my father did for thirty-seven years.

However, my circumstances changed when I was a sophomore in high school. That year, my father lost both of his legs in an accident at work. As I sat with him through his long stay in the hospital, I realized that I wanted a different future. I knew then that I had to go to college, but I didn't know how I could accomplish that seemingly impossible goal.

Timing is often miraculous. Soon after making the decision to pursue higher education, I was approached by a TRIO/Upward Bound counselor who asked me to consider participating in the program. I jumped at the opportunity. The TRIO student support services program gave me the support, encouragement, and skills I needed for college work, and I will always be deeply grateful for their help.

Juan Gonzalez
Vice President of
Student Affairs,
University of Texas,
Austin

Colleges / Degrees   B.A., Texas Tech University; M.Ed., University of Texas, San Antonio; Ph.D., University of Illinois, Urbana-Champaign.

Employer   University of Texas, Austin.

Writing at work   Most of the writing I do at work is in creating presentations for a variety of different audiences, reviewing and revising statements of school policy, and writing and updating various reports on student life at the school. I work closely with student leaders, and much of our communication is oral — shared exchanges of ideas during meetings. However, in those meetings I take minutes of what occurs so that I have accurate records. I maintain active correspondence with students, with administrators in other areas of the college, and with faculty. I also spend a good amount of time writing e-mail messages to people at the university, in the community, and to colleagues around the country.

How Juan uses illustration   In reports to administration and in presentations to parents, trustees, and students, I have to give detailed examples of the work that the Student Affairs office does.

Juan Gonzalez's Illustration

The following is from an address Dr. Gonzalez gave to a group of new students.

GUIDING QUESTION
What is the purpose of Student Affairs?

VOCABULARY
The following words are italicized in the excerpt: *embarking, striving, encapsulates, indicators, collaborative, integrated, aspire, complementing, facilitates, foster, engendering, status quo.* If you do not know their meanings, look them up in a dictionary or online.

CRITICAL
READING
■ Preview
■ Read
■ Pause
■ Review

PAUSE: Why is Gonzalez surprised by students?

As new students, you are *embarking* on an incredibly exciting and challenging time, a time of expanding knowledge, relationships, viewpoints, and achievements. In my role as vice president, I am constantly *striving* to match that energy level so that we can offer the highest level of service on this very diverse campus. I frequently marvel at college students who seem to have an unlimited amount of energy that allows them to attend classes, read and study, maintain a social life, run for political office, pursue a hobby, play an intramural sport, volunteer for a worthy cause, hold down a job. We in the Division of Student Affairs strongly encourage activities outside the classroom that enrich the academic experience, as we recognize that a university education is enhanced through involvement in our campus community.

Last November, a group of Student Affairs staff, students, and faculty began work on creating a strategic plan for the division. They have been laboring diligently on this document, and I am excited to share with you the fruit of that labor, our newly developed Student Affairs Strategic Plan, which has as its motto "Student Affairs: Where Life and Learning Intersect."

PAUSE: How does Gonzalez define success?

This phrase *encapsulates* the driving force behind the Division of Student Affairs. We exist, in essence, to help students succeed and grow, and we believe that growth and success must be measured in many ways. Academic success is one gauge of how well students are performing, but there are a variety of *indicators* other than grades. Those who take the most from their college experience are those who recognize that learning happens both inside and outside the classroom.

In fact, I recently had our units count the services they offer that are *collaborative* efforts with the academic side of the family, and a rough survey yielded 140 programs. This idea of *integrated* learning carries through most of what we do, whether it is a program to recruit the best students from around Texas like the Honors Colloquium, the increasingly popular "Academic Community Centers" for studying and advising on site in the residence halls, Summer Orientation, or the professor-led Freshman Reading Round-Up book discussions.

Our Vision Statement

Our vision statement lights the path we are following to where we *aspire* to be:

> The Division of Student Affairs at The University of Texas at Austin seeks to become the premier organization of its kind. We envision a network of programs and services that excels in meeting students' out-of-classroom needs, *complementing* their academic experiences, and building community on a diverse campus. In doing so, we will contribute to developing citizens and leaders who will thrive in and enrich an increasingly complex world.

Our Mission

Our mission, or the explanation of what we do, is described this way:

> The Division of Student Affairs *facilitates* students' discovery of self and the world in which they live. We enhance students' educational experiences through programs and services that support academic success. We provide for fundamental needs, including shelter, nourishment, and a sense of security. We create environments that *foster* physical, emotional, and psychological wellness, and advance healthy lifestyles. Student Affairs builds communities, both real and virtual, that encourage inclusiveness, invite communication, and add to the cultural richness of the institution. We focus on personal development, including career decision making, problem solving, and group dynamics, challenging students to work both independently and as part of a team.

PAUSE: How does this paragraph relate to the introductory paragraph?

The work group that wrote the strategic plan also composed a defining phrase to encapsulate Student Affairs: "Our passion is complete learning." These, I hope you will agree, are stirring words. We take our responsibility for providing an environment that is inclusive and promotes a healthy lifestyle seriously. We are committed to supporting you as you achieve your goals at this university.

PAUSE: What is "complete learning"?

Our Core Values

Sharing a fundamental belief in the value of Student Affairs and its ability to transform lives, we will pursue our vision by

- Focusing on the lifelong learning and personal growth of all members of the university community;
- *Engendering* a community that is inclusive, accessible, and secure;
- Conducting ourselves and our programs with the highest integrity;
- Enhancing our services by creating opportunities to collaborate and nurture partnerships;
- Challenging ourselves to move beyond the *status quo* and pursue higher levels of excellence with determination and enthusiasm;
- Strengthening a tradition of quality, compassion, and an unwavering belief in students and ourselves;
- Demonstrating the innovation and courage to adapt to changing conditions; and
- Realizing that both action and vision are necessary for a better future.

Our society benefits by having everyone educated, and education is a process that requires everyone to be engaged in the advancement of all peoples. The well-being of our state requires the next generation of leaders and scholars to understand our new world. This understanding means looking at the process of education as more than four years in college, the material in textbooks, or the contents of a classroom lecture but as a way to improve the world.

PAUSE: What is education, according to Gonzalez?

1. Who is the audience for Gonzalez's illustration? What is his purpose?
   Audience is students; purpose is to introduce them to Student Affairs, its strategic plan, and what it offers students.

2. Carefully reread the **Four Basics of Illustration** (p. 165) and determine if Gonzalez's essay is a good example of illustration. Make notes to support your opinion. *Answers will vary.*

174

3. What do you know about the services that are offered on your campus? If you know little, find out more, and comment on whether your college offers services like those that Gonzalez refers to. *Answers will vary.*

4. In your own words, state what you think Gonzalez says about what a good education is. Does he give you good examples? Do you agree with what he says? *Answers will vary.*

Illustration in Everyday Life

The following is from the *New York Times*.

Rob Walker

Stuck on You

GUIDING QUESTION
What examples of bumper stickers does Walker give?

VOCABULARY
The following words are *italicized* in the essay: *incredulous, inferences, plausible, delve, revelatory, benign, beguiling, paradox.* If you do not know their meanings, look them up in the dictionary or online.

1   My friend Scott once laughed in my face when I told him I did not like driving a car with Massachusetts plates in Texas. I am from Texas, you see, and when I visit my native state in a rental car, I don't want to be mistaken for a Yankee.[1] Scott, *incredulous* and logical, pointed out that it really did not make the slightest difference what *inferences* drivers on the roads I traveled might make about my geographical roots because I would never have any real-life dealings with them. Who cares what strangers in other cars think about you? One answer is that a lot of people must care or there would be no such thing as bumper stickers.

PAUSE: Why doesn't Walker want to be mistaken for a Yankee?

CRITICAL READING
■ Preview
■ Read
■ Pause
■ Review

1. Yankee: A Civil War term that means a person who lives in the northern United States and is assumed to have particular attitudes and beliefs

2   That doesn't mean that my friend didn't have a point, though: How much thought do we really put into the rather extraordinary number of identity signals that zoom by on highways or inch along in commuter traffic? It's possible that from time to time a Misfits or McCain message hits its mark, and somebody, somewhere, gives a thumbs up to another driver. (It's also *plausible* that some stickers inspire fellow motorists to extend another digit as a form of acknowledgment.) But the overwhelming majority of signals sent via bumper sticker almost certainly float unnoticed into the ether for the simple reason that nobody much cares. It's sad, really.

3   In addition to tribal-affiliation stickers — I Like This Band; I Root for That Sports Team; I Graduated From the Following Institution of Higher Learning — many bumper stickers attempt the more ambitious business of broadcasting some point of view on a matter of public contention, geopolitical policy, or even a philosophical mode of being. It's even more sad to conclude that nobody thinks about those either, but it turns out that somebody does or at least has: Jack Bowen, who teaches philosophy at Menlo School in Atherton, California. In a recent book called *If You Can Read This: The Philosophy of Bumper Stickers*, he not only thinks about bumper stickers but takes them seriously, evaluating the underlying worldviews they express.

4   Consider, for example, the sticker "Against Abortion? Then Don't Have One!" The political point of view there is obvious enough. But, Bowen says, if we *delve* deeper, we find the suggestion that morality itself is up for grabs, resolved on a person-by-person, situation-by-situation basis. "This is not at all what we want to say morality is," he says. "It would make the idea of morality completely pointless." He says he takes issue with about 70 percent of the broader conclusions implied by the many bumper stickers he evaluates.

5   Now, do we really need a philosopher to reveal that bumper stickers are simplistic? Probably not. We know that bumper stickers are about declaration, not dialogue; designed to end conversations, not start them. Possibly the most *revelatory* research to date on the subject was a 2008 Colorado State University study concluding that drivers who put bumper stickers and other decorations on their vehicles are 16 percent more likely to engage in road rage. It wasn't the message on the "territory markers," as a researcher called bumper stickers in an interview with *Nature News*, but the number of

PAUSE: What are tribal-affiliation stickers?

PAUSE: What political point of view does the sticker reveal?

PAUSE: What predicts road rage?

them that "predicted road rage better than vehicle value, condition or any of the things that we normally associate with aggressive driving."

6   Bowen concedes all this. But when he appears on radio call-in shows and the like to promote his book, he has learned that "people are really fired up about bumper stickers." Tellingly, however, the people he hears from almost never engage him with counter-interpretations of their own stickers (or even admit to having them). Instead they want explanations for messages they find baffling — or aggravating. "My Child Is an Honors Student" turns out to be one message that ticks off[2] a surprising number of people. As it happens, that one used to vaguely annoy Bowen too, but when he reflected on it for the book, he concluded that it was a perfectly reasonable thing to have on a car and not deserving of the "My Child Beat Up Your Honor Student" response stickers it has inspired.

PAUSE: What questions do callers ask Bowen?

7   Still, the general reaction to this *benign* message suggests that when the signals we send are noticed, we might not be happy with how they are received. This brings us to the most puzzling sticker Bowen evaluates: "Don't Judge Me." He argues that passing judgment is not such a bad thing. But this sticker struck me as an even more extreme version of my own silly worries about license-plate signifiers: Why would someone go out of the way to demand neutrality from strangers? And yet this *beguiling paradox* of a message might capture what bumper stickers are really about. Probably no one thinks about the signals sent along the highway more than those sending them. And bumper stickers are all about announcing judgments, not accepting them.

PAUSE: What sentence answers a question asked in paragraph 1?

TEACHING TIP
Have students work in groups to write.

1. Briefly summarize Walker's essay. What is his purpose? *Purpose is to entertain and explore what different bumper stickers mean to people.*

2. What examples does he give of bumper stickers? *Tribal affiliation, political point of view, other points of view, "My Child Is an Honor Student," "My Child Beat Up Your Honor Student," "Don't Judge Me."*

3. Write three questions that might be on a quiz of Walker's essay. *Answers will vary.*

4. What stereotype does Walker start the essay with? *Yankee, Texan*

2. **Ticks off:** slang for irritates, annoys

5. What is another good title for Walker's essay? <u>*Answers will vary.*</u>

6. What types of bumper stickers have you seen? What attitudes do they express? <u>*Answers will vary.*</u>

Write an Illustration Essay

In this section, you will write your own illustration essay based on one of the following assignments. Use the following tools to help you.

1. Review the Four Basics of Good Illustration (p. 165).
2. Use ▎**Illustration at a glance** ▎ as a basic organizer.
3. Use the Writing Guide: Illustration checklist as you write and revise (pp. 181–82).

Illustration at a glance

Introduction with thesis statement
Says what you want readers to know about the topic

↓

First example
Details about the example

↓

Second example
Details about the example

↓

Third example (often the most powerful)
Details about the example

↓

Conclusion
Reminds readers of the main point and makes an observation based on it

· ·

ASSIGNMENT 1   Writing about College, Work, and Everyday Life

Write an illustration essay on one of the following topics or on a topic of your own choice.

COLLEGE

- Discuss some of the activities, services, and programs offered on your campus.
- Write about what you expect to get out of college.
- Write about something you learned in another course, and give examples to explain it to a friend who has not taken the course.

WORK

- Tell someone applying for a job like yours what his or her typical responsibilities might be.
- Explain to your supervisor your claim that there is too much work to be done in the time allotted.
- Demonstrate to an interviewer the following statement: "I am a detail-oriented employee."

EVERYDAY LIFE

- Write a letter to your landlord about how your apartment's maintenance needs to be done more regularly.
- Write a letter to a friend in which you explain that your (mother, father, sibling, sweetheart) is the most (selfish, generous, irresponsible, capable) person you know.
- Name the most influential person in your life, and give examples of his or her characteristics.

ASSIGNMENT 2   Writing about an Image

Examples of giant pumpkins are evaluated on the basis of their shape, rind color, health, and, most of all, weight. The photo illustrates a prize winner. Choose an object or a type of object, and write an illustrative essay in which you give examples of the qualities that, in your view, make something "a prize winner."

ASSIGNMENT 3   Writing to Solve a Problem

THE PROBLEM: A good friend of yours is being sexually harassed at work by a supervisor who is not her boss. Although she has let the person know that the advances are not welcome, the offending behaviors have not stopped. Your friend is afraid that if she complains to her boss, she will be fired. She asks your advice about what to do.

THE ASSIGNMENT: Working on your own or with a small group, give your friend some advice about how she could handle the problem. Try to give her several good resources to think about or use. Do not forget to include resources that her company might offer.

RESOURCES
Additional Resources for Teaching Real Essays with Readings has visual planning forms for illustration and the other essays covered in Part 2. These forms are also online at bedfordstmartins .com/realessays.

Be sure to cite and document any sources you use in your papers. For advice, see Chapter 21.

RESOURCES: Review the chart on pages 840–41 for tips about problem solving. Also, check some Web sites for ideas about dealing with sexual harassment. You can start by typing *advice on sexual harassment* into a search engine. List any Web sites you use.

ASSIGNMENT 4 Writing about Connections

Read the following account of Lonza Fruitree before doing the assignment that follows.

COMMUNITY CONNECTIONS

**Lonza Fruitree,
Kennedy-King College**
Student government and Umoja

Lonza Fruitree is thirty years old and works part time while taking four classes. He got involved in student government because a friend was running for office and wanted Lonza's support. Lonza joined, became active, and also joined Umoja, a campus organization whose mission is to get more African Americans to attend college.

With Umoja, he does outreach to the community and has helped plan numerous activities, such as an AIDS Awareness Day with speakers, free testing, and candid conversations with experts. For such events, he creates announcements, pamphlets, and fliers to post on campus and in the surrounding community. His involvement has created in him a love of history and historical documents that reveal information about people and their cultures.

While Lonza has been involved with student government, he helped organize a question-and-answer forum with the president of the college and current students and other people interested in finding out more about Kennedy-King College.

He credits his experience in student government with making him better able to talk to different types of people, including strangers; to manage his time well; and to write more. More important, he knows that he has become a role model for others and tells them, "If I can do it, you can too. You can start, and you can finish. It's okay to stumble, but pick yourself up, and keep on pushing yourself. And if you are involved, you have others who will help you when you need it."

ASSIGNMENT: Choose one of the following and write an illustration essay. Work either on your own or with a partner.

▪ Find out about an organization on your campus and attend a meeting. What is the organization's purpose, and what kinds of activities are members involved in?

▪ Write about some examples of how you or others you know have "stumbled but picked yourself up."

▪ Go to the student center, the library, a mall, or some other public place. Consider how what you see and hear there reveals certain cultural messages. Assume you are writing for someone who is visiting this country for the first time.

ASSIGNMENT 5   Writing about Readings

Choose one of the following options:

▪ Read Kathleen Vail's essay, "Words That Wound" (p. 706), and review Juan Gonzalez's piece on page 172. Write a short essay explaining how schools can affect the quality of students' lives. Give examples of both positive and negative effects, drawing from Vail's essay and your own experience. You might want to write a thesis that makes use of Gonzalez's phrase "where life and learning intersect."

▪ Read Monique Rizer's essay, "When Students Are Parents" (p. 155), and Luz Medina's report (p. 169). Write a letter to Luz Medina that gives examples of programs that the Division of Student Affairs could offer to help students. Include examples from your own experience, too.

Use the steps in the Writing Guide that follows to help you prewrite, draft, revise, and edit your illustration. Check off each step as you complete it.

WRITING GUIDE: ILLUSTRATION	
STEPS IN ILLUSTRATION	**HOW TO DO THE STEPS**
☐ Focus.	• Think about your topic and what your audience knows about it.
☐ Explore your topic. See Chapter 5.	• Prewrite to give examples of your topic.
☐ Write a thesis statement. Topic + main point = Thesis See Chapter 6.	• Write a working thesis that includes your topic and main point about it. You might also include some examples you will give in your support paragraphs. →

STEPS IN ILLUSTRATION	HOW TO DO THE STEPS
☐ Support your thesis. See Chapter 7.	• Choose at least three examples that demonstrate your main point. • Consider what details about the examples your reader needs to know.
☐ Write a draft. See Chapter 8.	• Arrange your examples in order of importance or time. • Write topic sentences for each major example. • Write a paragraph for each example, giving details about the examples.
☐ Revise your draft. See Chapter 9.	• Get feedback using the peer-review guide for illustration at **bedfordstmartins.com/realessays**. • Make sure that your examples and details all relate to your main point. • Add transitions. • Improve your introduction, thesis, and conclusion.
☐ Edit your revised draft. See Parts 4 through 7.	• Correct errors in grammar, spelling, word use, and punctuation.
☐ Evaluate your writing.	• Does it have the Four Basics of Good Illustration? (p. 165) • Is this the best I can do?

> **reflect** Reread your responses to the "write" prompt on page 165 and revise what you wrote to include what you have learned about illustration. Adjust your statement of a main point, use of examples to prove the point, and supporting details as needed.

YOU KNOW THIS

You use description often.

- You tell one person about another.
- You write an ad to sell something online.
- You go somewhere new and let your friends know what it was like.

write about a place you are familiar with, and describe it well.

12

Description

Writing That Creates Pictures in Words

Understand What Description Is

Description is writing that creates a clear and vivid impression of the topic. Description translates your experience of a person, place, or thing into words, often by appealing to the senses — sight, hearing, smell, taste, and touch.

IDEA JOURNAL
Write about the most beautiful, the most interesting, or the ugliest chair, car, T-shirt, or other object you have ever seen.

Four Basics of Good Description

1. It creates a main impression — an overall effect, feeling, or image — about the topic.
2. It uses specific examples to support the main impression.
3. It supports those examples with details that appeal to the five senses.
4. It brings a person, place, or object to life for the reader.

In the following paragraph, each number corresponds to one of the Four Basics of Good Description.

1 Nojoqui Falls is a special place to me because its beauty provides a break from human worries. 2 At the start of the trail leading to the falls, the smell and sound of oak trees and pine trees make visitors feel they are up for the journey. 3 The sun hitting

4 All the details bring the falls to life.

the trees makes the air fresh with a leafy aroma. Overhead, the wind blows through the leaves, making a soft noise. **2** Closer to the waterfall, the shade from the trees creates a shielding blanket. When the sun comes out, it fills the place with light, showing the vapor coming out of the trees and plants. To the left of the trail are rocks that are positioned perfectly for viewing the waterfall. **3** Water splashes as it hits the rocks. **2** The waterfall itself is beautiful, like a transparent, sparkling window of diamonds. **3** The water is so clear that objects on the other side are visible. It is like a never-ending stream of water that splashes onto the rocks. **1** The total effect of these sights, sounds, and smells is a setting where daily cares can be set aside for a while.

— Liliana Ramirez, student

4 All the details bring the falls to life.

SEEING DESCRIPTION

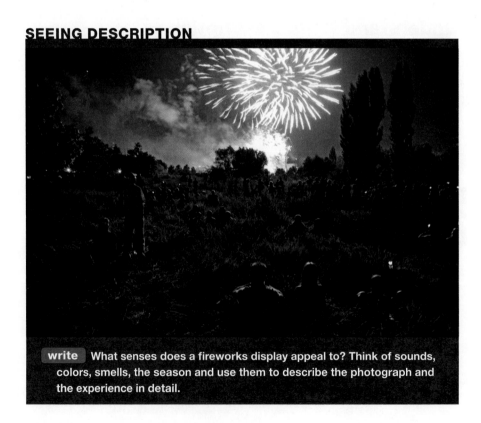

Crowd at a fireworks display in Bucharest, Romania.

write What senses does a fireworks display appeal to? Think of sounds, colors, smells, the season and use them to describe the photograph and the experience in detail.

Being able to describe something or someone accurately and in detail is important both in college and in other settings. Describing something well involves using specific, concrete details. Here are some ways that you might use description:

COLLEGE   For a science lab report, you describe the physical and chemical properties of an element.

WORK   You write a letter to your office manager describing the unacceptable conditions of the office refrigerator.

EVERYDAY LIFE   You describe a jacket that you left at the movies to the lost-and-found department.

Main Point in Description

In descriptive writing, your **main point** conveys the main impression you want your readers to see.

Take another look at the paragraph starting on page 183. What if the topic sentence had been

I love Nojoqui Falls.

You would not know why the writer likes the place. But the actual topic sentence conveys a main impression of the falls and lets you know why this place is important to the writer.

Nojoqui Falls is a special place to me because its beauty provides a break from human worries.

This statement provides a preview of what is to come, helping the audience read and understand the description.

The thesis statement in description essays typically includes the topic and the main impression about it that the writer wants to convey.

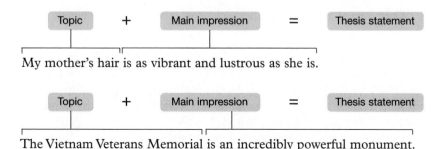

My mother's hair is as vibrant and lustrous as she is.

The Vietnam Veterans Memorial is an incredibly powerful monument.

For online exercises on main point and support, visit *Exercise Central* at **bedfordstmartins .com/realessays**.

Support in Description

Good description uses specific, concrete details to create the sights, sounds, smells, tastes, and textures that support and show your main impression.

SIGHT	SOUND	SMELL
Colors	Loud/soft	Sweet/sour
Shapes	Piercing/soothing	Sharp/mild
Sizes	Continuous/off-and-on	Good (like what?)
Patterns	Pleasant/unpleasant (how?)	Bad (rotten?)
Brightness	High/low	New (like what?)
Does it look like anything else?	Does it sound like anything else?	Does it smell like anything else?

TASTE	TOUCH
Good (What does *good* taste like?)	Hard/soft
Bad (What does *bad* taste like?)	Liquid/solid
Bitter/sugary	Rough/smooth
Metallic	Dry/oily
Burning/spicy	Textures
Does it taste like anything else?	Does it feel like anything else?

TEACHING TIP
Have students bring in descriptions of interesting places from books or newspapers. The Travel section of the *New York Times* (available on the Web at **www.nytimes .com/pages/travel/ index.html**) often has such descriptions.

TEAMWORK
Have students, working in small groups, choose an object from one group member's book bag or briefcase and agree on a main impression to use in describing that object.

RESOURCES
For online writing and grammar resources, go to bedfordstmartins .com/rewritingbasics.

As you think about the main impression you want to convey, ask yourself: What sensory details might bring this subject to life? Add additional details to convey each sensation more accurately or vividly.

For example, one student wrote this thesis statement:

When I wear my grandmother's old coat, she is standing beside me.

To support this main impression, the writer might include sensory details about the smell of the coat (*sweet like Grandma's perfume, with a faint odor of mothballs and home-baked bread*); the feel of the fabric (*nubby and rough, with some smooth spots where the fabric has worn thin*); and the candy in the pocket (*single pieces of butterscotch that rustle in their wrappings and a round cylinder that is a roll of wintergreen Life Savers*).

Organization in Description

Description may use any of the orders of organization, depending on the purpose of the description. If you are describing what someone or something looks like, you might use **spatial order,** the most common way to organize description. If you are describing something you want to sell, you might use **order of importance,** ending with the feature that would be most appealing to potential buyers.

Use transitions to help readers move smoothly from detail to detail.

Common Transitions in Description

TRANSITIONS TO SHOW SPATIAL ORDER	TRANSITIONS TO SHOW ORDER OF IMPORTANCE
above/underneath	even more
beyond	more
in front of/behind	the most
to the left/right	the most intense
	the strongest

Read and Analyze Description

Before writing a description essay, read the following three examples of description—from college, the workplace, and everyday life—and answer the questions that accompany them. For each essay, review the Four Basics of Good Description (p. 183) and practice your critical reading process by doing the following.

For more examples of description, see Chapter 43.

TEAMWORK
Have students work through the first essay together to apply the critical reading process and answer the questions after the essay.

2PR The Critical Reading Process

- **Preview** the reading, including the guiding question.

- **Read** the piece, double-underlining the thesis statement, underlining the major support, and circling the transitions. Consider the quality of the support.

- **Pause** to think during reading. Take notes and ask questions about what you are reading: Talk to the author.

- **Review** the reading, your guiding question, your marginal notes and questions, and your answers to the Pause prompts.

Description in College

The following description essay was written by a student for a course assignment.

Florence Bagley

Photograph of My Father

GUIDING QUESTION
What does Bagley see in the photo of her father?

PAUSE: Underline the sensory details in this paragraph.

1   This old black-and-white photograph of my father fills me with conflicting emotions. He died young, and this photo is one of the few that my family has of him. The picture seems to show a strong, happy man, young and smiling, but to me it also reveals his weakness.

2   Looking at this picture of my father, I feel how much I have lost. In it, my father is sitting upright in a worn plaid easy chair. It was "his" chair, and when he was at work, I'd curl up in it and smell his aftershave lotion and cigarette smoke. His pitch-black hair is so dark that it blends into the background of the photo. His eyes, though indistinct in this photo, were a deep, dark brown. Although the photo is faded around my father's face, I still can make out his strong jaw and the cleft in his chin. In the photo, my father is wearing a clean white T-shirt that reveals his thick, muscular arms. Resting in the crook of his left arm is my younger brother, who was about one year old at the time. Both of them are smiling.

PAUSE: What mood has Bagley created so far?

PAUSE: How has the mood changed and what transition signals the change?

3   However, when I study the photo, my eyes are drawn to the can of beer that sits on the table next to him. Against my will, I begin to feel resentful. I have so many wonderful memories of my father. Whether he was carrying me on his shoulders, picking me up from school, or teaching me to draw, he always made time for me. All of these memories fade when I see that beer. From what I remember, he always made time for that beer as well. The smell of beer was always on him, the cool, sweating can always within reach.

COMBINING MODES Note that the writer uses narration within her description.

4   In this photo, my father appears to be a strong man; however, looks are deceiving. My father died at the age of thirty-seven because he was an

alcoholic. I was eleven when he died, and I really did not understand that his drinking was the reason for his death. I just knew that he left me without a father and the possibility of more memories. He should have been strong enough to stop drinking.

PAUSE: What conflicting feelings does the picture create?

5   In spite of the resentment I may feel about his leaving me, this photo holds many loving memories as well. It is of my father — the strong, wonderful man and the alcoholic — and it is the most precious thing I own. Although I would much rather have him here, I stay connected to him when I look at it.

1. **Summarize.** Briefly summarize Bagley's essay, including her **main impression** and **major support**. What is her purpose? How does she feel about the photo and her father?

2. **Analyze.** How do the second and third paragraphs create different impressions? How do these paragraphs and paragraph 4 support the main impression in the first paragraph?

3. **Synthesize.** How does Bagley's essay prove the saying, "Photographs can be deceiving"? Find a photograph that deceives. How can you apply what you know about reading visuals to Bagley's essay and the photo you have found?

4. **Evaluate.** Does Bagley achieve her purpose? Can you visualize her father? Does her essay have the **Four Basics of Good Description** (see p. 183)? What do *you* think about her essay, and why?

CRITICAL THINKING
■ Summarize
■ Analyze
■ Synthesize
■ Evaluate

(More on p. 21.)

Description at Work

The following profile shows how a writer uses description in an excerpt from a novel.

Description in the Real World

Alex Espinoza
Writer and Assistant
Professor

RESOURCES
For a discussion of
how to use the
profiles in Part 2, see
*Practical Suggestions
for Teaching Real
Essays with Readings.*

**COMBINING
MODES** Note that
Espinoza uses narra-
tion within his
description.

Background   I was born in Mexico, the youngest of eleven children. My father was an alcoholic and was murdered when I was in high school. I didn't do well in school and was placed in the automotive program, where I barely passed my classes. At San Bernardino Community College, I discovered both writing and the Puenté Project. In writing, I found my voice; in Puenté, I found people who encouraged me academically. Although I had a low GPA, I had good recommendations and good grades in writing, so I was accepted at the University of California, Riverside, which has a great writing program. I then went on to get a master's degree in creative writing at the University of California, Irvine, which, although I didn't know it at the time, has one of the most selective creative writing programs in the country. My first novel, *Still Water Saints*, was published in 2007, and I have a contract for a second one.

Colleges / Degrees   A.A., San Bernardino Community College; B.A., University of California, Riverside; M.F.A., University of California, Irvine.

Employer   California State University, Fresno

Writing at work   My job is writing and teaching writing, so I'm always writing. Here's some advice I always give my students: When you write, you are putting yourself on the page, and you can control how you are perceived. If you ignore the conventions of writing (like grammar, spelling, and punctuation), you will in turn be ignored by those whose attention you want.

How Alex uses description   In my own writing, I have to create vivid scenes for my readers. In my teaching, I help students form vivid images in their own writing.

Alex Espinoza's Description

The following is from Espinoza's novel *Still Water Saints*. (For another example of Espinoza's descriptive writing, see pp. 723–25.) Note that there is no thesis statement because this is not an essay but rather part of a novel.

GUIDING QUESTION
What kinds of sensory details does Alex Espinoza use?

VOCABULARY
The following words are italicized in the excerpt: *bellows, padlock, massacred, lynched, opossum, dingy*. If you do not know their meanings, look them up in a dictionary or online.

The iron security gate unfolded like the *bellows* of an accordion as Perla pulled it along the rail in front of the door. She snapped the *padlock* shut, turned around the corner of the building, and headed home. Her house was close, just across the empty lot next to the shopping center. Wild sage and scrub grew beside the worn path that cut through the field. Boys sometimes rode their bikes there, doing tricks and wheelies as they bumped over mounds and breaks, falling down, laughing and scraping their knees, their faces coated with grime. Their tires left thin tracks that looped around the salt cedar trees, around the soiled mattresses and old washers and sinks that were dumped there.

CRITICAL
READING
■ Preview
■ Read
■ Pause
■ Review

People told of a curse on these grounds, a group of monks traveling through Agua Mansa in the days when California was still a part of Mexico, back before states were shapes on a map. They said a tribe of Indians *massacred* the monks; they skinned them and scattered their body parts around the lot for the crows. Still others said Mexican settlers had been *lynched* from the branches of the cedars by Anglos who stole their land for the railroads. Seeing a piece of stone, Perla wondered about the monks and those men dangling from branches. *A tooth? Part of a toe?* Empty soda cans and wrappers were caught under boulders and discarded car parts. *What would the monks think about having a tire for a headstone, a couch for a marker?* She thought of her husband, Guillermo, of his tombstone, of the thick, green lawns of the cemetery where he was buried.

When she reached her house and stepped inside, the air was warm and silent. Perla put her purse down on the rocking chair near the front door and went around, pushing the lace curtains back and cracking open the windows. She breathed in the scent of wood smoke from someone's fireplace down the street, a smell that reminded her of her father toasting garbanzo beans. She went into the kitchen and looked for something to eat.

Dinner was a bowl of oatmeal with two slices of toast, which she took out to the patio. The night was cold, and the steam from the oatmeal rose up and fogged her glasses as she spooned it in her mouth. Police sirens wailed down the street, and dogs answered, their cries lonely and beautiful. She looked up, and in the flashing lights saw a set of glowing red eyes.

PAUSE: What impression do you have of the area so far? Why?

PAUSE: How does this paragraph change the mood?

PAUSE: How does the impression change here? Why?

PAUSE: How does the last sentence change the mood of the scene?

PAUSE: Underline the sensory details in this paragraph.

Perla flicked on the porch light. It was an *opossum*, its <u>fur *dingy* and gray, the tips and insides of its ears bright pink.</u> <u>It stood motionless, behind the trunk of the organ pipe cactus, staring at her. It climbed to the top of the fence, making a low, faint jingle as it moved.</u> Perla looked again; <u>a small brass bell was tied to a piece of red yarn knotted around the opossum's tail.</u> She took her spoon and threw it. <u>When it hit the bottom of the fence, the animal darted, the clatter of the bell frantic.</u> The opossum disappeared behind the branches of the avocado tree and down the other side of the fence into the empty lot, <u>the ringing growing fainter and fainter.</u>

From under the kitchen sink, behind the pile of cloths and old sponges she could never bring herself to throw away, was a bottle of rum. She poured some into a cup and took a drink. Then she took another. The warmth calmed her nerves.

She imagined the ghosts of the dead monks and the lynched men rising up from the ground, awakened by her thoughts. Curls of gray smoke at first, they slowly took human form. They walked in a straight line, one in front of the other. A slow progression followed the opossum's tracks through the lot and back home.

She took another drink and closed her eyes. That animal was a messenger. It was letting her know that something was out there. It was coming.

PAUSE: What impression does the final paragraph create?

1. What is Espinoza's purpose? <u>*To create an impression of a place*</u>

2. What does he assume readers know about Agua Mansa? <u>*Nothing*</u>

3. How does the final paragraph contrast with the introductory one in terms of the impressions they create? <u>*The introductory paragraph creates a*</u> <u>*scene while the final one creates a feeling of something ominous.*</u>

4. How are you left feeling about the place? Why? Choose several details that give you that impression. <u>*Answers will vary.*</u>

Description in Everyday Life

The following is a letter that Jennifer Orlando wrote for a helium.com contest.

Jennifer Orlando

Rattlesnake Canyon: A Place of Peace and Beauty

CRITICAL
READING
■ Preview
■ Read
■ Pause
■ Review

GUIDING QUESTION
What impression does Orlando create?

VOCABULARY
The following words are *italicized* in the essay: *restorative, swarms, savory, perspective, eternity, surpass, humanity*. If you do not know their meanings, look them up in a dictionary or online.

1   Today I went for a hike in Rattlesnake Canyon in my hometown of Grand Junction, Colorado. I had been a little down and I just wanted to get out and forget my troubles. Instead, though, I came back happy and feeling really lucky to be alive. Rattlesnake Canyon is incredibly beautiful, peaceful, and *restorative*.

2   The hiking path is lined with gorgeous desert plants that go on for acres. There are many varieties of cactus, many with long white spines reaching out of the green "leaves." I never thought of cactus as being colorful, but there can be purple or about five shades of green. Some of them have "flowers" that look like huge, bright red radishes. Others have tiny yellow flowers growing beside the sharp spines, and still others have lavender flowers sprouting. There are all kinds of yellow flowering plants—some pale, and some darker, like an egg yolk. *Swarms* of yellow butterflies flutter around them, dancing in and out of the branches. I just started laughing when I saw them; it was so perfect. My favorite plant is sage, again lots of different kinds. Some have billions of little purple flowers, and they are about four feet tall. Others are a silvery green, and when you run your hand over the leaves, they give off this *savory* scent that is barely sweet and makes me think of my mother's stuffing at Thanksgiving. It is sage, the

PAUSE: What do you expect the rest of the essay will be about?

PAUSE: What impression does paragraph 2 create? Underline details that contribute.

herb. The air just smells all herby from sage, juniper, and other smells I cannot identify. Some low bushes have bright red flowers—some scarlet, some rust, and some orangy. The desert plants are beautiful. The desert is so much more than just sand.

PAUSE: How does the geography affect Orlando's sense of time?

3   As I went along, I was surrounded by the huge rocks of the canyon, like a mini-Grand Canyon. At the base, the rocks are a dark, rusty color. As they rise up, they have about ten different layers of color—from a kind of light grey, to darker grey, to pale red, and finally to a brilliant red that shines in the sunlight from flecks of mineral in them. Those layers of rock reveal the many different climates the area has experienced over billions of years, including being underwater several times. I was literally surrounded by these looming rocks, thousands of feet high.

4   Best of all, though, is the sky. The towering, multicolored cliffs are met by the bluest sky imaginable. There were no clouds, and this blue was dark and beautiful against the red of the rock. The sun was bright, as it usually is here, and everything was so big, so colorful, so intense that I felt lucky to be alive. There is something about all this beauty that has been here for billions of years that makes you feel as if your problems are unimportant: It gives peace.

PAUSE: What final impression does Orlando create?

5   Rattlesnake Canyon and places like it give us *perspective* on our lives. The beauty and *eternity* of nature assure us that so much in our lives is small compared with our surroundings. It opens our senses if we allow it to: We see, smell, hear, and feel more closely. These places restore our faith in forces that far *surpass* us in power and endurance. I left the canyon with my spirit restored. Nature is open to everyone, and we should take the time to let it work its wonders on our *humanity*.

1. Summarize Orlando's description of Rattlesnake Canyon and its effect on her. *Answers will vary.* _____

2. What details and impressions contribute to the effect? _____

3. What experience have you had of a place affecting you, either positively or negatively? What details caused your feeling? _____

4. Find a picture of a place and consider the effect or impression it creates. _____

TEACHING TIP
Bring in some pictures of places. Have students work in small groups to describe the places and their main impressions of them.

Write a Description Essay

In this section, you will write your own description essay based on one of the following assignments. Use the following tools to help you.

1. Review the Four Basics of Good Description (p. 183).
2. Use **Description at a glance** as a basic organizer.
3. Use the Writing Guide: Description checklist as you write and revise (pp. 199–200).

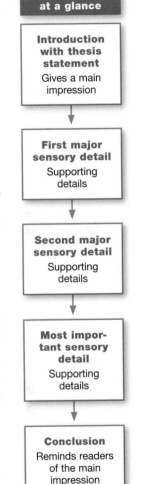

Description at a glance

Introduction with thesis statement
Gives a main impression

↓

First major sensory detail
Supporting details

↓

Second major sensory detail
Supporting details

↓

Most important sensory detail
Supporting details

↓

Conclusion
Reminds readers of the main impression
Makes an observation

ASSIGNMENT 1   Writing about College, Work, and Everyday Life

Write a description essay on *one* of the following topics or on a topic of your own choice.

COLLEGE
- Describe your favorite place on campus so that a reader understands why you like to be there.
- Describe what you imagine a character looks like in a novel you have read.
- Describe an event or a setting that you learned about in one of your courses.

WORK
- Describe an area of your workplace that is not worker friendly.
- Describe a product your company makes, or a service it provides.
- Describe a specific area at work that you see every day but have not really noticed. Look at it with new eyes.

EVERYDAY LIFE
- Describe a favorite photograph.
- Describe a favorite food without naming it. Include how it looks, smells, tastes, and what it means to you.
- Describe a place you have lived or visited.

ASSIGNMENT 2 Writing about an Image

Write a descriptive essay about the messy space shown below or about a similar space in your own home or workplace. Be sure to use plenty of details.

ASSIGNMENT 3 Writing to Solve a Problem

THE PROBLEM: A wealthy alumna has given your college money for a new student lounge. The president has selected a group of students (including you) to advise him on the lounge and has asked that the group be as specific as possible in its recommendations.

THE ASSIGNMENT: Working on your own or, preferably, in a small group, write a description of an ideal student lounge to send to the president. Be sure to think about what various purposes the lounge should serve, where it should be located, what it should have in it, and what it should look like.

RESOURCES: Review the chart on pages 840–41 for advice about problem solving. Also, search the Web using the words *student lounges* and *design*. You might also go to the library and look for design or architecture books and magazines. List any Web sites or publications that you consult.

....

ASSIGNMENT 4   Writing about Connections

Read the following account of Leandro Quispé before doing the assignment that follows.

COMMUNITY CONNECTIONS

Leandro Quispé, Western Nevada College (WNC)
Founder, Latino Club

Leandro Quispé (the student at the top left) moved to the United States from Peru when he was seventeen. He works at Domino's Pizza, but he wants more in his life here. He started taking developmental classes at WNC, and in his English class, he learned that Lupe Ramirez, the Executive Assistant to the Dean of Students, was interested in starting a club for Latino students. He and a friend met with Ms. Ramirez and officially started a club with the mission of representing and supporting Latino students at the college and in the community. Club members (and there are now many of them) visit schools to talk with students, and the club sponsors fund-raising events.

For their first event, a bake sale, members cooked and sold over a thousand tamales. The proceeds were used to start a scholarship fund for Latino

(continued)

students. A talent show event was wildly successful, and these funds, too, went into the scholarship fund. To publicize the event, Leandro created and distributed fliers, made radio announcements, and approached local businesses for sponsorship. Leandro spoke personally with the managers of local businesses, creating good relationships for his future.

Leandro loves his involvement in the club because he makes friends on campus as well as contacts in the community. He says participation makes him and others feel good. He says, "I am proud to be a Latino Club member and be surrounded by many wonderful people who want to achieve their dreams and meet their educational goals. Even though school is hard, my involvement in the club has also made my college experience fun and meaningful."

ASSIGNMENT: Choose one of the following and write a descriptive essay. Work either on your own or with a partner.

- Go to an event at the college and describe the scene.
- Go to the local library or museum and describe artwork that you see there.
- Go to a concert or talent show and describe the experience.

RESOURCES
Additional Resources for Teaching Real Essays with Readings has visual planning forms for description and the other essays covered in Part 2. These forms are also online at **bedfordstmartins .com/realessays.**

ASSIGNMENT 5 Writing about Readings

The assignments that follow ask you to read one or more different descriptions and draw from them to write an essay.

- Read Mary Brave Bird's "The Sweat Bath Ritual" (p. 727). Both Brave Bird's and Jennifer Orlando's (p. 193) essays describe experiences that transform the writers. Write your own descriptive essay about a transforming experience, drawing from these two essays as well as your own experience.

- Read Alex Espinoza's "An American in Mexico" (p. 723), and review his description on page 191. Are there similarities between the two pieces? Drawing from both pieces, write a more detailed description of the neighborhood in which Alex might have grown up. Use your imagination.

- Read Heaven Morrison's "My Kingdom" (p. 719). Both Morrison's and Jennifer Orlando's (p. 193) essays describe places that have had an impact on the writers. Write a descriptive essay about the power of a place, drawing from both of these essays and your own experience.

Use the steps in the Writing Guide that follows to help you prewrite, draft, revise, and edit your description. Check off each step as you complete it.

WRITING GUIDE: DESCRIPTION

STEPS IN DESCRIPTION	HOW TO DO THE STEPS
☐ Focus.	• Think about what you want to describe and who your readers are.
☐ Explore your topic. See Chapter 5.	• Make sure your topic can be described in a short essay. • Prewrite to generate sensory images and details.
☐ Write a thesis statement. [Topic] + <u>Main impression</u> = [Thesis] See Chapter 6.	• Decide your purpose for writing a description and what picture you want to create for your readers.
☐ Support your thesis. See Chapter 7.	• Add images and details that will bring what you are describing to life for your audience. • Use your senses to create the images.
☐ Write a draft. See Chapter 8.	• Arrange your main point and the images that help create it in a logical order. • Write topic sentences for the supporting images and details that show them. →

STEPS IN DESCRIPTION	HOW TO DO THE STEPS
☐ **Revise your draft.** See Chapter 9.	• Get feedback using the peer-review guide for description at **bedfordstmartins.com/realessays**. • Reread your essay, adding vivid details. • Add transitions to help show your reader your main impression of your topic. • Improve your introduction, thesis, and conclusion.
☐ **Edit your revised draft.** See Parts 4 through 7.	• Correct errors in grammar, spelling, word use, and punctuation.
☐ **Evaluate your writing.**	• Does it have the Four Basics of Good Description (p. 183)? • Is this the best I can do?

reflect Reread your response to the "write" prompt on page 183. Thinking back over what you have learned about description, revise what you wrote. As necessary, strengthen its main impression, add supporting examples and sensory details, and adjust the whole so it brings the place to life for your readers.

Process Analysis

Writing That Explains How Things Happen

Understand What Process Analysis Is

Process analysis explains either how to do something (so your readers can do it) or how something works (so your readers can understand it). Both types of process analysis present the steps involved in the process.

Four Basics of Good Process Analysis

1. It helps readers either perform the steps or understand how something works.
2. It presents the essential steps in the process.
3. It explains the steps in detail.
4. It arranges the steps in a logical order (usually in chronological order).

In the following paragraph, each number corresponds to one of the Four Basics of Good Process Analysis.

1 Two teenagers, Robbie and Brittany Bergquist, wanted to help American soldiers in combat zones call home, so in 2004 they founded the organization Cell Phones for Soldiers, which has proved to be extremely successful. 2 First, Robbie and Brittany pooled their own money, a total of $14. Realizing that would not go

4 Steps arranged in chronological order

201

far, they then decided to hold fund-raising events. **3** Next, they enlisted friends and family to help them organize a series of bake sales and car washes. As people learned about their efforts, more joined them, and they began to raise serious money to purchase phones. **2** Second, they started another fund-raising initiative: recycling old cell phones. **3** They collected old phones and brought them to a recycling company. **3** With this money, they purchased minutes on phone cards for the soldiers. **3** Then, they organized volunteers to wrap and send the cards to soldiers who had heard about their work and had contacted them. **2** To date, they have provided over 60 million minutes of phone time. Robbie and Brittany continue their efforts to include not only soldiers overseas but also returning veterans who are in the hospital.

4 Steps arranged in chronological order

SEEING PROCESS ANALYSIS

A container ship is unloaded in Long Beach, California.

write   In business, many processes involve figuring out the best way to transport cargo. List and describe the steps you or someone you know has taken to move something from one place to another.

Whenever you give someone directions about how to do something or explain how something works, you are using process analysis. Here are some ways you might use process analysis.

COLLEGE

In an information technology course, you write an essay explaining the process for implementing a new data management system.

WORK

The office has a new security system, and you are asked to write a memo to employees explaining how to access their work areas during and after normal business hours.

EVERYDAY LIFE

You write directions telling your child how to operate the washing machine.

PATTY MALONEY: The essence of good medicine is sound processes.

(See Patty Maloney's **PROFILE OF SUCCESS** on page 208.)

Main Point in Process Analysis

Your **purpose** in process analysis is to explain a process so that readers can either do it themselves or understand how it works. Your **main point** lets your readers know what you think about that process—for example, whether it is easy or complicated.

> The Web site *MapQuest.com* can get you from where you are to where you want to go in several easy steps.

A thesis statement for a process analysis usually identifies the process and the point you want to make about it. The thesis should also suggest what you want your readers to know or learn about the process.

For online exercises on main point and support, visit *Exercise Central* at bedfordstmartins .com/realessays.

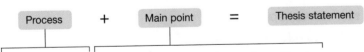

Painting a room takes careful preparation and application.

In process analysis, include your thesis statement in your introduction so that readers know from the start what the process and the purpose are.

Support in Process Analysis

A clear process analysis presents all the essential steps in the process; these steps constitute the **major support**. Each step is explained by supporting details. For example, the writer of the thesis *Successful weight loss is a* *challenge, but it starts with some simple steps* might use the following essential steps and details to explain the steps.

ESSENTIAL STEPS

STEP 1: Get rid of the junk food in your home and commit not to buy any.

   SUPPORTING DETAILS

   It is tempting and is not nutritional

   That includes chips, candy, and any other unhealthy foods you snack on

   Do not shop when you are hungry

   Stay away from the junk food aisles

STEP 2: Keep a list of everything you eat each day.

   SUPPORTING DETAILS

   When you are tempted, wait five minutes before eating

   Write each item just before or just after you eat it

   Include everything, even just tastes

STEP 3: Weigh yourself just once a week.

   SUPPORTING DETAILS

   Not daily because weight fluctuates

   Record your weight

STEP 4: Reward yourself, but not with food.

   SUPPORTING DETAILS

   Call a friend to share your success

   Go to a movie you want to see

RESOURCES
For online writing and grammar resources, go to bedford stmartins.com/ rewritingbasics.

Make sure to include all of the essential steps in the process, particularly if you want your readers to be able to do something using only your instructions. Read the following process analysis example. What essential step is missing?

TEAMWORK
Have students, in pairs, discuss whether any other steps are missing.

Please do the laundry before I get home. The clothes are in the baskets next to the machine. One of the baskets has all dark clothes. Put these in the washing machine, with the heaviest, biggest items on the bottom. You can fill the machine to the top, but do not mash the clothes down. (If you put in too many clothes, the machine will stall.) After all of the clothes are in, set the level on Extra High. Then, turn the knob on the left to Warm Wash, Cool Rinse. Press the Start button. After about half an hour, the laundry should be done, and you can transfer it to the dryer.

MISSING STEP: These directions cover loading the machine and operating it, but they leave out adding the soap.

Organization in Process Analysis

Because process analysis explains how to do something or how something works, it usually uses **chronological (time) order.** Start with the first step, and then explain each step in the order that it should occur.

Add transitional words and sentences to your essay to help readers follow each step in the process.

Common Transitions in Process Analysis

after	eventually	meanwhile	soon
as	finally	next	then
at last	first	now	when
before	last	second	while
during	later	since	

Read and Analyze Process Analysis

For each of the following three essays, review the Four Basics of Good Process Analysis (p. 201) and practice your critical reading process by doing the following.

For more examples of process analysis, see Chapter 44.

2PR   The Critical Reading Process

Preview the reading, including the guiding question.

Read the piece, double-underlining the thesis statement, underlining the major support, and circling the transitions. Consider the quality of the support.

Pause to think during reading. Take notes and ask questions about what you are reading: Talk to the author.

Review the reading, your guiding question, your marginal notes and questions, and your answers to the Pause prompts.

TEAMWORK
Have students work through the first essay together to apply the critical reading process and answer the questions after the essay.

Process Analysis in College

Daniel Flanagan

The Choice to Do It Over Again

GUIDING QUESTION
What did Flanagan do over?

VOCABULARY
The following words are *italicized* in the essay: *degenerate, spiral, consequence, fragile, shortcomings.* If you do not know their meanings, look them up in a dictionary or online.

PAUSE:
What does the second sentence mean?

1   I do not know why I came to the decision to become a loser, but I know I made the choice at a young age. Sometime in the middle of fourth grade, I stopped trying. By the time I was in seventh grade, I was your typical *degenerate*: lazy, rebellious, disrespectful. I had lost all social graces. I was terminally hip and fatally cool.

2   Not long after that, I dropped out of school and continued my downward *spiral*. Hard physical labor was the *consequence* for the choices I made as an adolescent. At the age of twenty-one, I was hopelessly lost and using drugs as a way to deal with the fact that I was illiterate and stuck in a dead-end job carrying roof shingles up a ladder all day.

3   But now I believe in do-overs, in the chance to do it all again. And I believe that do-overs can be made at any point in your life, if you have the right motivation. Mine came from a surprising source.

PAUSE:
Why did Flanagan decide to change his life?

4   It was September 21, 2002, when my son Blake was born. It's funny that after a life of avoiding responsibility, now I was in charge of something so *fragile*. Over the years, as I grew into the title of Dad, I began to learn something about myself. In a way, Blake and I were both learning to walk, talk, work, and play for the first time. I began my do-over.

PAUSE:
Underline the steps in Flanagan's do-over.

5   It took me almost three years to learn how to read. I started with my son's books. Over and over, I practiced reading books to him until I remembered all the words in every one of them. I began to wonder if it were possible for me to go back to school. I knew I wanted to be a good role model, so after a year-and-a-half and a lot of hard work, I passed my

GED[1] test on my son's fourth birthday. This may not sound like much, and I am not trying to get praise for doing something that should have been done in the first place, but all things considered it was one of the best days in my life. Today, I am a full-time college student, studying to become a sociologist.

6   Growing up, I always heard these great turn-around stories of triumph over *shortcomings*. But I never thought they applied to me. Now I believe it is a choice anyone can make: to do it all over again.

CRITICAL
THINKING
■ Summarize
■ Analyze
■ Synthesize
■ Evaluate

(More on p. 21.)

1. **Summarize.** Briefly summarize Flanagan's essay, including the process he describes and the major steps.

2. **Analyze.** How does the title set up the essay? Why do you think Flanagan placed his thesis somewhere other than the first paragraph? How is his concluding sentence tied to his thesis statement?

3. **Synthesize.** What has Flanagan learned about choices? How does this relate to other stories and choices you have experienced or read about?

4. **Evaluate.** What is Flanagan's purpose for writing, and does he achieve it? Does he give enough information? Is the process he went through clear? Does his essay use the **Four Basics of Good Process Analysis**?

Process Analysis at Work

The following profile shows how a nurse uses process analysis at work.

1. **GED:** General Education Development tests that substitute for high school graduation

Process Analysis in the Real World

Patty Maloney
Clinical Nurse
Specialist

Background   I was always a terrible student who was shy and lacking in confidence. After high school, I took one course at a community college but quit because I didn't think I could do it.

After working as a typist, I got a job as a nursing assistant at the Shriners Hospital in Boston, a thirty-bed pediatric burn hospital. This motivated me to become a licensed practical nurse (LPN).

As time went on, I wanted more responsibility, so I took courses that led, first, to a registered nurse (RN) degree and, finally, to a master's degree in nursing. In the various nursing degree programs I completed, I had to do lots of writing — long papers, summaries of articles, and analyses of diseases and of case studies.

Colleges / Degrees   Massachusetts Bay Community College, Labouré Junior College, Massachusetts College of Pharmacy (B.S.N.), Northeastern University (M.S.N.)

Employer   All Children's Hospital, St. Petersburg, Florida

Writing at work   Observations of patients, notes about patients, memos to colleagues, instructions for junior staff, lots of e-mail

How Patty uses process analysis   Notes on treatment are often process analyses. They need to be concise, precise, and clear because both I and others will need to refer to them for patients' further treatment.

Patty Maloney's Process Analysis

The following is from a report that Patty Maloney prepared for a patient's file to document the steps taken to treat her. The report shows that when a nurse on the team and a resident disagreed as to the treatment called for, the nurse called for another opinion. This type of communication is frequent among medical personnel.

GUIDING QUESTION
How did Maloney and others save a child's life?

VOCABULARY
The following words are *italicized* in the excerpt: *vital signs, pneumothorax, rupture, resident, attending physician.* If you do not know their meanings, look them up in a dictionary or online.

CRITICAL
READING
■ Preview
■ Read
■ Pause
■ Review

Patient: (name), female, age 8, with tumor and disease progression

Symptoms at arrival: Child had not eaten much for two days and was withdrawn and uncommunicative.

Treatment process: First, we needed to determine if the child was in immediate danger or in need of further medications for pain control. We took her *vital signs*, which were within the range of normal for her, with a slightly elevated heart rate. Then we interviewed the child's mother to see if she had administered any breakthrough pain medication during the last 24 hours. We gave the child a short-term pain medication.

As a next step, we had a discussion with the doctor in the unit, and we then administered a breakthrough pain medication. We closely monitored the patient's vital signs, particularly noting if the heart rate came down. We were documenting the signs every hour formally but also checked on the child's status in the Intensive Care Unit every 15 minutes.

During one check, one of our nurses noted that the child looked pale, and her breathing was somewhat shallow. The nurse knew that the child had fragile lungs and felt that she was at risk of the *pneumothorax* collecting fluid with a possible *rupture* of the lung lining and collapse of the lung. Following procedure, the nurse immediately alerted the *resident*, who felt that the child was fine and suggested that nothing but continued observation was necessary.

The nurse disagreed with the resident's diagnosis and at that point sent another nurse to page the *attending physician* for another opinion. In the meantime, while waiting for the attending, the nurse called for an x-ray. She then pulled the cart over to the patient in preparation for inserting a tube into the lung cavity to reinflate the lung. When the attending physician arrived and was briefed, he agreed with the nurse's diagnosis. The tube was quickly inserted, and the collapse of the lung was avoided.

The child continues in observation in the ICU. Her condition is stable.

COMBINING MODES: If you have already studied illustration, note that illustration is used here to give examples of steps in the process. Also, note that the report uses narration within the process.

PAUSE: What do you think will happen next?

1. Briefly summarize Maloney's report. *Answers will vary.*

2. Although a description of a treatment process, the report does not give many details. What is the purpose of the report? *Answers will vary but should include that it is for a record of the care that had been provided for this patient.*

3. How would the report differ if its purpose was to teach new nurses how to do a particular procedure? *It would give more details about the* *treatment.*

4. Write a possible **thesis statement** for the report. *Answers will vary.*

5. Write a possible **concluding statement**. *Answers will vary.*

Process Analysis in Everyday Life

Michael Gates Gill
How I Learned to Be a Barista[1]

CRITICAL
READING
■ Preview
■ Read
■ Pause
■ Review

For this reading, you do not need to underline the major support or circle transitions.

PAUSE: Why was Gill concerned about the kids from school coming in?

GUIDING QUESTION
What are the steps that Gill learns, and what else does he learn during his first day?

VOCABULARY
The following words are *italicized* in the essay: *combative, module, humiliating, literally, renewed, conspicuous.* If you do not know their meanings, look them up in a dictionary or online.

"Get out to the registers, Mike," my boss Crystal encouraged me. "And be sure to make eye contact and connect with conversation."

I had heard those words on the training video, but I was more concerned with just handling the cash so that I did not make a perfect fool of myself. Unfortunately, now the kids from school arrived.

Joann came over to me, though, and helped me put the drawer in.

"The computer will show you the correct change, and the great thing is that the Guest[2] will see the numbers, too, so they can catch you if you get it wrong. You will do fine, Mike."

5   "But I'm terrible with money."

"So were my first two husbands. Just let the register do the work."

I smiled. That was a good mantra.[3]

---

1. barista: Italian for "bartender." Starbucks servers are called *baristas.*
2. Guest: what Starbucks employees call their customers
3. mantra: a sound, word, or group of words that when repeated is supposed to be transformative

A guy stepped up to my register to order. He had no idea that he was dealing with a person who had never done this before.

"I want a Tall Mocha."

10 I called down to Tawana, an attractive but *combative* barista on the espresso bar: "Tall Mocha."

"Tall Mocha," Tawana called back to me, confirming that she had gotten the order right.

PAUSE: So far, what steps in the process has Gill presented?

I looked at the register. On the screen read the words "Tall" and "Mocha," just like on the computer training *module*. I jabbed at them with my finger. Sure enough, it worked, and the price came up on my screen.

The guy handed me five dollars.

The screen displayed the option "Five dollars" in a box, so I punched the box.

15 Then, the register opened, and the screen displayed the exact change I should hand the guy: $2.73. I dug out the change from my drawer. The guy looked at it and stuck it in his pocket and made his way to the espresso bar to pick up his drink.

My screen, about the size of a small television, read, "Close your drawer."

I closed my drawer, and said to myself, *Hey, you can do this!*

PAUSE: What steps does the register do for the barista?

Then, the next Guest stepped up, a young lady who was clearly pregnant.

"Just a Decaf Tall Coffee," she said.

20 I punched in Tall, took her money, gave her the change, closed the drawer, and turned to get a cup of coffee for her. Fresh coffee was right behind me, with the cups. I gave one to her.

She gave me a big smile, as though I were already a friend. "My name's Rachel. I have another child on the way. I have to stick to Decaf for a while. Can't wait to get back on the hard stuff."

I had a sudden realization that people might treat me the way they were said to treat bartenders. . . . They wanted to engage with someone serving them the good stuff. The afternoon went surprisingly well, despite the constant stream of customers.

PAUSE: What has Gill just realized?

As evening fell, it got even busier, but Joann came over a couple of times to help me out. The line moved smoothly, with people ordering Single Pump Mocha or Tall Latte. I was supposed to call out the size, name of drink, and any "customizing" such as One Tall One Pump Mocha. Often I would get the order wrong and start with One Pump Mocha, forgetting to call the size . . . or call for a Tall Latte forgetting to mention the Guest wanted it with skim milk. Sometimes, Guests would order Single Pump Mocha, or they would order a drink backward, starting with the milk, then the syrup, then the size, and I would repeat what they said and call it out to Tawana. Tawana would correct me at the top of her lungs, putting the order in the right way. It was *humiliating* for me, but I learned fast.

PAUSE: How does Tawana help Gill learn the job?

Also, it was a gift to me that Tawana had such a large, commanding voice. I had been worried about getting the orders straight, and I never missed Tawana's powerful calls. And I found that by leaning over the register, closer to the Guests, I could also hear them clearly.

25 "Ask if you have any questions," Joann said. "Just ask."

And I did. I found that the Guests didn't seem to mind helping me get their request just right.

That night, around 7:00 p.m., I was surprised to see the store grow really busy. I had thought coffee was something you picked up on the way to work, but it clearly was now an essential pick-me-up[4] on the way home as well. I noticed a businessman enter the store and join the growing line. When I had been on the *other* side of the bar, I had worked so hard just to get a prospective client like this well-dressed man to return a call. Now, my customers were *literally* waiting in line for my services, I thought to myself. How funny.

The businessman stepped up in line and told me, "Double Macchiato."

This was Starbucks language. I had a hard time figuring out what it translated to on the cash register screen. I started to feel flushed as I punched at various combinations incorrectly.

30 "You are new here, right?" the man asked. I looked at him. Was he going to complain to Crystal and get me fired on my first day at the register?

But he smiled at my look of panic.

---

4. pick-me-up: something that gives extra energy

"Don't worry, you'll get it."

He actually took the time to encourage me. Wow. I looked back at the screen with a *renewed* clarity of mind. Double Macchiato. Hit Tall, then Macchiato. Simple.

The businessman wasn't the only one to try to set me at ease.

35   "Welcome to the neighborhood," one lady said.

PAUSE: What has Gill learned about people getting coffee?

Another guy with an open shirt who looked like a hippie commented, "I'm glad to see they are hiring older people."

Older?! Okay, so I wasn't so happy with this comment, but I appreciated his attitude. There was no denying it: I was older, at least a generation or two older than most Partners[5] so it was good to be welcomed even if it was for my *conspicuous* seniority.

Around eight o'clock, it started to get even busier. I had not realized that people had made Starbucks a part of their nightlife. Crowds of young people were piling in to share time with one another over their Lattes.

Focus, I reminded myself: You know how this works. *Punch the right button, call out the order, make the right change, smile.*

1. Briefly summarize Gill's process. <u>Answers will vary.</u>

2. Were you surprised by anything in the essay? What and why?

   _____

3. In addition to the critical skills needed to do his new job, what else did Gill observe and learn? _____

4. Write three questions that might be on a quiz on this essay (and be prepared to answer them). _____

5. Does Gill's essay have the **Four Basics of Good Process Analysis** (p. 201)? Why or why not, specifically? _____

6. Of the three essays in this chapter, which do you think is the most effective model of process analysis? Is it the same one you like best? Why or why not? _____

5. **Partners:** what Starbucks baristas are called

Write a Process Analysis Essay

In this section, you will write your own process analysis essay based on one of the following assignments. Use these tools to help you.

1. Review the Four Basics of Good Process Analysis (p. 201).

2. Use Process analysis at a glance as a basic organizer.

3. Use the Writing Guide: Process Analysis checklist as you write and revise (pp. 218–19).

Process analysis at a glance

Introduction with thesis statement
Includes the process you are describing

↓

First step in process
Details about the first step (how to do it or how it works)

↓

Second step in process
Details about the second step

↓

Third step in process
Details about the third step

↓

Conclusion
Reminds readers of the process and makes an observation related to your main point

---

ASSIGNMENT 1   Writing about College, Work, and Everyday Life

Write a process analysis essay on *one* of the following topics or on a topic of your own choice.

COLLEGE
- How to apply for financial aid
- How to study for a test
- How (a process in your major field of study) works

WORK
- How to do one of your major tasks at work
- How to get a job at your place of work
- How to get fired or how to get promoted

EVERYDAY LIFE
- How to wake up or how to get to sleep
- How to do (something you do well)
- How to break up with someone

ASSIGNMENT 2   Writing about an Image

Many accomplishments require practice and hard work. In this photo, Indonesia's Hendra Setiawan celebrates victory in the doubles semifinal badminton match in the sixteenth Asian Games in China, in November 2010. Write an essay in which you analyze a process you or your friend went through that was either difficult or required a lot of practice.

ASSIGNMENT 3   Writing to Solve a Problem

THE PROBLEM: Your friend is in a terrible situation. Because of her great grades in high school, she was accepted at an excellent private university and received a lot of money in student aid. Even so, she could not manage work and class and had to drop out. At this point, her full loan payment came due. She wanted to transfer to a public university where the tuition was much lower; however, when she requested her transcript from the private university, she was told her records would not be sent until she had paid the charges on her loan. She wants to continue her studies but does not know how to manage this financially.

THE ASSIGNMENT: Working on your own or in a small group, research the options your friend has, and write some steps she could take to resolve her problem.

RESOURCES: Review the chart on pages 840–41 for advice on problem solving. The Internet also has many sites that offer advice on repayment of student loans. A good one to start with is at **www.finaid.org**. Or try typing *student loan repayment* into a search engine. List any Web sites that you use.

RESOURCES
Additional Resources for Teaching Real Essays with Readings has visual planning forms for process analysis and the other essays covered in Part 2.

TIP: When you refer to an outside source, document it in the text and in a list at the end of your essay.

··

ASSIGNMENT 4 Writing about Connections

Read the following account of Tiffany Ewigleben before doing the assignment that follows.

COMMUNITY CONNECTIONS

Tiffany Ewigleben, Grand Rapids Community College (GRCC)
Program Assistant, Academic Service Learning Center

A high school dropout, Tiffany Ewigleben never thought she would go to college, but she worked and got a GED when she was twenty-one. When she and her husband moved in with her in-laws so that her husband could attend a culinary program at GRCC, her mother-in-law sug-gested she take a class to see what college was like. The chil-dren's literature class she took had a service-learning component that sent students into an after-school program at an elementary school where she read to students. She says it brought what she was doing in the class to life. She so enjoyed her experience that she later volun-teered to help out at Family Promise, the only homeless shelter in the area that accepts whole families.

Tiffany noticed that the shelter had some children's books, but the director told her that parents did not read to their children. On her own, Tiffany bought books at the Salvation Army and created activities for vol-unteers to use with the children. She also got some early literacy materi-als donated for the parents. She needed volunteers and money, though, so she made a proposal to the director of the college's Academic Service Learning (ASL) Center. The director was so impressed with her work at Family Promise that she invited Tiffany to become a Student Scholar, a group of students who plan service events.

With the help of the director, Tiffany helped Family Promise get a grant of $1,700 for the reading program. Word of the literacy center spread, and students volunteered. Tiffany also applied for a community service work-study grant so that she could work at the ASL Center. She is now in the Honors Program at the college, a member of the student congress, and leader of a student organization on campus, the Center for Inquiry. She entered a scholarship contest and was awarded $1,300. Tiffany believes her journey from high school dropout to confident and successful student leader started with a few hours of community service.

ASSIGNMENT: Choose one of the following and write a process analysis essay.

- Go to one of the following Web sites: **literacysite.com**, **goodsitesforkids .org/literacy**. Write a process essay about either how the site works or how to promote reading in children.

- Find out if your local library has a literacy program or children's reading program. If so, write about how it works.

- Choose a community you are involved in (a church, a parent organization, a neighborhood, a sports group, even a family, for example) and write about an event in which you participated. Describe the process of the event.

ASSIGNMENT 5 Writing about Readings

Choose one of the following assignments and write a process analysis essay.

- Daniel Flanagan writes about how he became literate, a major change in his life. Reread his essay in this chapter (p. 206) and Jordan Brown's (p. 152) and Monique Rizer's (p. 155) essays in Chapter 10. Each essay deals with the author's decision to make life better. Drawing from at least two of the essays, write about each person's process, and include your own experience as well.

- Howard White's "The Power of Hello" (p. 157) and Michael Gates Gill's "How I Learned to Be a Barista" in this chapter (p. 210) both highlight some acts of basic human kindness and the response to it. Drawing from each of the essays, write about what the authors learned and how they learned it.

Use the steps in the Writing Guide that follows to help you prewrite, draft, revise, and edit your process analysis essay. Check off each step as you complete it.

WRITING GUIDE: PROCESS ANALYSIS

STEPS IN PROCESS ANALYSIS	HOW TO DO THE STEPS
☐ Focus.	• Think about a process and its essential steps.
☐ Explore your topic. See Chapter 5.	• Make sure your process can be explained in a short essay. • Prewrite to decide on the steps and how you will explain them to your audience.
☐ Write a thesis statement. Process + Main point = Thesis See Chapter 6.	• Decide what you want your readers to know or learn about this process and write a thesis statement.
☐ Support your thesis. See Chapter 7.	• List all of the essential steps and details to describe them for your readers. • Imagine you are not familiar with the process. Would you understand it from the support you have listed, or do you need more explanation?
☐ Write a draft. See Chapter 8.	• Arrange the steps in a logical order (often chronological). • Write topic sentences for each essential step and paragraphs that describe them in detail.
☐ Revise your draft. See Chapter 9.	• Get feedback using the peer review guide for process analysis at **bedfordstmartins.com/realessays**. • Ask another person to read and comment on your draft. • Read to make sure that all the steps are there and relate to the topic. • Add transitions (often chronological). • Improve your introduction, thesis, and conclusion.

STEPS IN PROCESS ANALYSIS	HOW TO DO THE STEPS
☐ Edit your draft. See Parts 4 through 7.	• Correct errors in grammar, spelling, word use, and punctuation.
☐ Evaluate your writing.	• Does it have the Four Basics of Good Process Analysis (p. 201)? • Is this the best I can do?

reflect Reread your response to the "write" prompt on page 201 and apply what you have learned about process analysis to revise what you wrote. As necessary, describe and explain for your reader the essential steps in the process, in detail and in a logical order. Is there anything that a reader might not understand that you can clarify?

14

Classification

Writing That Puts Things into Groups

YOU KNOW THIS

You already use classification.

- You use the college bookstore, where books are classified by discipline (English, biology, math, etc.) and by course number.
- You use catalogs organized by type of product.
- You organize your things into categories.

write about your responsibilities by sorting them into categories.

Understand What Classification Is

IDEA JOURNAL
Write about the different kinds of friends you have.

Classification is writing that organizes, or sorts, people or items into categories.

The **organizing principle** for a classification is *how* you sort the people or items, not the categories themselves. The organizing principle is directly related to the **purpose** of your classification. For example, you might sort clean laundry (your purpose) using one of the following organizing principles (how you achieve your purpose)—by ownership (yours, your roommate's, and so on) or by where it goes (the bedroom, the bathroom).

Four Basics of Good Classification

1. It makes sense of a group of people or items by organizing them into useful categories.

2. It has a purpose for sorting the people or items.

3. It uses a single organizing principle.

4. It gives detailed examples or explanations of the things that fit into each category.

In the following paragraph, each number corresponds to one of the Four Basics of Good Classification.

All people do not learn in the same way, and **2** it is helpful to know what learning style you prefer. How do you naturally take in and absorb new information? The VARK learning styles inventory is a thirteen-item questionnaire that reveals which **3** learning style a person favors. **1** The first of its four learning styles is visual (V). **4** Visual learners absorb information best by looking at images or by drawing or diagramming a concept. For example, a visual learner may learn more by studying a flowchart of information rather than reading that same information in paragraph form. **1** The second learning style is auditory (A). **4** Auditory learners take in information most efficiently by hearing and listening. They remember information that they hear better than they remember information that they read. Even reading aloud is better than reading silently because hearing is key. Auditory learners benefit from discussion with others rather than working alone silently. **1** The third learning style is read/write (R). **4** Read/write learners learn best by reading written material. They also benefit from writing about what they have read. For example, many read/write learners study by reading and then writing a summary of what they have just read. Many people who are not naturally read/write learners have used that learning style in school because schools are oriented toward reading and writing. For example, a person whose score on the VARK is split evenly between auditory and read/write is probably an auditory learner who has learned to use a read/write learning style for school. **1** The final learning style is kinesthetic (K). **4** Kinesthetic learners learn by doing and by being active. For these learners, experiments in science may be easier to understand than reading a chapter in a book, listening to a lecture, or looking at an image. Kinesthetic learners often need to create activity in order to learn well: They may make flash cards, walk around as they study, or make a static activity interactive in some other way. All learners benefit from learning techniques such as highlighting and making notes, though different kinds of notes work for different

WRITER AT WORK

REBEKA MAZZONE: I have to tell clients the types of financial options they have.

(See Rebeka Mazzone's **PROFILE OF SUCCESS** on page 229.)

learning styles. All learners are active learners: They learn best when they actively involve themselves in a task rather than passively observe it. **2** Taking a learning styles inventory is both fun and useful, particularly for students.

SEEING CLASSIFICATION

This photograph, titled *Uncle Timon's Keys,* is by Brooks Jensen.

write   What can keys tell you about their owner? What categories of keys do you own?

Whenever you organize or sort things to make sense of them, you are classifying them. Here are some ways that you might use classification:

COLLEGE   In a nursing course, you discuss three types of antibiotics used to treat infections.

For an example of a classification written for work, see page 230. The piece was written by the financial manager who is profiled in the box on page 229.

WORK   For a report on inventory at a software store, you list the types of software carried and report how many of each type you have in stock.

EVERYDAY LIFE   You look at the types of payment plans that are available for your car loan.

Main Point in Classification

The **main point** in classification uses a single **organizing principle** to sort items into useful categories that help achieve the **purpose** of the classification. Imagine the following situation, in which a classification system is not logical or useful.

You visit your movie rental store or online service to find that the movies have been rearranged. The comedy, drama, and action categories are gone. Instead, the movies are arranged either by length, starting with the shortest, or alphabetically by the lead actor's last name.

This new arrangement is confusing for three reasons.

1. It does not sort movies into **useful** categories. (Who chooses a movie based on its length?)

2. It does not serve the **purpose** of helping customers find the movies they want.

3. It does not have a **single organizing principle**. (You do not know whether to search by the length of the movie or the actor's last name.)

The diagram below shows how movies at most rental stores or online services are classified.

TEACHING TIP
Ask students to create another such chart for books, vehicles, music, or anything else they are interested in.

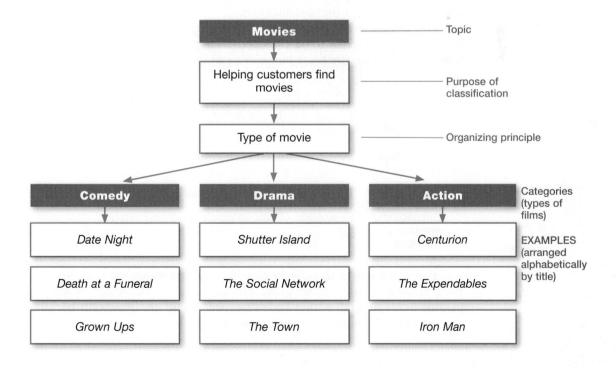

The following examples show how thesis statements for classification express the organizing principle and purpose.

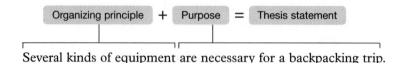

Several kinds of equipment are necessary for a backpacking trip.

In addition to the purpose and organizing principle, a thesis statement in a classification may also include the categories that will be explained.

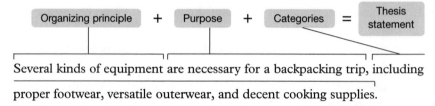

Several kinds of equipment are necessary for a backpacking trip, including proper footwear, versatile outerwear, and decent cooking supplies.

For online exercises on main point and support, visit *Exercise Central* at bedfordstmartins .com/realessays.

Support in Classification

The **primary support** in classification consists of the **categories** that serve the purpose of the classification.

The categories in classification are the "piles" into which the writer sorts a topic (the items to be classified). These categories will become the topic sentences for the body paragraphs of the essay.

TOPIC	College costs
THESIS STATEMENT	Tuition is only one of the many costs of going to college.
ORGANIZING PRINCIPLE	Types of costs other than tuition
PURPOSE	To show the different kinds of costs and their significance
CATEGORIES/ PRIMARY SUPPORT	Fees, costs of course materials, transportation expenses

RESOURCES
For online writing and grammar re- sources, go to bedfordstmartins .com/rewritingbasics.

The **supporting details** in classification are **examples** or explanations of what is in each category. The examples in classification are the various items that fall within each category. These are important because readers may not be familiar with your categories.

CATEGORY: Fees

EXAMPLES/SUPPORTING DETAILS: General student fee assessed to each student, lab fees, computer fees

CATEGORY: Costs of course materials

EXAMPLES/SUPPORTING DETAILS: Costs of books, lab manuals, software

CATEGORY: Transportation expenses

EXAMPLES/SUPPORTING DETAILS: Costs of gas, parking, train and bus fare

Organization in Classification

Classification can be organized in different ways depending on its purpose. For example, read the thesis statements and purposes that follow.

THESIS STATEMENT   The high costs of college make higher education impossible for many students.

PURPOSE   To argue that some costs should be reduced

How might this classification be organized? *Order of importance*

THESIS STATEMENT   My daughter has every kind of mess imaginable in her room, making it clear that she needs a lesson in taking care of her space and her things.

PURPOSE   To prove the need for the lesson by describing the messes

How might this classification be organized? *Spatial order*

THESIS STATEMENT   During my teenage years, I adopted three distinct clothing styles.

PURPOSE   To show how a person's style changed

How might this classification be organized? *Chronological order*

As you write your essay, you might find the following transitions helpful as you lead from one category to the next or from one example to another.

Common Transitions in Classification

another   first, second, third (and so on)

another kind   for example

for instance

Read and Analyze Classification

For more examples of classification, see Chapter 45.

Before writing a classification essay, read the following examples—one each from college, the workplace, and everyday life—and answer the questions that accompany them.

For each essay, review the Four Basics of Good Classification (p. 220) and practice your critical reading process by doing the following.

TEAMWORK
Have students work through the first essay together to apply the critical reading process and answer the questions after the essay.

2PR   The Critical Reading Process

Preview the reading, including the guiding question.

Read the piece, double-underlining the thesis statement, underlining the major support, and circling the transitions. Consider the quality of the support.

Pause to think during reading. Take notes and ask questions about what you are reading: Talk to the author.

Review the reading, your guiding question, your marginal notes and questions, and your answers to the Pause prompts.

TEACHING TIP
Read this essay aloud, give students a few minutes to respond to the questions in writing, and discuss the responses as a group. Ask students what other organizing principles they might use to classify personalities (for example, birth order).

Classification in College

The following student essay was written for an English class.

Josef Ameur

Videogame Genres

GUIDING QUESTION
What types of videogame genres does Ameur describe?

VOCABULARY
The following words are *italicized* in the essay: *accessible, arcade, genres, asteroids, attributes, charisma, embark, epic, quests*. If you do not know their meanings, look them up in a dictionary or online.

1   Video games are an easily *accessible* way to cure the effects of boredom. Ever since the late 1970s, video games have been extremely popular. They started out as *arcade* units, costing 25 cents to $1 per play. Kids would spend hundreds of dollars playing these games. The accessibility of video games has evolved over time from pay-to-play arcade units to personal home TV consoles. The *genres* of games have also evolved over time: shooter, role-playing, and strategy are just a few.

PAUSE:
Underline the sentence where Ameur presents his categories.

CRITICAL READING
- Preview
- Read
- Pause
- Review

2   Shooters are one of the oldest genres of games. This genre was born in arcade games such as *Asteroids* and *Galaga*. The early shooters were quite simple, and everything was on a two-dimensional plane. *Asteroids* consisted of a small spaceship avoiding *asteroids* by dodging and shooting at them. In *Galaga*, the players shot at enemy alien ships. Eventually, shooters evolved into third- and first-person shooters. In third-person, the player's view is from above, looking down at the character. In first-person, the player looks through the character's eyes. These shooters involve a character holding a gun shooting at enemies. Military, Sci-Fi, and Survival are a few sub-genres.

COMBINING MODES
Note that this classification essay also uses illustration.

3   Role-playing games (RPGs) started out on paper. *Dungeons & Dragons* was one of the more popular paper RPGs. Paper RPGs gave birth to computer-based ones. The benefit of computer-based RPGs is that with an Internet connection, they can be played with millions of other people. Players and their friends can create and control characters who live in a fantasy world. These characters are often class-based with classes such as thief, warrior, mage, and ranger. Players micromanage the *attributes* of their characters: *charisma*, strength, and magic, to name a few. Players *embark* on *epic quests*, slay beasts, find treasure, and fight in great battles.

PAUSE:
Note the detailed examples Ameur gives of each category.

4   Strategy games are similar to RPGs, but they are on a much larger scale. In strategy games, players often control a historic civilization. The three main components of strategy games are economy, military, and politics. There are usually several types of resources that the players manage such as gold, stone, wood, and food. Players control the villagers, assigning them to gather resources. In the military aspect of this genre, players control the army and train different types of soldiers, taking into consideration the strengths and weaknesses of the different units. Politics determines allies and enemies and who wars with whom. In strategy games, there is no such thing as peace.

PAUSE:
What sentence ties
the conclusion to the
thesis statement?

5   Many genres of games have been created to explore and play, but all videogames offer the same core benefit: They offer a brief moment in time to escape the world around you. Videogames not only cure boredom, but they also offer an experience that can rival that of books or films.

CRITICAL
THINKING
- Summarize
- Analyze
- Synthesize
- Evaluate

(More on p. 21.)

1. **Summarize.** Briefly summarize Ameur's essay, including what he is classifying and what categories he uses.

2. **Analyze.** Are the categories useful to Ameur's purpose of explaining videogame genres? Are all of the details clearly related to each category? How does Ameur's conclusion remind readers of the purpose? What system of organization does he use?

3. **Synthesize.** What else do you know about the topic? Do you agree that the reason people play videogames is to relieve boredom? What other ways are there to relieve boredom?

4. **Evaluate.** Does Ameur achieve his purpose? Do you agree that playing videogames rivals the experience of reading a book or seeing a film? Does the essay have the **Four Basics of Good Classification** (see p. 220)? What do you think of the essay?

Classification at Work

The following shows how a financial manager uses classification.

PROFILE OF SUCCESS

Classification in the Real World

Background   I was one of six daughters, and my mother was on welfare. I never knew my father. We lived in a housing project in upstate New York, and I dropped out of school and moved away. At seventeen, I got a job at a fancy restaurant, got my GED, and began hairdressing school. A customer at the restaurant encouraged me to go to college, which I hadn't even considered. But I went to Monroe Community College, worked several jobs, and graduated. Then, I transferred to St. John Fisher College and had a great mentor in the Accounting Department, who encouraged me to take the Certified Public Accountant (CPA) exam, which I did. I had to transform my image by learning to speak and write "proper" English; cutting and taming my big, long, platinum-blonde hair; and dressing more conservatively. Now I have a great job, a husband, and two children.

Rebeka Mazzone
Director, Rhode Island Region

Colleges/Degrees   Monroe Community College (A.S.), St. John Fisher College (B.S.)

Employer   Accounting Management Solutions (Note: Between the time of first interviewing Rebeka and the publication of this book, she started a new job as Director of Compliance and Internal Audit, at Johnson & Wales University. There she will create a new department, starting by hiring and training her own staff. She looks forward to this exciting new opportunity.)

Writing at work   People think accountants are numbers people, and we are, but much of what I do is writing: documenting my findings in words, for my clients, my colleagues, company management. So much is client communication. Only the accountant understands the numbers: I have to explain those numbers clearly. Like everyone else, I write lots of reports, memos, letters, proposals, and e-mails. I also give lots of presentations at conferences. I do not really like to write, but I do a lot of it—I have to—and I make sure that what I write is accurate and well written. It is essential to my success. I also do lots of speaking for the American Institute of Certified Public Accountants (AICPA), the professional organization for CPAs.

How Mazzone uses classification   I have to break complex financial strategies into categories that clients can understand, so that I can help them make good financial choices.

Rebeka Mazzone's Classification

Rebeka wrote the following for a presentation at the American Institute of Certified Public Accountants.

GUIDING QUESTION
What kinds of practices will help nonprofits?

VOCABULARY
The following words are *italicized* in the presentation: *laudable, scrutiny, onerous, intrusion, inventoried, strategic, surplus, adequate, assets, expenditures, mandatory.* If you do not know their meanings, look them up in a dictionary or online.

CRITICAL
READING
■ Preview
■ Read
■ Pause
■ Review

Serving on a Nonprofit Board Need Not Be Onerous

Doing good by serving on the board of nonprofit organizations, always *laudable*, is more demanding as public *scrutiny* of nonprofit financial management increases. But the job need not be *onerous*. A board member with a solid financial background can help a nonprofit achieve a sounder financial footing which will in turn help maintain its independence by minimizing potential legislative *intrusion*. Several types of sound financial management practices can benefit nonprofit organizations.

Documenting accounting and financial management practices. Organizations cannot know what needs improving until they understand how they currently operate. Everything the organization does should be *inventoried* and documented, including fund-raising, accounting, generating financial reports, interactions between senior management and the board, and when these actions occur.

Budgeting as part of *strategic* planning. Budgeting provides an opportunity to link the organization's operational plans with its strategy and financial success and growth. Before plunging into the budget process and assigning costs to program activities, all program and project managers should understand and discuss the organization's strategy. The time spent educating, communicating, and planning will get everyone to agree on organizational goals and how to achieve them.

Managing to the operating budget and audited financial statements. Frequently, management and the board look at cash budgets. Outsiders, including lenders, look at audited statements and can get a different picture. For example, depreciation expenses and vacation accruals can turn a $10,000 surplus on an operating budget into a $50,000 loss on an audited statement of activities.

Budget a surplus. Being around for the long term requires building reserves. Budget an annual *surplus*, even a minimal amount, to ensure that *adequate* resources exist to guard against unexpected shortfalls.

Project cash flow. An organization should have three to six months of current *assets* (cash, accounts receivable, and short-term investments) on hand. This policy and practice ensures enough cash to meet obligations throughout the year. It will help manage accounts receivable and accounts payable and the timing of budgeted *expenditures*.

PAUSE:
What is Mazzone classifying?

PAUSE:
According to Mazzone, what should the budgeting process do?

PAUSE:
How does this sound business practice relate to everyone?

With the nonprofit sector pumping more than $50 billion into the Massachusetts economy each year, solid financial management of nonprofit organizations is not simply nice to have. It is *mandatory*, and it need not be onerous for a person with financial acumen.

PAUSE:
How does Mazzone link the conclusion to the introduction?

1. Briefly summarize Mazzone's presentation, including what she is classifying and what categories she uses. *Answers will vary.* _____

2. What is her purpose? _____

3. Do you agree with her point of view? _____

4. Do you think Mazzone achieves her purpose? Why or why not? _____
   _____

Classification in Everyday Life

Dylan Marcos
Bad Roommates

GUIDING QUESTION
What kinds of bad roommates does Marcos classify?

VOCABULARY
The following words are *italicized* in the essay: *encountered, hounded, potential.* If you do not know their meanings, look them up in a dictionary or online.

1   Over the past few years, I have learned a lot about bad roommates. Although I doubt that I have *encountered* all types, I certainly know more now than I did before. I'll pass on to you some of what I have experienced, so you can try to avoid the following types of roommates—the romeos, the slugs, and the criminals.

2   The romeos are usually great guys and lots of fun, when they happen to be single—but they are usually not. They always seem to have

PAUSE: What is Marcos's purpose in writing the essay?

CRITICAL
READING
■ Preview
■ Read
■ Pause
■ Review

girlfriends, who basically become nonpaying roommates. The women are mostly nice, but they change the apartment in big ways. First, we have to watch how we act. We can't walk around half-dressed in the morning, for example. Also, we have to get used to sharing: The girlfriends spend hours at a time in the bathroom, doing their hair and putting on make-up. There are always more dishes in the sink when they are around, more food disappears, and even shampoo goes faster than normal. The romeos do not seem to understand that having semipermanent guests in the apartment really changes the way we live.

3   Another type, the slug, is even harder to live with than the romeo because the slugs are slobs. They never wash the dishes or put away food, they leave a trail of dirty clothes behind them, and they completely destroy the bathroom every time they use it. Slugs pretty much live in front of the television, so you will probably never have a chance to watch what *you* want. The slug is also sloppy about paying rent and bills. Although he usually has the money, he has to be reminded—no, *hounded*—before he will actually pay what he owes.

PAUSE: What categories does Marcos use?

4   The worst type of roommate is the criminal, for obvious reasons. I've had only one of these, but one was more than enough. He was a nice guy for about two weeks—clean, not around too much, but good to have a beer with when he was there. One day, though, I came home after work to find that he was gone, along with everything valuable in the apartment—our laptops, iPods, some cash, a bunch of CDs, and my favorite leather jacket. Although we called the police, I know I will never get back anything he stole.

PAUSE: What three types of roommate does Marcos identify? Which one does he like least?

5   What I have learned from my experience is that, when I interview *potential* roommates, I should ask for at least two references, preferably from former roommates, so I can weed out the romeos, slugs, and criminals. That should keep my living situation sane—at least until I meet someone who seems great at first but turns out to fall into another, equally bad category. I'll keep you posted.

PAUSE: How does Marcos tie the conclusion to the introduction?

1. What is Marcos's topic, and what categories does he use? *Answers will vary.*
    _____

2. Does he give enough detail about each category for you to understand it as he does? _____

3. Write three questions that might be on a quiz on Marcos's essay.

_____

4. Does the essay have the **Four Basics of Good Classification**

(p. 220)? _____

5. What other categories would you add based on your experience or

that of other people you know? _____

Write a Classification Essay

In this section, you will write your own classification essay. Use the following tools to help you.

1. Review the Four Basics of Good Classification (p. 220).
2. Use `Classification at a glance` as a basic organizer.
3. Use the Writing Guide: Classification checklist as you write and revise (pp. 238–39).

ASSIGNMENT 1   Writing about College, Work, and Everyday Life

Write a classification essay on one of the following topics or on a topic of your own choice.

COLLEGE
- Types of degree programs
- Types of students
- Skim a textbook from another class to find a topic that is broken into categories. Then, summarize the topic.

WORK
- Types of work spaces
- Types of customers or clients
- Types of skills needed for a particular job

EVERYDAY LIFE
- Types of drivers
- Types of restaurants in your town
- Types of cell phones

Classification at a glance

Introduction with thesis statement
Organizing principle + purpose OR Organizing principle + categories + purpose

↓

First category
Examples/ explanations

↓

Second category
Examples/ explanations

↓

Third category
Examples/ explanations

↓

Conclusion
Refers back to the classification's purpose and makes an observation

ASSIGNMENT 2   Writing about Images

All of us are members of a number of groupings. These three photographs are from a series by photographer Diane Meyers called "Without a Car in the World." Her series profiles a relatively small group of people who live in the Los Angeles area and who are, for various reasons, "car-less." She asked people who are "car-less" in Los Angeles about their motivations and impressions.

Write an essay in which you consider a decision you have made—either to own or not to own a commonly owned possession—that puts you in a particular category. Discuss what you have in common with others in this category, or how you differ from them, and how comfortable you are being considered a part of this category.

Because it's the car culture and most people don't think they can, right? And that's what we know as living in L.A. is; in L.A., you have to have a car. . . . [But] if you actually try to move around without one, it's actually not that difficult—it's quite easy. . . . It's really quite fun. . . . Don't get me wrong—the public transportation should be improved, but it has improved a lot in the past ten years.

—Melba Thorne, artist.
Car-less since 2008.

I wanted to get rid of all that stress around the cars and taking care of them and changing their parking spaces and so forth. And once one does that little twist in the head and is really getting rid of it . . . it is a very big piece of new-found freedom. And the walking, the biking, the intimacy of learning your neighborhood in ways that you may have not known it before is enormously gratifying. . . . That twist in one's head—the idea of sacrifice versus freedom [is important.] Getting rid of is getting free of, [while] giving up is sacrificing, and people who make that distinction are ultimately very happy about getting rid of the car.

—Lois Arkin, advocate and founder of the Cooperative
Resources and Services Project.
Car-less since 1991.

I think having a car in Los Angeles is a necessity. I really do.

—Jose Morgan, animal shelter employee.
Car-less since 2006.

ASSIGNMENT 3 Writing to Solve a Problem

THE PROBLEM: When you were starting college, you received many credit-card offers, and you signed up for three. Over time, you have run up a big debt, partly from the charges themselves and partly from the interest. Now you are seriously in debt and do not know how to get out of it.

THE ASSIGNMENT: Working on your own or in a small group, first classify your monthly expenses. Then, divide them into "necessary expenses" and "unnecessary expenses." Once you have done this, write an essay that classifies your expenses. Finally, cite some options you will pursue to pay down your debt.

RESOURCES: Review the chart on pages 840–41 for advice on problem solving. Also, check Web sites for advice about paying down debt without getting into even bigger trouble. You might start by typing in the words *advice on how to pay off credit cards* into a search engine. List any Web sites that you use.

RESOURCES
Additional Resources for Teaching Real Essays with Readings has visual planning forms for classification and the other essays covered in Part 2. These forms are also online at bedfordstmartins .com/realessays.

ASSIGNMENT 4   Writing about Connections

Read the following account of Maggie Gong before doing the assignment that follows.

COMMUNITY CONNECTIONS

Maggie Gong, Bergen Community College (BCC)
Cofounder, Community Service Club

Maggie Gong was the first in her family to go to college. She started at one college but did not feel that she fit in there, so she transferred to BCC, where she says that she gets great personal attention from her professors. Those connections with professors helped her to feel part of the college, and she decided to get more involved on campus. Maggie had done a little community service while she was in high school (she had partici-pated in a blood drive and a clothing drive), but she was not highly in-volved. However, she was interested, and, with faculty adviser Lori Talarico, she worked to establish the first community service club at BCC.

Events the first year included choosing a local agency to help: Chil-dren's Aid and Family Services. Club members "adopted" a family for the holidays, got lists of what the family needed and wanted, and bought gifts for them. They also gave the family gift cards for groceries, clothing, and transportation. To raise money, the club held fundraisers, such as a gift-wrapping event before the holidays. They also had a bake sale to raise money ($230), the proceeds from which were used to buy diapers of all sizes for one- to four-year-old children from low-income families.

Interest in the club has grown, and Gong continues to feel connected to and a part of the Bergen community.

ASSIGNMENT: Choose one of the following topics and write a classification essay.

- Go to your college's community service club or office if there is one. If there is not, use the search term "volunteer opportunities, [your town or city]." Then, write about the kinds of activities the club does or the opportu-nities in your area.

- If you did not do the activities in Chapter 1 (pp. 15–18) on finding out about resources and clubs on your campus, do so now. Write an essay about the types of resources or clubs.

- Write about the kinds of friends you have.

. . . .

ASSIGNMENT 5   Writing about Readings

In this chapter, Dylan Marcos writes about an element in his life (roommates) (p. 231). Read his essay and another selection that discusses elements of life today: Rob Walker's "Stuck on You" (p. 175), about bumper stickers. Then, drawing from the two essays and your own experience or that of others, write a classification essay describing the kinds of interests or activities that are representative of life today in the United States.

. . . .

Use the steps in the Writing Guide that follows to help you prewrite, draft, revise, and edit your classification essay. Check off each step as you complete it.

WRITING GUIDE: CLASSIFICATION

STEPS IN CLASSIFICATION	HOW TO DO THE STEPS
☐ **Focus.**	• Think about your topic and how you can sort it so that your audience will understand the categories.
☐ **Explore your topic.** See Chapter 5.	• Prewrite to find possible categories to use and examples that will explain each category.
☐ **Write a thesis statement.** Organizing principle + <u>Purpose</u> = Thesis Or Organizing principle + <u>Categories</u> = Thesis See Chapter 6.	• Include your topic and either the method you are using to sort (the organizing principle) or the categories you will describe.
☐ **Support your thesis.** See Chapter 7.	• Choose useful categories that will achieve your purpose. • Consider what your readers need to know to understand the categories.

STEPS IN CLASSIFICATION	HOW TO DO THE STEPS
☐ **Write a draft.** See Chapter 8.	• Arrange the categories logically. • Write topic sentences for each category and paragraphs giving examples of each of the categories.
☐ **Revise your draft.** See Chapter 9.	• Get feedback using the peer-review guide for classification at **bedfordstmartins.com/realessays**. • Add any examples that will help your readers understand. • Add transitions. • Improve your introduction, thesis, and conclusion.
☐ **Edit your revised draft.** See Parts 4 through 7.	• Correct errors in grammar, spelling, word use, and punctuation.
☐ **Evaluate your writing.**	• Does it have the Four Basics of Good Classification (p. 220)? • Is this the best I can do?

reflect Reread your response to the "write" prompt on page 220. How would you change what you wrote based on what you know about classification?

15

Definition

Writing That Tells What Something Means

YOU KNOW THIS

You already use definition.

- Your child hears the word *hurricane* and asks what it means. You then define it for him.
- You see a word you do not know, but figure out its meaning by reading the rest of the sentence or paragraph.
- You explain a slang term to someone who has not heard the term before.

write about a word you do not know. Look up its definition, then write an expanded definition with examples, explaining what it is and is not.

Understand What Definition Is

IDEA JOURNAL
Write about what *success* means.

Definition is writing that explains what a term or concept means.

Four Basics of Good Definition

1. It tells readers what term is being defined.
2. It presents a clear definition.
3. It uses examples to show what the writer means.
4. It gives details about the examples that readers will understand.

TEACHING TIP
Have several dictionaries in your classroom. Advise students to have their own dictionary as well.

In the following paragraph, each number corresponds to one of the Four Basics of Good Definition.

ESL Encourage ESL students to buy both an English dictionary and a bilingual dictionary.

1 Internet addiction is 2 chronic, compulsive use of the Internet that interferes with the addicts' lives or their relationships with others. 3 For example, addicts may spend so much time on-line that they are unable to perform as expected at home, work, or school. 4 These addicts may spend hours surfing the Web, playing games, or e-mailing friends and family. 3 In more serious cases, the Internet addiction can cause financial problems, or worse.

4 For example, online shoppers who go to extremes can find themselves in debt and, as a result, damage their credit, not to mention personal relationships. **3** Still other Internet addictions involve potentially dangerous or illegal activities. **4** These activities can include meeting people online, gambling, viewing pornography, and engaging in cybersex. However, for Internet addicts, the problem usually isn't *how* they use the Internet; the problem is that they cannot stop using it, even if they want to.

SEEING DEFINITION

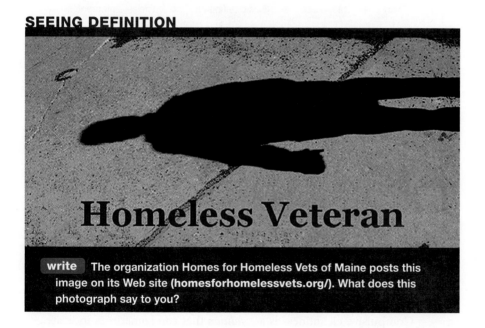

Homeless Veteran

write   The organization Homes for Homeless Vets of Maine posts this image on its Web site (**homesforhomelessvets.org/**). What does this photograph say to you?

Many situations require you to explain the meaning of a term, particularly how you are using it.

ESL Ask ESL students to define a term from their language.

| COLLEGE | On a U.S. history exam, you define the term *carpetbagger*. |
| WORK | You describe a coworker as a "slacker" to a human resources staffer, and the staffer asks what you mean exactly. |

EVERYDAY LIFE   You explain the term *fair* to your child in the context of games or sports.

Main Point in Definition

In definition essays, your **main point** typically defines your topic. The main point is directly related to your **purpose,** which is to get your readers to understand the way that you are using a term or concept in your essay. Although writers do not always define a term or concept in a thesis statement, it helps readers if they do.

A thesis statement in definition can follow a variety of different patterns, two of which include the term and its basic definition.

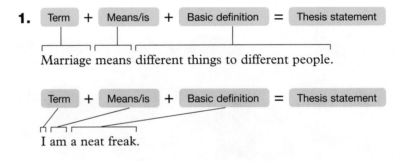

1.   Term   +   Means/is   +   Basic definition   =   Thesis statement

Marriage means different things to different people.

Term   +   Means/is   +   Basic definition   =   Thesis statement

I am a neat freak.

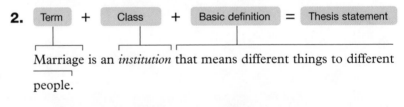

2.   Term   +   Class   +   Basic definition   =   Thesis statement

Marriage is an *institution* that means different things to different people.

Term   +   Class   +   Basic definition   =   Thesis statement

Compulsive cleanliness is a *condition* that can sometimes indicate a problem.

In essays based on the following thesis statements, readers would expect the italicized terms and concepts to be defined through examples that show the writer's meaning.

What does *marriage* mean today?

I am a *neat freak.*

Many people do not understand what *bullying* really means.

Support in Definition

If a friend says, "Summer in the city is awful," you do not know what she means by *awful.* Is it the weather? The people? The transportation? Until your friend explains what she means, you will not know whether you would agree that summer in the city is awful.

Support in definition provides specific examples of terms or concepts to help explain what they mean. Read the two thesis statements that follow and the lists of examples that could be used as support.

THESIS	Today, marriage means different things to different people.
SUPPORT	A union of one man and one woman
	A union of two people of either sex
	A union that is supported by state law
	A union that is supported by both civil and religious laws
THESIS	I am a neat freak.
SUPPORT	I clean compulsively.
	I am constantly buying new cleaning products.
	My cleaning habits have attracted the notice of friends and family.

In both of these examples, the writer would then go on to develop the examples with details.

THESIS	I am a neat freak.
SUPPORT	I clean compulsively.
	DETAILS: I clean in the morning and at night, and cannot let a spot on the counter go for a second.
SUPPORT	I am constantly buying new cleaning products.
	DETAILS: Every week, I buy new products, have a closet full of them, and believe every new sales pitch.
SUPPORT	My cleaning habits have attracted the notice of friends and family.
	DETAILS: Kids used to appreciate the clean house; now they complain that I am compulsive; friends tease me, but I wonder if they think I go too far.

DISCUSSION
Have students modify a dictionary definition for a variety of audiences.

Organization in Definition

The examples in a definition essay are often organized by **importance**, or the impact you think the examples will have on your readers. Save the most important example for last.

As you write, add transitions to connect one example to the next.

Common Transitions in Definition

another	for example
another kind	for instance
first, second, third, and so on	

Read and Analyze Definition

For more examples of definition, see Chapter 46.

TEAMWORK:
Have students work through the first essay together to apply the critical reading process and answer the questions after the essay.

Before writing a definition essay, read the following three examples—from college, the workplace, and everyday life—and answer the questions that accompany them.

For each of the following three essays, review the Four Basics of Good Definition (p. 240) and practice your critical reading process by doing the following.

2PR   The Critical Reading Process

■ **Preview** the reading, including the guiding question.

■ **Read** the piece, double-underlining the thesis statement, underlining the major support, and circling the transitions. Consider the quality of the support.

■ **Pause** to think during reading. Take notes and ask questions about what you are reading: Talk to the author.

■ **Review** the reading, your guiding question, your marginal notes and questions, and your answers to the Pause prompts.

Definition in College

The following essay was written for an English class. Note the use of outside sources and the documentation of them at the end.

Anna Puiia

What Is Hip?

CRITICAL
READING
■ Preview
■ Read
■ Pause
■ Review

GUIDING QUESTION

What examples does Puiia give to show her definition of *hip*?

VOCABULARY

The following words are *italicized* in the essay: *conspicuous, hodgepodge, conglomerate, dishevelment, aesthetic, amalgamated, apathy, nonchalance, ironic.* If you do not know their meanings, look them up in a dictionary or online.

1   You know who they are. You have seen their self-done haircuts, their skinny jeans, and their oversized sweaters and sunglasses. You have seen their bright colors, and mismatches, and secondhand store hand-me-downs. You have seen that guy with the faux—or maybe real—knuckle tattoos that either make no sense, or refer to something almost no one has heard of. You may spy them riding the bus wearing obnoxiously *conspicuous* headphones, which are blaring something that can only be described as "indie rock." You may catch them pining over some skinny boy in oxfords and a kaffiyeh.[1] Hipsters are the kids everyone loves to hate.

2   What is a hipster, anyway? Hipsterism, in general, is an to-each-his-own way of expressing oneself. Hipster fashion is a *hodgepodge* of past trends and styles; a recycled, updated *conglomerate* of former fashions. Hipsters combine elements of former subcultures to create their overall looks of *dishevelment.* Grunge's[2] flannel paired with skinny jeans and a book of Allen Ginsberg's[3] poetry, or a copy of *On The Road*[4] in your backpack could characterize a hipster. A hipster may frame his or her face in lens-less or non-prescription Buddy Holly glasses[5] or stomp around in an old pair of Converse sneakers.[6] With hipsters, it's all about seeming [effortlessly] cool, or as if they did not think or care about their outfits when they got dressed (Robie).

COMBINING MODES: Note that this definition also uses description.

PAUSE: Can you tell who Puiia is describing?

PAUSE: Underline the details Puiia gives.

1. **kaffiyeh:** a triangular-shaped Arab headdress
2. **grunge:** a style of dress, usually untidy
3. **Allen Ginsberg:** American poet and a leader of the 1950s Beat Generation
4. *On the Road:* a novel by Jack Kerouac, another leader of the Beat Generation
5. **Buddy Holly glasses:** thick-rimmed glasses worn by Buddy Holly, an American musician who was one of the first rock-and-roll artists
6. **Converse:** a brand of sneakers, particularly high tops

PAUSE:
How does Puiia move
the reader from one
paragraph to the
next?

3   But hipsterism goes beyond just fashion. The hipster subculture is very much defined by its musical tastes as well. The music of the hipster subculture is not defined by one genre. Most of the genres popularly associated with hipsters are combinations of other styles, and sometimes carry funny names, like shoegaze — a style of music characterized by the artists' use of effect pedals, which causes them to spend all of their live performances gazing at their feet (LaRose). Some hipsters prefer music of a moodier, folksier persuasion, while others prefer pure electronica and synthesizers. Some settle in between with bands that combine the simple, pretty melodies of folk with the intricate layering of electronica, creating an offbeat, experimental sound.

4   The hipster subculture is one of the most commonly criticized groups in American youth culture. A simple Google search of the word *hipster* provides one with links to pages and articles like, "Hipster Subculture Ripe for Parody," or "Why The Hipster Must Die." Another link is to an article entitled "Hipster: The Dead End of Western Civilization." This article by Douglas Haddow discusses hipsterism as the "dead end of western civilization" (Haddow), because he claims that the hipsters are no longer producing anything new. He attacks the recycled *aesthetic* and *amalgamated* music styles of the hipsters and points to the use of past trends in new ways as a lack of creativity. This lack of creativity is reflected, he says, in today's youth culture "simply consuming cool, rather than creating it," (Haddow) as though hipsters are not making the things they buy and wear and listen to cool, but are instead being told these things are cool, and then consuming them. This criticism is founded in most of the things that hipsterism, itself, is based in: a sense of *apathy*, a projected *nonchalance* about fashion, the idea of recycling the past.

PAUSE:
Do you agree with
Haddow's opinion?

5   I do not see hipsters as a dead end. I see them as making progress for the fashion world. Hipsters are taking the trends of the past and making them cool in a new way — giving them new life. They are taking the untrends of the past and making them cool for the first time. They are wearing the flaws of their predecessors on their sleeves, or in the soles of their run-down boots, or in place of the lenses in their giant glasses. Their recycling is moving fashion along in a different way. So the individual items they are wearing are not new, but they have created a completely new look.

6   [Now,] as I get dressed in my skinny jeans and my oversized ugly sweater, sliding on some thrift store loafers, I, a hipster, am wondering what the hippest response to being called a "dead end" would be. Maybe it was writing this paper, but I think I put in too much effort. It has to seem as if I did not care. Maybe it would be to laugh at it. Maybe I could name my band that, someday, when I have a band. Or maybe I should just make a T-shirt with the saying, "I Am the Dead End." That statement is simple, casual, and maybe even a little bit *ironic*. I like it.

Works Cited

Haddow, Douglas. "Hipster: The Dead End of Western Civilization Adbusters Culturejammer Headquarters." Adbusters Culturejammer Headquarters | Journal of the Mental Environment. 29 July 2008. Web 06 April 2011. <https://www.adbusters.org/magazine/79/hipster.html>.

LaRose, Philip. "Know Your Subgenres: Shoegazing." *The KEXP Blog.* 26 April 2009. Web 09 April 2011. <http://blog.kexp.org/blog/2009/04/26/know-your-subgenres-shoegazing/>.

Robie, Elizabeth. "Culture: Hipster Fashion: The Ultimate in Urban Cool." *Inside Vandy.* The Vanderbilt Hustler. 03 Jan. 2008. Web. 20 April 2011. <http://www.insidevandy.com/drupal/node/6260>.

1. **Summarize.** Briefly summarize Puiia's essay, including the term she is defining, her definition, and the examples she gives.

2. **Analyze.** In what paragraph does Puiia move toward her own definition of hipsterism, in contrast to Haddow's opinions? How does she mock his piece in the last paragraph?

3. **Synthesize.** Apart from Puiia's essay, what do you know about hipsters? Read Haddow's essay at **www.adbusters.org/magazine/79/hipster.html** and use both Puiia's essay and his to determine your own definition of *hip*.

4. **Evaluate.** Does Puiia give you the reader a clear idea of how she understands the term *hip*? What is her point of view? Do you think she is biased? If so, how? Does her essay have the **Four Basics of Good Definition** (p. 240)?

CRITICAL
THINKING
■ Summarize
■ Analyze
■ Synthesize
■ Evaluate

(More on p. 21.)

Definition at Work

The following profile shows how a business owner uses definition at work.

PROFILE OF SUCCESS

Definition in the Real World

Gary Knoblock
Business Owner

Background   I grew up in New Orleans, where, after high school, I tried college for a year but was told by a professor that I was not college material and should try manual labor. I left college and moved to Fort Worth, Texas, where I became a police officer. During my ten years with the force, I attended a junior college at night, earning an associate's degree. I received numerous promotions at work and eventually became a member of the force's SWAT team. In 1999, I decided to start my own business. I moved to Mississippi and started a sign company, Lightning Quick (LQ) Signs. Since then, the company has grown steadily into a successful business. It was destroyed by Hurricane Katrina in 2005, but I rebuilt and reopened it in 2007.

College / Degree   Tarrant County Junior College (A.A.)

Employer   Self

Writing at work   Proposals to get jobs, advertising copy, follow-up reports and letters, loan applications, correspondence with clients and prospective clients, precise and descriptive specifications for government jobs

How Gary uses definition   I often need to define terms for clients. In addition, the letter about the company that I use in sales situations defines how LQ Signs is customer-oriented.

Gary Knoblock's Definition

Gary Knoblock uses this mission statement to get contracts for his sign company.

GUIDING QUESTION
What does customer-oriented mean to Knoblock?

VOCABULARY
The following words are *italicized* in the excerpt: *fundamental, orientation, prospective, installation.* If you do not know their meanings, look them up in a dictionary or online.

CRITICAL
READING
■ Preview
■ Read
■ Pause
■ Review

> The *fundamental* principle of Lightning Quick (LQ) Signs is customer *orientation.* While most companies claim that they are customer-oriented, most have no idea what that really means. I tell my employees that I would like to have a customer giggle at the completion of the job, delighting in the product and service we have delivered, his every expectation met and

TEAMWORK
Have students read
this essay aloud and
respond to the
questions in pairs.

exceeded. For all of us at LQ Signs, *customer-oriented* means that from start to finish to follow-up, the customer comes first.

Our customer orientation begins before the job begins. Before doing anything, we interview the customer to learn what his or her needs are and to determine the most cost-effective route to meet those needs. No job for us is "standard." Each is unique.

Our customer orientation means that we produce high-quality products quickly. We keep signs simple because our customers want their *prospective* customers to be able to read the sign in a glance. We use the most current digital printing processes to produce sharp, readable signs quickly. Because we have previously determined, with the customer, the most cost-effective method of producing the signs, the high quality and rapid return do not come at extra cost.

Our customer orientation means that our products are thoroughly checked for flaws and installed at the customer's convenience. Our signs leave our workshop in perfect condition, as the customer has ordered. Our well-trained team of installers works with the customer to determine the *installation* schedule.

Finally, our customer orientation means that the job is not complete when the sign is in place. We follow up every sale to make sure that the product is in top shape and that the customer is pleased.

LQ Signs is truly customer-oriented, from start to finish to follow-up. Our customers are our partners.

---

1. What is Knoblock's **purpose**? *To persuade potential customers to use his company's services*

2. Briefly summarize the essay, including the term being defined and the definition and examples. *Answers will vary.*

3. Is Knoblock likely to be biased? Why or why not? _____

4. Does he do a good job of explaining the term? _____

Definition in Everyday Life

The following appeared originally in the *Boston Globe* newspaper.

Baxter Holmes

My Date with Fifteen Women

GUIDING QUESTION
How does the experience of judging a beauty pageant change Holmes's definition of *beauty*?

VOCABULARY
The following words are *italicized* in the essay: *innumerable, extracurricular, articulated, poise, segment.* If you do not know the meaning of these words, look them up in a dictionary or online.

CRITICAL READING
- Preview
- Read
- Pause
- Review

PAUSE: How would you define *beauty*?

1   There is a lot more to a beauty pageant than meets the eye. I know, after judging one myself. Beauty is a vague term often defined by first impressions. If you like what you see, it is beautiful. If not, it is not. For many people tuning in to the Miss America pageant, that will be their definition. It certainly was mine, until I judged a preliminary pageant for Miss New Hampshire last summer.

2   How did a twenty-one-year-old sportswriter on summer break from college get to be a tiny part of this glamorous slice of Americana? Given proper guidance on the rules, pretty much anyone can become a judge, and a former journalism professor of mine who has been involved in pageantry since 1986 signed me up to be on the panel for the twenty-second annual Miss Kingston/ Miss Seacoast scholarship pageant, partly because he thought it would be a good experience for me. He also thought it would be fun. So did I. It wasn't.

PAUSE: Why did seeing the contestants terrify Holmes?

3   As I entered the blue-gray antique home in Kingston, New Hampshire, where a preliminary session of private interviews would take place, I saw fifteen young women, all seventeen to twenty-one years old. I walked through the crowd, knowing I would be judging which one was most deserving of a scholarship; to me, in my own common sense terms, that meant picking who was most beautiful. It seemed so cool at the outset—there are far worse ways for a heterosexual male to spend a Sunday—but once I saw them and they saw me, it was terrifying. I was not the only judge (there were seven of us, all men), but because communication among judges is limited to avoid bias, I felt alone.

4   They walked in one by one, and, in ten-minute segments, we asked questions. It wasn't hard to decide who was the most physically attractive, but in those first ten minutes, I began to understand just how grossly misunderstood this whole pageantry thing is. Being a role model—and a pretty one at that—is hardly enough to win and advance. (The winners of this event would go on to prepare for the 2009 Miss New Hampshire contest, which leads to the Miss America pageant.) Each of the contestants had *innumerable* academic and *extracurricular* honors. Each had a thoroughly developed plan for advancing good causes, like awareness of Lyme disease, depression, and low self-esteem; or for donating blood; helping the elderly; or volunteering at local schools. To be sure, none of them was perfect. But they were mighty impressive human beings. And yet, what most of the typical observers will remember from a pageant is the swimsuit competition. If only they knew. After the interviews, the judges sat on a screened-in patio and ate lunch. I felt sick. Over and over in each interview, my definition of beauty was shattered, and I was ashamed.

PAUSE: Why does Holmes's definition of beauty start to change?

5   That night, the pageant moved to a nearby café for the talent, swim suit, onstage questioning, and evening-wear events. The contestants sang beautifully, danced gracefully, played violins and flutes, and recited poetry. They looked elegant in evening wear and *articulated* as best they could intelligent answers to the onstage questions, which were created by my former professor, a charming emcee if there ever was one.

6   And then the swimsuit competition began. On my drive to Kingston, I had looked forward to this event like Christmas morning. Now, I dreaded it. After seeing the contestants' smarts, skills, *poise*, and dedication, I couldn't help but wonder: What does a swimsuit have to do with any of this? Later, after the judging, I talked to KeriAnn Lynch, a former winner of this pageant, and Lindsey Graham, who was crowned Miss Seacoast that night, about whether pageants should drop this *segment*. Lynch said she "wouldn't shed a tear," while Graham said it would be a disservice if they did, because the contestants "need to represent what healthy is."

PAUSE: Why does Holmes dread the swimsuit segment?

7   But I guess that is a debate for another time. Each contestant crossed the stage in about fifteen seconds. I jotted a number from one to ten, and we moved on. The winners were crowned, and there was a dinner back at the blue-gray home. There, Graham told me she would not have gotten

through college without the nearly $30,000 she has won in pageants. She also admitted the difficulty of presenting herself. "You walk around in life trying not to think of people's opinions," she said, "but it's really hard when they are literally in front of you with numbers, judging you."

8   True enough, but it is not so easy on the other side, either. Beauty is not a simple matter.

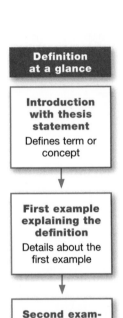

Definition at a glance

Introduction with thesis statement
Defines term or concept

First example explaining the definition
Details about the first example

Second example explaining the definition
Details about the second example

Third example explaining the definition
Details about the third example

Conclusion
Refers back to the defined term/ concept and makes an observation about it based on what you have written

1. Briefly summarize Holmes's essay including the term he is defining and how his experience affects his definition. *Answers will vary.*

2. What is his purpose in writing? Do you think he achieves it? _____

    _____

3. What does Holmes mean by his thesis, "There is a lot more to beauty than meets the eye"? What else is there? How does he tie his conclusion to his thesis statement? _____

4. Do you think the swimsuit competition in beauty pageants should be eliminated? Why or why not? _____

5. Think of other situations where you or others are judged by "what meets the eye." What are they? What is the danger in judging by what meets the eye? _____

Write a Definition Essay

In this section, you will write your own definition essay based on one of the following assignments. Use the following tools to help you.

1. Review the Four Basics of Good Definition (p. 240).

2. Use **Definition at a glance** as a basic organizer.

3. Use the Writing Guide: Definition checklist as you write and revise (pp. 256–57).

....

ASSIGNMENT 1   Writing about College, Work, and Everyday Life

Write a definition essay on *one* of the following topics or on a topic of your own choice.

COLLEGE
- A term or concept from another course you have taken
- Bullying
- Cheating

WORK
- Any term you use at work
- McJobs
- A model employee

EVERYDAY LIFE
- An attitude or behavior (such as assertiveness, generosity, negativity, optimism, and so on)
- Discrimination
- Road rage

ASSIGNMENT 2 Writing about an Image

What point is the woman in the following picture trying to make? How might she define *patriotism*? Write a definition essay presenting your definition of *patriotism*. What do you think is the setting for this picture?

· ·

ASSIGNMENT 3   Writing to Solve a Problem

THE PROBLEM: Your company is putting together a new employee handbook. To make the handbook both realistic and relevant, the company has decided that the contents will come directly from the employees. Your department has been assigned the section on communication.

THE ASSIGNMENT: Working on your own or with a small group, write a short piece defining *good communication skills*, giving detailed examples of how those skills should be applied in your company.

RESOURCES: Review the chart on pages 840–41 for advice on problem solving. You might also

- Set up an informational interview with a human resources worker to find out about your subject.

- Type *definition of good communication skills* into a search engine. Document any Web sites or references you use.

· ·

ASSIGNMENT 4   Writing about Connections

Read the account of Erick Traschikoff before doing the assignment that follows.

COMMUNITY CONNECTIONS

Erick Traschikoff, Santa Monica College
President, Rotaract Club

Erick Traschikoff was born in Mexico but came to the United States with his family. He never thought he would go to college because in high school he was a troublemaker, and no one else in his family had ever gone to college. But after graduating from high school, he realized that he would not have the kind of future he wanted if he did not get a college degree. He started at Santa Monica College taking developmental math and English and Introduction to Business while working at a real estate agency. He got involved in Rotaract (a college network of Rotary Clubs) mainly because he thought it might look good on his résumé to say he did something with the club. He also wanted to meet other people since he knew no one on campus. Although he had not planned to become involved, he found after attending a few meetings that he really liked the club. He became its public relations officer, producing newsletters, announcements, and publicity. He also set up an online network to connect some local Rotaract Clubs.

One of his first activities came about after a member of the local Rotary Club came to talk to the club about its work to help people in Papua, New Guinea, where malaria is widespread. Erick volunteered to help, did lots of research about the area and the disease, as well as how to prevent and treat malaria. He sponsored a car wash to raise funds and received matching funds from the Rotary Club.

Erick went on to become president of Rotaract and has benefited greatly from his involvement, including improved speaking, writing, and interviewing skills (including how to prepare and dress for an interview). He has become part not only of the college community, but also of the local business and Rotary communities, so he has good contacts for future jobs.

ASSIGNMENT: Write a definition essay on one of the following topics.

- Define *community*.

- Define *success* as you want it to apply to your future.

- Interview a member of any student organization on campus, and ask the person if involvement in the club builds *community*. Ask the person what he or she means by that, with examples.

- Many students who are involved in campus or community organizations say that volunteering makes them "feel good." Define *feeling good*.

RESOURCES

Additional Resources for Teaching Real Essays with Readings has visual planning forms for definition and the other essays covered in Part 2. These forms are also online at bedfordstmartins .com/realessays.

ASSIGNMENT 5   Writing about Readings

The assignments that follow ask you to read one or more different definition essays and draw from them to write your own essay.

- Reread Anna Puiia's essay "What Is Hip?" (p. 245) and Juliet Schor's "Age Compression" (p. 775). Drawing from both essays, write a definition essay starting with the thesis, "In many ways, what we consume defines who we are."

- Review Baxter Holmes's "My Date with Fifteen Women" (p. 250), and read Dave Barry's "The Ugly Truth about Beauty" (p. 787) and Amy L. Beck's "Struggling for Perfection" (p. 807). Drawing from these three selections to make your point, discuss the pressures that people who live in this society feel to be young and beautiful.

Use the steps in the Writing Guide that follows to help you prewrite, draft, revise, and edit your definition essay. Check off each step as you complete it.

WRITING GUIDE: DEFINITION

STEPS IN DEFINITION	HOW TO DO THE STEPS
☐ Focus.	• Think about the term you are going to define and how to get your readers to understand the term as you do.
☐ Explore your topic. See Chapter 5.	• Prewrite to get possible definitions and examples that will explain the definition.
☐ Write a thesis statement. Term + Definition = Thesis See Chapter 6.	• Include the term or concept you are defining and a basic definition of it.

STEPS IN DEFINITION	HOW TO DO THE STEPS
☐ **Support your thesis.** See Chapter 7.	• Choose examples of the definition and details about the examples that will show your reader how you "see" the term.
☐ **Write a draft.** See Chapter 8.	• Arrange your examples. • Write topic sentences for each example and paragraphs that give details about them.
☐ **Revise your draft.** See Chapter 9.	• Get feedback using the peer-review guide for definition at **bedfordstmartins.com/realessays**. • Make sure the examples explain your definition. • Think about what other details your readers might need to understand your definition. • Add transitions. • Improve your introduction, thesis, and conclusion.
☐ **Edit your revised draft.** See Parts 4 through 7.	• Correct errors in grammar, spelling, word use, and punctuation.
☐ **Evaluate your writing.**	• Does it have the Four Basics of Good Definition (p. 240)? • Is this the best I can do?

reflect Reread your response to the "write" prompt on page 240. Revise and edit the expanded definition that you wrote, adding new examples, supporting details, and transitions as needed. Then, exchange what you have written with a classmate and carefully read each other's definitions. How successful is each definition in clearly communicating the meaning of the difficult words being defined? Do you now understand the meaning of your classmate's word and does he or she now understand the word you defined?

16

Comparison and Contrast

Writing That Shows Similarities and Differences

YOU KNOW THIS

You use comparison and contrast to make decisions.

- You compare and contrast cell phone plans.
- You compare and contrast gasoline prices.
- You compare and contrast the nutritional value of your food options.

write about two seasons, comparing their meaning or appearance in your area. Alternatively, compare two times of day.

Understand What Comparison and Contrast Are

IDEA JOURNAL
Write about some differences you see between the movies that men and women like.

Comparison is writing that shows the similarities among subjects—people, ideas, situations, or items; **contrast** shows the differences. In conversation, we often use the word *compare* to mean either compare or contrast, but as you work through this chapter, the terms will be separated.

Four Basics of Good Comparison and Contrast

1 It uses subjects with enough in common to be usefully compared and contrasted.

2 It serves a purpose — either to help readers make a decision or to help them understand the subjects.

3 It presents several important, parallel points of comparison and/or contrast.

4 It is organized either point by point or whole to whole (see pp. 262–63).

In the following paragraph, which contrasts the subjects, each number corresponds to one of the Four Basics of Good Comparison and Contrast.

1 My current boyfriend **2** is a major improvement over **1** my ex-boyfriend **2** in terms of how he treats me. **3** One difference is that my current boyfriend opens the door when I get in the car as well as when I get out. In contrast, my ex-boyfriend never opened the door of the car or any other door. **3** My current boyfriend likes to tell me that he loves me. For example, we went to the beach, and he screamed that he loved me to the four winds so everyone could hear. My ex, on the other hand, always had a ready excuse for why he couldn't say that he loved me, ever. However, he wanted me to tell him I loved him all the time. **3** Another difference between the two is that my boyfriend spends money on me. When we go out to a restaurant, he pays for the meal. My ex just never seemed to have money to pay for dinner or anything else. He would say he forgot to bring his wallet, and I would have to pay for the food. **3** To me, the most important difference between the two guys is that my current boyfriend is honest. He never lies to me about anything, and he makes me feel confident about our relationship. In contrast, I never could tell if my ex was lying or telling the truth because he often lied about his family and other things, and I never knew what to believe. **2** To sum it all up, my current boyfriend is a gentleman, and my ex was a pig.

4 Uses point-by-point organization (see pp. 262–63).

—Liliana Ramirez, student

Many situations require you to use comparison and contrast.

COLLEGE — In a business course, you compare and contrast practices in e-commerce and traditional commerce.

WORK — You compare and contrast two health insurance options offered by your company in order to select the one that is best for you.

EVERYDAY LIFE — Before choosing a telephone plan, you compare and contrast the rates, services, and options each offers.

SEEING COMPARISON AND CONTRAST

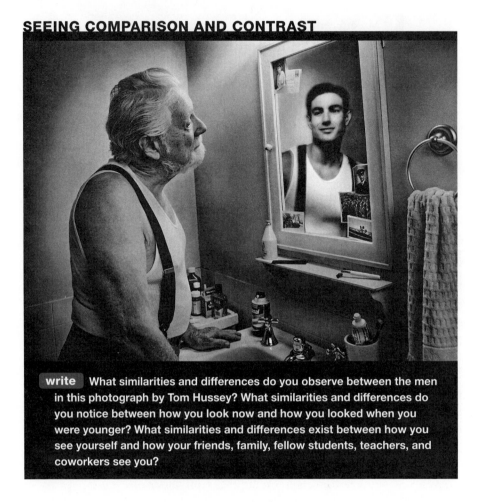

write What similarities and differences do you observe between the men in this photograph by Tom Hussey? What similarities and differences do you notice between how you look now and how you looked when you were younger? What similarities and differences exist between how you see yourself and how your friends, family, fellow students, teachers, and coworkers see you?

Main Point in Comparison and Contrast

A comparison and contrast essay shows readers how two or more subjects are alike or different. The **purpose** of a comparison and contrast essay may be to have readers understand the subjects or to help them make a decision.

In comparison and contrast, your **main point** expresses similarities or differences in your subjects. For example, in the paragraph on page 259, Liliana Ramirez contrasts the different ways that her two boyfriends treated her. Her purpose is to help readers understand why one became her "ex."

Typically, thesis statements in comparison and contrast essays present the central subjects and indicate whether the writer will show similarities, differences, or both.

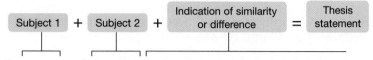

While my son and daughter both enjoy school, their educational experiences are very different.

[Purpose: To contrast educational experiences of her children.]

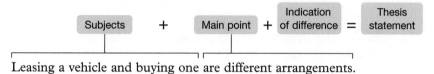

Leasing a vehicle and buying one are different arrangements.

[Purpose: to help readers decide whether to lease or buy]

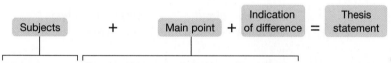

My twin sons have completely different personalities.

[Purpose: to help readers understand the sons' personalities and how they differ]

To determine your thesis in a comparison and contrast essay, decide whether you want to show similarities, differences, or both. To make this decision, you need to think about what your purpose is—what you want your readers to understand—and what will be meaningful to those readers.

Support in Comparison and Contrast

The **support** in comparison and contrast demonstrates your main point by showing how your subjects are the same or different. To find support, many people make a list with multiple columns—one for the points that will serve as the basis of the comparison or contrast and one for each of the subjects.

For example, one student, Daniel, wrote the following thesis statement, which indicates that his essay will focus on the differences between the ages of twenty and forty.

RESOURCES
For online writing and grammar resources, go to bedfordstmartins .com/rewritingbasics.

> *The ages of twenty and forty are both enjoyable, but they represent very different stages in life.*

To support this thesis, Daniel needs to find several points of contrast between twenty and forty. He generates the following list.

> DIFFERENCES BETWEEN TWENTY AND FORTY
> appearance
> place in life
> perspective

Then, for each point of comparison, Daniel lists some details that explain the differences.

	AGE TWENTY	AGE FORTY
APPEARANCE	smooth skin	some wrinkles
	trendy haircut	classic hairstyle
	rounded features	well-defined features
PLACE IN LIFE	just starting out	established
	single, no children	married with children
	living at home	own home
PERSPECTIVE	self-centered	more thoughtful
	choices to make	many choices made
	uncertainty	wisdom

Organization in Comparison and Contrast

TEACHING TIP
Remind students that a whole-to-whole essay must include a strong transition to move from subject 1 to subject 2.

A comparison and contrast essay can be organized in two basic ways: A **point-by-point** organization first compares or contrasts one point between the two subjects and then moves to the next point of comparison or contrast. A **whole-to-whole** organization first presents all the points of comparison or contrast for one subject and then all the points for the second. To decide which organization to use, consider which of the two will best serve your purpose of explaining similarities or differences to your readers. Once you choose an organization, stick with it throughout the essay.

The two organization types look like this.

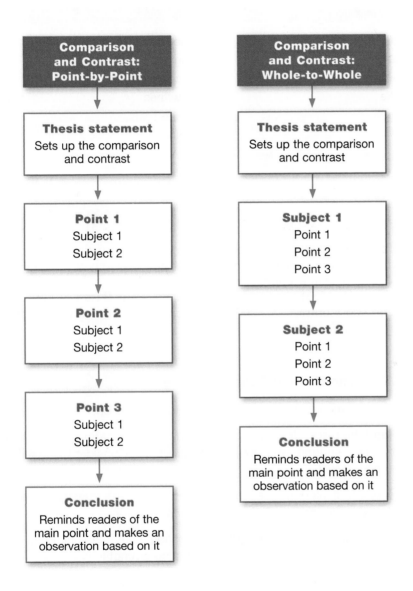

Using **transitions** in comparison and contrast essays is important to move readers from one subject to another and from one point of comparison to another.

Common Transitions in Comparison and Contrast

COMPARISON	CONTRAST
one similarity	one difference
another similarity	another difference
similarly	in contrast
like	now/then
both	unlike
	while

Read and Analyze Comparison and Contrast

For more examples of comparison and contrast, see Chapter 47.

Before writing a comparison and contrast essay, read the following three examples—from college, the workplace, and everyday life—and answer the questions that accompany them.

TEAMWORK
Have students work through the first essay together to apply the critical reading process and answer the questions after the essay.

For each of the three essays, review the Four Basics of Good Comparison and Contrast (p. 258) and practice your critical reading process by doing the following:

2PR The Critical Reading Process

■ **Preview** the reading, including the guiding question.

■ **Read** the piece, double-underlining the thesis statement, underlining the major support, and circling the transitions. Consider the quality of the support.

■ **Pause** to think during reading. Take notes and ask questions about what you are reading: Talk to the author.

■ **Review** the reading, your guiding question, your marginal notes and questions, and your answers to the Pause prompts.

Comparison and Contrast in College

The following is an excerpt from the textbook *Discovering Psychology*, Fifth Edition.

Don Hockenbury and Sandra Hockenbury

GUIDING QUESTION
How are anorexia nervosa and bulimia nervosa both alike and different?

VOCABULARY
The following words are *italicized* in the excerpt: *distorted, perception, emaciated, perfectionism, purging, preoccupation, compensates.* If you do not know their meanings, look them up in a dictionary or online.

CRITICAL
READING
■ Preview
■ Read
■ Pause
■ Review

1   **Anorexia nervosa** is life-threatening weight loss. Four key features define anorexia nervosa: First, the person refuses to maintain a normal body weight. With a body weight that is 15 percent or more below normal, body mass index can drop to 12 or lower. Second, despite being dangerously underweight, the person with anorexia is intensely afraid of gaining weight or becoming fat. Third, the anorexic has a *distorted perception* about the size of his or her body. Although *emaciated*, he or she looks in the mirror and sees someone fat or obese. And fourth, an anorexic denies the seriousness of his or her weight loss (American Psychiatric Association [APA], 2000).

2   *Perfectionism* and rigid thinking, poor peer relations, social isolation, and low self-esteem are common (Halmi et al., 2000). Although estimates vary, approximately 10 percent of people with anorexia nervosa die from starvation, suicide, or physical complications accompanying extreme weight loss (APA, 2000; Kaye, Klump, Frank, and Strober, 2000).

3   **Bulimia nervosa** is bingeing and *purging* of food. Like people with anorexia, people with bulimia nervosa fear gaining weight. Intense *preoccupation* and dissatisfaction with their bodies are also apparent. However, people with bulimia stay within a normal weight range or may even be slightly overweight. Another difference is that people with bulimia usually recognize that they have an eating disorder.

4   People with bulimia nervosa experience extreme episodes of binge eating, consuming as many as 50,000 calories in a single binge. Binges typically occur twice a week and are often triggered by negative feelings or hunger (Agras & Apple, 1997). During the binge, the person usually consumes sweet, high-calorie foods that can be swallowed quickly, such as ice cream, cake, and candy. Binges typically occur in secrecy, leaving the person feeling ashamed, guilty, and disgusted by his or her own behavior. After bingeing, the bulimic *compensates* by purging him- or herself of the excessive food by self-induced vomiting or by misuse of laxatives or enemas. After purging, he

PAUSE:
Underline or highlight the 4 key features of anorexia.

PAUSE:
How is bulimia similar to anorexia? How is it different?

or she often feels psychologically relieved. (Some) people with bulimia do not purge themselves of the excess food. Rather, they use fasting and excessive exercise to keep their body weight within the normal range (APA, 2000).

References

Agras, W. S., & Apple, R. F. (1997). *Overcoming eating disorders: A cognitive-behavioral treatment for bulimia nervosa and binge-eating.* San Antonio, TX: Harcourt Brace.

American Psychiatric Association. (2000). Practice guidelines for the treatment of patients with eating disorders (revision). *American Journal of Psychiatry, 157* (Suppl.), 1–39.

Halmi, K. A., Sunday, S. R., Strober, M., Kaplan, A., Woodside, D. B., Fichter, M., Treasure, J., . . . Kaye, W. H. (2000). Perfectionism in anorexia nervosa: Variation by clinical subtype, obsessionality, and pathological eating behavior. *American Journal of Psychiatry, 157,* 1799–1805.

Kaye, W. H., Klump, K. L., Frank, G. K., & Strober, M. (2000). Anorexia and bulimia nervosa. *Annual Review of Medicine, 51,* 299–313.

The documentation system used here is that of the American Psychological Association because the excerpt is from a psychology text. For English classes, use the MLA style (see Chapter 21).

CRITICAL THINKING
- Summarize
- Analyze
- Synthesize
- Evaluate

(More on p. 21.)

1. **Summarize.** Briefly summarize the text excerpt, including the conditions being compared or contrasted, the authors' purpose, and some of the points of comparison or contrast.

2. **Analyze.** Is the excerpt organized point-by-point or whole-to-whole? Why do you think there is no formal introduction or conclusion? If there were an introduction, what information might it include? If you were writing a concluding paragraph, what would you say? What might a good title be?

3. **Synthesize.** Do you know anyone who has an eating disorder such as those described? What behaviors or characteristics have you noticed about the person or people?

4. **Evaluate.** Does the excerpt have the **Four Basics of Good Comparison and Contrast** (p. 258)? Do the authors achieve their purpose?

Comparison and Contrast at Work

The profile on page 267 shows how a family-practice physician uses comparison and contrast in his work.

PROFILE OF SUCCESS

Comparison and Contrast in the Real World

Background   I was born in Jamaica, and at school, everyone thought I was lazy because I couldn't read. I knew I worked hard but didn't understand why I had such trouble reading. When it came time to go to high school, I dropped out and moved to Brooklyn, New York. Shortly thereafter, I was drafted and served as a medic in the military, where I got my GED. After completing my service, I went to Central Florida Community College and transferred to the University of Florida. I dropped out eventually and worked for a few years as an orderly.

Garth Vaz
Physician

I was accepted at the University of Florida Medical School but flunked out, at which point I finally discovered that my reading and writing problems were caused not by laziness but by dyslexia. I petitioned the school to return and passed my courses with the help of a note-taking service. But I failed the medical boards twice before I was allowed "accommodation" for dyslexia.

Today I am a doctor working at a community health clinic that, in addition to other medical services, provides care for migrant workers and their families. I also travel and speak extensively on learning behaviors, especially dyslexia and attention-deficit/hyperactivity disorder (ADHD).

Colleges/Degrees   A.A., Central Florida Community College; M.D., University of Florida

Employer   Community Health Centers of South Central Texas, Inc.

Writing at work   For work, I write patient reports, speeches, and papers for publication. As a dyslexic, writing is still very difficult for me, though I have learned how to compensate for the difficulty. Because I still make lots of spelling errors, I have to read very carefully and reread anything I write to correct the mistakes.

Garth Vaz's Comparison and Contrast

The following is excerpted from an article that Dr. Vaz published on the subject of dyslexia.

GUIDING QUESTION
How are dyslexia and ADHD different?

VOCABULARY
The following words are *italicized* in the excerpt: *dyslexics, misconceptions, misdiagnoses, abound, deficient, remediation, diligent, squirm, fidget, excessively, blurts, norms, alienates, shun, ostracism, labored, intervention, contemporary.* If you do not know their meanings, look them up in a dictionary or online.

267

CRITICAL
READING
■ Preview
■ Read
■ Pause
■ Review

For decades, *dyslexics* have been one of the most misunderstood groups in our society. *Misconceptions* and *misdiagnoses abound*, as when dyslexics are mislabeled stupid, retarded, or lazy and placed among the mentally *deficient*. Many dyslexics have been placed in special education programs along with the slow learners. Later, after appropriate *remediation*, these same students have gone on to become educators, lawyers, and doctors. It is therefore of great importance that we be aware of the sensitive nature of dealing with these prize products of our society, our dyslexic students. We must be *diligent* in our efforts to help them in their struggle for success.

Such misdiagnoses are due to the lack of understanding of dyslexia and conditions such as attention-deficit/hyperactivity disorder (ADHD), childhood depressive disorder (CDD), central auditory processing deficit (CAPD), and many others that share some similarities with common symptoms of dyslexia. I will now list, in brief, some of the differences in behaviors that characterize ADHD and dyslexia in children, particularly children in the elementary school classroom.

A young person with ADHD cannot easily sit still, certainly a problem in the classroom. He or she often leaves his assigned seat, running around and attempting to climb on shelves, desks, and the like. When told firmly to remain in his seat, the child will try to obey but will *squirm* and *fidget* almost constantly, clearly in a state of agitation. He acts as if he is driven by a motor.

A child with ADHD often talks *excessively* and is unable to wait to be called on: Instead, he *blurts* out answers and responses. He seems to just butt into games and conversations, not observing social *norms* that require a give-and-take among group members. Such behavior often *alienates* other children and frustrates teachers and others who try to maintain control. Other children may *shun* the child with ADHD. This *ostracism*, in turn, results in further negative effects, such as low self-esteem and greater isolation.

In contrast, a young person with dyslexia can sit still but has trouble organizing objects, belongings, and letters. She may mix up sounds, saying, for example, "plain" for "plan" or "seal" for "soul." She may have a stutter, furthering the frustration and embarrassment she already feels.

A dyslexic child typically reads poorly, confusing the order of letters, for example, in words such as "saw" and "was." Also, she may confuse words that have similar shapes or start and end with the same letters, as in "form" and "from" or the words cited in the last paragraph. While a dyslexic's reading is *labored*, his handwriting and spelling are usually worse. All of these symptoms of dyslexia, while quite different, often result in the same ostracism and loss of self-esteem. These problems then cause other behavior problems that are similar to those shown in children with ADHD and a number of other conditions. This explains why certain conditions are often confused. In addition, many children indeed have more than one condition. For example, over 40 percent of children with dyslexia have ADHD as well.

Unfortunately, because of budgeting restrictions, dyslexics are sometimes placed among the wrong group for remediation. In order for any *intervention* to succeed, it must be tailored specifically for the dyslexic. There are many improved techniques now being used successfully in reading remediation that are based on the Orton-Gillingham method. Many of these can be obtained on videocassettes and CDs. Arlene Sonday and the Scottish Rite Hospital have such programs on the market, and many other good ones can be located on the Internet (for example, **interdys.org/**, **dys.org/**, **kidshealth.org/**, and **ninds.hih.gov/disorders/dyslexia**, among many others).

There are many successful dyslexics in our society, some *contemporary* and others in the past. Albert Einstein, Benjamin Franklin, and General George Patton are a few who have made history. Athletes Bruce Jenner and Nolan Ryan and entertainers Whoopi Goldberg and Cher are among our contemporaries. Identifying with the successful dyslexic offers some hope to parents and children alike. The book *Succeeding with LD* is a collection of stories of successful dyslexics. The book was authored by Jill Lauren and published by Free Spirit Publishers. Each of these stories could make a book by itself but is short enough for the dyslexic to enjoy reading.

PAUSE: Summarize the characteristics of dyslexia.

1. Briefly summarize Vaz's essay, including the terms being compared or contrasted and the major similarities or differences. *Answers will vary.*

2. What organization does Vaz use? *Whole to whole*

3. Why is dyslexia so often misunderstood, according to Vaz?_____
Answers will vary.

4. Why is Vaz particularly interested in dyslexia? *He has it.*

Comparison and Contrast in Everyday Life

The following essay appeared in *Newsweek* in 2009.

Stephanie Lindsley

Autism and Education

GUIDING QUESTION
What are some differences between the educational resources Lindsley's son and daughter receive?

VOCABULARY
The following words are *italicized* in the essay: *intervention, attests, mandated, mediation, designated.* If you do not know their meanings, look them up in a dictionary or online.

CRITICAL READING
■ Preview
■ Read
■ Pause
■ Review

1   My son and my daughter are happy, active, healthy children who enjoy school and are lucky to have a solid family life, but they are very different. My autistic[1] son tests in the "severe" range in many subjects. At eight, he reads well but cannot answer basic questions about what he has read. He speaks at a three-year-old level, adores *Blue's Clues*, and is almost potty-trained.

PAUSE: What point is Lindsley making about her daughter?

2   My daughter, meanwhile, tests in the 95th percentile nationwide on standardized tests. At twelve, she shows an amazing ability to process information, taking complex ideas apart and putting them back together to form new thoughts. She reads an entire novel most Sunday afternoons, solves the Sudoku[2] puzzles in the paper, and memorizes the entire script— not just her own lines—for the school plays she loves to be in.

3   At school, my son spends a portion of his day in a regular classroom. But primarily he learns in a group of two to six children led by an *intervention* specialist, often accompanied by an aide. Even when he is in the regular classroom, he is never without an adult by his side. His intervention specialist records everything he does in daily logs that are required to ensure funding. She often presents me with new strategies to help him learn a difficult concept, which *attests* to the volumes of time she dedicates to addressing his unique needs.

1. autistic: a person with autism, a developmental disorder marked by poor communication skills, difficulties with social interaction, and other behavior patterns
2. Sudoku: a popular number puzzle

4   My son's teachers do their absolute best for him. I know they love him. But beyond that, his government-*mandated* Individualized Education Plan legally ensures that he gets every opportunity to excel. In addition, his teachers spend countless hours each year filling out detailed quarterly reports and other government-required paperwork. If I decide that the school district should pay for something extra to improve my son's education, I can appeal to an independent board for *mediation*.

PAUSE: What point is Lindsley making about her son?

5   My daughter spends all but three hours of her school week in a regular classroom, where she often hides a book in her desk and reads while the teacher talks. She complains to me when the teacher reteaches things she learned last year, and she resents being drilled over and over on something she learned in ten minutes. For three hours a week, she is pulled from her classroom for a "gifted" program with fifteen other children, where she works either on a group project with other students or independently on her own blog or a computer-based foreign-language program.

PAUSE: How is the daughter's experience different?

6   I can only imagine how much my daughter would excel if she had a program specifically geared to her strengths, one that challenged her creativity on a daily basis. Or if she received even half the individual attention my son receives every week. What if she had a person sitting next to her to encourage her to think of new ways of doing things? What if her teacher did not have to manage a large classroom full of kids, who did not scold her for "making things confusing for everyone else"? What would happen if she spent all day in a room with two to six other gifted children, along with a couple of adults who specialized in pushing them to realize their potential?

PAUSE: What does Lindsley imagine for her daughter?

7   There is no government mandate to fund gifted education. In 2008 there was only $7.5 million in federal grants available through the Jacob K. Javits[3] Gifted and Talented Students Education Program. All additional funding comes from states and private organizations. Compare that with the $24.5 billion allotted by No Child Left Behind, a federal program whose goal is to help every child, including the mentally disabled, meet minimum standards. But is that a wise investment? Wouldn't some of those billions be more wisely spent on special teachers and mandated

PAUSE: What is Lindsley's main point here?

---

3. Jacob K. Javits: longtime U.S. senator from New York

PAUSE: How does Lindsley justify her position?

programs for gifted children, who have the potential to make advances in science, technology, and the arts that would benefit everyone?

8   It pains me to suggest taking some of the federal money *designated* for my disabled son and spending it on my overperforming daughter. My son will probably meet minimum standards, but most parents of autistic children describe goals for their kids in much more modest terms: being able to bathe themselves, get a job, or live semi-independently. My daughter has the potential for much more. If she were given even a fraction of the customized education that my son receives, she could learn the skills needed to prevent the next worldwide flu pandemic, or invent a new form of nonpolluting transportation. Perhaps she could even discover a cure for autism.

1. Briefly summarize Lindsley's essay, including what she is comparing and what major point of contrast she uses.

    Answers will vary.

2. What is Lindsley's purpose? What is her point of view? *Her purpose is to question whether children with special needs should receive more educational resources than gifted children.*

3. What type of comparison/contrast organization does Lindsley use?

    Point by point

4. Do you agree or disagree with Lindsley? Why?

    Answers will vary.

5. Do you think this is a good contrast? Why or why not?

    Answers will vary.

Write a Comparison and Contrast Essay

In this section, you will write your own comparison and contrast essay based on *one* of the following assignments. Use the following tools to help you.

1. Review the Four Basics of Good Comparison and Contrast (p. 258).
2. Use the **Comparison and Contrast** charts on page 263 to help you with basic organization.

3. Use the Writing Guide: Comparison and Contrast checklist as you write and revise (pp. 277–78).

ASSIGNMENT 1   Writing about College, Work, and Everyday Life

Write a comparison and contrast essay on one of the following topics or on a topic of your own choice.

COLLEGE
- Two professors
- Two courses you are taking or have taken
- College and high school

WORK
- Two jobs you have had
- Two companies you have worked for
- A job and a career

EVERYDAY LIFE
- Two places you have lived
- Good customer service and bad customer service
- Two of your friends or relatives

TEAMWORK
Have students bring in advertisements from magazines, newspapers, or the Web that use comparison or contrast. Working in small groups, students can identify the subjects being compared or contrasted, the points of comparison or contrast, and the purpose.

ALTERNATIVE ASSIGNMENT 1   Writing about Comparison and Contrast in Everyday Life

THE PROBLEM: You need a computer, and you would also love to get a new TV. You decide you want to see the products and talk with someone who knows about them, so you want to go to a physical store rather than browse online. You do not have time to visit lots of places, and although online searches will show you comparative prices among stores, you know other factors also will influence where you make your purchase (for example, store location, return policy, and customer service).

ASSIGNMENT: Working on your own or in a small group, write a comparison and contrast essay using the ratings of electronics stores from *Consumer Reports* (see p. 274). Read the chart carefully.

- First, choose three stores from the ratings. Then, consider the survey results.
- Discuss the results in order of importance to you, ending with the most important.
- Decide whether to use point-by-point or whole-to-whole organization.
- In your concluding paragraph, indicate what store you will likely purchase from and why.

Use this ratings chart to write your comparison-and-contrast essay (see p. 273).

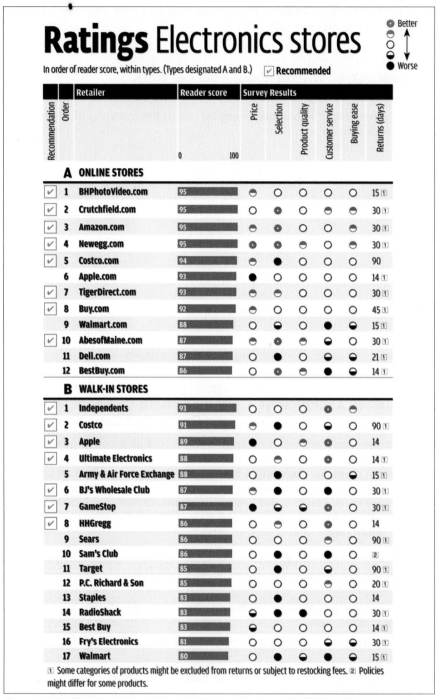

Ratings Electronics stores

In order of reader score, within types. (Types designated A and B.) ☑ Recommended

Better ● ↑ ↓ ● Worse

Recommendation	Order	Retailer	Reader score (0–100)	Price	Selection	Product quality	Customer service	Buying ease	Returns (days)
		A ONLINE STORES							
✓	1	BHPhotoVideo.com	95						15 [1]
✓	2	Crutchfield.com	95						30 [1]
✓	3	Amazon.com	95						30 [1]
✓	4	Newegg.com	95						30 [1]
✓	5	Costco.com	94						90
	6	Apple.com	93						14 [1]
✓	7	TigerDirect.com	93						30 [1]
✓	8	Buy.com	92						45 [1]
	9	Walmart.com	88						15 [1]
✓	10	AbesofMaine.com	87						30 [1]
	11	Dell.com	87						21 [1]
	12	BestBuy.com	86						14 [1]
		B WALK-IN STORES							
✓	1	Independents	93						
✓	2	Costco	91						90 [1]
✓	3	Apple	89						14
✓	4	Ultimate Electronics	88						14 [1]
	5	Army & Air Force Exchange	88						15 [1]
✓	6	BJ's Wholesale Club	87						30 [1]
✓	7	GameStop	87						30 [1]
✓	8	HHGregg	86						14
	9	Sears	86						90 [1]
	10	Sam's Club	86						[2]
	11	Target	85						90 [1]
	12	P.C. Richard & Son	85						20 [1]
	13	Staples	83						14
	14	RadioShack	83						30 [1]
	15	Best Buy	83						14 [1]
	16	Fry's Electronics	81						30 [1]
	17	Walmart	80						15 [1]

[1] Some categories of products might be excluded from returns or subject to restocking fees. [2] Policies might differ for some products.

ASSIGNMENT 2 Writing about Images

In 1961, Mattel Company launched a new product—a Ken doll—advertised as the perfect boyfriend for its popular Barbie doll. In the fifty years since then, Ken's appearance has evolved in an effort to keep pace with the times and to appeal to each new generation of children and the parents who make the purchases.

Choose two or more of the following images and compare and contrast the changing looks of Ken. In your essay, you might want to address how changes to Ken represent larger changes in society and culture. Also, answer this question: What do you think Ken might look like in ten or twenty years?

ASSIGNMENT 3 Writing about Connections

Read the account of Kathy Smiley before doing the assignment that follows.

COMMUNITY CONNECTIONS

Kathy Smiley, Georgia Perimeter College
President, Georgia Perimeter College Association of Nursing Students (GPCANS)

Kathy Smiley had started college after high school but dropped out. Years later and now the single mother of two children, she enrolled at Georgia Perimeter College taking one class at a time studying education. When she realized that she was more interested in nursing, she switched to that program, which is challenging and rigorous.

She became passionate about nursing and felt as if she finally knew what to do with her life. Motivated to find out as much as she could, she went to the college's Web site and found out about GPCANS, the college's association of nursing students. During her first year, she attended only a couple of meetings, but she found that she learned so much that the next year she ran for and was elected president. This has given her opportunities to meet people, speak publicly, run service events, handle publicity, and attend professional nursing conferences where she has made valuable contacts.

She has participated in many nursing-related service events, such as Hoops for Heart, a health day at an elementary school where the focus was on nutrition, exercise, and health, and students were given hula hoops. GPCANS also runs a mentoring program in which second-year nursing students help guide and support first-year students through difficult courses. The mentors also teach organizational skills, such as time management, which students will need to succeed in the nursing program. In the process, Kathy has developed her own skills, as she takes a full load of nursing courses and works in a restaurant at night. But her life is much richer and more rewarding than it was before she got involved with GPCANS.

ASSIGNMENT: Choose one of the following and write a comparison and contrast essay. Work either by yourself or with a partner.

- Interview a student who is an officer of a club or an organization on campus. Ask the person how his or her impression of college and academic achievement has changed since he or she became involved.

- If there is a new building on campus or in your community, interview someone who works there and ask how the new place compares with the old, including if it makes employees' jobs easier or better.

- Go to your college Web site and search for student organizations. Choose two or three, visit their respective Web sites, and read about their purpose and the events they have sponsored. How do they compare or contrast?

ASSIGNMENT 4   Writing about Readings

Read "The Ugly Truth about Beauty" by Dave Barry on page 787 and "Struggling for Perfection" by Amy L. Beck on page 807. Next, review the excerpt from the psychology textbook by Don H. Hockenbury and Sandra Hockenbury on page 265. Write a brief paper on one of the following.

RESOURCES
Additional Resources for Teaching Real Essays with Readings has visual planning forms for comparison and contrast essays and the other essays covered in Part 2. These forms are also online at bedfordstmartins .com/realessays.

- Although their tones are different, Barry, Beck, and the Hockenburys make a similar point about women's images of themselves. Explain that point, bringing in references from the three readings. In your concluding paragraph, indicate which of the three makes the point most effectively to you and why.

- Analyze why people are influenced by advertising images and why they hold unrealistic expectations for themselves. To do this, draw on the three sources and on experiences you or people you know have had.

Use the steps in the Writing Guide that follows to help you prewrite, draft, revise, and edit your comparison and contrast essay. Check off each step as you complete it.

WRITING GUIDE: COMPARISON AND CONTRAST	
STEPS IN COMPARISON AND CONTRAST	**HOW TO DO THE STEPS**
☐ Focus.	• Think about what you want to compare and contrast and your purpose for writing.
☐ Explore your topic. See Chapter 5.	• Make a side-by-side list of possible parallel points of comparison or contrast between your subjects. →

STEPS IN COMPARISON AND CONTRAST	HOW TO DO THE STEPS
☐ **Write a thesis statement.** Subjects + Main point = Thesis See Chapter 6.	• Include your subjects and some indication of whether you will be comparing or contrasting them.
☐ **Support your thesis.** See Chapter 7.	• Choose the points of comparison or contrast that your readers will understand and that will serve your purpose.
☐ **Write a draft.** See Chapter 8.	• Decide whether to use point-by-point or whole-to-whole organization and how to arrange your main points (by time, space, or importance). • Write topic sentences for your support paragraphs.
☐ **Revise your draft.** See Chapter 9.	• Get feedback from the peer-review guide for comparison and contrast at **bedfordstmartins .com/realessays**. • Reread to add any examples that will help your readers understand. • Add transitions. • Improve your introduction, thesis, and conclusion.
☐ **Edit your revised draft.** See Parts 4 through 7.	• Correct errors in grammar, spelling, word use, and punctuation.
☐ **Evaluate your writing.**	• Does it have the Four Basics of Good Comparison and Contrast (p. 258)? • Is this the best I can do?

> **reflect** Reread your response to the "write" prompt on page 258, and revise by adding a main point and thesis, improving the organization of points, and including new supporting details, examples, and transitions, as necessary.

Cause and Effect

Writing That Explains Reasons or Results

Understand What Cause and Effect Are

A **cause** is what makes an event happen. An **effect** is what happens as a result of an event.

Four Basics of Good Cause and Effect

1. The main point reflects the writer's purpose — to explain causes, effects, or both.
2. If the purpose is to explain causes, it presents real causes.
3. If the purpose is to explain effects, it presents real effects.
4. It gives clear and detailed examples or explanations of the causes and and/or effects.

In the following paragraph, each number corresponds to one of the Four Basics of Good Cause and Effect.

1 Little doubt remains that global warming is a threat to our world, but not everyone understands why it is happening and what the effects are. Many experts believe that this warming trend is largely the result of 2 greenhouse gases, including 4 carbon dioxide emissions, mainly from cars, and pollutants from industrial

processes. **2** Deforestation is another significant cause. If current warming trends continue, the United States is most at risk for **1** negative consequences, although the entire world will be affected. Scientists predict that **3** sea levels will rise dangerously and **4** flood coastal areas. There will also be **3** more droughts and changes in precipitation patterns, **4** such as more hurricanes and tornadoes. In addition and possibly most destructive is the **3** threat to plant and animal life and, consequently, to public health.

Analyzing causes and effects goes beyond asking "What happened?" to also ask "Why?" and "How?"

> **SITUATION:** On a hot summer day, you leave a rented DVD on the front seat of your car while you are at work. When you come out of work, you find that the DVD has melted.

The **cause** of the DVD's melting was **leaving it in a hot car all day**. The **effect** of leaving the DVD in a hot car all day was that **it melted**.

Jim Rice of Quinsigamond Community College helps his students visualize the cause-and-effect relationship by suggesting that they think of three linked rings.

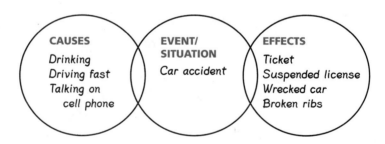

Many situations require you to determine causes or effects.

COLLEGE   In an information technology course, you must discuss the effects of a virus on a local-area computer network.

WORK   You analyze the likely effects of working five fewer hours per week.

EVERYDAY LIFE   You try to figure out what is causing your phone to need a battery charge so often.

SEEING CAUSE AND EFFECT

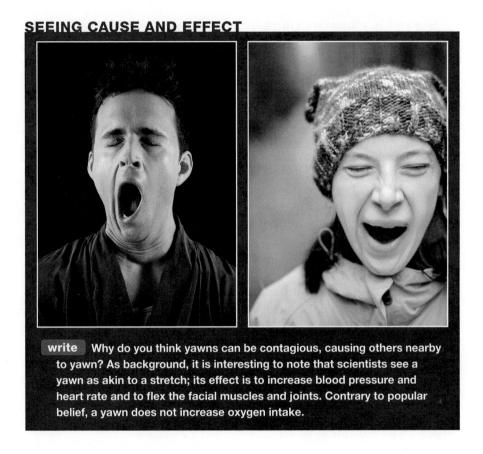

write Why do you think yawns can be contagious, causing others nearby to yawn? As background, it is interesting to note that scientists see a yawn as akin to a stretch; its effect is to increase blood pressure and heart rate and to flex the facial muscles and joints. Contrary to popular belief, a yawn does not increase oxygen intake.

Main Point in Cause and Effect

The **main point** in a cause-and-effect essay should reflect your **purpose**. For example, if you are writing about why a certain event in history happened, your main point would be to explain the causes. If you are writing about what happened as a result of that event, your main point would be to explain the effects. Consider the following thesis from an essay on drunk driving.

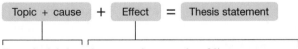

Topic + cause + Effect = Thesis statement

Drunk driving destroys thousands of lives every year.

The main point of the essay is to discuss the effects of drunk driving—thousands of destroyed lives. The body of the essay will give examples.

DISCUSSION
Ask students to identify a local or campus-related change and list its apparent causes and effects.

Sometimes a thesis statement for a cause-and-effect essay will include both what caused the topic and what resulted from the topic. The topic sentence below follows this pattern.

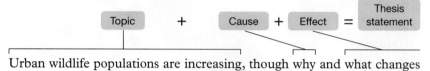

Urban wildlife populations are increasing, though why and what changes these different types of animals will bring to city life is not well understood.

Sometimes the writer does not directly indicate causes or effects in the thesis statement, as in the following example.

Until local police departments enforce restraining orders, women and children will continue to be the victims of violence.

For online exercises on main point and support, visit *Exercise Central* at **bedfordstmartins .com/realessays**. Also visit **bedfordstmartins .com/rewritingbasics**.

Although the writer does not indicate a specific cause or effect, the main point of the essay is clear—to discuss how unenforced restraining orders have resulted in violence. The body of the essay will likely give examples of such situations.

As you begin to write cause-and-effect essays, you might find it helpful to include both the topic and an indicator of cause or effect in your thesis statement.

Support in Cause and Effect

In a cause-and-effect essay, **support** consists of explanations of causes and effects, and it demonstrates the main point stated in your thesis. Take, for example, the following thesis statement.

Irresponsible behavior caused my car accident.

RESOURCES
To gauge students' understanding of main point, support, and other writing and grammar issues, use the *Testing Tool Kit* CD available with this book.

The writer supported this thesis by presenting the causes with details that explain them.

CAUSE	Driving too fast	CAUSE	On my cell phone
DETAILS	Rainy and slippery	DETAILS	Not paying close attention
	Going too fast to control car		Hit a curve while laughing
	Could not stop		Did not react fast enough

CAUSE	Drinking
DETAILS	Not focused
	Slowed reaction time

When you are writing about causes, be careful that you do not say something caused an event or situation just because it happened beforehand. For example, many of us have gotten sick after a meal and assumed that the food caused the sickness, only to find out that we had been coming down with the flu even before the meal.

When writing about effects, do not confuse something that happened after something else with an effect. In the previous example, just as the meal did not cause the illness, the illness was not the effect of the meal.

Organization in Cause and Effect

Cause-and-effect essays are organized in different ways depending on their purpose.

MAIN POINT	PURPOSE	ORGANIZATION
Global warming is a serious threat to life as we know it.	To explain the effects of global warming	Order of importance (saving the most serious effect for last)
Global warming will flood many coastal states.	To describe how the U.S. map eventually might look	Space order
Over the next century, the effects of global warming will be dramatic.	To describe the effects of global warming over the next 100 years	Time order

As you write your essay, add transitions to show how each cause or effect relates to your main point. Here are some common transitions that are used in cause-and-effect writing.

Common Transitions in Cause and Effect

one cause, reason, effect, result	as a result
also	because
another	thus
first, second, third, and so on	

Read and Analyze Cause and Effect

For more examples of cause and effect, see Chapter 48.

TEAMWORK
Have students work through the first essay together to apply the critical reading process and answer the questions after the essay.

Before writing your own cause-and-effect essay, read the following three examples—from college, the workplace, and everyday life—and answer the questions that accompany them.

For each of the following three essays, review the Four Basics of Good Cause and Effect (p. 279) and practice your critical reading process by doing the following.

2PR The Critical Reading Process

■ **Preview** the reading, including the guiding question.

■ **Read** the piece, double-underlining the thesis statement, underlining the major support, and circling the transitions. Consider the quality of the support.

■ **Pause** to think during reading. Take notes and ask questions about what you are reading: Talk to the author.

■ **Review** the reading, your guiding question, your marginal notes and questions, and your answers to the Pause prompts.

Cause and Effect in College

The following cause-and-effect essay was written for a child development course.

Jeanine Pepper

The Effects of Attachment Deprivation on Infants

CRITICAL
READING
■ Preview
■ Read
■ Pause
■ Review

GUIDING QUESTION
What are the effects of social deprivation on infants?

VOCABULARY
The following words are *italicized* in the essay: *instinct, deprivation, stimulation, juvenile.* If you do not know their meanings, look them up in a dictionary or online.

1   Infants are born with an *instinct* to attach themselves, to bond with, their caregivers, whether the caregiver is a parent or some other person. The instinct is so strong that experiments like Harlow's[1] have shown that infants will bond even with cloth substitutes. When infants are deprived of attachment, the effects are both immediate and long-ranging.

2   The immediate effects of attachment *deprivation* are obvious and sad. When babies are neglected or abused and deprived of any social *stimulation*, they are constantly afraid of their environment and others. Imagine being born and not being held or talked to: The world would be a pretty scary place. Another common effect is that they do not learn how to speak or communicate in any way. Because they never experience communication with others, they experience others as foreign and threatening. The infants often become totally withdrawn.

PAUSE:
Underline the two effects in this paragraph.

3   The effects of attachment deprivation often do not end with infancy. As the child grows older, he or she is still fearful, and that fear shows itself as anger. The child is often aggressive, defensive, and friendless. Many *juvenile* criminals have been shown to have been abused or neglected in infancy.

PAUSE:
Do any of these effects surprise you? Why or why not?

4   Individuals who are deprived of attachment in infancy are often depressed and more likely to develop drug and alcohol addictions, which in turn may lead to crime. The aggression they showed even as toddlers is more dangerous in adults, leading to fights, lost jobs, or unhealthy or abusive relationships.

5   The saddest long-range effect of attachment deprivation is when people carry on the pattern of abuse or neglect into another generation. Studies have shown that most child abusers were abused as children. That is the childhood they knew, and they repeat it.

6   Not all children who were abused or neglected grow up with these effects. Some are able to develop normally. However, many infants who experienced attachment deprivation grow up to be very troubled human beings. The effects are serious and spread into all areas of their lives and the lives of others around them.

1. Harlow: Harry Harlow, American psychologist famous for his work on social isolation

CRITICAL
THINKING
■ Summarize
■ Analyze
■ Synthesize
■ Evaluate

(More on p. 21.)

PAUSE:
The final question
after each reading in
this section makes a
good essay topic.

1. **Summarize.** Briefly summarize Pepper's essay, including her **audience** and **purpose** for writing and all of the major effects.

2. **Analyze.** How does Pepper organize the effects?

3. **Synthesize.** Did you know about the effects of social deprivation on children? What other kinds of negative behaviors are often carried from one generation to another? How do you know this?

4. **Evaluate.** Does Pepper clearly present the effects? What contributes to the clarity? Would an instructor reading the essay understand what Pepper has learned about the subject? Does the essay have the **Four Basics of Good Cause and Effect** (see p. 279)?

Cause and Effect at Work

The following profile shows how a lawyer, consultant, and city counselor uses cause and effect.

Cause and Effect in the Real World

Background   I grew up in a housing project in Houston, Texas, where I lost several relatives to street violence. I always did well in school, however, as a student and an athlete. I eventually graduated magna cum laude from the University of Houston, where I was a three-time NCAA heptathlon champion, and afterwards enrolled in law school. In 1996, I qualified for the U.S. Olympic Team trials, and I won the high jump, beating Jackie Joyner-Kersee, who went on to win the gold medal. However, my brother was murdered at about this time, and for a variety of reasons, I did not do well in the rest of the trials. In 2000, I received the NAACP's Award for Legal Excellence for dedication to community service. I started my own consulting business, along with a law practice, and in 2007, I won a highly contested seat on the Houston City Council. Along the way, I was a contestant in season 10 of *Survivor*.

Jolanda Jones
Attorney, Houston
City Councilor, and
Consultant

Colleges/Degrees   B.A., University of Houston; J.D.L., University of Houston, Bates School of Law

Employer   Self

Writing at work   Legal briefs, proposals, letters, Web site content, speeches, presentations

How Jolanda uses cause and effect   As part of my community service and consulting, I speak to inner-city youth. When I address students, I emphasize the importance of understanding that for every action they take, there is a consequence they should consider. During my election campaign, I emphasized to voters how a vote for me would result in many changes in the city of Houston.

Jolanda Jones's Cause and Effect

The following is a talk that Jolanda Jones gives to students.

GUIDING QUESTION
What does Jones want her audience to understand?

VOCABULARY
The following words are *italicized* in the essay: *consequences, abusive, coward, aspirations, humiliated,* and *capable.* If you do not know their meanings, look them up in a dictionary or online.

CRITICAL
READING
■ Preview
■ Read
■ Pause
■ Review

PAUSE:
What do you expect
the next paragraph to
be about?

**COMBINING
MODES**
Note the use of
narration within the
cause and effect.

Some of the worst life situations I've seen were caused simply by people failing to consider the effects of their actions. Each of you in this room must learn for yourselves that every single decision you make has *consequences*. It is important that you think about the decisions you make **before** you make them because if you don't, then you will end up somewhere you didn't plan for.

My best decisions are the ones I make when I think my grandmother might find out about them. If I would be proud for her to know the decision I've made, then it's probably a good decision. If I have to sneak or would be ashamed for her to know my decision, then it is probably a bad decision. In any case, here are some examples of the thought process in good decision making. They show what happens when you don't consider consequences.

Some of you girls might be getting pressured by your boyfriends to have sex. What should you think about? Well, you're probably wondering what he'll say if you don't sleep with him. Will he break up with you or call you "prude"? Well, don't let him define you. What if you get pregnant? What if you get a sexually transmitted disease? What if you get AIDS? What if you break up after you have sex with him? Will he tell everyone how good you were in bed? Will everyone know your business?

Single parenthood is hard. I know from personal experience. I had graduated from college, was working as a minority recruiter and admissions counselor, and was training for the Olympics. I also planned to go to law school at Stanford. Then, I got pregnant without planning for it. Suddenly, I was expecting a child with a man who was both *abusive* and unsupportive. I was not married. I was disappointed in myself. I was ashamed of the shame I brought on my grandmother. I was a *coward*. I fled the United States and hid my pregnancy in Spain. I absolutely love my son, but I gave up my Olympic *aspirations* and Stanford Law School.

Some of you might be thinking about using drugs. Think long and hard. I have crackheads in my family whose lives have been destroyed. Some are homeless. Some are dying of AIDS. My aunt was murdered in a drug house. My brother was murdered buying marijuana. I have an alcoholic cousin who does not take care of her children, and she is on welfare. People who do drugs come to love drugs more than they love anyone or anything else. Then, the drugs control you. You lose control of your life.

What about crime—just little stuff, like shoplifting that little pair of earrings at the neighborhood Target? When I was sixteen, I'd worked to earn money to buy stuff I wanted. I wanted a pair of jeans. Instead, my mother took my check for herself. I still thought I was entitled to the jeans, so I went to Target and took a pair. I got caught. I was arrested, handcuffed, put in the back of a patrol car, and detained. I ducked my head down in the back of the patrol car. I just knew the whole world was looking at me. I was *humiliated*. I should have thought about the consequences. It wasn't right to steal from Target even if my mother took my check. You best believe I've thought about that ever since that date because I've never shoplifted again. I even told my son about it. I don't want him to make the same mistake that I did.

You have choices in life, and it's up to you to make the decisions that will most positively benefit your life. We are all *capable* of thinking through stuff and making the right decision. The question is: Are you going to do it, or are you going to just take the easy road through life? My grandmother said, "If you make a bad decision, learn from it and move on; that way it's not your fault. If, however, you make the same mistake twice, you're stupid and it is your fault." I don't know about you, but I'm not stupid.

I've made good and bad decisions in my life. Thankfully, I've made more good ones than bad. I hope to continue to make good decisions by considering consequences and learning from my mistakes. I hope that's your philosophy too.

1. Briefly summarize Jones's essay, including her main point and purpose.

2. Use ring diagrams to show one of the situations Jones presents, along with the causes or effects.

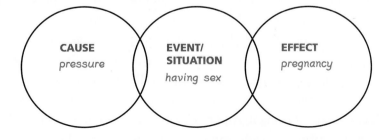

CAUSE
pressure

EVENT/ SITUATION
having sex

EFFECT
pregnancy

3. Review the Four Basics of Good Cause and Effect (p. 279) and determine whether Jones's writing is a good cause-and-effect essay. Make specific notes to support your opinion. *Answers will vary.*

4. What is your reaction to Jones's essay? What would you ask her if you could? _____

Cause and Effect in Everyday Life

The following example of cause-and-effect writing appeared in a *Boston Globe* article.

COMBINING
MODES
If you have studied
definition, point out to
students that while
this is a cause-and-
effect essay,
paragraph 2 uses
definition to explain
the term *social-norms
marketing.*

Christopher Shea

In Praise of Peer Pressure

GUIDING QUESTION
How can peer pressue have positive results?

VOCABULARY
The following words are *italicized* in the essay: *peer pressure, conserve, consumption, herd, intensifying, activists, oblivion, productive, insights, quirks, psyche, immobilize, irreplaceable, heritage, symbolically, compliance, manipulate, coincidentally,* and *scrupulous.* If you do not know their meanings, look them up in a dictionary or online.

CRITICAL
READING
■ Preview
■ Read
■ Pause
■ Review

1   *Peer pressure* gets bad press, but in some cases more of it might make the world a better place. In California, psychologists recently found that they could get people to *conserve* electricity with a simple notice, delivered to their doorstep, telling them how their *consumption* compared with the neighborhood average. In the weeks that followed, homeowners who were consuming more electricity than their neighbors cut back—presumably because they were embarrassed to be out of step with the *herd.*

PAUSE:
What is social-norms
marketing?

2   The research, reported in *Psychological Science*, reflects growing interest in what's known as "social-norms marketing"—attempting to change behavior by telling people what their peers do. The basic concept is about two decades old, but psychologists have been *intensifying* efforts to find more effective ways of using it. And now, with a growing recognition of the limits of browbeating, a wide range of groups—from climate-change

activists to college deans trying to keep students from drinking themselves to *oblivion*—have been making peer pressure their ally.

3   "The norm is like a magnet," says Robert Cialdini, a professor at Arizona State University who is an author of the new study. "What's appropriate to do, in most people's minds, is what other people like them do."

4   The social-norms approach is part of a general movement to make *productive* use of *insights* into the *quirks* of the human *psyche*. For example, psychologists have found that presenting people with a wide range of choices (about almost anything) can frustrate and *immobilize* them, so that they end up making no choice at all or a bad choice. Supermarket managers and policy experts designing health plans have taken note.

5   Cialdini's work tends to focus on the environment. In a paper from 2003, he identified a problem with signs in the Petrified Forest National Park, in Arizona, intended to discourage the theft of ancient, *irreplaceable* wood. The signs sternly warned that America's *"heritage"* was being "vandalized" by "theft losses of petrified wood of 14 tons a year."

6   That sent the message that pocketing souvenirs was the norm for tourists, Cialdini argues. In an on-site experiment, he and his coauthors demonstrated that by making use of new signs that stressed how few people removed items from the park and that by *symbolically* isolating those who do (on the sign, thieving stick figures had red slashes through them), the park could cut vandalism substantially.

7   In another experiment, Cialdini has shown that hotels will have more success encouraging their clients to reuse towels if they alter the wording of their appeals. "Join your fellow guests in helping to save the environment: A majority of our guests use their towels more than once" works better than any other approach.

8   In Minnesota, a study by the Department of Revenue found that informing taxpayers that most people don't cheat on their taxes improved tax *compliance* more than stressing the link between taxes and popular public programs.

9   The field is still in flux: The effects of peer pressure remain hard to measure and hard to *manipulate*—yet the tug of the herd mindset is everywhere. *Coincidentally,* I recently came across a survey that found that 80 percent of adult males in the United States have six or fewer drinks in

PAUSE:
Why would supermarket managers want to think about this?

PAUSE:
Can you think of an example of a positive effect of peer pressure?

a week. I was taken aback, assuming the average was higher. I skipped wine with dinner a few times that week.

10 ⟮Later that same week,⟯ I read in an economics journal that freelance businessmen—I'm a freelancer—report only about 60 percent of their income, according to IRS estimates. Yet I'm *scrupulous* to the penny. Do I want to remain abnormal? Does anyone? I filed for an extension, so I've got some time to think about it.

PAUSE:
What is he going to think about?

TEAMWORK
These questions, and the ones following the other readings in this chapter, can be answered in teams.

1. In your own words, describe the effects of peer pressure that Shea presents. *Answers will vary.* _____

2. Describe some effects of peer pressure that you have experienced or observed. _____

3. Do you think peer pressure is a good thing? How can it be negative? _____

4. Does Shea's essay have the **Four Basics of Good Cause and Effect** (p. 279)? Why or why not? _____

   _____

5. Which of the essays in this chapter do you think is the best model of cause-and-effect writing? Why? _____

   _____

ESL
Invite ESL students to write about the causes or effects of a cultural or linguistic misunderstanding. Native English-speaking students might focus on causes or effects of a misunderstanding based on race, social class, gender, or age.

Write a Cause and Effect Essay

In this section, you will write your own cause-and-effect essay based on *one* of the following assignments. Use the following tools to help you.

1. Review the Four Basics of Good Cause and Effect (p. 279).
2. Use Cause and Effect at a glance as a basic organizer.
3. Use the Writing Guide: Cause and Effect checklist as you write and revise (pp. 297–98).

ASSIGNMENT 1   Writing about College, Work, and Everyday Life

Write a cause-and-effect essay on *one* of the following topics or on a topic of your own choice.

COLLEGE
- The immediate effects of being in college or the desired long-term effects on your life of going to college
- Causes of a legitimate absence that resulted in your missing a test (directed to your professor)
- From another course you are taking, the causes or effects of something that was discussed in the course or the textbook

WORK
- Causes of low employee morale
- Causes, effects, or both of a situation in the workplace
- Effects of juggling work, school, and family

EVERYDAY LIFE
- Causes of an argument with a friend or a member of your family
- A good decision or a bad one, and its possible effects on your life
- Effects of sleep deprivation (look for articles or Web sites)

ASSIGNMENT 2   Writing about Images

After examining the photographs on page 294, write an essay that uses them as a jumping off place for your own thoughts on how a person can change and improve. Some questions you might wish to explore are:

- What are the causes of laziness? What are the effects?
- Is the voice of these signs nagging and critical, or is it positive, encouraging, and playful?
- What signs would you put up?
- Would reminder signs like Hanson's work for you, as a self-improvement method? If not, what methods have you found effective in helping you change your own behavior?

Cause and Effect at a glance

Thesis statement
Indicates causes, effects, or both

↓

Cause 1 or effect 1
Detailed explanation or example of the first cause or effect

↓

Cause 2 or effect 2
Detailed explanation or example of the second cause or effect

↓

Cause 3 or effect 3
Detailed explanation or example of the third cause or effect

↓

Conclusion
Reminds readers of your main point and makes an observation about it based on what you have written

"I believe we all are prey to bouts of laziness," writes photographer Erin Hanson, on her site, *Recovering Lazyholic* (**recoveringlazyholic.com**). The site features photos of the colorful, lettered reminders—in the style of schoolroom instructions—that she has placed around her house.

ASSIGNMENT 3   Writing to Solve a Problem

THE PROBLEM: Your child has been bullied at school, and you are deeply concerned about how it is affecting him or her. You have heard how desperate children can become in such circumstances, and you want to educate yourself on bullying in general and the situation in your child's school in particular. You have already contacted the principal, but so far, nothing has been done.

THE ASSIGNMENT: Read Kathleen Vail's "Words That Wound" (p. 706) to consider the causes and effects of bullying in that essay. Then, go online and search for articles about bullying. Look particularly for common situations (causes) and common effects on the victims. Write about these in a cause-and-effect essay.

ASSIGNMENT 4   Writing about Connections

Read the account of Stacy Gordon Welch before doing the assignment that follows.

COMMUNITY CONNECTIONS

Stacy Gordon Welch, Temple College
President, Sigma Zeta Tau, the local chapter of Lambda
Alpha Epsilon — the American Criminal Justice Association

Stacy Gordon Welch is thirty-one and the single mother of two children. She dropped out of school when she was fourteen, having run away from her alcoholic mother. At seventeen, she got her GED. While working as an apartment building manager, she suspected some tenants of dealing drugs, and as a result became interested in law enforcement and criminal justice and started taking courses at Temple College. Though she fell behind in her coursework and considered dropping out at one point, Leslie Keeling-Olson, chair of the Criminal Justice Department, helped her to stay in school. She also encouraged Welch to get involved with Lambda Alpha Epsilon, which Welch says has changed her life.

(continued)

> The organization made her feel that she was part of something use-
> ful. She participated in a forensic science conference where she heard
> many speakers and made great contacts. She believes her involvement in
> Lambda Alpha Epsilon has kept her in school: "The more involved I am,
> the better I do in school."

ASSIGNMENT: Choose one of the following topics and write a cause-and-effect
essay.

- Write about your involvement in something and its effect on you, either in a
  positive or negative way.

- Write about a time when your connection with another person changed
  your life in some way or when you changed someone else's life.

- Describe the various communities you belong to and the connections you
  have made as a result of your participation.

ASSIGNMENT 5   Writing about Readings

Society's (or a group's) standards of who and what are good or bad are
reflected in television, magazines, music, and virtually every other type of media.
Media images affect us all, whether or not we are aware of it, and several of the
readings in this book deal with how people can be harmed by them. Choose
one of the reading pairs below, and write an essay on the topic that follows it.

1. Amy L. Beck's "Struggling for Perfection" on page 807 and the
   excerpt from the psychology textbook by Don H. Hockenbury and
   Sandra Hockenbury on page 265

   - Discuss the issue that Beck raises and how the Hockenburys'
     piece on anorexia and bulimia supports her point. Refer to
     both readings, and bring in your own experiences with media
     portrayals as well, including how you or people you know have
     been affected.

2. Amy L. Beck's "Struggling for Perfection" on page 807 and Dave
   Barry's "The Ugly Truth about Beauty" on page 787

   - Discuss the authors' different approaches to a similar topic. Ana-
     lyze the differences, and discuss which piece is more effective to
     you and why.

3. Jolanda Jones's (p. 288) and Christopher Shea's (p. 290) essays in this chapter

   • How might the kind of peer pressure Shea presents be applied to what Jones discusses?

4. Amy L. Beck's "Struggling for Perfection" on page 807 and Brent Staples's "Just Walk on By: Black Men and Public Space" on page 802

   • How have the two different groups the authors portray been negatively affected by portrayals in the media? Bring in references from each reading along with your experiences of how the media can cause people to have incorrect, and sometimes dangerous, perceptions of themselves and others.

RESOURCES

Additional Resources for Teaching Real Essays with Readings has visual planning forms for cause and effect and the other essays covered in Part 2. These forms are also online at bedfordstmartins .com/realessays.

Use the steps in the Writing Guide that follows to help you prewrite, draft, revise, and edit your cause-and-effect essay. Check off each step as you complete it.

WRITING GUIDE: CAUSE AND EFFECT

STEPS IN CAUSE AND EFFECT	HOW TO DO THE STEPS
☐ Focus.	• Think about an event or a situation that had concrete causes and/or effects.
☐ Explore your topic. See Chapter 5.	• With your purpose in mind, prewrite or use the ring diagram to get ideas about causes and effects.
☐ Write a thesis statement. Topic + Indication of cause or effect = Thesis See Chapter 6.	• Write a thesis statement that includes your topic and an indication of whether you will be showing causes, effects, or both.
☐ Support your thesis. See Chapter 7.	• List the major causes and/or effects. • For each cause or effect, give details that will help your readers understand how they caused or affected an event.
☐ Write a draft. See Chapter 8.	• Arrange the causes and/or effects in a logical order (often chronological or by importance). • Write topic sentences for each major cause and/or effect and paragraphs that describe them in detail. →

STEPS IN CAUSE AND EFFECT	HOW TO DO THE STEPS
☐ Revise your draft. See Chapter 9.	• Get feedback using the peer-review guide for cause and effect at **bedfordstmartins.com/realessays**. • Ask another person to read and comment on your draft. • With your purpose and audience in mind, read to make sure the causes and effects are real, and if you have explained them adequately. • Add transitions. • Improve your introduction, thesis, and conclusion.
☐ Edit your draft. See Parts 4 through 7.	• Correct errors in grammar, spelling, word use, and punctuation.
☐ Evaluate your writing.	• Does it have the Four Basics of Good Cause and Effect (p. 279)? • Is this the best I can do?

> **reflect** Reread your response to the "write" prompt on p. 279. What would you change based on what you have learned about writing cause-and-effect pieces?

Argument

Writing That Persuades

Understand What Argument Is

Argument is writing that takes a position on an issue and offers reasons and supporting evidence to convince someone else to accept, or at least consider, that position. Argument is also used to persuade someone to take an action (or not to take an action).

Four Basics of Good Argument

1 It takes a strong, definite position on an issue or advises a particular action.

2 It gives good supporting evidence to defend the position or recommended action.

3 It considers opposing views.

4 It has enthusiasm and energy from start to finish.

In the following paragraph, each number corresponds to one of the Four Basics of Good Argument.

1 The drinking age should be lowered from twenty-one to eighteen. **2** The government gives eighteen-year-olds the right to vote. If they are adult enough to vote for the people and policies that run this country, they should be mature enough to have a

IDEA JOURNAL
Write about a time that you got something you wanted by giving someone good reasons and making a good case.

ESL Some students may come from a background in which direct argument is perceived as rude and points are therefore made indirectly.

drink. **2** The U.S. penal system also regards eighteen-year-olds as adults. If an eighteen-year-old commits a crime and goes to trial, he or she is tried and sentenced as an adult, not as a minor. That means that if the crime is murder, an eighteen-year-old could receive the death penalty. Eighteen-year-olds are not given special treatment. Most important is the fact that at eighteen, individuals can enlist in the armed forces and go to war. The government considers them old enough to die for their country but not old enough to have a drink? This makes no sense. **3** Opponents to lowering the drinking age justify their position by saying that if the age is lowered, teenagers will start drinking even earlier. However, there is no evidence to show that legal age is a major influence on teenage drinking. Other factors involved, such as peer pressure and the availability of fake IDs, have more impact on whether teenagers drink. While the government does need to address the issue of teenage drinking, forbidding eighteen-year-olds to drink while granting them other, more important rights and responsibilities at the same age is neither consistent nor reasonable.

4 Writing is enthusiastic and energetic.

DISCUSSION
Ask students to identify some issues — whether local, national, or international — that have more than two sides.

DISCUSSION
Ask students to give examples of situations in which they needed to defend a position.

Putting together a good argument is one of the most useful skills you can learn. Knowing how to argue well will equip you to defend effectively what you believe and to convince others to agree with you. We present an argument to persuade someone to give us a job, to buy something we are selling, or to give us more time to finish a task. And we argue when something important is at stake, like keeping a job or protecting our rights. To argue effectively, we need to do more than just say what we want or believe; we need to give solid reasons and evidence.

Argument is the method you use to persuade people to see things your way or at least to understand your position. Argument helps you to take action in problem situations rather than to stand by, silent and frustrated. Although knowing how to argue will not eliminate all such situations, it will help you to defend your position.

Many situations require good argument skills.

COLLEGE   An exit essay from a writing course contains the following instruction: "Develop a well-balanced argument on the subject of free speech on the Internet."

WORK   You present reasons why you should get a promotion.

EVERYDAY LIFE   You convince a large company that it has made a
                mistake on your bill.

SEEING ARGUMENT

write What issue might the photographer have had in mind with this
photo? What was his purpose in taking this photograph?

Main Point in Argument

Your **main point** in an argument is the position you take on the issue you are writing about. When you are free to choose an issue, choose something you care about. When you are assigned an issue, find something about it that you feel strongly about and take a definite position. You should approach your argument feeling committed to and enthusiastic about your position. To help you get there, consider the following tips.

Tips for Building Energy and Enthusiasm

- Imagine yourself arguing your position with someone who holds the opposite position.

- Imagine that your whole grade rests on persuading your teacher that your position is correct.

- Imagine how this issue could affect you or your family personally.

- Imagine that you are representing a large group of people who very much care about the issue and whose lives will be forever changed by it. It is up to you to win their case.

Take a few minutes to think about the issue, talk it over with a partner, or jot down ideas related to it. Once you have decided on your position and have built up some energy for it, write a thesis statement that includes the issue and your position on it.

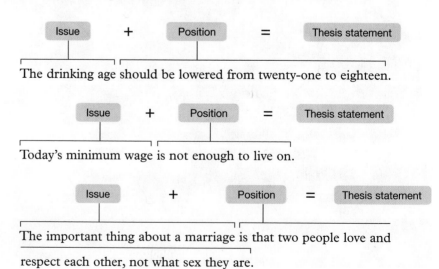

Issue + Position = Thesis statement

The drinking age should be lowered from twenty-one to eighteen.

Issue + Position = Thesis statement

Today's minimum wage is not enough to live on.

Issue + Position = Thesis statement

The important thing about a marriage is that two people love and respect each other, not what sex they are.

Sometimes the thesis combines the issue and the position, as in the following statements.

Issue/Position = Thesis statement

Soldiers should not be forced to stay in war zones beyond their terms.

Issue/Position = Thesis statement

All eighteen-year-olds should be drafted into the military.

Try to make the thesis statement for any argument as specific as possible to help guide your writing and your readers.

VAGUE	Our health-care system is disgraceful.
MORE SPECIFIC	Two key reforms would make health care more afford-able for all.

[The paper would detail the two reforms.]

Many thesis statements for arguments use words such as the following because they clearly express a position.

could (not)	ought (not)
must (not)	requires
must have	should (not)
needs	would

TEACHING TIP
Have students write at least three different versions of a position statement and then evaluate which they think is the most ef-fective, and why.

ESL Ask students how differences in languages and cul-tures help shape the presentation of an argument.

. . . .

PRACTICE 1 Writing a Statement of Your Position

Write your position on the following issues.

A ban on junk food and sugary drinks at elementary and high schools

Answers will vary.
_____

Mandatory drug testing as a requirement for employment

_____

Free college courses for prisoners

_____

DISCUSSION
Ask students to iden-tify a good argument or speech they have heard and explain what made it effective.

Now, take one of the position statements that you just wrote, and put more energy into it.

_____

_____

· ·

Support in Argument

However strongly you may feel about an issue, if you do not provide solid **support** for your position, you will not convince anyone to see it your way. As you develop support for your position, think carefully about your readers and the kind of information that will be most convincing to them.

Reasons and Evidence

For online exercises on main point and support, visit *Exercise Central* at bedfordstmartins .com/realessays.

The major support for your position consists of the **reasons** that you give for that position. These reasons must be backed up with **evidence**, such as facts, examples, and expert opinions. The success of your argument depends on the quality of the reasons and evidence that you present to support your position.

Facts are statements or observations that can be proved true. **Statistics**—numerical facts based on research—can be persuasive evidence to back up your position. **Examples** are specific experiences or pieces of information that support your position. **Expert opinion** is the opinion of someone who is considered an expert in the area you are writing about. *Note:* The fact that a person's opinion appears on a Web site does not necessarily mean that he or she has any expertise. When in doubt about a source's authority, consult your instructor or a research librarian.

For more on finding sources, using quotations, and citing sources, see Chapter 21.

POSITION	It pays to stay in college.
REASON	College graduates earn more than high school graduates.
EVIDENCE/ FACT	College graduates earn 55 percent more than high school graduates.
REASON	Students learn up-to-date skills that they will need to find a job.
EVIDENCE/ EXAMPLE	Understanding how to use technology in your field may make the difference between getting a job and coming in second.

TEACHING TIP
Have the class choose an issue, bring in evidence (facts, examples, expert opinions), and compare what they find.

REASON	Many jobs require college degrees.
EVIDENCE/ EXPERT OPINION	John Sterling, president of one of the largest recruiting agencies, said recently, "Ten years ago, a college degree was perceived as an advantage. Today, the college degree is the basic ticket of entry for the majority of jobs." [*Note:* When you use expert opinion, you need to identify the source of the quote.]

As you choose reasons and evidence to support your position, consider your readers. Are they likely to agree with you, to be uncommitted, or to be hostile? Choose the support that is most likely to convince them, drawing on outside sources (such as the library or Internet) as needed.

TEACHING TIP
Critique a misleading ad that uses weak evidence (such as a diet ad that promises instant weight loss). Ask students to bring in other examples.

Opposing Positions

Part of your support for your position involves the opposing position: Acknowledge it, and present some evidence against it. If, for example, you are arguing in favor of lowering the drinking age to eighteen, you should not ignore the position that it should be kept at age twenty-one. If you do not say anything about the other position, you are leaving your argument unprotected. To defend your own position, show some weakness in the opposing position.

The writer of the paragraph on pages 299–300 might consider the opposing position as follows.

DISCUSSION
Ask students to suggest a topic, a position, and some evidence. Then ask for ideas about how the opposition would try to knock down the evidence.

POSITION	The drinking age should be lowered from twenty-one to eighteen.
OPPOSING POSITION	The drinking age should not be lowered because people begin drinking before the legal age. If the age were lowered to eighteen, more sixteen-year-olds would drink.

ACKNOWLEDGING THE OPPOSING POSITION: First, laws should not be based on the extent to which they are likely to be abused or broken. They should be based on what's right. Even so, there is no evidence to show that legal age is a major influence on teenage drinking. Other factors involved, such as peer pressure and the availability of fake IDs, have more impact on whether teenagers drink.

As you gather support for your position, keep the opposing position in mind, and follow the tips given in the box on page 306.

> ## Tips for Supporting Your Position by Addressing the Opposing Position
>
> • Visualize someone who holds the opposing position and what that person would say to defend it.
>
> • In part of the body of your essay, acknowledge the opposing position. Do so politely; if you try to ridicule the opposing view, you will alienate people and immediately weaken your argument.
>
> • Address the opposing position directly and show what's wrong, or misguided, about it. Again, do this politely.
>
> • Return to the reasons and the evidence that support your position.

PRACTICE 2   Acknowledging and Addressing the Opposing View

TEAMWORK
Practice 2 works well in pairs.

For each of the following positions, in the spaces indicated, state the opposing position and at least one point someone holding the opposing view might make against your position. *Answers will vary. Suggested answers follow.*

ISSUE: The "Three Strikes and You're Out" rule in some high schools that requires students to be expelled after three serious offenses

POSITION: Against it

OPPOSING POSITION: *In favor of the rule*

POINT THAT SOMEONE HOLDING THE OPPOSING POSITION WOULD MAKE:

The rule serves as a deterrent.

ISSUE: Mandatory retirement at age sixty-seven

POSITION: In favor of it

OPPOSING POSITION: *Opposed to mandatory retirement at age sixty-seven*

POINT THAT SOMEONE HOLDING THE OPPOSING POSITION WOULD MAKE:

People live longer these days than they used to.

ISSUE: Stricter gun control laws

POSITION: Against it

OPPOSING POSITION: *In favor of stricter gun control laws*

POINT THAT SOMEONE HOLDING THE OPPOSING POSITION WOULD MAKE:

Stricter laws would decrease the number of accidental shootings.

Faulty Reasoning

As you write and review the support for your position, be sure that your evidence is good and your reasoning is logical. Unfortunately, we are exposed to **faulty reasoning** all the time, especially in advertising. Certain kinds of errors in logic are so common that there is a name for them—**logical fallacies**. Be aware of the common fallacies so you can avoid them. For a review of logical fallacies, see pages 32–34.

Organization in Argument

Argument most often uses **order of importance** to organize reasons for the writer's position on the issue. Consider what you think your readers will find your most convincing reason. Arrange your reasons and evidence so that they build the strongest case for your position, and save the most convincing reason for last. Do not forget to acknowledge and address the opposing position somewhere in your argument.

As you write your argument, use transitions such as those in the box below to move your readers from one reason or point to the next.

Common Transitions in Argument

FROM ONE POINT TO ANOTHER	TO ADD EMPHASIS
also	above all
another fact to consider	best of all
another reason	especially
another thing	in fact
consider that	in particular
for example	more important
in addition	most important
in the first place	remember
	the last point to consider
	worst of all

Read and Analyze Argument

Before writing your own argument essay, read the following three examples—from college, the workplace, and everyday life—and answer the questions that accompany them. As you read, notice that argument uses many of the other kinds of writing you have studied to support a

For more examples of argument, see Chapter 49.

position. It may tell a story, give examples, describe something, explain how something works, break a large point into categories, define a term, compare two or more things, or show cause and effect.

In learning how to construct a good argument you use everything you have learned about good writing. Being able to make a good case for or against something you believe may be the most important skill you learn in college and it can be applied to all other parts of your life.

For each of the following three essays, review the Four Basics of Good Argument (p. 299) and practice your critical reading process.

TEAMWORK Have students work through the first essay together to apply the critical reading process and answer the questions after the essay.

2PR   The Critical Reading Process

■ **Preview** the reading, including the guiding question.

■ **Read** the piece, double-underlining the <u>thesis statement</u>, underlining the <u>major support</u>, and circling the transitions. Consider the quality of the support.

■ **Pause** to think during reading. Take notes and ask questions about what you are reading: Talk to the author.

■ **Review** the reading, your guiding question, your marginal notes and questions, and your answers to the Pause prompts.

Argument in College

TEACHING TIP As an assignment, have students rewrite this argument, adding opposing positions, more support, and transitions.

The following essay was written in response to this assignment: *Take a position on some aspect of college life, and write a short essay defending that position.*

Donnie Ney

Attendance in College Classes

GUIDING QUESTION
What reasons does Ney give in support of his position?

VOCABULARY
The following words are *italicized* in Ney's essay: *mandatory, ratio, jeopardize, correspond,* and *penalized.* If you do not know their meanings, look them up in a dictionary or online.

CRITICAL
READING
■ Preview
■ Read
■ Pause
■ Review

1   Attendance in college classes should be optional, not *mandatory*. Students pay a lot of money for their courses, so they should be able to decide whether and how to take advantage of them. Also, although class participation can help many students, not all students learn through class participation. If they learn better on their own or if they already know the content of a course that is required for graduation, they should be able to decide for themselves whether to sit in class hearing about things they already have learned. Finally, optional attendance would benefit the students who want to go to class because the student-to-instructor *ratio* would be lower, and students would get more personal attention.

PAUSE: What reasons has Ney included in this paragraph?

2   First, students pay tuition, fees, and the cost of books and materials to enroll in a class. Because they have paid for the class, they should have the choice about whether to attend. Isn't it a basic right of a consumer to decide how to use the things he's bought and paid for? Also, students' lives are complicated, and there are many good reasons that they may have to miss classes, even if they want to attend. For example, this semester I have missed several classes because of my child's ongoing battle with severe asthma. I cannot *jeopardize* her health in order to get to a class. On the other hand, I do not want to fail because I have missed more than the allowed number of classes. Such a policy does not seem fair.

PAUSE: Note that Ney briefly uses narration here.

PAUSE: Do you agree that paying for the course should give students the right to attend or not without a penalty?

3   Also, it seems unfair to require students who already know the course content or who learn it on their own to waste their time hearing about it again. Although most students attend classes because they want to learn, there are some required courses that students have to take whether they want to or not. For example, I have had to attend basic computer classes to teach me procedures such as how to turn on a computer, what e-mail is, and how to access the Internet. I have known these things for years. Why should I sit through classes that repeat what I know when I could be spending my time doing the many things I really need to do? Why should I fail if I miss too many of these classes? Such policies do not benefit me or anyone else. In addition, although colleges do not like to admit this, attendance does not always *correspond* to grades. For example, some students can read and understand the materials assigned without any help from the teacher. If the goal of a college course is to learn, and a student can learn without attending class, why should that student need to attend lectures?

PAUSE: Where does Ney acknowledge the opposition?

PAUSE: Note that this benefit is an effect of Ney's position.

4   The best reason for making attendance optional is that students who do choose to attend could benefit from smaller classes and more personal attention. Classes could include more one-on-one instruction, which might improve students' grades and their ability to understand and retain course content. Many students struggle with course content and really need more of the instructor's time. However, with large classes, instructors do not have much chance to spend lots of time with individual students.

5   For all of these reasons, I believe that attendance should be optional in college courses. Students do not all learn in the same way. Some students learn best by studying a lot rather than sitting in class. With more study time and less class time, some students will achieve better results on tests. Attendance should be the students' choice. If they need to go to class to pass, they will attend; if they do not need to go to class to learn, they should not be *penalized*.

PAUSE: What, to you, is the most persuasive reason Ney gives?

CRITICAL THINKING
■ Summarize
■ Analyze
■ Synthesize
■ Evaluate

(More on p. 21.)

1. **Summarize.** Briefly summarize Ney's essay, including the topic, his position on it, and the main **support** he gives.

2. **Analyze.** How does Ney use **transitions** in his essay? How does he connect his concluding paragraph to his thesis statement? Is Ney biased or objective?

3. **Synthesize.** Read the attendance policy on the syllabus for this course. How would Ney respond to it? Have you had discussions about this topic with other students?

4. **Evaluate.** Does Ney make a good argument? Do you agree with him? Does his essay have the **Four Basics of Good Argument** (p. 299)? Are there any logical fallacies?

Argument at Work

The following profile shows how the director of a nonprofit organization uses argument in his work.

Argument in the Real World

Background   I had what is, unfortunately, a typical kind of life for many poor, urban youth who are caught up in gangs, drugs, and violence. My brother was murdered in a crossfire, and I lived with my mother with no father around. I was an athlete and got away with not doing much in school. I had my first kid at age fifteen and in that same year almost shot a rival who had disrespected me. I didn't, mainly because I remembered my coach, who'd warned me not to leave my son fatherless. This coach, Ed Powell, had a saying I still repeat often: "He who fails to plan, plans to fail." I was lucky to have Powell and a few other adults reach out to me, help me turn around, and get me on the track of education and a better life.

Shawn Brown
Founder, Diamond
Educators

A few years ago, I got together a group of my friends, all college-educated African American men with families and steady jobs. We talked about how many young black men have no positive role models and decided that we wanted to help them the way we had been helped. From that meeting came Diamond Educators, a nonprofit organization that starts working with kids in third grade by teaching them how to behave, speak, and "play the game" in a way that will lead to success in life. Teens who are in the program give back by mentoring elementary school boys. The program is growing and has a great success record.

College/Degree   B.A., Merrimack College

Employers   Diamond Educators, Boston Private Industry Council (PIC)

Writing at work   In both positions, I write a lot. For Diamond Educators, I've written a mission statement, research projects, proposals for funding and support, and many other kinds of writing. For the PIC, I write reports, e-mail, letters, and assessments.

How Shawn uses argument   I use argument in both speech and writing to persuade the boys, members of the community, legal bodies, and potential donors. I have to think about who the person is, what he or she thinks, and how I can best make my case.

Shawn Brown's Argument

Shawn Brown wrote this letter to support the parole request of a young man he had worked with.

GUIDING QUESTION
What is Brown's purpose, and what is his overall point?

VOCABULARY
The following words are *italicized* in the letter: *parole, mentor, multicultural, adverse, cope, invaluable, dedication, mentees, transform, jeopardize, essential,* and *incarcerated.* If you do not know their meanings, look them up in a dictionary or online.

CRITICAL
READING
■ Preview
■ Read
■ Pause
■ Review

PAUSE: What do you think the next paragraph will be about?

PAUSE: What conditions does Brown list as causes of bad life choices?

PAUSE: Why does Brown write about Diamond Educators here rather than talking about Rodney?

To Whom It May Concern:

It is with enthusiasm that I am writing to support *parole* for Rodney Strong. In his work for Diamond Educators as a *mentor* to young men, he has made a positive contribution to the at-risk youth in the city of Boston.

Diamond Educators is a nonprofit mentoring program that serves at-risk young males who attend Boston public schools or who live in the inner-city neighborhoods of Boston. The mentors of the Diamond Educators program are *multicultural* male educators and professionals who grew up in the city of Boston and who dealt with *adverse* conditions that the majority of our young minority males face every day, conditions that often result in bad life choices. The adverse conditions I refer to are living in an environment where young men *cope* with peer pressure to join a gang and involve themselves with drugs, crime, and violence; single-parent homes; and a lack of positive male role models. Our mentors help young men chart a course through their difficult situations. These mentors are an *invaluable* resource for our young, urban, minority males.

As a mentor, Rodney demonstrated commitment and *dedication* to our program and to our students. Rodney worked long hours, but he found time to meet and counsel his *mentees*. He showed his mentees the importance of meeting commitments, taking responsibility, and having a positive purpose in life. He was a good example of how positive peer relationships can *transform* lives.

Rodney gave these young boys hope. He showed his mentees that by applying themselves and taking advantage of the resources available to them, they could achieve success in life. Many of the boys otherwise live without hope of any kind and choose paths that *jeopardize* their own well-being and that of others in the community. That hope is *essential* to becoming a productive member of the human community. Rodney is a leader with a strong will to achieve his own success and to help others find theirs.

The path to success for urban minority males is extremely difficult, and, as with many difficult courses, progress is not always direct and uninterrupted. Rodney stepped off course and made a poor decision when he committed a crime. However, he has demonstrated that he has learned from his mistake and is ready to return to his community as a positive force. He is ready to contribute to society, and to keep him *incarcerated* deprives us of a good man, a good leader, and a good role model for young men. His release will show his mentees that there is hope of a good, lawful life after jail.

Rodney is dedicated to being a good father and a good community influence. Unlike many who return to the community after incarceration, Rodney will not persist in a life of crime; he will return to his path of success and contribution. Keeping him from that serves no purpose.

I support Rodney Strong and will continue to support him after his return to the community. I urge you to consider his good work and to allow him to continue it.

Sincerely,
Shawn Brown, Cofounder
Diamond Educators

PAUSE: Why is the last sentence here important to Brown's argument?

PAUSE: Note that Brown uses narration to suggest Rodney's future story.

1. Briefly summarize Brown's essay, including the topic, his position on it, and the main reasons he gives. _Answers will vary._

2. In what paragraph does Brown acknowledge and respond to an opposing view? _Paragraph 5_

3. If you were an officer of the court, would Brown's letter alone persuade you to support parole for Rodney Strong? Why or why not? What else would you want or need to know? _Answers will vary._

4. How might Brown's point of view differ from a member of the criminal justice system's?_____

5. What, to you, is the strongest reason Brown presents? Why? _____

_____

Argument in Everyday Life

After a class discussion and assignment on the unfairness of federal financial aid regulations, student John Around Him wrote the following letter to Senator John Kerry. Senator Kerry not only responded to the letter,

NOTE: Partly as a result of this letter and his internship, Around Him received a full scholarship to Dartmouth College.

promising to work to change the federal financial aid system, but he also visited Around Him's college class. Because of this contact, John Around Him was hired to work as a policy intern in Kerry's Massachusetts office.

GUIDING QUESTION

Why does the author think the financial aid system is not fair to many students?

VOCABULARY

The following words are *italicized* in the letter: *chaos, eligibility,* and *criteria.* If you do not know their meanings, look them up in a dictionary or online.

CRITICAL READING
■ Preview
■ Read
■ Pause
■ Review

Dear Senator Kerry:

1   My name is John Around Him, and I am a student at Bunker Hill Community College in Boston, Massachusetts. I am Native American and a veteran of the war in Iraq. I know that you, as a veteran of the Vietnam War, can relate to putting your life on the line in an environment of gunfire, explosions, *chaos*, and confusion, wondering if the next second might be your last. For most young people, being in the middle of a dangerous war—being shot at and surrounded by death and violence—is not an appealing way to earn money for college. However, for students like me who do not qualify for federal financial aid, it may be the only way to go to college, and this is why I am writing to you. The federal financial aid system needs to be changed because it is not effective in helping students, especially low-income and minority students, pay for college.

PAUSE: How does Around Him appeal to his audience here?

COMBINING MODES Note Around Him's use of narration within his argument.

2   I grew up on the Pine Ridge Reservation in South Dakota and graduated from Little Wound High School in 2001. I was an average student, with a grade-point average of just under 3.0. I always wanted to go to college, but I asked myself, "How would I pay for it?" I lived with a single-parent father and with two other families, and my father would often help others who needed it. My father was a language teacher, not highly paid, so for me family financial support for college was out of the question. I had to find another answer.

PAUSE: Note that Around Him uses narration in this paragraph.

3   When I turned to the federal financial aid system, I found that there is money to help some students pay for college, but none for a student like me. According to the College Board's report, "Trends in College Pricing, 2006," the average tuition, room, and board costs for public universities is $12,796 (though many are much more, as is the case here in Massachusetts)—way out of line for my family's finances. Yet according to the financial aid formula, my father made too much money.

4   The formulas used to determine a student's financial need are not real-istic: They do not represent the average student's situation. For example, according to the formula, to be considered independent (which largely determines *eligibility*) a student must meet one of the following *criteria*: He or she must be either twenty-four years of age or older, married, a veteran, or an orphan or ward of the court. Many students today, however, are financially independent as soon as they graduate from high school. In 2005, according to the National Center for Education Statistics, 64 per-cent of students at community colleges and 37 percent at public colleges and universities were financially independent. Fifty-eight percent of those students worked at least thirty-five hours per week, and 67 percent delayed entering college to earn money to help pay for it. Still, those under age twenty-four are not considered to be independent, and their family income is taken into consideration, even when the student receives no family sup-port. As a result, many students have to try to meet one of the other eligi-bility requirements. For too many, the answer is joining the military, going to war.

5   I am not saying that students should not enlist in the military. Would I have signed on if I had received financial aid? I don't know. I support our troops and enjoyed my time in the service. The military's values and dis-cipline and my experiences there have contributed to who I am today, and I am thankful for that. However, I don't believe that students should have to risk their lives to qualify for financial aid.

6   I am writing to you not only on my own behalf but for the well-being of my family and my country. The federal financial aid system ignores a majority of students in need of aid. Despite rising tuition costs, our finan-cial aid options are slim, and more and more students are not able to achieve a college education, our path to success. This problem is like a cancer; unless treated, it will spread and will hurt our nation's future.

Sincerely yours,
John Around Him

PAUSE: Summarize what Around Him says about the criteria for eligibility. What kind of evidence does he use in this paragraph?

PAUSE: Why is this conclusion effective?

1. Briefly summarize John Around Him's argument, including his main point and reasons. *Answers will vary.*

2. Where does Around Him acknowledge the opposing view? _____
Paragraph 5 _____

3. Write three questions you would ask for a quiz on this essay (and be able to answer your own questions). *Answers will vary.* _____

4. Is the argument a strong one? Why? _____

5. Which of the essays in this chapter is the best example of a good argument? Why? _____

Argument at a glance

Thesis statement
Includes the issue (topic) and your position on it

↓

Reason 1
Supporting examples, facts, and expert opinions

↓

Reason 2
Supporting examples, facts, and expert opinions

↓

Reason 3
Supporting examples, facts, and expert opinions

↓

Conclusion
Reminds readers of your position and makes a strong last attempt to convince them of that position

Write an Argument Essay

In this section you will write your own argument essay based on *one* of the following assignments. Use the following tools to help you.

1. Review the Four Basics of Good Argument (p. 299).
2. Use  as a basic organizer.
3. Use the Writing Guide: Argument checklist as you write and revise (pp. 321–22).

....

ASSIGNMENT 1 Writing about College, Work, and Everyday Life

Write an argument essay on one of the following topics or on a topic of your own choice. Select an issue that you care about so that you can argue powerfully.

COLLEGE
- Persuade one of your current instructors to raise the grade on your last assignment.
- Defend the following statement: "A college degree means something."
- Present your instructor with reasons why you should be able to make up a test that you missed.
- Write a letter to the Student Affairs office proposing a student service that does not currently exist.

WORK
- Argue against a company policy you find unfair.
- Argue that you should get a promotion.
- Argue that insurance companies should be allowed to use DNA testing.

- Argue that employers should or should not monitor employee e-mail use.

EVERYDAY LIFE
- Argue against a rent increase.

- Argue for or against McDonald's being sued by obese people who have eaten there regularly.

- Take a stand on a local issue or policy that you believe is unfair.

- Write a letter to your congressional representative asking him or her to work to change a law or policy that you believe is unfair.

ASSIGNMENT 2   Writing about Images

Artist Chris Jordan's photograph, "Prison Uniforms, 2007," is shown here in a close-up partial view and as the whole work appears on display on page 318 (**chrisjordan.com/gallery/rtn/prison-uniforms-set**). The entire photograph is

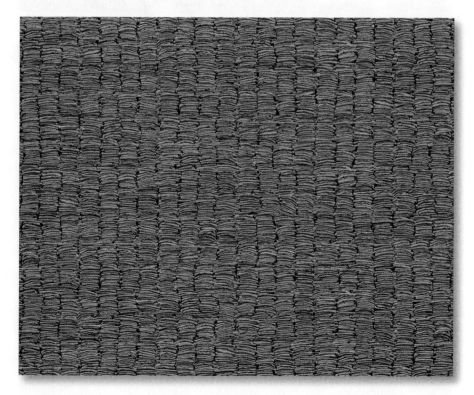

Copyright © Chris Jordan, Courtesy of Kopeikin Gallery.

Copyright ©
Chris Jordan,
Courtesy of
Kopeikin
Gallery.

10 x 23 feet in six vertical panels—in a word, *big*. It shows 2.3 million folded prison uniforms, one for each American in prison in 2005. (In 2011, that number remains approximately the same.) In part as a result of its particular laws and policies, the United States puts more of its population in prison, and keeps people in prison longer, than any other country. The number of inmates increased dramatically between 1980 and 2003, and the United States now has a problem with overcrowded prisons.

Write an essay in which you respond to Jordan's image and discuss the argument that you think he is making with it. How effective do you find his visual argument? Can a uniform stand for a person? Can an individual understand and connect with the giant numbers and statistics we face in today's society?

ASSIGNMENT 3 Writing to Solve a Problem

THE PROBLEM: An alumnus has given your college a large donation that is intended to improve the quality of student life. The president has set up a committee to determine several possible uses for the money, and you are one of the students on that committee.

ASSIGNMENT: Working either on your own or with a small group, first decide on three possible uses of the money that would improve the quality of student life. Then, choose one of them, and write a letter to the president arguing for this use of the donation. Be sure to include solid reasons for your choice.

RESOURCES: To help you decide which of the three possible uses you will argue for, you might type into a search engine key words related to areas in need of improvement at your college (for example, *[your college] computer center*). List any Web sites that you use.

....

ASSIGNMENT 4   Writing about Connections

Read the account of Yudi Romero before doing the assignment that follows.

COMMUNITY CONNECTIONS

Yudi Romero, Miami-Dade College
Vice-President, Lamba Omicron Delta

Yudi emigrated to Miami from Cuba with her mother and sister when she was young. At first, learning English was a struggle, but she graduated from high school and started college at Miami Dade. She knew that a college degree would help her in life, but she had no idea what to study. She was working and feeling removed from college life, "I just went to classes, to work, and home without ever meeting anyone." She had a friend who was also at the college and had become involved in Lambda Omicron Delta, a service society. Although she allowed her friend to bring her to a meeting, Yudi was reluctant to pledge because her life was already too busy. When she did pledge, she found that "being part of an organization that helps people is the best feeling in the world. My sorority sisters became like my family."

Yudi has been involved in many service events, many of which were fun as well as successful fundraisers for worthy causes. Being first a

(continued)

> member and then an officer of the sorority has built her leadership and or-
> ganizational skills. It has also helped her realize what she wants to study.
> She is now majoring in occupational therapy because she found, through
> her involvement with Lambda Omicron Delta, that she loves helping
> people. She wants other students to know, "In this life, you get what you
> give. Take advantage of the opportunities for participation that college of-
> fers every student. Don't miss out; this is your chance!"

TEACHING TIP
Have students read
and discuss their top-
ics and arguments
together.

ASSIGNMENT: Choose one of the following topics and write an argument essay.

■ Go to a meeting of a campus club or organization and ask a member why
he or she thinks students should be involved in that club or any other.
Then, write about the reasons he or she gives you. End with a statement of
whether you will attend another meeting or not, and why.

■ Read either the campus newspaper or a local one or listen to the local
news for several days. Choose an issue that you learn about there and
decide what your position is on that issue. Write an argument defending
your position.

■ Review your college's student handbook (if you do not have a copy, either
get one or read it online through the college's Web site). Choose a policy
that you do not agree with and write an argument supporting your position
on that policy.

ASSIGNMENT 5   Writing about Readings

RESOURCES
*Additional Resources
for Teaching Real
Essays with Readings*
has visual planning
forms for argument
and the other essays
covered in Part 2.
These forms are
also online at
bedfordstmartins
.com/realessays.

The examples of argument in this chapter cover the issues of lowering the
drinking age, eliminating mandatory class attendance in college, and revising
unfair federal financial aid provisions. At the heart of each of these issues is a
basic conflict between individual rights and institutional rules or laws. Keeping
this in mind, choose *one* of the following assignments.

■ Choose one of the issues covered in this chapter, and write your own pro
or con argument on the issue, using the evidence that the reading presents
but adding your own. Find at least one other source (either in print or
online) on the subject, and refer to that source to support your position. Be
sure to document your sources.

■ Choose a different issue that pits individual rights against institutional policies. Here are some examples of such topics.

— Should physician-assisted suicide be legal? (See the readings in
Chapter 49.)

— Should a college have the right to censor the contents of the college newspaper?

— Should military recruiters be allowed to visit high schools?

— Should same-sex marriage be banned?

— Should marijuana be legalized?

— Should the government be able to require that everyone have insurance coverage?

— Should students have to pass standardized tests to graduate from high school?

— Should junk food be banned from all public schools, including both elementary and high schools?

— Should college athletes be paid?

Write an essay responding to the question, and use at least one online or print source to support your position. Be sure to document the source.

■ Choose another issue that is important to you. (If you cannot think of one, try looking through a news magazine or newspaper, or go to **slate.com**, **salon.com**, **helium.com**, or **procon.org** or another news source.) Write an argument defending your position on the issue, using at least one source. Document any source that you use.

. . . .

Use the steps in the Writing Guide that follows to help you prewrite, draft, revise, and edit your argument. Check off each step as you complete it.

WRITING GUIDE: ARGUMENT	
STEPS IN ARGUMENT	**HOW TO DO THE STEPS**
☐ Focus.	• Think about your position on an issue and how you can persuade your readers of that position.
☐ Explore your topic. See Chapter 5.	• Think about why you have taken the position you have. • Prewrite to find good support for your argument.
☐ Write a thesis statement. Topic + Position = Thesis See Chapter 6.	• Write a thesis statement that includes your topic and your position. • Make sure it is a strong statement with a clear position. →

STEPS IN ARGUMENT	HOW TO DO THE STEPS
☐ Support your thesis. See Chapter 7.	• Provide facts, examples, and expert opinions to support your position. • Examine your reasons to make sure they are not faulty reasoning (see pp. 32–34). • Consider the opposing view. • Give details to strengthen each of your main points.
☐ Write a draft. See Chapter 8.	• Arrange your points by order of importance, leaving the one that will have the most impact until last. • Write topic sentences for each major point and paragraphs that demonstrate and prove them. • Write a conclusion that has energy and reminds your readers of your position and main support for it.
☐ Revise your draft. See Chapter 9.	• Get feedback using the peer-review guide for argument at **bedfordstmartins.com/realessays**. • With your audience in mind, read to make sure your supporting points are persuasive and complete. • Add transitions. • Improve your introduction, thesis, and conclusion.
☐ Edit your draft. See Parts 4 through 7.	• Correct errors in grammar, spelling, word use, and punctuation.
☐ Evaluate your writing.	• Does it have the Four Basics of Good Argument (p. 299)? • Is this the best I can do?

reflect Reread your response to the "write" prompt on page 299. Thinking back over what you have learned about effective argument, revise it as necessary to give good reasons and supporting evidence, consider opposing views, and show enthusiasm and energy from start to finish. Then exchange what you have written with a classmate, and see if you convince each other to try new points of view.

Part 3

Special College Writing Projects

Writing under Pressure

Tests and Essay Exams

You will need good reading and writing skills to do well on the many tests you will take in college. To become a good test-taker, you also need to develop good test-taking strategies.

Studying for Tests

Some students spend hours studying for a test that they then fail. Often, they have not studied efficiently. This chapter will give you tips on studying for tests and for taking essay exams and other types of timed writing assignments.

Here are four reliable tips to help you study for any exam.

TIPS FOR STUDYING

1. Ask about the test.
2. Predict what will be on the exam.
3. Use study aids.
4. Review actively.

Ask about the Test

Ask your instructor about an upcoming test. Just make sure you ask reasonable questions.

ASK	NOT
• What part of the course or what chapters of the text will it cover?	• What's on the test?
• Will the exam format be multiple choice, short answer, or essay?	• You're not going to give us essay questions, are you?
• Will we be allowed to use notes or books?	• We can just look up the answers, right?
• What percentage of my course grade will this count for?	• Is this test important?
• Can you recommend what to review?	• Do I need to read the book? Is the stuff you said in class important?
• Will we have the whole period to complete the test?	• How long is it?
• I know I have to miss class that day (give your reason). Can I arrange to take the test at another time?	• Is there a makeup test?

Write down your instructor's answers to your questions. Do not rely on your memory. You will be busy enough trying to remember the material you've studied for the exam without having to remember what your instructor said.

Predict What Will Be on the Exam

Whether you study with others or by yourself, make a list of what you think will be on the exam. Look over your notes, assignments, and any previous tests or quizzes. Try writing questions for that material, and then try answering your own questions.

If you are confused about any material, ask your instructor about it either in class, after class, or during your instructor's office hours. Your instructor will probably welcome questions by e-mail as well. Do not go into an exam knowing that you do not understand a major concept. Do not jeopardize your course grade when a few minutes of time may provide you with the information you need to pass the exam.

PRACTICE 1 Predicting the Content of a Test

Imagine that you are having a quiz in this class next week. With a partner or in a small group, identify three topics that might be on that quiz, and write one question for each.

TOPIC: Fragments

QUESTION: What are four kinds of sentence fragments?

TOPIC: *Answers will vary.* _____

QUESTION: _____

TOPIC: _____

QUESTION: _____

TOPIC: _____

QUESTION: _____

Use Study Aids

Use the following study aids to ensure your success.

- Reread your notes, looking especially for anything you have underlined or marked in some other way.

- If you are being tested on material from your textbook, reread chapter reviews, summaries, and boxes containing key concepts.

- Review handouts from your instructor.

- Review material in a variety of formats—videos, computer exercises, study guides, the course or textbook Web site, and so on.

Review Actively

The following are some suggestions for reviewing material actively.

- To review material from a book, take notes. Improve your retention by writing information in your own words.

- To review handouts, use a colored pen or highlighter to mark the most important ideas, most useful facts, and other key information.

- Say important material aloud. Many people learn well by hearing something in addition to seeing it. Discuss the material in a study group.

TEACHING TIP
Show students the study aids in a chapter of this book — the major headings, the boxed information, definitions, and so forth.

For more on active, critical reading, see Chapter 2.

- To review notes, rewrite them in other words or in another format. For example, if you have written an outline, transform it into a chart or diagram that shows the relationships among ideas (see, for example, the diagram on p. 67).

Test-Taking Strategies

Good test-takers know how to manage the test-taking process. They start with studying, and after they have studied, they move on to the next steps.

STRATEGIES FOR TAKING EXAMS

1. Be prepared.
2. Manage your nerves.
3. Understand the directions.
4. Survey the whole exam before starting.
5. Develop a plan.

Be Prepared

DISCUSSION
Early in the term, discuss how to prepare for an exam from the beginning of the course. Discuss the hazards of cramming for a test, and emphasize that college-level work requires consistent study over the course of the term.

If you have followed the advice in the first part of this chapter, you have already done the most important preparation. But do not arrive at the exam and discover that you have left something essential at home. Take some time the night before to think about what you need. Make a list of what to bring (pen? books? calculator? notebook? textbook? computer disk?), and assemble everything so that it is ready to go.

Manage Your Nerves

Get as much rest as possible the night before the exam, and allow extra time to get to class. Arrive early. Sit up straight, take a deep breath, and remind yourself that you know the material: You are prepared. If you are nervous, spend two minutes writing down what you are nervous about. Recent findings show that doing so helps nervous students do much better on tests. When your instructor starts to talk, look up and listen.

Understand the Directions

TEACHING TIP
Most people need to jot down directions that are given orally and highlight or make notes about written directions. Emphasize to students the importance of understanding directions.

Misunderstanding or ignoring directions is a major reason students do poorly on exams, so please pay attention to the advice here. First, listen to the **spoken directions** your instructor gives. It is tempting to start flipping through the exam as soon as you get it rather than listening to what your instructor is saying. Resist the temptation. Your instructor may be giving you key advice or information that is not written elsewhere, and you may miss it if you are not paying attention.

Second, when you begin the test, carefully read the **written directions** for each part of the test. Sometimes, students spend precious exam time answering all of the questions in a section only to find out afterward that the directions said to answer only one or two. If you find that you do not understand any part of the directions, be sure to ask your instructor for clarification.

Survey the Whole Exam before Starting

Look over the whole exam before doing anything. See how many parts the exam has, and make sure to look on both sides of all pages. Note the kinds of questions and the number of points each question or part is worth. The toughest questions (and the ones worth the most points) are often at the end, so leave enough time to answer those.

> **LANGUAGE NOTE:** Read the whole test through for any vocabulary you do not understand or cultural issues you are not familiar with. If you have questions, go to the teacher, and ask for clarification.

TEACHING TIP
Assure students that neither surveying nor developing a plan takes much time away from the test-taking process. Planning should take only three to five minutes.

Develop a Plan

First, **budget your time**. After surveying the whole test, write down how much time you will allow for each part. You might even find it helpful to calculate what time you want to start each section: Part 1 at 9:40, Part 2 at 9:55, and so on. Make sure you leave enough time for the parts with the highest point values, such as essay questions: They can take longer than you think they will. As you plan your time, keep in mind how much time you *really* have for the exam: A "two-hour" exam may be only one hour and fifty minutes once your instructor has finished giving directions. Remember also to leave a few minutes to check your work.

Second, **decide on an order**—where you should start, what you should do second, third, and so on. Start with the questions you can answer quickly and easily, but stay within your time budget on them, so you'll have time for sections you find more difficult.

Finally, **monitor your time** during the exam. If you find you are really stuck on a question and you are going way over your time budget, move on. If you have time at the end of the exam period, you can always go back to it.

DISCUSSION
Ask students to discuss their experiences with taking tests that have multiple parts (including standardized tests). What strategies not listed here did they find especially effective?

Answering an Essay Question

TEACHING TIP
Give students practice essay exams on topics that will allow them to determine how to focus their ideas.

An **essay question** requires writing several well-supported paragraphs in response to a question or prompt within a set amount of time.

Essay questions on an exam are usually worth more points than short-answer or multiple-choice questions, so they deserve special attention. Apply the following strategies to essay questions.

STRATEGIES FOR ANSWERING AN ESSAY QUESTION

1. Read and analyze the question.
2. Write a thesis statement.
3. Make an outline.
4. Write your answer.
5. Reread and revise your answer.

Read and Analyze the Question

Read an essay question carefully so that you know exactly what it calls for you to do. Look for three kinds of key words:

- Words that tell you *what subject* to write on.
- Words that tell you *how to write about it.*
- Words that tell you *how many parts* your answer should have.

Tells how many parts the answer should have

Discuss two major causes of personal bankruptcy in this country.

Tells how to write the response   Tells what subject to write about

Define and give examples of the phenomenon of global warming.

Tells how to write the response   Tells what subject to write about

The following chart translates some common types of essay questions into an action plan.

Analyzing Essay Questions

KEY WORDS	WHAT IS REQUIRED	SAMPLE ANSWER
"Analyze the theory of relativity."	Break into parts and discuss.	"The theory of relativity is made up of four components. . . ."
"Define *carpetbaggers*."	State the meaning, and give examples.	"*Carpetbaggers* were people who. . . ."
"Describe the steps in taking a blood pressure reading."	List and explain the steps.	"To take a person's blood pressure, first. . . . Next, ... Finally, ..."
"Discuss the causes of poor air quality."	List and explain the causes.	"Poor air quality is caused by several different factors. . . ."
"Discuss the effects of ozone levels."	List and explain the causes.	"Ozone levels affect air quality in several different ways. . . ."
"Discuss the meaning of obesity."	Define and give examples.	"Obesity, which the NIH defines as having a body mass index of 30 or higher, is reaching epidemic proportions in some parts of the industrialized world. . . ."
"Compare obsession and compulsion."	List and give examples of how the two items are similar. (Note: Sometimes the word *compare* can mean to write about *both* similarities and differences. When in doubt, ask.)	"Obsession and compulsion are both. . . ." "Obsession and compulsion share some traits such as . . . , but they differ in. . . ."

TEACHING TIP Ask students to bring in exams with essay questions from other classes. Look for the key words used on these exams — whether from this list or in addition to it — and discuss what they mean.

continued

KEY WORDS	WHAT IS REQUIRED	SAMPLE ANSWER
"Discuss the similarities and differences between obsession and compulsion."	List and give examples of how the two items are similar *and* how they are different.	"Obsession and compulsion share some traits such as . . . , but they differ in. . . ."
"Contrast obsession and compulsion." *or* **"Discuss the differences between** obsession and compulsion."	List and give examples of how the two items are different.	"Obsession and compulsion are related disorders, but they are not the same. . . ."
"Evaluate John Smith's argument."	Make a judgment about the subject, and support that judgment with reasons, opinions, and evidence.	"John Smith's argument in favor of *X* has several weaknesses. . . ."
"Explain the term *hyperactivity*."	Define and give examples.	"*Hyperactivity* is characterized by. . . ."
"Trace the development of the Industrial Revolution."	Explain the sequence of steps or stages of the subject.	"The Industrial Revolution in the United States began. . . ."
"Identify and discuss the major causes of *X*."	List and give examples.	"The major causes of *X* are. . . ."
"Should sex education be taught?"	Argue for or against with reasons, opinions, and evidence.	"Sex education is essential to . . . because. . . ."
"Summarize the concept of equal rights."	Give a brief overview.	"In the United States, the concept of equal rights is. . . ."

. . . .

PRACTICE 2 Identifying Key Words

Read the following essay questions, and then circle the key words that tell what subject to write about, how to write about it, and how many parts to write. In the space below each item, explain what the question is asking the writer to do.

TEAMWORK
This practice works well in pairs. Have students discuss the reasons for their responses.

> EXAMPLE: Define and illustrate dependency.
> *Give the meaning of the term dependency and give examples of it.*

1. Identify three causes of World War II.
List and explain three major causes of World War II.

2. Trace the stages of grieving.
Explain the steps in the grieving process.

3. Discuss the problem of the current energy crisis.
Identify and explain the problem of the current energy crisis.

4. Should drivers be banned from using handheld cell phones while driving? Why or why not?
Argue for or against banning drivers from using handheld cell phones.

. . . .

Write a Thesis Statement

Your response should include a thesis statement that is simple and clear. In the thesis statement, you may want to preview what you plan to cover in your answer because sometimes an instructor will give partial credit for information contained in the thesis even if you run out of time to explain fully.

For more on writing a thesis statement, see Chapter 6.

The best way to stay on track in an essay exam is to write a thesis statement that contains the key words from the essay question and restates the question as a main idea. It also helps to reread your thesis statement several times as you write your exam response.

The following are possible thesis statements for the four essay questions from Practice 2. (Because answers would vary, we have left blanks in these statements.)

There were three major causes of World War II: _____, _____, and _____.

People normally move through _____ stages of grieving: _____, _____, _____, (and however many there are).

The current energy crisis is a problem because it _____, _____, and _____.

Drivers should be banned from using handheld cell phones while driving because of _____ and _____ (or however many reasons).

· ·

PRACTICE 3   Writing Thesis Statements

TEAMWORK
This practice works well in pairs. Have students create at least two different thesis statements for each prompt.

Write possible thesis statements in response to the following sample essay exam questions. Even if you do not know the answer to the question, write a thesis statement that responds to the question and lets the reader know what you will cover (as in the possible answers above).

ESSAY EXAM QUESTION: Discuss the concept of First Amendment (free speech) protection as it relates to government document leaks on the Internet.

POSSIBLE THESIS STATEMENT: The protection of First Amendment rights is often cited as a reason not to ban government document leaks on the Internet.

1. Discuss the causes of the decline of the traditional "nuclear family" (two married parents and their children living under the same roof, without others).

   Answers will vary. _____

2. Explain the effects of binge drinking.

   _____

3. Trace the development of social networks.

   _____

4. Describe the atmospheric conditions in a thunderstorm that precede a tornado.

   _____

5. Discuss three advantages or three disadvantages of reliance on Twitter.

   _____

· ·

Make an Outline

Make a short, informal outline to map out your answer to an essay question or writing prompt. Include any important names, dates, or facts that occur to you. This outline will help you stick to your main points and remember essential details as you write.

For more on outlining, see Chapter 8.

The following short outline is for a possible essay on the causes for the decline of the traditional "nuclear family" (item 1 in Practice 3 on p. 334).

Thesis: Many forces have combined to cause a decline in the traditional "nuclear family," and they are not all negative.

Cause 1:	High rate of divorce
	Percentage of marriages that end in divorce
Cause 2:	Not as much social pressure to marry
	Many famous couples have children without being married.
Cause 3:	Families are defined in broader ways.
	Blended families
	Single parents
	Gay parents

Conclusion: Many reasons: Restate causes; make an observation (concept of "family" has evolved)

Write Your Answer

Your answer to an essay question should always be in essay form, with an introductory paragraph, several support points, and a concluding paragraph. It is a good idea to list all of your key points before providing details. Some teachers give partial credit for points that reflect your understanding of the topic, even if the points have not been developed. At the least, get down the thesis statement and then the first sentence of each support paragraph.

For more on the parts of an essay, see pages 51–52 and Chapters 7 and 8.

Here is an essay written by Meagan Willey, the student whose outline appeared in the previous section.

At least two factors, the high rate of divorce and the lessening social pressure to marry, have contributed to a decline in the traditional "nuclear family," which was once defined as a mother, a father, and their children. Today a family can consist of different configurations. The change came about gradually, but has resulted in a broader definition of *family*.

Introduction includes thesis statement and previews support points.

Support point 1 ——————   One factor was the high rate of divorce. As our book indicates, 50 percent of all marriages end in failure. That then results in different family configurations, with more blended families, parents and children from more than one marriage. The high rate of divorce has also caused many people to wait to marry until a later age or not to marry at all.

Support point 2 ——————   Another factor is that there is not as much social pressure to marry as there once was. Many people live together and have children without being married or marry after one or more of their children are born. Although this was happening anyway, some people believe that celebrities started the trend, or at least made it seem more common. Now there is not much social stigma attached to having children without being married.

New definition ——————   These two factors have resulted in a more inclusive definition of *family*. There are blended families as mentioned above, families with a single parent and children, families with same-sex parents and children, families with a mix of biological and adopted children, and families with a grandparent and grandchildren.

Reread and Revise Your Answer

After you have finished writing your answer to an essay question, reread it carefully. Then, revise your response to make it clearer, more precise, and more detailed.

Instructors sometimes use a *scoring rubric*, which consists of the criteria—or standards—they use to judge the quality of an essay. Although scoring rubrics vary from one instructor to the next, most rubrics used to evaluate writing include the following basic elements.

TEACHING TIP
If your department, university, or state has a rubric for grading standardized essay exams, distribute it to the students, and explain each point so that students will have a better sense of their audience's expectations.

- Fulfills the assignment. (Has the writer followed the assignment and answered the question? Does the essay stay focused on the topic?)

- Contains a thesis statement. (Does the essay clearly state the topic and the writer's main point about it?)

- Contains accurate information. (Does the essay include correct answers or reliable information?)

- Provides adequate support for the thesis. (Is the thesis backed by major support points, which are in turn supported by examples and details?)

- Uses correct language and expression. (Is the essay free of major errors in grammar, mechanics, and usage?)

Scoring rubrics often have points or percentages attached to each element. A typical scoring rubric might look like this.

RESOURCES
For advice on creating and using scoring rubrics, see *Practical Suggestions for Teaching Real Essays with Readings*.

ELEMENT	TOTAL POINTS POSSIBLE	STUDENT SCORE
Adherence to assignment	20	18
Thesis statement	15	15
Accurate information	30	25
Development of ideas	25	20
Language and expression	10	10
TOTAL POINTS	**100**	**88**

If your instructor provides you with a rubric, use it to set priorities as you review and revise your essay. Otherwise, consider the elements in the sample rubric as you revise your essay exam.

For more on revising, see Chapter 9.

Writing an Essay for a Writing Test

In college, mainly you will be writing responses to essays as part of course exams. However, you may also have to write an essay as part of an entrance or exit exam or a state test: to place in a course, to demonstrate your ability to move on to the next course, or to graduate. For the most part, the same strategies apply to these essays as to those for course exams, so use the same ones you have just learned in this chapter. However, there are some differences worth noting.

One difference between an essay for a course exam and an essay that is a writing test is the audience and purpose. In a course exam, the course instructor (your audience) will read your essay to determine if you have learned and understood certain concepts in the course, often those covered in a textbook or in class discussions. In this case, the purpose of your writing is to demonstrate your familiarity with course content. In an entrance, exit, or state exam, several people (your audience) may read your essay to determine your ability to present a main point and develop support for the main point in an organized, logical way in writing that is largely free of serious grammar errors. In this case, the whole purpose of the essay is to demonstrate that you can write clearly and correctly. This kind of essay is not to test your knowledge of specific course content but to see how well you can present your ideas. Your audience here will also be more sensitive to correct grammar (though instructors in any course will deduct points for poor writing), so you will need to leave some time to carefully revise and edit your essay.

The other difference, very much related to the purpose of the test, is that entrance, exit, and state exam questions are often more open-ended because their purpose is not to test your understanding of specific course content but to test your writing ability. Course exam essay question are designed to elicit specific information, and are like the ones in the chart on pages 331–32. Writing test questions more often draw on personal opinion, experience, and general knowledge. Sometimes, the questions call for you to construct an argument and ask you to respond to a question that starts with should, such as the following ones.

Should the government meddle in our dietary choices?

Should health insurance be mandatory for everyone?

Does education rely too much on standardized testing?

Are professional athletes paid too much?

Does sex education promote teen sex?

Are violent videogames dangerous?

Should the drinking age be lowered?

Should service learning be part of a college education?

Do social networks collect too much information about their users?

Should bullying be against the law?

For questions such as these, which ask your opinion, first decide what your position is on the issue. Write a thesis that contains your position and a preview of your reasons for your position. Answer the question posed.

ESSAY QUESTION: Should bullying be against the law?

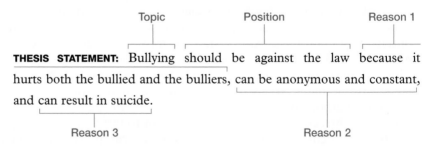

Then, your essay should go on to support the three reasons in your thesis statement.

Other open-ended questions may ask you to draw on personal experience or general knowledge, such as these.

What is the greatest lesson you have learned in life so far, and how did you learn it?

What do you think being a good citizen is?

What do you think the biggest problem facing your generation is, and why?

What is your biggest goal in life, and why?

Who has most influenced you, and how?

Who is a hero?

What does *having good character* mean to you?

Discuss how a particular book, film, or piece of music has had an impact on you.

What would people be surprised to know about you?

Discuss how your biggest strength may also be your biggest weakness.

To answer questions such as these, you will draw on different kinds of writing: narration, illustration, classification, definition, and so on. Take a few minutes to decide what your main point should be and then write a working thesis statement such as the ones that follow. Once again, your thesis should include the essay question.

ESSAY QUESTION: What is the greatest lesson you have learned in life?

Topic (includes question)

THESIS STATEMENT: The greatest lesson I have learned in life is that it is not what happens to you but what you learn from what happens that is important.

Main point (answers question)

Then, your response would give examples of how you have learned that lesson. Again, for a writing test essay, make sure to leave time to revise and edit since your essay will be evaluated for thesis, support, and correctness.

20

Finding and Evaluating Outside Sources

Preparing to Write a Research Essay

YOU KNOW THIS

You have done your own research.

- You go online to learn more about a product you are interested in.
- You ask friends about their jobs, courses, or instructors.

write about your experience doing research for a class or in everyday life. How did you find reliable information?

Most of your college classes will require you to write papers that draw not only on what you have observed, learned, and experienced but also on the knowledge of others, especially experts on the topic you are writing about. Using the knowledge of others to inform your work and to support the points you make is called using outside sources. Today, we have all kinds of information available to us, and finding information is usually easy. Your task, though, is not just to *find* information, but to find information that is reliable, objective, and relevant to your purpose. This chapter gives you the tools you will need to find and evaluate the vast information resources available to you before using it in your writing, or in any situation that requires you to make decisions or opinions based on information. You will use outside sources of information in such situations as the following.

COLLEGE   You are assigned a paper on targeting consumer preferences in a marketing course.

WORK   You want to find out what kinds of employment opportunities a new geographic area has. You also want to know what average salaries are for specific kinds of work.

EVERYDAY LIFE   You need information about a particular illness: its causes, symptoms, and treatments and questions you should ask a doctor.

Find Sources

Turn first to your college's library. Before even visiting the library, find its Web site by using a search engine and typing in your college's name and the word *library* (for example, "Santa Monica College library"). That will bring up the home page for the library. Look at the example of the Santa Monica College library's Web page, annotated to show the various entries there. Note that not only is there source material available (books, media, articles, and electronic), but also (in the left column) specific help on using the library and research topics.

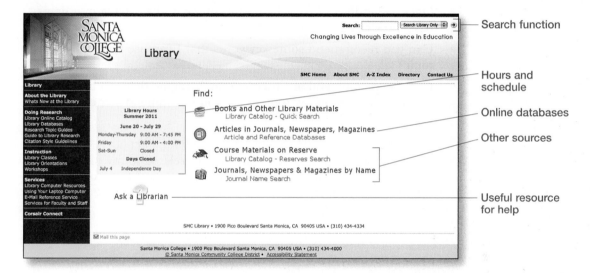

Next, visit the library in person. Most college (and public) libraries have hours that allow people with different schedules to use them.

Consult a Librarian

Librarians are essential resources to help you find appropriate information in both print and electronic forms. If your library allows it, make an appointment with a librarian to discuss your project and information needs. Or, you and some other students might arrange to go together for a helpful orientation. Note in the lists of useful resources on the left side of the Santa Monica College Library page that users can schedule a library class. Your college library's Web site may have the same option, but if not, visit the library to schedule the appointment. Before your appointment, make a list of questions you would like to ask, either based on what you have seen on the library Web site or some of the following questions.

QUESTIONS FOR THE LIBRARIAN

- Can you show me how to use the library catalog? How do I use the information I find there?

- What are databases? How does database information differ from what I can find in the library catalog?

- Can I access the library catalog and article databases when I'm not on campus?

- Based on my topic, what other reference tools would you recommend that I use for my research?

- Once I identify a potentially useful source in the catalog or a database, how can I find the material?

- Can you recommend some keywords that I can use for my particular topic?

- Can you recommend an Internet search engine that will help me find information on my topic? Can you recommend some useful reference sites for my topic?

- How can I tell whether an online source is reliable?

- I have already found some online articles related to my topic. Can you suggest some other places to look? How can I find good print sources on my topic?

Use Library Resources

Books

To find books on your topic, use the library catalog, which is likely to be online. Look at the Santa Monica College Library Web site on page 341, and see the "Library Catalog" link under the "Books and Other Library Materials" heading. When you are beginning your research, using a keyword as your search term can often be more effective than a subject search.

Keyword Searches

Keywords are the different words that can be used to name your topic. You type these keywords into the library catalog, online database, or search engine to find material on your topic. When you first look for sources, your keywords can be fairly general, such as those used by Michael McQuiston, a Temple College student whose research essay on using native plants for landscaping appears on page 373: *green landscaping*. When McQuiston searched his library's online card catalog for books, using the keywords *green landscaping*, he found:

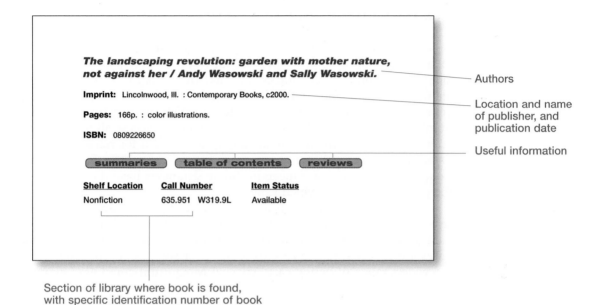

The landscaping revolution: garden with mother nature, not against her / Andy Wasowski and Sally Wasowski. — Authors

Imprint: Lincolnwood, Ill. : Contemporary Books, c2000. — Location and name of publisher, and publication date

Pages: 166p. : color illustrations.

ISBN: 0809226650

— Useful information

summaries   table of contents   reviews

Shelf Location	Call Number	Item Status
Nonfiction	635.951 W319.9L	Available

Section of library where book is found, with specific identification number of book

The entry has lots of information, such as the author and the publisher (the imprint), information McQuiston will need if he uses this book in his paper. It also offers reviews, a table of contents that shows what is in the book, and summaries, all of which will help McQuiston decide if this book is relevant to his research.

Along the bottom of the entry, McQuiston could see that the book was located in the nonfiction area of the library. The **call number** is a book's library identification number. With that information, McQuiston could go to the nonfiction section and, within that section, look for the book's number (635.951 W318.9L). Since library holdings are organized by subject matter, the books on either side of the one you want may also be related to your research subject. Most libraries are also able to transfer books without charge from other libraries, so if your library does not have a book, see if the librarian can order it via interlibrary loan. You can also usually log in to the library's Web site and request a book from another library. Just because a source is not found in your library does not mean it is unavailable. Again, consult a reference librarian if you have questions about what you find in the library catalog.

As you narrow your topic and search, you will use more specific keywords, as McQuiston does in the next chapter, which describes the process of writing a research essay.

NOTE For a complete online research guide, visit bedfordstmartins .com/researchroom.

Online Databases/Periodical Indexes

Most libraries, and college libraries in particular, subscribe to online **databases**, which are lists of all **periodical** (journal, newspaper, and magazine) articles on different topics. Because the library pays a subscription fee for these databases, only library members may them. By entering your student number on the college library Web site or your library card number on the public library's Web site, you can access all these helpful reference sources, which have already been checked for reliability. Some databases are general; some are more specialized with a focus on, for example, psychology or education. Some databases have the full texts of the periodicals online, which is handy.

Most college libraries subscribe to the most popular and comprehensive subscription databases: **Academic Search Premier**, **LexisNexis Academic**, **ProQuest Research Library**, and **InfoTrac**. These databases are excellent places to start looking for sources because they cover the widest range of periodicals. Michael McQuiston could search any of these databases, using his keywords, and immediately be referred to a variety of good sources on his topic.

NOTE Most resources referred to here can be accessed through a print reference guide as well as online. A librarian can direct you to the right area of the library and help you find good sources to start your research.

Because these databases include so many sources, a first search for McQuiston might show thousands of sites that included *green* and *landscaping*. An easy way to limit a keyword search is to enclose your topic in quotations ("green landscaping"). The search then shows only sources that include the two words together, making the search more specific.

Some specialized subscription online databases might also be useful in your search. These include newspaper Web sites (such as the *New York Times* and the *Wall Street Journal*) and topical sites such as AccessScience, Business Source Premier, and Criminal Justice Index.

The Santa Monica College Library site (see p. 341) also provides links to journals, newspapers, and magazines. While every library Web site is a little different, by looking at the Santa Monica College Library site, you can see what to look for and how to navigate your own library's resources.

Encyclopedias

NOTE Do not rely on Wikipedia for accurate information.

Encyclopedias give brief, basic information on a wide range of subjects. Like databases, encyclopedias can be general or specialized. A reliable general encyclopedia, the *Encyclopedia Britannica*, is usually available in print in the reference section of the library and online (**www.britannica .com**). Specialized encyclopedias exist for almost any subject you can imagine; you can find them in the reference section or in the online catalog. Encyclopedias might be a good place to get an overview of your topic, but many instructors want students to use more specialized sources in their writing.

Use Other Resources

Although your library is the best place to find good sources, other ways can work well too. But you should always make sure these types of sources are reliable.

Open Databases

Many databases, both general and specialized, are free and open. Some particularly good ones are InfoPlease (**www.infoplease.com**), the Librarian's Internet Index (**www.ipl.org**), the Library of Congress Online (**www.catalog.loc.gov/**), and Martindale's Reference Desk (**www.martindale center.com**). To use these, follow the same search and keyword instructions covered earlier in this chapter.

Search Engines

Using a general search engine to search the Web will bring you more sources on your topic, some reliable and some not. Some of the most popular search engines are

- Google (**www.google.com**)
- Bing (**www.bing.com**)
- Ask.com (**www.ask.com**)
- AltaVista (**www.altavista.com**)

To use a search engine, enter your keywords in the subject box. Michael McQuiston, the Temple College student, used Google and tried several variations on his search keywords, which netted the following results.

KEYWORDS	SEARCH RETURNS
green landscaping	More than 19 million results
"green landscaping"	More than 500,000 results
"green landscaping in dry areas"	0 results
green landscaping in dry areas	More than 3 million results

These figures are a little surprising: Putting the keywords *green landscaping* in quotations narrowed the number of entries, but adding the words *in dry areas* within the quotation marks did not further narrow the search; instead, it provided no entries at all. Taking away the quotations produced even more entries than "green landscaping." In this case, narrowing the search terms while using a general search engine resulted in the unwanted inclusion of many commercial sites, such as businesses that provide green landscaping services in dry areas. Finding good sites can require a long process of sifting through inappropriate sources for your research essay. Therefore, using library sources is often a better strategy than using general sources.

Statistical Sources

Statistical data are facts and figures. When they are directly related to the thesis of your research essay and are from a reliable source, they can provide very strong support. One good source of statistical data is the *Statistical Abstract of the United States,* published annually by the U.S. Census Bureau. It can help you find useful statistics related to social trends, social issues, population trends, economics, demographics, and other topics.

Online Research Sites

Online research sites constitute another valuable source of information on how to do research. At **bedfordstmartins.com/researchroom** (see p. 347), the publisher of this book hosts the *Bedford Research Room,* which includes guided tutorials on research processes; advice on finding, evaluating, and documenting sources; tips on avoiding plagiarism; and more. Other useful sites include Purdue University's Online Writing Lab (OWL) at **http://owl.english.purdue.edu**. This site offers a variety of materials and resources for writers, including research information.

Interview People

TEAMWORK
Have students interview each other on their research topics. They can write a short summary of the interview using both direct quotations and paraphrases.

Personal interviews can be excellent sources of information. Before interviewing anyone, however, plan carefully. First, consider what kind of person to interview. Do you want information from an expert on the subject or from someone directly affected by the issue? How would the experience or comments of each person help support your points? The person should be knowledgeable about the subject and have firsthand experience. When you have decided whom to interview, schedule an appointment.

Next, to get ready for the interview, prepare a list of five to ten questions. Ask open-ended questions (What is your position on regulating cell-phone use by drivers?) rather than questions that require only a simple yes-or-no response (Do you favor regulating cell-phone use by drivers?). Leave space for notes about the person's responses and for additional questions that may occur to you during the interview. Include in your notes the person's full name and qualifications and the date of the interview.

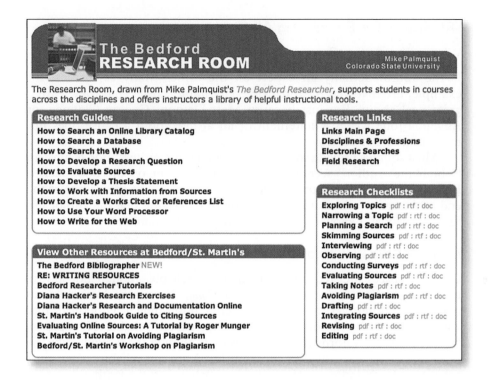

The Bedford
RESEARCH ROOM

Mike Palmquist
Colorado State University

The Research Room, drawn from Mike Palmquist's *The Bedford Researcher*, supports students in courses across the disciplines and offers instructors a library of helpful instructional tools.

Research Guides

How to Search an Online Library Catalog
How to Search a Database
How to Search the Web
How to Develop a Research Question
How to Evaluate Sources
How to Develop a Thesis Statement
How to Work with Information from Sources
How to Create a Works Cited or References List
How to Use Your Word Processor
How to Write for the Web

View Other Resources at Bedford/St. Martin's

The Bedford Bibliographer NEW!
RE: WRITING RESOURCES
Bedford Researcher Tutorials
Diana Hacker's Research Exercises
Diana Hacker's Research and Documentation Online
St. Martin's Handbook Guide to Citing Sources
Evaluating Online Sources: A Tutorial by Roger Munger
St. Martin's Tutorial on Avoiding Plagiarism
Bedford/St. Martin's Workshop on Plagiarism

Research Links

Links Main Page
Disciplines & Professions
Electronic Searches
Field Research

Research Checklists

Exploring Topics pdf : rtf : doc
Narrowing a Topic pdf : rtf : doc
Planning a Search pdf : rtf : doc
Skimming Sources pdf : rtf : doc
Interviewing pdf : rtf : doc
Observing pdf : rtf : doc
Conducting Surveys pdf : rtf : doc
Evaluating Sources pdf : rtf : doc
Taking Notes pdf : rtf : doc
Avoiding Plagiarism pdf : rtf : doc
Drafting pdf : rtf : doc
Integrating Sources pdf : rtf : doc
Revising pdf : rtf : doc
Editing pdf : rtf : doc

As you conduct the interview, listen carefully, and write down any important ideas. If you plan to use any of the interviewee's exact words, put them in quotation marks in your notes. Confirm the wording with the interviewee to be sure you have it correctly in your notes. (For more on using direct quotations, see page 360 of Chapter 21 and Chapter 39.)

NOTE: If you plan to record an interview (whether on tape, or using a digital recorder), get your subject's permission first. Recording what a person says without being granted permission is unethical and, in some states, against the law.

Evaluate Sources

Evaluating sources means judging them to determine how reliable and appropriate they are for your topic, your assignment, your purpose, and your audience. To evaluate sources, use the critical thinking and reading skills you have learned and used in earlier chapters. Before using a source for your paper, apply the following questions to all sources: print, electronic, and open access Web.

Questions for Evaluating All Sources

Who Is the Author?

Is the author actually an expert on the topic? Many celebrities, for example, are involved in worthwhile charitable causes that they learn a great deal about. But just because Matt Damon, George Clooney, or Angelina Jolie writes a statement or an article about a cause does not make him or her an expert.

Most sources provide some information about authors. Books have an "About the Author" section, usually at the end or on the book jacket. Periodicals have biographical headnotes or notes about the author at the end of the article. Read this information to make sure that the author has the authority and knowledge to make the source reliable.

Is the Source Well Known and Respected?

Certain sources are generally agreed to be reliable, though not always unbiased. National magazines such as *Time, Newsweek, National Geographic,* and others verify information before publishing it. Periodicals that you find on a subscription database are also usually reliable. Newspapers too usually verify information before using it, though the tabloids (like the ones sold in the supermarket checkout lines) are not reliable. Their purpose is to shock and entertain, not necessarily to tell the truth.

Is the Source Up-to-Date?

Look to see when a source was published. If your topic is in a rapidly changing field (for example, science or medicine), your source should be as recent as possible to include the most current knowledge. On the other hand, if you learn about a person or a work that is considered classic (something that has been respected for a long time), the publication date is not as important. For example, Michael McQuiston's topic, green landscaping, is a relatively new practice, so he should be looking for works that have been published recently. In his reading, however, if he learns of a practice that changed the whole direction of landscaping, that would be considered classic work. Depending on his purpose, he might want to include a reference to that work, in addition to new findings. Whatever your topic is, judge each possible source for how current the information is.

Is the Source Unbiased?

Every writer reflects some personal opinion on the subject he or she writes about. However, a good source balances those opinions with reasonable evidence. But facts and numbers can be used differently by people with different biases. For example, a researcher who believes in strict gun control may cite statistics about how many children are killed each year in gun accidents. A researcher who believes in the individual right to own guns may use statistics about how many people are killed in robberies or burglaries. Both writers use accurate numbers to argue different positions.

Consider the author's background to determine if he or she is likely to be biased in a way that interferes with reliability. In the gun issue, if an author is president of an organization named CeaseFire, he has a bias toward gun control. If an author is president of the National Rifle Association, she has a bias toward gun ownership. If you think an author is strongly advocating one side of an issue without addressing the other side, move on to another source, or include both sides in your essay.

Questions for Evaluating Web Sites

The Web is open to anyone with Internet access, which is one of the great things about it. Anyone can develop a Web site to promote anything he or she wants. That very openness means, though, that you have to be even more critical in evaluating information that you find on a Web site, especially if you are using a general search engine such as Google, Bing, or others.

The extension to the Uniform Resource Locator (URL) is the letters after the first period (or "dot"). Different extensions convey information about the site's sponsor.

EXTENSION	INDICATES
.com	a commercial or personal site
.edu	an educational institution's site
.gov	a government agency's site
.net	a commercial or personal site
.org	a nonprofit group's site

As a general rule, educational (.edu) and government (.gov) sites are likely to be reliable. The commercial and personal sites (.com, .net) may be good sources, but they may also be promoting the opinions of a biased person or group of people. A nonprofit group's site (.org) also may present either good or biased information. When a search brings you to Web sites with *.com, .net,* or *.org* extensions, find out about the sponsors of the sites and examine the sites for evidence of strong bias.

In addition to the questions that you would ask to evaluate any source, add the following, which use your critical reading and thinking skills.

QUESTIONS TO ASK IN EVALUATING A WEB SITE

- What is the URL extension?
- Who sponsors the site?

- Is there an "About" link? What does it tell me when I click on it?
- What is the purpose of the site?
- What kind of information is on the site?
- Does the site material indicate a bias? What is it?
- Based on the answers to the above, do I think information on the site is reliable and appropriate for my research essay?

PRACTICE   Look carefully at the two Web sites that Michael McQuiston found on his topic. In the space provided next to each number, explain what the corresponding numbered element tells you about the site.

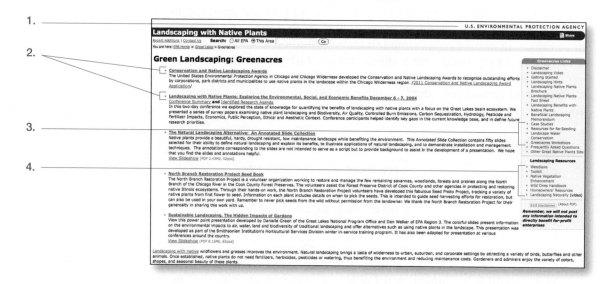

1. <u>name of government agency (U.S. Environmental Protection Agency)</u>

2. <u>links to information related to topic</u>

3. <u>reports on native landscaping</u>

4. <u>links to information about landscaping resources</u>

Other things I found out by going to the Web site: <u>Answers will vary.</u>

My evaluation of site: <u>Answers will vary.</u>

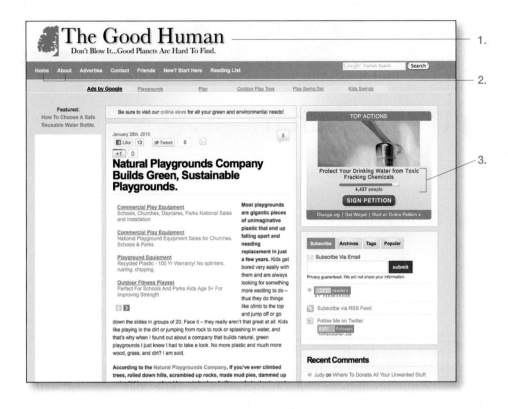

1. *Banner heading indicates purpose of site.*

2. What do I learn from going to the "Home" and "About" pages?
   Answers will vary.

3. *Petition box provides visual, allows interactivity, and facilitates activism among like-minded site visitors.*

   My evaluation of site: *Answers will vary.*

. . . .

   This chapter helps you find and locate good sources for a research essay. The next chapter will show you how to plan and write your research essay.

---

reflect Given what you have learned about how to find and evaluate sources, how would you change previous searches for information?

21

Writing the Research Essay

Using Outside Sources

This chapter will guide you through the process of writing a research essay. Throughout the chapter, we show how one student, Michael McQuiston, worked through key steps in the process. Michael's completed research essay appears on pages 373–77.

To write your research essay, follow these steps:

STEPS TO WRITING A GOOD RESEARCH ESSAY

1. Make a schedule.
2. Choose a topic.
3. Find sources (see Chapter 20).
4. Evaluate sources (see Chapter 20).
5. Avoid plagiarism by taking careful notes.
6. Write a thesis statement.
7. Make an outline.
8. Write your essay.
9. Cite and document your sources.
10. Revise and edit your essay.

Make a Schedule

After you receive your assignment, make a schedule that divides your research assignment into small, manageable tasks. There is no way that you can do every step the day (or even a few days) before the assignment is due, so give yourself a reasonable amount of time.

For more information on research papers, visit **bedfordstmartins** .com/researchroom.

You can use the following schedule as a model for making your own.

SAMPLE RESEARCH ESSAY SCHEDULE

Assignment: _____

(Write out what your instructor has assigned.)

Length: _____

Draft due date: _____

Final due date: _____

My general topic: _____

My narrowed topic: _____

TEACHING TIP
Walk students through the process of creating a schedule, starting with the date the essay is due and working backward. Suggest and discuss the amount of time they should allow for each key step.

STEP	DO BY
Choose a topic.	_____
Find and evaluate sources.	_____
Take notes, keeping publication information for each source.	_____
Write a working thesis statement by answering a research question.	_____
Review all notes; choose the best support for your working thesis.	_____
Make an outline that includes your thesis and support.	_____
Write a draft, including a title.	_____
Review the draft; get feedback; add more support if needed.	_____
Revise the draft.	_____
Prepare a works cited list using correct documentation form.	_____
Edit the revised draft.	_____
Submit the final copy.	_____

Choose a Topic

Your instructor may assign a topic, or you might be expected to think of your own. If you are free to choose your own topic, find a subject that you are personally interested in or curious about. If you need help, try asking yourself some of the following questions.

1. What is going on in my own life that I want to know more about?

2. What have I heard about lately that I would like to know more about?

3. What am I interested in doing in the future, either personally or professionally, that I could investigate?

4. What famous person—living or deceased—most interests me?

5. What do I daydream about? What frightens me? What do I see as a threat to me or my family? What inspires or encourages me?

6. Is there something I do in my spare time (sports, music, computer games) that I would like to know more about?

POSSIBLE TOPICS FOR A RESEARCH ESSAY

TEACHING TIP
Have students select three of these topics to write about in their journals. Their journal entries should answer the following questions: Why does this topic interest me? What would be my purpose in writing about this topic? What audience would be interested in reading about this topic? Why?

Animal rescue	Local community service options
Assisted suicide	Mandatory drug testing
Banning texting (in class, while driving)	Mandatory medical insurance
	Mandatory school uniforms
Causes of stress	Marijuana for medical purposes
Dieting/eating disorders	The minimum wage
Environmental issues	Music downloading
Ethics: business/political/personal	Obesity in the United States
Executive salaries	Online dating services
The family in America	Outsourcing jobs to foreign countries
Gambling	Patients' rights
Gay/lesbian marriage/adoption	Pets and mental health
Global warming	Presidential campaigns
Gun control	Reality television programs
Healthy eating	Rights of children of illegal immigrants
Identity theft	
An illness	Road rage
Limiting cell-phone use	Scams

Sexual harassment	Violence in the media
Standardized testing	Volunteerism
Veterans' issues	Women in military combat
Video games	

When you have chosen a general topic, you will need to narrow it using the same process you learned about in Chapter 5. Although a research essay may be longer than some of the other essays you have written, the topic still needs to be narrow enough to write about in the assigned length. It would be impossible, for example, to write a good five-page paper on "The Family in America Today." That general topic could be narrowed, as shown in the following diagram. The three topics in the second row are narrower than the main topic "family." See how two of the three are further narrowed:

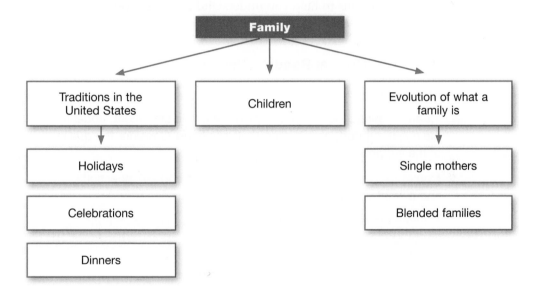

Next, the writer could try out one of the narrowed topics or further narrow those. Before moving ahead with a topic, check its appropriateness with your instructor if you have any doubt. You might also check library resources to see if information is available on your planned topic. You do not need to actually look at the sources at this point, but you should assure yourself that a reasonable number of sources exist on your topic.

Before writing a working thesis statement, choose a **guiding research question** about your narrowed topic. For example, a writer using one of the narrowed topics on "family," "celebrations," might start with a question like, "What functions do common family celebrations serve in the life of a family?"

In this chapter, you will see how Michael McQuiston's paper on green landscaping developed.

MICHAEL MCQUISTON'S GUIDING RESEARCH QUESTION

> What are the benefits of green landscaping?

In Chapter 20, you learned how to find and evaluate sources for a research essay. After choosing and narrowing a topic and developing a guiding research question, you are ready to find sources that you will use. As you read through a variety of sources to find ones that you will use and as you then more carefully read the sources you have chosen, use your critical reading skills to help you understand and effectively use the information in your research essay. Remember **2PR**.

2PR   The Critical Reading Process

- **Preview** the reading.

- **Read** the piece, double underlining the <u><u>thesis statement</u></u>, underlining the <u>major support</u>, and circling the transitions. Consider the quality of the support.

- **Pause** to think during reading to take notes and ask questions about what you are reading: Talk to the author.

- **Review** the reading, your marginal notes, and your questions.

Avoid Plagiarism

ESL In some cultures, copying someone else's work is a gesture of respect. Be clear with students about what constitutes plagiarism.

Plagiarism is passing off someone else's ideas and information as your own. Turning in a paper written by someone else, whether it is from the Internet or written by a friend or family member who gives you permission, is deliberate plagiarism. Sometimes, however, students plagiarize by mistake because they have taken notes that do not distinguish a source's ideas from their own or that do not fully record source information, including publication data. As you find information for your research essay, do not rely on your memory to recall details about your sources; take good notes from the start. For more on how to avoid plagiarism, visit the Bedford Research Room at **bedfordstmartins .com/researchroom**.

NOTE: This section's advice on recording, citing, and documenting sources reflects Modern Language Association (MLA) style, the preferred style for the humanities.

Keep a Running Bibliography

A **bibliography** is a complete list, alphabetized by author, of the outside sources you consult. A **list of works cited** is a complete list, alphabetized by author, of the outside sources that you actually use in your essay. Most instructors require a list of works cited at the end of a research essay. Some may require a bibliography as well.

You can keep information for your bibliography and list of works cited on notecards or on your computer. Whatever method you use, be sure to record complete publication information for each source at the time you consult it; this will save you from having to look up this information again when you are preparing your list of works cited.

The following is a list of information to record for each source.

TEACHING TIP
Ask students to bring in a draft bibliography after they have gathered and read their sources but before they finish writing the research paper. This will allow you to make sure they are compiling one.

BOOKS	ARTICLES	WEB PAGES/OTHER ELECTRONIC SOURCES
Author name(s)	Author name(s)	Author name(s)
Title and subtitle	Title of article	Title of Web page/online material
—	Title of magazine, journal, or newspaper	Title of site/larger work (e.g., online periodical)
City of publication and publisher	—	Name of sponsoring organization OR name of database
Year of publication	Date of publication	Date of publication or latest update
—	Page number(s)	Page, section, or paragraph numbers (if provided)
—	Volume number	Date you accessed the site
Medium (print)	Medium (print or Web)	Medium (Web/URL, CD)

TEACHING TIP
Have students practice citing and documenting sources throughout the semester. For example, if they write summaries of readings from this textbook, articles, or Web sites, ask them to use in-text citations and to include a list of works cited at the end of each summary.

Create Clear, Complete Records of Source Information

For each source that you take notes on, create an individual notecard or file on your computer. It should include the source's author(s) and title, the page number(s) where you found the specific information, and what method you are using to present it: summary or paraphrase (which are called **indirect quotations**) or **direct quotation** (which is word for word what the source says). A sample card or entry might look like this.

Last name(s) of author(s): List as in works cited list.

Category of information: McQuiston is sorting information into categories, each a benefit of green landscaping.

Information: Fact or idea to include in his paper.

Information source

Method used to record information: Direct quotation, summary, or paraphrase.

Welsh, Welch, Duble
Water Conservation
"In urban areas of Texas about 25 percent of the water supply is used for landscape and garden watering."
"Landscape Water Conservation: Xeriscape." *Aggie Horticulture.*
http://aggie-horticulture.tamu.edu/extension/xeriscape/xeriscope.html.
Direct Quotation

It is essential to note how you have recorded the information you might use in your paper. For example, if you transfer the exact wording of your note to your paper but have not recorded whether the note was a summary, a paraphrase, or an exact quotation, you risk plagiarizing the author. Even when you do not quote a source directly, you still must cite the source both in the text of your essay and at the end in the works cited list. The numbers after the indirect and direct quotations in the examples that follow indicate the page number where the words or ideas appear in the original work.

Indirect Quotation: Summary

TEACHING TIP
Remind students that they must cite source information even when they summarize and paraphrase. Students often think they need to cite only when quoting directly.

As you learned in Chapter 2, a summary is your condensed version of a longer piece of writing, which should include the main point of what you are summarizing. It should also be written as much as possible in your own words, and not by using many of the same words or phrases from the longer source.

One way to include outside source material as evidence or support in your own writing is to summarize. Look back at "Attendance in College Classes" on page 308, and then read the two summaries that follow here. The first is unacceptable because it uses too many words and phrases from the original. The second is an acceptable summary.

UNACCEPTABLE SUMMARY

> In his essay "Attendance in College Classes" (308), Donnie Ney argues that attendance in college classes should be optional, not mandatory. One reason he gives is that because students have paid for the class, they should have the right to decide whether to attend or not, particularly since their lives are often complicated. He also says that many students already know the course content and should not have to waste time hearing about it again. He also argues that optional attendance would result in smaller classes with more personal attention, which would be good for students who do choose to attend class.

Direct quotation should be in quotation marks.

Phrase is a common expression, though it is from the original; here, however, it is part of a pattern of using exact phrases from the original, and so should be in quotation marks.

Exact wording of original; should be in quotation marks.

ACCEPTABLE SUMMARY

> In his essay "Attendance in College Classes" (308), Donnie Ney argues that college students should not be required to attend classes because since they have paid for the course, like a consumer purchase, it should be up to the purchaser to use or not use it. He goes on to give other reasons that expand on his basic assumption that students have the right to choose if and when they should attend a class.

This summary does not use the language of the original, other than those words that refer to the topic. It also focuses on the main point of the piece rather than including all the specific support points. This summary gives the "big picture" of the essay in a condensed form.

Indirect Quotation: Paraphrase

A paraphrase restates another person's idea in your own words. Unlike a summary, a paraphrase is not necessarily a condensed version of the original; it is the idea expressed in your own words. You cannot paraphrase a whole essay or article. Again, you should not use the same wording or phrasing that is in the original. For example, the unacceptable summary above would also be an unacceptable paraphrase.

Because paraphrasing is a bit tricky, it may be easier for you to quote directly from the original piece. When you are taking notes from a source and find an idea that you might want to use, try writing the idea in your own words, and then look back at the original piece. If what you have written is too close to the words or phrases in the original, either try again or use a direct quotation.

Look back at the essay comparing anorexia and bulimia on page 265. The unacceptable and acceptable paraphrases are of information in the first paragraph.

Each of the shaded words and phrases are too close to the original. Though not direct quotes, the wording is close enough and the pattern of the phrases is the same as in the original.

UNACCEPTABLE PARAPHRASE

According to the authors (Hockenbury, 593–94), anorexia nervosa is weight loss that makes a person dangerously underweight. It is characterized by four key features that include a person refusing to keep a normal weight, having an intense fear of getting fat, being unable to see how she really looks, and denying how much weight she has lost.

ACCEPTABLE PARAPHRASE

According to the authors (Hockenbury, 593–94), the behaviors that characterize anorexics are an unwillingness to eat enough to be healthy because they believe they will get fat, and a lack of understanding that they are endangering themselves.

The ideas in this paraphrase are the authors', but the wording is very different from the original.

Direct Quotation

A direct quotation uses information from an outside source word for word, enclosing it in quotation marks (" "). Use a direct quotation when it is the best way to support your thesis. Avoid using long direct quotations in a short research essay, however, since most of what you write should be your own words. If you do use a direct quotation that is more than about forty words or four typed lines, indent the whole quotation, and do not use quotation marks.

SHORT DIRECT QUOTATION

According to psychologists Don Hockenbury and Sandra Hockenbury, "four key features define anorexia nervosa" (593).

LONGER DIRECT QUOTATION

> Psychologists Don Hockenbury and Sandra Hockenbury explain the disorder of anorexia nervosa this way:
>
> > Four key features define anorexia nervosa. First, the person refuses to maintain a minimally normal body weight. With a body weight that is 15 percent or more below normal, body mass index can drop to 12 or lower. Second, despite being dangerously underweight, the person with anorexia is intensely afraid of gaining weight or becoming fat. Third, she has a distorted perception about the size of her body. Although emaciated, she looks in the mirror and sees herself as fat or obese. And fourth, she denies the seriousness of her weight loss. (593–94)

Again, be certain to include how the information on your notecards is recorded (summary, paraphrase, or direct quotation) and the page number. You may think you will remember, but honestly, you will not. No one does. Rather than preparing good paraphrases, it may be easier to record the idea as a direct quotation. As you draft your essay, you will see that the material is a direct quotation, and you can then take the time to paraphrase carefully.

For more on using quotations correctly, see Chapter 38.

Write a Thesis Statement

After you have taken notes on the sources you gathered, you should be ready to write a thesis statement, which states the main idea of your research essay. You can start by turning your guiding research question into a statement that answers the question, as Michael McQuiston does below. Note how he revises his thesis to make it more forceful and concrete.

For more on writing a thesis statement, see Chapter 6.

> **MICHAEL MCQUISTON'S GUIDING RESEARCH QUESTION:** *What are the benefits of green landscaping?*
>
> **DRAFT THESIS STATEMENT:** *There are many clear benefits of green landscaping.*
>
> **REVISED AFTER TAKING NOTES FROM SOURCES:** *Landscaping with drought-tolerant native plants conserves water, reduces the use of toxic soil conditioners, and makes maintenance easier.*

As you write and revise your essay, your thesis statement may change, but having a good working one helps you focus your writing and see where you might need to do additional research.

For more on outlining,
see Chapter 8.

Make an Outline

To organize your notes, you need to make an outline that shows how
you will support your thesis. First, write down your thesis statement.
Then, review your notes to decide what your three or four major support points will be. Write these under your thesis statement and number
them. Under each of your major support points, write two or three supporting details, and number them.

As you read McQuiston's outline, note that although he started with
four benefits of green landscaping (*water conservation, fertilizers/safety,
effect on wildlife, maintenance*), as he read and took notes, he decided to
put "effect on wildlife" into the "fertilizers/safety" category. Note also
that he is reviewing his organized notes and sources and trying to fit
them into appropriate places in his essay (the names in parentheses and
boldface).

MICHAEL MCQUISTON'S OUTLINE

   I.   **Thesis Statement (introductory paragraph):** Landscaping with
        drought-tolerant native plants conserves water, reduces the use of
        toxic soil conditioners, and makes maintenance easier.

First support point — II. **Water Use**

Supporting details —   A. A limited natural resource already strained
                             B. Landscaping uses lots of water **(Welsh?)**
                             C. Native plants **(Tufts?)**
                                 1. use less water, drought-tolerant
                                 2. many kinds
                                 3. lower water bills/save money and water

Second support
point —   III. **Fertilizers/Pest Control/Safety**

                             A. Poisonous, kids, pets **(Native Plant, Texas Wildscapes?)**
Supporting details —   B. Good bugs/wildlife
                             C. Native plants use little or none

Third support point — IV. **Maintenance**

Supporting details —   A. Foreign plants, lots of water, lots of time and money
                             B. Native plants, not much maintenance **(Lueck?)**

                        V. **Conclusion**
                             A. Review benefits
                             B. Observation

Write Your Essay

Using your outline, write a draft of your research essay. (For more information on writing a draft, see Chapter 8.)

Your **introduction** should include your thesis statement and a preview of the support you will provide in the body of the essay. If you are
taking a stand on an issue, the introduction should let your readers know
what your position is. The **body** of the essay will present your major support points for your thesis backed by supporting details from your research.
The **conclusion** will remind readers of your main point and make a further observation based on the information you have presented.

As you write, incorporate your sources into your paper with **introductory phrases**. Most often, you will state the name of the source or
author before adding the information you are using. Use a comma after
the introductory phrases.

INTRODUCTORY PHRASE IDENTIFYING SOURCE

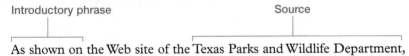

Introductory phrase   Source

As shown on the Web site of the Texas Parks and Wildlife Department,

INTRODUCTORY PHRASE IDENTIFYING AUTHOR AND SOURCE

In his article "Sustaining Mother Nature with Native Plants," Bill Ward
states,

Common Introductory Phrases

according to [source]

as [source] claims   says

          explains   shows

          notes   states

          points out   writes

When you have finished writing your draft essay, take a break from it.
Then, definitely allow time to reread, revise, and edit it. At this point, you
might read the draft essay and see that you need a bit more support from
outside sources. Perhaps you can find more in the sources you have already
been using, or you may want to find another source to support your thesis
statement.

All the sources that you use must be cited correctly where you use them in your paper, as well as at the end of the paper, in the Works Cited list. The sections that follow give you the correct format for documenting in-text citation and works cited. If you are using a type of source that you do not find in these sections, visit **bedfordstmartins.com/ researchroom** where you will find the documentation format for every kind of source imaginable.

For more information on documenting sources, visit bedfordstmartins .com/researchroom.

Cite and Document Your Sources

You need to include **in-text citations** of sources as you use them in the essay. You also need to document, or give credit to, your sources at the end of your research essay in a **list of works cited**.

Few people can remember the specifics of correct citation and documentation, so be sure to refer to this section or the reference text that your instructor prefers. Be sure to include all of the correct information, and pay attention to where punctuation marks such as commas, periods, and quotation marks should go.

There are several different systems of documentation. Most English professors prefer the Modern Language Association (MLA) system, which is used in this chapter. However, when you are writing a research paper in another course, you may be required to use another system. When in doubt, always ask your instructor.

Use In-Text Citations within Your Essay

Along with an introductory phrase that smoothly incorporates information from an outside source into your writing, your sources need to be cited where they are used and according to correct documentation format. In-text citations are shorter than Works Cited citations, but each must correspond to an entry in the Works Cited list.

The following section shows you what you need to include in an in-text citation for various kinds of sources. Use this format for any source material you are using: a summary, a paraphrase, or a direct quotation. In every case, insert the citation after the material you have used. If you use a direct quotation, the citation comes after the end quote and before the period ending the sentence.

NOTE: The formats given below are for print sources. When you cite a Web source, use page numbers if available. If the source is not paged, use the paragraph number instead. If there are no paragraphs, cite the author, title of the part of the Web site, or the Web site's sponsor.

The series of dots (called ellipses) in the following examples indicate that words have been left out.

Two examples are provided for each citation:

1. The author is named in an introductory phrase, with the page or paragraph number in parentheses.

2. The author is not named in the introductory phrase, and the author's name and page or paragraph number appear in parentheses.

One Author

> As David Shipler states, ". . ." (16).

> The number of people who work and fall below the poverty line has increased dramatically (Shipler 16).

Two or Three Authors   Use all authors' last names.

> Quigley and Morrison found that . . . (243).

> Banks and credit card companies are charging many more fees . . . (Quigley and Morrison 243).

Four or More Authors   Use the first author's last name and the words *et al.* (*et al.* means "and others").

> According to Sen et al., . . . (659).

> The overuse of antibiotics can result in . . . (Sen et al. 659).

Group, Corporation, or Government Agency   Use the name of the group, corporation, or government agency. The source can be abbreviated in the parentheses, as shown in the second example.

> The Texas Parks and Wildlife Department offers guidelines for landscaping . . . (26).

> Texas has more native plants than any other . . . (Texas Parks and Wildlife Dept. 26).

Author Not Named   Use the article title in quotations, shortened if it is a long title.

> In the article "Texas Wildscapes," . . . (7).

> Many areas of Texas are filled with drought-tolerant native . . . ("Texas Wildscapes" 7).

Encyclopedia or Other Reference Work   Use the name of the entry you are using as a source.

> In its entry on xeriscaping, the *Landscape Encyclopedia* claims that . . . ("Xeriscaping").

> Xeriscaping is often used in . . . ("Xeriscaping").

Work in an Anthology   Use the name of the author(s) of the piece you are using as a source.

> As Rich Chiappone believes, . . . (200).

> Fly fishing is as much a spiritual . . . (Chiappone 200).

Interview, E-mail, Speech   Use the name of the person interviewed or the author of an e-mail.

> As University of Texas Vice President of Student Affairs Juan Gonzalez said in an interview. . . .

> Students have many resources available to . . . (Gonzalez).

Use a Works Cited List at the End of Your Essay

DIRECTORY OF MLA WORKS CITED

Books

One author   367

Two or three authors   368

Four or more authors   368

Group, corporation, or government agency   368

Editor   368

Work in an anthology   368

Encyclopedia   369

Periodicals

Magazine article   369

Newspaper article   369

Editorial in a magazine or newspaper, author known   369

Editorial in a magazine or newspaper, author unknown   369

Article, scholarly journal with numbered volumes   370

Article, scholarly journal without numbered volumes   370

Electronic Sources

Work from a library subscription database (such as InfoTrac)   370

Online periodical   370

Short work from a Web site   371

Other Sources

Personal interview   371

E-mail   371

NOTE: Works cited entries that have a month and day as part of the publication date are formatted so that the date appears before the month; the month is abbreviated (Jan., Apr., Sept.); and there is no comma between the month and year:

WORKS CITED DATE STYLE: 14 Mar. 2011

Books

One Author

Author's Last Name, First Name. *Title of Book.* Publisher Location: Name of Publisher, Publication Date. Medium of Publication.

Shipler, David K. *The Working Poor: Invisible in America.* New York: Knopf, 2004. Print.

For each set of entries, the first example shows the format; the second is an example of the format.

Note that titles of books are in *italics*.

Two or Three Authors

Author's Last Name, First Name, and Other Authors' First and Last Names. *Title of Book.* Publisher Location: Name of Publisher, Publication Date. Medium of Publication.

Picciotto, Richard, and Daniel Paisner. *Last Man Down: A New York City Fire Chief and the Collapse of the World Trade Center.* New York: Berkeley, 2002. Print.

Four or More Authors

Author's Last Name, First Name, et al. *Title of Book.* Publisher Location: Name of Publisher, Publication Date. Medium of Publication.

Roark, James L., et al. *The American Promise: A History of the United States.* 4th ed. Boston: Bedford/St. Martin's, 2009. Print.

Group, Corporation, or Government Agency

Name of Group, Corporation, or Agency. *Title of Book.* Publisher Location: Name of Publisher, Publication Date. Medium of Publication.

American Cancer Society. *The American Cancer Society's Guide to Pain Control.* New York: McGraw-Hill, 2004. Print.

Editor

Editor's Last Name, First Name, ed. *Title of Book.* Publisher Location: Name of Publisher, Publication Date. Medium of Publication.

Canellos, Peter S., ed. *The Last Lion.* New York: Simon & Schuster, 2009. Print.

Work in an Anthology

Selection Author's Last Name, First Name. "Title of Selection in the Anthology." *Anthology Title.* Ed. First and Last Name of Anthology Editor. Publisher Location: Name of Publisher, Publication Date. Pages of Selection. Medium of Publication.

Brown, Sterling A. "Riverbank Blues." *250 Poems: A Portable Anthology.* 2nd ed. Boston: Bedford/St. Martin's, 2009. 141-42. Print.

Encyclopedia

Entry Author's Last Name, First Name. "Title of Entry." *Title of Encyclopedia.* Edition Number [1st, 2nd, 3rd] ed. Date of publication. Medium of Publication.

Araya, Yoseph. "Ecology of Water Relations in Plants." *Encyclopedia of Life Sciences.* Apr. 2007. Web. 4 Apr. 2010.

NOTE The citation here is for an online encyclopedia. Note that the entry includes the date the article was accessed (4 Apr. 2010).

Periodicals

Magazine Article

Author's Last Name, First Name. "Title of Article." *Title of Magazine* Day Month Year of Publication: Medium of Publication.

Kluger, Jeffrey. "One Weird Dinosaur." *Time* 11 Oct. 2010: 44-45. Print.

Note that titles of periodicals are in italics.

Newspaper Article

Author's Last Name, First Name. "Title of Article." *Title of Newspaper* Day Month Year of Publication: Page Number [if Print]. Medium of Publication.

Barringer, Felicity. "Indians Join Fight for an Oklahoma Lake's Flow." *New York Times* 12 Apr. 2011: A1+. Print.

Editorial in a Magazine or Newspaper, Author Known

Author's Last Name, First Name. "Title of Article." *Title of Newspaper* Day Month Year of Publication: Page Number [if Print]. Medium of Publication.

Udall, Don. "When Someone Is Alive but Not Living." Editorial. *Newsweek* 14 June 1999: 12. Print.

Editorial in a Magazine or Newspaper, Author Unknown

"Title of Article." Editorial. *Title of Magazine or Newspaper* Day Month Year of Publication: Page Number [if Print]. Medium of Publication.

"Growing Smart." Editorial. *Miami Herald* 29 Apr. 2010. Web. 20 May 2010.

Article, Scholarly Journal with Numbered Volumes

Author's Last Name, First Name. "Title of Article." *Title of Journal* Volume Number. Issue Number (Year of Publication): Page Number [if Print]. Medium of Publication.

Fountain, Glinda H. "Inverting the Southern Belle: Romance Writers Redefine Gender Myths." *Journal of Popular Culture* Volume 41. 1 (2008): 37-55. Print.

Article, Scholarly Journal without Numbered Volumes

Author's Last Name, First Name. "Title of Article." *Title of Journal* Issue Number (Year of Publication): Page Number [if Print]. Medium of Publication.

Thiel, Peter. "The Optimistic Though Experiment." *Policy Review* 147 (2008): 17-37. Print.

Electronic Sources

The format for citing electronic periodicals follows much of the same format as for print periodicals, so refer to the entries in the previous section for journals with numbered volumes.

Work from a Library Subscription Database (such as InfoTrac)

Author's Last Name, First Name. "Title of Article." *Title of Periodical* Volume number. Issue number (Year of Publication): Page Numbers. *Name of Database.* Web. Date of access.

McManus, John F. "Global Warming Skeptic Remains Adamant." *New American* 27.2 (2011): 9. *InfoTrac.* Web. 31 Mar. 2011.

Online Periodical

Author's Last Name, First Name. "Title of Article." *Title of Online Periodical.* Name of Periodical Publisher, Day Month Year of Article Publication. Web. Day Month Year of Access.

Manjoo, Farhad. "Is Something Rotten at Apple?" *Slate.* Slate Group, 25 Aug. 2008. Web. 14 Feb. 2011.

Short Work from a Web site   If no author is given, omit this information. If no site sponsor is listed, use N.p. If no date of publication is available, use n.d.

> Author's Last Name, First Name. "Title of Work." *Title of Web Site.* Name of Site Sponsor, Day Month Year of Publication. Web. Day Month Year of Access.

> "In Her Own Words." *Lady Bird Johnson Wildflower Center.* Univ. of Texas at Austin, 2010. Web. 4 Apr. 2011.

Note that titles of Web sites are in italics.

Other Sources

Personal Interview

> Last Name, First Name of Person Interviewed. Personal interview. Day Month Year of Interview.

> Okayo, Margaret. Personal interview. 16 Apr. 2009.

E-mail

> Last Name, First Name of Author of E-mail Message. "Subject of E-mail." Name of Person Who Received E-mail. Day Month Year E-mail Received. E-mail.

> Willey, Liz. "Happy Holidays from Paraguay." Message to Susan Anker. 4 Jan. 2011. E-mail.

For citation examples for other electronic sources, visit bedfordstmartins .com/researchroom.

Revise and Edit Your Essay

After a break, reread your draft with fresh eyes and an open mind. Then, ask yourself these questions.

- Does my introduction state my thesis?
- Does each of the body paragraphs contain a topic sentence that directly supports my thesis? Do the supporting details in each paragraph relate to and explain the topic sentence?

- Do I provide a conclusion that reminds readers of my main point and makes a further observation?

- Have I included enough support for the thesis that readers are likely to see my topic the way I do? Is there anything else I could add to make my point?

- Do transitions help readers move from one idea to the next?

- Have I integrated source material smoothly into the essay? Do I need to smooth out anything that seems to be just dumped in?

- Have I reread the essay carefully, looking for errors in grammar, spelling, and punctuation?

- Have I cited and documented my sources?

- Are all of my citations and Works Cited entries in correct form (MLA or whatever style the instructor specifies)?

- Is this the best I can do?

For more on revising, see Chapter 9. When checking for grammar, spelling, and punctuation errors, consult Parts 4 through 7 of this book.

After reading the annotated student essay that follows, use the Writing Guide on page 378 to write your research essay.

Sample Student Research Essay

The student essay that follows is annotated to show both typical features of research essays (such as references to sources) and elements of good writing (such as the thesis statement and topic sentences). The paper also shows formatting (such as margins, spacing between lines, and placement of the title). Your instructor may specify different or additional formatting in class or in your syllabus.

McQuiston 1 — Student's last name and page number at top of each page.

Michael McQuiston
Professor Bicknell
Composition 1 ——————————————— Course
21 Apr. 2010 ——————————————— Date

To Be Green or Not to Be Green — Title centered

 When people make landscaping decisions, many do not realize that the choices they make affect not just the immediate appearance of their yard, but also the present and future environment. Lady Bird Johnson, a champion of — Introductory phrase native landscaping, once said, "My special cause, the one that alerts my interest and quickens the pace of my life, is to preserve the wildflowers and native plants that define the regions of our land—to encourage and promote — Direct quotation their use in appropriate areas" ("In Her Own"). Many people share her feelings — Introduction and might want to know how landscaping can accomplish such preservation. When planning your landscaping, it is important to choose plants that will not only be aesthetically pleasing, but low-maintenance and cost-effective as well. After owning a lawn care and landscape business in Texas for six years, I am a firm believer in green landscaping. <u>Landscaping with drought-tolerant native plants conserves water, reduces the use of toxic soil conditioners, and requires</u> — Thesis statement <u>little maintenance.</u>

 As the world's population grows, it strains our earth's limited supply of natural resources. One resource essential to both plants and animals is water. Many cities and towns already restrict watering during the hot summer months to certain days of the week or certain times of day. In an online article written for Texas A&M University, Welsh, Welch, and Duble state that "in urban areas of Texas about 25 percent of the water supply is used for landscape and garden — Body paragraphs watering." Some homeowners argue that water is necessary to ensure the survival of the plants in their yards.

 However, part of the problem lies with the types of flowering plants, trees, and grass used in urban and suburban landscaping, many of them to achieve a certain "look." But these plants can require a great deal of water, as they often originate in areas with much higher rainfall per year or a more

McQuiston 2

constant amount of rain throughout the year. In order to sustain plants native to a climate zone that gets more rain, many homeowners not only see their water bills double during the arid summer months, but also contribute to the overall potential environmental water-shortage problem.

First support point

In-text citation

Fortunately, there is a way to have a beautiful yard in Texas without depleting our water supply: use plants that are drought-tolerant or native to the area. The nonprofit organization Wild Ones Natural Landscapers defines *native plants* as "those that were growing naturally in the area before humans introduced plants from a distant place" ("Landscaping"). Plants native to a certain area can survive with the amount of water available through local bodies of water and rainfall. Some native Texas plants that will still look beautiful in the midsummer after two weeks of record-high temperatures and drought include flowers such as the Bluebonnet, Indian Blanket, Indian Paintbrush, Lantana, and many others, as well as many shrubs and trees. Homeowners need only ask at their local nursery or ask a landscape

Body paragraphs

Support point

professional to find out what plants, grass, and trees are native and drought-tolerant. Many respected Web sites also provide similar advice. Green landscaping significantly reduces people's water bills and at the same time conserves water, a limited natural resource.

On a typical Saturday in suburbia, one might hear, "Don't let the kids go in the yard today. I put down fertilizer." But, wait — aren't the pets and other wildlife out there too? Although many homeowners and landscape services recognize the harmful effects of fertilizer and pesticides, they think having the "best-looking yard on the block" is worth the risk. According to the California Department of Pesticide Regulation's "Community Guide to Recognizing and Reporting Pesticide Problems," pesticides are safest if used properly, but they are still dangerous. Children and people with asthma or other chronic diseases are much more likely to get sick from pesticides than healthy adults, and "some individuals are also more sensitive to the odor or other irritant effects of certain pesticides" (29).

In-text citation

Using native plants and grasses instead of turf grass in the landscape eliminates the need for fertilizers and pesticides, making the yard a safer place

McQuiston 3

for both people and beneficial insects. Jane Scott, a gardener and naturalist, argues in her book *Field and Forest* that although the creation of a landscape of any kind causes some disturbance of land and soil, not all the harm landscaping and gardening does is necessary, and native plants would help reduce our environmental impact (4). Native plants do not need fertilizer to condition the soil because it is the soil they will naturally grow best in; there is no need to worry about the correct Ph balance or the perfect balance of nitrogen-potash-iron in the fertilizer. The need for pesticides is also diminished because plants that grow naturally in an area have developed defenses against harmful local insects.

Green landscaping also saves local wildlife, which can have a hard time finding food and water in the hot, dry summer months. Natural vegetation not only provides a safe haven for these creatures, but also nourishes them. Planting native and drought-tolerant vegetation in the yard transforms it into an extension of these creatures' homes, and in exchange for food, water, and shelter, the creatures offer homeowners an exclusive peek into the wild world around them. The Texas Parks and Wildlife Department recognizes the importance of native plants in providing food for native species of animals, birds, and butterflies, even going so far as to offer a "habitat restoration and conservation plan for rural and urban areas" ("Texas Wildscapes"). Bill Ward's article "Sustaining Mother Nature with Native Plants" illustrates the necessity of native plants for insect life. Monarch butterfly larvae depend on the milkweed for their survival, but as can be gathered from its name, this Texas native is often eradicated because it is considered a weed. "Bugs in native plant gardens," Ward states, "are helping to sustain the ecosystem by supporting a diverse and balanced food web. The same cannot be said about yards landscaped with predominantly exotic plants."

In addition to the environmental effects of nonnative landscape plantings, the regular upkeep of a nonnative lawn can prove too much for busy homeowners. What began as the best-looking yard on the block can quickly deteriorate into the neighborhood eyesore without the necessary maintenance and regular application of extra water and pesticides. While all plants require

Paraphrase

Body paragraphs

McQuiston 4

Body paragraphs

some care, native plants require far less than the transplanted ones, and Jane Scott argues that native plants are just as attractive as common exotics: "The more we know about the native plant communities that surround us, the more we will come to appreciate their inherent beauty and diversity and the more effectively we can accommodate them in the places where we live" (4). So, native plants offer peace of mind that the yard will look good season after season without constant daily care.

Observation

In this time of growing environmental awareness, planting nonnative, high-maintenance plants is irresponsible. Native plants do not strain the environment, and they provide food and shelter for various species of wildlife.

Review of support

The low-maintenance nature of native plants makes them friendly to the busy homeowner concerned about the environment. With less fertilizer and pesticide on the lawn, the yard will be a healthier place for families to spend their time and enjoy the outdoors. Green landscaping makes sense for everyone, for now and for the future. Be green.

McQuiston 5

Works Cited

"Community Guide to Recognizing and Reporting Pesticide Problems."
     California Department of Pesticide Regulation. State of California,
     Apr. 2008. Web. 11 Apr. 2011. <http://www.cdpr.ca.gov/docs/dept/
     comguide/index.htm>.

"In Her Own Words." *Lady Bird Johnson Wildflower Center.* Univ. of
     Texas at Austin, 2010. Web. 4 Apr. 2011. <http://www.wildflower
     .org/herownwords/>.

"Landscaping with Native Plants." *Wild Ones.* Wild Ones Natural
     Landscapers, May 2008. Web. 3 Apr. 2011. <http://www.for-wild
     .org/landscap.html>.

Scott, Jane. *Field and Forest.* New York: Walker, 1992. Print.

"Texas Wildscapes: Gardening for Wildlife in Backyards, Schoolyards,
     and Corporate Parks." *Texas Parks and Wildlife.* Texas Parks &
     Wildlife Department, Feb. 2010. Web. 2 Apr. 2011. <http://www
     .tpwd.state.tx.us/huntwild/wild/wildscapes/>.

Ward, Bill. "Sustaining Mother Nature with Native Plants." *Native Plant
     Society of Texas.* Native Plant Soc. of Texas, 29 May 2010. Web. 11
     Apr. 2011. <http://npsot.org/wp/story/2010/436/>.

Welsh, Douglas F., William C. Welch, and Richard L. Duble.
     "Landscape Water Conservation: Xeriscape." *Aggie Horticulture.*
     Texas A&M Univ. Dept. of Horticultural Science, 26 Oct. 2000. Web.
     3 April 2011. <http://aggie-horticulture.tamu.edu/extension/
     xeriscape/xeriscape.html>.

Note that in works
cited entries, all lines
after the first are
indented.

Source without
author

After you have taken notes, found outside sources, and written a draft thesis statement, use the writing guide that follows to help you write your research essay.

WRITING GUIDE: RESEARCH ESSAY

STEPS	HOW TO DO THE STEPS
☐ **Make a schedule.** See page 353.	• Include the due date and dates for doing research, finishing a draft, revising, documenting sources, and editing.
☐ **Choose a topic.** See pages 354–55.	• Choose a topic that interests you. • Make sure the topic is narrow enough to cover in the assigned length of the paper.
☐ **Ask a guiding question.** See pages 355–56.	• Ask a question that will guide your research.
☐ **Find and evaluate sources.** See Chapter 20.	• Use library resources. • Consider the reliability of each source.
☐ **Take notes to avoid plagiarism.** See pages 356–61.	• Note the publication information. • Make an entry for each piece of information (p. 358).
☐ **Write a thesis statement.** See Chapter 6.	• Based on what you have read, write a thesis statement that includes the main point of your essay. • Turn your research question into a statement: **RESEARCH QUESTION:** What are the benefits of green landscaping? **THESIS STATEMENT:** There are many clear benefits of green landscaping. **REVISED AFTER TAKING NOTES FROM SOURCES:** Landscaping with drought-tolerant native plants conserves water, reduces the use of toxic soil conditioners, and requires little maintenance.
☐ **Support your thesis.** See Chapter 7.	• Review all notes to choose the best points. • Do further research if you do not have enough support to convince your readers of your main point. →

STEPS	HOW TO DO THE STEPS
☐ Write a draft essay. See Chapter 8.	• Make an outline that organizes your support. • Write an introduction that includes your thesis statement. • Write topic sentences and paragraphs that give support and supporting details. • Work in your outside sources using introductory phrases (see p. 363). • Write a conclusion that reminds your readers of your main point and support and makes an observation. • Title your essay.
☐ Revise your draft. See Chapter 9.	• Is the thesis clear? • Do I have enough support? • Do I end strongly? • Have I integrated outside sources smoothly in the essay (and cited them)? • Are all sources documented correctly?
☐ Cite and document your sources. For in-text citations, see pages 365–66. For works cited entries, see pages 367–71.	
☐ Edit your essay.	• Reread your essay, looking for errors in grammar, spelling, and punctuation.

Part 4

The Four Most Serious Errors

22

The Basic Sentence

An Overview

The Four Most Serious Errors

This book emphasizes the four grammar errors that people most often notice.

These four errors may make your meaning harder to understand, and they definitely give readers a bad impression of you. It is like going for a job interview in pajamas. People *will* notice. Learning how to correct these errors will make a big difference in your writing.

1. Fragments (see Chapter 23)
2. Run-ons (see Chapter 24)
3. Problems with subject-verb agreement (see Chapter 25)
4. Problems with verb form and tense (see Chapter 26)

This chapter will review the basic elements of the sentence; the next four chapters cover the four most serious errors.

IDEA JOURNAL
Write about any problems you have had with grammar in the past.

DISCUSSION
Ask students how much time they leave for editing their papers before turning them in. Remind them that even the most experienced writers leave time for editing and proofreading.

The Parts of Speech

There are seven basic parts of speech in English:

1. A **noun** names a person, place, or thing.

   Heroin <u>is</u> a drug.

In the examples in this chapter, <u>subjects</u> are underlined once and <u>verbs</u> are underlined twice.

2. A **pronoun** replaces a noun in a sentence. A pronoun can be the subject of a sentence (*I, you, he, she, it, we, they*), or it can be the object of a sentence (*me, you, him, her, us, them*). A pronoun can also show possession (*mine, yours, his, her, its, our, their*).

It causes addiction.

3. A **verb** tells what the subject does, or it links a subject to another word that describes it.

Heroin *causes* addiction.   [The verb *causes* is what the subject *Heroin* does.]

It *is* dangerous.   [The verb *is* links the subject *It* to a word that describes it: *dangerous*.]

4. An **adjective** describes a noun or pronoun.

Heroin is *dangerous*.   [The adjective *dangerous* describes the noun *Heroin*.]

It is *lethal*.   [The adjective *lethal* describes the pronoun *It*.]

5. An **adverb** describes an adjective, a verb, or another adverb. Many adverbs end in *-ly*.

Heroin is *very* dangerous.   [The adverb *very* describes the adjective *dangerous*.]

Addiction occurs *quickly*.   [The adverb *quickly* describes the verb *occurs*.]

Addiction occurs *very* quickly.   [The adverb *very* describes the adverb *quickly*.]

6. A **preposition** connects a noun, pronoun, or verb with some other information about it (*across, at, in, of, on, around, over*, and *to* are some prepositions).

Dealers often sell drugs *around* schools.   [The preposition *around* connects the noun *drugs* with the noun *school*.]

7. A **conjunction** (*for, and, nor, but, or, yet, so*) connects words.

> **LANGUAGE NOTE:** Any idea that ends with a period needs a subject and a verb to be a complete sentence. For a review of subjects and verbs, see pages 386–91.
>
> If you are not sure about the order in which words in a sentence usually appear, see Chapter 33.

· ·

PRACTICE 1   Using the Parts of Speech

In the following sentences, fill in each blank with a word that is the part of speech called for in parentheses after the blank. *Note:* Some verbs may be in the past tense, and some verbs may use a helping verb such as *is* or *was*. *Answers will vary. Possible edits shown.*

> **EXAMPLE:** The ___soccer___ (*adjective*) ___coach___ (*noun*), a for-
>
> mer drill sergeant, _demanded_ (*verb*) that _____she_____
>
> (*pronoun*) arrive _promptly_ (*adverb*) _____for_____
>
> (*preposition*) practice.

1. The young ___student___ (*noun*), who was new _at_ (*preposition*) the school, _wanted_ (*verb*) to join the debating _and_ (*conjunction*) fencing clubs.

2. _Her_ (*pronoun*) dream _was_ (*verb*) to play the _trumpet_ (*noun*) _in_ (*preposition*) the _state_ (*adjective*) band.

3. The _cars_ (*noun*) that _continually_ (*adverb*) went by _made_ (*verb*) it difficult for the hotel's _angry_ (*adjective*) customers to sleep.

4. The _small_ (*adjective*) _store_ (*noun*), a recent addition _to_ (*preposition*) the neighborhood, _had_ (*verb*) the freshest fruit _and_ (*conjunction*) vegetables that _he_ (*pronoun*) had ever seen.

5. Shaking his head _decisively_ (*adverb*), _he_ (*pronoun*) looked up and _refused_ (*verb*) to get out _of_ (*preposition*) the car.

· ·

The Basic Sentence

A **sentence** is the basic unit of written communication. A complete sentence written in standard English must have three elements:

- A **subject**
- A **verb**
- A **complete thought**

TEACHING TIP
Consider having students use different-colored highlighters to mark subjects and verbs.

To edit your writing, you need a clear understanding of what a sentence *is* and what a sentence *is not*. You can find out if a group of words is a complete sentence by checking to see if it has a subject, a verb, and a complete thought.

For a list of pronoun types, see page 496.

Subjects

The **subject** of a sentence is the person, place, or thing that the sentence is about. The subject of the sentence can be a noun (a word that names the person, place, or thing) or a pronoun (a word that replaces the noun, such as *I, you, she,* or *they*).

> **LANGUAGE NOTE:** English sentences always have a subject.
>
> **INCORRECT**   Is hot outside.
>
> **CORRECT**   It is hot outside.

To find the subject, ask yourself, "Who or what is the sentence about?"

PERSON AS SUBJECT   Vivian works for the police department.

[*Who* is the sentence about? *Vivian*]

THING AS SUBJECT   The tickets cost $65 apiece.

[*What* is the sentence about? The *tickets*]

> **LANGUAGE NOTE:** The two sentences above use the word *the* before the noun (*the police department, the tickets*). *The, a,* and *an* are called *articles*. If you have trouble deciding which article to use with which nouns or if you often forget to use an article, see page 596.

A **compound subject** consists of two (or more) subjects joined by *and, or,* or *nor.*

TWO SUBJECTS   Nick and Chelsea have a new baby girl.

SEVERAL SUBJECTS   The jacket, pants, and sweater match perfectly.

SEVERAL SUBJECTS   Kim, Juan, or Melba will bring dessert.

A **prepositional phrase** is a word group that begins with a preposition and ends with a noun or pronoun. A **preposition** is a word that connects a noun, pronoun, or verb with some other information about it.

The subject of a sentence is *never* in a prepositional phrase.

> **LANGUAGE NOTE:** If you have trouble deciding which prepositions to use, see page 599.

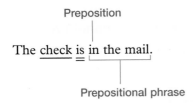

The subject of the sentence is *check*. The subject cannot be the word *mail,* which is in the prepositional phrase *in the mail.*

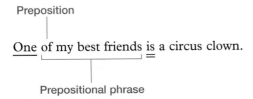

Although the word *friends* may seem to be the subject of the sentence, it is not. *One* is the subject. The word *friends* is not the subject because it is in the prepositional phrase *of my best friends.*

When you are looking for the subject of a sentence in your writing, it may help to cross out any prepositional phrases, as in the following sentences.

The rules about smoking are posted everywhere.

The sound of lightning striking a tree is like gunfire.

Many of the students work part-time.

Common Prepositions

about	beneath	like	to
above	beside	near	toward
across	between	next to	under
after	by	of	until
against	down	off	up
along	during	on	upon
among	except	out	with
around	for	outside	within
at	from	over	without
before	in	past	
behind	inside	since	
below	into	through	

....

PRACTICE 2   Identifying Subjects and Prepositional Phrases

In each of the following sentences, cross out any prepositional phrases, and underline the subject of the sentence.

> EXAMPLE: ~~For several months~~, <u>Ronald</u> has been raising a guide dog ~~for the blind~~.

1. Many other <u>people</u> ~~around the country~~ are raising guide dog puppies.

2. However, Ronald's <u>situation</u> is unusual because he is ~~in prison~~.

3. <u>Ronald</u> is participating ~~in a program called Puppies Behind Bars~~.

4. The <u>dog</u> he is raising, a black Labrador puppy named Cooper, lives ~~with Ronald~~ twenty-four hours a day.

5. Whenever Ronald's cell is locked, <u>Cooper</u> stays ~~in the cell with him~~.

6. In the cell, <u>Ronald</u> plays ~~with the dog~~, rolling ~~on the floor with him~~ and talking ~~to him in a high voice~~.

7. <u>Ronald</u> teaches Cooper manners and obedience ~~before the start of Cooper's formal guide dog training~~.

8. ~~In return~~, <u>Ronald</u> gains a sense ~~of responsibility~~.

9. When he finishes his formal training, <u>Cooper</u> will be matched ~~with a blind person~~.

For more practice, visit *Exercise Central* at bedfordstmartins .com/realessays.

10. <u>Ronald</u> believes that he and Cooper are contributing an important service ~~to society~~.

....

Verbs

Every sentence has a **main verb,** the word or words that tell what the subject does or that link the subject to another word that describes it. Verbs do not always immediately follow the subject: Other words may come between the subject and the verb.

There are three kinds of verbs—action verbs, linking verbs, and helping verbs.

LANGUAGE NOTE: Be careful with -*ing* and *to* forms of verbs (*reading, to read*).

INCORRECT   Terence loves to be reading.

CORRECT   Terence loves reading. *or* Terence loves to read.

If you make errors like this, see page 594.

Action Verbs

An **action verb** tells what action the subject performs.

To find the main action verb in a sentence, ask yourself, "What action does the subject perform?"

ACTION VERBS

The baby cried all night.

The building collapsed around midnight.

After work, we often go to Tallie's.

My aunt and uncle train service dogs.

Linking Verbs

A **linking verb** connects (links) the subject to a word or group of words that describes the subject. Linking verbs show no action. The most common linking verb is *be,* along with all its forms (*am, is, are,* and so on). Other linking verbs, such as *seem* and *become,* can usually be replaced by the corresponding form of *be,* and the sentence will still make sense.

To find linking verbs, ask yourself, "What word joins the subject and the words that describe the subject?"

LINKING VERBS

The dinner is delicious.

I felt great this morning.

This lasagna tastes just like my mother's.

The doctor looks extremely tired.

Some words can be either action verbs or linking verbs, depending on how they are used in a particular sentence.

ACTION VERB   The dog smelled Jake's shoes.

LINKING VERB   The dog smelled terrible.

Common Linking Verbs

FORMS OF *BE*	FORMS OF *BECOME* AND *SEEM*	FORMS OF SENSE VERBS
am	become, becomes	appear, appears
are	became	appeared
is	seem, seems	feel, feels, felt
was	seemed	look, looks
were		looked
		smell, smells
		smelled
		taste, tastes, tasted

LANGUAGE NOTE: The verb *be* cannot be left out of sentences in English.

INCORRECT   Tonya well now.

CORRECT   Tonya **is** well now.

Helping Verbs

A **helping verb** joins with the main verb in the sentence to form the **complete verb**. The helping verb is often a form of the verb *be, have,* or *do*. A sentence may have more than one helping verb along with the main verb.

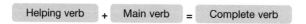

Helping verb **+** Main verb **=** Complete verb

HELPING VERBS + MAIN VERBS

Sunil <u>was talking</u> on his cell phone.

[The helping verb is *was*, and the main verb is *talking*. The complete verb is *was talking*.]

Charisse <u>is taking</u> three courses this semester.

Tomas <u>has missed</u> the last four meetings.

My <u>brother</u> <u>might have passed</u> the test.

Common Helping Verbs

FORMS OF *BE*	FORMS OF *HAVE*	FORMS OF *DO*	OTHER
am	have	do	can
are	has	does	could
been	had	did	may
being			might
is			must
was			should
were			will
			would

LANGUAGE NOTE: The verb *be* cannot be left out when forming sentences in English.

INCORRECT   Greg studying tonight.

CORRECT   Greg **is** studying tonight.

. . . .

PRACTICE 3   **Identifying the Verb
(Action, Linking, or Helping + Main)**

In the following sentences, underline each subject and double-underline each verb. Then, identify each verb as an action verb, a linking verb, or a helping verb + a main verb.

EXAMPLE: At first, Miguel did not want to attend his high school

reunion. *helping verb + main verb*

1. Miguel's family moved to Ohio from Escuintla, Guatemala, ten

   years ago. *action verb*

2. He was the new kid at his high school that fall. *linking verb*

3. Miguel was learning English at that time. *helping verb + main verb*

4. The football <u>players</u> <u>teased</u> small, quiet boys like him. *action verb*

5. After graduation, <u>he</u> <u>was</u> delighted to leave that part of his life behind. *linking verb*

6. Recently, the planning <u>committee</u> <u>sent</u> Miguel an invitation to his high school reunion. *action verb*

7. His original <u>plan</u> <u>had been</u> to throw the invitation straight into the trash. *helping verb + main verb*

8. Instead, <u>he</u> <u>is going</u> to the reunion to satisfy his curiosity about how his former classmates are doing. *helping verb + main verb*

9. His <u>family</u> <u>is</u> proud of Miguel's college degree and his new career as a graphic artist. *linking verb*

10. Perhaps <u>some</u> of the other students at the reunion <u>will</u> finally <u>get</u> to know the real Miguel. *helping verb + main verb*

Complete Thoughts

A **complete thought** is an idea that is expressed in a sentence and that makes sense by itself, without other sentences. An incomplete thought leaves readers wondering what is going on.

DISCUSSION
Have students discuss the differences between a complete thought in speaking and one in writing. Remind them that the context for speaking can be different from that for writing — and that in writing, a complete sentence always needs a subject and a verb.

INCOMPLETE THOUGHT	as I was leaving [*What is going on?*]
COMPLETE THOUGHT	The <u>phone</u> <u>rang</u> as I was leaving.
INCOMPLETE THOUGHT	the <u>people</u> selling the car [*What is going on?*]
COMPLETE THOUGHT	The <u>people</u> selling the car <u>placed</u> the ad.

To identify a complete thought, ask yourself, "Do I know what is going on, or do I have to ask a question to understand?"

INCOMPLETE THOUGHT   in the apartment next door

[Do I know what is going on, or do I have to ask a question to understand? *You would have to ask a question, so this is not a complete thought.*]

COMPLETE THOUGHT   <u>Carlos</u> <u>lives</u> in the apartment next door.

PRACTICE 4   **Identifying Complete Thoughts**

Some of the following items contain complete thoughts, and others do not. In the space to the left of each item, write either "C" for complete thought or "I" for incomplete thought. If you write "I," add words to make a sentence. *Answers will vary. Possible edits shown.*

has surprised some people.

EXAMPLE: *I* The success of recent 3-D movies~

, many viewers are happy to pay more.

 I **1.** Although 3-D movies are more expensive~

enjoy the feeling of being in the scene.

 I **2.** People in the audience~

 C **3.** They are thrilled.

Some people complain

 I **4.** ~~Complain~~ about wearing the special glasses.

 C **5.** The glasses can be uncomfortable.

 I **6.** However, if people have a choice between watching *Avatar*
in 2-D or 3-D~
, they tend to choose 3-D.

Today's 3-D technology is much

 I **7.** ~~Much~~ better than it used to be.

 C **8.** It is more expensive, too.

It is hard to tell if

 I **9.** ~~If~~ 3-D is just a fad or not.

 C **10.** Time will tell.

Six Basic Sentence Patterns

In English, there are six basic sentence patterns, some of which you have already worked with in this chapter. Although there are other patterns, they build on these six.

1. Subject-Verb (S-V)

This is the most basic pattern, as you have already seen.

           S   V

Airplanes pollute.

2. Subject-Linking Verb-Noun (S-LV-N)

S LV   N
Fuel is a pollutant.

3. Subject-Linking Verb-Adjective (S-LV-ADJ)

S   LV   ADJ
Travel seems cheap.

4. Subject-Verb-Adverb (S-V-ADV)

S   V   ADV
Pollution costs dearly.

5. Subject-Verb-Direct Object (S-V-DO)

A *direct object* directly receives the action of the verb.

S   V   DO
It degrades ozone.

6. Subject-Verb-Indirect Object-Direct Object

An *indirect object* does not directly receive the action of the verb.

S   V IO DO
Biofuels offer us hope.

....

PRACTICE 5 Identifying Basic Sentence Patterns

In each of the following sentences, identify the basic sentence pattern by writing "S" above the subject, "V" above a verb, "LV" above a linking verb, "N" above a noun, "ADJ" above an adjective, "ADV" above an adverb, "DO" above a direct object, and "IO" above an indirect object.

              S   V   IO   DO
EXAMPLE: Dogs teach people manners.

      S   V
1. Dogs teach.

      S   LV (ADJ)   N
2. Dogs are natural coaches.

      S   LV   ADJ
3. Dogs appear submissive.

      S   V   IO   DO
4. They teach people lessons.

        S   LV   ADV
5. They instruct unintentionally.
        S   ADV   V
6. They clearly teach.
        S   V   IO   (ADJ)   DO
7. Dogs give owners valuable lessons.
        S   V   DO   (ADV)
8. Dogs greet owners excitedly.
        S   V   ADV
9. Dogs respond promptly.
        S   LV   (ADV)   ADJ
10. Dogs are extremely alert.

Edit Paragraphs and Your Own Writing

EDITING REVIEW 1

Underline each subject, double-underline each verb, and correct the six incomplete thoughts. *Answers will vary. Possible edits shown.*

(1) It is easier to help others than many people think. (2) For example,
a person can donate his or her
~~donating hair.~~ (3) Some people need donated hair in the form of wigs. (4)
Who uses these wigs? (5) Mostly, children with cancer or other diseases
need wigs
that cause hair loss. (6) Donating is popular, especially with young girls.
(7) More and more frequently, though, men and boys are contributing
organization receives
hair. (8) For example, one nonprofit ~~organization. (9) It receives~~ up to
2,000 locks of hair every week. (10) Unfortunately, most of the donated
The
hair is unusable for this charity's wigs. (11) ~~Because the~~ charity's
The organization must reject
guidelines are quite strict. (12) ~~Rejecting~~ hair that is gray, wet, moldy, too
short, or too processed. (13) It is able to sell some rejected hair to help
the organization
meet the group's costs. (14) ~~But~~ continues to encourage donations. (15)
Obviously, contributors feel they are getting more than they are giving.

··

EDITING REVIEW 2

Underline each subject, double-underline each verb, and correct the six incomplete thoughts.

(1) New <u>parents</u> commonly <u>dress</u> their baby boys in ~~blue. (2) And~~ *blue and* their girls in pink. (3) Now, a recent <u>study</u> <u>suggests</u> that males actually do prefer blue and females prefer ~~pink. (4) Or~~ *pink, or* at least a redder shade of blue. (5) The <u>study</u> <u>involved</u> 208 men and women ages 20 to 26./ ~~(6) Who~~ *, who* were asked to quickly select their preferred color./ ~~(7) Choosing~~ from about 1,000 colored rectangles on a computer screen. (8) <u>Women</u> and <u>men</u> like <u>blue</u>./ ~~(9) According~~ *, according* to the study. (10) However, <u>women</u> clearly <u>express</u> a greater preference for the pinker end of the blue color spectrum. (11) The <u>researchers</u> <u>think</u> that females may have developed a preference for more reddish colors./ ~~(12) Which~~ *, which* resemble riper fruit and healthier faces.

··

EDITING REVIEW 3

In each blank, fill in a word that is the appropriate part of speech.

(1) Taking a peek _at_ a fellow passenger's computer screen is OK to do, right? (2) This is a serious question at a time when airplane flights _are_ tightly packed _and_ laptop use is common. (3) What if the _person_ in the next seat is watching an offensive movie _without_ headphones? (4) A recent survey _showed_ that 45 percent _of_ business travelers admit to peeking at someone else's laptop in a public place. (5) In many cases, it is _nearly_ impossible to avoid getting a glimpse of a nearby screen. (6) So, what is the _proper_ etiquette for in-flight laptop use? (7) If you are using _your_ laptop, bring headphones. (8) Do not watch _movies_ that are in poor taste. (9) If a neighbor seems interested, invite _him or her_ to watch. (10) If you are sitting next to a laptop user, don't peek.

(11) However, if the movie _he or she_ is watching looks interesting, it is OK to ask _politely_ to watch. (12) If the sound is _too_ high _or_ the content offensive, tell the laptop user. (13) If that does not work, _ask_ a flight attendant for assistance.

EDITING REVIEW 4

In each sentence of the following paragraph, identify the basic sentence pattern by writing "S" above the subject, "V" above a verb, "LV" above a linking verb, "DO" above a direct object, and "IO" above an indirect object.

(1) It is afternoon. (2) At this hour, many people become drowsy. (3) Most fight this "post-lunch dip." (4) Some people nap. (5) Others give themselves a coffee transfusion. (6) Some try exercise. (7) The cleverest, however, use simple planning. (8) For these people, the "dip" is the time for simple, non-creative tasks. (9) They give their brains a well-deserved break. (10) Later in the afternoon, their energy returns. (11) At this point, they resume more complex tasks. (12) Sometimes, the path of least resistance is best.

23

Fragments

Incomplete Sentences

Understand What Fragments Are

IDEA JOURNAL
Without looking at
this chapter, how
would you define
a fragment? How
do you find a
fragment in your
writing?

A **sentence** is a group of words that has a subject and a verb and expresses a complete thought, independent of other sentences. A **fragment** is a group of words that is missing a subject or a verb or that does not express a complete thought.

> **SENTENCE** I <u>am going</u> to a concert on Friday at Memorial Arena.
>
> **FRAGMENT** I <u>am going</u> to a concert on Friday. *At Memorial Arena.*
>
> [*At Memorial Arena* does not have a subject or a verb.]

In the examples in this chapter, <u>subjects</u> are underlined once and <u>verbs</u> are underlined twice.

LANGUAGE NOTE: Remember that any idea that ends with a period needs a subject and a verb to be complete. For a review of subjects and verbs, see pages 386–91.

In the Real World, Why Is It Important to Correct Fragments?

A fragment is one of the grammatical errors that people notice most, as the following example shows.

SITUATION: A student responds to an ad for a work-study position at the college.

Dear Professor Espinoza:

I am interested in the position for an assistant that I saw. <u>On the work-study Web site.</u> I have attached a résumé for you to review. <u>That describes my experience.</u> I would very much like to work for you next semester. <u>Helping with your writing and research.</u> I type very fast.

Thank you for your consideration.

Sincerely,
Carson Watson

DISCUSSION
Distribute and discuss "What Business People Think about Grammar and Usage" by Maxine Hairston, available on the Web at www.d .umn.edu/cla/faculty/ troufs/comp3160/ Hairston.Business_ People.html.

WRITER AT WORK

Alex Espinoza, the college professor, read Carson's letter and made the following comments.

ALEX ESPINOZA'S RESPONSE: If I had received this letter, I would not hire the writer. If Carson doesn't care about writing, why should I hire him? Bad writing is like walking out the door in your pajamas, unshaven, unshowered, and gross.

(See Alex Espinoza's **PROFILE OF SUCCESS** on page 190.)

Find and Correct Fragments

To find fragments in your own writing, look for the five kinds of fragments in this chapter. They represent common trouble spots.

When you find a fragment, you can usually correct it in one of two ways.

RESOURCES For more practice and instructions, refer students to *Exercise Central* at bedfordstmartins .com/realessays.

WAYS TO CORRECT FRAGMENTS

- Add what is missing (a subject, a verb, or both).
- Attach the fragment to the sentence before or after it.

PRACTICE 1   Finding and Correcting Fragments

Underline the three fragments in Carson Watson's letter above.

Fragments That Start with Prepositions

For a list of common prepositions, see page 387.

Whenever a preposition starts what you think is a sentence, check for a subject, a verb, and a complete thought. If any one of those is missing, you have a fragment.

FRAGMENT   The <u>plane</u> <u>crashed</u> into the house. *With a deafening roar.*

[*With a deafening roar* is a prepositional phrase that starts with the preposition *with* and ends with the noun *roar*. The phrase has neither a subject nor a verb. It is a fragment.]

FRAGMENT   You <u>should take</u> the second left and head west. *Toward the highway.*

[*Toward the highway* is a prepositional phrase that starts with the preposition *toward* and ends with the noun *highway*. The phrase has neither a subject nor a verb. It is a fragment.]

Remember, the subject of a sentence is *never* in a prepositional phrase (see p. 386).

Correct a fragment that starts with a preposition by connecting the fragment to the sentence either before or after it. If you connect a fragment to the sentence after it, put a comma after the fragment to join it to the sentence.

TEACHING TIP Have students read a piece of their writing and underline any of the common prepositions listed on page 387. Then, have them highlight any fragments that start with a preposition. Ask students to give examples of fragments from their papers, and copy the fragments on the board. Have the whole class work together to create complete sentences from the fragments.

FRAGMENT   The <u>plane</u> <u>crashed</u> into the house. *From a height of eight hundred feet.*

CORRECTED   The <u>plane</u> <u>crashed</u> into the house, ᶠFrom a height of eight hundred feet.

CORRECTED   From a height of eight hundred feet, the <u>plane</u> <u>crashed</u> into the house.

Fragments That Start with Dependent Words

DISCUSSION Ask students what the word *dependent* means in the real world. Then, ask them how that definition will help them remember what a *dependent clause* is.

A **dependent word** is the first word in a dependent clause, which does not express a complete thought even though it has a subject and a verb. Whenever a dependent word starts what you think is a sentence, look for a subject, a verb, and, especially, a complete thought.

Some dependent words are **subordinating conjunctions** (*after, because, before, since, until,* and so on).

FRAGMENT   I took the bus. *Because* I missed my ride.

[*Because* is a dependent word introducing the dependent clause *because I missed my ride*. The clause has a subject, *I*, and a verb, *missed*, but it does not express a complete thought.]

CORRECTED   I took the bus because I missed my ride.

[The dependent clause is attached to the sentence before it.]

CORRECTED   Because I missed my ride, I took the bus.

[The dependent clause is in front of the sentence. Note that when the dependent clause comes at the beginning of the sentence, it needs a comma after it.]

For more practice with correcting fragments, visit *Exercise Central* at bedfordstmartins .com/realessays.

Common Dependent Words

after	if	what(ever)
although	since	when(ever)
as	so that	where
because	that	whether
before	though	which(ever)
even though	unless	while
how	until	who/whose

Some dependent words are **relative pronouns** (*who, whose, which*). When a word group starts with *who, whose,* or *which*, it is not a complete sentence unless it is a question.

FRAGMENT   I visited my friend John. *Whose* brother is an astronaut.

[*Whose* is a relative pronoun starting a word group, so it is a fragment. If this phrase ended with a question mark ("Whose brother is an astronaut?"), it would be correct, but the writer is not asking a question.]

CORRECTED   I visited my friend John, whose brother is an astronaut.

LANGUAGE NOTE: For help with forming questions with pronouns, see Chapters 26 and 33.

....

PRACTICE 2 Correcting Fragments That Start with Prepositions or Dependent Words

In the following items, circle any prepositions or dependent words starting a fragment. Then, correct the fragments by connecting them to the previous or next sentence.

EXAMPLE: Most dogs are content to have a daily ~~walk. While~~ *walk, while* some dogs need more.

1. (Even after) having a walk, These dogs become nervous and overly excited.

2. This, of course, greatly upsets the dogs' owners, (Who) have to deal with the messes that these agitated dogs leave around the home.

3. (To) address this growing need, A new type of service is springing up, especially in the larger cities of the country.

4. (Because) walking does not offer enough exercise for these high-spirited dogs, This new service provides someone to run with the dogs.

5. A runner will come to the owner's home and take the dog out for some vigorous exercise, (At) a price of around thirty to forty dollars.

6. Many of the runners are marathoners, (With) a large number also being actors, singers, writers, and students.

7. The runners have the chance to earn some much-needed cash, (While) they get some great exercise for both the dogs and themselves.

8. Some dogs, such as English bulldogs, are not good candidates for this service, (Since) they are not built for running.

9. But the larger dogs, especially young retrievers, Dalmatians, and Weimaraners, are perfect for this, (If) they are strong and healthy.

10. Many dog owners who use this service say it has solved a huge problem for them, (With) their exhausted dogs eagerly packing away their dinners and then lying down for the entire night.

PRACTICE 3   Correcting Fragments That Start with Prepositions or Dependent Words

Read the following paragraph, and circle the ten fragments that start with prepositions or dependent words. Then, correct the fragments.

For decades, scholars have argued, About when and how chickens reached the Americas. One theory is that Portuguese and Spanish settlers brought them, When they arrived after 1500. Another suggests that the chickens were brought over by Polynesian visitors before Columbus's voyages. Most scholars once believed that the Portuguese and Spanish brought chickens to the Americas, Along with seeds, medicinal plants, and other necessities. Now, researchers think they finally know what happened, Thanks to some revealing evidence found on the coast of Chile, where chicken bones were discovered, Along with some pottery that was definitely dated between 1304 and 1424, or even earlier. Anthropologists performed a DNA analysis on the bones, Which revealed that the chickens from Chile had a close genetic relationship to chickens from several Polynesian sites, On the islands of Tonga and American Samoa. When these findings were published, Some anthropologists said the discovery supports the idea that Polynesians had by that time populated the Pacific and had even reached the Americas. Though the chicken bones matched Polynesian chickens, The pottery found with the bones was of the local Chilean style. However, it is still unclear whether it was the local Chileans or the visiting Polynesians, Who ate the chickens back then.

Fragments That Start with *-ing* Verb Forms

An ***-ing* verb form** (also called a **gerund**) is the form of a verb that ends in *-ing: walking, writing, swimming*. Unless it has a helping verb (*was walking, was writing, was swimming*), it is not a complete verb in a sentence. Sometimes an *-ing* verb form is used as a subject at the beginning of a complete sentence.

-ING FORM USED AS A SUBJECT

Swimming is a wonderful form of exercise.

[In this sentence, *swimming* is the subject and *is* is the verb.]

Running strains the knees.

[In this sentence, *running* is the subject, not the verb; *strains* is the verb.]

-ING FORM USED WITH A HELPING VERB AS A VERB

I *am working* full-time this semester.

[In this sentence, *am* is the helping verb; *am working* is the complete verb.]

Tom *was running* when he saw the accident.

[In this sentence, *was* is the helping verb; *was running* is the complete verb.]

> **LANGUAGE NOTE:** English uses both *-ing* verb forms (*Kara loves **singing***) and *infinitives* (*to* before the verb) (*Kara loves **to sing***). If these forms confuse you, pay special attention to this section and see also page 406.

Whenever a word group begins with a word in *-ing* form, look carefully to see if the word group contains a subject and a verb and if it expresses a complete thought.

FRAGMENT   Snoring so loudly I couldn't sleep.

[If *snoring* is the main verb, what is the subject? There isn't one. Is there a helping verb used with *snoring*? No. It is a fragment.]

FRAGMENT   *Hoping for a faster route.* I took a back road to school.

[If *hoping* is the main verb, what is the subject? There isn't one. Is there a helping verb used with *hoping*? No. It is a fragment.]

Correct a fragment that starts with an *-ing* verb form either by adding whatever sentence elements are missing (usually a subject and a helping verb) or by connecting the fragment to the sentence before or after it. Usually, you will need to put a comma before or after the fragment to join it to the complete sentence.

-ING FRAGMENT   The audience applauded for ten minutes. *Whistling and cheering wildly.*

CORRECTED   The audience applauded for ten minutes, whistling and cheering wildly.

CORRECTED   The audience <u>applauded</u> for ten minutes. ~~Whistling~~ *They were whistling* and cheering wildly.

-ING FRAGMENT   *Working two jobs and going to school.* <u>I am</u> tired all the time.

CORRECTED   Working two jobs and going to school, <u>I am</u> tired all the time.

CORRECTED   ~~Working~~ *I am working* two jobs and going to school. <u>I am</u> tired all the time.

....

PRACTICE 4   Correcting Fragments That Start with *-ing* Verb Forms

In the following items, circle any *-ing* verb that appears at the beginning of a word group. Then, correct any fragment either by adding the missing sentence elements or by connecting it to the sentence before or after it.

EXAMPLE: (Quilting) with a group of other women, *m* /My grandmother found a social life and a creative outlet. *Answers may vary. Possible edits shown.*

1. My grandmother spent her entire life, (Living) on a farm in eastern Wyoming.

2. (Growing) up during World War II, *s* /She learned from her mother how to sew her own clothes.

3. She was a natural seamstress. *My grandmother created* (Creating) shirts and dresses more beautiful than anything available in a store.

4. (Joining) a quilting circle at the age of twenty, *m* /My grandmother learned how to make quilts.

5. The quilting circle made quilts for special occasions, *u* /(Using) scraps of cloth left over from other sewing projects.

6. *The quilters laid* (Laying) the scraps out in an interesting pattern. The women then chose a traditional design for the stitching that joined the top and bottom parts of the quilt.

7. ~~Celebrating~~ the birth of her first child, my father,/ ~~T~~he quilting
   circle gave my grandmother a baby quilt that is now a treasured
   heirloom.

8. She told me that the quilt was made of memories. ~~Incorporating~~ *It incorporated*
   fabric from her wedding dress, her maternity outfits, and all of the
   baby clothes she had stitched.

9. ~~Looking~~ at each bit of cloth in that quilt,/ ~~M~~y grandmother could
   still describe, years later, the garment she had made from it.

10. ~~Trying~~ to ensure that those memories would survive,/ I asked
    her to write down everything she recalled about the quilt.

Fragments That Start with *to* and a Verb

An **infinitive** is the word *to* plus a verb—*to hire, to eat, to study*. These
phrases are all called *infinitive forms*. Although they contain verbs, infinitive forms function as nouns, adjectives, or adverbs.

If a word group begins with *to* and a verb, it must have another verb
or it is not a complete sentence.

> **FRAGMENT**   I will go to the store later. *To buy a card.*

[The first word group is a sentence, with *I* as the subject and *will go* as the verb.
There is no subject in the word group *to buy a card*, and there is no verb outside
of the infinitive.]

> **FRAGMENT**   Last week, a couple in New York fulfilled their wedding
>   fantasy. *To get married on the top of the Empire State*
>   *Building.*

[The first word group is a sentence, with *couple* as the subject, and *fulfilled* as
the verb. In the second word group, there is no subject or verb outside of the
infinitive.]

Correct a fragment that starts with *to* and a verb by connecting it to the
sentence before or after it or by adding the missing sentence elements (a
subject and a verb).

> **FRAGMENT**   Geri climbed on the roof. *To watch the fireworks.*

CORRECTED   Geri climbed on the roof./To watch the fireworks.
(t above the slash)

CORRECTED   Geri climbed on the roof. ~~To~~ watch the fireworks.
(She wanted to, inserted above)

FRAGMENT   *To save on her monthly gas bills.* Tammy sold her SUV and got a hybrid car.

CORRECTED   To save on her monthly gas bills,/Tammy sold her SUV and got a hybrid car.

CORRECTED   ~~To~~ save on her monthly gas bills. ~~Tammy~~ sold her SUV and got a hybrid car.
(Tammy wanted to, inserted above "To"; She inserted above "Tammy")

LANGUAGE NOTE: Do not confuse the infinitive (*to* before the verb) with *that*.

INCORRECT   My brother wants *that* his girlfriend cook.

CORRECT   My brother wants his girlfriend *to cook*.

PRACTICE 5   Finding and Correcting Fragments That Start with *to* and a Verb

In the following items, circle any examples of *to* and a verb that begin a word group. Then, correct each fragment either by adding the missing sentence elements or by connecting it to the previous or the next sentence.

EXAMPLE: In the 1940s, Joe Gold decided/(To become) a member
(t above the slash)

of the Muscle Beach Weightlifting Club. *Answers may vary. Possible edits shown.*

1. (To lift weights,) Bodybuilders then met at the Muscle Beach of Santa Monica in Los Angeles.
(b marked above)

2. When Joe Gold thought of opening a gym in 1965, he knew exactly where,(To locate) it.
(t marked above)

3. Muscle Beach had become known as Venice by then, but bodybuilders still went there,(To lift) railroad ties and buckets filled with concrete.
(t marked above)

4. Gold invented several new workout machines,(To give) the bodybuilders more useful exercise.
(t marked above)

5. (To get) the best possible workout, Arnold Schwarzenegger regularly went to Gold's Gym in Venice.

6. Schwarzenegger won the title of Mr. Universe and later successfully ran in an election, (To become) governor of California.

7. (To have) a realistic setting for the 1977 movie *Pumping Iron*, The filmmaker selected Gold's Gym.

8. *Pumping Iron*, featuring Schwarzenegger and other weight lifters, helped, (To make) Gold's Gym famous.

9. In the early 1970s, however, Joe Gold made a decision, (To sell) his original business along with the name *Gold's Gym* to another company.

10. Later, Gold went on, (To create) World Gym, which now has more than three hundred locations around the world.

···

Fragments That Start with Examples or Explanations

As you edit your writing, pay special attention to groups of words that are examples or explanations of information you presented in the previous sentences. These word groups may be fragments.

> **FRAGMENT**   <u>Shoppers</u> <u>find</u> many ways to save money on food bills.
>
> *For example, using double coupons.*

[The second word group has no subject and no verb. The word *using* is an *-ing* verb form that needs either to be the subject of a sentence or to have a helping verb with it.]

> **FRAGMENT**   <u>Parking</u> on this campus <u>is</u> a real nightmare. *Especially between 8:00 and 8:30 a.m.*

[The second word group has no subject and no verb.]

Finding fragments that start with examples or explanations can be difficult, because there is no single kind of word to look for. The following are a few starting words that may signal an example or explanation, but fragments that are examples or explanations do not always start with these words:

especially	for example	like	such as

When a group of words that you think is a sentence gives an example or explanation of information in the previous sentence, stop to see if it has a subject and a verb and if it expresses a complete thought. If it is missing any of these elements, it is a fragment.

FRAGMENT   The <u>Web</u> <u>has</u> many job search sites. *Such as Monster.com.*

[Does the second word group have a subject? No. A verb? No. It is a fragment.]

FRAGMENT   <u>I</u> <u>wish</u> I had something to eat from Chipotle's right now. *A giant burrito, for example.*

[Does the second word group have a subject? Yes, *burrito.* A verb? No. It is a fragment.]

FRAGMENT   <u>I</u> <u>pushed</u> seven different voice-mail buttons before I spoke to a real person. *Not a helpful one, though.*

[Does the second word group have a subject? Yes, *one.* A verb? No. It is a fragment.]

To correct a fragment that starts with an example or an explanation, connect it either to the previous sentence or to the next one. Sometimes, you can add the missing sentence elements (a subject, a verb, or both) instead. When you connect the fragment to a sentence, you may need to reword or to change some punctuation. For example, fragments that are examples and fragments that are negatives are often set off by commas.

FRAGMENT   The <u>Web</u> <u>has</u> many job search sites. *Such as Monster.com.*

CORRECTED   The <u>Web</u> <u>has</u> many job search sites, such as Monster.com.

FRAGMENT   I <u>pushed</u> seven different voice-mail buttons before I spoke to a real person. *Not a helpful one, though.*

CORRECTED   I <u>pushed</u> seven different voice-mail buttons before I spoke to a real person, though not a helpful one.

CORRECTED   I <u>pushed</u> seven different voice-mail buttons before I spoke to a real person. He was not a helpful one, though.

PRACTICE 6   Correcting Fragments That Are Examples or Explanations

In the following items, circle any word groups that are examples or explanations. Then, correct each fragment either by connecting it to the previous sentence or by adding the missing sentence elements.

EXAMPLE: Some studies estimate that the number of teenage girls suffering dating abuse is very high. Perhaps as many as one out of three girls, *experiences some type of abuse from her boyfriend.*
^ Answers may vary. Possible edits shown.

1. Many parents believe that they would know if their daughters were being abused, Either physically or emotionally.

2. Most parents would certainly be concerned to see signs of violence on their children, Such as bruises or scratches.

3. A young man can be abusive without laying a finger on his girl-friend. *He might* A guy who monitors her actions and keeps her from spend-ing time with other friends.

4. Abusive boyfriends often want to control their partners. *They may want to make* Make sure that their girlfriends dress a certain way, for example.

5. Around her parents, a teenager's boyfriend may act like a perfect gentleman. *He may be polite,* Polite, attentive, and kind to the young woman.

6. When the couple is alone, however, he may be giving her verbal abuse, Like telling her that she is fat, stupid, and ugly.

7. A young woman with an abusive boyfriend may develop psychological problems that will be difficult to treat, Such as low self-esteem.

8. Parents should look for signs that their daughter needs help, Like slipping grades, loss of interest in her friends, and unwillingness to confide in parents.

9. Friends who think that a young woman is involved in an abusive relationship should try to be supportive of her, Not turn away even if she refuses to leave her boyfriend.

10. Young women need to know that help is available. From parents, guidance counselors, women's support services, and even the police, if necessary.

Edit Paragraphs and Your Own Writing

As you edit the following paragraphs and your own writing, use the checklist that follows. You may also want to refer to the chart on page 414.

CHECKLIST

Editing for Fragments

FOCUS

☐ Whenever you see one of the five trouble spots in your writing, stop to check for a possible fragment.

ASK

☐ Does the word group have a subject?

☐ Does it have a verb?

☐ Does it express a complete thought?

EDIT

☐ If your answer to any of these questions is "no," you have a fragment that you must correct.

Find and correct any fragments in the following paragraphs. *Answers may vary. Possible edits shown.*

RESOURCES For cumulative Editing Review Tests, see pages 667–83.

EDITING REVIEW 1 (5 fragments)

(1) Genetically modified foods are being marketed, (2) As the foods of the future. (3) For the past decade, gene technology has been advancing dramatically. (4) Inserting a gene from one species into the DNA of another species is easily possible. (5) A gene from a fish may be found, (6) To make tomatoes more resistant to disease. (7) Of course, genetic modification may have unintended effects, (8) As in the case of geneti-

TEAMWORK Divide the class into small groups and have each group present a corrected Editing Review. Compare the different ways in which the groups correct the fragments.

cally modified corn, (9) Which may harm monarch butterfly caterpillars. (10) Arguing that the long-term effects of genetic modification may not be known for years to come, (11) Some scientists urge caution before marketing genetically modified foods.

- -

EDITING REVIEW 2 (4 Fragments)

(1) The term *organic* means different things, (2) To different people. (3) Organic foods are supposed to be grown without pesticides, (4) A method that reduces a farm's impact on the environment. (5) But is organic food a healthier choice for the person eating it? (6) Most people who buy organic food think so. (7) They pay premium prices for organic products because they think the food is good for their own well-being, (8) Not just that of the environment. (9) Surprisingly, however, some foods labeled organic today are highly processed. (10) The label merely means that the ingredients meet a certain government standard, (11) While guaranteeing nothing about the nutritional content or health benefits of the food.

- -

EDITING REVIEW 3 (5 fragments)

(1) For several years, (2) The U.S. Department of Agriculture has permitted the irradiation of certain foods sold in American supermarkets. (3) Irradiating produce kills bacteria on the food, (4) Increasing its shelf life. (5) Without irradiation, a strawberry may last only a day or two after being purchased. (6) An irradiated strawberry, in contrast, can last a week or more, (7) Because the bacteria that would cause it to spoil are killed by radiation. (8) While some consumers worry about buying irradiated food, (9) Others dismiss these concerns as the effect of too

many science-fiction movies. (10) In stores where irradiated fruits and vegetables are sold under banners announcing the radiation treatment‚ (11) The owners report a booming market.

EDITING REVIEW 4 (4 fragments and 4 formal English errors)

(1) Bacteria that resist antibiotics could be a real health threat in the next century. (2) ~~Doctrz~~ *Doctors* have begun 2 *to* explain 2 *to* their patients‚ (3) That antibiotics are useful only for certain kinds of infections and that patients must finish every course of antibiotics they start. (4) Antibiotic use in agriculture, however, has continued‚ (5) To increase. (6) The government does not even keep records‚ (7) Of antibiotic use in farm animals. (8) ~~Mne~~ *Many* cattle, pigs, and chickens get antibiotics for economic reasons‚ (9) Such as to keep them healthy and to make them grow faster. (10) Many scientists fear that antibiotic residue in the meat Americans eat may contribute to antibiotic resistance. (11) If so, agricultural antibiotics could eventually endanger human health.

PRACTICE 7   Editing Your Own Writing for Fragments

As a final practice, edit fragments in a piece of your own writing — a paper you are working on for this class, a paper you've already finished, a paper for another course, or a recent piece of writing from your work or everyday life. Use the checklist on page 411 and the chart below to help you.

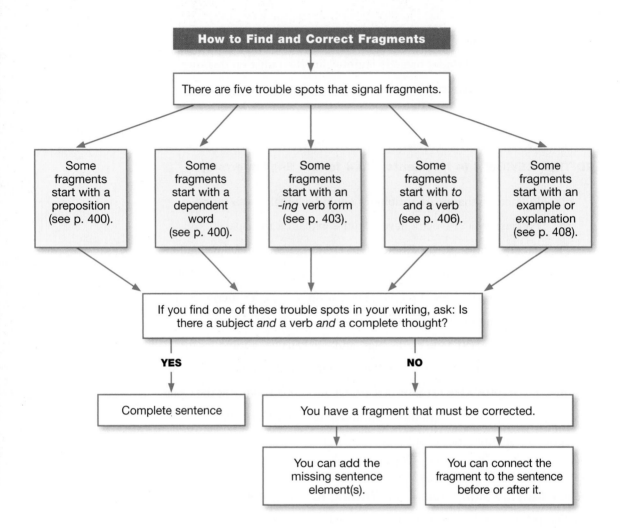

24

Run-Ons

Two Sentences Joined Incorrectly

Understand What Run-Ons Are

A sentence is also called an **independent clause**, a group of words with a subject and a verb that expresses a complete thought. Sometimes, two independent clauses can be joined correctly in one sentence.

SENTENCES WITH TWO INDEPENDENT CLAUSES

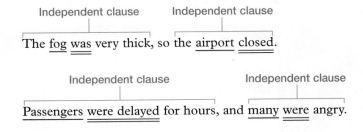

Independent clause   Independent clause

The fog was very thick, so the airport closed.

Independent clause   Independent clause

Passengers were delayed for hours, and many were angry.

A **run-on** is two sentences (each containing a subject and a verb and expressing a complete thought) that are joined incorrectly and written as one sentence. There are two kinds of run-ons—**fused sentences** and **comma splices**.

A **fused sentence** is two complete sentences joined without any punctuation.

In the examples throughout this section, the <u>subject</u> is underlined once, and the <u>verb</u> is underlined twice.

Independent clause   Independent clause

FUSED SENTENCE   Anger is a dangerous emotion it has many bad effects.

No punctuation

A **comma splice** is two complete sentences joined by only a comma instead of a comma and one of these words: *and, but, for, nor, or, so, yet.*

COMMA SPLICE   Anger is a dangerous emotion, it has many bad effects.

Comma

In the Real World, Why Is It Important to Correct Run-Ons?

Run-ons are errors that many people, including instructors and employers, will notice, as the following example shows.

SITUATION: Marion is new to her position as a licensed practical nurse at a large hospital. Each day, she updates patients' records and writes brief summaries of their progress for other nurses. The following is a report that Marion wrote in her first week on the job.

Trudari Kami is a premature infant she was born with a birth weight of 1.7 pounds her lungs were not fully developed, she was not able to breathe on her own. As of 2:15 a.m. on Thursday, April 6, she remains in stable condition her condition is still critical though she is being carefully monitored.

WRITER AT WORK

Patty Maloney, a clinical nurse specialist, read Marion's report.

PATTY MALONEY'S RESPONSE: I met with Marion to explain that what she had written was difficult to understand, and I worked with her on editing the report. The reports must be clear; otherwise, the next person might not be sure how to treat the baby.

(See Patty Maloney's **PROFILE OF SUCCESS** on page 208.)

Find and Correct Run-Ons

To find run-ons, focus on each sentence in your writing one at a time. Until you get used to finding run-ons, this step will take time, but after a while you will not make the error as often.

Read the paragraph below. Does it include any run-ons? ___*yes*___
If so, how many? ___2___

The concert to benefit AIDS research included fabulous musicians and songs. One of the guitarists had six different <u>guitars they were all acoustic</u>. One had a shiny engraved silver shield on it, <u>it flashed in the lights</u>. The riffs the group played were fantastic. All of the songs were original, and many had to do with the loss of loved ones. At the end of some songs, the audience was hushed, too moved with emotion to begin the applause right away. When the concert was over, the listeners, many of them in tears, gave the performers a standing ovation.

. . . .

PRACTICE 1   Finding Run-ons

Find and underline the four run-ons in Marion's report on page 416.

. . . .

When you find a run-on in your writing, you can correct it in one of four ways.

WAYS TO CORRECT A RUN-ON

- Add a period.
- Add a semicolon.
- Add a comma and a coordinating conjunction.
- Add a dependent word.

Add a Period

You can correct a run-on by adding a period to make two separate sentences.

Independent clause   Independent clause

FUSED SENTENCES (corrected)

I called about my bill. I got four useless recorded messages.

I finally hung up my question remained unanswered.

COMMA SPLICES (corrected)

My sister found a guy she likes in a chat room she plans to meet him
tomorrow.

I warned her that she should choose a public place Applebee's at lunch
would be good.

Add a Semicolon

A second way to correct a run-on is to join the two independent clauses
into one sentence by adding a semicolon (;). Use a semicolon only when
the two independent clauses express closely related ideas that make sense
in a single combined sentence.

S + V ;	S + V .
Independent clause	Independent clause

FUSED SENTENCES (corrected)

My father had a heart attack he is in the hospital.

My mother called 911 the ambulance was there in just under four
minutes.

COMMA SPLICES (corrected)

The emergency room was like the one on the show *Grey's Anatomy*
the doctors and nurses were efficient.

He was in the emergency room for over three hours there was no bed
for him.

A semicolon is sometimes used before a transition from one independent clause to another, and the transition word is followed by a comma.

TRANSITION BETWEEN SENTENCES

Transition

I tried to visit my father; however, I had no ride.

Semicolon   Comma

PRACTICE 2   Correcting a Run-on by Adding a Period or a Semicolon

For each of the following run-ons, indicate in the space to the left whether it is a fused sentence (FS) or a comma splice (CS). Then, correct the run-on by adding a period or a semicolon. *Answers may vary. Possible edits shown.*

EXAMPLE: __CS__ Social networking sites allow users to connect

with one another; the sites also allow users to access

each other's personal information.

__CS__ **1.** Online profiles often include photographs, group associa-

tions, and personal preferences; this information can some-

times be embarrassing.

__FS__ **2.** Many sites, like Facebook, allow users to choose their

own privacy settings. Users can limit how much information

they want to share and who has access to their personal

data.

__CS__ **3.** Some people take steps to protect their privacy; they actively

monitor their information and protect their online

reputations.

__CS__ **4.** Most people assume that younger social networkers are

freer with their personal information. Young people, how-

ever, are more likely than older people to limit what they

share online.

FS   **5.** In a recent survey, 44 percent of Internet users ages eighteen to twenty-nine reported limiting the information available about themselves online;only 25 percent of users ages fifty to sixty-four reported doing so.

CS   **6.** Some people argue that older users are simply less knowl-edgeable about how to protect themselves, younger users are more likely to know how to adjust settings and remove unwanted information.

For more practice correcting run-ons, visit *Exercise Central* at **bedfordstmartins .com/realessays**.

FS   **7.** On the other hand, many observers note that security policies at sites like Facebook change frequently;even young people struggle to keep up with complicated and confusing privacy controls.

RESOURCES To gauge students' skills in correcting run-ons, use the *Testing Tool Kit* CD available with this book.

FS   **8.** The survey also reported that younger people are generally less trusting of social networking sites. More than a quarter of them said they "never" trust such sites.

CS   **9.** The truth is that younger users spend much more time on social networking sites than older users do; twenty-somethings simply have more information online to protect and more reason to be concerned.

CS   **10.** Fortunately, few of the people surveyed reported problems with private information being released. Taking precautions, as the younger users do, still seems wise.

Add a Comma and a Coordinating Conjunction

TIP Note that there is no comma *after* a coordinating conjunction.

A third way to correct a run-on is to add a comma and a **coordinating conjunction**: a link that joins independent clauses to form one sentence. Some people remember the seven coordinating conjunctions (*and, but, for, nor, or, so, yet*) by using the memory device of *fanboys*, for **f**or, **a**nd, **n**or, **b**ut, **o**r, **y**et, **s**o.

To correct a fused sentence, add both a comma and a coordinating conjunction. A comma splice already has a comma, so just add a coordinating conjunction that makes sense in the sentence.

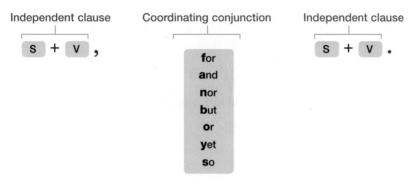

FUSED SENTENCES (corrected)

We warned Tim to wear a seat belt *, but* he refused.

He hit another car *, and* he went through the windshield.

COMMA SPLICES (corrected)

He was unbelievably lucky, *for* he got just scrapes and bruises.

He is driving again, *but* he always buckles his seat belt before starting the car.

LANGUAGE NOTE: **Coordinating** conjunctions need to connect two independent clauses. They are not used to join a dependent and an independent clause.

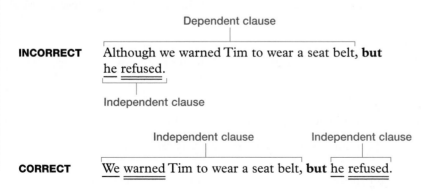

....

PRACTICE 3   Correcting a Run-on by Adding a Comma and a Coordinating Conjunction

Correct each of the following run-ons. First, underline the subjects and double-underline the verbs to find the separate sentences. Then, add a comma (unless the run-on already includes one) and a coordinating conjunction.

> **EXAMPLE:** Tasmania, an island off the coast of Australia, is the home
> *but*
> of many unusual kinds of wildlife, it also has been the site
> of several oil spills.   *Answers may vary. Possible edits shown.*

1. Fairy penguins, a small breed of penguin, live in Tasmania *, and* these
    birds have often been the victims of oil spills.

2. The birds clean their feathers with their beaks *, and* they swallow the oil
    on their feathers.

3. Unfortunately, the penguins' attempts to clean off their feathers can
    be fatal *, for* crude oil is poisonous to penguins.

4. Wildlife conservationists in Tasmania expected future spills, *so* they
    created a plan to save the penguins.

5. One of the conservationists created a pattern for a sweater for the
    penguins *, and* volunteers from around the world knitted these unusual
    sweaters.

6. The sweaters cover everything but the penguins' heads and feet, *so*
    they cannot lick the oil-poisoned feathers.

7. Most of the sweaters were made by elderly nursing-home residents
    in Tasmania, *but* some were sent from as far away as Japan.

8. After future spills, a fairy penguin may wear a sweater *, or* it also might
    wear a tiny football jersey.

9. Some creative <u>knitters</u> <u>made</u> tuxedo-patterned sweaters _∧*, and* a <u>few</u> of

　　these penguin suits even <u>have</u> bow ties.

10. The <u>penguins</u> <u>have</u> a variety of protective outfits _∧*, but* they <u>do not like</u>

　　any of the garments.

....

Add a Dependent Word

The fourth way to correct a run-on is to make one of the complete sentences a dependent clause by adding a dependent word (a **subordinating conjunction** or a **relative pronoun**), such as *after, because, before, even though, if, though, unless,* or *when.* Choose the dependent word that best expresses the relationship between the two clauses.

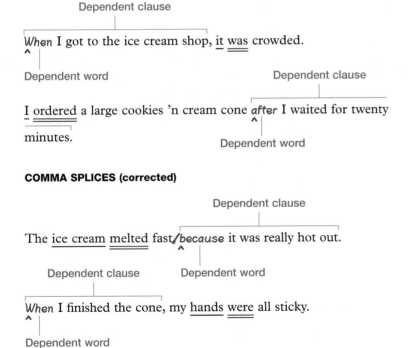

FUSED SENTENCES (corrected)

Dependent clause

When I got to the ice cream shop, <u>it</u> <u>was</u> crowded.
∧

Dependent word

Dependent clause

<u>I</u> ordered a large cookies 'n cream cone *after* I waited for twenty

minutes.

Dependent word

COMMA SPLICES (corrected)

Dependent clause

The <u>ice cream</u> <u>melted</u> fast/*because* it was really hot out.
∧

Dependent clause　　　　Dependent word

When I finished the cone, my <u>hands</u> <u>were</u> all sticky.
∧

Dependent word

When the dependent clause starts off the sentence, you need to add a comma after it, as in the first and fourth sentences in the preceding examples. When the dependent clause is after the independent clause, there is no comma, as in the second and third examples.

Common Dependent Words

after	if	what(ever)
although	since	when(ever)
as	so that	where
because	that	whether
before	though	which(ever)
even though	unless	while
how	until	who/whose

PRACTICE 4   Correcting a Run-On by Making a Dependent Clause

Correct each of the following run-ons. First, underline the subjects and double-underline the verbs to find the separate sentences. Then, make one of the clauses dependent by adding a dependent word. Add a comma after the dependent clause if it comes first in the sentence.

EXAMPLE: Everyone knows where a compass points, ~~it points~~
            which is
          ^toward the north.   *Answers may vary. Possible edits shown.*

 Although this
1. ~~This~~ phenomenon is something we take for granted, it may be changing.

                                     because
2. A change in magnetism is possible ^the earth's magnetic field is getting weaker.

                                            when
3. Such a change happened before in the earth's history, ^magnetic materials pointed south instead of north for long periods.

  Although a
4. ^A complete reversal could take thousands of years, some effects of the weaker magnetic field are already apparent.

                                         which
5. The change in magnetism has affected some satellites, ~~the satellites~~^ have been damaged.

6. Animals <u>may</u> also <u>be affected</u> some of them <u>use</u> the earth's

   magnetic field to sense where they are located.

   because (above "some of them")

7. *Because bees*

   ~~Bees~~, pigeons, salmon, turtles, whales, newts, and even <u>bacteria</u>

   <u>need</u> the magnetic field to navigate, <u>they</u> <u>will adjust</u> to the magnetic

   change.

8. However, <u>it</u> <u>could take</u> five thousand to seven thousand years

   before

   compasses <u>would point</u> south instead of north.

9. The processes affecting magnetism <u>may unfold</u> much more slowly,

   so that

   the magnetic <u>change</u> <u>may</u> not <u>occur</u> for millions of years.

10. *While the*

    ~~The~~ dinosaurs <u>roamed</u> the earth for about thirty-five million years,

    the earth's magnetic <u>field</u> <u>did</u> not <u>change</u> during all this time.

···

A Word That Can Cause Run-Ons: *Then*

Many run-ons are caused by the word *then.* You can use *then* to join two sentences, but if you add it without the correct punctuation and/or joining word, the resulting sentence will be a run-on. Often, writers mistakenly use just a comma before *then,* but that makes a comma splice. To correct a run-on caused by the word *then,* you can use any of the four methods presented in this chapter.

COMMA SPLICE	I <u>grabbed</u> the remote, then <u>I</u> <u>ate</u> my pizza.
CORRECTED	I <u>grabbed</u> the remote. Then <u>I</u> <u>ate</u> my pizza.
	[period added]
CORRECTED	I <u>grabbed</u> the remote; then <u>I</u> <u>ate</u> my pizza.
	[semicolon added]
CORRECTED	I <u>grabbed</u> the remote, and then <u>I</u> <u>ate</u> my pizza.
	[coordinating conjunction *and* added]
CORRECTED	I <u>grabbed</u> the remote before ~~then~~ <u>I</u> <u>ate</u> my pizza.
	[dependent word *before* added to make a dependent clause]

Edit Paragraphs and Your Own Writing

TEACHING TIP
Have students review
a rough draft and
highlight problem
sentences. Then,
have them edit each
sentence systemati-
cally to make sure it
has one subject and
one verb and ex-
presses a single
complete thought.

As you edit the following paragraphs and your own writing, use the check-list that follows. You may also want to refer to the chart on page 430.

CHECKLIST: EDITING FOR RUN-ONS

FOCUS

☐ Read each sentence aloud, and listen carefully as you read.

ASK

☐ Am I pausing in the middle of the sentence?

☐ If so, are there two subjects and two verbs?

☐ If so, are there two complete sentences in this sentence?

☐ If there are two sentences (independent clauses), are they separated by punctuation? If the answer is "no," the sentence is a **fused sentence**.

☐ If there is punctuation between the two independent clauses, is it a comma only, with no coordinating conjunction? If the answer is "yes," the sentence is a **comma splice**.

EDIT

☐ If the sentence is a run-on, correct it using one of the four methods for editing run-ons.

RESOURCES
For cumulative Editing
Review Tests, see
pages 667–83.

Find and correct any run-ons in the following paragraphs. Use whichever of the four methods of correcting run-ons that seems best to you. *Answers may vary. Possible edits shown.*

· ·

EDITING REVIEW 1 (6 run-ons)

(1) Your memory can play tricks on you. (2) It is often easy to forget
when
things ͜ you want desperately to remember them. (3) You have probably
which
had the experience of forgetting an acquaintance's name ~~the name,~~ ͜
comes to your mind only when it is too late. (4) You have also probably
because
been unable to find your keys once in a while͜ you put them down
somewhere without thinking. (5) At other times, however, you may find
even though
it difficult to forget some things͜ you wish you could never think of them
again. (6) If you have an annoying song in your mind, you may spend
hours wishing desperately to forget it. (7) Sometimes, you may find

yourself forced to relive your most embarrassing moment over and over again in your mind your memory will not let you leave that part of your past behind. (8) Some scholars believe that these annoying habits of memory evolved for a reason, it is hard to imagine, though, any good reason for developing the ability to forget where you left your keys.

· ·

EDITING REVIEW 2 (10 run-ons)

(1) There is one primary rule about cooking for astronauts, never make food that crumbles. (2) Looking for crumbs in a space station is no fun for the same reason, salt and pepper for astronauts are always in liquid form. (3) Space cuisine has come a long way since the first astronauts went up in 1961 those *Gemini* astronauts primarily had gelatin-coated food cubes and aluminum tubes of apple sauce. (4) They now get fresh fruit on occasion as well as such choices as shrimp cocktail, mashed potatoes with bacon, green beans with garlic, and New Orleans jambalaya, they have to be especially careful with some food choices, though. (5) For example, the Russians often bring tomatoes when it is their turn to supply the space station it is not wise to bite right into a fresh tomato because it can squirt out juice which then has to be tracked down. (6) Every dish is eventually consumed, even if it is not liked, wasting food makes no sense when anything can happen in space. (7) NASA's current challenge is preparing and packaging food for the planned expeditions to Mars this food will have to have a five-year shelf life. (8) The food will be shot into space before the astronauts are first the food will go up, which will take six months. (9) Getting the astronauts to Mars will take another six months, returning adds yet another six months, and delays have to be anticipated due to possible weather or mechanical problems. (10) A lot of thought is going into

minimizing bacterial growth in the food *, for* bacteria is the last thing one

wants on a space mission.

. . . .

EDITING REVIEW 3 (12 run-ons)

(1) The number of bike riders is growing, especially in American cities *because* increasing numbers of people are riding bikes to work and for exercise. (2) This makes it all the more important for drivers and bike riders to learn to share the road *.E* every year, approximately 46,000 bike riders are injured in crashes with motor vehicles. (3) The good news is that most of these accidents are preventable, *but* it takes special care on the part of both drivers and riders. (4) Car drivers need to recognize that bicycles have a legal right to use most roads *, although* bikes must ride on the shoulder when the speed limit is over fifty miles per hour. (5) When coming up on a cyclist, slow down *;* when passing, give the bike at least three feet of clearance. (6) Be especially careful with young cyclists, even those on the sidewalks, *because* they can suddenly dart out in traffic without looking. (7) When making a right turn, make sure there is no bicycle on the right *;* when waiting to turn left or at a stop sign, yield to a bicycle that has the right of way. (8) Check carefully for bicycles before opening a car door *. C* cyclists have been killed by headlong crashes into suddenly opened car doors. (9) Bike riders need to follow the same traffic rules that apply to drivers *. W* wait for a green light before crossing intersections and signal before all turns and stops. (10) Try to ride at least three feet from parked cars *;* do not weave in and out between parked cars. (11) Do not ride wearing headphones or while talking on a cell phone *, and* always wear a properly fitted bike helmet. (12) Increasing bike riding is a good sign for the environment and for Americans' expanding waistlines, *but* for everyone's safety, both drivers and riders must vigilantly follow the rules of road-sharing.

EDITING REVIEW 4 (10 run-ons and 7 formal English errors)

(1) In times past, when a Ping-Pong player could not find someone to play against, that meant there was no Ping-Pong, *. T* ^those times are now over. (2) More and more, people are installing in their basements and garages the perfect Ping-Pong partner ~~it~~ *, which* ^is a robot that endlessly serves fast-moving Ping-Pong balls. (3) There ~~R~~ *^are* several ~~dfrnt~~ *different* Ping-Pong robots on the market, *but* ^they all do basically the same thing. (4) They pitch balls one by one to the person on the other side of the table *;* ^the fancier ones have nets that can catch return balls and funnel them back to the automatic server. (5) The human player ~~cn~~ *can* control the speed, placement, *and* ^and spin of the balls, ^the more elaborate models allow random serves or a programmed series of serves that can, for example, go ~~2~~ *to* ^alternate sides of the table. (6) Some players feel that the robots ~~cn b mo~~ *can be more* ^ ^ ^challenging to play against than a human opponent *because* ^it is hard to see where the ball is coming from. (7) Human players partially give away their intentions with their body position, the angle of the paddle, and the type of stroke *;* ^none of these cues is visible with a robot server. (8) The ability of some robots to spin balls is also helpful, say some players *, for* ^the machine can be set to replay the exact same spinned serve repeatedly, allowing the person to better learn how to counter it. (9) The Ping-Pong robots with retrieving nets can save the human player time and effort *; however,* ^some humans appreciate the break to pick up balls. (10) The relentless machine can provide an exhausting workout, *which* ^of course, for many robot owners, is the whole point.

PRACTICE 5   Editing Your Own Writing for Run-Ons

As a final practice, edit run-ons in a piece of your own writing — a paper you are working on for this class, a paper you've already finished, a paper for another course, or a recent piece of writing from your work or everyday life. Use the checklist on page 426 and the chart on page 430 to help you.

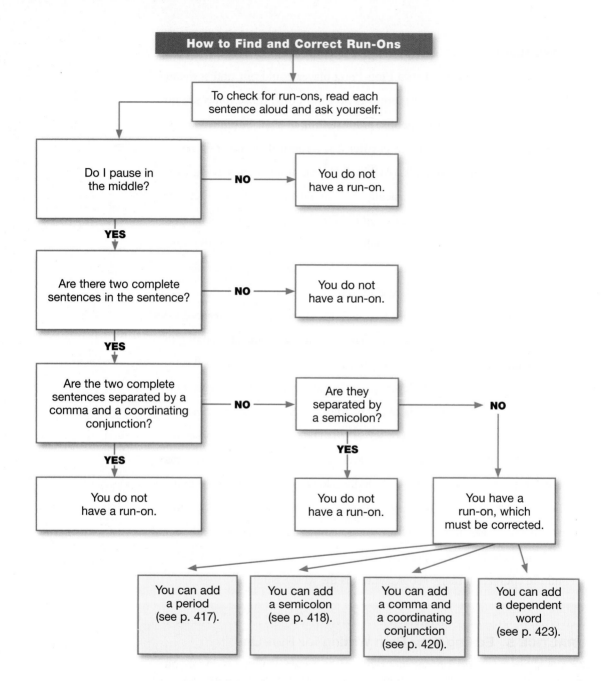

Problems with Subject-Verb Agreement

When Subjects and Verbs Do Not Match

Understand What Subject-Verb Agreement Is

In any sentence, **the subject and the verb must match—or agree—in number**. If the subject is singular (one person, place, or thing), then the verb must also be singular. If the subject is plural (more than one), the verb must also be plural.

> **SINGULAR**   The <u>phone</u> <u><u>rings</u></u> constantly at work.
>
> [The subject, *phone,* is singular—just one phone—so the verb must take the singular form: *rings.*]
>
> **PLURAL**   The <u>phones</u> <u><u>ring</u></u> constantly at work.
>
> [The subject, *phones,* is plural—more than one phone—so the verb must take the plural form: *ring.*]

Regular verbs, verbs that follow standard English patterns, have two forms in the present tense: one that does not add an ending and one that ends in *-s.* First-person (*I, we*) subjects, second-person (*you*) subjects, and plural subjects (more than one person, place, or thing) have verbs with no *-s* ending. Third-person singular subjects (*he, she, it,* and singular nouns) always have a verb that ends in *-s.* The chart that follows shows the differences.

IDEA JOURNAL
Write about a major disagreement you had with someone.

In the examples throughout this chapter, the <u>subject</u> is underlined once, and the <u>verb</u> is underlined twice.

For more on regular verbs and how they differ from irregular verbs, see Chapter 26.

431

Regular Verbs, Present Tense

	SINGULAR FORM	PLURAL FORM
First person	I walk.	We walk.
Second person	You walk.	You walk.
Third person	He/she/it walks.	They walk.
	Percy walks.	Percy and Don walk.
	The dog walks.	The dogs walk.

LANGUAGE NOTE: Some nouns that do not end in -*s* are plural, so they need plural verbs. For example, *children* and *people* do not end in -*s*, but they mean more than one child or person, so they are plural.

INCORRECT   The people owns their apartments.

CORRECT   The people own their apartments.

In the Real World, Why Is It Important to Correct Subject-Verb Agreement Problems?

Like fragments and run-ons, subject-verb agreement errors are significant problems that can make a bad impression with instructors, employers, and others.

SITUATION: Part of Monique's work at the National Military Family Association involves helping people find and apply for various kinds of assistance. Below is a letter from a woman seeking help for her son who has returned from deployment in Iraq with symptoms of post-traumatic stress disorder.

Dear X:
My son, Corporal Jonas Brown, were in Iraq. Now he is home, and he have many problems that is getting worse. He wake up every night screaming, and he cry and hold his head in his hands. Jonas, a young man who always work very hard, have not been able to hold a job. He is changed, and he need help before he hurt himself. His friends from the army talks to me and says as a veteran he are able to get free help. Please tell me what I should do.

WRITER AT WORK

Monique Rizer, a journalist and development associate, read the woman's letter and made the following comments.

MONIQUE RIZER'S RESPONSE: Many veterans suffer from post-traumatic stress disorder, and military resources are stretched thin. Unfortunately, the people most likely to get the help they need are those who can present their case well in writing. For someone like the mother who wrote this letter, the chances are not good.

(See Monique Rizer's **PROFILE OF SUCCESS** on page 154.)

(See Monique Rizer's **PROFILE OF SUCCESS** on page 154.)

Find and Correct Errors in Subject-Verb Agreement

To find problems with subject-verb agreement in your own writing, read carefully, and look for the five trouble spots covered in this chapter.

> **TEACHING TIP** Remind students that correcting each of the four most serious grammar errors depends on being able to identify the subject and the verb in a sentence.

. . . .

PRACTICE 1   Finding Subject-Verb Agreement Problems

Find and underline the thirteen subject-verb agreement problems in the letter about Corporal Jonas Brown on page 432.

. . . .

The Verb Is a Form of *Be, Have,* or *Do*

The verbs *be, have,* and *do* do not follow the regular patterns for forming singular and plural forms; they are **irregular verbs**.

These verbs cause problems for people who use only one form of the verb in casual conversation: *You be the richest* (incorrect). *You are the richest* (correct). In college and at work, use the correct form of the verbs *be, have,* and *do* as shown in the charts on the next page.

<u>You</u> ~~is~~ *are* the craziest person I have ever known.

<u>Johnson</u> ~~have~~ *has* the best car in the lot.

<u>Valery</u> ~~do~~ *does* the bill paying on the first of every month.

Forms of the Verb *Be*

PRESENT TENSE	SINGULAR	PLURAL
First person	I am	we are
Second person	you are	you are
Third person	she/he/it is	they are
	the student/Joe is	the students are

PAST TENSE		
First person	I was	we were
Second person	you were	you were
Third person	she/he/it was	they were
	the student/Joe was	the students were

Forms of the Verb *Have*, Present Tense

	SINGULAR	PLURAL
First person	I have	we have
Second person	you have	you have
Third person	she/he/it has	they have
	the student/Joe has	the students have

Forms of the Verb *Do*, Present Tense

	SINGULAR	PLURAL
First person	I do	we do
Second person	you do	you do
Third person	she/he/it does	they do
	the student/Joe does	the students do

PRACTICE 2   Choosing the Correct Form of *Be, Have,* or *Do*

In each sentence, underline the subject of the verb *be, have,* or *do,* and circle the correct form of the verb.

> **EXAMPLE:** The microwave <u>oven</u> (am /(is)/ are) a common fixture in most American homes.

1. Yet many <u>people</u> (has /(have)) concerns about the safety of this standard appliance.

2. <u>They</u> (am / is /(are)) worried that standing close to an operating microwave oven can expose them to harmful radiation.

3. Some microwave <u>ovens</u> (does /(do)) in fact leak radiation, but the levels that might be released are quite small.

4. The <u>Center for Devices and Radiological Health</u>, a unit of the U.S. Food and Drug Administration, ((has)/ have) responsibility for regulating microwave oven safety.

5. According to the Center, the allowed <u>amount</u> of leakage from each microwave oven that reaches the market (am /(is)/ are) far below the level of radiation that is harmful to humans.

6. <u>Manufacturers</u> of microwave ovens (does /(do)) even more to assure the safety of their products.

7. All microwave <u>ovens</u> (has /(have)) a type of door latch that prevents the production of microwaves whenever the latch is released.

8. Also, the <u>doors</u> of microwave ovens (am / is /(are)) lined with a metal mesh that stops microwaves from escaping.

9. Furthermore, the radiation <u>level</u> from a microwave oven (am /(is)/ are) extremely low at a distance of even a foot from the oven.

10. Therefore, the <u>radiation</u> from an operating microwave oven (do / (does)) not pose a threat to anyone.

TEACHING TIP
Complete the practices in this chapter as a group, and ask students to read the sentences aloud. What differences do they find in formal versus informal communication? How do they account for those differences?

For more practice with subject-verb agreement, visit *Exercise Central* at bedfordstmartins .com/realessays.

RESOURCES
To gauge students' skills in correcting subject-verb agreement problems, use the *Testing Tool Kit* CD available with this book.

· ·

PRACTICE 3   Using the Correct Form of *Be, Have,* or *Do*

In each sentence, underline the subject and fill in the correct form of the verb (*be, have,* or *do*) indicated in parentheses.

> **EXAMPLE:** Our <u>professor</u> <u>*has*</u> (*have*) forty papers to grade this weekend.

1. Most <u>students</u> <u>*are*</u> (*be*) used to the idea that computers sometimes grade tests.

2. <u>You</u> <u>*have*</u> (*have*) probably taken standardized tests and filled in small ovals with a pencil.

3. A <u>computer</u> <u>*does*</u> (*do*) not have to be sophisticated to read the results of such tests.

4. Surprisingly, one software <u>program</u> <u>*is*</u> (*be*) designed to grade student essays.

5. The <u>program</u> <u>*has*</u> (*have*) the ability to sort words in an essay and compare the essay to others in its database.

6. The <u>software</u> <u>*does*</u> (*do*) not check grammar or spelling.

7. <u>Teachers</u> <u>*are*</u> (*be*) still needed to supplement the computer grade, according to the software manufacturer.

8. If a computer grades your essay, <u>you</u> <u>*have*</u> (*have*) to write about one of five hundred specified topics.

9. A <u>computer</u> <u>*does*</u> (*do*) check the organization, clarity, and style of your writing.

10. Some <u>teachers</u> <u>*are*</u> (*be*) excited about their computerized assistant, but <u>I</u> <u>*do*</u> (*do*) not like the idea of a computer grading my essays.

· ·

Words Come between the Subject and the Verb

When the subject and the verb are not right next to each other, it can be difficult to make sure that they agree. Most often, what comes between the subject and the verb is either a prepositional phrase or a dependent clause.

Prepositional Phrase between the Subject and the Verb

A **prepositional phrase** starts with a preposition and ends with a noun or pronoun: The line *for the movie* went *around the corner*.

For a list of common prepositions, see page 387.

Remember, the subject of a sentence is never in a prepositional phrase. When you are looking for the subject, you can cross out any prepositional phrases. This strategy should help you find the real subject and decide whether it agrees with the verb.

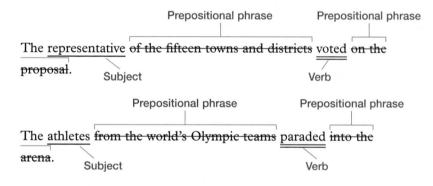

PRACTICE 4   Making Subjects and Verbs Agree When They Are Separated by a Prepositional Phrase

In each of the following sentences, first cross out the prepositional phrase between the subject and the verb, and then circle the correct form of the verb. Remember, the subject of a sentence is never in a prepositional phrase.

> **EXAMPLE:** Twenty-eight million people ~~in the United States~~ (am /
>
> is /(are)) deaf or hard of hearing.

1. Most parents ~~with hearing loss~~ (has /(have)) children who can hear.

2. Many ~~of these children~~ (learns /(learn)) sign language as a first language.

3. Communication ~~with words~~ (comes / come) later.

4. Few people ~~in the hearing world~~ (understands / understand) the lives of deaf people completely.

5. Many deaf people ~~in this country~~ (feels / feel) closer to deaf people from other parts of the world than to hearing Americans.

6. The hearing children ~~of deaf parents~~ (comes / come) closer to understanding deaf culture than most hearing people.

7. A hearing child ~~in a deaf household~~ (resembles / resemble) a child of immigrant parents in many ways.

8. Adapting ~~to two different cultures~~ (makes / make) fitting in difficult for some young people.

9. Sometimes, ties ~~to the hearing world and the deaf world~~ (pulls / pull) in opposite directions.

10. Bridges ~~between cultures~~ (am / is / are) more easily built by people who understand both sides.

Dependent Clause between the Subject and the Verb

A **dependent clause** has a subject and a verb, but it does not express a complete thought. When a dependent clause comes between the subject and the verb, it usually starts with the word *who, whose, whom, that,* or *which.*

The subject of a sentence is never in the dependent clause. When you are looking for the subject, you can cross out any dependent clauses.

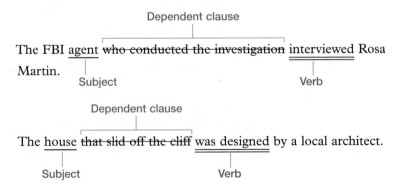

Dependent clause

The FBI agent ~~who conducted the investigation~~ interviewed Rosa Martin.
      Subject   Verb

Dependent clause

The house ~~that slid off the cliff~~ was designed by a local architect.
   Subject   Verb

PRACTICE 5 **Making Subjects and Verbs Agree When They Are Separated by a Dependent Clause**

In each of the following sentences, cross out any dependent clauses. Then, correct any problems with subject-verb agreement. If a sentence has no problem, write "OK" next to it.

EXAMPLE: A person ~~who lies in job applications~~ *is* ~~are~~ likely to get

caught.

1. A résumé, ~~which is a job applicant's first contact with many prospective employers,~~ *contains* ~~contain~~ details about past work experience and education.

2. Many people ~~who write résumés~~ are tempted to exaggerate. *OK*

3. Perhaps an applicant ~~who held a previous job for two months~~ *claims* ~~claim~~ to have spent a year there.

4. A job title ~~that sounds impressive~~ *looks* ~~look~~ good on a résumé, whether or not it is accurate.

5. Often, a person ~~who never received a college degree~~ wants to add it to a résumé anyway. *OK*

6. A person ~~who is considering untrue résumé additions~~ *needs* ~~need~~ to think twice.

7. Employers ~~who like a résumé~~ *check* ~~checks~~ the information provided by the applicant.

8. A résumé ~~that contains false information~~ goes in the reject pile. *OK*

9. In addition, many people ~~who invent material on a résumé~~ *forget* ~~forgets~~ the inventions when they face a prospective employer in an interview.

10. Even a company ~~that does not check all of the information on résumés~~ pays attention when interviewees seem to forget some of their qualifications. *OK*

The Sentence Has a Compound Subject

A **compound subject** consists of two (or more) subjects connected by *and, or,* or *nor* (as in *neither/nor* expressions). If two subjects are joined by *and,* they combine to become a plural subject, and the verb must take a plural form as well.

Subject *and*   Subject   Plural form of verb

The <u>director</u> *and* the <u>producer</u> <u>decide</u> how the film will be made.

If two subjects are connected by *or* or *nor,* they are considered separate, and the verb should agree with the subject closest to it.

Subject *or* Singular subject   Singular form of verb

The <u>director</u> *or* the <u>producer</u> <u>decides</u> how the film will be made.

Subject *nor* Singular subject Singular form of verb

Neither the <u>director</u> *nor* the <u>producer</u> <u>wants</u> to give up control.

Subject *or*   Plural subject   Plural form of verb

The <u>director</u> *or* his <u>assistants</u> <u>decide</u> how the film will be made.

Subject *nor*   Plural subject   Plural form of verb

Neither the <u>director</u> *nor* his <u>assistants</u> <u>want</u> to give up control.

· ·

PRACTICE 6   **Choosing the Correct Verb in a Sentence with a Compound Subject**

In each of the following sentences, underline the word (*and, or,* or *nor*) that joins the parts of the compound subject. Then, circle the correct form of the verb.

EXAMPLE: A child <u>and</u> an adult (has /(have)) different nutritional needs.

1. Fruits <u>and</u> vegetables (does /(do)) not make up enough of most Americans' diets.

2. The U.S. government <u>and</u> other organizations concerned with health and nutrition (recommends /<u>recommend</u>) that people eat at least five servings of fruits and vegetables a day.

3. Whole-grain cereal <u>or</u> bread (<u>is</u>/ are) another important part of a healthy diet.

4. Neither vitamins <u>nor</u> fiber (<u>is</u>/ are) found in many popular snack foods.

5. Potato chips <u>and</u> candy (contains /<u>contain</u>) few useful nutrients.

6. Neither fat <u>nor</u> sugar (<u>helps</u> / help) build a healthy body.

7. However, in small amounts, fat <u>and</u> sugar (contributes /<u>contribute</u>) beneficially by making food taste good.

8. Motivated dieters <u>and</u> certain health fanatics (eats /<u>eat</u>) nutritious food that tastes terrible.

9. Neither dieters <u>nor</u> health fanatics (is /<u>are</u>) likely to keep eating the unappetizing food for a lifetime.

10. Choosing nutritious food <u>and</u> preparing it well (allows /<u>allow</u>) a person to feel healthy and satisfied.

The Subject Is an Indefinite Pronoun

Indefinite pronouns, which refer to unspecified people or objects, are often singular, although there are exceptions.

When you find an indefinite pronoun in your writing, use the table on the next page to help you determine the correct verb form, singular or plural. If the pronoun may be singular or plural, you will need to check whether the word it refers to is singular or plural to determine what verb form to use.

<u>Everyone</u> <u>loves</u> vacations.

[*Everyone* is always singular, so it takes the singular verb *loves.*]

<u>Some</u> of the wreckage <u>was recovered</u> after the crash.

[In this case, *some* is singular, referring to *wreckage,* so it takes the singular verb *was recovered.*]

Indefinite Pronouns

ALWAYS SINGULAR

anybody	everyone	nothing
anyone	everything	one (of)
anything	much	somebody
each (of)	neither (of)	someone
either (of)	nobody	something
everybody	no one	

MAY BE SINGULAR OR PLURAL

all	none
any	some

Some of the workers <u>were delayed</u> by the storm.

[In this case, *some* is plural, referring to *workers*, so it takes the plural verb *were delayed*.]

Often, an indefinite pronoun is followed by a prepositional phrase or a dependent clause; remember that the subject of a sentence is never found in either of these. To choose the correct verb, you can cross out the prepositional phrase or dependent clause to focus on the indefinite pronoun.

All ~~of my first day on the job~~ <u>was devoted</u> to filling out forms.

Some ~~who are longtime residents~~ <u>recommend</u> a rent strike.

· ·

PRACTICE 7 Choosing the Correct Verb When the Subject Is an Indefinite Pronoun

In each of the following sentences, underline the indefinite pronoun that is the subject, and cross out any prepositional phrases or dependent clauses that come between the subject and the verb. Then, circle the correct verb.

EXAMPLE: <u>One</u> ~~of the oldest types of exercise that people use to stay in shape~~ ((is)/ are) once again fashionable.

1. <u>Many</u> ~~who choose this newly trendy type of exercise, which is walking,~~ (is /(are)) middle-aged or older.

2. Someone ~~with aching joints, past injuries, or an aging body~~ (want / (wants)) a relatively gentle form of exercise.

3. But everybody~~, even people who are young and in great shape,~~ (need / (needs)) exercise that is safe, practical, and enjoyable.

4. Those ~~who walk for aerobic exercise~~ ((sustain) / sustains), on average, fewer fitness-related injuries than people who run.

5. Nobody ~~with good sense or serious concern for his or her health~~ (pursue / (pursues)) activities that might risk bodily damage.

6. Furthermore, anyone ~~who sets aside the time and makes the effort to walk regularly~~ (benefit / (benefits)) in several ways.

7. Some ~~of today's active walkers~~ ((do) / does) it to lose weight.

8. Anybody ~~with a waistline problem, which is a category that includes too many people these days,~~ (appreciate / (appreciates)) the opportunity to shed 300 calories by walking briskly for an hour.

9. Others ~~who have the time for an energetic yet leisurely walk~~ ((enjoy) / enjoys) looking at people, stores, and the outdoors as they exercise and observing the new and unusual around them.

10. Depending on their specific situations and preferences, many people want a steady, low-impact type of exercise, like walking, and many others choose something more strenuous and demanding, such as running; either ~~type of exercise~~ (help / (helps)) them to have a more active and healthy life.

The Verb Comes before the Subject

In most sentences, the subject comes before the verb. Two kinds of sentences reverse that order — questions and sentences that begin with *here* or *there*. In these two types of sentences, you need to check carefully for errors in subject-verb agreement.

Questions

In questions, the verb or part of the verb comes before the subject. To find the subject and verb, you can turn the question around as if you were going to answer it.

Where is the nearest gas station? The nearest gas station is . . .

Are the keys in the car? The keys are in the car.

> **LANGUAGE NOTE:** Forming questions correctly is difficult for many people, especially those whose first language is not English. For charts that summarize how to correctly form questions, see Chapter 26.

Sentences That Begin with Here or There

When a sentence begins with *here* or *there,* the subject always follows the verb. Turn the sentence around to find the subject and verb.

Here are the hot dog rolls. The hot dog rolls are here.

There is a fly in my soup. A fly is in my soup.

> **LANGUAGE NOTE:** *There is* and *there are* are common in English. If you have trouble using these expressions, see pages 583–84.

....

PRACTICE 8 Correcting a Sentence When the Verb Comes before the Subject

Correct any problems with subject-verb agreement in the following sentences. If a sentence is already correct, write "OK" next to it.

> *are*
> **EXAMPLE:** There ~~is~~ several openings for bilingual applicants.
>   ^

are
1. Where ~~is~~ the corporation's main offices located?
                 ^

are
2. There ~~is~~ branch offices in Paris, Singapore, and Tokyo.
             ^

           does
3. How well ~~do~~ the average employee abroad speak English?

       does ^
4. What ~~do~~ the company manufacture?
         ^

                            is
5. How many languages ~~are~~ the manual written in?
                          ^

6. Does the company employ college graduates as entry-level translators? *OK*

7. There _are_ ~~is~~ some machines that can do translation.
        ^

8. Does learning a second language give an applicant an advantage? _OK_

9. There is never a disadvantage in knowing another language. _OK_

10. Here _are_ ~~is~~ the names of several qualified people.
        ^

Edit Paragraphs and Your Own Writing

As you edit the following paragraphs and your own writing, use the check-list that follows. You may also want to refer to the chart on page 448.

CHECKLIST

EDITING FOR SUBJECT-VERB AGREEMENT

FOCUS

☐ Whenever you see one of the five trouble spots in your writing, stop to check that the subject and the verb agree.

ASK

☐ Where is the subject in this sentence? Where is the verb?

☐ Do the subject and verb agree in number? (Are they both singular or both plural?)

EDIT

☐ If you answer "no" to the agreement question, you need to correct the sentence.

Find and correct any problems with subject-verb agreement that you find in the following paragraphs.

EDITING REVIEW 1 (7 errors)

(1) School systems around the country _are_ ~~is~~ embracing educational
standards. (2) The idea of standards _sounds_ ~~sound~~ reasonable. (3) Does anyone
                                          ^
want to argue that students should not have to meet certain requirements to graduate? (4) A national standard for all American students
has
~~have~~ many supporters, too. (5) If the requirements for graduation in
  ^

RESOURCES
For cumulative Editing Review Tests, see pages 667–83.

                 are

Oregon and Tennessee ~~is~~ the same, everyone with a high school diploma

gets a similar education. (6) There is a catch, of course. (7) Not every-

one with a professional or personal interest in school quality is able to

                               are

agree on these requirements. (8) Mathematics and writing ~~is~~ important,

   are   *are*

but so ~~is~~ music and physical education. (9) How ~~is~~ parents, teachers,

and administrators ever going to find standards that everyone accepts?

....

EDITING REVIEW 2 (9 errors)

                          is

    (1) Agreeing on school standards ~~are~~ only part of the battle over

              are

education. (2) How ~~is~~ students going to prove that they have met the

                                   is

standards before graduation? (3) The answer, in many cases, ~~are~~ testing.

                             are

(4) School tests that are required by state law ~~is~~ becoming more and

more common. (5) These tests are standardized, so all of the students

                       are

taking an eighth-grade test in a particular state ~~is~~ given the same test.

                                        are

(6) Both the individual student and his or her school district ~~is~~ evalu-

                              learn

ated by the scores. (7) The parents of a student ~~learns~~ not only what

their child's score is but also how the school compares with others

                              are

around the state. (8) Then, children who need extra help ~~is~~ supposed to

                                   become

receive it, and schools with very low scores year after year ~~becomes~~

eligible for additional resources.

....

EDITING REVIEW 3 (6 errors)

    (1) In reality, standardized tests for schools have many problems.

                                   use

(2) Most school districts that have a testing program ~~uses~~ tests that can

be scored by a computer. (3) Computers cannot read, so the tests that

                 offer

they grade usually ~~offers~~ multiple-choice questions. (4) A multiple-

                             does

choice test in science or mathematics ~~do~~ not allow students to

                        do

demonstrate critical thinking. (5) How ~~does~~ students show their writing

                        are

ability on such a test? (6) There ~~is~~ tricks to answering multiple-choice questions that many students learn. (7) Frequently, a high score on such a test says more about the student's test-taking ability than about his or her knowledge of a subject. (8) Nevertheless, the quick results and low cost of a computer-graded multiple-choice test ~~means~~ *mean* that this imperfect testing system is used in many school systems.

EDITING REVIEW 4 (7 errors and 4 formal English errors)

(1) Another problem with standardized tests ~~are~~ *is* that test material ~~en~~ *can* begin to change the curriculum. (2) Everyone who teaches ~~want~~ *wants* his or her students *to* 2 get high scores on the tests. (3) For one thing, a teacher of underperforming students ~~are~~ *is* likely to be criticized for not preparing them ~~btr.~~ *better* (4) One result of teachers' fears ~~are~~ *is* that they spend most of the class time preparing students for the test. (5) In some cases, the phenomenon of "teaching to the test" ~~become~~ *becomes* school policy. (6) A creative teacher or one who has been teaching for years ~~are~~ *is* no longer trusted to engage students with a subject. (7) ~~Skul~~ *School* officials, who also want high scores for their districts, encourage teachers to focus on material that the test will cover. (8) Other material, which may be fascinating to students, ~~are~~ *is* ignored because the test does not require it.

PRACTICE 9 Editing Your Own Writing for Subject-Verb Agreement

As a final practice, edit for subject-verb agreement in a piece of your own writing — a paper you are working on for this class, a paper you have already finished, a paper for another course, or a recent piece of writing from your work or everyday life. Use the checklist on page 445 and the chart on page 448 to help you.

TEAMWORK
Have students exchange and read drafts of their writing, focusing on subject-verb agreement.

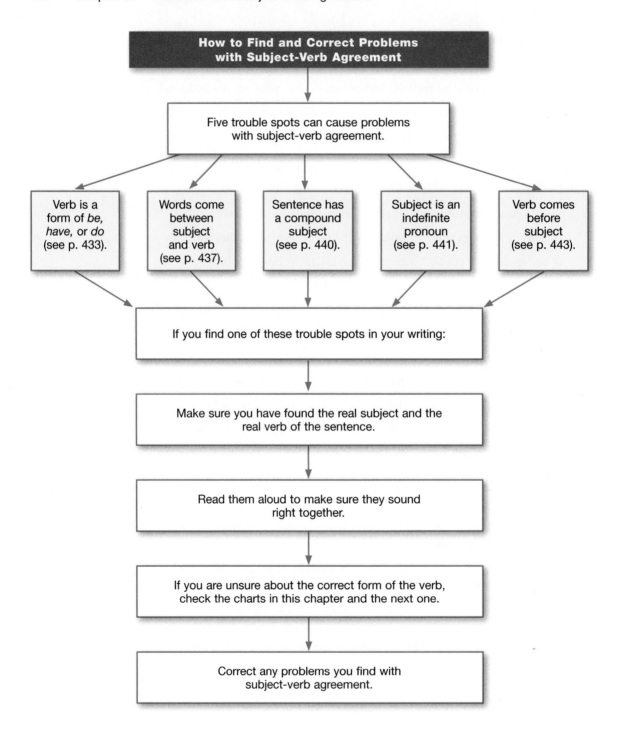

How to Find and Correct Problems with Subject-Verb Agreement

Five trouble spots can cause problems with subject-verb agreement.

Verb is a form of *be, have,* or *do* (see p. 433).

Words come between subject and verb (see p. 437).

Sentence has a compound subject (see p. 440).

Subject is an indefinite pronoun (see p. 441).

Verb comes before subject (see p. 443).

If you find one of these trouble spots in your writing:

Make sure you have found the real subject and the real verb of the sentence.

Read them aloud to make sure they sound right together.

If you are unsure about the correct form of the verb, check the charts in this chapter and the next one.

Correct any problems you find with subject-verb agreement.

26

Verb Problems

Avoiding Mistakes in Verb Tense

Understand What Verb Tense Is

Verb tense tells *when* the action of a sentence occurs—in the present, in the past, or in the future. Verbs change their form and use the helping verbs *have* or *be* to indicate different tenses.

To choose the correct form and tense, consider whether the subject is singular or plural *and* when the action occurs.

PRESENT TENSE	Teresa and I talk every day. [Plural subject]
PRESENT TENSE	She also talks to her mother every morning. [Singular subject]
PAST TENSE	Yesterday, they talked for two hours. [Plural subject]
FUTURE TENSE	Tomorrow, they will talk again. [Plural subject]

LANGUAGE NOTE: Remember to add the endings on present-tense and past-tense verbs, even if they cannot be heard in speech.

PRESENT TENSE	Krystal plays varsity basketball.
PAST TENSE	She rode downtown on her bike.

IDEA JOURNAL Write about something you did yesterday. Then, write about it again as if you are going to do it tomorrow.

In the examples throughout this chapter, the subject is underlined once, and the verb is underlined twice.

449

For more on subject-
verb agreement and
singular versus plural
verb forms, see
Chapter 25.

Regular verbs follow a few standard patterns in the present and past tenses, and their past-tense and past-participle forms end in *-ed* or *-d*.

Irregular verbs change spelling in the past-tense and past-participle forms. (For more on irregular verbs, see pp. 464–72.)

	REGULAR VERB: *WALK*	IRREGULAR VERB: *EAT*
Past tense	walked [I walk**ed**.]	ate [I ate.]
Past participle	walked [I have/had walk**ed**.]	eaten [I have/had eaten.]

In the Real World, Why Is It Important to Use Correct Verbs?

Errors in verb tense can create a negative impression of the writer, as the following example shows.

SITUATION: A student that Shawn has been working with shows him the script for an oral presentation he has to give in school the following week. Here is what the student wrote as an introduction.

> Last week I done gone to the awards day for Diamond Educators and receive my first prize ever. I receive the prize because last semester I work with younger kids to help them do things right, like doing their homework and why it be important to go to school. Before I meet people at Diamond, I never understand why school matter. I believe that only fools cared about school, but now I know education can change my life. Trying to get a good education don't mean selling out: It mean making something of myself.

WRITER AT WORK

Shawn Brown, founder of Diamond Educators, read the student's introduction, and
made the following comments.

SHAWN BROWN'S RESPONSE: The
student has great ideas here, but there are
lots of errors that will make people ignore his
good ideas. He is writing more like he talks
informally, and I tell people over and over
that they need to know how and when to
use "formal" English. It is important to
achieving their own goals and to getting a
better life.

(See Shawn Brown's **PROFILE OF SUCCESS** on page 311.)

Use Correct Verbs

Verbs have several tenses to express past, present, and future time. This section will explain what those tenses are and how to use them correctly when you write.

Regular Verbs

To avoid mistakes with regular verbs, understand the basic patterns for forming the present, past, and future tenses.

Present Tense

The **simple present tense** is used for actions that are happening at the same time that you are writing about them and about actions that are ongoing. There are two forms for the simple present tense of regular verbs—**-s ending** or **no added ending**. Use the -s ending when the subject is *she, he,* or *it,* or the name of one person or thing. Do not add any ending for other subjects.

Regular Verbs in the Simple Present Tense

	SINGULAR	PLURAL
First person	I laugh.	We laugh.
Second person	You laugh.	You laugh.
Third person	She/he/it laugh**s**.	They laugh.
	The baby laugh**s**.	The babies laugh.

....

PRACTICE 1   **Finding Verb Errors**

Find and underline the eleven errors in the student's writing on page 450.

....

PRACTICE 2   **Using the Simple Present Tense
of Regular Verbs**

In each of the following sentences, first underline the subject, and then circle the correct verb form.

> **EXAMPLE:** Most elevator <u>riders</u> ((share) / shares) a common
> complaint.

For more practice
with verbs, visit
Exercise Central at
bedfordstmartins
.com/realessays.

1. Too often, elevator <u>doors</u> ((open) / opens) at practically every floor even when there are just a few people in the car.

2. Now, <u>guests</u> at one big hotel ((enjoy) / enjoys) faster, more direct elevator rides, thanks to a new "smart elevator" system.

3. The <u>system</u> (work / (works)) so well because it knows where people want to go before they get into their elevator car.

4. Whenever <u>someone</u> (want / (wants)) to take an elevator, he or she must first punch in the desired floor number at a keypad in the lobby.

5. A digital <u>display</u> then (indicate / (indicates)) the letter of the elevator car that will directly go to a floor close to the person's destination.

6. To ensure that guests do not get confused with the new system, <u>employees</u> of the hotel ((help) / helps) guests to use it correctly.

7. The hotel's <u>managers</u> ((claim) / claims) that the system reduces the average trip time by up to 30 percent.

8. However, some <u>guests</u> ((express) / expresses) irritation with the system.

9. <u>They</u> sometimes ((wait) / waits) a long time for an elevator, and then they cannot get into the first car that comes because it is not going near their floor.

RESOURCES
To gauge students'
verb skills, use the
Testing Tool Kit CD
available with this
book.

10. Still, most <u>people</u> who use the system ((consider) / considers) it to be a welcome improvement in elevator technology.

. . . .

Two other present-tense forms are the present progressive tense and the present perfect tense. The **present progressive tense** is used to describe actions that are in progress. It is formed as follows:

Present-tense form of *be* (helping verb)	+	Main verb with *-ing* ending

Present Progressive Tense

	SINGULAR	PLURAL
First person	I am laughing.	We are laughing.
Second person	You are laughing.	You are laughing.
Third person	She/he/it is laughing.	They are laughing.
	The baby is laughing.	The babies are laughing.

LANGUAGE NOTE: Some languages, such as Russian, do not use the progressive tense. If your first language does not use the progressive tense, pay special attention to this section.

PRACTICE 3   Using the Present Progressive Tense

In each of the following sentences, underline the helping verb (a form of *be*), and fill in the correct form of the verb in parentheses.

> **EXAMPLE:** My grandmother is ___looking___ (*look*) into our family history.

1. She is ___starting___ (*start*) with my grandfather's side of the family, the Mancinis.

2. To learn more about the Mancinis, she is ___contacting___ (*contact*) several of my grandfather's relatives to get birth documents and other information.

3. Also, she is ___gathering___ (*gather*) information about the Mancinis through genealogy sites on the Internet.

4. She is ___learning___ (*learn*) a lot about my grandfather's ancestors; for instance, they were peasants who fled Italy around 1910 because of difficult living conditions.

5. My sister and I are _helping_ (*help*) our grandmother by looking at online records from Ellis Island.

6. Also, we are _thinking_ (*think*) of taking a course in genealogical research at a local college.

7. Even our mother is _pitching_ (*pitch*) in.

8. For example, she is _calling_ (*call*) older Mancinis to get family stories.

9. She is constantly _sharing_ (*share*) the stories with my sister and me; for instance, she learned that our great-grandfather helped to organize a coal-miner strike soon after coming to America.

10. "These stories are _reminding_ (*remind*) me of some modern Mancinis," she said. "We like to stir things up."

··

The **present perfect tense** is used for an action that started in the past and is ongoing into the present or that was completed at some unspecified time in the past. It is formed by using a **past participle**, a verb form that uses the helping verb *have*. The past participle of the verb *play*, for example, is *has played* or *have played*. The **present perfect** is formed as follows:

Be and *have* are irregular verbs. For more details on irregular verbs, see pages 464–72.

| Present-tense form of *have* (helping verb) | + | Past participle |

Present Perfect Tense

	SINGULAR	PLURAL
First person	I have laughed.	We have laughed.
Second person	You have laughed.	You have laughed.
Third person	She/he/it has laughed.	They have laughed.
	The baby has laughed.	The babies have laughed.

> **LANGUAGE NOTE:** Be careful not to leave out *have* when it is needed for the present perfect. Time-signal words like *since* or *for* may mean that the present perfect is needed.

INCORRECT	Krystal *played* basketball since she was ten.
CORRECT	Krystal *has played* basketball since she was ten.

· ·

PRACTICE 4   Using the Present Perfect Tense

In each of the following sentences, underline the helping verb (a form of *have*), and fill in the correct form of the verb in parentheses.

> **EXAMPLE:** My father has ___served___ (*serve*) in the army for twenty
> years.

1. My father's military career has ___forced___ (*force*) our family to move many times.

2. We have ___lived___ (*live*) in seven towns that I remember.

3. I have ___attended___ (*attend*) three different high schools.

4. None of the towns has ever really ___seemed___ (*seem*) like home.

5. I have never ___objected___ (*object*) to my family's traveling life.

6. None of us has ever ___expected___ (*expect*) to stay in one place for long.

7. My closest friends have all ___traveled___ (*travel*) a lot, too.

8. One of them has ___visited___ (*visit*) Egypt, Australia, Turkey, Pakistan, and seventeen other countries.

9. She has always ___liked___ (*like*) the idea of becoming a travel agent.

10. But she has ___decided___ (*decide*) to accept a position with a large international corporation that will allow her to travel.

· ·

Past Tense

The **simple past tense** is used for actions that have already happened. An **-ed ending** is needed for all regular verbs in the past tense.

	SIMPLE PRESENT	SIMPLE PAST
First person	I rush to work.	I rushed to work.
Second person	You lock the door.	You locked the door.
Third person	Rufus seems strange.	Rufus seemed strange.

PRACTICE 5   Using the Simple Past Tense

In each of the following sentences, fill in the correct past-tense form of the verb in parentheses.

> **EXAMPLE:** After the Revolutionary War __ended__ (*end*), American politicians __turned__ (*turn*) their anger against each other.

(1) In general, politicians after the war __decided__ (*decide*) to support either Alexander Hamilton, who favored a strong central government, or Thomas Jefferson, who advocated states' rights. (2) Rival politicians were __concerned__ (*concern*) about the direction of the new democracy, so they __attacked__ (*attack*) each other with great passion. (3) Few people __cared__ (*care*) about facts or honesty in their attacks. (4) Some politicians eagerly __challenged__ (*challenge*) President George Washington and __called__ (*call*) him a would-be king. (5) Hamilton __engaged__ (*engage*) in personal attacks that were especially nasty. (6) In return, Hamilton's enemies __accused__ (*accuse*) him of planning to bring back the British monarchy.

(7) In six different instances, Hamilton __participated__ (*participate*) in fierce arguments that __stopped__ (*stop*) just short of causing a duel. (8) He __failed__ (*fail*) to avoid a duel in his long dispute with Vice President Aaron Burr. (9) For years, Hamilton __charged__ (*charge*) Burr with being corrupt and dishonest. (10) When they __dueled__ (*duel*) in 1804, each __fired__ (*fire*) a shot from a pistol. (11) Burr was not hit, but Hamilton was seriously wounded, and he __died__ (*die*) the next day.

TEACHING TIP
Have students write a paragraph about something annoying they experienced in the past week. Ask each student to write one sentence from his or her paragraph on the board. As a class, edit for correct past-tense verb forms.

SIMPLE PAST TENSE   My <u>car</u> <u>stalled</u>.

[The car stalled at some point in the past but does not stall now, in the present.]

PRESENT PERFECT TENSE   My <u>car</u> <u>has stalled</u> often.

[The car began to stall in the past but may continue to do so into the present.]

Be careful not to confuse the simple past tense with the present perfect tense (see p. 454).

PRACTICE 6   Using the Simple Past Tense and Present Perfect Tense

In each of the following sentences, circle the correct verb form.

> **EXAMPLE:** Within the last twenty years, racial profiling (became / (has become)) a significant source of disagreement between law enforcement agencies and some communities of color.

1. Numerous charges of racial profiling (increased / (have increased)) the tension between local police and members of various ethnic groups.

2. Law enforcement agencies (used / (have used)) profiling for a long time.

3. With this practice, they (attempted / (have attempted)) to identify people who might be participating in criminal activity by their behavior and the conditions of a particular situation.

4. Once these "profiled" individuals ((were singled out) / have been singled out), the police questioned or searched them for drugs, guns, or other illegal material.

5. In 1998, an investigation of the New Jersey State Police ((raised) / has raised) the public's awareness of this issue.

6. The extensive publicity from this investigation ((defined) / has defined) racial profiling as the separating out of members of racial or ethnic groups for minor traffic or criminal offenses.

7. Investigators reviewing past law-enforcement activity concluded that the New Jersey State Police ((violated) / have violated) civil rights on numerous occasions.

8. Since this case was made public, other police departments (initiated / have initiated) investigations into their own possible profiling activities.

9. Similarly, communities (started / have started) to demand that the
police be more accountable in their relationships with members of
minority racial or ethnic groups.

10. The issue of profiling (endured / has endured) in the public mind
and continues to be controversial.

··

Two other past-tense forms are the past progressive tense and the past
perfect tense. The **past progressive tense** is used to describe actions that
were ongoing in the past. It is formed as follows.

Past-tense form of *be* (helping verb)	+	Main verb with *-ing* ending

Past Progressive Tense

	SINGULAR	PLURAL
First person	I was laughing.	We were laughing.
Second person	You were laughing.	You were laughing.
Third person	She/he/it was laughing.	They were laughing.
	The baby was laughing.	The babies were laughing.

··

PRACTICE 7   Using the Past Progressive Tense

In each of the following sentences, first underline the helping verb (a form of
be), and then fill in the correct form(s) of the verb in parentheses.

> **EXAMPLE:** When Victoria graduated from college, she was *looking*
> (*look*) for a good job.

1. Because she was not sure exactly what kind of job she wanted, she

was *hoping* (*hope*) to find a city with a lot of opportunities.

2. However, because she had college loans to repay, she was _looking_ (*look*) to find a city that was not too expensive.

3. Discouraged by the recession, many of her friends were _struggling_ (*struggle*) to figure out where to go.

4. After doing some research, Victoria discovered that some cities were _experiencing_ (*experience*) growth in both population and employment.

5. Many of these cities were _drawing_ (*draw*) large numbers of young people in their twenties and early thirties as well.

6. Soon, Victoria was _focusing_ (*focus*) her attention on three cities.

7. According to a 2010 study, Austin, Texas; Washington, D.C.; and Raleigh, North Carolina, were _providing_ (*provide*) the best market for young adults.

8. Victoria was _having_ (*have*) trouble deciding among the three cities until she read about Austin's South-by-Southwest Festival.

9. A city that supported music, film, and technology was _going_ (*go*) to make her happy.

10. Before long, Victoria was _trying_ (*try*) to convince several of her friends to move to Austin with her.

· ·

The **past perfect tense** is used for an action that began and ended in the past before some other past action took place. It is formed as follows.

| Past-tense form of *have* | + | Past participle |

Past tense of *have*   Past participle

PAST PERFECT TENSE My head had ached for a week before I called a doctor.

[Both of the actions (*head ached* and *I called*) happened in the past, but the ache happened before the calling.]

Be and *have* are irregular verbs. For more details on irregular verbs, see pages 464–72.

Be careful not to confuse the simple past tense with the past perfect tense.

SIMPLE PAST TENSE My <u>daughter</u> <u><u>left</u></u>.

[One action (the daughter leaving) occurred in the past.]

PAST PERFECT TENSE By the time Jill arrived, my <u>daughter</u> <u><u>had left</u></u>.

[Two actions (Jill's arrival and the daughter leaving) occurred in the past, but the daughter left before Jill's arrival.]

· ·

PRACTICE 8 Using the Past Perfect Tense

In each of the following sentences, circle the correct verb form. Note that some of the verbs are irregular. For a chart showing forms of these verbs, see pages 467–69.

> **EXAMPLE:** By the time I reached home, rolling blackouts
>
> (darkened /(had darkened)) the city.

For more practice on the past and perfect tenses, see Chapter 33.

1. The temperature was unseasonably hot when I ((got)/ had gotten) out of bed that morning.

2. By noon, the air conditioners at the office (were running /(had been running)) at high power for three hours.

3. My boss told me that she (heard /(had heard)) that energy use that day was skyrocketing.

4. I ((asked)/ had asked) how we could conserve energy.

5. I mentioned that I (just learned /(had just learned)) that some household and office machines use power even when they are turned off.

6. My boss (read /(had read)) the same information, so we unplugged computers in the office that were not in use.

7. We also ((raised)/ had raised) the office temperature from sixty-eight degrees to seventy-two, and then we turned off some of the lights.

8. By late afternoon, we (did /(had done)) everything we could think of to save energy, but it was not enough.

9. We knew that the city (warned /(had warned)) residents that rolling blackouts were possible.

10. However, when the office ((suddenly darkened)/ had suddenly darkened), everyone was stunned.

··

Future Tense

The **simple future tense** is used for actions that will happen in the future. It is formed with the helping verb *will*.

Simple Future Tense

	SINGULAR	PLURAL
First person	I will graduate in May.	We will graduate in May.
Second person	You will graduate in May.	You will graduate in May.
Third person	She/he/it will graduate in May.	They will graduate in May.
	My son will graduate in May.	My sons will graduate in May.

Two other future tense forms to be familiar with are the future progressive tense and the future perfect tense. The **future progressive tense** is used to describe actions that will be ongoing in the future. It is formed as follows.

Will + Be + Main verb with *-ing* ending

Future Progressive Tense

	SINGULAR	PLURAL
First person	I will be working Friday.	We will be working Friday.
Second person	You will be working Friday.	You will be working Friday.
Third person	She/he/it will be working Friday.	They will be working Friday.
	The boss will be working Friday.	The bosses will be working Friday.

The **future perfect tense** is used to describe actions that will be completed in the future before another action in the future. It is formed as follows.

$$\boxed{\textit{Will have}} \ + \ \boxed{\text{Past participle}}$$

Future Perfect Tense

	SINGULAR	PLURAL
First person	I will have finished by 10:00.	We will have finished by 10:00.
Second person	You will have finished by 10:00.	You will have finished by 10:00.
Third person	She/he/it will have finished by 10:00.	They will have finished by 10:00.
	The painter will have finished by 10:00.	The painters will have finished by 10:00.

PRACTICE 9   Using the Future Perfect Tense

The future perfect tense is formed with helping verbs "will have" plus a verb's past participle. Using the list of past participles on pages 467–469 (see the third column in the boxed chart), circle the correct form of the past participle in the following sentences.

> **EXAMPLE:** Rebekah will have ((woken)/ woke) with the roosters and eaten a hearty breakfast.

1. A student in the year-long Learn to Farm program in Athol, Massachusetts, Rebekah will have (rose /(risen)) early to give the sheep some garlic oil, a natural deworming agent.

2. Rebekah's fellow student Lee will have ((chosen)/ chose) which sheep from the herd to put in the holding pen for treatment.

3. Their instructor, Josh, will have (gave /(given)) them tips on how to get the animals to hold still and swallow the deworming medicine.

4. Josh's instructions will have (came /(come)) with a lot of encouragement.

5. For these experiences, Lee, Rebekah, and eleven other college students will have ((paid)/ pay) $12,500 tuition to the Farm School, for lessons, room, and board.

6. Students who graduate from the program will have ((driven)/ drove) diesel tractors and operated other large pieces of farm equipment.

7. They will have ((ridden)/ rode) horses, planted beans, weeded fields of broccoli, and met many new friends.

8. In the coming years, the director of the Farm School, Patrick Connors, will have (grew /(grown)) more confident and seen enrollments increase.

9. Some graduates of the Learn to Farm program will have ((taken)/ took) jobs on farms or gone on to study veterinary medicine.

10. Other graduates will have ((seen)/ saw) how satisfying it is, in hard economic times, to be able to grow their own food.

Irregular Verbs

Unlike regular verbs, which have past-tense and past-participle forms that end in *-ed* or *-d*, **irregular verbs** change spelling in the past-tense and past-participle forms.

Present-Tense Irregular Verbs

Only a few verbs are irregular in the present tense. The ones most commonly used are the verbs *be* and *have*.

The Verb *Be*, Present Tense

	SINGULAR	PLURAL
First person	I am	we are
Second person	you are	you are
Third person	he/she/it is	they are
	the dog is	the dogs are
	Chris is	Chris and Dan are

The Verb *Have*, Present Tense

	SINGULAR	PLURAL
First person	I have	we have
Second person	you have	you have
Third person	he/she/it has	they have
	the dog has	the dogs have
	Chris has	Chris and Dan have

PRACTICE 10   Using *Be* and *Have* in the Present Tense

In each of the following sentences, fill in the correct form of the verb indicated in parentheses.

> **EXAMPLE:** Disc golf ___is___ (*be*) played with Frisbees.

1. I ___am___ (*be*) a fanatical disc golfer.

2. The game ___has___ (*have*) eighteen holes, like regular golf, but uses a Frisbee instead of a ball.

3. A disc golf course ___has___ (*have*) fairways and holes.

4. A tee ___is___ (*be*) at the beginning of each fairway.

5. Players ___are___ (*be*) eager to get the Frisbee from the tee into a metal basket in the fewest possible throws.

6. Some disc golfers ___have___ (*have*) special Frisbees for teeing off and putting.

7. My brother, who also plays disc golf, ___has___ (*have*) thirty different Frisbees for the game.

8. His wife ___is___ (*be*) surprisingly patient with his enthusiasm for the sport.

9. "You ___are___ (*be*) in the middle of a second adolescence," she tells him.

10. However, she, too, ___has___ (*have*) formidable Frisbee technique.

Past-Tense Irregular Verbs

As discussed earlier, the past-tense and past-participle forms of irregular verbs do not follow a standard pattern. For example, they do not use the -*ed* ending for past tense, although the past participle uses a helping verb, just as regular verbs do.

PRESENT TENSE	PAST TENSE	PAST PARTICIPLE
Tony makes hats.	Tony made hats.	Tony has/had made hats.
You write well.	You wrote well.	You have/had written well.
I ride a bike.	I rode a bike.	I have/had ridden a bike.

The verb *be* is tricky because it has two different forms for the past tense—*was* and *were*.

The Verb *Be*, Past Tense

	SINGULAR	PLURAL
First person	I was	we were
Second person	you were	you were
Third person	she/he/it was	they were
	the car was	the cars were
	Jolanda was	Jolanda and Ti were

. . . .

PRACTICE 11   Using Past-Tense Forms of the Verb *Be*

In the paragraph that follows, fill in each blank with the correct past-tense form of the verb *be*.

> **EXAMPLE:** The many visitors to President Lincoln's White House __were__ generally polite.

(1) Lincoln __was__ respectful of his visitors as well, but they took up a great deal of his time. (2) Most of his visitors __were__ politicians, army generals, journalists, job seekers, and relatives of Mrs. Lincoln. (3) Nearly every visitor __was__ seeking something from the president, such as promotions, policy changes, or pardons. (4) Whenever a visitor came asking for nothing, Lincoln __was__ clearly relieved. (5) Mrs. Lincoln's relatives __were__ especially troublesome for the president. (6) Many of the Todds __were__ Confederate sympathizers or even Confederate combatants. (7) Usually, though, a Todd visiting

Lincoln ___was___ looking for a job. (8) Nearly everyone who had known
Lincoln at some point in his life ___was___ welcomed by the president.
(9) His manner ___was___ almost always so friendly and gracious that his
visitors ___were___ quickly put at ease. (10) Contrary to the serious face
in the Lincoln Memorial, whenever the president greeted a visitor, he
___was___ usually smiling.

As you write and edit, consult the following chart to make sure that you
use the correct form of irregular verbs.

Irregular Verb Forms

PRESENT TENSE	PAST TENSE	PAST PARTICIPLE (with helping verb)
be (am/are/is)	was/were	been
become	became	become
begin	began	begun
bite	bit	bitten
blow	blew	blown
break	broke	broken
bring	brought	brought
build	built	built
buy	bought	bought
catch	caught	caught
choose	chose	chosen
come	came	come
cost	cost	cost
dive	dived, dove	dived
do	did	done
draw	drew	drawn
drink	drank	drunk
drive	drove	driven
eat	ate	eaten

(continued)

PRESENT TENSE	PAST TENSE	PAST PARTICIPLE (with helping verb)
fall	fell	fallen
feed	fed	fed
feel	felt	felt
fight	fought	fought
find	found	found
fly	flew	flown
forget	forgot	forgotten
freeze	froze	frozen
get	got	gotten
give	gave	given
go	went	gone
grow	grew	grown
have/has	had	had
hear	heard	heard
hide	hid	hidden
hit	hit	hit
hold	held	held
hurt	hurt	hurt
keep	kept	kept
know	knew	known
lay	laid	laid
leave	left	left
let	let	let
lie	lay	lain
light	lit	lit
lose	lost	lost
make	made	made
mean	meant	meant
meet	met	met
pay	paid	paid
put	put	put
quit	quit	quit
read	read	read
ride	rode	ridden
ring	rang	rung

PRESENT TENSE	PAST TENSE	PAST PARTICIPLE (with helping verb)
rise	rose	risen
run	ran	run
say	said	said
see	saw	seen
sell	sold	sold
send	sent	sent
set (to place)	set	set
shake	shook	shaken
show	showed	shown
shrink	shrank	shrunk
shut	shut	shut
sing	sang	sung
sink	sank	sunk
sit (to be seated)	sat	sat
sleep	slept	slept
speak	spoke	spoken
spend	spent	spent
stand	stood	stood
steal	stole	stolen
stick	stuck	stuck
sting	stung	stung
strike	struck	struck, stricken
swim	swam	swum
take	took	taken
teach	taught	taught
tear	tore	torn
tell	told	told
think	thought	thought
throw	threw	thrown
understand	understood	understood
wake	woke	woken
wear	wore	worn
win	won	won
write	wrote	written

PRACTICE 12   Using Past-Tense Irregular Verbs

In each of the following sentences, fill in the correct past-tense form of the irregular verb in parentheses. If you do not know the answer, find the word in the chart of irregular verb forms on pages 467–69.

> **EXAMPLE:** The *Titanic* __set__ (*set*) out from Southampton, England, in 1912.

1. The White Star Line __built__ (*build*) the *Titanic*, which was the biggest moving object in the world at that time.

2. The huge ship __held__ (*hold*) over 2,200 passengers on its maiden voyage.

3. The newspapers __wrote__ (*write*) that twenty lifeboats, which could hold 1,178 people altogether, hung from the upper deck of the *Titanic*.

4. The shipbuilders __felt__ (*feel*) that the giant liner was the safest ship in the world and that more lifeboats were simply unnecessary.

5. On April 14, 1912, during its first trip across the Atlantic, the *Titanic* __struck__ (*strike*) an iceberg.

6. The sharp ice __tore__ (*tear*) a gaping hole in the bottom of the ship.

7. Icy ocean water __began__ (*begin*) to pour into the hold, dragging the *Titanic* down in the water.

8. Few passengers __understood__ (*understand*) the danger at first.

9. Half-empty lifeboats __left__ (*leave*) the sinking ship while other passengers __stood__ (*stand*) on deck, refusing to depart.

10. Hundreds of people __froze__ (*freeze*) to death in the ocean before the nearest ship __came__ (*come*) to rescue the *Titanic*'s 705 survivors.

PRACTICE 13   **Using Past-Tense Irregular Verbs**

In the following paragraph, replace any incorrect present-tense verb forms with the correct past-tense form of the verb. If you do not know the answer, look up the verbs in the chart of irregular verb forms on pages 467–69.

> **EXAMPLE:** Dewayne faced a judge and jury of his fellow high school
> students after he ~~hits~~ *hit* a boy in the classroom.
> ^

(1) Two years ago, my high school ~~sets~~ *set* up a student court to give students a voice in disciplining rule breakers. (2) Before the court opened its doors, adults ~~teach~~ *taught* students about decision making and about courtroom procedures. (3) Some of us served as members of juries, and others ~~become~~ *became* advocates or even judges. (4) I ~~sit~~ *sat* on a jury twice when I was a junior. (5) Then, last spring, my friend Dewayne appeared before the student court after he ~~loses~~ *lost* his temper and ~~strikes~~ *struck* a fellow student. (6) I agreed to be his advocate because I ~~think~~ *thought* he truly regretted his behavior. (7) I ~~tell~~ *told* the jury that he knew his violent reaction was a mistake. (8) The jury ~~sends~~ *sent* Dewayne for counseling to learn to manage his anger and made him write an apology to the other student. (9) After hearing the verdict, Dewayne ~~shakes~~ *shook* hands with all the jurors and thanked them for their fairness. (10) The experience ~~makes~~ *made* me eager to learn more about America's system of justice.

PRACTICE 14   **Using Past-Participle Forms for Irregular Verbs**

In each of the following sentences, underline the helping verb (a form of *have*) and fill in the correct past-participle form of the verb in parentheses. If you do not know the correct form, find the word in the chart on pages 467–69.

> **EXAMPLE:** Because many of the city's jobs had ___been___ (*be*) in the auto industry, Detroit's economy suffered when the car factories closed.

1. Over the last fifty years, the population of Detroit has ___shrunk___ (*shrink*) by 50 percent.

2. Many people have ___begun___ (*begin*) to argue that the city itself needs to shrink as well.

3. The mayor of Detroit has ___said___ (*say*) that the city needs to take drastic measures to save itself.

4. In the past, urban renewal has ___meant___ (*mean*) new buildings and fancy projects.

5. However, despite such efforts, Detroit has ___fallen___ (*fall*) further into decline.

6. Now, the mayor says the time has ___come___ (*come*) to close schools, cut services, and bulldoze neighborhoods.

7. A third of the city has ___become___ (*become*) vacant.

For more practice on using past forms of irregular verbs, see Chapter 33.

8. Even some who had ___held___ (*hold*) out hope that Detroit might regain its old size and strength agreed with the mayor when he presented his plan.

9. Others have ___grown___ (*grow*) angry and scared that their neighborhoods will be the ones destroyed.

10. However, given the failure of previous renewal strategies, "right-sizing" has ___won___ (*win*) many supporters.

Passive Voice

A sentence that is written in the **passive voice** has a subject that performs no action. Instead, the subject is acted upon. To create the passive voice, combine a form of the verb *be* with a past participle.

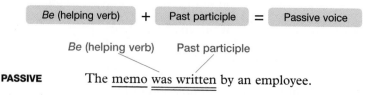

Be (helping verb) + Past participle = Passive voice

        Be (helping verb)   Past participle

PASSIVE   The <u>memo</u> <u>was written</u> by an employee.

[The subject, *memo*, did not write itself. An employee wrote the memo, but the subject in the sentence, *memo*, performs no action.]

In sentences that use the **active voice**, the subject performs the action.

ACTIVE   An <u>employee</u> <u>wrote</u> the memo.

Use the passive voice when no one person performed the action, when you don't know who performed the action, or when you want to emphasize the receiver of the action. Use the active voice whenever possible, and use passive voice sparingly.

PASSIVE   The <u>dog</u> <u>was hit</u> by a passing car.

[If the writer wants to focus on the dog as the receiver of the action, the passive voice is acceptable.]

ACTIVE   A passing <u>car</u> <u>hit</u> the dog.

TEACHING TIP
Encourage students to identify the nouns in a passive-voice sentence. Remind them that they usually can change the sentence to active voice by exchanging the noun that comes before the verb and the noun that comes after the verb. They will also need to change the form of the verb.

LANGUAGE NOTE: Do not confuse the passive voice with the present-perfect tense or past-perfect tense. The passive uses a form of the verb *be* (*is, was, were*), and the subject performs no action. The present-perfect tense and the past-perfect tense have subjects that perform an action, and they use a form of the verb *have*.

**PASSIVE
CORRECT**   The <u>boat</u> <u>was crushed</u> by huge waves.

[The subject *boat* performs no action. The verb uses *was,* a form of *be.*]

**PASSIVE
INCORRECT**   The <u>boat</u> <u>was been</u> crushed by huge waves.

[The verb in the passive voice should not use *two* forms of *be* (*was, been*). Use *was.*]

**PRESENT
PERFECT**   Huge <u>waves</u> <u>have crushed</u> all the boats.

[The subject *waves* performs the action, *crushed,* using the present form of *have.*]

**PAST
PERFECT**   Huge <u>waves</u> <u>had crushed</u> all the boats.

[The subject *waves* performed the action, *crushed,* using the past form of *have.*]

···

PRACTICE 15 Changing from Passive Voice to Active Voice

Rewrite the following sentences in the active voice.

Officers control the

EXAMPLE: ~~The~~ *Queen Mary 2*, one of the world's largest cruise
ships, ~~can be controlled~~ with a joystick. *Answers may*
vary. Possible edits shown.

has

1. The *Queen Mary 2* ~~is equipped with~~ a grand lobby and an old-style

   three-story restaurant.

   features

2. Its bridge, however, ~~is filled with~~ advanced consoles, screens, and

   joysticks.

   The ship's computer systems can automatically correct the

3. ~~The~~ effects of the wind, waves, and ocean currents ~~can be~~

   ~~automatically corrected by the ship's computer systems.~~

   captain did not touch the

4. During the ship's first docking in New York, the joystick ~~was not~~

   ~~touched by the captain.~~

   he would probably use

5. He said the joystick ~~would probably be used~~ more ~~by him~~ in the

   future.

···

Consistency of Verb Tense

Consistency of verb tense means that all the actions in a sentence that
happen (or happened) at the same time are in the same tense. If all of the
actions happen in the present, use the present tense for all verbs in the
sentence. If all of the actions happened in the past, use the past tense for
all verbs in the sentence.

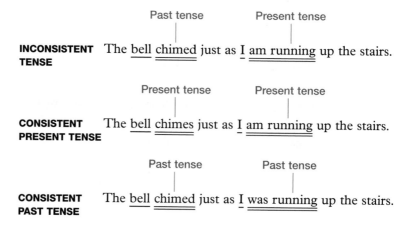

PRACTICE 16 Using Consistent Tense

In each of the following items, double-underline the verbs in the sentence, and correct any unnecessary shifts in verb tense by writing the correct form of any incorrect verb in the blank space provided.

> EXAMPLE: ___use___ People either ride bicycles for leisurely journeys, or they used bikes for serious exercise.

1. ___need___ Those who want a good workout needed different kinds of equipment than those interested in an easy ride.

2. ___have___ For example, serious cyclists who had bikes with wide padded seats face the chance of injuries.

3. ___causes___ A wide seat makes the rider shift from side to side, and it caused painful rubbing.

4. ___should be___ In addition, the seat should have been high enough so that the rider cannot put his or her feet on the ground.

5. ___wear___ Serious riders wore special shoes that snap onto the pedals to allow pushing up as well as pushing down.

6. ___are___ Serious money is also a factor because custom bicycles were expensive.

7. ___chooses___ Once an experienced cyclist chose the proper bicycle, he or she knows how to ride it properly.

8. ___exercise___ For instance, knowledgeable riders move around as they ride so that they exercised different muscle groups.

9. ___keeps___ The smart rider also kept his or her knees slightly bent, which eases the strain on the knees.

10. ___wish___ Of course, those who just wished to have a fun ride through the park ignore all of this advice.

Edit Paragraphs and Your Own Writing

As you edit the following paragraphs and your own writing, use the checklist below and the Verb Tense Reference Charts that begin on page 480.

CHECKLIST

EDITING FOR VERB PROBLEMS

FOCUS

☐ Read all of your sentences carefully, looking for verb problems.

ASK

☐ Is my sentence about the present? About the past? About something that happened before something else?

☐ Is each verb a regular verb or an irregular verb?

☐ Have I used the tense that tells the reader when the action happened?

☐ Have I used the correct form of the verb?

☐ If the verbs in the sentence are not all in the same tense, is it because the actions actually happened at different times?

EDIT

☐ Edit to correct any problems with verb form or verb tense.

Find and correct any problems with verb form or tense in the following paragraphs.

RESOURCES
For cumulative Editing Review Tests, see pages 667–83.

EDITING REVIEW 1 (7 errors)

(1) Since 1835, trapeze artists *consider* the triple somersault the [*have considered*] most dangerous maneuver. (2) That year, a performer tried to do a triple somersault on a trapeze for the first time and *dies* in the attempt. [*died*] (3) Only one person *has* managed to do the trick successfully in the next sixty-three years. (4) That man, a trapeze artist named Armor, did a triple somersault in 1860 and *is* afraid to try it again. [*was*] (5) According to circus legend, the second person to survive the triple, Ernie Clarke, once *done* a quadruple somersault in private. [*did*] (6) Ernie Lane, the third

person to complete a triple somersault, was later killed by the maneuver.

(7) Circus historians now ~~believed~~ *believe* that Alfredo Codona, a performer in the 1920s and 1930s, was the greatest master of the triple somersault.

(8) He has ~~went~~ *gone* down in history as the King of Trapeze.

....

EDITING REVIEW 2 (8 errors)

(1) Many people go through life without even knowing that there is a record for peeling an apple or hopping on a pogo stick. (2) However, some people are very aware of such records, and ordinary folks around the world have ~~did~~ *done* some peculiar things to qualify for the *Guinness Book of World Records*. (3) For example, a New Zealand disc jockey, Nikora Curtis, recently ~~setted~~ *set* a new record for the longest continuous radio broadcast. (4) In the summer of 2010, he ~~has~~ stayed on the air for one hundred and seventy-six hours with no sleep. (5) Another world record, for hopping up steps on a bicycle, is ~~hold~~ *held* by Javier Zapata of Colombia. (6) He climbed 943 steps without letting his feet touch the ground, breaking a record that he ~~has~~ *had* previously set. (7) Ashrita Furman of New York also ~~be~~ *is* a record breaker. (8) He balanced a milk bottle on his head and then ~~walks~~ *walked* almost eighty-one miles around a track. (9) These strange endurance contests may not make Curtis, Zapata, and Furman famous, but their names ~~had~~ *have* entered the record book.

....

EDITING REVIEW 3 (9 errors)

(1) The Olympic Games first let women compete in swimming events in 1912, and with that, the swimsuit revolution ~~begun~~ *began*. (2) In 1913, the first mass-produced women's swimsuit hit the market.

(3) Before that year, women ~~have~~ *had* only been able to wade at the beach

in bathing costumes with long, baggy legs. (4) The 1913 suits, designed
by Carl Jantzen, *were* ~~was~~ ribbed one-piece outfits that allowed actual swimming. (5) An engineer, Louis Réard, *came* ~~comed~~ up with the next major
development in swimwear in 1946 while working in the lingerie business. (6) He ~~has~~ called it the "bikini," after a Pacific island used for
testing the atomic bomb. (7) In the 1950s, few Americans ~~had~~ dared to
wear bikinis, which *were* ~~was~~ considered scandalous. (8) Two-piece swimsuits
caught ~~catch~~ on in the 1960s and 1970s. (9) The bikini *lost* ~~losted~~ some popularity
in the last decades of the twentieth century, but it has made a trium-
phant return in the new millennium.

....

EDITING REVIEW 4 (14 errors and 6 formal English errors)

(1) Located in southern Utah, Best Friends Animal Sanctuary *is* ~~are~~
the largest "no-kill" animal shelter in the United States. (2) For over
twenty-five years, the sanctuary *has* ~~had~~ provided a refuge *for* 4 unwanted,
abused, and neglected animals^,^ and has promoted spay and neuter programs. (3) Dogs *and* 'n cats, as well as birds, *pigs* ~~piggies~~, horses, and rabbits,
come to the sanctuary ~~were coming there~~ from all over the country. (4) The organization *takes* ~~took~~
in animals from other shelters *and* ~~but~~ also *rescues* ~~rescue~~ animals from disaster
areas and inhumane situations. (5) After Hurricane Katrina, volunteers
from Best Friends *found* ~~find~~, *rescued* ~~rescue~~, *cared* ~~care~~ for, and transported many lost or
abandoned *animals* ~~critters~~. (6) In 2008, twenty-two of football player Michael
Vick's fighting dogs were taken in by the sanctuary. (7) Best Friends'
goal is ~~being~~ to rehabilitate animals so that they *can* ~~could~~ find new homes.
(8) *Because* ~~Cuz~~ the animals often need to learn how to be around people, the
sanctuary *encourages* ~~was encouraging~~ visitors. (9) Visitors can even take a dog or
cat home overnight. (10) These home visits *are* ~~had been~~ fun for the *people* ~~peeps~~,
help the animals get used to new environments, and sometimes lead to
adoption.

- -

**PRACTICE 17   Editing Your Own Writing for
Correct Verb Tense and Form**

As a final practice, edit for verb problems in a piece of your own writing —
a paper you are working on for this class, a paper you have already finished, a paper for another course, or a recent piece of writing from your
work or everyday life. Use the Verb Tense Reference Charts starting on
page 480.

- -

Verb Tense Reference Charts

English verbs, like verbs in most other languages, have different tenses to
show when something happened: in the past, present, or future.

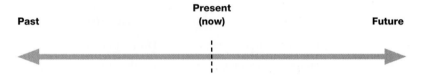

	Present	
Past	**(now)**	**Future**

This section covers the most common tenses. The discussions of each
tense start with a chart that tells you what time the tense is used for. The
chart then shows how to use the tense in statements, negative sentences,
and questions. You can use the verb charts both to learn tenses and to edit
your own writing. Following the charts are lists of common errors
to avoid.

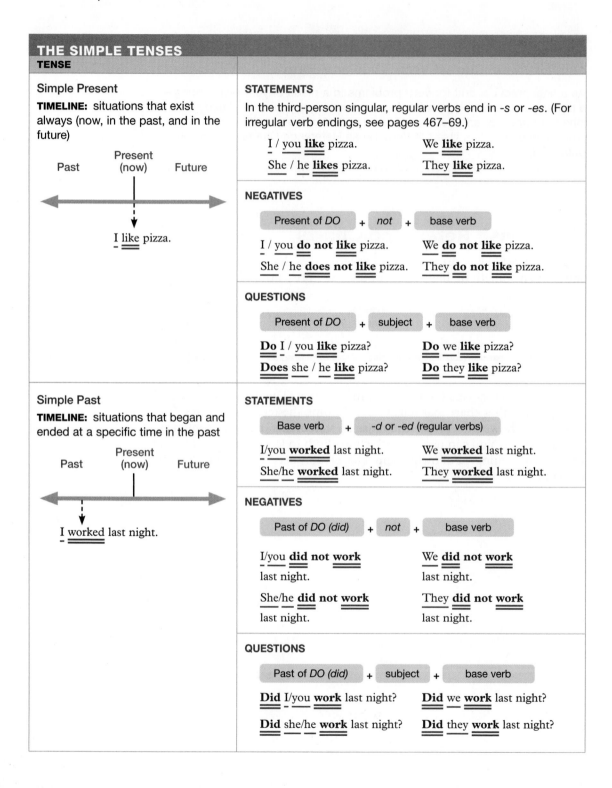

THE SIMPLE TENSES

TENSE

Simple Present

TIMELINE: situations that exist always (now, in the past, and in the future)

Past   Present (now)   Future

I like pizza.

STATEMENTS

In the third-person singular, regular verbs end in *-s* or *-es*. (For irregular verb endings, see pages 467–69.)

I / you **like** pizza.   We **like** pizza.

She / he **likes** pizza.   They **like** pizza.

NEGATIVES

Present of *DO* + *not* + base verb

I / you **do not like** pizza.   We **do not like** pizza.

She / he **does not like** pizza.   They **do not like** pizza.

QUESTIONS

Present of *DO* + subject + base verb

Do I / you **like** pizza?   **Do** we **like** pizza?

Does she / he **like** pizza?   **Do** they **like** pizza?

Simple Past

TIMELINE: situations that began and ended at a specific time in the past

Past   Present (now)   Future

I worked last night.

STATEMENTS

Base verb + *-d* or *-ed* (regular verbs)

I/you **worked** last night.   We **worked** last night.

She/he **worked** last night.   They **worked** last night.

NEGATIVES

Past of *DO (did)* + *not* + base verb

I/you **did not work** last night.   We **did not work** last night.

She/he **did not work** last night.   They **did not work** last night.

QUESTIONS

Past of *DO (did)* + subject + base verb

Did I/you **work** last night?   **Did** we **work** last night?

Did she/he **work** last night?   **Did** they **work** last night?

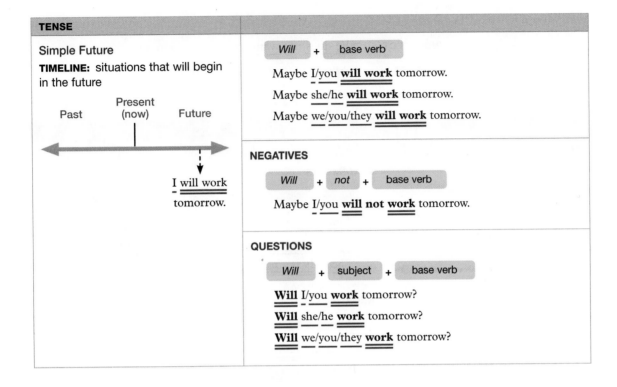

TENSE		
Simple Future **TIMELINE:** situations that will begin in the future	Will + base verb Maybe I/you **will work** tomorrow. Maybe she/he **will work** tomorrow. Maybe we/you/they **will work** tomorrow.	
	NEGATIVES Will + not + base verb Maybe I/you **will not work** tomorrow.	
	QUESTIONS Will + subject + base verb **Will** I/you **work** tomorrow? **Will** she/he **work** tomorrow? **Will** we/you/they **work** tomorrow?	

Common Errors Forming Simple Present

Forgetting to add -s or -es to verbs that go with third-person singular subjects (*she/he/it*):

INCORRECT   She know the manager.

CORRECT   She knows the manager.

Common Errors Forming Simple Past

Forgetting to add -d or -ed to regular verbs:

INCORRECT   Gina work late last night.

CORRECT   Gina worked late last night.

Forgetting to use the correct past form of irregular verbs (see the chart of irregular verb forms on pages 467–69):

INCORRECT   Gerard speaked to her about the problem.

CORRECT   Gerard **spoke** to her about the problem.

Forgetting to use the base verb without an ending for negative sentences:

INCORRECT	She does not wants money for helping.
CORRECT	She does not **want** money for helping.

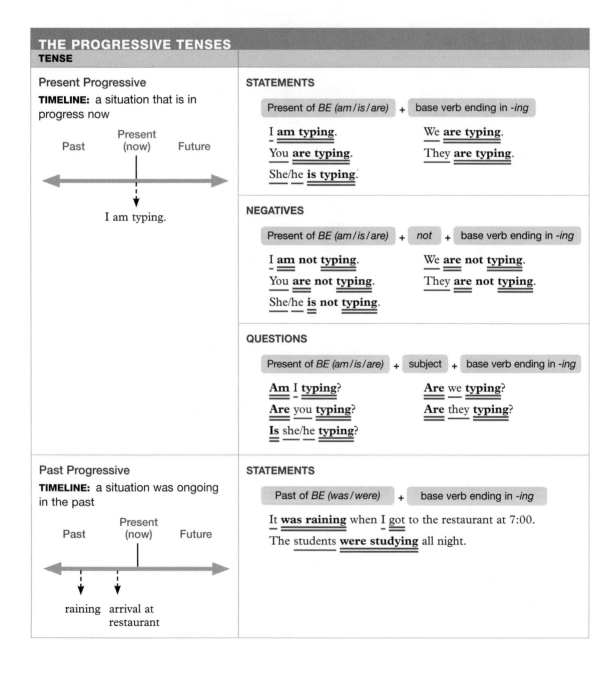

THE PROGRESSIVE TENSES

TENSE

Present Progressive

TIMELINE: a situation that is in progress now

Past   Present (now)   Future

I am typing.

STATEMENTS

Present of *BE (am/is/are)* + base verb ending in *-ing*

I **am typing**.   We **are typing**.
You **are typing**.   They **are typing**.
She/he **is typing**.

NEGATIVES

Present of *BE (am/is/are)* + *not* + base verb ending in *-ing*

I **am not typing**.   We **are not typing**.
You **are not typing**.   They **are not typing**.
She/he **is not typing**.

QUESTIONS

Present of *BE (am/is/are)* + subject + base verb ending in *-ing*

Am I **typing**?   **Are** we **typing**?
Are you **typing**?   **Are** they **typing**?
Is she/he **typing**?

Past Progressive

TIMELINE: a situation was ongoing in the past

Past   Present (now)   Future

raining   arrival at restaurant

STATEMENTS

Past of *BE (was/were)* + base verb ending in *-ing*

It **was raining** when I got to the restaurant at 7:00.
The students **were studying** all night.

TENSE	

NEGATIVES

| Past of *BE (was/were)* | + | *not* | + | base verb ending in *-ing* |

It **was not raining** when I got to the restaurant at 7:00.

The students **were not studying** all night.

QUESTIONS

| Past of *BE (was/were)* | + | subject | + | base verb ending in *-ing* |

Was it **raining** when I got to the restaurant at 7:00?

Were the students **studying** all night?

Future Progressive

TIMELINE: a situation that will be ongoing at some point in the future

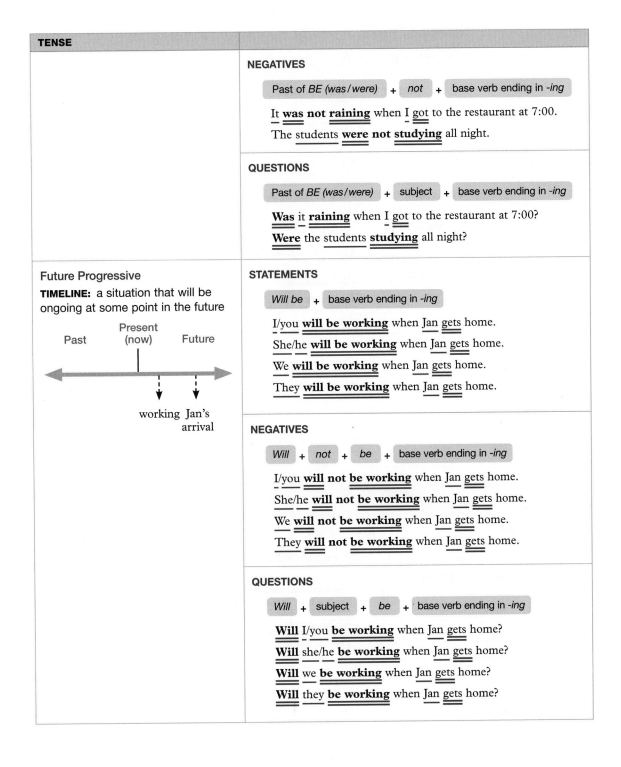

Past   Present (now)   Future

working   Jan's arrival

STATEMENTS

| *Will be* | + | base verb ending in *-ing* |

I/you **will be working** when Jan gets home.

She/he **will be working** when Jan gets home.

We **will be working** when Jan gets home.

They **will be working** when Jan gets home.

NEGATIVES

| *Will* | + | *not* | + | *be* | + | base verb ending in *-ing* |

I/you **will not be working** when Jan gets home.

She/he **will not be working** when Jan gets home.

We **will not be working** when Jan gets home.

They **will not be working** when Jan gets home.

QUESTIONS

| *Will* | + | subject | + | *be* | + | base verb ending in *-ing* |

Will I/you **be working** when Jan gets home?

Will she/he **be working** when Jan gets home?

Will we **be working** when Jan gets home?

Will they **be working** when Jan gets home?

Common Errors Forming the Present Progressive

Forgetting to add *-ing* to the verb:

INCORRECT	I am type now.
	She/he is not work now.
CORRECT	I am typ**ing** now.
	She/he is not work**ing** now.

Forgetting to include a form of *be* (*am/is/are*):

INCORRECT	He typing now.
	They typing now.
CORRECT	He **is** typing now.
	They **are** typing now.

Forgetting to use a form of *be* (*am/is/are*) to start questions:

INCORRECT	They typing now?
CORRECT	**Are** they typing now?

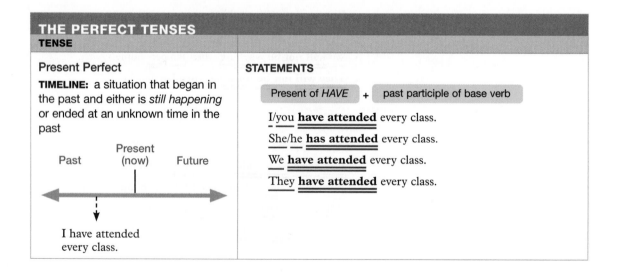

THE PERFECT TENSES

TENSE	
Present Perfect **TIMELINE:** a situation that began in the past and either is *still happening* or ended at an unknown time in the past	**STATEMENTS**

Present of *HAVE*	+	past participle of base verb

I/you **have attended** every class.

She/he **has attended** every class.

We **have attended** every class.

They **have attended** every class.

Past   Present (now)   Future

I have attended every class.

TENSE	

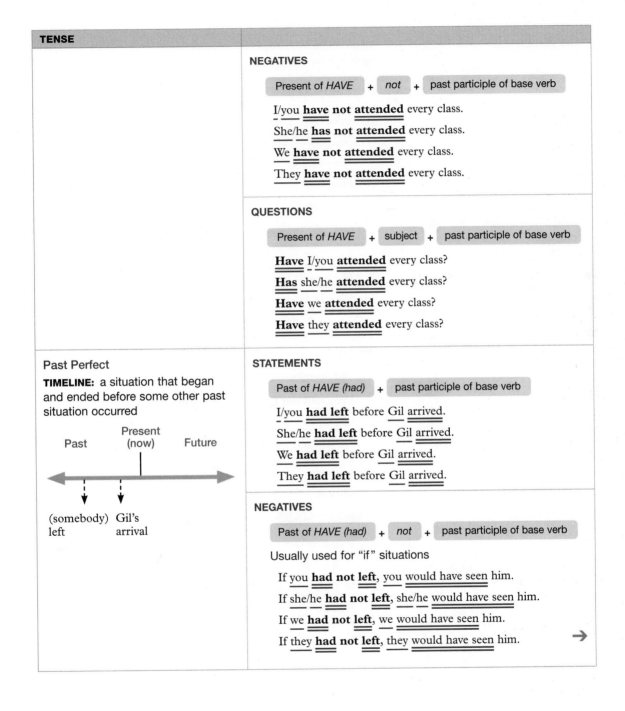

NEGATIVES

Present of *HAVE* + *not* + past participle of base verb

I/you **have not attended** every class.

She/he **has not attended** every class.

We **have not attended** every class.

They **have not attended** every class.

QUESTIONS

Present of *HAVE* + subject + past participle of base verb

Have I/you **attended** every class?

Has she/he **attended** every class?

Have we **attended** every class?

Have they **attended** every class?

Past Perfect

TIMELINE: a situation that began and ended before some other past situation occurred

Past   Present (now)   Future

(somebody) left   Gil's arrival

STATEMENTS

Past of *HAVE (had)* + past participle of base verb

I/you **had left** before Gil arrived.

She/he **had left** before Gil arrived.

We **had left** before Gil arrived.

They **had left** before Gil arrived.

NEGATIVES

Past of *HAVE (had)* + *not* + past participle of base verb

Usually used for "if" situations

If you **had not left**, you would have seen him.

If she/he **had not left**, she/he would have seen him.

If we **had not left**, we would have seen him.

If they **had not left**, they would have seen him.

→

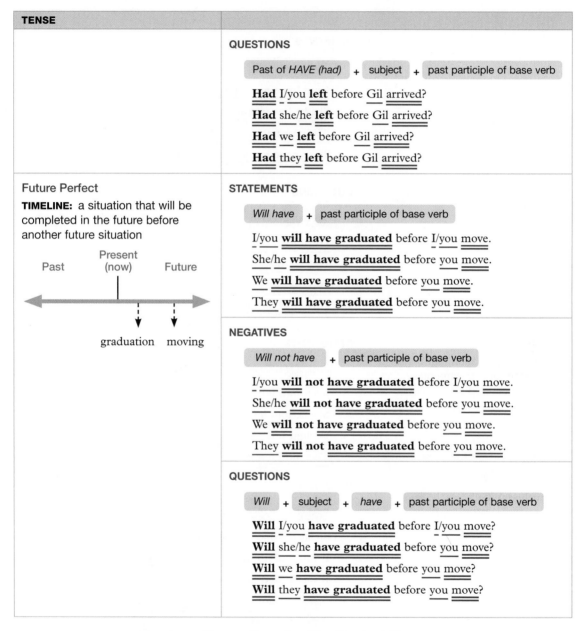

TENSE	
	QUESTIONS Past of *HAVE (had)* + subject + past participle of base verb **Had** I/you **left** before Gil arrived? **Had** she/he **left** before Gil arrived? **Had** we **left** before Gil arrived? **Had** they **left** before Gil arrived?
Future Perfect **TIMELINE:** a situation that will be completed in the future before another future situation Past Present (now) Future graduation moving	**STATEMENTS** *Will have* + past participle of base verb I/you **will have graduated** before I/you move. She/he **will have graduated** before you move. We **will have graduated** before you move. They **will have graduated** before you move. **NEGATIVES** *Will not have* + past participle of base verb I/you **will not have graduated** before I/you move. She/he **will not have graduated** before you move. We **will not have graduated** before you move. They **will not have graduated** before you move. **QUESTIONS** *Will* + subject + *have* + past participle of base verb **Will** I/you **have graduated** before I/you move? **Will** she/he **have graduated** before you move? **Will** we **have graduated** before you move? **Will** they **have graduated** before you move?

Common Errors Forming the Perfect Tense

Using *had* instead of *has* or *have* for the present perfect:

INCORRECT   We **had** lived here since 2003.

CORRECT   We **have** lived here since 2003.

Forgetting to use past participles (with *-d* or *-ed* endings for regular verbs):

INCORRECT	She has attend every class.
CORRECT	She has attend**ed** every class.

Using *been* between *have* or *has* and the past participle of a base verb:

INCORRECT	I have **been** attended every class.
CORRECT	I have attended every class.

INCORRECT	I will have **been** graduated before I move.
CORRECT	I will have graduated before I move.

MODAL AUXILIARIES/HELPING VERBS

HELPING VERB (MODAL AUXILIARY)

Modal auxiliaries join with a main (base) verb to make a complete verb.	**STATEMENTS**
	Subject + helping verb + base verb
	PRESENT Dumbo can fly.
	PAST Forms vary—see below.
	NEGATIVES
	Subject + helping verb + *not* + base verb
	PRESENT Dumbo cannot fly.
	PAST Forms vary—see below.
	QUESTIONS
	Helping verb + subject + base verb
	PRESENT Can Dumbo fly?
	PAST Forms vary—see below.
Can Means *ability*	**STATEMENTS**
	PRESENT Beth **can** work fast.
	PAST Beth **could** work fast. →

HELPING VERB (MODAL AUXILIARY)	
Can (cont.)	**NEGATIVES** **PRESENT** Beth **can**not work fast. **PAST** Beth **could** not work fast.
	QUESTIONS **PRESENT** **Can** Beth work fast? **PAST** **Could** Beth work fast?
Could Means *possibility*. It can also be the past tense of *can*.	**STATEMENTS** **PRESENT** Beth **could** work fast if she had more time. **PAST** Beth **could** have worked fast if she had more time.
	NEGATIVES *Can* is used for present negatives. (See above.) **PAST** Beth **could** not have worked fast.
	QUESTIONS **PRESENT** **Could** Beth work fast? **PAST** **Could** Beth have worked fast?
May Means *permission* For past-tense forms, see *might*.	**STATEMENTS** **PRESENT** You **may** borrow my car.
	NEGATIVES **PRESENT** You **may** not borrow my car.
	QUESTIONS **PRESENT** **May** I borrow your car?
Might Means *possibility*. It can also be the past tense of *may*.	**STATEMENTS** **PRESENT (with *be*):** Lou **might** be asleep. **PAST (with *have* + past participle of *be*):** Lou **might** have been asleep. **FUTURE:** Lou **might** sleep.

HELPING VERB (MODAL AUXILIARY)	
Might (cont.)	**NEGATIVES** **PRESENT (with *be*):** Lou **might** not be asleep. **PAST (with *have* + past participle of *be*):** Lou **might** not have been asleep. **FUTURE:** Lou **might** not sleep.
	QUESTIONS *Might* in questions is notably formal and not often used.
Must Means *necessary*	**STATEMENTS** **PRESENT:** We **must** try. **PAST (with *have* + past participle of base verb):** We **must** have tried.
	NEGATIVES **PRESENT:** We **must** not try. **PAST (with *have* + past participle of base verb):** We **must** not have tried.
	QUESTIONS **PRESENT: Must** we try? (Past-tense questions with *must* are unusual.)
Should Means *duty* or *expectation*	**STATEMENTS** **PRESENT:** They **should** call. **PAST (with *have* + past participle of base verb):** They **should** have called.
	NEGATIVES **PRESENT:** They **should** not call. **PAST (with *have* + past participle of base verb):** They **should** not have called. →

HELPING VERB (MODAL AUXILIARY)	STATEMENTS
Should (cont.)	**QUESTIONS** **PRESENT:** **Should** they call? **PAST (with *have* + past participle of base verb):** **Should** they have called?
Will Means *intend to* (future) For past-tense forms, see *might*.	**STATEMENTS** **FUTURE:** I **will** succeed.
	NEGATIVES **FUTURE:** I **will** not succeed.
	QUESTIONS **FUTURE:** **Will** I succeed?
Would Means *prefer* or is used to start a future request. It can also be the past tense of *will*.	**STATEMENTS** **PRESENT:** I **would** like to travel. **PAST (with *have* + past participle of base verb):** I **would** have traveled if I had the money.
	NEGATIVES **PRESENT:** I **would** not like to travel. **PAST (with *have* + past participle of base verb):** I **would** not have traveled if it had not been for you.
	QUESTIONS **PRESENT:** **Would** you like to travel? *Or* to start a request: **Would** you help me? **PAST (with *have* + past participle of base verb):** **Would** you have traveled with me if I had asked you?

Common Errors Using Modal Auxiliaries

For more on the modal auxiliaries, see Chapter 33.

Using more than one helping verb:

INCORRECT	They **will can** help.
CORRECT	They **will** help. (future intention)
	They **can** help. (are able to)

Using *to* between the helping verb and the main (base) verb:

INCORRECT	Emilio **might to** come with us.
CORRECT	Emilio **might** come with us.

Using *must* instead of *had to* in the past:

INCORRECT	She **must** work yesterday.
CORRECT	She **had to** work yesterday.

Forgetting to change *can* to *could* in the past negative:

INCORRECT	Last night, I **can**not sleep.
CORRECT	Last night, I **could** not sleep.

Forgetting to use *have* with *could/should/would* in the past tense:

INCORRECT	Tara **should** called last night.
CORRECT	Tara **should have** called last night.

Using *will* instead of *would* to express a preference in the present tense:

INCORRECT	I **will** like to travel.
CORRECT	I **would** like to travel.

"I write e-mails to my friends and family."

—Jonatan T., student

Part 5

Other Grammar Concerns

27

Pronouns

Using Substitutes for Nouns

Understand What Pronouns Are

Pronouns replace nouns (or other pronouns) in a sentence so that you do not have to repeat the nouns.

> *her*
> Tessa let me borrow ~~Tessa's~~ jacket.
> *He^*
> You have met Carl. ~~Carl~~ is my cousin.
> ^

The noun (or pronoun) that a pronoun replaces is called the **antecedent**. The word *antecedent* means "something that comes before." In most cases, a pronoun refers to a specific antecedent nearby. In the second example above, "Carl" is the antecedent and "He" is the pronoun that replaces "Carl."

There are three basic types of pronouns—**subject** pronouns, **object** pronouns, and **possessive** pronouns. Note the pronouns in the following sentences.

> Object   Subject
> | |
> The linebacker tackled him, and he went down hard.

> Possessive
> |
> His shoulder was injured.

IDEA JOURNAL
Write about something you did with friends recently.

ESL Students may have particular trouble with pronouns and would benefit from extra practice. Encourage these students to pay special attention to pronouns as they revise their own writing.

Pronoun Types

	SUBJECT	OBJECT	POSSESSIVE
First person (singular/plural)	I/we	me/us	my, mine/ our, ours
Second person (singular/plural)	you/you	you/you	your, yours/ your, yours
Third person (singular)	he, she, it	him, her, it	his, her, hers, its
Third person (plural)	they who/who	them whom/whom	their, theirs whose

LANGUAGE NOTE: Notice that pronouns have gender (*he/she, him/her, his/her/ hers*). The pronoun must agree with the gender of the noun it refers to.

INCORRECT   Tonya lives with *his* cousin.

CORRECT   Tonya lives with *her* cousin.

Also, notice that English has different forms for subject and object pronouns, as shown in the preceding chart.

PRACTICE 1   Identifying Pronouns

In each of the following sentences, circle the pronoun, underline the antecedent (the noun to which the pronoun refers), and draw an arrow from the pronoun to the antecedent.

EXAMPLE: My uncle is a hardworking entrepreneur who knew he could succeed with a business loan.

1. Many poor people do not feel as if they can depend on big banks.

2. A bank in an underdeveloped area, however, needs to find customers wherever it can.

For more practice with pronouns, visit *Exercise Central* at bedfordstmartins .com/realessays.

3. Microlending has become a popular banking trend. It has helped people in impoverished neighborhoods all over the world.

For more help with pronouns, see Chapter 33.

4. Microlending has succeeded because it involves lending very small amounts of money.

5. Many poor owners of small businesses use microlending to help them get their start.

6. For example, street vendors sell small quantities and earn small profits, so they may never save up enough to expand.

7. Yet a woman selling tacos from a cart may have enough experience to manage her own business successfully.

8. If the taco vendor gets a microloan, she may be able to open a storefront restaurant and earn larger profits.

9. After receiving a small loan, a young entrepreneur can make his or her business more successful.

10. According to my uncle, getting a microloan allowed him to pursue a childhood dream.

Practice Using Pronouns Correctly

Check for Pronoun Agreement

A pronoun must agree with (match) the noun or pronoun it refers to in number: It must be singular (one) or plural (more than one). If it is singular, it must also match its noun or pronoun in gender (*he, she,* or *it*).

> **CONSISTENT**   Sherry talked to *her* aunt.
>
> [*Her* agrees with *Sherry* because both are singular and feminine.]

> **CONSISTENT**   The Romanos sold *their* restaurant.
>
> [*Their* agrees with *Romanos* because both are plural.]

Watch out for singular nouns that are not specific. If a noun is singular, the pronoun must be singular as well.

> **INCONSISTENT**   Any athlete can tell you about *their* commitment to practice.

[*Athlete* is singular, but the pronoun *their* is plural.]

> **CONSISTENT**   Any athlete can tell you about *his* or *her* commitment to practice.

[*Athlete* is singular, and so are the pronouns *his* and *her.*]

As an alternative to using the phrase *his or her,* make the subject plural if you can. (For more on this, see the note below.)

> **CONSISTENT**   All athletes can tell you about *their* commitment to practice.

Two types of words often cause errors in pronoun agreement—indefinite pronouns and collective nouns.

Indefinite Pronouns

TIP Focus on the "significant seven" indefinite pronouns: *any, each, either, neither,* and words ending in *-one, -thing,* or *-body.*

An **indefinite pronoun** does not refer to a specific person, place, or thing; it is general. Indefinite pronouns often take singular verbs. Whenever a pronoun refers to an indefinite person, place, or thing, check for agreement.

>   his
> Someone forgot ~~their~~ coat.
>   ^

>   his or her
> Everybody practiced ~~their~~ lines.
>   ^

NOTE: Although it is grammatically correct, using a masculine pronoun (*he, his,* or *him*) alone to refer to a singular indefinite pronoun such as *everyone* is now considered sexist. Here are two ways to avoid this problem:

1. Use *his or her.*

   Someone forgot his or her coat.

2. Change the sentence so that the pronoun refers to a plural noun or pronoun.

   The children forgot their coats.

Indefinite Pronouns

ALWAYS SINGULAR

anybody	everyone	nothing
anyone	everything	one (of)
anything	much	somebody
each (of)	neither (of)	someone
either (of)	nobody	something
everybody	no one	

MAY BE SINGULAR OR PLURAL

all	none
any	some

PRACTICE 2 Using Indefinite Pronouns

Circle the correct pronoun or group of words in parentheses.

(1) Everyone who has battled an addiction to alcohol has (his or her /
their) own view of the best ways to stop drinking. (2) Millions of former
problem drinkers have quit, and many have made (his or her /their) way
through recovery programs. (3) Few begin the road to recovery without
attending (his or her /their) first Alcoholics Anonymous (AA) meeting.
(4) With its famous twelve-step program, AA has helped countless alcoholics, but someone who is not religious may find that (he or she / they)
has difficulty with one of the twelve steps. (5) No one can complete the
whole AA recovery program without turning (himself or herself/ themselves) over to a "higher power." (6) In addition, everybody who joins
AA is asked to admit that (he or she is/ they are) powerless over alcohol.
(7) Many object that (he or she needs /they need) to feel empowered
rather than powerless in order to recover. (8) Anyone who does not feel
that (he or she/ they) can believe in a higher power might participate

instead in a group like Secular Organizations for Sobriety. (9) Some can take responsibility for (his or her / their) drinking and stop more easily with groups such as Smart Recovery. (10) Different approaches work for different people, but former problem drinkers offer this sober advice to others with alcohol problems: Anyone can quit drinking if (he or she wants / they want) to stop badly enough.

Collective Nouns

A **collective noun** names a group that acts as a single unit.

Common Collective Nouns

audience	company	group
class	crowd	jury
college	family	society
committee	government	team

Collective nouns are usually singular, so when you use a pronoun to refer to a collective noun, it too must usually be singular.

The class had ~~their~~ *its* final exam at 8:00 a.m.

The group turned in ~~their~~ *its* report.

If the people in a group are acting as individuals, however, the noun is plural and should be used with a plural pronoun.

The audience took *their* seats.

The drenched crowd huddled under *their* umbrellas.

PRACTICE 3   Using Collective Nouns and Pronouns

Fill in the correct pronoun (*their* or *its*) in each of the following sentences.

EXAMPLE: The basketball team was playing all of ___*its*___ games in a damp, dark gymnasium.

1. The downtown branch of the university needed to overhaul several buildings on ___*its*___ campus.

2. The theater department wanted to enlarge the auditorium used for ___*its*___ productions.

3. In the present theater, the audience had to wait in ___*their*___ seats until the performance was over and then exit through the stage door.

4. A sorority also needed more space to house ___*its*___ members.

5. In addition, the football team could not go to any out-of-town games because ___*its*___ bus had broken down.

6. The science teachers had to hold ___*their*___ office hours in the student cafeteria.

7. The university president appointed a commission to study renovations and agreed to abide by ___*its*___ findings.

8. The graduating class agreed to step up ___*its*___ fund-raising campaign.

9. One wealthy family donated ___*its*___ slightly used luxury car to a fundraising auction.

10. A record homecoming crowd shouted ___*its*___ approval as the renovation plans were announced.

Make Pronoun Reference Clear

If the reader isn't sure what a pronoun refers to, the sentence may be confusing.

Avoid Ambiguous or Vague Pronoun References

In an **ambiguous pronoun reference**, the pronoun could refer to more than one noun.

> **AMBIGUOUS**   Michelle told Carla that she needed new shoes.
>
> [Did Michelle tell Carla that Michelle herself needed new shoes? Or did Michelle tell Carla that Carla needed new shoes?]

EDITED	Michelle needed new shoes. She told her friend Carla.

AMBIGUOUS	I threw my present on the table, and it broke.

[Was it the present or the table that broke?]

EDITED	My present broke when I threw it on the table.

In a **vague pronoun reference**, the pronoun does not refer clearly to any particular person or thing. To correct a vague pronoun reference, substitute a more specific noun for the pronoun.

VAGUE	After an accident at the intersection, they installed a traffic light.

[Who installed the traffic light?]

EDITED	After an accident at the intersection, the highway department installed a traffic light.

VAGUE	When I heard it, I laughed.

[Heard what?]

EDITED	When I heard the message, I laughed.

....

PRACTICE 4   Avoiding Ambiguous or Vague Pronoun References

Edit each of the following sentences to eliminate any ambiguous or vague pronoun references. Some sentences may be revised correctly in more than one way. *Possible edits shown.*

scientists
EXAMPLE: In a recent study, ~~they~~ found that people do not always
          see objects that are in unexpected places.

who
1. In a psychology study, volunteers watched a video of two basketball

   teams, ~~and they~~ had to count the number of passes.

Focusing   *the volunteers*
2. ~~As the volunteers focused~~ on the players, some of ~~them~~ did not

   notice a person in a gorilla suit walking onto the basketball court.

meeting   *the volunteers*
3. Later, when ~~the volunteers met~~ with the researchers, many of ~~them~~

   asked, "What gorilla?"

an object
4. By the end of the study, the researchers had learned that if ~~it~~ was

   unexpected, many people simply could not see it.

5. The way the human brain processes visual information may keep
people from using ~~it~~ *that information* wisely.

6. For example, if a car crosses into the lane facing oncoming traffic, ~~it~~ *the danger*
may not register in the mind of a driver who expects a routine trip.

7. A stop sign appearing at an intersection cannot prevent an accident
if drivers do not see ~~it~~ *the sign*.

8. Before the psychology study, ~~they~~ *most people* thought that drivers who missed
signs of danger were simply not paying attention.

9. However, the study indicates that drivers make mistakes because
they may not see ~~them~~ *problems* ahead.

10. Traffic safety regulations cannot make people's brains and eyes
work differently, but ~~they~~ *laws* can make ~~them~~ *people* wear seat belts.

Avoid Repetitious Pronoun References

In a **repetitious pronoun reference**, the pronoun repeats a reference to
a noun rather than replacing the noun. Remove the repetitious pronoun.

> The police officer ~~he~~ told me I had not stopped at the sign.
>
> The sign ~~/it~~ was hidden by a tree.

> **LANGUAGE NOTE:** In some languages, like Spanish, it is correct to repeat
> the noun with a pronoun. In formal English, however, a pronoun is used
> to replace a noun, not to repeat it.
>
> **INCORRECT**   My son he is a police officer.
>
> **CORRECT**   My son is a police officer.

ESL Read aloud
some sentences from
ESL students' writing,
and ask them to raise
their hands when they
hear a repetitious ref-
erence. Then, ask
students to edit the
sentence for clarity.

PRACTICE 5   Avoiding Repetitious Prounoun References

Correct any repetitious pronoun references in the following sentences.

> **EXAMPLE:** The science of robotics ~~it~~ already has practical
> applications.

1. Robots ~~they~~ have been part of many science-fiction classics, from
The Jetsons to *Star Wars*.

2. Is there any child who ~~he~~ has not wished for a robot friend, a robot tutor, or a robot maid?

3. In some industries, robots ~~they~~ are already part of the workforce.

4. Robots ~~they~~ make sushi for some Japanese fast-food restaurant chains.

5. Additionally, a factory might use robots to handle substances that ~~they~~ are dangerous for humans to touch.

6. But business ~~it~~ is not the only area in which the robot population is increasing.

7. Some children who ~~they~~ wanted a robot friend have already gotten their wish.

8. Toy manufacturers have created a robot dog that ~~it~~ can respond to human commands.

9. The robot dog ~~it~~ was on many holiday and birthday gift lists for children.

10. Also, some house-cleaning robots ~~they~~ are on the market; for example, one vacuums floors.

Use the Right Type of Pronoun

As you can see on the chart on page 496, there are several types of pronouns—*subject* pronouns, *object* pronouns, and *possessive* pronouns, each of which has a different function.

Subject Pronouns

For more on subjects, see Chapter 22.

Subject pronouns serve as the subject of a verb.

> *She* took my parking space.

> *I* honked my horn.

> **LANGUAGE NOTE:** Some languages omit subject pronouns, but English sentences always have a stated or written subject.
>
> **INCORRECT**   Hates cleaning.
>
> **CORRECT**   *He* hates cleaning.

Object Pronouns

Object pronouns either receive the action of a verb (the object of the verb) or are part of a prepositional phrase (the object of the preposition).

OBJECT OF THE VERB	Carolyn asked *me* to drive.
	Carolyn gave *me* the keys.
OBJECT OF THE PREPOSITION	Carolyn gave the keys to *me*.

Possessive Pronouns

Possessive pronouns show ownership. Note that you never need an apostrophe with a possessive pronoun.

Giselle is *my* best friend.

That jacket is *hers*.

Certain kinds of sentences can make choosing the right type of pronoun a little more difficult—ones that have compound subjects or objects; ones that make a comparison; and ones where you have to choose between *who* or *whom*.

Pronouns Used with Compound Subjects and Objects

A **compound subject** has more than one subject joined by a conjunction such as *and* or *or*. A **compound object** has more than one object joined by a conjunction.

COMPOUND SUBJECT	Tim and *I* work together.
COMPOUND OBJECT	Kayla baked the cookies for Jim and *me*.

To decide what type of pronoun to use in a compound construction, try leaving out the other part of the compound and the conjunction. Then, say the sentence aloud to yourself.

~~Jerome and~~ (me / I̲) like chili dogs.

[Think: *I* like chili dogs.]

The package was for ~~Karen and~~ (she / her̲).

[Think: The package was for *her*.]

When you are writing about yourself and others, always put the others first, choosing the correct type of pronoun.

> **INCORRECT**   *Me* and my friends went to the movies.
>
> **CORRECT**   My friends and *I* went to the movies.
>
> [Sentence puts others first and uses the subject pronoun, *I*]
>
> **INCORRECT**   Gene bought the tickets for *I* and my friends.
>
> **CORRECT**   Gene bought the tickets for my friends and *me*.
>
> [Sentence puts others first and uses the object pronoun, *me*]

If a pronoun is part of a compound object in a prepositional phrase, use an object pronoun.

> Please keep that information just between you and *me*.
>
> [*Between you and me* is a prepositional phrase, so it uses the object pronoun, *me*.]

Many people make the mistake of writing *between you and I*. The correct pronoun is the object pronoun, *me*.

· ·

PRACTICE 6   Editing Pronouns in Compound Constructions

Edit each sentence using the proper type of pronoun. If a sentence is already correct, write "C" next to it.

> EXAMPLE: Megan and I love soda, and ~~her~~ and ~~me~~ regularly have
> *she*   *I*
>
> two cans a day each.

1. However, a TV program on dental health started making ~~she~~ and ~~I~~
   her   *me*
   rethink our soda-drinking habit.

2. ~~Her~~ and ~~me~~ paid close attention as we watched a dentist, Dr. Jenine
   She   *I*
   Summers, and her assistant, Ian, conduct an experiment.

3. Dr. Summers asked Ian to place a tooth in a bottle of soda, and ~~her~~
   she
   and ~~him~~ observed what happened to the tooth.
   he

4. Megan and ~~me~~ watched as time-lapse photography showed how the
   I
   tooth changed from day to day.

5. The result of the experiment surprised her and ~~I~~. *me*

6. At the end of the experiment, Dr. Summers and Ian looked in the bottle of soda for the tooth, and she and he showed that it had disappeared. *C*

7. ~~Them~~ and ~~us~~ said "Wow" at the same time. *They* *we*

8. Dr. Summers explained how acids in the soda broke down the tooth; her comments about soda's sugar content were equally shocking to Megan and me. *C*

9. Megan and ~~me~~ learned that each can of soda we drink contains about ten teaspoons of sugar, which creates even more tooth-dissolving acid and contributes to weight gain. *I*

10. Therefore, ~~us~~ and some other friends have decided to ban soda from our refrigerators. *we*

. . . .

Pronouns Used in Comparisons

Using the wrong type of pronoun in comparisons can give a sentence an unintended meaning. Editing sentences that contain comparisons can be tricky because comparisons often imply words that are not actually included in the sentence.

To find comparisons, look for the words *than* or *as*. To decide whether to use a subject or object pronoun in a comparison, try adding the implied words and saying the sentence aloud.

Bill likes Chinese food more than *I*.

[This sentence means Bill likes Chinese food more than I like it. The implied word after *I* is *do*.]

Bill likes Chinese food more than *me*.

[This sentence means Bill likes Chinese food more than he likes me. The implied words after *than* are *he likes*.]

The professor knows more than (us / we).

[Think: The professor knows more than *we know*.]

Jen likes other professors more than (he / him).

[Think: Jen likes other professors more than *she likes him*.]

....

PRACTICE 7   Editing Pronouns in Comparisons

Edit each sentence using the correct pronoun type. If a sentence is correct, put a "C" next to it.

> **EXAMPLE:** I chose to go to a private university instead of a public one
>
> like my brother Anthony, and, as a result, I had to take out
>
> *he*
> more student loans than ~~him~~.

1. Our parents are worried because when they went to college they

   I
   did not need to borrow as much as he or ~~me~~.

2. However, we know better than ~~them~~ what is necessary to get an
   they

   education these days.

3. For Anthony as well as for ~~I~~, borrowing money is part of today's
   me

   reality.

4. More than two-thirds of American college students are in the same

   position as we. *C*

5. The average college student will graduate with $24,000 in debt, a

   I
   little more than Anthony but a little less than ~~me~~.

6. No one is more confident than ~~me~~, though, that I can repay the
   I

   loans quickly.

7. Even though the average graduate takes fifteen years to repay his or

   me
   her loans, I think getting out of debt will be easier for ~~I~~ than for the

   average graduate.

8. Balancing several jobs is not as difficult for ~~I~~ as for some people.
   me

9. Anthony will probably take longer than ~~me~~ to pay back his
   I

   loans because he plans to go to graduate school and defer

   payment.

10. However, getting out of debt before I am thirty means more to me

    than to him. *C*

....

Choosing between Who and Whom

Who is always a subject; use it if the pronoun performs an action. *Whom* is always an object; use it if the pronoun does not perform any action.

WHO = SUBJECT   Janis is the friend *who* introduced me to Billy.

WHOM = OBJECT   Billy is the man *whom* I met last night.

In most cases, for sentences where the pronoun is followed by a verb, use *who*. When the pronoun is followed by a noun or pronoun, use *whom*.

The person (who / whom) spoke was boring.

[The pronoun is followed by the verb *spoke*. Use *who*.]

The person (who / whom) I met was boring.

[The pronoun is followed by another pronoun: *I*. Use *whom*.]

Whoever is a subject pronoun; *whomever* is an object pronoun.

. . . .

PRACTICE 8   Choosing Between *Who* and *Whom*

In each sentence, circle the correct word, *who* or *whom*.

> **EXAMPLE:** Most people think it was Thomas Alva Edison (who / whom) invented the electric light bulb. *Answers may vary. Possible edits shown.*

1. Edison is certainly the one (who / whom) became famous for his electric light bulb, but he did not invent it.

2. The inventor to (who / whom) this credit belongs is the English chemist Humphry Davy.

3. It was Davy for (who / whom), in 1809, a charged strip of charcoal took on a satisfying glow after he connected it to a battery with wires.

4. An English physicist named Joseph Wilson Swan, (who / whom) is also largely unknown, advanced this development in 1878 by creating an electric light bulb that glowed for 13.5 hours.

5. Three years earlier, Henry Woodward and Matthew Evans had patented a light bulb, and it was then Edison (who / whom) purchased their patent and in 1879 devised a carbon filament that burned for 40 hours.

Make Pronouns Consistent

Pronouns have to be consistent in **person**, which is the point of view a writer uses. Pronouns may be in first person (*I, we*); second person (*you*); or third person (*he, she, it,* or *they*). (See the chart on page 496.)

INCONSISTENT PERSON   *I* wanted to use the copier, but the attendant said *you* had to have an access code.

[The sentence starts in the first person (*I*) but shifts to the second person (*you*).]

CONSISTENT PERSON   *I* wanted to use the copier, but the attendant said *I* had to have an access code.

[The sentence stays with the first person, *I*.]

INCONSISTENT PERSON   After *a caller* presses 1, *you* get a recording.

[The sentence starts with the third person (*a caller*) but shifts to the second person (*you*).]

CONSISTENT PERSON   After *a caller* presses 1, *he or she* gets a recording.

CONSISTENT PERSON, PLURAL   After *callers* press 1, *they* get a recording.

[In these last two examples, the sentence stays with the third person.]

PRACTICE 9   Making Pronouns Consistent in Person

In the following items, correct the shifts in person. There may be more than one way to correct some sentences. *Possible edits shown.*

EXAMPLE: I have a younger brother with an allergy to peanuts, so
                                                    I
~~you~~ have to be very careful with his food.
               ^

1. Experts agree that the percentage of people with allergies to foods is rising, but ~~we~~ *they* don't know why.

2. Someone who has a mild allergic reaction the first time ~~you eat~~ *he or she eats* a food may develop more severe allergies from future contacts with the food.

3. If a person has a severe allergy to a food and unknowingly eats even a small amount of that food, ~~you~~ *her or she* could die.

4. However, if people with allergies are protected from any contact with the food for several years, ~~his or her~~ *their* allergies may disappear or become milder.

5. When ~~a child has~~ *children have* severe allergies, their parents can be extremely cautious.

6. My little brother is severely allergic to peanuts, so ~~you are~~ *I am* not allowed to eat anything containing peanuts while he is nearby.

7. He carries an adrenaline pen that can save ~~your~~ *his* life if ~~you go~~ *he goes* into shock from a food allergy.

8. I love peanut butter, but ~~you~~ *I* can't eat a peanut butter sandwich in my house.

9. My mother will not take my brother to any public place where ~~you~~ *she* can even smell peanuts.

10. Some people think that her precautions are extreme, but she knows that ~~you~~ *she* can't be too careful when ~~your~~ *her* child's life is at stake.

....

Edit Paragraphs and Your Own Writing

Edit the following paragraphs for pronoun errors, referring to the chart on page 515 as you need to. *Answers may vary. Possible edits shown.*

RESOURCES For cumulative Editing Review Tests, see pages 667–83.

....

EDITING REVIEW 1 (13 errors)

(1) 1977 ~~it~~ was the first year a woman driver qualified for the

Indianapolis 500. (2) Janet Guthrie, *who* ~~whom~~ also competed in the Daytona

500 that year, became a role model for aspiring female drivers. (3)

Though progress has been slow, the sport has become more welcoming

to women drivers, and audiences now see many more women competing

in the big races. (4) These days, fans have several strong female drivers

to follow, one of *whom* ~~who~~ is the famous Danica Patrick. (5) Danica Patrick

has made a name for *herself* ~~himself~~ by being a strong competitor. (6) In

particular, she has shown male racers that women can be as ambitious

and talented as *they* ~~them~~. (7) Because of her talent and perhaps her willing-

ness to promote herself, no female car racer receives as much attention

as *she* ~~her~~. (8) However, other women drivers ~~they~~ have joined Patrick at the

big Indianapolis races. (9) In 2010, *she* ~~her~~ and three other women qualified

for and raced in the Indianapolis 500. (10) For driver Sarah Fisher, the

2010 race was her ninth time competing in the "Indy 500." (11) Though

none of them placed in the top five, each of the four women said *she* ~~they~~

was ~~were~~ there to win. (12) The car-racing audience now has *its* ~~their~~ eyes on

NASCAR. (13) Few female racers have appeared in NASCAR races,

and many say *NASCAR needs* ~~they need~~ to focus more on diversity and encourage more

women to join *its* ~~their~~ ranks.

....

EDITING REVIEW 2 (12 errors)

(1) If someone arrives home carrying a heavy bag of groceries,

he or she often has ~~they often have~~ to struggle to find and get out the house keys to open

the door. (2) A person in this situation can use a type of door lock that

allows *him or her* ~~he or she~~ to enter with just the swipe of a finger. (3) The lock is a

scanner that stores the fingerprints of those *who* ~~whom~~ are authorized to

have access. (4) If the person's fingerprint matches a stored print, the lock ~~it~~ slides open. (5) The user does not need to do any wiring to install

the lock, and *he or she needs* ~~it needs~~ only four AA batteries to operate it. (6) Using

radio waves, the lock detects distances between ridges and valleys of a

finger just below the skin's surface, so it doesn't even matter if *the user has* ~~they have~~

a minor cut or scratch. (7) While it may be possible for criminals to

somehow get a photocopy of a homeowner's fingerprint, *they are* ~~him or her is~~

unlikely to get this opportunity. (8) Furthermore, the person *for whom* ~~who~~ the

lock is intended ~~for~~ will never have this fingerprint information hacked

because it is stored only by the lock itself and not in a central computer.

(9) Homeowners with this device no longer need to remember their

house keys because *their* ~~his or her~~ fingerprints are always with *them* ~~him or her~~.

(10) There is one thing homeowners do have to remember, though; *they* ~~you~~

have to make sure there are always fresh batteries in the lock.

EDITING REVIEW 3 (11 errors)

(1) In 2006, NASA had trouble finding enough volunteers for ex-

periments designed to test how well *they* ~~you~~ could counteract the effects of

weightlessness. (2) The recruits were asked if *they* ~~he or she~~ would lie down

in bed for three weeks. (3) *The volunteers* ~~Each volunteer~~ also had to have their feet

about five inches higher than their heads. (4) The subjects ~~they~~ could

not get up, ate while supported by one elbow, used bedpans, and show-

ered lying down on a waterproof cart. (5) When people lie down for

three weeks, *their* ~~your~~ muscles and bones can weaken, just as in real weight-

lessness. (6) To see if this weakening can be counteracted, *the researchers* ~~they~~ had

some subjects spin around on a centrifuge bed for thirty times a minute

for one hour each day, which simulated gravity. (7) In order to test the

comparative effects of the centrifuge on men and women, subjects

were studied in male-female pairs, but only one such pair showed any

difference. (8) (He was affected more than *she* ~~her~~.) (9) From the start, the

the researchers'
project was hampered by ~~their~~ inability to recruit more than ten
                           ^
                                              who
subjects. (10) Most of the researchers, ~~whom~~ had hoped for thirty
                                           ^
participants, were puzzled by the small number of volunteers. (11) But
                 whom
one scientist, for ~~who~~ this was no surprise, noted that the centrifuge
                     ^
experience, combined with three weeks of lying in bed, probably scared

off a lot of people. (12) She also wondered if many people could take so
                                      their jobs
much time off from ~~his or her job~~.
                        ^

. . . .

EDITING REVIEW 4 (12 errors)
                            who
(1) For those ~~whom~~ have some clothes they no longer want, there
                  ^
is now a new way to put those clothes to use. (2) A trend called clothes
                                          his or her
swapping allows a person to donate ~~their~~ unwanted but still usable
                                       ^
clothing in exchange for someone else's clothes. (3) People ~~they~~ are

swapping clothes in many American cities and even in other countries.

(4) It started in the 1990s when groups of women would get together
                              her
and someone would bring along ~~their~~ unwanted clothes to see if anyone
                                  ^
else wanted them. (5) But now there are advertised clothes swaps, and
they draw   *Some swap events*
~~it draws~~ men as well as women. (6) ~~At some swap events, they~~ require a
    ^   ^
donation of clothes in order to enter; at others, there might be an admis-

sion fee. (7) There is also the chance of finding a smelly or dirty tee shirt
while rummaging
~~as you rummage~~ through a stack of clothing. (8) But most swaps have
      ^   *their*
a rule that participants clean and press ~~his or her~~ donated clothing.
                                              ^
(9) The attraction ~~it~~ is a combination of the thrill of bartering and the

anticipation of coming across some free clothes that fit one's size and
                                                     participants
personality. (10) Swaps do not have changing rooms, so ~~they~~ just put on
                                                            ^
                                                      who
an item over the clothes they are already wearing and ask others ~~whom~~
                                                                     ^
are nearby how it looks. (11) Getting clothes at no cost is, of course, the
                                                  the clothes
main advantage, but participants are also aware that, if ~~they~~ look awful
                                                             ^
when tried on at home, they can simply be donated at the next swap.

···

PRACTICE 10   Editing Your Own Writing for Pronoun Use

As a final practice, edit for pronoun use in a piece of your own writing — a paper you are working on for this course, a paper you have already finished, a paper for another course, a recent piece of writing from your work or everyday life, or your idea journal entry. You may want to use the following chart as you edit.

TEACHING TIP Have students underline all of the pronouns in the piece they choose and draw arrows to the antecedents.

···

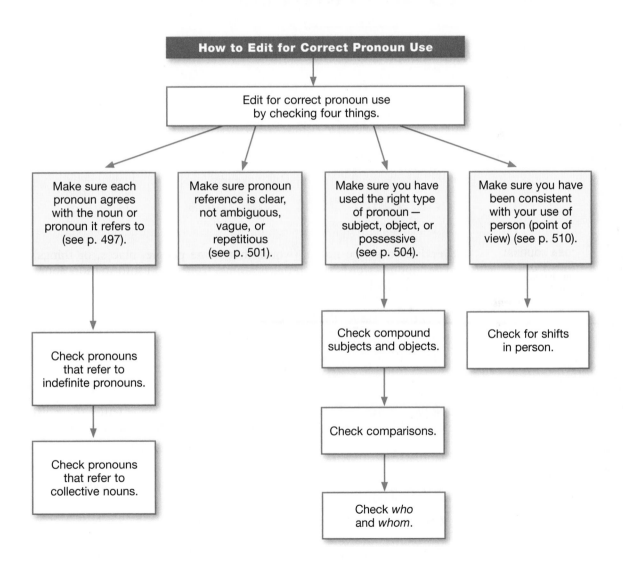

How to Edit for Correct Pronoun Use

Edit for correct pronoun use by checking four things.

Make sure each pronoun agrees with the noun or pronoun it refers to (see p. 497).

Make sure pronoun reference is clear, not ambiguous, vague, or repetitious (see p. 501).

Make sure you have used the right type of pronoun — subject, object, or possessive (see p. 504).

Make sure you have been consistent with your use of person (point of view) (see p. 510).

Check pronouns that refer to indefinite pronouns.

Check pronouns that refer to collective nouns.

Check compound subjects and objects.

Check for shifts in person.

Check comparisons.

Check *who* and *whom*.

28

Adjectives and Adverbs

Describing Which One? *or* How?

Understand What Adjectives and Adverbs Are

IDEA JOURNAL
Describe—in as much detail as possible—either a person or a room.

Adjectives describe nouns (words that name people, places, or things) and pronouns (words that replace nouns). They add information about what kind, which one, or how many.

City traffic was *terrible* last night.

The highway was *congested* for *three* miles.

Two huge old tractor trailers had collided.

> **LANGUAGE NOTE:** In English, adjectives do not indicate whether the word they modify is singular or plural, unless the adjective is a number.
>
> **INCORRECT**   My two new classes are *hards*.
>
> [The adjective *two* is fine because it is a number, but the adjective *hard* should not end in *s*.]
>
> **CORRECT**   My two new classes are *hard*.

DISCUSSION
Make two columns on the board—one for adjectives and one for adverbs. In each column, have students list words describing a common subject, such as your classroom or the weather outside.

Adverbs describe verbs (words that tell what happens in a sentence), adjectives, or other adverbs. They add information about how, how much, when, where, why, or to what degree. Adverbs often end with *-ly*.

MODIFYING VERB   Dave drives *aggressively*.

MODIFYING ADJECTIVE   The *extremely* old woman swims every day.

MODIFYING ANOTHER ADVERB Dave drives *very* aggressively.

Adjectives usually come *before* the words they modify; adverbs come either before or after. You can also use more than one adjective or adverb to modify a word.

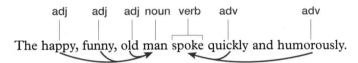

adj   adj   adj noun verb   adv   adv

The happy, funny, old man spoke quickly and humorously.

LANGUAGE NOTE: Sometimes, students confuse the *-ed* and *-ing* forms of adjectives. Common examples are *bored/boring, confused/confusing, excited/exciting*, and *interested/interesting*. Often, the *-ed* form describes a person's reaction, while the *-ing* form describes the thing being reacted to.

INCORRECT   James is *interesting* in all sports. [James is not interesting; sports are.]

CORRECT   James *is interested* in all sports. [*Is interested* describes James's reaction to sports.]

Another common confusion is between when to use an adjective and when to use an adverb. Remember that adverbs modify verbs, adjectives, and other adverbs but not nouns. Adverbs often end in *-ly*.

INCORRECT   James is a *carefully* driver.

[The word *carefully* should not be used to describe a noun, *driver*. The noun *driver* should be modified by an adjective, *careful*. The adverb *carefully* can be used to modify a verb, *drives*.]

CORRECT   James is a *careful* driver.   *or*   James drives *carefully*.

Practice Using Adjectives
and Adverbs Correctly

Choosing between Adjective and Adverb Forms

Many adverbs are formed by adding *-ly* to the end of an adjective. To decide whether to use an adjective form or an adverb form, find the word you want to describe. If that word is a noun or a pronoun, use the

For coordinate adjectives, see Chapter 36.

adjective form. If it is a verb, an adjective, or another adverb, use the adverb form.

ADJECTIVE	ADVERB
The *new* student introduced himself.	The couple is *newly* married.
That is an *honest* answer.	Please answer *honestly*.

. . . .

PRACTICE 1   Choosing between Adjective and Adverb Forms

In each sentence, underline the word or phrase in the sentence that is being described, and then circle the correct word in parentheses.

> **EXAMPLE:** Recent research indicates that some dinosaurs were (beautiful /(beautifully)) colored.

For more practice
with adjectives
and adverbs, visit
Exercise Central at
bedfordstmartins
.com/realessays.

1. Scientists were ((excited)/ excitedly) to discover something new about these ancient creatures.

2. Before this discovery, people could offer only ((rough)/ roughly) guesses about dinosaurs' colors.

3. Now, research (strong /(strongly)) suggests that some dinosaurs had red, gray, black, and white feathers.

4. Scientists determined this by (close /(closely)) analyzing dinosaur fossils.

5. The fossils themselves are ((dull)/ dully) in color.

6. However, when scientists use a microscope, they can (easy /(easily)) see tiny structures called melanosomes.

7. Melanosomes make birds' feathers ((colorful)/ colorfully), so scientists speculate that melanosomes also made dinosaurs' feathers colorful.

8. Like birds, dinosaurs may have used their ((brilliant)/ brilliantly) feathers to attract mates or scare away enemies.

9. Some <u>scientists</u> remain (skeptical / skeptically) about these recent

discoveries.

10. Others see them as (valuable / valuably) <u>contributions</u> to the study

of dinosaurs.

Using Adjectives and Adverbs in Comparisons

To compare two persons, places, or things, use the **comparative** form of
adjectives or adverbs.

Sheehan drives *faster* than I do.

Francis is *more talkative* than Destina is.

Comparative and Superlative Forms

ADJECTIVE OR ADVERB	COMPARATIVE	SUPERLATIVE
ADVERBS AND ADJECTIVES OF ONE SYLLABLE		
tall	taller	tallest
fast	faster	fastest
ADJECTIVES ENDING IN Y		
happy	happier	happiest
silly	sillier	silliest
ADVERBS AND ADJECTIVES OF MORE THAN ONE SYLLABLE		
graceful	more graceful	most graceful
gracefully	more gracefully	most gracefully
intelligent	more intelligent	most intelligent
intelligently	more intelligently	most intelligently

To compare three or more persons, places, or things, use the **superlative** form of adjectives or adverbs.

Sheehan drives the *fastest* of all our friends.

Francis is the *most talkative* of the children.

Comparatives and superlatives can be formed either by adding an ending to an adjective or adverb or by adding a word.

DESCRIPTION OF ADJECTIVE OR ADVERB	COMPARATIVE	SUPERLATIVE
Short (one syllable): tall	Add -er: taller	Add -est: tallest
Adjective ends in -y: silly	Change -y to -i and add -er: sillier	Change -y to -i and add -est: silliest
More than one syllable: intelligent	Add the word more: more intelligent	Add the word most: most intelligent

Use either an ending (-er or -est) or an extra word (more or most) to form a comparative or superlative—not both at once.

One of the ~~most~~ easiest ways to beat stress is to exercise regularly.

It is ~~more~~ harder to study late at night than during the day.

· ·

PRACTICE 2 Using Comparatives and Superlatives

In the space provided in each sentence, write the correct form of the adjective or adverb in parentheses. You may need to add more or most to some adjectives and adverbs.

TEACHING TIP Go over this practice together as a class. Then, have students proofread a piece of their own writing to make sure that they have used comparatives and superlatives correctly.

EXAMPLE: One of the ___most loved___ (loved) treats is chocolate.

1. Some people think that Americans are the __biggest__ (*big*) consumers of chocolate in the world.

2. Actually, the people who eat the __greatest__ (*great*) amount of chocolate are the British.

3. In fact, the British are nearly 40 percent __fonder__ (*fond*) of chocolate than Americans are.

4. British chocolate makers are concerned because they expected British people's chocolate consumption to grow __more robustly__ (*robustly*) than it has in recent years.

5. However, a small company that makes chocolate with organically
    grown ingredients has experienced some of the ___*healthiest*___
    (*healthy*) sales of all chocolate manufacturers in recent years.

6. Even though this organic chocolate is ___*more expensive*___ (*expensive*)
    than regular chocolate, people are willing to pay the price.

7. People have come to expect that organic foods will carry a ___*higher*___
    (*high*) price than conventional foods.

8. Another type of chocolate is also enjoying ___*stronger*___ (*strong*) sales in
    Britain than regular chocolate.

9. This chocolate does not contain the vegetable solids found in most
    British chocolate; therefore, it is considered by some chocolate lov-
    ers to be ___*purer*___ (*pure*) than the standard product.

10. This "real" chocolate is expensive, but its sales are expected to con-
    tinue to grow ___*faster*___ (*fast*) than sales of other premium chocolates.

Using *Good, Well, Bad,* and *Badly*

Four common adjectives and adverbs have irregular forms—*good, well,
bad,* and *badly.*

People often are confused about whether to use *good* or *well. Good* is
an adjective, so use it to describe a noun or pronoun. *Well* is an adverb, so
use it to describe a verb or an adjective.

Forms of *Good, Well, Bad,* and *Badly*

	COMPARATIVE	SUPERLATIVE
ADJECTIVE		
good	better	best
bad	worse	worst
ADVERB		
well	better	best
badly	worse	worst

TEAMWORK Using an article from the newspaper, a Web site, or some other source, have students draw arrows from the adjectives and adverbs to the words they modify. This activity can be done in small groups or assigned as homework and reviewed in teams the next day.

ADJECTIVE   She is a *good* friend.

ADVERB   He works *well* with his colleagues.

Well can also be an adjective to describe someone's health:

I am not feeling *well* today.

PRACTICE 3 Using *Good* and *Well*

Complete each sentence by circling the correct word in parentheses. Underline the word that *good* or *well* modifies.

> **EXAMPLE:** A ((good)/ well) storyteller can hold an audience's attention.

1. Mark Twain's ability to tell an amusing story is (good /(well)) known.

2. Twain's famous story "The Celebrated Jumping Frog of Calaveras County" is a ((good)/ well) example of traditional American tale-telling.

3. The story is narrated by an Easterner whose proper speech contrasts (good /(well)) with the country dialect of Simon Wheeler, a storyteller he meets.

4. Wheeler may not be (good /(well)) educated, but he is a master of the tall tale.

5. The narrator claims that Wheeler has told him a "monotonous" story, but the tale is apparently ((good)/ well) enough for the narrator to repeat.

6. The frog in the story is famous for being a ((good)/ well) jumper.

7. Wheeler explains that the frog's owner lives (good /(well)) by gambling on the frog's jumping ability.

8. The frog's owner, Jim Smiley, makes the mistake of leaving the frog with a man whom Smiley does not know (good /(well)).

9. The stranger makes the frog swallow heavy shot so that he can no longer <u>jump</u> (good /(well)).

10. In Twain's story, Simon Wheeler has such a ((good)/ well) <u>time</u> telling stories that the narrator has to escape from him at the end.

. . . .

PRACTICE 4   Using Comparative and Superlative Forms of *Good* and *Bad*

Complete each sentence by circling the correct comparative or superlative form of *good* or *bad* in parentheses.

EXAMPLE: The (better /(best)) way my family found to learn about another culture was to allow an exchange student to live in our home.

1. Simone, a French high school student, spent last summer getting to know the United States ((better)/ best) by living with my family.

2. She had studied English since the age of five, and her understanding of grammar was ((better)/ best) than mine.

3. She told me that she had the (worse /(worst)) accent of any student in her English classes, but I liked the way she spoke.

4. Her accent was certainly no ((worse)/ worst) than mine would be if I tried to speak French.

5. My (worse /(worst)) fear was that she would find our lives boring.

6. However, the exchange program's administrator explained that the (better /(best)) way for Simone to learn about our country was for us to do ordinary things.

7. For me, the (better /(best)) part of Simone's visit was the chance to see my world through fresh eyes.

8. I felt ((better)/ best) about my summer job, trips to the supermarket, and afternoon swims at the pool because Simone found all of these things exotic and fascinating.

9. Simone even liked summer reruns on television; she claimed that French television was much (worse / worst).

10. The (worse / worst) part of the visit was having to say goodbye to Simone at the end of the summer.

RESOURCES For cumulative Editing Review Tests, see pages 667–83.

Edit Paragraphs and Your Own Writing

Edit the following paragraphs for adjective and adverb errors, referring to the chart on page 528 as you need to.

EDITING REVIEW 1 (9 errors)

(1) For an average European in the Middle Ages, wearing stripes was not ~~simple~~ *simply* a fashion mistake. (2) According to Michel Pastoureau, a scholar of the medieval period, wearing stripes was one of the ~~worse~~ *worst* things a European Christian could do in the thirteenth and fourteenth centuries. (3) Stripes might be taken as a sign that the wearer was ~~more~~ sillier than other people; jesters, for example, often wore them. (4) Prostitutes also wore striped clothes, so stripes might be seen as an indication that the person was ~~sinfuller~~ *more sinful* than others. (5) Wearing stripes was ~~dangerousest~~ *most dangerous* for clergymen. (6) At least one clergyman in fourteenth-century France was executed because he had been ~~foolishly~~ *foolish* enough to wear striped clothes. (7) Carmelite monks who wore striped cloaks were ~~frequent~~ *frequently* attacked, and several popes insisted that the monks change to a ~~more simple~~ *simpler* costume. (8) People in medieval Europe certainly took their clothing ~~serious.~~ *seriously.* (9) The only reason some people don't wear stripes today is that they are afraid of looking fat.

EDITING REVIEW 2 (14 errors)

(1) Many people no longer find it ~~embarrassingly~~ *embarrassing* to admit that they have seen a psychotherapist. (2) Some patients argue that it is ~~gooder~~ *better* to seek mental help than to suffer silently. (3) Others seem to feel that needing a therapist is a sign that their lives are ~~interestinger~~ *more interesting* than other people's. (4) At any rate, the stigma that some people once attached to psychotherapy is disappearing ~~quick.~~ *quickly* (5) Therapists have lately become ~~visibler~~ *more visible* in popular culture, and this visibility may result in even wider acceptance of psychotherapy. (6) For example, when a mobster on the cable television show *The Sopranos* asked a therapist to treat his panic attacks, viewers saw that the ~~most tough~~ *toughest* of men was still able to discuss his relationships and feelings with a mental health specialist. (7) If Tony Soprano could do it, what ordinary person is going to feel ~~badly~~ *bad* about seeking help for ordinary problems?

(8) However, people considering seeing a therapist are not the only ones who loved to watch Tony Soprano trying to work through his problems. (9) Indeed, *The Sopranos,* which was one of the ~~bigger~~ *biggest* hits ever on cable television, included many psychologists in its audience. (10) One online magazine ~~regular~~ *regularly* published a therapist's analysis of each episode. (11) Other therapists chatted online about whether or not the psychologist on the television show was practicing psychology. (12) The audiences of psychological professionals seem to agree that therapy was portrayed ~~accurater~~ *more accurately* on the show than in many popular films. (13) As they pointed out, at least the therapist was not in love with her patient, unlike several psychiatrists in ~~recently~~ *recent* movies. (14) Although Mr. Soprano, like many actual therapy patients, did things that were not good for his mental health, his therapist thought that he was functioning ~~best~~ *better* than before. (15) If he ever ~~honest~~ *honestly*

discussed his criminal day job with her, even the therapists tuning in

might have had trouble figuring out the ~~bestest~~ _best_ possible response.

EDITING REVIEW 3 (12 errors)

(1) Many people assume that today's college students are
~~traditionaler~~ _more traditional_ than they really are. (2) Seventy-five percent of today's
college students ~~actual~~ _actually_ do not go to college right after high school, live
in the dorms, or finish in four years. (3) For many people, waiting a few
years before starting college is not a ~~worst~~ _bad_ choice. (4) Some also find
that taking ~~more long~~ _longer_ than four years to finish is ~~more good~~ _better_ than trying
to rush through school. (5) Almost half of today's students find that going
to school part-time is the ~~goodest~~ _best_ plan. (6) One of the ~~interestingest~~ _most interesting_
statistics shows that half of today's students support themselves and do
not receive money from family. (7) In fact, because school is ~~surprising~~ _surprisingly_
expensive, 38 percent of college students work full-time. (8) Some students are able to balance work and school ~~good~~ _well_, but many struggle.
(9) One of the ~~more~~ sadder statistics shows that less than half of students
finish their schooling. (10) The truth is that older students tend to
have more ~~complicate~~ _complicated_ lives with more distractions and responsibilities.
(11) When colleges and universities offer flexible schedules and requirements, students have a better chance of ~~successful~~ _successfully_ finishing school.

EDITING REVIEW 4 (14 errors)

(1) In large and small parks across the country, a common sight is
a pair of chess players ~~quiet~~ _quietly_ and ~~intent~~ _intently_ studying the pieces on the board
between them. (2) But lately, chess in the park has been taken to a ~~newest~~ _new_
level. (3) "Street chess," as it is ~~typical~~ _typically_ called, is no longer recreation;
instead, it is ~~most~~ _more_ like a business. (4) ~~Normal~~ _Normally_, it is the same people,

mainly men, who are at their chess boards every day. (5) These players—

some call them hustlers—take on anybody who is willing to try to beat

them, ~~usual~~ *usually* for a wager of about $5. (6) Most of them are ~~real~~ *very* skilled

and able to defeat just about any opponent who challenges them.

(7) Some play ~~bad~~ *badly* sometimes and lose a game ~~deliberate~~ *deliberately* so that their

regular customers will keep coming back. (8) But most hustlers play to

win all the time, even if they hold back sometimes to avoid embarrassing

or discouraging their customers. (9) Players say that, ~~general~~ *generally (or "in general")*, the police

do not bother them, but most hustlers still find it ~~best~~ *better* to use street

aliases than their real names. (10) One player claims never to play for

money, adding that he gives lessons for $45 an hour. (11) Some players

treat the pastime ~~casual~~ *casually*, playing only when they're in the mood.

(12) But for many hustlers, street chess is their life; they start during the

day, every day, and continue ~~good~~ *well* into the next morning.

- -

PRACTICE 5   Editing Your Own Writing for Correct Adjectives and Adverbs

As a final practice, edit a piece of your own writing for correct use of adjectives and adverbs. It can be a paper you are working on for this course, a paper you have already finished, a paper for another course, a recent piece of writing from your work or everyday life, or your idea journal entry. You may want to use the chart on page 528 as you edit.

- -

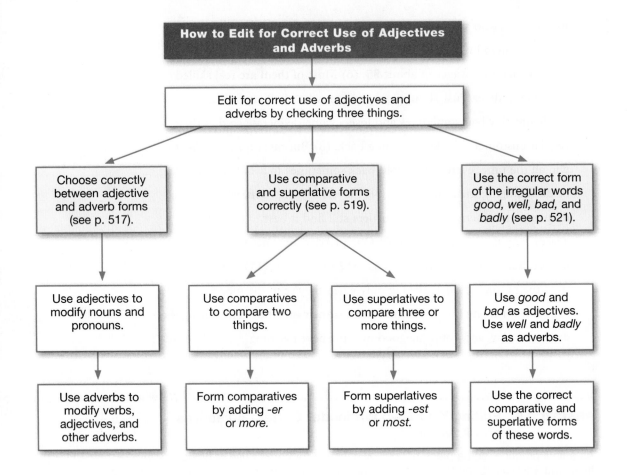

How to Edit for Correct Use of Adjectives and Adverbs

Edit for correct use of adjectives and adverbs by checking three things.

Choose correctly between adjective and adverb forms (see p. 517).

Use comparative and superlative forms correctly (see p. 519).

Use the correct form of the irregular words *good, well, bad,* and *badly* (see p. 521).

Use adjectives to modify nouns and pronouns.

Use comparatives to compare two things.

Use superlatives to compare three or more things.

Use *good* and *bad* as adjectives. Use *well* and *badly* as adverbs.

Use adverbs to modify verbs, adjectives, and other adverbs.

Form comparatives by adding *-er* or *more.*

Form superlatives by adding *-est* or *most.*

Use the correct comparative and superlative forms of these words.

29

Misplaced and Dangling Modifiers

Avoiding Confusing Descriptions

Understand What Misplaced and Dangling Modifiers Are

Modifiers are words or word groups that describe other words in a sentence. Unless the modifier is near the words it modifies, the sentence can be misleading or unintentionally funny.

Misplaced Modifiers

A **misplaced modifier**, because it is not correctly placed in the sentence, describes the wrong word or words. To correct a misplaced modifier, move the modifier as close as possible to the word or words it modifies. The safest choice is often to put the modifier directly before the sentence element it modifies.

MISPLACED   Rudy saw my dog *driving his car on the highway*.

[Was my dog driving a car? No, Rudy was, so the modifier must come right before or right after his name.]

CORRECT   *Driving his car on the highway*, Rudy saw my dog.

MISPLACED   Claudia could not see the stop sign *without sunglasses*.

[Did the sign need sunglasses? No, Claudia did.]

CORRECT   *Without sunglasses*, Claudia could not see the stop sign.

529

Four sentence constructions in particular often lead to misplaced modifiers:

1. Modifiers such as *only, almost, hardly, nearly,* and *just*

I ~~only ordered~~ half a pound. ordered only

Molly ~~almost~~ slept for ten hours. almost

2. Modifiers that start with *-ing* verbs

Using cash,
Timothy bought the car. ~~using cash.~~

Wearing an oven mitt,
Elena took out the hot pizza. ~~wearing an oven mitt.~~

[Note that when you move the phrase beginning with an *-ing* verb to the beginning of the sentence, you need to follow it with a comma.]

Looking out the window of the plane, they
~~They~~ saw the Statue of Liberty. ~~looking out the window of the plane.~~

3. Modifiers that are prepositional phrases

to the house for his sister.
Jim was carrying the bags ~~for his sister to the house.~~

for ice cream in her glove compartment.
Julie found money ~~in her glove compartment for ice cream.~~

With binoculars, we
~~We~~ saw the rare bird. ~~with binoculars.~~

For more on how to use relative pronouns — *who, which,* and *that* — see page 586.

4. Modifiers that are clauses starting with *who, whose, that,* or *which*

that was missing
I finally found the sock stuck to a T-shirt. ~~that was missing.~~

who call people during dinner
Telemarketers are sure to be annoying. ~~who call people during dinner.~~

that I recently bought
The computer died. ~~that I recently bought.~~

Dangling Modifiers

A **dangling modifier** "dangles" because the word or words it is supposed to modify are not in the sentence. Dangling modifiers usually appear at the beginning of a sentence and may seem to modify the noun or pronoun that immediately follows—but they do not.

Correct dangling modifiers either by adding the word being modified right after the opening modifier or by adding the word being modified to the opening modifier. Note that to correct a dangling modifier, you might have to reword the sentence.

DANGLING	*Talking on the telephone,* the dinner burned.

[Was the dinner talking on the telephone? No.]

CORRECT	*While Sharon was talking on the telephone,* the dinner burned.
	The dinner burned *while Sharon was talking on the telephone.*

DANGLING	*While waiting in line,* the alarms went off.

[Were the alarms waiting in line? No.]

CORRECT	*While waiting in line,* I heard the alarms go off.
	While I was waiting in line, the alarms went off.

Even if readers can guess what you are trying to say, misplaced and dangling modifiers are awkward. Be sure to look for and correct any misplaced and dangling modifiers in your writing.

Practice Correcting Misplaced and Dangling Modifiers

. . . .

PRACTICE 1   Correcting Misplaced Modifiers

Find and correct any misplaced modifiers in the following sentences. If a sentence is correct, write a "C" next to it.

EXAMPLE: Many nurses *who work in U.S. hospitals* are being trained to perform therapeutic touch. ~~who work in U.S. hospitals.~~

For more practice
with correcting mis-
placed and dangling
modifiers, visit
Exercise Central at
bedfordstmartins
.com/realessays.

1. Are there energy fields that can be touched by trained professionals *in a human body* ?
~~in a human body?~~

2. People claim to be able to feel and move invisible energy fields *who practice therapeutic touch* . ~~who practice therapeutic touch~~.

3. According to believers in therapeutic touch, an energy field *that is out of alignment* can cause pain and illness. ~~that is out of alignment~~.

4. A practitioner treating a patient does not touch the sick person. *C*

5. After a session of therapeutic touch, many patients ~~just~~ report that *just* they felt better without knowing why.

6. Emily Rosa, the twelve-year-old daughter of a nurse, made news *to test practitioners of therapeutic touch* when her experiment appeared in an important medical journal. ~~to test practitioners of therapeutic touch~~.

7. In her experiment, practitioners *who could not see Emily* were supposed to use the invisible energy field to determine when her hands were near theirs. ~~who could not see Emily~~.

8. Even though guessing should have allowed a 50 percent accuracy rate, the practitioners were correct only 44 percent of the time. *C*

9. Anyone who can demonstrate the ability to detect a human energy *in a similar experiment* field can claim a million-dollar prize. ~~in a similar experiment~~.

10. The prize has not been awarded yet, *, which is offered by a foundation that investigates supernatural claims,* ~~which is offered by a foundation that investigates supernatural claims~~.

RESOURCES
To gauge students'
skills in correcting
misplaced and
dangling modifiers,
use the *Testing Tool
Kit* CD available with
this book.

TEACHING TIP
Have students try this
practice on their own
and discuss the
results with a class-
mate. Then, go over
the practice with
everyone so that stu-
dents can explain
their corrections.

· ·

PRACTICE 2   Correcting Dangling Modifiers

Find and correct any dangling modifiers in the following sentences. If a sentence is correct, write "C" next to it. It may be necessary to add new words or ideas to some sentences.

the owner will get a better price for
EXAMPLE: Selling a used car, a resale ~~will bring a better price~~ than a trade-in. *Answers may vary. Possible edits shown.*

1. Trading in a used car, a ~~buyer will offer~~ *seller will get* a better price if the car is

    clean.

2. ~~Hiring~~ *If the owner hires* a professional detailer, a used car can be given a more pol-

    ished appearance.

3. ~~Looking~~ *With the used car looking* like new, the owner can get the best price for a trade-in or

    a resale.

4. With essential repairs completed, a used car should be in good

    working order to be sold. *C*

5. Approved as safe and drivable by a reputable mechanic, *a used car may still have* minor

    mechanical problems ~~may~~ *that do* not have to be fixed.

6. Winning points for honesty, ~~prospective buyers should know~~ *sellers should tell prospective buyers* about

    a used car's minor problems.

7. ~~Deducted~~ *By deducting the cost of repairing minor problems* from the asking price, the owner can be fair with a

    buyer.

8. No matter how expensive, decorative lighting and other details usu-

    ally do not add to the value of a car. *C*

9. With higher than usual mileage, ~~the owner may have to reduce the~~ *a used car might need a reduced*

    asking price.

10. Advertising in a local newspaper, *the owner of* a used car is likely to reach ~~its~~ *his or her*

    target market.

• •

Edit Paragraphs and Your Own Writing

Edit the following paragraphs for misplaced and dangling modifiers, referring to the chart on page 536 as you need to. *Answers may vary. Possible
edits shown.*

RESOURCES
For cumulative Editing
Review Tests, see
pages 667–83.

EDITING REVIEW 1

(1) ~~When ordering items online,~~ shipping [S] and handling costs can make or break a business. *[that sells online]* *[a site may force customers to]* (2) By charging too much, ~~customers may~~ *[who feels that shipping and handling charges are too high]* abandon their order. (3) A customer may never return to the site ~~who feels that shipping and handling charges are too high.~~ (4) Most people have shipped packages, *[at least occasionally,]* so they know how much shipping costs ~~at least occasionally.~~ (5) Going too far in the other direction, some online *[sites offer their customers]* ~~customers get~~ free shipping and handling. (6) The sites lose money ~~that offer free shipping~~ *[that offer free shipping]* and may have to either close down for good or start charging shipping fees. (7) Most shipping companies charge by weight. (8) ~~Buying from the sites that use~~ *[Using]* these shippers, the online sites must either charge a flat fee, which may be too much or too little, or make the customer wait until the order is complete to find out the shipping fee. (9) Neither option is perfect, so a business *[that wants to keep expanding its online customer base]* must choose the least unattractive solution ~~that wants to keep expanding its online customer base.~~

EDITING REVIEW 2

MEMO

To: All staff

From: Sara Hollister

Re: Dress code

(1) After ~~encouraging employees~~ *[employees were encouraged]* to wear casual clothing on Fridays, the casual dress code was soon in force all week long. (2) With some uncertainty about what was appropriate casual wear, ~~a memo was circulated~~ *[employees received a memo]* last year with guidelines for dress. (3) ~~Wearing~~ *[When all of the staff members began wearing]* khakis and polo shirts, suits and ties became rare in the halls of Wilson and Hollister. (4) Some younger staff members almost never wore anything

but jeans. (5) ~~Arriving~~ *When Mr. Wilson arrived* in the office in a Hawaiian shirt, some employees hardly recognized ~~Mr. Wilson~~ *him* without his trademark pinstriped suit. (6) Believing that informality improved productivity and morale, *the company felt that* the casual dress code was well liked.

(7) The company must recommend ~~for several reasons~~ changes in the dress policy now*, for several reasons.* (8) The human resources department feels that the relaxed attitude toward dress may have contributed to the recent increases in absenteeism and lateness at Wilson and Hollister. (9) Other problems have also surfaced. (10) Clients *who have dropped in unexpectedly* have sometimes expressed surprise.~~who have dropped in unexpectedly.~~ (11) Hoping to keep their respect and their business, *we have observed that* the clients appear to feel more comfortable with employees in suits. (12) Finally, fearing an increase in sexual harassment, *Wilson and Hollister will no longer permit* sleeveless shirts, shorts, miniskirts, and halter tops.~~will no longer be permitted.~~ (13) Human resources ~~almost~~ recommends a~~a~~ *an almost* complete change in the casual-dress policy. (14) While ~~continuing~~ *employees may continue* to wear casual clothing on Friday, *they must wear* business attire Monday through Thursday, ~~is~~ effective immediately. (15) As an employee who prefers casual clothing, *I find* this news ~~is~~ rather sad, but the decision is for the best. (16) Certain that you will understand the necessity for these changes, *I appreciate* your cooperation.~~is appreciated.~~

· ·

PRACTICE 3 Editing Your Own Writing for Misplaced and Dangling Modifiers

As a final practice, edit a piece of your own writing for misplaced and dangling modifiers. It can be a paper you are working on for this course, a paper you have already finished, a paper for another course, a recent piece of writing from your work or everyday life, or your idea journal entry. You may want to use the chart on page 536 as you edit.

· ·

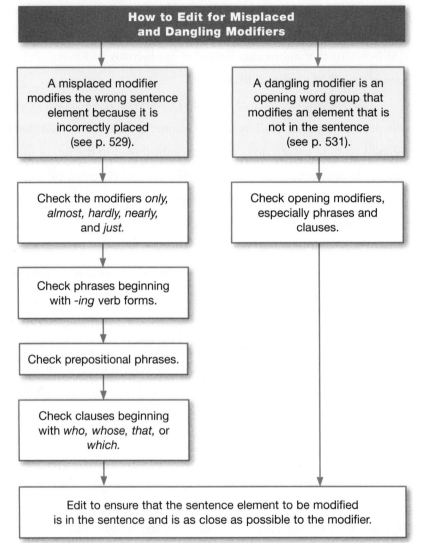

How to Edit for Misplaced and Dangling Modifiers

A misplaced modifier modifies the wrong sentence element because it is incorrectly placed (see p. 529).

A dangling modifier is an opening word group that modifies an element that is not in the sentence (see p. 531).

Check the modifiers *only, almost, hardly, nearly,* and *just.*

Check opening modifiers, especially phrases and clauses.

Check phrases beginning with *-ing* verb forms.

Check prepositional phrases.

Check clauses beginning with *who, whose, that,* or *which.*

Edit to ensure that the sentence element to be modified is in the sentence and is as close as possible to the modifier.

30

Coordination and Subordination

Joining Ideas

Understand Coordination and Subordination

Coordination is used to join two sentences with related ideas, using *for, and, nor, but, or, so,* or *yet*. The two sentences you join will still be independent clauses—complete sentences—joined with a comma and a coordinating conjunction.

IDEA JOURNAL
Write about a family story—an incident that is told repeatedly.

TWO SENTENCES   The internship at the magazine is very prestigious. Many interns have gone on to get good jobs.

Independent clause

JOINED THROUGH   The internship at the magazine is very prestigious,
COORDINATION   *and* many interns have gone on to get good jobs.

Independent clause

Subordination is also used to join two sentences with related ideas, using a dependent word such as *although, because, if,* or *that*. The resulting sentence will have one independent clause (a complete sentence) and one dependent clause (not a complete sentence).

TWO SENTENCES   The internship was advertised last week. The magazine received many calls about it.

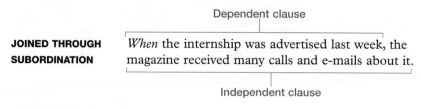

Dependent clause

JOINED THROUGH SUBORDINATION *When* the internship was advertised last week, the magazine received many calls and e-mails about it.

Independent clause

[Adding the word *when* makes the first sentence dependent, or subordinate, to the second sentence.]

Both coordination and subordination are ways to join short, choppy sentences to get better rhythm and flow in your writing.

Practice Using Coordination and Subordination

Using Coordinating Conjunctions

Conjunctions join words, phrases, or clauses. **Coordinating conjunctions** (*and, but, for, nor, or, so,* and *yet*) join independent clauses. You can remember them by keeping the word *fanboys* in mind: **f**or, **a**nd, **n**or, **b**ut, **o**r, **y**et, **s**o. Choose the conjunction that makes the most sense, and make sure to put a comma before it when joining two independent clauses.

Coordinating conjunction

, for
, and
, nor
, but
, or
, yet
, so

Independent clause   Independent clause

My friend is coming   , and   I'm excited to see her.

[*And* simply joins two ideas.]

We were best friends   , but   I haven't seen her for years.

[*But* indicates a contrast.]

I am a little nervous   , for   we may be late.

[*For* indicates a reason or cause.]

We haven't talked much   , nor   have we been in touch
                                                online.
[*Nor* indicates a negative.]

Maybe we will pick   , or   we may be like strangers.
up our friendship
                    [*Or* indicates alternatives.]

We are meeting tonight   , so   we will know soon.

[*So* indicates a result.]

It is hard to keep old   , yet   they are very important.
friends
                    [*Yet* indicates a reason.]

TEACHING TIP
Emphasize that con-
junctions are not
interchangeable. Write
two independent
clauses on the board
(*Lucy was hungry/
She ate an apple*).
Ask students which
conjunctions would
work and how the
sentence would have
to change to use
others.

PRACTICE 1   Joining Ideas with Coordinating Conjunctions

In each of the following sentences, fill in the blank with an appropriate coordinating conjunction. There may be more than one correct answer for some
sentences.

For more practice
with coordination and
subordination, visit
Exercise Central at
bedfordstmartins
.com/realessays.

> **EXAMPLE:** Millions of people get motion sickness while traveling,
> __and__ it can turn an enjoyable experience into a
> nightmare. *Possible answers shown.*

1. Nearly 60 percent of children get carsick or airsick, __and__ many
   also get sick on amusement park rides.

2. Some amusement park operators are aware of this, __for__ a
   major theme park recently handed out "stomach distress" bags to
   customers.

3. Most people have experienced motion sickness at one time or
   another, __yet__ there are ways of easing or even avoiding its effects.

4. Motion sickness happens when a person's eyes and ears sense that
   she is moving one way, __but__ her brain detects movement in
   another way.

5. When in a car, you want to see the car's movement while you are
   feeling it, __so__ sit in the front seat and watch the road.

6. On a ship, you need to find a level point to focus on, _____*so*_____ you should keep your eyes on the horizon.

7. When you are flying, choose a window seat, _____*and*_____ look outside to watch and sense the plane's movement.

8. You can get a prescription for medication to prevent motion sickness, _____*but*_____ you can also find some effective over-the-counter medications.

RESOURCES
To gauge students' skills in coordination and subordination, use the *Testing Tool Kit* CD available with this book.

9. Taking ginger may be an even better way to prevent motion sickness, _____*for*_____ you can simply buy ginger tea or raw ginger at a supermarket.

10. If you use a medication, be sure to take it one hour before you travel, _____*or*_____ there may not be enough time for it to take effect.

···

PRACTICE 2   Combining Sentences with Coordinating Conjunctions

Combine each pair of sentences into a single sentence by using a comma and a coordinating conjunction. In some cases, there may be more than one correct answer.

> **EXAMPLE:** For years, researchers have been trying to prove that media
> , *yet some*
> images have negative effects on women's body image. ~~Some~~
>   ^
> people are not convinced. *Possible edits shown.*

1. Recently, two researchers decided to try and convince people
   , *so they*
   once and for all. ~~They~~ collected all the reliable research they
                     ^
   could find.
                                                                , *and they*
2. They found seventy-seven trustworthy studies on the subject. ~~They~~
                                                                 ^
   analyzed the data.

3. The studies looked at different subjects and used a variety of
   , *but the*
   methods. ~~The~~ findings were consistent.
            ^

4. Seeing super-thin models does make women feel dissatisfied with
   their own bodies/ ~~This~~ dissatisfaction is causing problems.
   , and this

5. Women with poor body image are at risk for depression and low
   self-esteem/ ~~They~~ do not have the "ideal" body and therefore see
   , for they
   themselves as flawed.

6. However, the super-thin body they see in advertisements is not
   realistic/ ~~That~~ body ~~is not~~ always healthy.
   , nor is that

7. Many women who strive for this "ideal" body will often engage in
   unhealthy dieting/ ~~They~~ may develop a more serious eating
   , and some
   disorder.

8. Many women are aware that media images are unrealistic and
   manipulative/ ~~That~~ awareness does not protect women from being
   , but that
   influenced.

9. Education is not enough/ ~~The~~ images are simply too powerful.
   , for the

10. People need to acknowledge the problems these dangerous images
    are causing/ ~~Society~~ needs to develop solutions.
    , and society

···

Using Semicolons

A **semicolon** is a punctuation mark that can join two sentences through coordination. When you use a semicolon, make sure that the ideas in the two sentences are closely related.

EQUAL IDEA	;	EQUAL IDEA
My computer crashed	;	I lost all of my files.
I had just finished my paper	;	I will have to redo it.

A semicolon alone does not tell readers much about the relationship between the two ideas. Use a **conjunctive adverb** after the semicolon to give more information about the relationship. Put a comma after the conjunctive adverb.

The following are some of the most common conjunctive adverbs, along with a few examples of how they are used.

Independent clause	; afterward, ; also, ; as a result, ; besides, ; consequently, ; frequently, ; however, ; in addition, ; in fact, ; instead, ; still, ; then, ; therefore,	Independent clause

TEACHING TIP
Remind students that a semicolon balances two independent clauses. What is on either side must be able to stand alone as a complete sentence.

My computer crashed	; as a result,	I lost all my files.
I should have made backup files	; however,	I had not.
The information is lost	; therefore,	I will have to try to rebuild the files.

· ·

PRACTICE 3   Joining Ideas with Semicolons

Join each pair of sentences by using a semicolon alone.

> **EXAMPLE:** In the wake of corporate scandals, many businesses
>
> are using new techniques to identify questionable job
>
> candidates/ ~~Graphology~~ is one such technique.
>   *; graphology*

1. Graphology involves identifying personality features on the basis of a person's handwriting/ ~~These~~ features include honesty, responsibility, and loyalty.
                    ; these

2. Graphology is now used widely in Europe/ ~~Many~~ American graphologists, too, say their business has grown significantly in recent years.
                    ; many

3. An owner of a jewelry store turned to a graphology consultant following an increase in employee theft. *; he* He says that handwriting analysis helped to identify the thieves.

4. Many scientists and doctors, however, believe that graphology is not reliable or scientific at all. *; they* They state that there is no evidence that graphology can uncover a person's true character.

5. Nevertheless, even some job seekers are beginning to use graphology to help them find work. *; one* One says he submitted his handwriting analysis report along with his résumé and got the job he wanted.

. . . .

PRACTICE 4 Combining Sentences with Semicolons and Connecting Words (Conjunctive adverbs)

Combine each pair of sentences by using a semicolon and a connecting word followed by a comma. Choose a conjunctive adverb that makes sense for the relationship between the two ideas. In some cases, there may be more than one correct answer. *Possible edits shown.*

EXAMPLE: Most people do not own a gas mask. *; however, after* After 9/11, some may have felt more comfortable having one available.

1. Two inventors believed that Americans would welcome the opportunity to have a gas mask. *; as a result, they* They invented one that is part of a baseball cap.

2. Professional gas masks are costly, heavy, and hard to use. *; therefore, most* Most consumers did not find them appealing.

3. The new baseball-cap gas mask was small and lightweight. *; in fact, it* It could fit in the corner of a drawer, in a coat pocket, or in a briefcase.

4. This mask could easily fit children as well as adults. *; in addition, it* It may have sold for as little as twenty dollars.

5. The wearer slipped a thin sheet of transparent plastic attached to the hat over his or her head. *; then, the* The plastic sheet could be tied shut at the back of the neck.

6. Air from the outside was pulled in by a tiny fan. *; afterward, the* ~~The~~ air was forced

    through a filter of activated carbon in the hat's brim.

7. The inventors said that the plastic sheet allowed the wearer to see

    clearly. *; also, it* ~~It~~ did not make the wearer feel too closed in.

8. The mask was not intended for long-term use. *; instead, it* ~~It~~ was meant to be

    worn for about fifteen to thirty minutes.

9. The goal was to allow the wearer to get out of the contaminated

    area quickly. *; consequently, the* ~~The~~ wearer could simply slip on the mask and then

    move into fresh air.

10. The inventors then looked for a company to make the new gas

    mask. *; afterward, consumers* ~~Consumers~~ would be able to obtain the gas masks from the

    manufacturer.

Using Subordinating Conjunctions

Conjunctions join words, phrases, or clauses. **Subordinating conjunctions** join two sentences, making the one after the dependent word a dependent clause.

Choose the conjunction that makes the most sense with the two sentences. Here are some of the most common subordinating conjunctions.

Independent clause	after	once	Dependent clause
	although	since	
	as	so that	
	as if	unless	
	because	until	
	before	when	
	even though	whenever	
	if	where	
	if only	while	
	now that		

I decided to go to work   although   I had a terrible cold.

I hate to miss a day   unless   I absolutely cannot get there.

When the dependent clause ends a sentence (as in the preceding examples), it usually does not need to be preceded by a comma unless it is showing a contrast. When the dependent clause begins a sentence, use a comma to separate it from the rest of the sentence.

Subordinating conjunction	Subordinate idea	,	Main idea
Although	I had a terrible cold	,	I decided to go to work.
Unless	I absolutely cannot get there	,	I hate to miss a day.

TEACHING TIP
Write two sentences on the board, and ask students how they would have to edit them to accommodate different subordinating conjunctions.

PRACTICE 5   Joining Ideas through Subordination

In the following sentences, fill in the blank with an appropriate subordinating conjunction. In some cases, there may be more than one correct answer.

> **EXAMPLE:** Smokey Bear spent most of his life in the National Zoo in Washington, D.C., ___*where*___ he received so much mail that he had his own zip code. *Possible answers shown.*

1. Smokey Bear began reminding people that "Only you can prevent forest fires" in 1944 _*because*_ government officials during World War II were concerned about preserving valuable resources like trees.

2. However, Smokey Bear existed only as a cartoon _*until*_ a tragedy occurred six years later.

3. _*After*_ a fire destroyed part of Lincoln National Forest in 1950, forest rangers found a badly burned bear cub clinging to a tree.

4. The "real" Smokey Bear became a celebrity _*when*_ the public heard his story.

5. After his death, Smokey Bear's body was returned to New Mexico _*so*_ _*that*_ he could be buried near his former home.

6. The character of Smokey Bear has been used continuously in U.S. fire safety campaigns _*since*_ it first appeared more than sixty years ago.

7. Smokey has also appeared in public service announcements in Mexico, __*where*__ he is known as Simon.

8. Recently, Smokey's famous line was changed to "Only you can prevent wildfires" __*because*__ research indicated that most adults did not believe they could cause a wildfire.

9. However, humans can easily set fires ____*if*____ they discard cigarettes carelessly, burn trash on windy days, or even park a car with a catalytic converter in a dry field.

10. ____*As*____ the campaign heads into its seventh decade, Smokey is as recognizable to most Americans as Mickey Mouse and Santa Claus.

· ·

PRACTICE 6 Combining Sentences through Subordination

Combine each pair of sentences into a single sentence by using an appropriate subordinating conjunction either at the beginning or between the two sentences.

EXAMPLE:
Although
‸Michael had heard about lengthy delays for some air
travelers, he
~~travelers. He~~ had never experienced one himself. *Answers*
‸ *may vary. Possible edits shown.*

1. His turn came on a flight back to school in Austin from
Minneapolis, where he
~~Minneapolis. He~~ was staying with his family during winter break.
‸
Even though the   *smoothly, he*
2. ~~The~~ flight took off on time and was going ~~smoothly. He~~ had heard
‸   ‸
some fellow passengers talking about a possible storm in the Austin area.
rumors until the
3. He paid no attention to the ~~rumors. The~~ pilot announced to the
‸
passengers that the flight was landing in Wichita, Kansas, due to severe weather in Austin.
soon because he
4. According to the pilot, they would be taking off again ~~soon. He~~
‸
expected the weather in Texas to clear.

TEAMWORK Have students in small groups write five sentences that use coordinaation and/or subordination. Then, ask them to copy half of each sentence (without conjunctions, punctuation, or beginning capital letters) on a slip of paper. Have the groups shuffle the slips and give them to another group. Each group then puts the pieces together and reads the sentences aloud.

As

5. Michael sat in his seat and tried to ~~sleep. He~~ heard some people   *sleep, he*

ask the flight attendants to allow the passengers to wait in the air

terminal.
After everyone   *hours, the*

6. ~~Everyone~~ had waited over two ~~hours. The~~ flight crew told the

passengers to go out to the air terminal.

7. Five hours later, Michael and his fellow passengers still did not
                                                    flight, since there
know when they would be able to resume their ~~flight. There~~ were

no announcements from anybody about what would happen next.
When an   *came, the*
8. ~~An~~ announcement finally ~~came. The~~ passengers learned that the bad

weather in Texas prevented the flight from continuing on to Austin.
If
9. Michael was already upset by the hours-long delay with no
       announcements, he
~~announcements. He~~ was even angrier at the thought of sleeping

overnight in the air terminal.
While he   *hopeless, a*
10. ~~He~~ was sitting uncomfortably in his terminal seat, feeling ~~hopeless.~~

~~A~~ few other passengers asked him if he wanted to join them in

renting a car to complete the trip to Austin, which he did.

Edit Paragraphs and Your Own Writing

Join the underlined sentences by using either coordination or subordination, referring to the chart on page 550 as you need to. Be sure to punctuate correctly. *Answers may vary. Possible edits shown.*

RESOURCES
For cumulative Editing Review Tests, see pages 667–83.

EDITING REVIEW 1 (6 sets of sentences to be joined)

Whenever a

(1) <u>A patient misunderstands a doctor's explanation and recommen-</u>
              , there
<u>dations.</u> (2) <u>~~There~~ can be serious consequences.</u> (3) If medications are

not properly used or preventive measures are not taken, health risks

increase. (4) <u>These problems are common with people of all ages, races,</u>
                                        , but they
<u>and educational levels.</u> (5) <u>~~They~~ are especially prevalent among the</u>

elderly. (6) The individual patient, of course, is affected in a personal and sometimes life-threatening way, but society in general also has to pay for the resulting increased medical costs. (7) <u>A patient follows these</u> _{If a} <u>simple guidelines</u>, (8) <u>He</u> _{he} <u>or she can better understand what is wrong and what to do about it.</u> (9) First of all, make absolutely sure that the doctor's instructions are understandable. (10) <u>The doctor will probably ask if there are any questions</u>, (11) <s>Think</s> _{so think} <u>over each step of the instructions, and ask for a clearer explanation of anything that's confusing.</u> (12) Repeat the instructions back to the doctor and ask, "Is that right?" (13) <u>Another tip is to take notes on what the doctor recommends</u>; (14) <s>Either</s> _{either} <u>write the notes yourself or bring along someone else to jot them down.</u> (15) It is easy to feel intimidated by being partially unclothed in the examination room. (16) <u>Ask to hear the necessary instructions in the doctor's office</u>, (17) <s>You</s> _{when you} <u>are fully clothed.</u> (18) Finally, follow the doctor's instructions carefully, for recovery depends just as much on the patient as on the doctor.

. . . .

EDITING REVIEW 2 (7 sets of sentences to be joined)

(1) Al-Qurain is a community in the small Middle Eastern country of Kuwait. (2) <u>Forty years ago, Kuwait City officials began to use an abandoned quarry in al-Qurain as a garbage dump</u>, (3) <s>None</s> _{because none} <u>of them thought the area would ever be populated.</u> (4) Twenty-five years ago, the government began to build subsidized housing in al-Qurain. (5) <u>The dump was supposed to be closed</u>, _{but} (6) <u>Kuwaitis continued to use the al-Qurain landfill.</u> (7) People soon lived all around the foul-smelling garbage pit. (8) <u>Residents of the area were teased and insulted for living in the neighborhood</u>, (9) <s>Al-Qurain</s> _{which} <u>housed sixty thousand people.</u>

(10) For years, the dump sickened people around it; (11) ~~Sometimes~~ *sometimes* the garbage caught fire and sent fumes into the homes nearby. (12) Finally, the Kuwaiti Environment Public Authority decided to try to help. (13) The agency gets little government funding, (14) ~~It~~ *so it* needed to rely on donations for the cleanup effort. (15) Soon, a mountain of garbage had been removed, (16) ~~The~~ *and the* leveled site was covered with pebbles from the desert. (17) Engineers found a way to siphon methane gas from the seventy-five-foot-deep garbage pit. (18) Kuwait is famous for oil production, (19) ~~A~~ *yet a* methane-powered generator was proposed to provide electricity for al-Qurain residents. (20) The air in the neighborhood now ranks among the country's cleanest. (21) For many environmentalists and residents of this neighborhood, the cleanup of al-Qurain is almost a miracle.

· ·

PRACTICE 7   **Editing Your Own Writing for Coordination and Subordination**

As a final practice, edit a piece of your own writing for coordination and subordination. It can be a paper you are working on for this course, a paper you have already finished, a paper for another course, a recent piece of writing from your work or everyday life, or your idea journal entry. You may want to use the chart on page 550 as you edit.

· ·

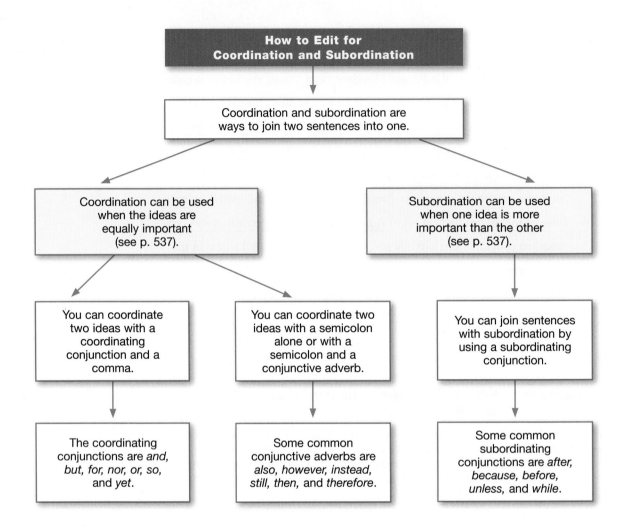

31

Parallelism

Balancing Ideas

Understand What Parallelism Is

Parallelism in writing means that similar parts in a sentence are balanced by having the same structure. Put nouns with nouns, verbs with verbs, and phrases with phrases.

NOT PARALLEL   I like <u>math</u> more than <u>studying English</u>.

[*Math* is a noun, but *studying English* is a phrase.]

PARALLEL   I like <u>math</u> more than <u>English</u>.

NOT PARALLEL   In class, we <u>read</u>, <u>worked</u> in groups, and <u>were writing</u> an essay.

[Verbs must be in the same tense to be parallel.]

PARALLEL   In class, we <u>read</u>, <u>worked</u> in groups, and <u>wrote</u> an essay.

NOT PARALLEL   Last night we went <u>to a movie</u> and <u>dancing at a club</u>.

[*To a movie* and *dancing at a club* are both phrases, but they have different forms. *To a movie* should be paired with another prepositional phrase: *to a dance club*.]

PARALLEL   Last night we went <u>to a movie</u> and <u>to a dance club</u>.

IDEA JOURNAL
Write about a movie you saw recently, and explain why you liked or disliked it.

ESL Tell students that parallel constructions often depend on using infinitives and idioms correctly. See Chapter 33 for details.

Practice Writing Parallel Sentences

Parallelism in Pairs and Lists

When two or more items in a series are joined by the word *and* or *or,* use a similar form for each item.

TEACHING TIP
Review these examples with students, and ask them to explain why each of the nonparallel sentences needs correction.

NOT PARALLEL	The fund-raiser included a bake sale and also holding an auction.
PARALLEL	The fund-raiser included a bake sale and an auction.
NOT PARALLEL	Students got items for the auction from local businesses, from their families, and ran an advertisement in the newspaper.
PARALLEL	Students got items for the auction from local businesses, from their families, and from people who responded to a newspaper advertisement.

· ·

PRACTICE 1 Making Pairs and Lists Parallel

In each sentence, underline the parts of the sentence that should be parallel. Then, edit the sentence to make it parallel.

> **EXAMPLE:** Being a single parent can make the morning routine
> *and stressful*
> difficult, and it can be stressful without the proper
> organization. *Answers may vary. Possible edits shown.*

1. This is important because the beginning of the day affects you,
   and your children.
   and your children are affected as well.

2. Get a good start by planning ahead, setting a few rules, and also
   keeping a cool head.
   be sure to keep a cool head.

3. On the night before, make as many preparations for morning as
   possible, including preparing lunches, getting out clothes, and
   organizing schoolbooks.
   it's important to organize schoolbooks.

RESOURCES To gauge students' skills in using parallelism, use the *Testing Tool Kit* CD available with this book.

4. A quick cold breakfast can be easy, tasty, and it can provide good
   nutritious.
   nutrition.

For more practice
with parallelism, visit
Exercise Central at
bedfordstmartins
.com/realessays.

5. Cold cereal with milk and fruit, for example, is <u>delicious</u> and <s>has</s> ^*vitamin- and mineral-rich.*

   <s>the added advantage of giving you plenty of vitamins and minerals.</s>

6. Allowing the kids to watch TV in the morning <u>can cause all sorts of</u>
   it can work to your advantage.
   <u>problems,</u> or <s>you can let the TV work to your advantage.</s>

7. Set a rule that the kids must <u>eat breakfast,</u> <u>wash up,</u> *brush their teeth,* <s>be sure of</s>

   <s>brushing their teeth,</s> <u>get dressed,</u> and <u>put their shoes on</u> before they

   turn on the TV.

8. Prevent frantic, last-minute searches by establishing specific places

   for the items each of you needs for the day, such as <u>car keys,</u>
   shoes
   <u>backpacks,</u> <s>all pairs of shoes that the kids will wear during the day,</s>

   and <u>coats.</u>

9. Save for the evening time-consuming, stressful tasks such as <u>teaching</u>
   refereeing a dispute.
   <u>a child to tie shoes</u> or <s>becoming a referee who can objectively discuss</s>

   <s>both sides in a dispute between kids.</s>

10. Set aside some "myself time," in which you <u>stop rushing around,</u>
    take a deep breath,
    <s>taking a deep breath,</s> and <u>calmly prepare for your day.</u>

Parallelism in Comparisons

In comparisons, the items being compared should have parallel structures.
Comparisons often use the words *than* or *as.* When you edit for parallelism, make sure that the items on either side of the comparison word are
parallel.

NOT PARALLEL   <u>Driving downtown</u> is as fast as <u>the bus.</u>

PARALLEL   <u>Driving downtown</u> is as fast as <u>taking the bus.</u>

NOT PARALLEL   <u>Running</u> is more tiring than <u>walks.</u>

PARALLEL   <u>Running</u> is more tiring than <u>walking.</u> *Or,*

   A <u>run</u> is more tiring than a <u>walk.</u>

To make the parts of a sentence parallel, you may need to add or drop a word or two.

NOT PARALLEL	A <u>multiple-choice test</u> is easier than <u>answering an essay question</u>.
PARALLEL, WORD ADDED	*Taking* <u>a multiple-choice test</u> is easier than <u>answering an essay question</u>.
NOT PARALLEL	<u>The cost</u> of a train ticket is less than <u>to pay the cost</u> of a plane ticket.
PARALLEL, WORDS DROPPED	<u>The cost</u> of a train ticket is less than <u>the cost</u> of a plane ticket.

· ·

PRACTICE 2   Making Comparisons Parallel

In each sentence, underline the parts of the sentence that should be parallel. Then, edit the sentence to make it parallel.

> **EXAMPLE:** New appliances are usually much more energy-efficient than ~~running~~ <u>old ones.</u> *Answers may vary. Possible edits shown.*

1. For many people, <u>getting the household electric bill</u> is more
   worrisome than ^{paying} <u>~~to pay~~ the rent</u> each month.

2. <u>The amount of the rent bill</u> usually changes much less from month
   to month than ^{the amount of the energy bill.} <u>~~what an energy company charges.~~</u>

3. <u>Saving money</u> appeals to many consumers more than ^{using} <u>~~to use~~ less</u>
   <u>electricity.</u>

4. Compact fluorescent light bulbs use <u>less energy</u> than <u>~~continuing to use~~</u>
   <u>regular incandescent bulbs.</u>

5. In most households, <u>running the refrigerator</u> uses more energy than
   ^{using} <u>~~the use of~~ all other appliances.</u>

6. Many people worry that <u>buying a new refrigerator</u> is more
   ^{simply keeping} expensive than <u>~~if they simply keep~~ the old one.</u>

7. However, an energy-efficient new refrigerator uses much less
electricity than running an inefficient older model.
   running ^

8. Some new refrigerators use only as much energy as ~~keeping~~ a
75-watt light bulb ~~burning.~~ ^

9. Householders might spend less money to buy an efficient new
refrigerator than ~~it would take~~ to run the old one for another five
years.

10. Researching information about energy efficiency can save consumers as much money as ~~when they remember~~ to turn off lights and
air conditioners.
    remembering ^

....

Parallelism with Certain Paired Words

When a sentence uses certain paired words called **correlative conjunctions**, the items joined by these paired words must be parallel. Correlative
conjunctions, shown below, link two equal elements and show the relationship between them.

both . . . and	neither . . . nor	rather . . . than
either . . . or	not only . . . but also	

NOT PARALLEL Brianna dislikes *both* fruit *and* eating vegetables.

PARALLEL Brianna dislikes *both* fruit *and* vegetables.

NOT PARALLEL She would *rather* eat popcorn every night *than* to cook.

PARALLEL She would *rather* eat popcorn every night *than* cook.

....

PRACTICE 3 Making Sentences with Paired Words Parallel

In each sentence, circle the paired words and underline the parts of the sentence that should be parallel. Then, edit the sentence to make it parallel. You
may need to change the second part of the correlative conjunction.

EXAMPLE: A recent survey of young women reported that a majority of them would (rather) lose twenty pounds permanently
(than) ~~to~~ live to be ninety. *Answers may vary. Possible edits
shown.*

1. People in the United States are (both) pressed for time (and) ~~have gotten~~ used to convenient but fattening foods.

2. Many Americans are (neither) willing to exercise regularly (nor) ~~do they have~~ to do anything physical during a normal day.
  _{*required*}

3. Being overweight can be unhealthy, but many Americans would (rather) look thinner (than) ~~to~~ stay the same size and get in better shape.

4. In fact, some Americans are (not only) out of shape (but) ~~are~~ dangerously obsessed with being thin.

5. The idea that thinner is better affects (both) overweight people (and) ~~it even influences~~ people of normal weight.

6. In their quest to lose weight, many Americans have tried (either) fad diets (or) ~~have taken~~ prescription drugs.

7. Dozens of healthy, average-sized Americans in the past ten years have died from (either) surgical procedures to remove fat (or) ~~they have died from~~ dangerous diet drugs.

8. A thin person is (neither) guaranteed to be attractive (nor) ~~is he or she~~ necessarily healthy.

9. Some people who are larger than average are (not only) in good health (but also) ~~can be~~ physically fit.

10. Americans who would (rather) pay for risky drugs and surgery (than) ~~eating moderately and exercising~~ may have hazardous priorities.
  eat moderately and exercise

· ·

PRACTICE 4   Completing Sentences with Paired Words

The following items contain only the first part of a correlative conjunction. Complete the correlative conjunction, and add more information to form a whole sentence. Make sure that the structures on both sides of the correlative conjunction are parallel. *Answers may vary. Possible answers shown.*

   EXAMPLE: I am both enthusiastic about your company ___*and eager to work for you*___.

1. I could bring to this job not only youthful enthusiasm <u>*but also*</u>

   <u>*leadership experience*</u>   .

2. I am willing to work either in your Chicago office <u>*or in your San*</u>

   <u>*Francisco office*</u>   .

3. My current job neither encourages creativity <u>*nor allows flexibility*</u> .

4. I would rather work in a difficult job <u>*than work in an unchallenging one*</u>.

5. In college I learned a lot both from my classes <u>*and from other*</u>

   <u>*students*</u>   .

Edit Paragraphs and Your Own Writing

Edit the following paragraphs for parallelism, referring to the chart on page 559 as you need to. *Answers may vary. Possible edits shown.*

RESOURCES For cumulative Editing Review Tests, see pages 667–83.

EDITING REVIEW 1 (8 errors)

(1) Some employees who want to advance their careers would rather transfer within their company than ~~looking~~ *look* for a new job else-where. (2) In-house job changes are possible, but employees should be sure that they both meet the criteria of the job and ~~to~~ avoid making their present boss angry. (3) Because businesses invest money in each person they hire, many companies would rather hire from within ~~and not~~ *than* bring an outsider into a position. (4) By hiring an employee from another department, a company neither needs to make an investment in a new employee ~~but may also prevent the current employee from leaving.~~ *nor loses a current employee.* (5) Transfers usually go more smoothly now than in the past; however, an in-house job move can still require diplomacy and ~~being honest.~~ *honesty.* (6) Experts caution employees who are considering an in-house transfer to tell their current manager the truth and ~~that they should~~ *to* discuss their wish to transfer with the potential new manager. (7) Employees should

neither threaten to quit if they do not get the new job nor ~~is it a good idea to~~ spread the word around the department that they are anxious to leave their present job. (8) Employees' goals for in-house transfers should be *advancing their careers* ~~career advancement~~ and making sure that they create no bad feelings with the move.

....

EDITING REVIEW 2 (10 errors)

(1) Black motorists frequently arouse police suspicion either when driving in neighborhoods that are mainly white or when ~~they are~~ driving an expensive car. (2) A higher percentage of African Americans than *whites* ~~among people who are white~~ are pulled over by the police. (3) Many African Americans feel insulted, endangered, and *angry* ~~react with anger~~ when they are stopped randomly. (4) African Americans are liable to be singled out by police who suspect they are criminals not only while in a car but ~~African Americans~~ also *while* ~~report being wrongly stopped~~ on foot. (5) Racial profiling is illegal yet ~~a~~ fairly common ~~phenomenon.~~ (6) According to a 2001 poll, ~~among black women the figure is~~ 25 percent *of black women* and 52 percent of black men have been stopped by police. (7) Victims of racial profiling have done nothing wrong, yet they are made to feel that others are either afraid *of them* or do not trust them. (8) Law-abiding African Americans should neither expect such treatment nor ~~should they~~ put up with it from public officials who are supposed to protect citizens. (9) Police departments around the country must make their employees aware that automatically stopping, *questioning,* ~~asking them questions,~~ and searching African Americans will not be tolerated. (10) *Fair treatment of all citizens* ~~Treating all citizens fairly~~ is a more important American value than ~~that there is~~ a high arrest rate for the police.

....

PRACTICE 5   Editing Your Own Writing for Parallelism

As a final practice, edit a piece of your own writing for parallelism. It can be a paper you are working on for this course, a paper you have already finished, a paper for another course, a recent piece of writing from your work or everyday life, or your idea journal entry. You may want to use the chart below as you edit.

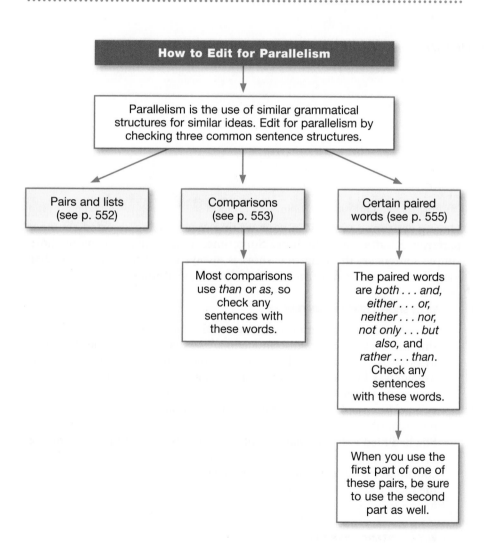

How to Edit for Parallelism

Parallelism is the use of similar grammatical structures for similar ideas. Edit for parallelism by checking three common sentence structures.

Pairs and lists (see p. 552)

Comparisons (see p. 553)

Certain paired words (see p. 555)

Most comparisons use *than* or *as,* so check any sentences with these words.

The paired words are *both . . . and, either . . . or, neither . . . nor, not only . . . but also,* and *rather . . . than.* Check any sentences with these words.

When you use the first part of one of these pairs, be sure to use the second part as well.

32

Sentence Variety

Putting Rhythm in Your Writing

Understand What Sentence Variety Is

Having **sentence variety** in your writing means using assorted sentence patterns, lengths, and rhythms. Sometimes writers use too many short, simple sentences, thinking that short is always easier to understand than long. In fact, that is not true, as the following examples show.

WITH SHORT, SIMPLE SENTENCES

Age discrimination can exist even in unpaid jobs. In 2002, a magazine was accused of age discrimination. The magazine was the *Atlantic Monthly*. A woman was told she was too old to be an unpaid intern. The woman was forty-one. The position was for a senior in college. The woman was a senior. She had raised three children before going to college. She sued the magazine. The next day, another woman, age fifty-one, reported that the same thing had happened to her a year earlier. She had filed a discrimination suit. The suit was brought to court by the Council on Age Discrimination. The magazine never showed up. The court never took any follow-up action against the magazine. Apparently, the matter was not of great importance to either the magazine or the justice system.

WITH SENTENCE VARIETY

Age discrimination can exist even in unpaid jobs. In 2002, a forty-one-year-old woman accused a magazine, the *Atlantic Monthly*, of age discrimination. This woman, who raised three children before going to college and was then in her senior year, was told she was too old to be an unpaid intern, even though the position was for a college senior. She sued the magazine. The next day, another woman, age fifty-one, reported that the same thing had happened to her a year earlier, and she, too, had filed an age discrimination suit. The suit was brought to court by the Council on Age Discrimination, but the magazine did not appear for the court date, and the court never took any follow-up action. Apparently, the matter was not of great importance to either the magazine or the justice system.

Too many short sentences make your writing sound like a list of ideas rather than a presentation of them. Sentence variety is what gives your writing good rhythm and flow.

TEAMWORK
After completing the chapter, students can work in small groups to reexamine this paragraph. Have them identify which kinds of sentence variety the writer has used.

Practice Creating Sentence Variety

To create sentence variety, write sentences of different types and lengths. Because many writers tend to write short sentences that start with the subject, this chapter will focus on techniques for starting with something other than the subject and for writing a variety of longer sentences.

Remember that the goal is to use variety to achieve a good rhythm. Do not simply change all your sentences from one pattern to another, or you still will not have variety.

For two additional techniques used to achieve sentence variety, coordination and subordination, see Chapter 30.

Start Some Sentences with Adverbs

Adverbs are words that describe verbs, adjectives, or other adverbs; they often end with *-ly*. As long as the meaning is clear, you can place an adverb at the beginning of a sentence or near the word it describes. An adverb at the beginning is usually followed by a comma.

For more about adverbs, see Chapter 28.

ADVERB AT BEGINNING	*Frequently,* stories about haunted houses surface at Halloween.
ADVERB NEAR A VERB	Stories about haunted houses *frequently* surface at Halloween.
ADVERB AT BEGINNING	*Often,* these tales reveal the life stories of former inhabitants.
ADVERB NEAR A VERB	These tales *often* reveal the life stories of former inhabitants.

For more practice
with sentence variety,
visit *Exercise Central*
at **bedfordstmartins**
.com/realessays.

PRACTICE 1   Starting Sentences with an Adverb

In each sentence, fill in the blank with an adverb that makes sense, adding a
comma when necessary. There may be several good choices for each item.
Possible answers shown.

EXAMPLE: ___*Frequently,*___ hurricanes hit barrier islands.

1. ___*Suddenly,*___ a hurricane can destroy land and houses.

2. ___*Overnight,*___ most houses on an island are washed away.

3. ___*Quickly,*___ the ocean sweeps away the land under the houses.

4. ___*Now,*___ the island is a different shape.

5. ___*Later,*___ maps will have to be redrawn with the new

configuration.

RESOURCES
To gauge students'
skills in sentence
variety, use the
Testing Tool Kit
CD available with
this book.

PRACTICE 2   Writing Sentences That Start with an Adverb

Write three more sentences that start with an adverb, using commas as
necessary. Choose from the following adverbs: *amazingly, frequently, gently,
lovingly, luckily, often, quietly, sadly, stupidly.*

EXAMPLE: ___*Luckily, I remembered to save my file on a disk.*___

1. *Answers will vary.*

2. _____

3. _____

Join Ideas Using an *-ing* Verb Form

TEACHING TIP
Explain to students
that in their own writ-
ing they will need to
consider the context
when deciding which
sentence contains the
more important idea.

One way to combine sentences is to turn one of them into a phrase using an
-ing verb form (such as *walking* or *racing*). The *-ing* verb form indicates that
the two parts of the sentence are happening at the same time. The more
important idea (the one you want to emphasize) should be in the main clause,
not in the phrase you make by adding the *-ing* verb form. In the examples that
follow, the idea the writer wanted to emphasize is underlined.

TWO SENTENCES   Jonah did well in the high jump. He came in second.

JOINED WITH   Jonah did well in the high jump, coming in second.
-*ING* VERB FORM

Doing well in he high jump, Jonah came in second.

To combine sentences this way, add *-ing* to the verb in one of the sentences and delete the subject. You now have a phrase that can be added to the beginning or the end of the other sentence, depending on what makes sense.

He also won the long jump/~~He broke~~ *, breaking* the record.

If you add the phrase to the end of a sentence, you will usually need to put a comma before it unless the phrase is essential to the meaning of the sentence, as in the following example.

The thief broke into the apartment/~~The thief used~~ *using* a crowbar.

If you add a phrase starting with an *-ing* verb form to the beginning of a sentence, put a comma after it. Be sure that the word being modified follows immediately after the phrase. Otherwise, you will create a dangling modifier.

TWO SENTENCES	I dropped my bag. My groceries spilled.
DANGLING MODIFIER	Dropping my bag, my groceries spilled.
EDITED	Dropping my bag, I spilled my groceries.

ESL Remind students that an *-ing* verb form that modifies the subject cannot be the main verb in the sentence.

··

PRACTICE 3 Joining Ideas Using an *-ing* Verb Form

Combine each pair of sentences into a single sentence by using an *-ing* verb form. Add or delete words if necessary. *Answers may vary. Possible edits shown.*

EXAMPLE: ~~Many fans of~~ *Imagining that* rap music ~~imagine it~~ is a recent development. ~~They~~ *, many fans* are not aware that the roots of this music go back centuries.

1. ~~Folk poets wandered~~ *Wandering* from village to village in West Africa hundreds of years before the birth of the United States/ ~~They~~ *, folk poets* rhythmically recited stories and tales with the accompaniment of a drum and a few instruments.

2. ~~Rap music uses~~ *Using* rhymes and wordplay with a rhythmic delivery to build on this heritage/ ~~Its~~ *, rap music's* lyrics often deal with matters of race, socioeconomic class, and gender.

Tracing

3. ~~Many fans trace~~ the beginning of modern-day rap to a Jamaican
   ^   , *many fans*
   immigrant to the Bronx in New York, ~~They~~ still revere Kool Herc,
   ^
   a DJ in the 1970s who originated the new sound in America.

Reciting

4. ~~Kool Herc recited~~ lyrics to go along with the songs that he was
   ^   , *Kool Herc*
   playing as a DJ. ~~He~~ introduced this innovative music at private par-
   ^
   ties and then later at well-known dance halls.

5. In the 1980s, rappers' lyrics focused on sharp sociopolitical con-
   , *captivating*
   tent. ~~They captivated~~ listeners with increasingly creative wordplay.
   ^

Developing

6. ~~Rap songwriters developed~~ a rougher, more sinister edge in the
   ^   , *rap songwriters*
   1990s, ~~They~~ began narrating personal street experiences mixed
   ^
   with social commentary.

Branching   , *rap music today*

7. ~~Today, rap music has branched~~ out in several directions, ~~Today, it~~
   ^   ^
   has southern, northern, midwestern, and even international rap
   forms alongside the more established styles.

8. Perhaps consciously and perhaps not, rappers extensively use forms of
                                            , *calling*
   wordplay that are also found in classical poetry, ~~They call~~ on such lit-
   ^
   erary devices as double meanings, alliteration, similes, and metaphors.

Emphasizing

9. ~~Rap artists emphasize~~ frequently the themes of wealth and class,
   ^, *nearly*
   ~~Nearly~~ all popular rappers in the United States are African
   ^
   American.

Having   , *rap*

10. ~~Rap has~~ gained a solid foothold in American culture, ~~It~~ is now
    ^   ^
    widely accepted as a form of mainstream American music.

• •

PRACTICE 4   Joining Ideas Using an *-ing* Verb Form

Fill in the blank in each sentence with an appropriate *-ing* verb form. There are
many possible ways to complete each sentence.

    EXAMPLE: <u>*Owning*</u>   the rights to the character Spider-Man,
                       Marvel Enterprises has been making big money lately.
                       Possible answers shown.

1. _Switching_ from losses of tens of millions of dollars a year, Marvel now turns a profit of more than $150 million a year, thanks to Spider-Man.

2. Marvel dominates the comic-book market, _producing_ sixty comic books a month.

3. _Earning_ 83 percent of its profits from licensing its characters for films and related merchandise, Marvel makes only 15 percent of its profits from comic-book sales.

4. Marvel keeps tight control of the characters it licenses to filmmakers, _allowing_ no costume changes or added superpowers without Marvel's approval.

5. _Preventing_ any film studio from having Spider-Man kill anyone, for example, Marvel maintains the character as it believes he should be.

....

PRACTICE 5   Joining Ideas Using an *-ing* Verb Form

Write two sets of sentences, and join each set of sentences using an *-ing* verb form.

EXAMPLE: a. _Teresa signed on to eBay.com._

b. _She used her password._

COMBINED: _Using her password, Teresa signed on to eBay.com._

Teresa signed on to eBay.com using her password.

1. a. _Answers will vary._

b. _____

COMBINED: _____

_____

2. a. _____

   b. _____

   COMBINED: _____

   _____

....

Join Ideas Using an *-ed* Verb Form

For more on helping verbs, see Chapters 22, 26, and 33.

Another way to combine sentences is to turn one of them into a phrase using an **-ed verb form** (such as *waited* or *walked*). You can join sentences this way if one of them has a form of *be* as a helping verb along with the *-ed* verb form.

TWO SENTENCES	Leonardo da Vinci was a man of many talents. He was noted most often for his painting.
JOINED WITH -ED VERB FORM	Noted most often for his painting, Leonardo da Vinci was a man of many talents.

To combine sentences this way, drop the subject and the helping verb from a sentence that has an *-ed* verb form. You now have a modifying phrase that can be added to the beginning or the end of the other sentence, depending on what makes the most sense.

Interested   *, Leonardo*
~~Leonardo was interested~~ in many areas./~~He~~ investigated problems of

geology, botany, mechanics, and hydraulics.

For more on finding and correcting dangling modifiers, see Chapter 29.

If you add a phrase that begins with an *-ed* verb form to the beginning of a sentence, put a comma after it. Be sure the word that the phrase modified follows immediately, or you will create a dangling modifier. Sometimes, you will need to change the word that the phrase modifies from a pronoun to a noun, as in the previous example.

TWO SENTENCES	Marie paused at the podium. She was exhilarated by her achievement.
DANGLING MODIFIER	Exhilarated by her achievement at the podium, Marie paused.
CORRECT	Exhilarated by her achievement, Marie paused at the podium.

....

PRACTICE 6 Joining Ideas Using an *-ed* Verb Form

Combine each pair of sentences into a single sentence by using an *-ed* verb form.

Hatched

EXAMPLE: ~~Alligators are hatched~~ from eggs when they are only a few
                ^   *, alligators*
inches long. ~~Alligators~~ can reach a length of ten feet or
                   ^
more as adults.   *Answers may vary. Possible edits shown.*

1. ~~An alligator was spotted in a pond in Central Park in New York~~
                                                       an
~~City.~~ Many New Yorkers refused to believe in the existence of ~~the~~ alli-
       spotted in a pond in Central Park in New York City.   ^
gator.
       ^
Released
2. ~~Alligators were released~~ by their owners for growing too large to be
       ^
pets. ~~These~~ alligators were sometimes said to be living in New York
         ^
City sewers.
Believed   *, the*
3. ~~Rumors were believed~~ by some gullible people. ~~The~~ rumors about
       ^   ^
giant sewer alligators were untrue.
Denied
4. ~~The story of the alligator in Central Park was denied~~ by city offi-
       ^   *, the*   *of the alligator in Central Park*
cials. ~~The~~ story sounded like another wild rumor.
         ^   ^
Reported
5. ~~Central Park alligator sightings were reported~~ by several New
       ^   *the Central Park alligator*
Yorkers. ~~The~~ sightings were confirmed when a television news crew
           ^   ^
filmed a reptile in the pond.
Hired   *, a professional alligator wrestler*
6. ~~A professional alligator wrestler was hired~~ to catch the reptile. ~~He~~
       ^   ^
came to New York from Florida.
Surrounded
7. ~~The pond in Central Park was surrounded~~ by news cameras and
       ^   *, the pond in Central Park*
curious onlookers. ~~It~~ was brightly lit just before 11:00 p.m. on the
                     ^
day the alligator wrestler arrived.
Captured
8. ~~The creature was captured~~ in just a few minutes by the alligator
       ^   *, the*
wrestler's wife. ~~The~~ so-called alligator turned out to be a spectacled
                   ^
caiman, a species native to Central and South America.

Surprised

9. ~~Some New Yorkers were surprised~~ to find that the caiman was only
   ^
                          , some New Yorkers
   two feet long, ~~They~~ may have felt a bit foolish for expecting to see
                    ^
   a giant alligator in the park.
   Removed   *, the caiman*
10. ~~The caiman was removed~~ from Central Park, ~~It~~ soon found a home
    ^   ^
    in a warmer climate.

· ·

**PRACTICE 7   Joining Ideas Using
an *-ed* Verb Form**

Fill in the blank in each sentence with an appropriate *-ed* verb form. There are
several possible ways to complete each sentence.

> **EXAMPLE:** *Enjoyed* by many people around the world, online
> gambling is an increasingly popular recreational
> option. *Answers may vary. Possible edits shown.*

1. ___*Used*___ regularly by Europeans, this venue for gambling is
   more difficult for Americans to access.

2. ___*Prohibited*___ by some U.S. states, online gambling is a major worry
   of the government.

3. ___*Concerned*___ that Internet gambling can be used for hiding large
   exchanges of money, the U.S. Justice Department has asked major
   Internet search engines to remove advertising for online gambling
   operations.

4. Also ___*opposed*___ to legalizing online gambling in the United
   States, some antigambling activists think the speed of the Internet
   makes it more likely for problem gamblers to give in to their
   addiction.

5. ___*Considered*___ a harmless pastime by some, easy-access online gambling can arguably ruin even more lives than it already has.

PRACTICE 8   Joining Ideas Using an -ed Verb Form

Write two sets of sentences, and join them using an -ed verb form.

EXAMPLE: a. _Lee is training for the Boston Marathon._

b. _It is believed to have the most difficult hill to run._

COMBINED: _Lee is training for the Boston Marathon, believed to have the most difficult hill to run._

1. a. _Answers will vary._

b. _____

COMBINED: _____

_____

2. a. _____

b. _____

COMBINED: _____

_____

Join Ideas Using an Appositive

An **appositive** is a phrase that renames a noun. Appositives, which are nouns or noun phrases, can be used to combine two sentences into one.

TWO SENTENCES	Elvis Presley continues to be popular many years after his death. He is "the King."
JOINED WITH AN APPOSITIVE	Elvis Presley, "the King," continues to be popular many years after his death.

[The phrase *"the King"* renames the noun *Elvis Presley*.]

To combine two sentences by using an appositive, turn the sentence that renames the noun into a phrase by dropping its subject and verb. The appositive phrase can appear anywhere in the sentence, but it should be placed before or after the noun it renames. Use a comma or commas to set off the appositive.

, Graceland,

Millions of people make a special trip to visit Elvis's home each year. ~~It is called Graceland.~~

··

PRACTICE 9 Joining Ideas Using an Appositive

Combine each pair of sentences into a single sentence by using an appositive. Be sure to use a comma or commas to set off the appositive.

, one of the greatest writers in the English language,

EXAMPLE: William Shakespeare was famous and financially comfortable during his lifetime. ~~Shakespeare was one of the greatest writers in the English language.~~

, the son of a former town leader,

1. Shakespeare grew up in Stratford, England. ~~He was the son of a former town leader.~~

, a poor manager of money,

2. Shakespeare attended the local grammar school until his father could no longer afford it. ~~His father was a poor manager of money.~~

3. In 1582, Shakespeare, just eighteen, married twenty-six-year-old Anne Hathaway, ~~She was~~ a farmer's daughter.

4. Three years later, he left for London, ~~London was~~ the center of England's theater world.

5. Young Shakespeare, ~~was~~ once a simple country boy, ~~He~~ soon became involved in acting, writing, and managing for one of London's theater companies.

6. By 1592, he was famous enough to be criticized in writing by one of the leading playwrights of the time, ~~This playwright was~~ Robert Greene.

7. Greene's publisher soon printed a public apology for the criticism, ~~This was~~ proof that Shakespeare had won the respect of some influential figures.

8. Shakespeare is said to have performed for Queen Elizabeth I, ~~She was~~ a theater fan and supporter.

9. Eventually, Shakespeare returned to Stratford and purchased a large home *, New Place,* where he lived until his death in 1616. ~~The house was called New Place.~~

10. Shakespeare remains highly popular today, and more than 250 movies have been made of his plays or about his life, ~~His life is~~ a rich enough source of drama for any movie producer.

. . . .

PRACTICE 10   Joining Ideas Using an Appositive

Fill in the blank in each sentence with an appropriate appositive. There are many possible ways to complete each sentence.

> **EXAMPLE:** My sister Clara, <u>*a busy mother of three*</u>, loves to watch soap operas. *Possible answers shown.*

1. Clara's favorite show, <u>*Love and Desire*</u>, comes on at three o'clock in the afternoon.

2. Clara, <u>*a hardworking seamstress*</u>, rarely has the time to sit down in front of the television for the broadcast.

3. Instead, she programs her VCR, <u>*an aging but reliable machine*</u>, and tapes the show for later.

4. Clara's husband, <u>*her childhood sweetheart*</u>, used to tease her for watching the soaps.

5. But while he was recovering from the flu recently, he found her stack of tapes, <u>*a pile over two feet high*</u>, and Clara insists that he watched every show of the previous season.

. . . .

Join Ideas Using an Adjective Clause

An **adjective clause** is a group of words with a subject and a verb that describes a noun. Adjective clauses often begin with the word *who, which,* or *that* and can be used to combine two sentences into one.

TWO SENTENCES	Lorene owns an art and framing store. She is a good friend of mine.
JOINED WITH AN ADJECTIVE CLAUSE	Lorene, who is a good friend of mine, owns an art and framing store.

Use *who* to refer to a person, *which* to refer to places or things (but not to people), and *that* for places or things.

To join sentences this way, use *who, which,* or *that* to replace the subject of a sentence that describes a noun that is in the other sentence. Once you have made this change, you have an adjective clause that you can move so that it follows the noun it describes. The sentence with the idea you want to emphasize should become the main clause. The less important idea should be in the adjective clause.

TWO SENTENCES	Rosalind is director of human services for the town of Marlborough. Marlborough is her hometown.

[The more important idea here is that Rosalind is director of human services. The less important idea is that the town is her hometown.]

JOINED WITH AN ADJECTIVE CLAUSE	Rosalind is director of human services for the town of Marlborough, which is her hometown.

NOTE: If an adjective clause can be taken out of a sentence without completely changing the meaning of the sentence, put commas around the clause.

Lorene, who is a good friend of mine, owns an art and framing store.

[The phrase *who is a good friend of mine* adds information about Lorene, but it is not essential; the sentence *Lorene owns an art and framing store* means almost the same thing as the sentence in the example.]

If an adjective clause is essential to the meaning of a sentence, do not put commas around it.

The meat was recalled for possible salmonella poisoning. I ate it yesterday.

The meat that I ate yesterday was recalled for possible salmonella poisoning.

[The clause *that I ate yesterday* is an essential piece of information. The sentence *The meat was recalled for possible salmonella poisoning* changes significantly with the adjective clause *that I ate yesterday*.]

· ·

PRACTICE 11   Joining Ideas Using an Adjective Clause

Combine each pair of sentences into a single sentence by using an adjective clause beginning with *who*, *which*, or *that*.

Allergies that

EXAMPLE: ~~Some allergies~~ cause sneezing, itching, and watery eyes/

~~They~~ can make people very uncomfortable.

1. Cats produce a protein/ *that* ~~It~~ keeps their skin soft.

2. This protein makes some people itch and sneeze/ *, which* ~~The protein~~ is the reason for most allergic reactions to cats.

3. Some cat lovers are allergic to cats/ *who* ~~They~~ can control their allergies with medication.

4. Allergic cat lovers may get another option from a new company/ *that* ~~The company~~ wants to create a genetically engineered cat.

5. Scientists have successfully cloned mice/ *that* ~~Some mice~~ have been genetically engineered for scientific study.

6. Researchers may soon have the technology to clone cats/ *, which* ~~Cats~~ could be genetically engineered to remove the allergen.

7. ~~Many people have allergic reactions to cats.~~ According to cat experts, more than 10 percent of those people *who have allergic reactions to cats* are allergic to something other than the skin-softening protein.

8. ~~A single gene produces a cat's skin-softening protein.~~ Scientists are not sure whether the gene *that produces a cat's skin-softening protein* is necessary for the cat's good health.

9. However, owning a genetically engineered cat would allow an allergic person to avoid taking allergy medications/ *, which* ~~The medications~~ can sometimes cause dangerous side effects.

10. Cloning and genetic engineering raise ethical questions/ *that* ~~These~~ are difficult to answer.

··

PRACTICE 12   Joining Ideas Using an Adjective Clause

Fill in the blank in each of the following sentences with an appropriate adjective clause. Add commas, if necessary. There are many possible ways to complete each sentence.

EXAMPLE: Interactive television ___*, which has started to become avail-*

*able to consumers,*___ is a potential threat to viewers'

privacy.   *Possible answers shown.*

1. Many Web sites _*that receive hundreds or thousands of hits each day*_

    try to make a profit by selling information about visitors to the site.

2. Consumers ___*who buy products online*___ must provide informa-

    tion to retail Web sites before being allowed to complete a purchase.

3. Consumer privacy _*, which is becoming rarer every day,*_ is suffering

    further with interactive television.

4. A viewer _*who tunes in to an interactive television program*_ may not

    realize that the broadcaster is collecting information about him or her.

5. The sale of personal information *, which companies use to target*

    potential customers, can bring huge profits.

··

Edit Paragraphs and Your Own Writing

RESOURCES
For cumulative Editing
Review Tests, see
pages 667–83.

Create sentence variety in the following paragraphs by joining at least two sentences in each of the paragraphs. Try to use several of the techniques discussed in this chapter. There are many possible ways to edit each paragraph. You may want to refer to the chart on page 578. *Answers will vary. Possible edits shown.*

··

EDITING REVIEW 1

, which   *, are*
(1) Rats might be nicer creatures than people think, (2) It's cer-
                                            Not only do they
tainly hard to love and appreciate. rats. (3) They carry serious diseases

like typhus, salmonella poisoning, and bubonic plague *, but rats* (4) ~~Rats~~ have such huge appetites that it has been estimated that they destroy as much as one-third of humans' food supplies every year. (5) It has been estimated that rats have been responsible for ten million deaths over the past century alone *; however, rats* (6) ~~Rats~~ in the laboratory should probably be given credit for saving as many lives as wild rats have taken.

(7) *Used* ~~Rats are used~~ widely in laboratory research *, rats* (8) ~~Rats~~ have many similarities to humans. (9) *Being* ~~Young rats are~~ ticklish *, when* (10) ~~When~~ a rat pup is gently scratched at certain spots, such as the nape of the neck, *, which* it will squeal. (11) The squeal can be heard only with an ultrasound scan *,* (12) ~~The squeal~~ has a similar soundgram pattern to that of a human giggle. (13) Rats can get addicted to the same drugs that humans do *, craving* (14) ~~Rats crave~~ alcohol, nicotine, amphetamine, and cocaine. (15) *Capable of overindulging,* ~~Rats can also overindulge.~~ (16) *rats* ~~They~~ can continue consuming food or drugs until they die.

(17) Studies also show that rats, similar to humans, have personalities *, being* (18) ~~They can be~~ sad or cheerful depending on how they were raised and their circumstances. (19) *Raised* ~~Rats that have been raised~~ in stable, caring conditions tend to be optimists *, rats* *, while rats* (20) ~~Rats~~ reared in uneven and unreliable conditions are likely to be pessimists. (21) Both types of rats can learn to connect a certain sound with getting food *, and they* (22) ~~They~~ also can associate another sound with no food. (23) However, when they hear a new sound, *not associated with either food or no food,* the two types of rats react differently. (24) ~~The new sound is not associated with either food or no food.~~ (25) The optimist will run to the food dispenser *,* (26) ~~It is~~ expecting to be fed. (27) The pessimist will go somewhere else *, expecting nothing,* (28) ~~It is expecting nothing.~~

(29) *Demonstrating that rats* ~~Rats~~ can express kindness *, researchers* (30) ~~Researchers~~ put pairs of female rats *who were* littermates in a cage but separated by wire mesh. (31) *Trained so that in* ~~In~~ each half of the cage, a rat could pull a lever that would deliver

food to her sister but not to herself_, (32) ~~Each~~ *each* rat learned to be a giver of food and a recipient of a gift of food from her sister. (33) Then, one of the rats was replaced by an unfamiliar and unrelated rat that had never learned about the food gift process_, (34) ~~Those~~ *revealing that those* rats who had recently received food gifts were 21 percent more likely to pull the lever to give food to their new, unknown partners. (35) The researchers ~~believe~~ *, believing* that these rats were generous only because another rat had just been kind to them_, (36) ~~Perhaps~~ *show us that perhaps* there is more to the rodents than previously thought.

....

EDITING REVIEW 2

(1) Employees once wanted nothing more than to stay at their jobs as long as possible_, (2) ~~They also viewed~~ *viewing* career advancement as a high priority. (3) The optimal situation was to be valued on the job_, (4) ~~This~~ *which* brought rewards of satisfaction and money as well as the attainment of higher rungs on the corporate ladder. (5) ~~Today's young employees are going~~ *Headed* in a different direction_, (6) ~~Young~~ *young* workers these days have some expectations that few, if any, jobs could satisfy.

(7) A twenty-eight-year-old designer at an architecture firm had two weeks of vacation every year_, (8) ~~This is~~ the standard vacation for most young employees. (9) ~~Employees are commonly~~ *Commonly* encouraged to take only one of these weeks off at a time_, (10) ~~Many~~ *many employees* have trouble finding time to take any vacation at all. (11) ~~The designer arranged~~ *Arranging* to take a job with another firm_, (12) ~~He~~ *the designer* then resigned from his current firm.
(13) ~~His~~ *After his* new firm agreed that he could begin work in four weeks_,
(14) ~~He~~ *he* then left on a leisurely motorcycle trip beginning in the South, swinging over to the Rocky Mountains and returning across the Great Plains. (15) ~~He chose~~ *Choosing* an alternative to the entry-level two-week vacation_, (16) ~~He~~ *he* quit, went on an adventure, and then started a new job.

(17) *Focused on a similar quest, a* ~~A~~ thirty-three-year-old bankruptcy lawyer ~~was focused on a similar quest.~~ (18) ~~She~~ quit her job, had an extended visit with her family, traveled for four months through New Zealand, Australia, Southeast Asia, and central Europe and then found a new job at a different law firm. (19) In another telling example, ~~a software engineer, thirty-two,~~ *having* worked hard with little vacation during the ten years he was with his company*,* *a software engineer, thirty-two,* (20) ~~He~~ quit to live his dream of visiting all fifty-eight national parks. (21) *Equipped with* ~~His~~ skills were in demand*,* *that* (22) ~~He~~ *he* did not worry about finding another job but was concerned about getting burned out again. (23) Growing up in a time of relative prosperity and economic stability, these workers can usually find new jobs*,* (24) ~~This is~~ perhaps a major difference between today's young employees and the generation before them.

(25) *When a* ~~A~~ twenty-seven-year-old minister and his wife left their posts in Colorado Springs for new positions at a church in Philadelphia*,* (26) ~~They~~ *they* took six weeks off between jobs. (27) ~~They say~~ *Saying* the six weeks of unemployment was healthy*,* (28) ~~They~~ *they* maintain that they are not defined by what they do but by who they are. (29) ~~They are emblematic~~ *Emblematic* of their generation of workers*,* (30) ~~They~~ *they* took time off to renew relationships and pursue experiences that helped them reach a comfortable balance between work and life.

··

PRACTICE 13   Editing Your Own Writing for Sentence Variety

As a final practice, edit a piece of your own writing for sentence variety. It can be a paper you are working on for this course, a paper you have already finished, a paper for another course, a recent piece of writing from your work or everyday life, or your idea journal entry. You may want to use the chart on page 578 as you edit.

··

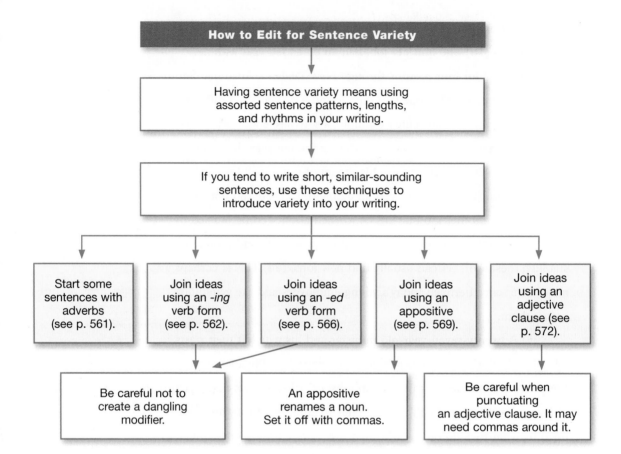

How to Edit for Sentence Variety

Having sentence variety means using assorted sentence patterns, lengths, and rhythms in your writing.

If you tend to write short, similar-sounding sentences, use these techniques to introduce variety into your writing.

Start some sentences with adverbs (see p. 561).

Join ideas using an *-ing* verb form (see p. 562).

Join ideas using an *-ed* verb form (see p. 566).

Join ideas using an appositive (see p. 569).

Join ideas using an adjective clause (see p. 572).

Be careful not to create a dangling modifier.

An appositive renames a noun. Set it off with commas.

Be careful when punctuating an adjective clause. It may need commas around it.

33

Formal English and ESL

Grammar Trouble Spots for Multilingual Students

Academic, or formal, English is the English you will be expected to use in college and in most work situations, especially in writing. If you are not used to speaking and writing formal English or if English is not your first language, this chapter will help you with the most common problems students have.

NOTE: In this chapter, the word *English* means formal English.

IDEA JOURNAL
Write about a cultural or religious family tradition.

Basic Sentence Patterns

Statements

Every sentence in English must have at least one subject and one verb **(S-V)** that together express a complete idea. (Some languages, such as Spanish and Italian, do not always use a subject because the subject is implied by the verb. In English, always include a subject.) The subject performs the action, and the verb names the action, as in the sentence that follows.

TEACHING TIP
For practice with ESL grammar issues, visit *Exercise Central* at bedfordstmartins .com/realessays.

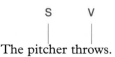

The pitcher throws.

Other English sentence patterns build on that structure. One of the most common patterns is subject-verb-object **(S-V-O)**.

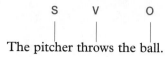

The pitcher throws the ball.

There are two kinds of **objects:**

A **direct object** receives the action of the verb.

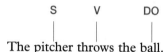

The pitcher throws the ball.

[The ball directly receives the action of the verb *throws*.]

An **indirect object** does not receive the action of the verb. Instead, the action is performed *for* or *to* the person.

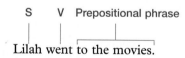

The pitcher throws me the ball.

[In this sentence, the word *me* does not receive the action of the verb, *throws*. The action is performed *to* the person.]

For other common English sentence patterns, see Chapter 22.

Note that the **S-V-O** pattern differs from the sentence patterns in some other languages. For example, in some languages (like Arabic) the pattern may be **S-O-V**; other languages do not have as strictly defined a word order (Spanish, Italian, and Russian, for example).

Another common sentence pattern is subject-verb-prepositional phrase. In standard English, the prepositional phrase typically follows the subject and verb.

For more on prepositions, see pages 599–600. For more on the parts of sentences, see Chapter 22.

S   V   Prepositional phrase

Lilah went to the movies.

RESOURCES For tests on particular ESL trouble spots, see the *Testing Tool Kit* CD available with this book.

Negatives

To form a negative statement, use one of these words, often with a helping verb such as *can/could*, *does/did*, *has/have*, or *should/will/would*.

never	nobody	no one	nowhere
no	none	not	

Notice in the examples that the word *not* comes *after* the helping verb.

SENTENCE	The baby can talk.
NEGATIVE	The baby ~~no can~~ talk. *(cannot)*
SENTENCE	The store sells cigarettes.
NEGATIVE	The store ~~no~~ sell~~s~~ cigarettes. *(does not)*
SENTENCE	Jonah talks too much.
NEGATIVE	Jonah not talk~~s~~ too much. *(does)*
SENTENCE	Johnetta will call.
NEGATIVE	Johnetta ~~no~~ will call. *(not)*
SENTENCE	Caroline called.
NEGATIVE	Caroline ~~no~~ did call. *(not)*
SENTENCE	Paul will come.
NEGATIVE	Paul ~~no~~ will come. *(not)*

Common Helping Verbs

FORMS OF *BE*	FORMS OF *HAVE*	FORMS OF *DO*	OTHER VERBS
am	have	do	can
are	has	does	could
been	had	did	may
being			might
is			must
was			should
were			will
			would

The helping verb cannot be omitted in expressions using *not*.

For more on helping
verbs and their forms,
see Chapter 22.

INCORRECT	The store *not sell* cigarettes.
CORRECT	The store *does not sell* cigarettes.

[*Does*, a form of the helping verb *do*, must come before *not*.]

CORRECT   The store *is not selling* cigarettes.

[*Is,* a form of *be,* must come before *not.*]

Double negatives are not standard in English.

INCORRECT   Johnetta *will not call no one.*

CORRECT   Johnetta *will not call anyone.*

CORRECT   Johnetta *will call no one.*

INCORRECT   Shane *does not have no* ride.

CORRECT   Shane *does not have a* ride.

CORRECT   Shane *has no* ride.

When forming a negative in the simple past tense, use the past tense of the helping verb *do.*

did	+	not	+	base verb without an -ed	=	negative past tense

SENTENCE   I *talked* to Kayla last night.

[*Talked* is the past tense.]

NEGATIVE   I *did not* talk to Kayla last night.

For forming negatives in other tenses, see pages 480–90.

[Note that *talk* in this sentence does not have an *-ed* ending because the helping verb *did* conveys that past.]

SENTENCE   Kerry *passed* the test.

NEGATIVE   Kerry *did not* pass the test.

Questions

To turn a statement into a question, move the helping verb so that it comes before the subject. Add a question mark (**?**) to the end of the question.

STATEMENT   Danh *can work* late.

QUESTION   *Can* Danh *work* late?

If the only verb in the statement is a form of *be,* it should be moved before the subject.

STATEMENT	Phuong *is* smart. Jamie *is* at work.
QUESTION	*Is* Phuong smart? *Is* Jamie at work?

If there is no helping verb or form of *be* in the statement, add a form of *do* and put it before the subject. Be sure to end the question with a question mark (**?**).

STATEMENT	Norah sings in the choir.
QUESTION	*Does* Norah sing in the choir?
STATEMENT	Amy visited the elderly woman.
QUESTION	*Did* Amy visit the elderly woman?
STATEMENT	The building burned.
QUESTION	*Did* the building burn?

Notice that the verb *visited* changed to *visit* and the verb *burned* to *burn* once the helping verb *did* was added.

For more on questions, see Chapters 25 and 26.

LANGUAGE NOTE: *Do* is used with *I, you, we,* and *they. Does* is used with *he, she,* and *it.*

EXAMPLES	*Do* [I, you, we, they] practice every day?
	Does [he, she, it] sound terrible?

There Is and There Are

English sentences often include *there is* or *there are* to indicate the existence of something.

There is a man at the door.   [You could also say, *A man is at the door.*]

There are many men in the class.   [You could also say, *Many men are in the class.*]

When a sentence includes the words *there is* or *there are,* the verb (*is, are*) comes before the noun it goes with. The verb must agree with the noun in number. For example, the first sentence at the bottom of page 583 uses the singular verb *is* to agree with the singular noun *man,* and the second sentence uses the plural verb *are* to agree with the plural noun *men.*

> **LANGUAGE NOTE:** The *there is/there are* structure does not exist in some other languages, so speakers of those languages sometimes leave out these words when writing in English.
>
> | | |
> |---|---|
> | **INCORRECT** | My mother said much work to do. |
> | | Much work to do. |
> | **CORRECT** | My mother said *there is* much work to do. |
> | | *There is* much work to do. |

In questions, the word order in *there is* and *there are* is inverted.

STATEMENTS	*There is* plenty to eat.
	There are some things to do.
QUESTIONS	*Is there* plenty to eat?
	Are there some things to do?

Pronouns

For more on pronouns, see Chapter 27.

Pronouns replace nouns or other pronouns in a sentence so that you do not have to repeat them. There are three types of pronouns:

Subject pronouns serve as the subject of the verb (and every English sentence must have a subject).

              He
Jonah is my cousin. ~~Jonah~~ lives next door to me.

Object pronouns receive the action of the verb or are part of a prepositional phrase.

Jonah asked *me* for a ride.

[The object pronoun *me* receives the action of the verb, *asked.*]

Jonah is my cousin. He lives next door *to me.*

[*To me* is the prepositional phrase; *me* is the object pronoun.]

Possessive pronouns show ownership.

Jonah is *my* cousin.

Use the following chart to check which type of pronoun to use.

Pronoun Types

SUBJECT		OBJECT		POSSESSIVE	
SINGULAR	**PLURAL**	**SINGULAR**	**PLURAL**	**SINGULAR**	**PLURAL**
I	we	me	us	my/mine	our/ours
you	you	you	you	your/yours	your/yours
he/she/it	they	him/her/it	them	his/her/hers/its	theirs

RELATIVE PRONOUNS					
who, which, that					

The singular pronouns *he/she*, *him/her*, and *his/hers* show gender. *He, him,* and *his* are masculine pronouns; *she, her,* and *hers* are feminine.
Here are some examples of common pronoun errors, with corrections.

Confusing Subject and Object Pronouns

Use a subject pronoun for the word that *performs* the action of the verb, and use an object pronoun for the word that *receives* the action.

                                  She
Dora is a good student. ~~Her~~ gets all A's.

[The pronoun performs the action *gets,* so it should be the subject pronoun, *she.*]

                                 her
Tomas gave the keys to ~~she.~~

[The pronoun receives the action of *gave,* so it should be the object pronoun, *her.*]

Confusing Gender

Use masculine pronouns to replace masculine nouns and feminine pronouns to replace feminine nouns.

                              He
Gordon passed the test. ~~She~~ got a B.

[*Gordon* is a masculine noun, so the pronoun must be masculine.]

The iPod belongs to Michael. Carla gave it to ~~her~~. *him*

[*Michael* is masculine, so the pronoun must be masculine.]

Leaving Out a Pronoun

Some sentences use the pronoun *it* as the subject or object. Do not leave *it* out of the sentence.

It is
~~Is~~ my birthday today.

Annahita will travel by bus. ~~Will~~ arrive at 3:00. *It will*

I tried calamari last night and liked very much. *it*

Using a Pronoun to Repeat a Subject

Pronouns *replace* a noun, so do not use both a subject noun and a pronoun.

The boss ~~he~~ is very mean.

[*Boss* is the subject noun, so the sentence does not also need a subject pronoun.]

The baseball ~~it~~ broke the window.

[*Baseball* is the subject, so no pronoun is needed.]

Using Relative Pronouns

The words *who, which,* and *that* are **relative pronouns**. Use relative pronouns in a phrase or clause that gives more information about the subject.

Use *who* to refer to a person or people.

The man *who* owns the building is strange.

Use *which* to refer to nonliving things.

The building, *which* was just painted, is for sale.

Use *that* to refer to either people or nonliving things. (Note that *who* is the preferred pronoun to refer to a person or people.)

The building *that* my uncle owns is for sale.

The present *that* you gave me is great.

Verbs

Verbs have different tenses to show when something happened: in the past, present, or future.

Learning how to use the various verb tenses is a challenge for everyone (I know from trying to learn Spanish). This section will give you examples that build on what you learned in Chapter 26.

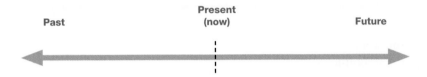

This section covers some common errors in verb usage and also has full coverage of the progressive tenses. In addition, this section contains timelines, examples, and common errors for the simple, perfect, and progressive tenses. For full coverage of verbs and complete verb charts, see Chapter 26.

The Simple Tenses

Simple Present

Use the simple present to describe situations that exist now.

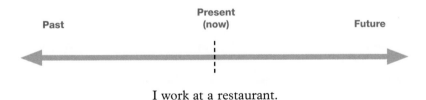

I work at a restaurant.

I/You/We/They <u>work</u> at a restaurant.

She/He <u>works</u> at a restaurant.

The third-person singular (*she/he*) of regular verbs ends in *-s* or *-es*. For irregular verb endings, see pages 467–69.

Simple Past

Use the simple past to describe situations that began and ended in the past.

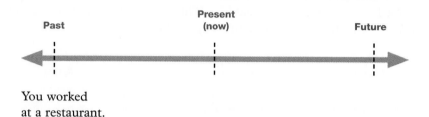

You worked
at a restaurant.

I/You/She/He/We/They work**ed** at a restaurant.

For regular verbs, the simple past is formed by adding either -*d* or -*ed* to the verb. For the past forms of irregular verbs, see the chart on pages 467–69.

Simple Future

TIP
For charts, explanations, and practices on the simple tense, including how to use it to form negatives and questions, see Chapter 26.

Use the simple future to describe situations that will happen in the future. It is easier to form than the past tense. Use this formula for forming the future tense.

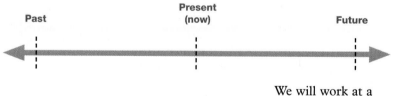

We will work at a
restaurant next semester.

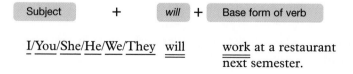

| Subject | + | *will* | + | Base form of verb |

I/You/She/He/We/They will   work at a restaurant
next semester.

The Progressive Tenses

Present Progressive

Use the present progressive to describe situations that are happening now but began in the past.

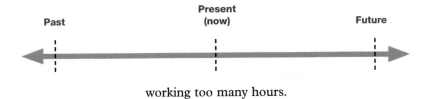

working too many hours.

We are working too many hours.

Use this formula to form the present progressive tense:

For examples, explanations, and practices on the progressive tenses, along with a chart showing negatives and questions, see Chapter 26.

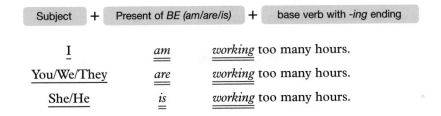

| Subject | + | Present of *BE (am/are/is)* | + | base verb with *-ing* ending |

I	*am*	*working* too many hours.
You/We/They	*are*	*working* too many hours.
She/He	*is*	*working* too many hours.

Past Progressive

Use the past progressive to describe situations that were going on in the past.

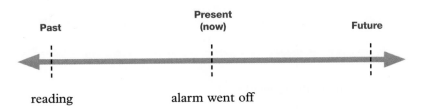

reading   alarm went off

I was reading when the alarm went off.

Use this formula to form the past progressive tense:

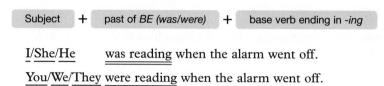

I/She/He   was reading when the alarm went off.

You/We/They were reading when the alarm went off.

Future Progressive

Use the future progressive to describe situations that began and ended before some other situation happened.

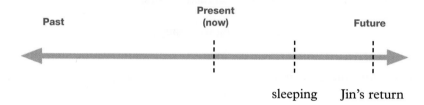

I will be sleeping when Jin returns.

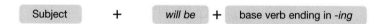

I/You/She/He/We/They will be sleeping when Jin returns.

The Perfect Tenses

Present Perfect

TIP
For charts, explanations, and practices on the perfect tense, including how to use it to form negatives and questions, see Chapter 26.

Use the present perfect to describe situations that started in the past and are still happening.

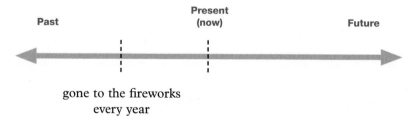

We have gone to the fireworks every year.

To form the present perfect tense, use this formula:

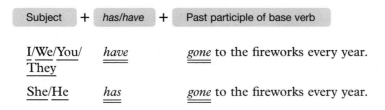

| I/We/You/They | *have* | *gone* to the fireworks every year. |
| She/He | *has* | *gone* to the fireworks every year. |

Past Perfect

Use the past perfect to describe situations that began and ended before some other situation happened.

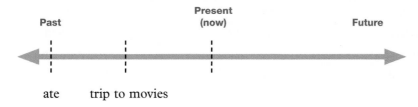

I had eaten before I went to the movies.

To form the past perfect tense, use this formula:

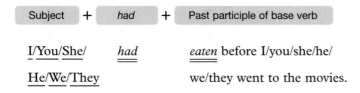

| I/You/She/ | *had* | *eaten* before I/you/she/he/ |
| He/We/They | | we/they went to the movies. |

Future Perfect

Use the future perfect to describe siuations that begin and end before another situation begins.

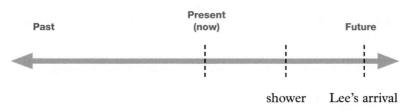

I will have showered before Lee's arrival.

TIP For more on the perfect tense, see Chapter 26. For a list of irregular verbs and their forms, see pages 467-69.

Use this formula to form the future perfect tense:

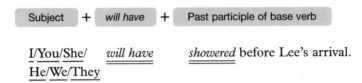

I/You/She/   *will have*   *showered* before Lee's arrival.
He/We/They

Modal Auxiliaries

Modal verbs are helping verbs that express the writer's attitude about an action. There aren't many of them to learn—see the chart below.

MODAL AUXILIARY	MEANING	EXAMPLE
can	ability	I can sing.
could	possibility	I could sing.
may	permission	You may sing.
might	possibility	I might sing.
must	obligation	I must sing.
should	advice or expectation	I should sing.
will	intention	I will sing.
would (often with the verb *like*)	desire, intention	I would sing.

For this section, you will need to refer to the charts on pages 487–90, which list statements, negatives, and questions for all of the modal auxiliaries.

Should/Must

As you see in the chart, *should* means that an action is expected or recommended. *Must* means that an action is required; it is an obligation.

Tomorrow, I *should* go to class.   [The writer has a choice about whether to go or not.]

Tomorrow, I *must* go to class.   [The writer has no choice about going to class: It is necessary.]

Read the two sentences that follow, and explain their meaning.

My grandmother *should* eat more.

My grandmother *must* eat more.

Two common student errors when using *should* or *must* are the following:

Using the Infinitive Instead of the Base Verb.   The infinitive is *to + the base verb*. The base verb does not have *to* before it. When using *should* and *must*, use the base verb.

INCORRECT	Children should *to obey* their parents.
CORRECT	Children should *obey* their parents.
INCORRECT	They must *to work* late.
CORRECT	They must *work* late.

Using Two Modals.   Using two modal auxiliaries together in a sentence is incorrect in English. Use only one.

INCORRECT	I *must should* study harder.
CORRECT	I *must* study harder. *Or* I *should* study harder.

Could/Would

Could means a possibility that an action will happen; *would* means an intention that an action happen. The meanings are similar, but the words are not interchangeable.

Gina *could* go to bed early.   [Gina has the ability to go to bed early; it is possible that she will.]

Gina *would* like to go to bed early.   [Gina has the wish and intention to go to bed early, but she might not be able to.]

Read the two sentences that follow, and explain their meaning.

Next semester, I *could* take two courses.

Next semester, I *would* like to take two courses.

Two common student errors when using *could* or *would* are the following:

Using a Gerund Instead of an Infinitive or the Base Verb.   A gerund is a verb form that ends in *-ing* and functions as a noun in a sentence. When using the modal auxiliary *could*, follow it with the base verb. When using *would*, follow it with the infinitive (*to* + base verb), not a gerund.

INCORRECT	Today, I could *winning* the lottery.
CORRECT	Today, I could *win* the lottery.
INCORRECT	I would like *graduating* in 2015.
CORRECT	I would like *to graduate* in 2015.

Omitting the Modal.   Just as you don't want to use two modal auxiliaries together in a sentence, you also don't want to forget a modal when it is required to show intention.

INCORRECT	Next month, I *like* to take a vacation.
CORRECT	Next month, I *would like* to take a vacation.
INCORRECT	Tomorrow, I *help* you.
CORRECT	Tomorrow, I *could help* you. *Or* Tomorrow, I *can help* you.

Gerunds and Infinitives

A **gerund** is a verb form that ends in *-ing* and acts as a noun. An **infinitive** is a verb form that is preceded by the word *to*. Gerunds and infinitives cannot be the main verbs in sentences; each sentence must have another word that is the main verb.

GERUND	I like *running*.

[*Like* is the main verb, and *running* is a gerund.]

INFINITIVE	I like *to run*.

[*Like* is the main verb, and *to run* is an infinitive.]

To improve your ability to write and speak standard English, read magazines and your local newspaper, and listen to television and radio news programs. Read magazines and newspaper articles aloud; it will help your pronunciation.

How do you decide whether to use a gerund or an infinitive? The decision often depends on the main verb in a sentence. Some verbs can be followed by either a gerund or an infinitive.

Verbs That Are Followed by Either a Gerund or an Infinitive

begin	forget	like	remember	stop
continue	hate	love	start	try

Sometimes, using an infinitive or gerund after one of the verbs listed in the preceding box results in the same meaning.

GERUND   I love *listening* to Ray Charles.

INFINITIVE   I love *to listen* to Ray Charles.

Other times, however, the meaning changes depending on whether you use an infinitive or a gerund.

INFINITIVE   Mario stopped to smoke.

[This sentence means that Mario stopped what he was doing and smoked a cigarette.]

GERUND   Mario stopped smoking.

[This sentence means that Mario no longer smokes cigarettes.]

Verbs That Are Followed by an Infinitive

agree	decide	need	refuse
ask	expect	offer	want
beg	fail	plan	
choose	hope	pretend	
claim	manage	promise	

Tony *expects to get* a raise.

Lana *plans to adopt* a child.

Verbs That Are Followed by a Gerund

admit	discuss	keep	risk
avoid	enjoy	miss	suggest
consider	finish	practice	
deny	imagine	quit	

Football players *avoid injuring* themselves.

Imagine sitting on a beach in Hawaii.

Do not use the base form of the verb when you need a gerund or an infinitive.

| INCORRECT | *Cook* is my favorite activity. |

[*Cook* is the base form of the verb, not a noun; it can't function as the subject of the sentence.]

| CORRECT GERUND: | *Cooking* is my favorite activity. |

[*Cooking* is a gerund that can serve as the subject of the sentence.]

| INCORRECT | *Play* piano is fun. |
| CORRECT GERUND: | *Playing* piano is fun. |

| INCORRECT | My goal is *graduate* from college. |
| CORRECT INFINITIVE: | My goal is *to graduate* from college. |

[*To graduate* is an infinitive that can serve as the subject of the sentence.]

| INCORRECT | I need take vacation. |

[There is already a verb, *need,* in the sentence, so there can't be another verb that shows the action of the subject, *I.*]

| CORRECT INFINITIVE: | I need *to take* a vacation. |

Articles

Articles announce a noun. English uses only three articles: *a, an,* and *the.* The same articles are used for both masculine and feminine nouns.

> **LANGUAGE NOTE:** Articles (*a, an, the*) are not used in Russian or in many Asian languages. If you are not sure when to use an article or which one to use, pay close attention to this section.

Using Definite and Indefinite Articles

The is a **definite article** and is used before a specific person, place, or thing. *A* and *an* are **indefinite articles** and are used with a person, place, or thing whose specific identity is not known.

| DEFINITE ARTICLE | *The* man knocked on *the* door. |

[A specific man knocked on a specific door.]

INDEFINITE ARTICLE   *A* man knocked on *a* door.

[Some man knocked on some door. We don't know what man or what door.]

DEFINITE ARTICLE   *The* hostess showed us to our seats.

INDEFINITE ARTICLE   *A* hostess showed us to our seats.

When the word following the article begins with a vowel (*a, e, i, o, u*), use *an* instead of *a*.

An energetic hostess showed us to our seats.

Using Articles with Count and Noncount Nouns

To use the correct article, you need to know what count and noncount nouns are. **Count nouns** name things that can be counted. **Noncount nouns** name things that cannot be counted.

COUNT NOUN   I sold ten of my old *CDs* on eBay.

NONCOUNT NOUN   I sold lots of *music* on eBay. [A *CD* can be counted; *music* cannot.]

Here are some examples of count and noncount nouns. This is just a brief list; all nouns in English are either count or noncount. To help determine if a noun is count or noncount, try adding *s*. Most count nouns form a plural by adding *s*; noncount nouns do not have plural forms.

COUNT	NONCOUNT		
apple/apples	advice	homework	rain
chair/chairs	beauty	honey	rice
dollar/dollars	equipment	information	salt
letter/letters	flour	jewelry	sand
smile/smiles	furniture	mail	spaghetti
tree/trees	grass	milk	sunlight
	grief	money	thunder
	happiness	postage	wealth
	health	poverty	

Articles with Count and Noncount Nouns

COUNT NOUNS	ARTICLE USED
SINGULAR **Specific →**	**the** I want to read *the book* on taxes that you recommended. [The sentence refers to one particular book — the one that was recommended.] I can't stay in *the sun* very long. [There is only one sun.]
Not specific →	**a** or **an** I want to read *a book* on taxes. [It could be any book on taxes.]
PLURAL **Specific →**	**the** I enjoyed *the books* we read. [The sentence refers to a particular group of books — the ones we read.]
Not specific →	**no article** or **some** I usually enjoy *books*. [The sentence refers to books in general.] She found *some books*. [We do not know which books she found.]

NONCOUNT NOUNS	ARTICLE USED
SINGULAR **Specific →**	**the** My son ate all *the food* we bought. [The sentence refers to particular food — the food we bought.]
Not specific →	**no article** or **some** There is *food* all over the kitchen. [The reader does not know what food the sentence refers to.] Give *some food* to the neighbors. [The sentence refers to an indefinite quantity of food.]

Prepositions

A **preposition** is a word (such as *of, above, between, about*) that connects a noun, pronoun, or verb with other information about it. The correct preposition to use is often determined by idiom or common practice rather than by the preposition's actual meaning.

An **idiom** is any combination of words that is always used the same way, even though there is no logical or grammatical explanation for it. The best way to learn English idioms is to listen and read as much as possible and then to practice writing and speaking the correct forms.

For more on prepositions, see Chapter 22. For a list of prepositions, see page 387.

Prepositions after Adjectives

Certain prepositions often come after certain adjectives. Here are some common examples:

afraid of	full of	responsible for
ashamed of	happy about	scared of
aware of	interested in	sorry about/sorry for
confused by	nervous about	tired of
embarrassed about	proud of	worried about
excited about	reminded of	

about
Tanya is excited ~~of~~ going to Mexico.

of
However, she is afraid ~~by~~ taking time off.

Prepositions after Verbs

Many verbs in English consist of a verb plus a preposition (or an adverb). The meaning of these combinations is not usually the literal meaning the verb and the preposition would each have on its own. Often, the meaning of the verb changes completely depending on which preposition is used with it.

You must *take out* the trash.   [*take out* = bring to a different location]

You must *take in* the exciting sights of New York City.   [*take in* = observe]

Here are a few common examples:

call in (telephone)	You can *call in* your order.
call off (cancel)	They *called off* the pool party.
call on (choose)	The teacher always *calls on* me.
drop in (visit)	*Drop in* when you are in the area.
drop off (leave behind)	Cherry will *drop off* the car.
drop out (quit)	Too many students *drop out* of school.
fight against (combat)	He tried to *fight against* the proposal.
fight for (defend)	We need to *fight for* our rights.
fill in (refill)	Please *fill in* the holes in the ground.
fill out (complete)	Please *fill out* this application form.
fill up (make something full)	Don't *fill up* with junk food.
find out (discover)	Did you *find out* what happened?
give up (forfeit)	Don't *give up* your place in line.
go over (review)	He wants to *go over* our speeches.
grow up (mature)	All children *grow up*.
hand in (submit)	You may *hand in* your homework now.
lock up (secure)	Don't forget to *lock up* before you go to bed.
look up (check)	I *looked up* the word in the dictionary.
pick out (choose)	Sandy *picked out* a puppy.
pick up (take or collect)	When do you *pick up* the keys?
put off (postpone)	I often *put off* doing dishes.
sign in (register, leaving name)	I have to *sign in* to work.
sign out (borrow, leaving name)	I want to *sign out* a book.
sign up (register for)	Cressia *signed up* for three classes.
think about (consider)	Patsy sometimes *thinks about* moving.
turn in (submit)	Please *turn in* your homework now.

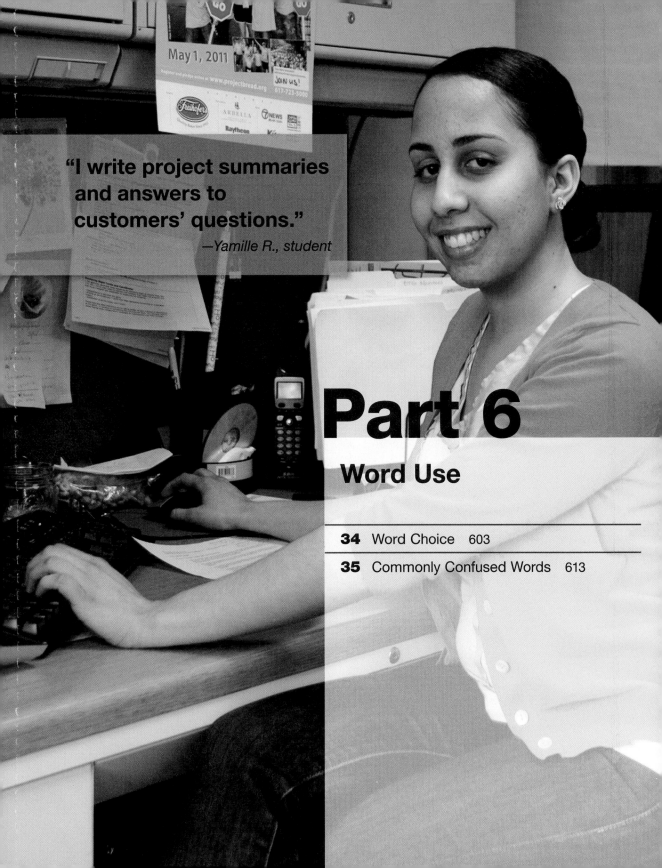

May 1, 2011

"I write project summaries and answers to customers' questions."

—Yamille R., student

Part 6
Word Use

34

Word Choice

Avoiding Language Pitfalls

Understand the Importance of Choosing Words Carefully

In conversation, much of your meaning is conveyed by your facial expression, your tone of voice, and your gestures. In writing, you have only the words on the page to make your point, so you must choose them carefully. If you use vague or inappropriate words, your readers may not understand you. Carefully chosen, precise words tell your readers exactly what you mean.

Two resources will help you find the best words for your meaning—a dictionary and a thesaurus. Both of these reference works are available in print and online forms.

IDEA JOURNAL
Describe your working habits.

Dictionary

A dictionary provides all kinds of useful information about words—spelling, division of words into syllables, pronunciation, parts of speech, other forms of words, definitions, and examples of use.

ESL students can use a dictionary written especially for nonnative speakers (such as the *Longman Dictionary of American English*) in addition to a standard English dictionary.

The following is a part of a dictionary entry:

Spelling and
end-of-line
division   Pronunciation   Parts of
                                                                        speech

Other forms ———

Definition ———

Example ———

con • crete (kon´ krēt, kong´- krēt, kon krēt´, kong- kret´), *adj., n., v.*
-cret • ed, -cret • ing, *adj.* **1.** constituting an actual thing or instance;
real; perceptible; substantial: *concrete proof.* **2.** pertaining to or concerned
with realities or actual instances rather than abstractions; particular as
opposed to general: *concrete proposals.* **3.** referring to an actual substance
or thing, as opposed to an abstract quality: The words *cat, water,* and
teacher are concrete, whereas the words *truth, excellence,* and *adulthood*
are abstract. . . .

—*Random House Webster's College
Dictionary*

Thesaurus

To look up words in
both the dictionary
and the thesaurus,
visit Merriam-Webster
Online at www.m-w
.com.

A thesaurus gives *synonyms* (words that have the same meaning) for the
words you look up. Use a thesaurus when you cannot find the right word
for what you mean or to avoid repeating the same word too often.

Concrete, *adj.* 1. Particular, specific, single, certain, special, unique,
sole, peculiar, individual, separate, isolated, distinct, exact, precise,
direct, strict, minute; definite, plain, evident, obvious; pointed,
emphasized; restrictive, limiting, limited, well-defined, clear-cut, fixed,
finite; determining, conclusive, decided.

—J. I. Rodale, *The Synonym
Finder*

Practice Avoiding Four Common
Word-Choice Problems

Four common problems with word choice can make it difficult for readers
to understand your point. You can avoid them by using specific words
that fit your meaning and make your writing clearer.

LANGUAGE NOTE: Make sure to use the right kinds of words—nouns to name a person, place, or thing; adjectives to describe nouns; adverbs to describe adjectives or other adverbs.

                            N

INCORRECT   Tyra seems *sadness.*

[*Sadness* is a noun. The kind of word needed to modify the noun, *Tyra, is an* adjective.]

                           ADJ

CORRECT   Tyra seems *sad.*

Vague and Abstract Words

Your words need to create a clear picture for your readers. **Vague and abstract words** are too general to make an impression. Here are some common vague and abstract words.

Vague and Abstract Words

a lot	dumb	OK (okay)	stuff
awesome	good	old	thing
awful	great	person	very
bad	happy	pretty	whatever
beautiful	house	sad	young
big	job	school	
car	nice	small	

TEAMWORK
Form groups, assign each group a column of words, and have them come up with more specific words to replace the words that you've given them.

When you see one of these words or another general word in your writing, try to replace it with a concrete or more specific word. A **concrete word** names something that can be seen, heard, felt, tasted, or smelled. A **specific word** names a particular individual or quality. Compare these two sentences:

TEACHING TIP
Encourage students to look up in a dictionary words that they find in the thesaurus. Remind students that not all thesaurus words are interchangeable. Model specific examples of this problem for the class.

VAGUE AND ABSTRACT	It was a beautiful day.
CONCRETE AND SPECIFIC	The sky was a bright, cloudless blue; the sun was shimmering; and the temperature was a perfect 78 degrees.

The first version is too general to be interesting. The second version creates a clear, strong image.

Some words are so vague that it is best to avoid them altogether.

VAGUE AND ABSTRACT   It's like *whatever*.

[This sentence is neither concrete nor specific.]

Slang

For practice with word choice, visit *Exercise Central* at bedfordstmartins .com/realessays.

Slang, the informal and casual language shared by a particular group, should be used only in informal and casual situations. Avoid it when you write, especially for college classes or at work. Use language that is appropriate for your audience and purpose.

SLANG	EDITED
I'm going to *chill* at home.	I'm going to relax at home.
I *dumped* Destina.	I ended my relationship with Destina.
I've been working *crazy* hard on my research project.	I've been working extremely hard on my research project.

If you are not sure if a word is slang, check an online source, such as **slangsite.com** or **manythings.org/slang**.

Wordy Language

RESOURCES
To gauge students' skills in word choice, use the *Testing Tool Kit* CD available with this book.

Sometimes people think that using more words or using big words will make them sound smart and important. But using too many words in a piece of writing can obscure or weaken the point.

Wordy language includes phrases that contain too many words, unnecessarily modify a statement, or use slightly different words without adding any new ideas. It also includes overblown language—unnecessarily complicated words and phrases that are often used to make the writer or writing sound important.

WORDY   We have no openings *at this point in time*.

EDITED   We have no openings now.

[The phrase *at this point in time* uses five words to express what could be said in one word—*now*.]

WORDY   *In the opinion of this writer*, tuition is too high.

EDITED   Tuition is too high.

[The qualifying phrase *in the opinion of this writer* is not necessary and weakens the statement.]

WORDY   In our advertising, we will *utilize* the *superlative photographic images* of ArtSense.

EDITED   Our advertising will use ArtSense photographs.

[The words *utilize* and *superlative photographic images* are overblown.]

Common Wordy Expressions

WORDY	EDITED
A great number of	Many
A large number of	Many
As a result of	Because
At that time	Then
At the conclusion of	At the end
At this point in time	Now
Due to the fact that	Because
In order to	To
In spite of the fact that	Although
In the event that	If
In this day and age	Now
In this paper I will show that	(Just make the point; don't announce it.)
It is my opinion that	I think (or just make the point)
The fact of the matter is that	(Just state the point.)

Clichés

Clichés are phrases used so often that people no longer pay attention to them. To get your point across and to get your readers' attention, replace clichés with fresh language that precisely expresses your meaning.

CLICHÉS	EDITED
Passing the state police exam is no *walk in the park*.	Passing the state police exam requires careful preparation.
I was *sweating bullets* until the grades were posted.	I was anxious until the grades were posted.

COMMON CLICHÉS	
as big as a house	last but not least
as hard as a rock	more trouble than it's worth
as light as a feather	no way on earth
best/worst of times	110 percent
better late than never	playing with fire
break the ice	spoiled brat
climb the corporate ladder	spoiled rotten
crystal clear	starting from scratch
drop in the bucket	sweating blood/bullets
easier said than done	24/7
hell on earth	work like a dog

There are hundreds of clichés. To check if you have used a cliché, go to **clichesite.com.**

Edit Paragraphs and Your Own Writing

Edit the following paragraphs for vague and abstract language, slang, wordiness, or clichés, referring to the chart on page 612 as you need to. *Answers will vary. Possible edits shown.*

....

EDITING REVIEW 1 (24 possible edits)

RESOURCES
For cumulative Editing
Review Tests, see
pages 667–83.

(1) Although people don't hear much about hobos in ~~this day and~~ *these days* ~~age~~ of tightly sealed boxcars, there was a time not long ago when hobos were a distinct segment of American culture. (2) Even then, however, few knew the ~~handles~~ *names* of any hobos. (3) But to those who followed such social currents, there was one hobo who ~~stood above the crowd~~ *stood out*—Steam Train Maury. (4) By the time he ~~hung up his spurs~~ *retired* from his hobo wanderings, he was crowned the king of the hobos five times, and eventually he achieved the status of Grand Patriarch of the Hobos.

(5) ~~Hailing from~~ *Born in* Kansas in 1917 as Maurice W. Graham, Steam Train Maury was the product of a troubled family. (6) He spent much of his youth shifting ~~from here to there~~ *among parents and various relatives*. (7) In 1931, at the age of fourteen, he jumped on a train and ~~at this point in time he~~ began his first time as a hobo. (8) After ~~riding the rails and bouncing about~~ *hopping on trains and wandering* for several years, he became a cement mason, operated his own school for masons in Toledo, Ohio, and later served as a medical technician during World War II. (9) By 1971, he ~~hooked up with a wife~~ *had married* and had two children, but he also developed hip problems and was unable to work much, and he became dissatisfied with his life. (10) Now fifty-four, he hopped on a freight train ~~with the vague intention and confused impression that~~ *thinking* he'd just relive his hobo life for a few weeks and then return home. (11) Those two weeks ~~morphed~~ *turned* into ten years during which Steam Train Maury became a hobo legend. (12) By 1981, Mr. Graham had cowritten a book about his ~~sometimes exciting, sometimes boring, and sometimes frightening~~ *eventful* life as a hobo, helped to found the Hobo Foundation, and took part in establishing the Hobo Museum in Britt, Iowa. (13) At the *annual* National Hobo Convention held in Britt, ~~which was celebrated every single year,~~ he was named the hobo king in 1973, 1975, 1976, 1978, and 1981. (14) In 2004, he was crowned as the Grand Patriarch of the Hobos, ~~a title so prized that he was~~ the only person ever to have won ~~it.~~ *that title*.

(15) Hobos have been hopping trains for free rides ever since the Civil War, when wandering field workers and laborers ~~took a significant and some say vital role in building~~ *helped to build* the American West. (16) ~~Later,~~ *Toward the end of the nineteenth century,* some hobos, as a joke, named themselves "Tourist Union Local 63." (17) In 1900, ~~the big shots~~ *officials* from Britt, Iowa, offered their town for Local 63's hobo convention. (18) In the following decades, Britt became known as the "hobo town," and by 1933, it was widely publicizing its four-day

hobo convention and drawing tens of thousands to the ~~several widely~~ *festivities.* ^ ~~varied events that were created just for the occasion.~~ (19) This was during the Great Depression, when more than a million people were sneaking onto trains in a ~~no-win~~ *desperate* search for work.

(20) Mr. Graham always emphasized ~~a gussied-up~~ *an idealized* view of the hobo existence, the perspective that moved author John Steinbeck to call hobos "the last free men." (21) ~~One of the typical and often-repeated~~ *Typical* ~~examples~~ of Mr. Graham's stories was that of a character called the Pennsylvania Kid, who shaved with a piece of glass from a Coke bottle. (22) When asked if it was true that some hobos used deodorant, Mr. Graham ~~cracked~~ *commented* that it was a shame but he didn't know what to do about it. (23) Steam Train Maury ~~croaked~~ *died* of a stroke in 2006 at the age of eighty-nine. (24) ~~Making a fitting and appropriate use of~~ *Using* the hobos' term for death, he had "taken the westbound."

···

EDITING REVIEW 2 (22 possible edits)

(1) Do humans have ~~a thing or two~~ *something* to learn from honeybees? (2) A research study suggests that these hard-working insects may be ~~hotshots~~ *experts* at decision making. (3) This becomes evident when a hive of honeybees ~~keeps growing and growing so much~~ *becomes so large* that it eventually outgrows its home. (4) When that happens, the old queen ~~shoves off,~~ *flies away,* accompanied by a swarm of about 10,000 bees. (5) Their challenge ~~at this critical and decisive moment~~ *then* is to find the best possible location for the new hive. (6) According to the study, the bees, ~~in the vast majority of cases in~~ *almost always* ~~which this happens,~~ end up making good decisions.

(7) How do they ~~swing~~ *manage* that? (8) Do they ~~in one way or another~~ *somehow* vote or have a method of coming to a consensus? (9) ~~As a means of~~ *To find out,* ~~discerning the answer to this,~~ the researchers conducted several experiments as they observed the honeybees making their decision. (10) While

the swarm ~~took a breather~~ *waited,* huddling together on a tree branch, scout
bees searched for suitable locations. (11) As the scout bees ~~wended their~~ *returned,*
~~way back,~~ each scout did a waggle dance to highlight what she had
found. (12) Apparently, during this process, some scouts ~~flip flopped~~ *changed their minds*
and ended up dancing to support other scouts' finds. (13) The research-
ers concluded that the swarm doesn't wait for ~~each and every one of~~ *all* the
scouts to settle on one location. (14) Instead, the swarm senses when
~~a sufficient and satisfactory number of~~ *enough* scouts, perhaps fifteen or twenty,
have agreed on one site. (15) At that point, the entire swarm gets ready
to ~~make their move.~~ *go.* (16) For ~~an approximate period of~~ *about* an hour, the
bees warm up their flight muscles, and during this time, the remaining
scouts usually decide to support the chosen site. (17) In this way, a solid
consensus is achieved, and, in most cases, it is the ~~coolest~~ *best* possible location for the new hive.
        (18) ~~As a result of these experiments, the~~ *The* researchers note that the
bees' process works because it makes sense. (19) ~~The inside story~~ *Information* is
brought to the group by independent individuals. (20) In the free
marketplace of waggle dancing, they openly ~~chew the fat over it~~ *confer* and
eventually arrive at a mutual decision. (21) ~~The fact of the matter is that~~ *It*
~~it~~ is almost always the right decision. (22) Are humans capable of
~~pulling this off?~~ *doing this?*

....

PRACTICE   Editing Your Own Writing for Word Choice

As a final practice, edit a piece of your own writing for word choice. It can be
a paper you are working on for this course, a paper you have already finished,
a paper for another course, a recent piece of writing from your work or everyday life, or your idea journal entry. You may want to use the following chart as
you edit.

....

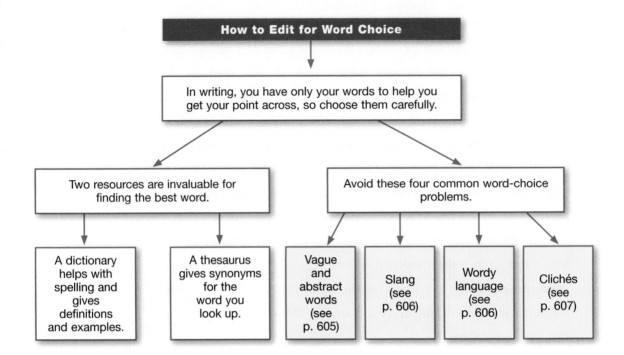

How to Edit for Word Choice

In writing, you have only your words to help you get your point across, so choose them carefully.

Two resources are invaluable for finding the best word.

Avoid these four common word-choice problems.

A dictionary helps with spelling and gives definitions and examples.

A thesaurus gives synonyms for the word you look up.

Vague and abstract words (see p. 605)

Slang (see p. 606)

Wordy language (see p. 606)

Clichés (see p. 607)

35

Commonly Confused Words

Avoiding Mistakes with Sound-Alikes

Understand Why Certain Words Are Commonly Confused

Certain words in English are confusing because they sound alike and may have similar meanings. In writing, words that sound alike may be spelled differently, and readers rely on the spelling to understand what you mean. Edit your writing carefully to make sure that you have used the correct words.

IDEA JOURNAL
Write about something you and a friend or family member disagree about. Explain your friend's opinion as well as your own.

For a list of commonly misspelled words and spelling strategies, visit **bedford stmartins.com/ realessays**.

Practice Using Commonly Confused Words Correctly

Study the different meanings and spellings of these twenty-seven sets of commonly confused words. Complete the sentence after each set of words, filling in each blank with the correct word.

A / An / And

a: used before a word that begins with a consonant sound

an: used before a word that begins with a vowel sound

and: used to join two words

TEACHING TIP
Have students read the sentences in this section aloud so that they can focus on differences in pronunciation. Encourage them to exaggerate the pronunciation of words that do not sound exactly alike.

A friend *and* I got lost in *an* old maze.

Most classrooms have ___*a*___ worn-out chair ___*and*___ ___*an*___ old desk for the teacher.

Accept / Except

accept: to agree to receive or admit (verb)

except: but, other than (conjunction)

I *accept* all your requests *except* the one to borrow my car.

Do not ___*accept*___ anything from people at airports ___*except*___ from family members.

Advice / Advise

advice: opinion (noun)

advise: to give an opinion (verb)

Please *advise* me what to do; your *advice* is always helpful.

___*Advise*___ me of your plans, particularly if you don't follow my ___*advice*___.

Affect / Effect

affect: to have an impact on, to change something (verb)

effect: a result (noun)

The sunny weather has had a positive *effect* on people's moods, but it will negatively *affect* the economy.

Since this year's drought will ___*affect*___ the cost of food, we'll be feeling its ___*effect*___ personally.

Are / Our

are: a form of the verb *be*

our: a pronoun showing ownership

Gardens *are* rare in *our* neighborhood.

___*Our*___ bulbs ___*are*___ arriving this week.

By / Buy

by: next to or before

buy: to purchase (verb)

By the time I'm ready to leave the dollar store, I have found too much I want to *buy.*

I have decided to ___*buy*___ the model ___*by*___ the showroom entrance.

Conscience / Conscious

conscience: a personal sense of right and wrong (noun)

conscious: awake, aware (adjective)

Danny made a *conscious* decision to listen to his *conscience.*

The burglar was _*conscious*_ that someone else was in the house and for

a moment felt a twinge of _*conscience*_.

Remember that one of the words is *con-science*; the other is not.

Fine / Find

fine: of high quality (adjective); feeling well (adverb); a penalty for breaking a law (noun)

find: to locate, discover (verb)

You will *find* a *fine* leather jacket in the coat department.

A ___*fine*___ partner is hard to ___*find*___.

Some commonly confused words — such as *conscience* and *conscious*, *loose* and *lose*, and *of* and *have* — sound similar but not exactly alike. To avoid confusing these words, practice pronouncing them correctly.

Its / It's

its: a pronoun showing ownership

it's: a contraction of the words *it is*

It's amazing to see a butterfly come out of *its* cocoon.

___*It's*___ good news for us that the bus changed ___*its*___ route.

If you are not sure whether to use *its* or *it's* in a sentence, try substituting *it is*. If the sentence does not make sense with *it is*, use *its*.

Knew / New / Know / No

knew: understood; recognized (past tense of the verb *know*)

new: unused, recent (adjective)

know: to understand, to have knowledge of (verb)

no: used to form a negative

I *knew* that Jason would need *new* shoes.

The ___*new*___ employee already ___*knew*___ some of the other employees.

There is *no* way to *know* what will happen.

Do you ___*know*___ what ___*"no"*___ means?

Loose / Lose

loose: baggy, not fixed in place (adjective)

lose: to misplace, to forfeit possession of (verb)

If the muffler is *loose,* you might *lose* it.

You will ____*lose*____ that bracelet if it's too ____*loose*____ .

Mind / Mine

mind: to object to (verb); the thinking or feeling part of one's brain (noun)

mine: belonging to me (pronoun); a source of ore and minerals (noun)

Keep in *mind* that the sweater is *mine.*

Your ____*mind*____ is a lot sharper than ____*mine*____ .

Of / Have

Do not use *of* after *would, should, could,* and *might.* Use *have* after those words.

of: coming from; caused by; part of a group; made from (preposition)

have: to possess (verb; also used as a helping verb)

I would *have* helped if you had told me you were out *of* change.

Joe might ____*have*____ been part ____*of*____ the band.

Passed / Past

passed: went by or went ahead (past tense of the verb *pass*)

past: time that has gone by (noun); gone by, over, just beyond (preposition)

This *past* school year, I *passed* all of my exams.

If you go ____*past*____ the church, you have ____*passed*____ the right turn.

Peace / Piece

peace: no disagreement; calm

piece: a part of something larger

We will have no *peace* until we give the dog a *piece* of that bread.

Selling his ____*piece*____ of land will give Uncle Joe ____*peace*____ of mind.

Principal / Principle

principal: main or chief (adjective); head of a school or a leader of an organization (noun)

principle: a standard of beliefs or behaviors (noun)

The *principle* at stake is the *principal* issue of the court case.

The _principal_ problem with many criminals is that they do not have good _principles_.

Quiet / Quite / Quit

quiet: soft in sound; not noisy (adjective)

quite: completely, very (adverb)

quit: to stop (verb)

It is not *quite* time to *quit* yet.

The machine ___quit___ running, and the office was ___quiet___.

Right / Write

right: correct; in a direction opposite from left (adjective)

write: to put words on paper (verb)

Please be sure to *write* the *right* address.

___Write___ your name in the ___right___ column.

Set / Sit

set: a collection of something (noun); to place an object somewhere (verb)

sit: to rest with one's rear end supported by a chair or other surface

Set your coat down before you *sit.*

Let's ___sit___ and look over my ___set___ of travel photos.

Suppose / Supposed

suppose: to imagine or assume to be true

supposed: past tense of *suppose;* intended

You are *supposed* to call when you are going to be late, but I *suppose* that's too much to expect.

I was _supposed_ to take the ten o'clock train, but I _suppose_ the eleven o'clock is okay.

Than / Then

than: a word used to compare two or more things or persons

then: at a certain time

I weigh a lot more *than* I used to back *then*.

If you want to lose weight, ___then___ you will have to eat less ___than___ you do now.

Their / There / They're

If you are not sure whether to use *their* or *they're*, substitute *they are*. If the sentence does not make sense, use *their*.

their: a pronoun showing ownership

there: a word indicating location or existence

they're: a contraction of the words *they are*

Their windows are open, and *there* is a breeze, so *they're* not hot.

___They're___ going to be away, so my friend will be staying ___there___ and

taking care of ___their___ cat.

Though / Through / Threw

though: however; nevertheless; in spite of (conjunction)

through: finished with (adjective); from one side to the other (preposition)

threw: hurled, tossed (past tense of the verb *throw*)

Jimmy *threw* the ball, and it went *through* the window, *though* he had not aimed it there.

___Though___ Amanda loved the shoes, she ___threw___ them out because

she could not go ___through___ any more foot pain.

To / Too / Two

to: a word indicating a direction or movement (preposition); part of the infinitive form of a verb

too: also; more than enough; very (adverb)

two: the number between one and three

They went *to* a restaurant and ordered *too* much food for *two* people.

The ___two___ friends started ___to___ dance, but it was ___too___ crowded to move.

Use / Used

use: to employ or put into service (verb)

used: past tense of the verb *use*. *Used to* can indicate a past fact or state, or it can mean "familiar with."

Paolo *used* to be a farmer, so he knows how to *use* all the equipment.

When you last ___*used*___ the oven, what did you ___*use*___ it for?

Who's / Whose

who's: a contraction of the words *who is* or *who has*

whose: a pronoun showing ownership

The person *whose* name is first on the list is the one *who's* going next.

___*Who's*___ the man ___*whose*___ shoes are on the table?

> If you are not sure whether to use *whose* or *who's*, substitute *who is*. If the sentence does not make sense, use *whose*.

Your / You're

your: a pronoun showing ownership

you're: a contraction of the words *you are*

You're about to get paint all over *your* hands.

___*Your*___ teacher says ___*you're*___ always late to class.

> If you are not sure whether to use *your* or *you're*, substitute *you are*. If the sentence does not make sense, use *your*.

Edit Paragraphs and Your Own Writing

Edit the following paragraphs for commonly confused words.

....

EDITING REVIEW 1 (18 errors)

(1) Most people ~~no~~ *know* that Americans love to drive ~~there~~ *their* cars.
(2) However, many people may not be ~~conscience~~ *conscious* of how much the government does to support our car culture. (3) For instance, the United States would never ~~of~~ *have* had so many good highways without federal and state assistance for road construction and maintenance.
(4) New highways are usually paid for mainly ~~buy~~ *by* tax money. (5) It is

RESOURCES
For cumulative Editing Review Tests, see pages 667–83.

to
rare for a new road ~~too~~ be paid for with tolls, which would come

exclusively from the people driving on it. (6) Americans also expect
their   *write*
~~they're~~ roads to be well maintained, and they may ~~right~~ to their repre-

sentatives to complain about aging road surfaces. (7) The government
                                        than
even keeps gas prices lower here ~~then~~ in most other nations.
                        mind
    (8) Few people ~~mine~~ that the government assists drivers in these
                                it's
ways. (9) Some would argue that ~~its~~ a government's job to help pay for

transportation. (10) However, other forms of transportation in this
                        passed
country are often ~~past~~ over when Congress hands out funds. (11) Am-
                                lose
trak, the U.S. railroad, may soon ~~loose~~ virtually all government funds,
                                                            its
even though many government officials are skeptical of ~~it's~~ ability to
                                                Except
keep operating without government assistance. (12) ~~Accept~~ for a few

places like New York and San Francisco, most U.S. cities do not have
                                        whose
good mass transit systems. (13) Americans ~~who's~~ travels have taken

them to certain parts of the world praise the national train systems and

city transit systems they find there. (14) As traffic gets worse in our na-
                                                find
tion's urban and suburban areas, some people ~~fine~~ it odd that the

United States does not invest more in transportation that would allow
                        their
people to leave ~~there~~ cars at home.

· ·

EDITING REVIEW 2 (14 errors)

                our
    (1) Hoping to keep ~~are~~ nation's blood supply safe, the U.S. govern-
                                                        who's
ment has placed restrictions on donating blood. (2) Anyone ~~whose~~ spent

more than five years in Europe or more than three months in England

since 1980 is not allowed to give blood. (3) Officials hope that asking
                                find   *have*
about time in Europe will help them ~~fine~~ people who might ~~of~~ been

exposed to mad cow disease. (4) Men are also asked whether they have
                                        past
had sexual relations with other men in the ~~passed~~ ten years. (5) If they
        they're   *supposed*
have, ~~their~~ asked not to give blood. (6) This is ~~suppose~~ to protect the

blood supply from the AIDS virus. (7) Of course, ~~they're~~ *there* are some prob-

lems with these restrictions. (8) First, ~~know~~ *no* one knows how much

exposure to infected meat can give a person mad cow disease, and ~~know~~ *no*

one is sure how long the disease can hide in a human body. (9) Second,

many gay men ~~our~~ *are* not infected with HIV, and many women, who are

not asked about sexual activity, are infected. (10) Restricting certain

groups of people from giving blood may not do anything to protect the

blood supply, but it will certainly ~~effect~~ *affect* the amount of blood available.

(11) Is it better to allow the blood supply to become dangerously low

~~then~~ *than* to allow people ~~who's~~ *whose* blood might carry a disease to donate blood?

· ·

**PRACTICE   Editing Your Own Writing
for Commonly Confused Words**

As a final practice, edit a piece of your own writing for commonly confused
words. It can be a paper you are working on for this course, a paper you have
already finished, a paper for another course, a recent piece of writing from
your work or everyday life, or your idea journal entry. Add any misused words
you find to your personal list of confusing words.

· ·

"I write short stories."

—Elijah M., student

Part 7

Punctuation and Capitalization

36

Commas (,)

Understand What Commas Do

Commas (,) are punctuation marks that help readers understand a sentence by introducing a pause at key points. Read aloud the following three sentences. How does the use of commas change the meaning?

NO COMMA   After you call Jim I'll leave for the restaurant.

ONE COMMA   After you call Jim, I'll leave for the restaurant.

TWO COMMAS   After you call, Jim, I'll leave for the restaurant.

Commas signal particular meanings to your readers, so it is important that you understand when and how to use them.

IDEA JOURNAL
Write about some things you enjoy doing.

TEACHING TIP
Have a student read these sentences aloud, and ask the class to tell how they differ.

Practice Using Commas Correctly

Commas between Items in a Series

Use commas to separate three or more items in a series. This includes the last item in the series, which usually has *and* before it.

item , item , item , and item

When you go to the store, please pick up *milk, bread, orange juice,* and *bananas.*

Last semester I took *math, reading,* and *composition.*

Students may take the course as a *regular classroom course,* as an *online course,* or as a *distance learning course.*

A comma is not always used before the final item in a series. In college writing, however, it is always best to include it.

Commas between Coordinate Adjectives

Coordinate adjectives are two or more adjectives that independently modify the same noun and are separated by commas. Coordinate adjectives can be separated by the word *and.*

We had an entire month of *cold, damp, grey* weather.

The car is *old, battered,* and *rusty.*

Do *not* use a comma between the final adjective and the noun it modifies.

INCORRECT	It was a *long, hard, complicated,* test.
CORRECT	It was a *long, hard, complicated* test.

Cumulative adjectives modify the same noun but form a unit and are not separated by commas. Cumulative adjectives cannot be joined by the word *and.*

Our team wants to win the *big regional sales* trophy.

All of the words in italics are adjectives, but they build on each other. Moving left from *trophy,* each adjective becomes part of a larger unit.

1. *Sales* describes the trophy.
2. The next word to the left, *regional,* describes not just the trophy but the *sales* trophy.
3. The next word to the left, *big,* describes the *regional sales* trophy.

The team did not want to win just a *big* trophy or just a *regional* trophy or just a *sales* trophy. The team wanted the *big regional sales* trophy.

To summarize the rule: Use a comma to separate two or more coordinate adjectives. Do not use commas to separate cumulative adjectives.

PRACTICE 1   Using Commas in a Series and with Adjectives

Add commas where they are needed in the following sentences. If the sentence is correct, write "C" next to it.

> **EXAMPLE:** The short, slim conductor stepped up to the elaborate, colorful podium.

1. We had prepared a wholesome, flavorful meal for the children, their parents, and their friends.

2. Lucas has painted three large pictures for the unfurnished, boring living room.

3. The huge, confusing, and annoying airport desperately needed renovating.

4. I have several urgent e-mail messages from Mr. Toland, Ms. Fry, and my father.

5. Our scholarly English professor was once a professional baseball player. C

6. She loves to take long, slow walks in the rain.

7. My peer editor posts comments on my paper before I leave for my session in the writing lab. C

8. Driving on this endless, dull, unsafe highway can be unpleasant.

9. The funny animated movie was based on a well-written graphic novel. C

10. We always buy rich, high-calorie candy bars when we go to the movies.

For more practice using commas, visit *Exercise Central* at bedfordstmartins .com/realessays.

RESOURCES
To gauge students' skills with comma usage, use the *Testing Tool Kit* CD available with this book.

Commas in Compound Sentences

A **compound sentence** contains two independent clauses (sentences) joined by one of these words—*and, but, for, nor, or, so, yet.* Use a comma before the joining word to separate the two clauses.

The words *and, but, for, nor, or, so,* and *yet* are called coordinating conjunctions. See Chapter 30 for more details.

Sentence **,** *and / but / for / nor / or / so / yet* sentence.

Tom missed class yesterday, *and* he texted me to ask what he missed.

I would have been happy to help him, *but* I was absent too.

I told him I wasn't there, *so* he said he would e-mail the professor.

A comma is not needed if the word *and, but, for, nor, or, so,* or *yet* joins two sentence elements that are not independent clauses.

> **LANGUAGE NOTE:** A comma by itself cannot separate two sentences: Doing so creates a run-on (see Chapter 24).

PRACTICE 2 Using Commas in Compound Sentences

Edit the following compound sentences by adding commas where they are needed. If a sentence is already correct, put a "C" next to it.

EXAMPLE: The U.S. population is getting older, but the number of

people trained to care for the elderly is declining.

1. Working in a nursing home is a difficult job, for elderly patients can seldom do much for themselves.

2. The labor is physically difficult, and it can also be mentally draining.

3. Few trained nurses and nurse's aides want nursing-home jobs, for the pay is also usually lower than that offered by hospitals.

4. Nursing-home workers have high turnover rates, and the facilities are constantly in need of new personnel.

5. More workers will be needed as the baby boomers become elderly, yet there is already a shortage of people willing to do the work.

6. A director sometimes must hire undertrained workers, or the nursing home will face a severe staff shortage.

7. Workers without education and training may have difficulty understanding a doctor's orders, so the patients' care may suffer. C

8. Home health aides and hospice workers are also in short supply, and the need for such workers is growing every day.

9. Solving these problems will be difficult, for long-term care for the elderly is already very expensive.

10. People caring for elderly patients must get better pay, or no one will be available to do the work in a few years.

Commas after Introductory Word Groups

Use a comma after an introductory word or word group. An introductory word group can be a word, a phrase, or a clause. The comma lets your readers know when the main part of the sentence is starting.

| Introductory word or word group | , | main part of sentence. |

INTRODUCTORY WORD   *Finally,* I finished the job.

INTRODUCTORY PHRASE   *According to the paper,* the crime rate went down.

INTRODUCTORY CLAUSE   *As you know,* the store is going out of business.

PRACTICE 3   **Using Commas after Introductory Word Groups**

In each item, underline any introductory word or word group. Then, add commas after introductory word groups where they are needed.

EXAMPLE: Every year, more than two hundred motorists die in collisions with animals.

1. Along roadsides all across the country, drivers see the bodies of animals hit by cars.

2. Usually, the victims are common species, such as deer and raccoons.

3. Of course, hitting a deer is not only disturbing but also potentially harmful or fatal to the occupants of a car.

4. However, the deer population has not suffered much of a decline from traffic accidents.

5. On the other hand, drivers in wilderness areas may accidentally kill endangered species.

6. For instance, experts believe that 65 percent of the population of Florida panthers has been killed on highways in the past twenty years.

7. Maintaining the world's largest network of roads, the U.S. Forest Service tries to balance the needs of humans and wildlife.

8. To get access to wilderness areas, humans, many of whom strongly favor protecting the environment, need roads.

9. Unfortunately, wilderness roads may isolate populations of animals that will not cross them and kill animals that make the attempt.

10. Although expensive, underpasses and overpasses have been successful in some areas at reducing human collisions with animals.

Commas around Appositives and Interrupters

For more on appositives, see pages 569–70.

An **appositive,** a phrase that renames a noun, comes directly before or after the noun.

> Dick, *my neighbor,* has a new job.
>
> Apartment prices are high at Riverview, *the new complex.*

An **interrupter** is an aside or transition that interrupts the flow of a sentence and does not affect its meaning.

> Campus parking fees, *you should know,* are going up by 30 percent.
>
> A six-month sticker will now be $75, *if you can believe it.*

An interrupter that appears at the beginning of a sentence can be treated the same as an introductory word group.

> *As a matter of fact,* the fees are the highest of any of the campuses in the city.

Putting commas around appositives and interrupters tells readers that these elements give extra information but are not essential to the meaning of a sentence. If an appositive or interrupter is in the middle of a sentence, set it off with a pair of commas, one before and one after. If an appositive or interrupter comes at the beginning or end of a sentence, separate it from the rest of the sentence with one comma.

Incidentally, your raise has been approved.

Your raise, *incidentally,* has been approved.

Your raise has been approved, *incidentally.*

Sometimes, an appositive is essential to the meaning of a sentence. When a sentence would not have the same meaning without the appositive, the appositive should not be set off with commas.

The actor *John Travolta* has never won an Academy Award.

[The sentence *The actor has never won an Academy Award* does not have the same meaning.]

The lawyer *Clarence Darrow* was one of history's greatest speakers.

[The sentence *The lawyer was one of history's greatest speakers* does not have the same meaning.]

. . . .

PRACTICE 4   Using Commas to Set Off Appositives and Interrupters

Underline any appositives or interrupters in the following sentences. Then use commas to set them off.

EXAMPLE: The reason for the delay, a mechanical problem with the airplane, was not mentioned.

1. Road rage, as most people know, occurs when angry drivers overreact.

2. Another phenomenon, air rage, involves out-of-control and often intoxicated passengers on an airplane.

3. One famous air rage incident, a confrontation between a drunken businessman and a flight attendant, ended with the passenger tied to his seat for the rest of the flight.

4. Ground rage, like air rage, is a term used for incidents between airline passengers and airline employees.

5. Ground rage, as the name suggests, occurs in the terminal, not in the air.

6. Gate agents, the people who check tickets and allow passengers to board the plane, are frequent victims of ground rage.

7. Oversold seats, a common occurrence in air travel, can mean that some passengers are forced to miss a flight.

8. Passengers, many of whom are on a tight schedule or have a connecting flight to catch, find delayed flights infuriating as well.

9. Some delayed or bumped passengers take out their anger on the gate agent, a convenient target.

10. Although some airline employees may not be helpful or friendly, their attitudes do not excuse passengers who commit assault, a serious crime.

Commas around Adjective Clauses

An **adjective clause** is a group of words that often begins with *who, which,* or *that;* has a subject and verb; and describes the noun that comes before it in a sentence. An adjective clause may or may not be set off from the rest of the sentence by commas depending on its meaning in the sentence.

If an adjective clause can be taken out of a sentence without completely changing the meaning, put commas around the clause.

The mayor, *who was recently elected,* has no political experience.

SuperShop, *which is the largest supermarket in town,* was recently bought by Big Boy Markets.

I have an appointment with Dr. Kling, *who is the specialist.*

If an adjective clause is essential to the meaning of a sentence, do not put commas around it. You can tell whether a clause is essential by taking it out and seeing if the meaning of the sentence changes significantly, as it would if you took the clauses out of the following examples:

The hair salon *that I liked* recently closed.

Salesclerks *who sell liquor to minors* are breaking the law.

| Noun | adjective clause essential to meaning | rest of sentence. |

| Noun , | adjective clause not essential to meaning , | rest of sentence. |

Use *who* to refer to a person; *which* to refer to places or things (but not to people); and *that* for people, places, or things. When referring to a person, *who* is preferable to *that*.

For more on adjective clauses, see page 572.

PRACTICE 5   Using Commas to Set Off Adjective Clauses

Edit the following sentences by putting any needed commas around adjective clauses. Remember that if an adjective clause is essential to the meaning of the sentence, you should not use commas. If a sentence is already correct, put a "C" next to it.

> **EXAMPLE:** Stephen King,who understands how to frighten his
>
> readers,has depicted evil clowns in his work.

1. The only thing that terrifies Maria is a person dressed as a clown. C

2. The fear of clowns, which is called *coulrophobia*, is fairly common.

3. Some young children who develop this fear are not prepared adequately before seeing a clown for the first time. C

4. Clowns, who usually wear heavy makeup and brightly colored wigs, do not look like ordinary people.

5. Clowns also make sudden movements that can frighten children. C

6. Most children who fear clowns will get over their phobia as they grow up. C

7. Such people, who may never love clowns, will still be able to tolerate having them around.

8. Many adults have seen movies that show clowns as evil killers. C

9. Few adults admit to having coulrophobia, which is most effectively treated when the sufferer confronts the fear.

10. Unlike some other phobias‚which can trap people in their homes or make them unable to work‚coulrophobia has little effect on most sufferers, who are not likely to meet clowns frequently in everyday life.

Other Uses for Commas

Commas with Quotation Marks

For more on quotation marks, see Chapter 38.

Quotation marks are used to show that you are using a direct quotation, repeating exactly what someone said or wrote. Generally, use commas to set off the words inside quotation marks from the rest of the sentence.

> "Excuse me‚" said the old woman in back of me. "Did you know‚" she asked‚ "that you just cut in front of me?"

> I exclaimed‚ "Oh, no. I'm so sorry!"

Notice that a comma never comes directly *after* a quotation mark.

Commas in Addresses

Use commas to separate the elements of an address included in a sentence. However, do not use a comma before a zip code.

> My address is 4498 Main Street‚ Bolton‚ Massachusetts 01740.

If a sentence continues after the address, put a comma after the address. Also, use a comma after individual elements used to name a geographical location such as a city and state.

> The house was moved from Cripple Creek‚ Colorado‚ to the lot on Forest Street.

Commas in Dates

Separate the day from the year with a comma. If you give only the month and year, do not separate them with a comma.

> She wrote the letter on April 1‚ 2009.

> The next session is in January 2011.

If a sentence continues after a date that includes the day, put a comma after the date.

> He waited until April 15, 2010, to file his 2008 tax return.

Commas with Names

Put commas around the name of someone you are addressing by name.

> Don, I want you to come look at this.
>
> Unfortunately, Marie, you need to finish the report by next week.

Commas with Yes or No

Put a comma after the word *yes* or *no* in response to a question.

> No, that isn't what I meant.
>
> [To express a strong emotion, an exclamation mark is sometimes used instead of a comma: *No! That is not what I meant.* A word or phrase that expresses emotion and stands alone (like *No!*) is called an interjection.]

- -

PRACTICE 6   Using Commas

Edit the following sentences by adding commas where they are needed. If a sentence is already correct, put a "C" next to it.

> **EXAMPLE:** Strict telemarketing laws took effect on April 1,2001.

1. My sister asked, "James, do you get a lot of telemarketing calls?"

2. "Yes, I do," I replied "and they always come at dinnertime."

3. She told me that I could add my name to a list of those people not wanting calls from telemarketers. C

4. I wrote to the governor's office in Albany, New York, for information about the telemarketing registry.

5. My address, which is 21 Highland Road, Binghamton, New York, has now been added to the state registry.

6. For a while, I still got occasional calls that began with an unfamiliar voice saying, "James, I have an exciting offer for you."

7. I simply replied, "No, I have news for you."

8. I pointed out that on August 11, 2010, I had added my name and address to a list of people who do not want to receive calls about exciting offers.

9. "As you probably know," I told my unwanted callers, "it is illegal for you to contact me in this way."

10. The marketing calls had stopped completely by November 1. C

· ·

RESOURCES
For cumulative Editing Review Tests, see pages 667–83.

Edit Paragraphs and Your Own Writing

Edit the following paragraphs by adding commas where they are needed.

· ·

EDITING REVIEW 1 (17 commas)

(1) Everyone who uses cleaning products at home has probably seen warning labels on those products, for most household cleaners contain harsh chemicals. (2) The warnings, which are required by law, are so common that many users probably ignore them. (3) However, all cleaning products should be used with care, and some of them can seriously injure children or anyone else who misuses them. (4) Drain cleaners, toilet bowl cleaners, and chlorine bleach can all cause serious damage to skin, eyes, and other sensitive tissue. (5) Glass cleaners can react with bleach to produce toxic fumes. (6) Alternative cleansers, nontoxic products that can be made from items in an average kitchen, are cheaper than brand-name cleaning products and usually work just as well. (7) For most cleaning jobs, a solution of vinegar and water or baking soda and water is effective. (8) A plunger can often fix a clogged drain as well as a drain cleaner can, and club soda cleans windows nicely. (9) As for air fresheners, one expert advises, "Open your windows." (10) Economy, efficiency, and safety are great reasons to choose homemade cleansers.

EDITING REVIEW 2 (39 commas)

(1) A few days ago, I received an e-mail that told a terrifying story.
(2) At a large discount store in Austin, Texas, a four-year-old girl had disappeared, and her mother had asked for the store employees' help in finding the child. (3) Thinking quickly, the employees locked all of the doors, posted an employee at every exit, and systematically searched the store. (4) The child, who was found in a bathroom, was safe, but half of her head had been shaved. (5) In addition, someone had changed her clothes, so it seemed obvious that an abductor had been trying to slip her out of the store unnoticed. (6) The e-mail message, which came from a distant acquaintance, ended by advising me, "Don't let your children out of your sight!"

(7) Later that day, I was talking to my neighbor, and I happened to mention the message. (8) She too had seen it, and the story had shocked her. (9) Something about the story made me suspicious, however, so I decided to do some Internet research. (10) I found a site that discussed urban legends, Internet hoaxes, and chain letters. (11) On the site, I discovered an exact copy of the e-mail I had received. (12) I also learned that my neighbor and I were not the first people to fall for this hoax, for Ann Landers had even printed a version of it years earlier. (13) When she learned that she had been fooled, she printed a retraction, a column explaining that the story was fictional. (14) A reader wrote to her and said, "Reminding people to be cautious is one thing. Scaring them is another."

(15) After doing the research, I felt better about the scary e-mail story, but I felt sad that we are so distrustful of one another. (16) Such stories can make us fear that potential abductors are everywhere.
(17) Thirty years ago, most parents were not usually afraid to let children walk to school alone or play outside, but today's parents rarely let

children out of their sight until the kids are in their teens. (18) The difference is not in the number of abductions of children, a very small number that has remained nearly constant over the decades. (19) No, the difference is that people now hear about these unusual and terrifying instances over and over. (20) Eventually, they reach the conclusion that these stories must be true, and they are convinced that such dreadful things must happen frequently. (21) The e-mail I had received was contributing, I decided, to this climate of irrational fear. (22) "Ann Landers's reader was right," I said to myself. (23) "We should teach our children caution, but we can harm them and ourselves by making them believe that evil strangers are lurking around every corner."

TEAMWORK
Put students in small groups, and give each group one paragraph to edit. Then, have a member of each group read the edited paragraph aloud.

PRACTICE 7   Editing Your Own Writing for Commas

As a final practice, edit a piece of your own writing for commas. It can be a paper you are working on for this course, a paper you have already finished, a paper for another course, a recent piece of writing from your work or everyday life, or your idea journal entry.

37

Apostrophes (')

Understand What Apostrophes Do

An **apostrophe (')** is a punctuation mark that either shows ownership (*Susan's*) or indicates that a letter has been intentionally left out to form a contraction (*I'm, that's, they're*). Although an apostrophe looks like a comma **(,)**, it is not used for the same purpose, and it is written higher on the line than commas are.

apostrophe**'**   comma**,**

IDEA JOURNAL
Write about some possessions that you and others in your family value.

Practice Using Apostrophes Correctly

Apostrophes to Show Ownership

- **Add 's to a singular noun to show ownership even if the noun already ends in s.**

  Darcy**'s** car is being repaired.

  Joan got all the information she needed from the hotel**'s** Web site.

To understand this chapter, you need to know what nouns and pronouns are. For a review, see Chapters 22, 27, and 33.

- **If a noun is plural and ends in *s*, just add an apostrophe to show ownership. If it is plural but does not end in *s*, add *'s*.**

  Seven boys' coats were left at the school.

  The children's toys were all broken.

- **The placement of an apostrophe makes a difference in meaning.**

  My neighbor's twelve cats are howling. [One neighbor who has twelve cats]

  My neighbors' twelve cats are howling. [Two or more neighbors who together have twelve cats]

TEACHING TIP
Tell students to be especially careful of using an apostrophe with a possessive pronoun. Have them discuss why this error is so common. What is it about words like *yours* and *ours* that seem to need an apostrophe?

- **Do not use an apostrophe to form the plural of a noun.**

  Use the stair's or the elevator.

- **Do not use an apostrophe with a possessive pronoun. These pronouns already show ownership (possession).**

  That basket is our's.

DISCUSSION
Ask students to brainstorm some sentences that include *its* and some that include *it's*. After discussing these sentences, have the students create a tip or two about *its* versus *it's* that they can use when editing their own papers.

Possessive Pronouns

my	his	its	their
mine	her	our	theirs
your	hers	ours	whose
yours			

Its *or* It's

The single most common error with apostrophes and pronouns is confusing *its* (a possessive pronoun) with *it's* (a contraction meaning "it is"). Whenever you write *it's*, test to see if it's correct by reading it aloud as *it is*.

. . . .

PRACTICE 1   Using Apostrophes to Show Ownership

Edit the following sentences by adding *'s* or an apostrophe alone to show ownership and by crossing out any incorrect use of an apostrophe or *'s*.

EXAMPLE: *Fevers*
Fever's are an important part of the human bodys *body's*

system of defense against infection.

1. A ~~thermometers~~ *thermometer's* indicator mark at 98.6 degrees is supposed to show a ~~persons~~ *person's* normal body temperature.

2. However, normal body temperature can range from 97 degrees to 100.4 degrees, so most ~~doctors~~ *doctors'* view of a temperature lower than 100.5 is that ~~its~~ *it's* not a fever at all.

3. ~~Fever's~~ *Fevers* help the body combat ~~virus's~~ *viruses* and stimulate the immune system.

4. Unless a ~~persons~~ *person's* temperature is raised by an outside source, the ~~bodys~~ *body's* regulatory system will not usually let a fever go higher than 106 degrees.

5. A ~~fevers~~ *fever's* appearance is not necessarily a reason to take fever-reducing ~~medication's~~ *medications*, which can lower a ~~bodys~~ *body's* temperature without doing anything to fight the infection.

6. Taking fever-reducing ~~drug's~~ *drugs* can actually make an illness take longer to run ~~it's~~ *its* course.

7. Many ~~doctors~~ *doctors* do not recommend using any drugs to treat a fever if ~~its~~ *it's* lower than 102 degrees.

8. Parents should know that ~~childrens~~ *children's* fevers can go higher than ~~their's~~ *theirs.*

9. Some ~~parents~~ *parents'* fears of fever are so intense that they suffer from "fever phobia" and overreact to their ~~childrens~~ *children's* symptoms.

10. Fever phobia can cause ~~parent's~~ *parents* to give their child extra medicine, but overdoses of ibuprofen and other fever reducers can impair the ~~livers~~ *liver's* ability to work properly and can therefore complicate the ~~childs~~ *child's* sickness.

For more practice with apostrophe usage, visit *Exercise Central* at bedfordstmartins .com/realessays.

Apostrophes in Contractions

A **contraction** is formed by joining two words and leaving out one or more of the letters. When writing a contraction, put an apostrophe where the letter or letters have been left out, not between the two words.

NOTE: In academic writing, contractions are rarely used.

I'll go when you come back. = *I will* go when you come back.

Be sure to put the apostrophe in the right place.

Don does'n't work here anymore.

Do not use contractions in papers or reports for college or work.

Common Contractions

aren't = are not	she'll = she will
can't = cannot	she's = she is, she has
couldn't = could not	there's = there is, there has
didn't = did not	they'd = they would, they had
doesn't = does not	they'll = they will
don't = do not	they're = they are
he'd = he would, he had	they've = they have
he'll = he will	who'd = who would, who had
he's = he is, he has	who'll = who will
I'd = I would, I had	who's = who is, who has
I'll = I will	won't = will not
I'm = I am	wouldn't = would not
I've = I have	you'd = you would, you had
isn't = is not	you'll = you will
it's = it is, it has	you're = you are
let's = let us	you've = you have
she'd = she would, she had	

LANGUAGE NOTE: Contractions that include a *be* verb cannot be followed by the base verb or the helping verbs *can, does,* or *has.*

INCORRECT   She's *work* late. Dan's *has* sick.

CORRECT   She's *working* late. Dan's sick.

. . . .

PRACTICE 2   Using Apostrophes in Contractions

Read each sentence carefully, looking for any words that have missing letters. Edit these words by adding apostrophes where needed. Or, if apostrophes are misplaced, cross out and correct the error.

It's
EXAMPLE: ~~Its~~ sadly true that some athletes will use performance-
^

enhancing drugs if they can get away with it.

they're
1. Those who do often say ~~theyre~~ using these drugs because their
^

competitors are probably using them too.

2. Performance-enhancing drugs help some athletes win competitions,
aren't
but for other athletes, these drugs ~~arent~~ enough to ensure victory.
^

3. Most athletes taking steroids and other substances say they
wouldn't
~~would'nt~~ use these drugs if they could be certain that their oppo-
^   *aren't*
nents ~~are'nt~~ using them.
Who'll ^
4. ~~Wholl~~ be the one to put a stop to this drug use?
^
don't   *who's*
5. If sports organizations ~~do'nt~~ eliminate drug use, we all know ~~whos~~
^   ^

the loser.
You're   *I'm*
6. ~~Youre~~ the loser, ~~Im~~ the loser, and all athletes are the losers.
^   ^
can't
7. When even one athlete gets away with using drugs, we ~~ca'nt~~ trust
^

that any athletic competition has been won fairly.
You've   *I've*
8. ~~Youve~~ got to take a stand, ~~Ive~~ got to take a stand, and anyone who
^   ^

believes in fairness has got to take a stand.
Let's
9. ~~Lets~~ eliminate performance-enhancing drugs now.
^   *aren't*
10. If we all ~~are'nt~~ ready to unite against drug use in sports, we might
^

as well change the word *athlete* to *actor*.

....

Apostrophes with Letters, Numbers, and Time

■ **Use 's to make letters and numbers plural. The apostrophe**
prevents confusion or misreading.

Mississippi has four i's.

In women's shoes, size 8's are more common than size 10's.

■ **Use an apostrophe or *'s* in certain expressions in which time nouns are treated as if they possess something.**

I get two weeks' vacation next year.

Last year's prices were very good.

. . . .

PRACTICE 3   **Using Apostrophes with Letters, Numbers, and Time**

Edit the following sentences by adding apostrophes where needed and fixing incorrectly used apostrophes.

> **EXAMPLE:** I just updated my blog by entering the last three ~~week's~~ *weeks'* worth of entries.

1. Next ~~months~~ *month's* schedule is less busy, so I think I'll be able to keep my blog current then.

2. Arthur's blog offers an entire ~~winters~~ *winter's* worth of detail on his social life.

3. His blog is a little hard to read because he always leaves out certain letters, such as ~~as~~ *a's*, ~~es~~ *e's*, and ~~os.~~ *o's.*

4. Katie's blog also gets confusing when she puts all of her ~~4s~~ *4's* and ~~8s~~ *8's* in Roman numerals.

5. When Manny's computer was stolen, he lost notes for his blog and two ~~year's~~ *years'* work on his novel.

. . . .

Edit Paragraphs and Your Own Writing

RESOURCES
For cumulative Editing
Review Tests, see
pages 667–83.

Edit the following paragraphs by adding apostrophes where needed and crossing out incorrectly used apostrophes. If a sentence is already correct, put a "C" after it.

EDITING REVIEW 1 (15 errors)

(1) Some of the first ~~discussion's~~ *discussions* of global warming focused attention on one of the gases that contributes to the greenhouse effect: methane. (2) Like other greenhouse gases, methane helps to keep the ~~earths'~~ *earth's* heat trapped in our atmosphere, and the temperature of the earth goes up as a result. (3) Humans ~~are'nt~~ *aren't* the only producers of methane; ~~its~~ *it's* also a by-product of ~~cow's~~ *cows'* digestion of their food. (4) For a while, many ~~Americans~~ *Americans'* knowledge of global warming ~~didnt~~ *didn't* go much further than cow jokes. (5) As ~~scientists'~~ *scientists* have become more convinced that global warming is real and a potential threat to ~~human's,~~ *humans,* our knowledge of the causes of the greenhouse effect has expanded. (6) Cows ~~arent~~ *aren't* completely off the hook, but ~~theyre~~ *they're* far less guilty of contributing to global warming than humans and cars are. (7) The amount of methane produced by ~~cows'~~ *cows* adds up to about 3 percent of the total amount of greenhouse gases produced by people. (8) Getting a cow to change ~~it's~~ *its* diet ~~wo'nt~~ *won't* solve the ~~worlds~~ *world's* warming problem.

EDITING REVIEW 2 (11 errors)

(1) In March of 2001, the keyless entry systems of cars in Bremerton, Washington, suddenly stopped working, and still no one knows why. *C* (2) The ~~cars~~ *cars'* locks were supposed to respond when their ~~owner's~~ *owners* pushed a button, and all at once they ~~wouldnt.~~ *wouldn't.* (3) After a few ~~days~~ *days'* wait, the entry systems began functioning again. (4) Many ~~resident's~~ *residents* of Bremerton, the home of a Navy shipyard, were convinced that the ~~militarys~~ *military's* technological activity had affected the locks, but Navy ~~official's~~ *officials* denied it. (5) Other people wondered if radio transmissions might have

jammed the frequency and prevented the keyless ~~systems'~~ *systems* from func-

tioning. (6) Fortunately, people whose cars had keyless entry systems ~~were'nt~~ *weren't* locked out for those days. (7) These owners simply resorted to a backup system to open and lock their ~~car's~~ *cars* — ~~its~~ *it's* called a "key." (8) To this day, the mystery ~~remain's~~ *remains* unsolved and still happens occasionally, in Bremerton and other ~~place's~~ *places*.

....

PRACTICE 4   Editing Your Own Writing for Apostrophes

As a final practice, edit a piece of your own writing for apostrophes. It can be a paper you are working on for this course, a paper you have already finished, a paper for another course, a recent piece of writing from your work or every-day life, or your idea journal entry.

....

Quotation Marks (" ")

Understand What Quotation Marks Do

Quotation marks (" ") are punctuation marks with two common uses in college writing: They are used with some quotations, and they are used to set off titles. They always appear in pairs.

A **quotation** is the report of another person's words. There are two types of quotations: **direct quotations** (the exact repetition, word for word, of what someone said or wrote) and **indirect quotations** (a restatement of what someone said or wrote, not word for word). Quotation marks are used only for direct quotations.

IDEA JOURNAL
Write about a conversation you had today.

DIRECT QUOTATION   George said, "I'm getting a haircut."

INDIRECT QUOTATION   George said that he was getting a haircut.

To understand this chapter, you need to know what a sentence is. For a review, see Chapter 22.

Practice Using Quotation Marks Correctly

Quotation Marks for Direct Quotations

When you write a direct quotation, you need to use quotation marks around the quoted words. These marks tell readers that the words used are exactly what was said or written.

Quoted words are usually combined with words that identify who is speaking. The identifying words can come after the quoted words, before them, or in the middle. Here are some guidelines for capitalization and punctuation.

■ Capitalize the first letter in a complete sentence that's being quoted, even if it comes after some identifying words.

Quotation mark   Quotation mark

The teacher said, "This assignment is due next Monday."

Capital letter for complete sentence

■ Do not capitalize the first letter in a quotation if it is not the first word in the complete sentence.

Quotation marks

"If anyone needs help with it," she said, "see me during office hours."

Not the first word in the complete sentence, no capital letter

■ If it is a complete sentence and its source is clear, you can let a quotation stand on its own, without any identifying words.

Speaker (teacher) known

"My office hours are on the first page of your syllabus."

■ Attach identifying words to a quotation with a comma; these identifying words cannot be a sentence on their own.

Identifying words attached with comma

A student asked, "May we e-mail questions?"

For more on commas with quotation marks, see page 634.

■ Always put quotation marks *after* commas and periods. Put quotation marks after question marks and exclamation points if they are part of the quoted sentence.

Quotation mark   Quotation mark

The teacher replied, "Yes. Do you all have my address?"

Comma   Question mark

- If a question mark or exclamation point is part of your own sentence, put it after the quotation mark.

When you quote the exact words of an outside source in a paper, use quotation marks. You also need to cite, or give credit to, the source.

> The government needs to ensure that when a company fails, employees' pensions are protected. An article in the *Boston Globe* reported, "When Polaroid collapsed, pension funds and employee stock programs were suddenly worthless. At the same time, however, the chief financial officer walked away with a package worth more than $2 million" (Richardson B3).

For information about how to use quotations in research papers, see Chapter 21.

For more on citing and documenting sources, see pages 364–71.

Setting Off a Quotation within Another Quotation

Sometimes you may directly quote someone who quotes what someone else said or wrote. Put **single quotation marks** (' ') around the quotation within a quotation so that readers understand who said what.

> The student handbook reads, "Students must be given the opportunity to make up work missed for excused absences."

> Terry told his instructor, "I'm sorry I missed the exam, but I would like to take a makeup exam. According to our student handbook, 'Students must be given the opportunity to make up work missed for excused absences,' and I have a good reason."

Terry's entire quotation

Here, Terry is quoting from the student handbook.

PRACTICE 1   Punctuating Direct Quotations

Edit the following sentences by adding quotation marks and commas where needed.

> **EXAMPLE:** At a meeting of a self-help group, the leader, Brooke, stood up and said, "We are all here because each of us is suffering from an eating disorder."

1. Looking around the room, Allison said, "I thought only teenage girls had eating disorders. There are people here of all ages, including several men."

2. "Yes, there are men here," said Brooke. "Only some of us are teenage girls."

3. "I'm forty years old, not a teenager, and not a girl," Patrick said. "However, I have an eating disorder."

4. Allison said, "You don't look like you have an eating disorder. You are not super skinny."

5. "I eat too much," said Patrick. "I'm a compulsive eater."

6. "When you say, 'I'm a compulsive eater,' I don't know what you mean," said Allison.

7. "The dictionary defines *compulsive* as 'related to a psychological obsession,'" said Brooke.

8. Evan suddenly shouted, "We're all doing this because we're trying to hurt our families and friends!"

9. "That is one myth we're going to talk about," said Brooke. "In fact, people with eating disorders are hurting themselves. They are usually upset that their families and friends are worried about them."

10. Why did it suddenly get quiet when Brooke said, "Does this sound right to any of you?"

For more practice with quotation marks, visit *Exercise Central* at bedfordstmartins .com/realessays.

RESOURCES
To gauge students' skills with using quotation marks, use the *Testing Tool Kit* CD available with this book.

TEAMWORK Ask students to pair off, interview each other on a predetermined topic, and then write a one-paragraph report that includes at least one direct quotation and one indirect quotation. Photocopy several of these reports to use for a whole-class workshop on quotation marks.

No Quotation Marks for Indirect Quotations

When you report what someone said or wrote but do not use the person's exact words, you are writing an indirect quotation. Do not use quotation marks for indirect quotations. Indirect quotations often begin with the word *that*.

> **INDIRECT QUOTATION** Sophie said that the exam was postponed.
>
> **DIRECT QUOTATION** Sophie said, "The exam was postponed."

INDIRECT QUOTATION Carolyn told me that she had an accident.

DIRECT QUOTATION   Carolyn told me, "I had an accident."

. . . .

PRACTICE 2 Punctuating Direct and Indirect Quotations

Edit the following sentences by adding quotation marks where needed and crossing out quotation marks that are incorrectly used. If a sentence is already correct, put a "C" next to it.

> **EXAMPLE:** Sarita told me that ~~"~~she met her new boyfriend through an online dating service.~~"~~

1. "I never thought I would use the Internet for dating, but it really worked," she said.

2. Sarita remembered ~~"~~how easy it was to look up profiles of men with her interests and to pick the best candidates.~~"~~

3. She said, "I could tell right away if I wasn't going to have anything in common with a person."

4. "I could also tell a lot about a guy's personality by the way he expressed himself," she added. *C*

5. Sarita said the hardest part of the experience was going on trial dates to see if her original impressions of candidates were correct. *C*

6. She knew that there was no future with one man when he arrived a half hour late and told her, "I had something else to do first."

7. "He apparently thought that I was happy to wait around for him forever," she said exasperatedly. *C*

8. Sarita told me that ~~"~~I should think about online dating.~~"~~

9. "I found a great person," she said, "and you could too."

10. I told her that I appreciated the advice but that I'm happy being single right now. *C*

. . . .

Quotation Marks for Certain Titles

When referring to a short work such as a magazine or newspaper article, a chapter in a book, a short story, an essay, a song, or a poem, put quotation marks around the title of the work.

NEWSPAPER ARTICLE	"Mayor Warns of Budget Cuts"
SHORT STORY	"Everyday Use"
ESSAY	"Mother Tongue"

Usually, titles of longer works—such as novels, books, magazines, newspapers, movies, television programs, and CDs—are italicized. The titles of sacred books such as the Bible or the Koran are neither italicized nor surrounded by quotation marks.

BOOK	*The Chocolate War*
NEWSPAPER	the *Washington Post*

[Do not italicize or capitalize the word *the* before the name of a newspaper or magazine, even if it is part of the title. But do capitalize *The* when it is the first word in titles of books, movies, and other sources.]

If you are writing a paper with many outside sources, your instructor will probably refer you to a particular system of citing sources. Follow that system's guidelines when you use titles in your paper.

NOTE: Do not put quotation marks around the title of a paper you write.

· ·

PRACTICE 3 Using Quotation Marks for Titles

Edit the following sentences by adding quotation marks around titles as needed. Underline any book, magazine, or newspaper titles.

> **EXAMPLE:** Tyler walked down the aisle of the bus, humming "When
>
> the Saints Go Marching In" and wondering how he would
>
> keep from getting bored on the long bus ride home.

1. He sat down and noticed that the woman sitting next to him was holding the <u>Dallas Morning News</u>.

2. Glancing at his neighbor's newspaper, he saw that she was reading an article called "Best Bets for Winter Gardening."

3. He noticed that the passenger sitting directly in front of him was carefully going through "Imitation of Spenser," John Keats's first poem.

4. The boy sitting in front of his neighbor was working on exercises from a book titled <u>Rapid Math Tips and Tricks</u>, and he suddenly cried out, "I won!"

5. Tiring of his little game, Tyler took out his sociology textbook and began reading his next assigned chapter, "The Economy and Politics."

Edit Paragraphs and Your Own Writing

Edit the following paragraphs by adding quotation marks where needed and crossing out any incorrectly used quotation marks. Underline any book, magazine, or newspaper titles. Correct any errors in punctuation.

RESOURCES
For cumulative Editing Review Tests, see pages 667–83.

EDITING REVIEW 1 (17 errors)

(1) "Here is one I've loved for years," said Evi, as she held up a CD called "Kind of Blue" by the "jazz trumpeter" Miles Davis. (2) Charlie, who was also flipping through the jazz CDs, said that "he had gone through a Miles Davis phase but wasn't so interested in Miles's music now." (3) Shortly after they moved into the main section of the store, Charlie pulled out a book and opened it to an essay titled ~~Shooting an Elephant~~. "Shooting an Elephant." (4) "Reading this had a big effect on me," he said, adding that "he eventually read most of what George Orwell had written." (5) They were browsing through the rows of books when Evi stopped and said, "This ~~this~~ is what led me to read all of Dylan Thomas's poetry." (6) Taking a book from the shelf, she opened it to a poem titled "Do Not Go Gentle into That Good Night," noting that "It ~~it~~ was written for Thomas's dying father." (7) Pointing to a line in the poem, she said, "When ~~when~~ Thomas

writes 'Rage, rage against the dying of the light,' he is talking to his father, to himself, and to me, bringing all of us into that special moment." (8) They continued on silently until Charlie exclaimed, "Look at this—a book about the making of the Beatles's <u>Sgt. Pepper's Lonely Hearts Club Band!</u>" (9) Evi reached for another copy of the book, saying that "her father had introduced her to the Beatles's music when she was ten and that it had been one of her favorite albums ever since." (10) Charlie picked up a copy of "<u>Rolling Stone</u> magazine" as they walked to the checkout counter, and he said, "A trip to the bookstore turned out to be a lot more fun than I thought it would be."

....

EDITING REVIEW 2 (18 errors)

(1) "Did you know that people our age could experience a life crisis?" my twenty-five-year-old friend Beth asked as we browsed at the newsstand. (2) She showed me an article called "The Trouble with Being 25" in a magazine she was looking at.

(3) I told her that "she was crazy." (4) "You wait until midlife for your crisis, silly," I said. (5) I was imagining a middle-aged businessman suddenly buying an expensive sports car and driving around listening to Prince singing "Little Red Corvette."

(6) Beth pointed out that she had plenty of anxiety about being twenty-five. (7) "It's as if people look at me and think I'm still basically a teenager, yet I have a grown-up job and grown-up responsibilities to go with it," she said.

(8) I asked her "what kinds of responsibilities she was talking about." (9) "I have rent and bills to pay," she said, "and I'm trying to decide if I should take a couple of classes at night to get a better job." (10) She thought for a moment and then added, "And sooner or later I'll need to figure out whether I want to get married and have children."

(11) She picked up a newspaper and idly turned the pages until she found a headline that said, "Confusion Reigns among Young Singles."

(12) "Wow! You're right!" I blurted out. (13) "It's a good thing you read those stupid magazines," I said to Beth. (14) I was only partly kidding when I added that "she and I would never have realized that we were supposed to be having a crisis if we hadn't read about it."

(15) "Let's do something to celebrate," said Beth. (16) That's why we spent the rest of the afternoon sitting around my kitchen table drinking coffee, listening to Beck singing "Loser," and reading out loud to each other from "How to Tell If You're Ready to Settle Down" in the new issue of <u>Cosmopolitan</u>.

PRACTICE 4   Editing Your Own Writing for Quotation Marks

As a final practice, edit a piece of your own writing for quotation marks. It can be a paper you are working on for this course, a paper you have already finished, a paper for another course, a recent piece of writing from your work or everyday life, or your idea journal entry.

39

Other Punctuation

(; : () — -)

Understand What Punctuation Does

IDEA JOURNAL
Write to someone
about to enter
your college,
giving him or her
five good pieces
of advice.

To understand
this chapter, you
need to know what
sentences and
independent
clauses are. For
a review, see
Chapters 22
and 24.

Punctuation helps readers understand your writing. If you use punctuation incorrectly, you send readers a confusing message—or, even worse, a wrong one. This chapter covers five marks of punctuation that people sometimes use incorrectly. Knowing what these marks do in a sentence can help you avoid such mistakes.

SEMICOLON ;	Joins two independent clauses into one sentence
	Separates complete items in a list that already has commas within individual items
COLON :	Introduces a list
	Announces an explanation or example
PARENTHESES ( )	Set off extra information that is not essential to the sentence
DASH —	Sets off words for emphasis
	Indicates a pause
HYPHEN -	Joins two or more words that together form a single description
	Shows a word break at the end of a line

Practice Using Punctuation Correctly

Semicolon ;

Semicolons to Join Independent Clauses (Sentences)

Use a semicolon to join very closely related sentences and make them into one sentence.

> In an interview, hold your head up and don't slouch; it is important to look alert.

> Make good eye contact; looking down is not appropriate in an interview.

> **LANGUAGE NOTE:** Do not use a comma instead of a semicolon to join two independent clauses: That would create a run-on (see Chapter 24).

Semicolons When Items in a Series Contain Commas

Use a semicolon to separate list items that themselves contain commas. Otherwise, it is difficult for readers to tell where one item ends and another begins.

> I have a cousin who lives in Devon, England; another cousin who lives in Derry, New Hampshire; and a third cousin who lives in Freeport, Maine.

Colon :

Colons before Lists

Use a colon to introduce a list after an independent clause.

> In the United States, three ice cream flavors are the most popular: vanilla, chocolate, and strawberry.

Colons before Explanations or Examples

Use a colon after an independent clause to let readers know that you are about to provide an explanation or example of what you just wrote. If the explanation or example is also an independent clause, capitalize the first letter after the colon.

> Sometimes, the choice of cereals is overwhelming: My supermarket carries at least five different types of raisin bran.

> I use one criterion to choose a cereal: price.

TEACHING TIP
Caution students not to use semicolons as a default solution when trying to increase sentence complexity; overuse and misuse are common.

For more on using semicolons to join sentences, see Chapter 30.

TEACHING TIP
After each of the explanations and examples in this chapter, ask students to write examples of their own.

TEACHING TIP
It may help students
to think of the colon
as a spotlight, espe-
cially in sentences
where an example fol-
lows the colon *(The
plan has one major
problem: cost).*

NOTE: A colon in a sentence must follow an independent clause. A common misuse is to place a colon after a phrase instead of an independent clause. Watch out especially for colons following the phrases *such as* or *for example.*

An independent clause contains a subject and a verb, and it expresses a complete thought. It can stand on its own as a sentence.

INCORRECT	The resort offers many activities, such as: snorkeling, golf, and windsurfing.
CORRECT	The resort offers many activities: snorkeling, golf, and windsurfing.
CORRECT	The resort offers many activities, such as snorkeling, golf, and windsurfing.
INCORRECT	Suzy has many talents. For example: writing, drawing, and painting.
CORRECT	Suzy has many talents: writing, drawing, and painting.

Colons in Business Correspondence

Use a colon after a greeting (called a *salutation*) in a business letter and after the standard heading lines at the beginning of a memorandum.

Dear Mr. Latimer:

To: Craig Kleinman

From: Susan Anker

Parentheses ( )

TEACHING TIP
Have students find
examples of the over-
use of parentheses
from newspapers,
magazines, or Web
sites; edit these as a
class.

Use two parentheses to set off information that is not essential to the meaning of a sentence. Parentheses are always used in pairs and should be used sparingly.

My grandfather's most successful invention (his first) was the electric blanket.

My worst habit (and also the hardest to break) is interrupting.

Dash —

Use dashes as you use parentheses: to set off additional information, particularly information that you want to emphasize.

> The essay question — worth 50 percent of the whole exam — will be open book.

> Your answers should be well developed, and points — 2 per error — will be deducted for major grammar mistakes.

A dash can also indicate a pause, much as a comma does.

> My son wants to buy a car — if he can find an affordable one.

Make a dash by typing two hyphens together. Do not leave any extra spaces around a dash.

Hyphen -

Hyphens to Join Words That Form a Single Description

Use a hyphen to join words that together form a single description of a person, place, or thing.

> The eighty-year-old smoker was considered a high-risk patient.

> I followed the company's decision-making procedure.

If you are unsure about whether or how to hyphenate a word or phrase, consult a dictionary or your instructor.

Hyphens to Divide a Word at the End of a Line

Use a hyphen to divide a word when part of the word must continue on the next line. Most word-processing programs do this automatically, but if you are writing by hand, you need to insert hyphens yourself.

> If you give me the receipt for your purchase, I will imme-
> diately issue a refund.

> If you are not sure where to break a word, look it up in a dictionary. The word's main entry will show you where you can break the word: *dic • tio • nary.*

Edit Paragraphs and Your Own Writing

RESOURCES For
cumulative Editing
Review Tests, see
pages 667–83.

Edit the following paragraphs by adding semicolons, colons, parentheses, dashes, and hyphens where needed. Keep in mind that more than one type of punctuation may be acceptable in some places.

Answers may vary. Possible edits shown.

EDITING REVIEW (15 errors)

For more practice
with the punctuation
covered in this
chapter, visit
bedfordstmartins
.com/realessays.

RESOURCES To
gauge students' skills
with the punctuation
covered in this chap-
ter, use the *Testing
Tool Kit* CD available
with this book.

(1) To avoid predators, many butterflies and moths randomly change directions as they fly about, but this is not their only strategy; they also display striking colors (like radiant and shiny reds, oranges, and blues) and camouflage themselves in effective disguises. (2) For example, some butterflies have streaks composed of many dazzling colors across their wings to emphasize the speed of their flight—sending a message that they're hard to catch. (3) Other butterflies use bold, attention-getting color patterns to signal that they are poisonous to eat: Some are truly poisonous and some are faking. (4) There are also species that attempt to look distasteful by imitating something that is not nutritious—a bit of bird dropping, a dead leaf, or rotting vegetation. (5) One moth, *Oxytenis modestia*, is especially enterprising in its disguises: In its first four caterpillar stages it looks like a bird dropping, even including fake seeds in it; the fifth stage imitates a green snake with a fake large head and two fake eyes; and the adult *Oxytenis* moth looks like a leaf, and because it breeds twice a year, mimics the appropriate leaf for the season. (6) *Oxytenis* moths that hatch in the dry season look like dry dead leaves; those hatching in the rainy season look dark and moldy. (7) Several butterflies combine camouflage with eye-catching display; for example, *Pieria helvetia* has front wings that are bland and dull, but its hind wings are bright red. (8) When it is resting, its wings are closed, and it can hardly be seen, but when a predator threatens, it bursts into rapid, dramatic flight—its red patches make it conspicuously visible. (9) However, then it

suddenly sets down again, folds its wings in, and seemingly disappears a
clever magic act. (10) Birds and monkeys do their best to see past these
disguises because, according to one researcher one who will do anything
for his research, moths taste something like raw shrimp.

. . . .

PRACTICE   **Editing Your Own Writing for Other
                 Punctuation Marks**

Edit a piece of your own writing for semicolons, colons, parentheses, dashes,
and hyphens. It can be a paper you are working on for this course, a paper
you have already finished, a paper for another course, a piece of writing from
your work or everyday life, or your idea journal entry. You may want to try
more than one way to use these marks of punctuation in your writing.

. . . .

40

Capitalization

Using Capital Letters

Understand Capitalization

IDEA JOURNAL
Write a guide to your family: their names, where they live, where they grew up, and where they work.

There are three basic rules of capitalization: Capitalize the first letter of

- every new sentence.
- names of specific people, places, dates, and things.
- important words in titles.

TEACHING TIP
Remind students that their papers should not be written in all capital letters.

If you can remember these three rules, you will avoid the most common errors in capitalization.

Practice Capitalization

Capitalization of Sentences

Capitalize the first letter in each new sentence, including the first word in a direct quotation.

Mary was surprised when she saw all the people.

She asked, "What's going on here?"

Capitalization of Names of Specific People, Places, Dates, and Things

Capitalize the first letter in names of specific people, places, dates, and things. Do not capitalize general words such as *college* as opposed to the specific name: *Lincoln College*. Look at the examples for each group.

For more practice with capitalization, visit *Exercise Central* at bedfordstmartins .com/realessays.

People

Capitalize the first letter in names of specific people and in titles used with names of specific people.

The word *president* is not capitalized unless it comes directly before a name as part of that person's title: President Barack Obama.

SPECIFIC	NOT SPECIFIC
Carol Schopfer	my friend
Dr. D'Ambrosio	the physician
Professor Shute	your professor
Aunt Jane, Mother	my aunt, my mother

The name of a family member is capitalized when the family member is being addressed directly or when the family title is standing in for a first name.

Good to see you, Dad.   Mother is taking classes.

In other instances, do not capitalize.

It is my father's birthday.   My mother is taking classes.

RESOURCES
To gauge students' capitalization skills, use the *Testing Tool Kit* CD available with this book.

Places

Capitalize the first letter in names of specific buildings, streets, cities, states, regions, and countries.

DISCUSSION
Have students come up with their own examples of people, places, and so forth that are "specific" and "not specific."

SPECIFIC	NOT SPECIFIC
Bolton Police Department	the police department
Washington Street	our street
Boston, Massachusetts	my hometown
Texas	this state
the West	the western part of the country
Italy	that country

Do not capitalize directions in a sentence: *Drive south for five blocks.*

Dates

Ask ESL students to identify any English capitalization rules that differ from the rules in the other languages that they speak and write. Invite students to write any examples they want to share on the board.

Capitalize the first letter in the names of days, months, and holidays. Do not capitalize the names of the seasons (winter, spring, summer, fall).

SPECIFIC	NOT SPECIFIC
Monday	today
January 4	winter
Presidents' Day	my birthday

LANGUAGE NOTE: The first letter of all days, months, and proper names is capitalized.

Today is Tuesday, March 10.

Organizations, Companies, and Groups

SPECIFIC	NOT SPECIFIC
Santa Monica College	my college
Toys"R"Us	the toy store
Merrimack Players	the theater group

Languages, Nationalities, and Religions

The names of languages should be capitalized even if you are not referring to a specific course: *I am taking nutrition and Spanish.*

SPECIFIC	NOT SPECIFIC
English, Greek, Spanish	my first language
Christianity, Buddhism	your religion

LANGUAGE NOTE: The first letter of all languages and nationalities is capitalized.

Gina speaks Italian, but she is Chinese.

Courses

SPECIFIC	NOT SPECIFIC
Nutrition 100	the basic nutrition course

Commercial Products

SPECIFIC	NOT SPECIFIC
Diet Coke	a diet cola

Capitalization of Titles

Capitalize the first word and all other important words in titles of books, movies, television programs, magazines, newspapers, articles, stories, songs, papers, poems, legislation, and so on. Words that do not need to be capitalized (unless they are the first word) include articles (*the, a, an*); coordinating conjunctions (*and, but, for, nor, or, so, yet*); and prepositions.

For more on punctuating titles, see page 652. For a list of common prepositions, see page 387.

American Idol is a popular television program.

Newsweek and *Time* often have similar cover stories.

"Once More to the Lake" is one of Chuck's favorite essays.

Edit Paragraphs and Your Own Writing

Edit the following paragraphs by capitalizing as needed and removing any unnecessary capitalization.

RESOURCES
For cumulative Editing Review Tests, see pages 667–83.

EDITING REVIEW (88 errors)

(1) in Robert Louis Stevenson's 1886 novella "the strange case of dr. jekyll and mr. hyde," a doctor uses Himself as the subject of an experiment and the results are Disastrous. (2) The novella was a Great Success, but stevenson didn't originate the idea of Doctors experimenting on themselves.

(3) one of the earliest known examples of self-experimentation goes back to the sixteenth Century, when santorio santorio, of padua, italy, weighed himself every Day for thirty Years. (4) By weighing everything he ate and drank as well as his Bodily Discharges, Santorio discovered that the Human body continually and imperceptibly loses large amounts of Fluid. (5) today, that Loss, called *insensible perspiration*, is routinely measured in Hospital patients.

(6) A Key Breakthrough to the modern age of Cardiology was made in 1929 by a german, dr. werner forssmann, who as a Surgical Resident at a medical facility called the august victoria home, near berlin, conducted

a daring self-experiment by inserting a thin tube into one of his Veins and slid the tube into his own Heart. (7) This idea was later developed by other Researchers into the Technique of cardiac catheterization. (8) Dr. forssmann, who used catheters on himself nine times, shared a nobel prize in 1956 for his Pioneering Experiments.

(9) An important innovation in Anesthesia occurred when a Dentist in connecticut, Horace wells, watched a demonstration in which a Volunteer inhaled Nitrous Oxide, cut his own leg, and felt no pain until the effects of the Gas wore off. (10) dr. wells then had one of his own teeth extracted after he had inhaled the Chemical, which people later commonly called "Laughing Gas." (11) he was amazed to have no Pain during his extraction, declaring, "it is the greatest discovery ever made." (12) Others' self-experimentation later aided the Development of ether, chloroform, and additional Anesthetics.

(13) In Medical circles, many people believe that major walter reed experimented on himself in the early 1900s as the Leader of the group in cuba that discovered that Mosquitoes transmit yellow fever. (14) in fact, Dr. reed said he would allow mosquitoes to infect him to test the Theory, but he returned to the united states before this was done. (15) Instead, other Members of his Team conducted the mosquito experiment on themselves, with one dying and another barely surviving. (16) after these self-experimenters proved the crucial Connection between mosquitoes and yellow fever, dr. reed returned to Cuba, but he never did perform the experiment on himself.

···

PRACTICE Editing Your Own Writing for Capitalization

Edit a piece of your own writing for capitalization. It can be a paper for this course, a paper for another course, a recent piece of writing from your work or everyday life, or your idea journal entry.

···

Editing Review Test 1
The Four Most Serious Errors (Chapters 22–26)

1

DIRECTIONS: Each of the underlined word groups contains one or more errors. As you identify each error, write in the space the number of the word group containing the error. Then, edit the underlined word groups to correct the errors. If you need help, turn back to the chapters indicated above. *Answers may vary. Possible edits shown.*

Two fragments <u>3, 13</u>   Two verb problems <u>5, 9</u>

Two run-ons <u>1, 10</u>   Four subject-verb
                                           agreement errors <u>1, 7, 14, 15</u>

  and
 1 One opponent faces the other, during their personal battle, nobody else in
  exists.
the universe ~~exist~~. **2** An attack prompts an immediate defense, often followed by a
    , *starting*
counterattack. **3** ~~Starting~~ the cycle again. **4** In an age of precision-guided, pilotless

missiles and laser weapons, there would seem to be no place for fencing. **5** Yet in
     has
recent years, fencing ~~had~~ been experiencing a surge in popularity among women and

men of all ages. **6** That is partly because, with training and dedicated practice, even

someone who is elderly or not adept at other sports can often learn to hold his or her

own quite well in a fencing encounter.

 7 Most beginning fencers are equipped with a training sword and protective
    includes
equipment that ~~include~~ a glove, face mask, knee socks, knickers, and a special gray

jacket. **8** The jacket is woven with wire mesh for use with an electronic scoreboard.
     is   *and*
9 At the tip of the sword ~~will be~~ a button instead of a sharp point. **10** This is for safety,

it is also useful for keeping track of valid hits. **11** When the button contacts a valid

target on the jacket of an opponent, an electric signal courses through the sword to a

wire in the attacker's hand guard. **12** From the hand guard the wire runs to the back

of the fencer's jacket up to an apparatus mounted on the ceiling where the hit is
   , *causing*
registered, **13** ~~Causing~~ a red light to go on. **14** In a typical match, the first fencer to
           wins.   *provides*
score five valid hits on an opponent ~~win~~. **15** All in all, fencing ~~provide~~ strenuous

exercise, competition, excitement, and a never-ending challenge.

2

Editing Review Test 2
The Four Most Serious Errors (Chapters 22–26)

DIRECTIONS: Each of the underlined word groups contains one or more errors. As you identify each error, write in the space the number of the word group containing the error. Then, edit the underlined word groups to correct the errors. If you need help, turn back to the chapters indicated above. *Answers may vary. Possible edits shown.*

Two fragments _10, 17_____   Two verb problems _5, 11_____

Two run-ons _1, 3_____   Four subject-verb
                                        agreement errors _7, 8, 13, 14_____

1 Finding a poisonous snake is not something most people go out of their way to
, but
do that is exactly the goal of some scientists. 2 They are looking for precisely what
everyone else wants to avoid: the snakes' venom. 3 This is not a hunt for excitement or
;
a dangerous thrill, it is a search for a medical breakthrough. 4 For over thirty years,
scientists have been using snake venom to create new drugs. 5 One type of venom, for
provided
example, has provide a key ingredient for treating congestive heart failure.

6 A snake creates venom in special glands in its upper jaw. 7 In latching onto prey,
releases
the snake squeezes these glands and release the venom. 8 Molecules from the venom
attack
then attacks the prey from the inside. 9 Some venom molecules cause muscle cells to
which   induce
relax. 10 Which cuts off the victim's oxygen supply. 11 Other molecules will have
induced the victim's immune system to attack its own organs. 12 Most venoms contain
a combination of such molecules.

13 In recent years, researchers have discovered how certain genes in venom
relax
relaxes the muscles in the prey's aorta, which pumps blood to the body's organs.
prevents
14 Relaxing these muscles prevent the aorta from contracting, which lowers the
blood pressure and allows time for deadly toxins to attack the victim's bloodstream.

15 Scientists are now trying to use these muscle-relaxing toxins to humans' advantage.

16 Controlled relaxation of the blood vessels around the heart helps blood flow more
, reducing
easily. 17 Reducing the effects of congestive heart failure.

Editing Review Test 3
The Four Most Serious Errors (Chapters 22–26)
Other Grammar Concerns (Chapters 27–33)

3

DIRECTIONS: Each of the underlined word groups contains one or more errors. As you identify each error, write in the space the number of the word group containing the error. Then, edit the underlined word groups to correct the errors. If you need help, turn back to the chapters indicated above. *Answers may vary. Possible edits shown.*

Two fragments *9, 14* _____   One verb problem *2* _____

One run-on *4* _____   One pronoun error *6* _____

One adjective error *4* _____   One parallelism error *2* _____

Three subject-verb
agreement errors *6, 7, 12* _____

1 Anyone who has ever gotten lost in a maze knows what a frightening experience

it can be. 2 But it is also challenging, exciting, and ~~there is no problem with safety~~ *safe*

because few people ever ~~got~~ *get* lost in them for long. 3 Mazes have become more popular

than ever in recent years in the United States and in many countries around the world.

4 Mazes can be made of many different types of materials *, but* perhaps the ~~larger~~ *largest*

number of them are made of corn stalks. 5 Corn mazes have become big business in

some farming communities. 6 Building mazes ~~are~~ *is* one way for farmers to market ~~his~~ *their*

farms as popular entertainment.

7 The point of this for some farmers ~~are~~ *is* to adapt the small farm so that it can

remain competitive in today's economy. 8 Some farms are expanding on the maze idea

by turning a section of land into small theme ~~parks. 9 Complete~~ *parks, complete* with hay rides, petting

zoos, and pig races. 10 Mazes are usually the major attraction, however, and many

are quite elaborate. 11 There are mazes shaped like butterflies, crowns, and sheriff's

badges. 12 Some mazes even ~~includes~~ *include* such features as double-decker bridges.

13 Other mazes are designed to teach people about various farm crops and how

they are grown. 14 Whether entertaining, educational, or both. ~~15 Mazes~~ *, mazes* have become

a significant way of raising people's awareness of and interest in farming.

Editing Review Test 4

The Four Most Serious Errors (Chapters 22–26)
Other Grammar Concerns (Chapters 27–33)

DIRECTIONS: Each of the underlined word groups contains one or more errors. As you identify each error, write in the space the number of the word group containing the error. Then, edit the underlined word groups to correct the errors. If you need help, turn back to the chapters indicated above. *Answers may vary. Possible edits shown.*

Two fragments _2, 9_   One run-on _5_

One subject-verb agreement error _4_   Two pronoun errors _4, 6_

One misplaced/dangling modifier _4_   Two coordination/subordination

Two uses of inappropriately informal or errors _3, 12_
casual language _7, 16_

    1 Many Internet users are not aware of the current debate over network neutrality,
or what
2 ~~What~~ some call the argument over who owns the Internet. 3 People assume that
                                                                       , but
open and equal access to Web content is a protected right, some companies are trying

to change the way users access online information.
                                                           that   *want*
    4 Companies like Comcast and AT&T, (who provide Internet service,) ~~wants~~ greater

control over the data that travels through their lines and cables. 5 The companies argue
                          , so
that they built the roads they should be able to control who uses those roads. 6 By
                                                       the Internet providers
allowing some Web sites to pay more for faster transmission, ~~they~~ can earn more

money. 7 The companies say they would like to use that money to develop new
                                    better
networks and ultimately provide ~~killer~~ service.

    8 Supporters of network neutrality argue that consumers should have equal
                         , not
access to all Web sites. 9 ~~Not~~ just to those Web sites that pay more for faster delivery.

10 Internet service providers should not have the power to restrict, block, or slow down

the delivery of any content. 11 Network neutrality advocates want to see the Internet

remain free, open, and democratic.

12 The federal government supports network neutrality in theory; *however,* ~~passing laws that protect network neutrality has been difficult.~~ 13 Critics have found many flaws in the proposed legislation. 14 For example, without the power to filter content, unwanted material like spam cannot be prevented. 15 Nevertheless, many still hope that the government will find a way to protect users' rights. 16 If service providers become "gatekeepers" of the Web, many fear that users are the ones who will ~~get the shaft.~~ *be negatively affected.*

Editing Review Test 5

The Four Most Serious Errors (Chapters 22–26)
Other Grammar Concerns (Chapters 27–33)
Word Use (Chapters 34–35)

DIRECTIONS: Each of the underlined word groups contains one or more errors. As you identify each error, write in the space the number of the word group containing the error. Then, edit the underlined word groups to correct the errors. If you need help, turn back to the chapters indicated above. *Answers may vary. Possible edits shown.*

One run-on _8_

One word choice error _10_

One adjective error _15_

One subject-verb agreement error _1_

Two commonly confused word errors _3, 12_

One verb problem _4_

Two pronoun errors _4, 14_

One misplaced/dangling modifier _6_

1 Nobody ~~want~~ *wants* to go through life frightened that criminals might be lurking around every corner. 2 But criminals do exist, and it makes sense to take precautions to avoid being victimized. 3 There are prudent measures that you can work into ~~you're~~ *your* everyday routines that can help prevent you from becoming a victim to some common scams.

4 First of all, don't give out financial information, such as your bank account or Social Security number, to anyone ~~who~~ *whom* you ~~didn't~~ *don't* know and trust. 5 It is surprisingly easy to create a fake Social Security card and then a fake birth certificate to go with it. 6 Using these fake documents, *a criminal can ask* the local motor vehicle department ~~will~~ *to* issue a new driver's license with your name and the criminal's photo.

7 You have probably heard of some of the standard e-mail scams, one of which involves a so-called deposed Nigerian leader who offers to pay you a substantial sum if you help him transfer his fortune out of his country. 8 Many of these scams use the same trick to get people to believe the sender is ~~honest, the~~ *honest. The* criminal will send a postdated check for a share in the fortune in return for a check from the victim that is allegedly necessary to unfreeze the funds. 9 Needless to say, the criminal's checks always bounce. 10 If you receive e-mail solicitations of any kind, ~~don't play with fire.~~ *use extreme caution.*

11 Do thorough background checks on the sender before sending any money or information. **12** In addition, when ~~its~~ *it's* time to discard your old computer, remove the hard drive first to prevent thieves from recovering any vital data.

    13 On the positive side, you can relax a bit about your household trash. **14** Most identity theft cases ~~they~~ do not start with scammers rummaging through trash **15** Instead, scammers use computer spyware or steal outgoing mail because they find these methods ~~more easy.~~ *easier.*

Editing Review Test 6

The Four Most Serious Errors (Chapters 22–26)
Other Grammar Concerns (Chapters 27–33)
Word Use (Chapters 34–35)

DIRECTIONS: Each of the underlined word groups contains one or more errors. As you identify each error, write in the space the number of the word group containing the error. Then,
edit the underlined word groups to correct the errors. If you need help, turn back to the
chapters indicated above. *Answers may vary. Possible edits shown.*

Two run-ons 4, 11 _____

One subject-verb agreement error 14 _____

One parallelism error 7 _____

Two commonly confused
words errors 2, 8 _____

One use of inappropriately informal
or casual language 6 _____

One verb problem 2 _____

One pronoun error 11 _____

1 Eastern Egg Rock, a remote, treeless island off the coast of southern Maine, was

for much of the twentieth century inhabited by a huge population of gulls. 2 By the

mid-1980s, the gulls ~~have~~ <u>had</u> been the dominant bird species ~~they're~~ <u>there</u> for about a hundred

years. 3 But before that, the island was primarily the home of arctic terns and puffins.

4 By the late nineteenth century, hunting had reduced the tern and puffin populations

to nonviable levels, <u>and</u> the gulls had taken over. 5 In 1973, the National Audubon Society

decided to launch an experiment to try to bring puffins and terns back to Eastern Egg

Rock. 6 Since then, Project Puffin has proven so successful that biologists from all over

the world now come to ~~check it out.~~ <u>study it.</u>

7 The Audubon's team focused on restoring the nesting environment and ~~to control~~ <u>controlling</u>

predators. 8 The team moved puffin chicks from successful colonies in Newfoundland

~~too~~ <u>to</u> carefully built burrows and fed them by hand. 9 Decoys and recorded calls helped

to attract puffins and terns to the nests. 10 Team members stayed on the island during

every breeding season. 11 The large gulls don't like to nest around people<u>, so</u> this helped

prevent ~~them~~ <u>the gulls</u> from returning. 12 There are now more than one hundred pairs of breeding puffins on Eastern Egg Rock. **13** In addition, there are sizable populations of terns, storm petrels, and black guillemots.

    14 Birdlife conservation efforts like Project Puffin ~~seems~~ *seem* to be having a significant effect worldwide. **15** A recent study found that, in the last century, thirty-one species of birds were saved from extinction due to conservation programs.

Editing Review Test 7

7

The Four Most Serious Errors (Chapters 22–26)
Other Grammar Concerns (Chapters 27–33)
Word Use (Chapters 34–35)
Punctuation and Capitalization (Chapters 36–40)

DIRECTIONS: Each of the underlined word groups contains one or more errors. As you identify each error, write in the space the number of the word group containing the error. Then,
edit the underlined word groups to correct the errors. If you need help, turn back to the
chapters indicated above. *Answers may vary. Possible edits shown.*

One run-on _8_____   One verb problem _7_____

Two apostrophe errors _3, 11_____   One pronoun error _14_____

One adverb error _11_____   One quotation mark error _12_____

One subject-verb agreement error _9_____   One capitalization error _8_____

One commonly confused word error _4_____   One comma error _3_____

One semicolon error _2_____

1 Many engineering students nationwide belong to a group called Engineers

Without Borders-USA (EWB-USA). 2 EWB-USA is a nonprofit organization that allows

engineering students and professionals to volunteer in developing countries; and to use

their knowledge to help communities meet basic needs. 3 In particular volunteer's work

to improve shelter, water, sanitation, and energy systems.

    4 One of the goals of EWB-USA is to train socially ~~conscience~~ *conscious* engineers. 5 By

offering their skills in places where those skills are most needed, students see how

their education can help people in very direct ways. 6 When designing projects,

students work with local communities to understand what the communities' needs are

and to ensure that the local people can maintain the projects once EWB volunteers

have left. 7 Throughout the process, professional engineers ~~acted~~ *act* as mentors and

technical consultants.

    8 Currently, EWB-USA is working on projects in more than forty-five developing

countries. ~~these~~ *These* projects range from building bridges in El Salvador and Guatemala to digging wells in ~~t~~*T*anzania. **9** One group from Iowa State University ~~are~~ *is* even helping local schools in ^Belize build solar fruit dryers. **10** The dried fruit will provide the local children with healthy, inexpensive snacks throughout the school year and will make use of the country's large supply of fresh fruit. **11** Most of ~~EWBs~~ *EWB's* projects have multiple benefits; for example, one project might ~~simultaneous~~ *simultaneously*^ reduce disease, decrease labor, allow children to spend more time in school, and improve living conditions.

12 Bernard Amadei, who founded EWB-USA in 2002, has explained "how billions of people all over the world are in need of basic services." **13** Given how popular EWB-USA has become, it appears that many engineers and engineering students agree with Amadei. **14** The organization now has more than twelve thousand members in ~~their~~ *its* two hundred and fifty chapters and is present on one hundred and eighty campuses in the United States.

Editing Review Test 8

The Four Most Serious Errors (Chapters 22–26)
Other Grammar Concerns (Chapters 27–33)
Word Use (Chapters 34–35)
Punctuation and Capitalization (Chapters 36–40)

DIRECTIONS: Each of the underlined word groups contains one or more errors. As you iden-tify each error, write in the space the number of the word group containing the error. Then, edit the underlined word groups to correct the errors. If you need help, turn back to the chapters indicated above. *Answers may vary. Possible edits shown.*

One run-on 6

One pronoun error 1

Two comma errors 2, 7

One apostrophe error 8

One use of inappropriately
informal or casual language 11

One capitalization error 3

One commonly confused words error 6

One semicolon error 10

One verb problem 2

Two adverb errors 10, 12

One misplaced/dangling modifier 3

Two hyphen errors 7, 9

1 Some parents buy turtles for their children to keep as pets, but, apart from that, most adults probably don't think about ~~them~~ *turtles* at all. **2** Yet, these slow͵ clumsy creatures possess two remarkable qualities that many people *would* love to have. **3** Turtles are *nearly* indestructible, and they can ~~nearly~~ live for ~~Centuries.~~ *centuries.*

4 Most people attribute turtles' sturdiness to their tough shells, but turtles are tough in other important ways as well. **5** A turtle can go without food or liquid for months at a time. **6** ~~It's~~ *Its* heart doesn't need to beat constantly, so a turtle can virtually turn it on (or off) whenever it ~~wants, turtles~~ *wants. Turtles* are built to survive through floods, heat waves, famines, ice ages, and predators' attacks.

7 In March͵ 2006, a 250 year old turtle died in a zoo in Calcutta. **8** Scientists have recently discovered that, unlike nearly every other animal studied, a ~~turtles~~ *turtle's* organs resist breaking down or becoming less efficient over time. **9** A turtle that is over

100 *years old*
~~100 years old~~ can have a liver, lungs, and kidneys that are nearly identical to those of
^
a turtle in its teens.

    10 Although turtles resist disease and predators extremely *well,* ~~good,~~ many turtle
^
populations are now facing dire threats they have never had to deal with before; threats

from humans. 11 Every year, *many* ~~zillions of~~ turtles are killed by automobiles on new roads
^
built across turtles' migrational pathways. 12 People are also steadily encroaching on
^
turtle habitats and, in some areas, hunting them near *ly* to extinction in order to sell their
^
valuable shells and meat. 13 The resilient turtle might finally have met its match in
^
humans.

Editing Review Test 9

The Four Most Serious Errors (Chapters 22–26)
Other Grammar Concerns (Chapters 27–33)
Word Use (Chapters 34–35)
Punctuation and Capitalization (Chapters 36–40)

9

DIRECTIONS: Each of the underlined word groups contains one or more errors. As you identify each error, write in the space the number of the word group containing the error. Then, edit the underlined word groups to correct the errors. If you need help, turn back to the chapters indicated above. *Answers may vary. Possible edits shown.*

One fragment _15_

One run-on _2_

One pronoun error _2_

One parallelism error _12_

One apostrophe error _6_

One dash error _10_

One semicolon error _9_

One parentheses error _6_

One use of inappropriately informal or casual language _4_

1 One of the most common afflictions people have is an allergy to pets. 2 Some ~~whom~~ *who* are allergic simply refuse to have pets that can trigger a ~~reaction, these~~ *reaction. These* pets include cats, dogs, birds, rabbits, gerbils, hamsters, and horses. 3 Instead, allergic people may keep pets that do not ordinarily cause an allergic reaction, such as fish, turtles, frogs, and lizards. 4 However, most pet-allergic people who ~~are ga-ga about~~ *love* pets just go ahead and bring them into their homes anyway. 5 For these pet-allergic pet lovers, there are some good ways to reduce the allergens in a home to tolerable levels.

6 Allergens are spread from a ~~pets~~ *pet's* saliva, urine, skin secretions, and dander (the dead skin particles that animals continually shed.) 7 These allergens disperse directly into the air. 8 The best way to minimize pet allergies is to limit where the pet goes in the home. 9 Here is the single most important rule : no pets in the bedroom. 10 Also, keep pets off of the furniture; instead , get a dog or cat its own floor cushion, and choose a cushion with a washable cover. 11 Rabbits, birds, gerbils, and hamsters need

to be in their cages. **12** <u>Another key is to thoroughly and frequently clean the pet, the areas where it spends most of its time, and</u> ~~it's extremely important to clean~~ the <u>bedrooms.</u> **13** Install an air purifier in your bedroom and, if necesary, in other rooms where the pet is allowed. **14** Regularly clean the top blades of ceiling <u>~~fans. 15 Which~~</u> *fans, which* <u>are one of the main spreaders of allergens.</u> **16** In many cases, with sufficient care and effort, pets and pet-allergic humans can coexist.

Editing Review Test 10

The Four Most Serious Errors (Chapters 22–26)
Other Grammar Concerns (Chapters 27–33)
Word Use (Chapters 34–35)
Punctuation and Capitalization (Chapters 36–40)

10

DIRECTIONS: Each of the underlined word groups contains one or more errors. As you identify each error, write in the space the number of the word group containing the error. Then, edit the underlined word groups to correct the errors. If you need help, turn back to the chapters indicated above. *Answers may vary. Possible edits shown.*

One fragment 8

One pronoun error 7

One coordination/subordination error 2

One subject-verb agreement error 2

One commonly confused words error 1

One comma error 5

One semicolon error 13

One colon error 11

One apostrophe error 13

                                             than
   1 People are arriving at airports earlier ~~then~~ they used to and spending more time there, and that has created an unexpected problem for travelers and airport managers.
As people
2 ~~People~~ wait in security lines and for their flights*;* most of them ~~is~~ *are* using their cell phones and laptops. **3** This is not a problem in terms of cell phone and wireless Internet access because most airports can easily make these networks available. **4** The problem occurs when cell phone and laptop users run out of battery power and need to plug into an electrical outlet. **5** In many airports*,* including some of the most heavily used ones, there are not many outlets to go around.

   6 Despite travelers' annoyance, many don't complain to airport personnel about
                                          they
not having enough outlets. **7** Most travelers mistakenly think that ~~he or she~~ are not
                     outlets, assuming
allowed to use the ~~outlets. 8 Assuming~~ the outlets are only for airport management and cleaning staff. **9** Airport managers are definitely aware of the problem and have tried various ways of resolving it, including adding outlets in public seating areas and even in snack bars.

10 In the meantime, it's not unusual to see airport travelers carefully searching all the walls around them for a free outlet. **11** One experienced airport user offers other travelers this advice: Think like airport cleaning staff. **12** Look for the best place to plug in a vacuum cleaner. **13** Often, he says, there's an outlet in a pillar, or behind some seats on a wall. **14** An especially kind traveler brings along an extension cord with three extra outlets and invites others to share in the connection. **15** Until the airports catch up on outlet availability, these makeshift solutions will have to do.

Part 8

Readings
for Writers

41

Narration

This part of the book (this chapter through Chapter 49) contains twenty-nine essays that demonstrate the types of writing you learned in Part 2. The first essay in each chapter was written by a student; the next two were written by professional writers.

These essays are more than just good models of writing. They tell great stories, argue passionately about different issues, and present a wide range of perspectives and information. These essays can also provide you with ideas for your own writing. Most important, they offer you the opportunity to become a better reader and writer by reading and analyzing how others write.

Each essay in this chapter uses narration to make its main point. As you read these essays, consider how they achieve the four basics of good narration that are listed below and discussed in Chapter 10 of this book.

IDEA JOURNAL
Write about something you did because of peer or family pressure.

Four Basics of Good Narration

1   It reveals something of importance to your reader (your **main point**).

2   It includes all the major events of the story (**primary support**).

3   It uses details to bring the story to life for your audience (**secondary support**).

4   It presents the events in a clear order, usually according to when they happened.

Beth Trimmer

Birdshot

Beth Trimmer is currently pursuing a degree in general business from the Technical College of the Lowcountry in Beaufort, South Carolina. Her narration essay, "Birdshot," tells the story of a life-changing experience. Since receiving feedback on her writing, Trimmer remarks that "I have realized that I am a stronger writer than I thought," and she encourages other students to "never give up."

CRITICAL READING
■ Preview
■ Read
■ Pause
■ Review

(More on p. 28.)

PAUSE: Based on the first paragraph, what do you think will happen to the narrator?

PAUSE: Underline the details in this paragraph that create a dominant impression of confusion and shock.

GUIDING QUESTION
What effect did this experience have on Trimmer?

1   It was a cool October morning. I had awakened to pack my gear for yet another weekend hunting trip with my boyfriend, James, and his father, Lou. We went outside on the front porch to feel the temperature in order to dress appropriately for the field. The day was unusually cold, so I added another two layers of clothing. Then, we set off for our camp site to set up. My guardian angel must have been watching over me on this trip, which would affect the rest of my life.

2   Later that day, I sat in the middle of the field in my deer stand, just waiting for the perfect buck to come by. It was getting late, the temperature was dropping quickly, and there were not any buck in sight. I went back to camp to sit by the fire and get warm. In a matter of minutes, the flames exploded in front of my face and lit up the night sky. Sparks from the fire surrounded me, and a loud piercing noise erupted past my ears. Startled, I turned to see where the sound came from. In the distance, I saw Lou, saying something that I could not hear. I sat for a moment trying to piece together what had happened. Suddenly, intense pain shot through my whole body, as if I had been hit, hard, by a giant hammer. I realized my body was not working properly, and I fell, hands first, into the blazing fire. The next thing I knew, James was carrying me to his truck. He and his father stripped me down to my underwear. When the headlights exposed my skin, all that was visible was blood; it covered every inch of my body. I had been shot with birdshot, which has many points of penetration. At that moment, I realized that this was not going to be good, but I somehow felt that I would be alright.

3   We tried to use the Citizens' Band (CB) radio to call for help, but we were out of the range of reception. Lou and James decided to take me to the nearest hospital and got reception after ten miles. I sat in the back of the truck wrapped in a blanket as we drove for two hours to reach the

hospital. The pain was almost unbearable, causing me to fade in and out of consciousness and experience intense nausea. Then, shock set in. When we arrived at the hospital, the nurses were waiting outside with a wheelchair and took me straight to the emergency room. After they had cleaned my wounds, they took me to radiology. There, the technicians took sixteen x-rays of my legs and feet, twelve of my arms and hands, and four of my torso. They determined that surgery was not necessary because the pellets had not been imbedded in a vital organ or joint. I was given numerous prescriptions and extensive directions for caring for my wounds.

PAUSE: What are the physical consequences of this accident?

4   Now, five pellets remain in my right leg. The nurses were able to scrub the pellet fragments out of my arms, back, and left leg. One of the pellets in my right calf caused extensive muscle damage and atrophy. Another pierced my Achilles' tendon, leaving only half of the tendon intact. Another pellet went into a bone in my ankle, causing it to crack, while the two remaining pellets are floating dangerously close to the joint. If one of the pellets moves into my ankle, emergency surgery will have to be performed in order to save my joint. I am unable to run, jump, or stand for long durations. I wear a leg brace when I walk any distance, and my leg aches badly during damp weather. The birdshot was made of lead, so I must get tetanus shots every two years, and I will always set off metal detectors at the airport or courthouse.

5   As I reflect on this experience, I wonder how I could have remained calm and have found the patience and strength required to recover. It is then that I feel most strongly that someone was watching over and protecting me. My accident could have been worse: I could easily have died. The chair that I had been sitting in was completely destroyed. I believe that my guardian angel helped me survive my wounds and the resulting shock. My traumatic experience has significantly affected me, but not all in a bad way. From it, I have learned to be more patient on my own and to practice a life of positive thinking. These lessons will guide the rest of my life.

PAUSE: Summarize the narrator's attitude toward the experience.

. . . .

SUMMARIZE AND RESPOND

In your reading journal or elsewhere, summarize the main point of "Birdshot." Then, go back and check off support for this main idea. Next, write a brief summary (three to five sentences) of the essay. Finally, jot down your initial responses to the reading. What do you think Trimmer wanted to communicate to her readers? What do you learn about the narrator from her account of this experience?

CHECK YOUR COMPREHENSION

1. Which of the following would be the best alternative title for this essay?

   a. "A Trip with My Boyfriend"

   b. "My Guardian Angel Was Watching Over Me"

   c. "The Need for Gun Control Laws"

   d. "The Dangers of Hunting"

2. The main idea of this essay is that

   a. the narrator had a good relationship with her boyfriend.

   b. physical injuries can lead a person to depression.

   c. the narrator will never go hunting again.

   d. people can remain positive and grateful, even after a traumatic experience.

3. According to Trimmer, her boyfriend and her boyfriend's father

   a. drove her two hours to a hospital after the accident.

   b. gave her first aid at the camp site instead of seeking professional medical attention.

   c. were reluctant to bring Trimmer along on the hunting trip.

   d. called an ambulance after the accident.

4. If you are unfamiliar with the following words, use a dictionary to check their meanings: piercing (para. 2); radiology (3); durations (4); tetanus (4); traumatic (5).

READ CRITICALLY

1. What does this experience lead the writer to believe?

2. What is your overall impression of the narrator?

3. Where in the essay does Trimmer use transitions? How do they help the writer present the story in a clear order? Underline specific examples.

4. How does Trimmer's secondary support make her narrative vivid and lively for readers? Point to a specific example.

5. How does the essay's conclusion refer to the essay's introduction? Do you find this choice effective? Why or why not?

. . . .

WRITE AN ESSAY
Trimmer's traumatic experience affected the rest of her life. For example, it made her realize the importance of a positive attitude. Write about a traumatic, painful, or difficult experience in your own life. How did it change you? Did you learn anything from it? Share your thoughts and feelings about the experience. Are they different now than they were at the time?

. . . .

Langston Hughes

Salvation

Langston Hughes (1902–1967) was born in Joplin, Missouri, and spent his high school years in Cleveland, Ohio. Later, he studied engineering at Columbia University, but he eventually dropped out, soon becoming a central figure in the Harlem Renaissance, a period of creative innovation by writers, artists, and musicians in the African American section of New York. While he is primarily known as a poet, he was also a prolific writer of stories, plays, and essays.

In this excerpt from his autobiography, *The Big Sea* (1940), Hughes recounts a childhood struggle to fulfill others' expectations while remaining true to his own ideas about being "saved."

CRITICAL
READING
■ Preview
■ Read
■ Pause
■ Review

(More on p. 28.)

GUIDING QUESTION
Was Hughes saved, or not?

1   I was saved from sin when I was going on thirteen. But not really saved. It happened like this. There was a big revival at my Auntie Reed's church. Every night for weeks there had been much preaching, singing, praying, and shouting, and some very hardened sinners had been brought to Christ, and the membership of the church had grown by leaps and bounds. Then just before the revival ended, they held a special meeting for children, "to bring the young lambs to the fold." My aunt spoke of it for days ahead. That night I was escorted to the front row and placed on the mourners' bench with all the other young sinners, who had not yet been brought to Jesus.

PAUSE: Based on the first paragraph, predict what this essay will be about.

TEACHING TIP
This essay is an excellent model of concrete language used to bring a narration vividly to life. Have students consider Hughes's use of specific nouns, verbs, adjectives, and adverbs in several paragraphs.

DISCUSSION
Ask students about initiation practices in their own faiths. How do they respond to the practices within Hughes's Christian church?

PAUSE: What do you think Hughes might do next?

2   My aunt told me that when you were saved you saw a light, and something happened to you inside! And Jesus came into your life! And God was with you from then on! She said you could see and hear and feel Jesus in your soul. I believed her. I had heard a great many old people say the same thing and it seemed to me they ought to know. So I sat there calmly in the hot, crowded church, waiting for Jesus to come to me.

3   The preacher preached a wonderful rhythmical sermon, all moans and shouts and lonely cries and dire pictures of hell, and then he sang a song about the ninety and nine safe in the fold, but one little lamb was left out in the cold. Then he said: "Won't you come? Won't you come to Jesus? Young lambs, won't you come?" And he held out his arms to all us young sinners there on the mourners' bench. And the little girls cried. And some of them jumped up and went to Jesus right away. But most of us just sat there.

4   A great many old people came and knelt around us and prayed, old women with jet-black faces and braided hair, old men with work-gnarled hands. And the church sang a song about the lower lights are burning, some poor sinners to be saved. And the whole building rocked with prayer and song.

5   Still I kept waiting to *see* Jesus.

6   Finally all the young people had gone to the altar and were saved, but one boy and me. He was a rounder's[1] son named Westley. Westley and I were surrounded by sisters and deacons praying. It was very hot in the church, and getting late now. Finally Westley said to me in a whisper: "God damn! I'm tired o' sitting here. Let's get up and be saved." So he got up and was saved.

7   Then I was left all alone on the mourners' bench. My aunt came and knelt at my knees and cried, while prayers and songs swirled all around me in the little church. The whole congregation prayed for me alone, in a mighty wail of moans and voices. And I kept waiting serenely for Jesus, waiting, waiting—but he didn't come. I wanted to see him, but nothing happened to me. Nothing! I wanted something to happen to me, but nothing happened.

8   I heard the songs and the minister saying: "Why don't you come? My dear child, why don't you come to Jesus? Jesus is waiting for you. He wants you. Why don't you come? Sister Reed, what is this child's name?"

9   "Langston," my aunt sobbed.

10   "Langston, why don't you come? Why don't you come and be saved? Oh, Lamb of God! Why don't you come?"

11   Now it was really getting late. I began to be ashamed of myself, holding everything up so long. I began to wonder what God thought about Westley, who certainly hadn't seen Jesus either, but who was now sitting

---

1. rounder: a man with a bad character

proudly on the platform, swinging his knickerbockered[2] legs and grinning down at me, surrounded by deacons and old women on their knees praying. God had not struck Westley dead for taking his name in vain or for lying in the temple. So I decided that maybe to save further trouble, I'd better lie, too, and say that Jesus had come, and get up and be saved.

12   So I got up.

13   Suddenly the whole room broke into a sea of shouting, as they saw me rise. Waves of rejoicing swept the place. Women leaped in the air. My aunt threw her arms around me. The minister took me by the hand and led me to the platform.

14   When things quieted down, in a hushed silence, punctuated by a few ecstatic "Amens," all the new young lambs were blessed in the name of God. Then joyous singing filled the room.

15   That night, for the last time in my life but one—for I was a big boy twelve years old—I cried. I cried, in bed alone, and couldn't stop. I buried my head under the quilts, but my aunt heard me. She woke up and told my uncle I was crying because the Holy Ghost had come into my life, and because I had seen Jesus. But I was really crying because I couldn't bear to tell her that I had lied, that I had deceived everybody in the church, and I hadn't seen Jesus, and that now I didn't believe there was a Jesus any more, since he didn't come to help me.

PAUSE: Why did Hughes get up to be saved?

PAUSE: Summarize Hughes's feelings.

2. **knickerbockered:** wearing a pair of knee-length pants popular for boys in the early twentieth century

· ·

SUMMARIZE AND RESPOND

In your reading journal or elsewhere, summarize the main point of "Salvation." Then, go back and check off support for this main idea. Next, write a brief summary (three to five sentences) of the essay. Finally, jot down your initial response to the essay. What do you think Hughes wanted to communicate to readers by relating this story from his youth? What did you learn about Hughes as a young person?

· ·

CHECK YOUR COMPREHENSION

1. Which of the following would be the best alternative title for this essay?

   a. "Auntie Reed's Church"

   b. "The Power of Prayer"

   c. "Waiting for Jesus"

   d. "Westley and Me"

2. The main idea of this essay is that
   a. most religious people are hypocrites.
   b. a good preacher can stir a congregation to be saved.
   c. Hughes had a very religious upbringing that affected him throughout his lifetime.
   d. Hughes lost his faith because he didn't see Jesus when he pretended to be saved.

3. According to Hughes, his aunt
   a. deeply wanted him to be saved.
   b. raised him for most of his childhood.
   c. was herself saved when she was twelve years old.
   d. knew the real reason Hughes was crying after the revival meeting.

4. If you are unfamiliar with the following words, use a dictionary to check their meanings: escorted (para. 1); dire (3); gnarled (4); congregation, serenely (7); deacons (11); deceived (15).

READ CRITICALLY

1. How can you tell that Hughes truly wanted to be "brought to Christ" (para. 1)?

2. Why did Hughes finally join the other children who had been "saved"?

3. What does the fact that Hughes cried after the revival service tell you about him?

4. What is the purpose of the exclamation points after the first three sentences of paragraph 2?

5. Note where Hughes uses direct quotation in the essay. What is the effect of these quotations?

WRITE AN ESSAY

Write an essay about a time in your youth when you desperately wanted to experience or achieve something but failed to do so, or missed your opportunity. In addition to narrating the events that occurred, share the thoughts and feelings you had at the time.

M. Catherine Maternowska
Truck-Stop Girls

Having earned a doctorate in anthropology and sociomedical sciences from Columbia University, M. Catherine Maternowska is now an assistant professor at the University of California, San Francisco, and currently director of the International Centre for Reproductive Health in Kenya. In 2006, she wrote *Reproducing Inequalities: Poverty and the Politics of Population in Haiti*, and in 2010 was chosen as a child protection specialist and gender-based advisor to UNICEF in Haiti. Maternowska first published "Truck-Stop Girls" in the *New York Times* in 2009 after returning from a fact-finding trip to Swaziland, where one in three people is infected with HIV.

CRITICAL
READING
■ Preview
■ Read
■ Pause
■ Review

(More on p. 28.)

GUIDING QUESTION
Why is Maternowska so affected by Mbali's story?

1   In May, I was traveling down a South African highway with a colleague and a driver, headed toward Swaziland.[1] A private foundation had assigned me to assess a health clinic that it set up for truckers and the girls and women who trade sex with them for cash and goods. Truckers are well known to transmit HIV up and down the highways. And Swaziland, a small, landlocked country dependent on its busy trucking corridors, is particularly troublesome. It has the highest HIV rate in the world: One in three people is infected.

PAUSE: What is the writer trying to find out by her trip to Swaziland?

2   When we reached the Osheok[2] border post, the Swazi official welcomed us, inspecting the vehicle efficiently. Apart from a gas station, a dozen roadside vegetable stands, and some dingy bars, there was little activity in the little border town. Adjacent to the customs office, there was a small building fashioned from a shipping container with a hand-painted sign outside: "Truckers Wellness Center." It's an innovative way to set up a clinic. While papers are processed at customs, truckers use the clinic to obtain medications for "hot urine"[3] and other sexually transmitted diseases.

3   We watched truckers filing into the clinic throughout the evening, but there were no girls. So I wandered up and chatted with the border official, who said, "You want girls? Then go to Matsapha. They'll attack your car!"

---

1. Swaziland: a small country in southeast Africa   **2. Osheok:** a region of Swaziland   **3. hot urine:** a possible indicator of sexually transmitted disease

PAUSE: How does the quotation from the guidebook contribute to the narrative?

PAUSE: Why might the girls run away from Maternowska and her colleague?

Matsapha is the main overnight hub for truckers. It was well past 11 p.m., but we decided to go there. As we drove, the "majestic mountains, fertile valleys and lush forests" described in Swaziland guidebooks appeared only as shadows.

4   Matsapha was still, almost abandoned. A lone gas attendant directed us to the edge of town and an old sign on a hill for the Economy Flats motel. The driver slowed, and as the official predicted, about ten girls in tiny dresses and little shorts swarmed around our vehicle. But when they saw my female colleague and me, they screamed and went off. I sent the driver out to negotiate. "Tell them we just want to talk," I said. "I'll buy them dinner." The lure of food was enough. Three girls got in the car, and we drove down a narrow, beaten track through the trees to a rundown complex of rough cement-block buildings. This was their home. This was where the truckers slept and the girls earned their meals.

5   We sat on stones outside the barren rooms and talked with the young women. Dozens of girls, between the ages of fourteen and twenty-four, were hanging around the compound. Men smoking cigarettes and drinking liquor walked up and down the path and in and out of the cement-block buildings. The girls were alert to one another's needs, listening for sounds of violence in the rooms or the shouts of the younger girls closer to the road.

6   I met eyes with a sixteen-year-old named Mbali. She was thin, with close-cropped hair and a beautiful smile. I offered her a packet of crackers, which she ripped open with her teeth. After wolfing them down, she looked at me and said, "I hate having sex." Her parents were dead; she was unable to pay her school fees, had been abused by an overburdened aunt—and now, like many of the girls, she was a runaway. Nearly one in four Swazi girls is HIV positive, and Mbali is one of them. Her treatment options are limited. "I have nowhere to sleep unless I find a man," she said. "Sometimes I don't have money and food for two days. A man without a condom will pay more, so obviously I say O.K. because I need money."

7   She continued: "I am so tired. These men are so rough."

PAUSE: What makes the writer "suddenly burst into tears"?

8   I've been working with women and girls for over two decades now—in Haiti, in Zimbabwe, in Tanzania, and in Kenya—and I have heard this story often. But this one, deep in the forest of Swaziland, seemed so desperate. I was as surprised as she was when I suddenly burst into tears.

9   Mbali held my face and said, "Don't cry!" She hugged me. How absurd can life be? A sixteen-year-old, HIV-positive orphan was comforting me while I wept. It was a strange way to carry on an interview, but that's what we did. I asked her what she needed most. "Someplace safe," she said. "Someplace to be a girl. Someplace where I won't have to have sex with men anymore."

10   The driver of our car appeared, carrying takeout food from a nearby bar. I could hear trucks speeding along the highway through the forest. I kept thinking about what Mbali asked for: a safe place to be a girl. How strange. How simple.

··

SUMMARIZE AND RESPOND

In your reading journal or elsewhere, summarize the main point of "Truck-Stop Girls." Then, go back and check off support for this main idea. Next, write a brief summary (three to five sentences) of the essay. Finally, jot down your initial response to the reading. What impression of the "truck-stop girls" did you come away with? Do you understand why they do what they do? What is your impression of the narrator?

··

CHECK YOUR COMPREHENSION

1. Which of the following would be the best alternative title for this essay?

   a. "My Travels in the Majestic Mountains and Lush Forests of Swaziland"

   b. "A Road Trip in Africa"

   c. "African Truckers Face HIV Risk"

   d. "Tears for Mbali"

2. What is the main idea of this essay?

   a. The author wants to show the desperate lives and hopes of truck-stop girls, and highlight the terrible conditions that force them to work as they do.

   b. The author wants to encourage Americans to give more financial support to charities operating in countries like Swaziland.

   c. The author hopes to show that, despite its many problems, Swaziland is a pleasant place for tourists to visit.

   d. The author wishes to highlight how Mbali and the other truck-stop girls lack personal responsibility.

3. The narrator is surprised at her own emotional response to Mbali because

   a. Mbali is not a sympathetic figure.

   b. writers are never supposed to show any emotion in their work.

   c. Maternowska has worked with similar women and often heard stories like Mbali's.

   d. Mbali seemed so happy with her life as a "truck-stop girl."

4. If you are unfamiliar with the following words, use a dictionary to check their meanings: corridors (para. 1); efficiently, dingy, adjacent (2); negotiate, complex (4); wolfing, condom (6); absurd (9).

READ CRITICALLY

1. Note the writer's use of direct quotations. How do they contribute to the narrative? Point to a specific example.

2. Underline the secondary support in paragraph 6. How do these details help bring the narrative to life?

3. In paragraph 9, Maternowska asks, "How absurd can life be?" What does she mean by this? What seems absurd?

4. How does the writer show the passage of time in this narrative?

5. Maternowska suggests that Mbali's needs were "strange" and "simple." What does this mean?

WRITE AN ESSAY

Write an essay about a time when you had a strong and surprising emotional response to something or someone. In addition to narrating the experience, share the thoughts and feelings you had at the time.

Narration: Linked Readings

THE PRESSURE TO CONFORM

Each of the following readings focuses on various aspects of the pressures people feel to conform.

Langston Hughes, "Salvation" (this chapter, p. 691)

Kathleen Vail, "Words That Wound" (Chapter 42, p. 706)

Malcolm X, "My First Conk" (Chapter 44, p. 741)

Read the selections, and draw from at least one in addition to "Salvation" to write an essay entitled "The Pressure to Conform in Our Society." You can refer to your own experience, but make sure to use material from the essays as well.

OVERCOMING ADVERSITY AND TRAUMA

Each of the following readings shows people overcoming adversity or trauma in different ways.

Beth Trimmer, "Birdshot" (this chapter, p. 688)

Daniel Flanagan, "The Choice to Do It Over Again" (Chapter 13, p. 206)

Michael Jernigan, "Living the Dream" (Chapter 48, p. 798)

Read the selections, and draw from at least one in addition to "Birdshot" to write an essay titled "Overcoming Adversity." You can refer to your own experience, but make sure to use material from the essays as well.

CONCEPTIONS OF GENDER

Each of the following readings focuses on various aspects of the effects of gender on people's behavior and lives.

M. Catherine Maternowska, "Truck-Stop Girls" (this chapter, p. 695)

Deborah L. Rhode, "Why Looks Are the Last Bastion of Discrimination" (Chapter 42, p. 711)

Dave Barry, "The Ugly Truth about Beauty" (Chapter 47, p. 787)

Amy L. Beck, "Struggling for Perfection" (Chapter 48, p. 807)

Read the selections, and draw from at least one in addition to "Truck-Stop Girls" to write an essay titled "How Gender Affects Behavior." You can refer to your own experience, but make sure to use material from your essays as well.

42

Illustration

Each essay in this chapter uses illustration to get its main point across. As you read these essays, consider how they achieve the four basics of good illustration that are listed below and discussed in Chapter 11 of this book.

IDEA JOURNAL
Write about a time when you were bullied or hurt by what someone said about you.

Four Basics of Good Illustration

1 It has a point.

2 It gives specific examples to show, explain, or prove the point.

3 It gives details to support the examples.

4 It uses enough examples to get the point across to the reader.

Tam Nguyen

Reflection

Tam Nguyen wrote this essay while she was a student at Bunker Hill Community College in Boston, Massachusetts. "Reflection" records a campus visit by writer Tim O'Brien to address almost four hundred veterans and explores her own emotional connections to the Vietnam War. Nguyen is Vietnamese, and her grandfather fought against the United States as a Viet Cong general in the Vietnam War. Because she was on the waiting list for Mount Holyoke College, one of her professors encouraged Nguyen to write about the event and send it in as a supplement to her application. Not only was she later accepted at Mount Holyoke, but *Insider Higher Ed* also featured her piece in an article titled "The Story of an Essay."

CRITICAL READING
■ Preview
■ Read
■ Pause
■ Review

(More on p. 28.)

COMBINING MODES: Notice that the author uses narration within her illustration essay.

PAUSE: What effect does O'Brien have on the audience?

GUIDING QUESTION

Why does the writer feel such a deep connection to O'Brien?

1   The author Tim O'Brien[1] came to Bunker Hill Community College for an event hosted by the Veterans Club. The event drew so many people that the A Lounge, where it took place, was overcrowded. People were standing wherever they could find a spot and those who wanted to attend spilled out into the hallway leading to the lounge. Despite the mass of people, the audience was silent. As I came into the room, I was drawn into an invisible circle that trapped me, and the force drawing the audience and me in was Tim O'Brien. He was casually dressed in jeans, a T-shirt, and his favorite baseball cap. He spoke slowly and quietly. Every word he uttered was clear, concise, factual, and devoid of excess emotion. Each word, however, trapped the audience in an emotion, and besides me, I saw a few others shedding tears from his presentation.

2   I joined the audience in the middle of the event, after finishing up at work. When I came, O'Brien was discussing "The Man I Killed," one of the most famous stories in his novel *The Things They Carried.* "The Man I Killed" describes O'Brien's reaction when he looked at the dead body of an enemy he just killed. O'Brien looked at the man's wounds and imagined different stories about him. He was a young boy with a typical life who wished every day that the Americans would leave, so he would not have to join the war. The story, at every moment it was discussed, evoked many personal feelings and memories from me.

1. Tim O'Brien: American novelist (b. 1946) and Vietnam War veteran who writes about the effects of war on those who fought

3   It is commonly said that war distorts[2] all the values of humanity. War allows only action, which is that a man kills another man, so he will not be killed himself. But to learn this deconstruction of humanity from a soldier who was put in a situation where it was either kill or be killed brings the cruelty of war to a new dimension. This extreme situation pushes a human into a dead end; it traps him or her in a corner where the only choice is either to give up on conscience or to die. Why does this type of situation dominate war, when people all across the world are taught not to kill? We understand that when a soldier kills another human, he has a good reason to do so: He is trying to protect himself and survive.

4   However, war causes combatants to lose sight of the value of humanity. The act of killing another human crosses a line which devalues the life of another human being. Once the line is crossed, what the soldiers see and feel becomes the hidden part of war that only a soldier, not an outsider, can tell. And this hidden part has been covered in the darkness of war trauma, which Vietnamese and American soldiers all experienced. At least, that is what I found out from my family members and friends.

5   My family has many members who were devoted to the war. They fought and killed to survive and contribute to a Vietnamese victory. They were honored and received many medals and awards which they should be proud of. Yet, besides their accomplishments, I have never heard a specific war story vividly describing a battle.

PAUSE: Why do you think her family members avoid telling "specific" war stories?

6   For example, my uncle often used words like "we fought," "we won," and "we lost." He never told stories about what actually happened: whom he met, how he fought, or what he thought about the war. In fact, my uncle and the millions of participants, real people, are hidden behind characters. There is a key emotion that is always missing from history texts, novels, and movies, seemingly because no one really knows the truth or they just never tell. I wanted to get the answer from my uncle, but he usually stayed quiet and immersed himself in deep thought whenever I asked him about the battles he participated in. He would never tell me anything, and I could feel that the war created a secret circle around him which would haunt him for the rest of his life.

PAUSE: What, exactly, does the writer want to know from her uncle?

7   Another person that the war will bother for eternity is my friend Arthur. He is an American veteran of the Vietnam War who is devoted to obtaining an education and helping his fellow veterans. After leaving the war, he suffered for many years. In spite of the trauma plaguing Arthur, he fights the pain with optimism, which has gotten him through all his days.

PAUSE: What qualities does Arthur illustrate?

8   One day, I asked him about his time in Vietnam. He smiled and joked about the "lousy" food he ate and the deep forests he had been through. But just like my uncle, he would not talk about the enemies he faced and how he fought. Again, the war remains hidden! How amazing it is that two

2. **distorts:** twists

individuals from two opposite cultures, who fought on opposing sides in a horrible war, share the same feelings.

9   Throughout the event, these experiences and connections were running through my head, and the stories were capturing me in the invisible circle. I wondered why, when Tim O'Brien was speaking about his own experiences, I couldn't get away from the similarities to my own experiences. The presentation came to an end, and I decided to stay afterward. I joined the line, which was meant for Tim O'Brien to sign his books, even though I didn't have one of his books and couldn't buy one, either. I just thought that I had to talk to him.

10   While I was waiting in line, memories again encircled me, and many thoughts came into my mind. I kept thinking about my grandfather who passed away. He was a general in the American War, and if all the soldiers I know keep the war hidden, my grandfather—who had more war stories than anyone in my family—also had more secrets as well. Then my mind wandered to my high school literature teacher who lost her whole family in the war and was disabled by a bomb in 1972. I also recalled a taxi driver whom I met last year, who was laughing when he told me that the Vietnam War cost him his two brothers. And right before I got to Tim O'Brien, I thought about my friend Arthur, who came back with a hidden part of his life which he barely shares with others. I wanted to tell Tim O'Brien all I knew and to express to him all my emotions. But once I came up to him all I could say was my name and that with all that I have heard, we, both Vietnamese and Americans, share the same feelings. The moment was unforgettable. We hugged each other, and just like the shared emotions, we both cried.

11   I was drawn to Tim O'Brien by an invisible circle of war experiences and memories, probably because I somehow felt its existence by my own experiences and memories. He was the first one to open up and share such intensive stories of the war, and gave me the emotions that I have been searching for. I cried hard, as I felt connected to O'Brien and the soldiers on both sides. But above all, it was the greater understanding of my uncle, my grandfather, and Arthur that I appreciated the most. We know that nothing can be changed about the war. Time can never be turned back. There are wounds to be healed and others that won't disappear. However, we move on and find peace of mind by knowing that we at least share the same feelings with someone, somewhere.

PAUSE: What is significant about the fact that the author's grandfather was a Viet Cong general? How does it affect her perception?

PAUSE: What does Nguyen realize when she finally speaks to O'Brien?

SUMMARIZE AND RESPOND

In your reading journal or elsewhere, summarize the main point of "Reflection." Then, go back and check off support for the main idea. Next, write a brief summary (three to five sentences) of the reading. Finally, jot down your initial response to the selection. Does the essay give you any insight into the effects of war, even for those who are not direct participants?

CHECK YOUR COMPREHENSION

1. Which of the following would be the best alternative title for the essay?
   a. "How America Lost the Vietnam War"
   b. "My Friend Arthur"
   c. "The Hidden Truths of War"
   d. "A War for Justice"

2. The main idea of this essay is that
   a. many Vietnamese people still resent Americans because of the Vietnam War.
   b. war is destructive, dehumanizing, and irreversible, but we can find healing and peace of mind by understanding the feelings of those affected by it.
   c. Tim O'Brien's short stories give an unfair and one-sided account of the American involvement in the Vietnam War.
   d. Nguyen resented members of her own family because they would not tell her exactly what happened during the Vietnam War.

3. According to Nguyen, wars
   a. force soldiers into situations where they must kill or be killed.
   b. provide an opportunity for people to prove their courage.
   c. only serve to benefit the wealthy and powerful.
   d. are brutal but necessary.

4. If you are unfamiliar with the following words, use a dictionary to check their meanings: concise, devoid (1); evoked (2); conscience, dominate (3); trauma (4); immersed (6); optimism (7).

READ CRITICALLY

1. Identify three examples in the essay. Are they effective? Do you think Nguyen uses enough examples?

2. According to Nguyen, what do Vietnamese and American soldiers have in common, even though they fought on opposite sides in the war?

3. The narrator writes that the truths of war are often hidden. How can people who did not fight directly in a war better understand such truths?

4. When Nguyen asked her friend Arthur about the war, the veteran only "smiled and joked about the 'lousy' food he ate and the deep forests he had been through" (para. 8). Why do you think Arthur responds this way?

5. Is Nguyen's conclusion effective? Explain your answer.

WRITE AN ESSAY

Nguyen illustrates how war can distort the "values of humanity," as well as how shared memories and experiences can help heal war's victims. Write your own essay illustrating the meaning and effects of war—whether on individuals or entire societies and countries. You may use examples from your own observations, current events, history, films, books, and other accounts.

Kathleen Vail

Words That Wound

Kathleen Vail was born in Pittsburgh, Pennsylvania, and received a bachelor's degree in journalism from California University of Pennsylvania. She has worked as an education reporter at daily newspapers in Pennsylvania, North Carolina, and Virginia, and in 1994 she became an assistant editor at the *American School Board Journal: The Source for School Leaders.* She has been managing editor there since 2006. Vail lives in Springfield, Virginia, with her husband and two sons. Originally published in the *American School Board Journal,* "Words That Wound" focuses on school bullying and its sometimes devastating consequences.

CRITICAL
READING
■ Preview
■ Read
■ Pause
■ Review

(More on p. 28.)

PAUSE: Based on these two opening paragraphs, what do you predict that this essay will be about?

GUIDING QUESTION
What examples of bullying does Vail give?

1   Brian Head saw only one way out. On the final day of his life, during economics class, the fifteen-year-old stood up and pointed a semiautomatic handgun at himself. Before he pulled the trigger, he said his last words, "I can't take this anymore."

2   Brian's father, William Head, has no doubt why his child chose to take his life in front of a classroom full of students five years ago. Brian wanted everyone to know the source of his pain, the suffering he could no longer endure. The Woodstock, GA, teen, overweight with thick glasses, had been systematically abused by school bullies since elementary school. Death was the only relief he could imagine. "Children can't vote or organize, leave or run away," says Head. "They are trapped."

DISCUSSION
Do members of your
class think that Vail's
phrase "torture cham-
ber" (para. 3) is too
strong or essentially
accurate?

3   For many students, school is a torture chamber from which there is no escape. Every day, 160,000 children stay home from school because they are afraid of being bullied, according to the National Association of School Psychologists. In a study of junior high school students from small Midwestern towns, nearly 77 percent of the students reported they'd been victims of bullies at school — 14 percent saying they'd experienced severe reactions to the abuse. "Bullying is a crime of violence," says June Arnette, associate director of the National School Safety Center. "It's an imbalance of power, sustained over a period of time."

4   Yet even in the face of this suffering, even after Brian Head's suicide five years ago, even after it was revealed this past spring that a culture of bullying might have played a part in the Columbine High School shootings,[1] bullying remains for the most part unacknowledged, underreported, and minimized by schools. Adults are unaware of the extent and nature of the problem, says Nancy Mullin-Rindler, associate director of the Project on Teasing and Bullying in the Elementary Grades at Wellesley College Center for Research for Women. "They underestimate the import. They feel it's a normal part of growing up, that it's character-building."

5   After his son's death, William Head became a crusader against bullying, founding an effort called Kids Hope to prevent others from suffering as Brian had. Unfortunately, bullying claimed another victim in the small town of Woodstock: thirteen-year-old Josh Belluardo. Last November, on the bus ride home from school, Josh's neighbor, fifteen-year-old Jonathan Miller, taunted him and threw wads of paper at him. He followed Josh off the school bus, hit the younger boy in the back of the head, and kicked him in the stomach. Josh spent the last two days of his life in a coma before dying of his injuries. Miller, it turns out, had been suspended nearly twenty times for offenses such as pushing and taunting other students and cursing at a teacher. He's now serving a life sentence for felony murder while his case is on appeal.

6   Bullying doesn't have to result in death to be harmful. Bullying and harassment are major distractions from learning, according to the National School Safety Center. Victims' grades suffer, and fear can lead to chronic absenteeism, truancy, or dropping out. Bullies also affect children who aren't victimized: Bystanders feel guilty and helpless for not standing up to the bully. They feel unsafe, unable to take action. They also can be drawn into bullying behavior by peer pressure. "Any time there is a climate of fear, the learning process will be compromised," says Arnette.

PAUSE: Underline
the ways that bullying
can be harmful, ac-
cording to Vail.

7   A full 70 percent of children believe teachers handle episodes of bullying "poorly," according to a study by John Hoover at the University of North Dakota at Grand Forks. It's no wonder kids are reluctant to tell adults about bullying incidents. "Children feel no one will take them seriously," says Robin

1. **Columbine High School shootings:** the April 1999 shootings at Columbine High School in Littleton, Colorado, in which two male students killed twelve students and a teacher, injured twenty-three others, and then killed themselves

Kowalski, professor of psychology at Western Carolina University, Cullo-whee, NC, who's done research on teasing behavior.

8   Martha Rizzo, who lives in a suburb of Cincinnati, calls bullying the "dirty little secret" of her school district. Both her son and daughter were teased in school. Two boys in her son's sixth-grade class began taunting him because he wore sweatpants instead of jeans. They began to intimidate him during class. Once they knocked the pencil out of his hand during a spelling test when the teacher's back was turned. He failed the test. Rizzo made an appointment with the school counselor. The counselor told her he could do nothing about the behavior of the bullies and suggested she get counseling for her son instead. "Schools say they do something, but they don't, and it continues," says Rizzo. "We go in with the same problem over and over again."

9   Anna Billoit of Louisiana went to her son's middle school teachers when her son, who had asthma and was overweight, was being bullied by his classmates. Some of the teachers made the situation worse, she says. One male teacher suggested to her that the teasing would help her son mature. "His attitude was, 'Suck it up, take it like a man,'" says Billoit.

PAUSE: Why can confronting bullies in front of their peers be counterproductive, according to Vail?

10   Much bullying goes on in so-called transition areas where there is little or no adult supervision: hallways, locker rooms, restrooms, cafeterias, playgrounds, buses, and bus stops. When abuse happens away from adult eyes, it's hard to prove that the abuse occurred. Often, though, bullies harass their victims in the open, in full view of teachers and other adults. Some teachers will ignore the behavior, silently condoning.[2] But even when adults try to deal with the problem, they sometimes make things worse for the victim by not handling the situation properly. Confronting bullies in front of their peers only enhances the bullies' prestige and power. And bullies often step up the abuse after being disciplined. "People know it happens, but there's no structured way to deal with it," says Mullin-Rindler. "There's lots of confusion about what to do and what is the best approach."

11   Societal expectations play a part in adult reactions to childhood bullying. Many teachers and administrators buy into a widespread belief that bullying is a normal part of childhood and that children are better off working out such problems on their own. But this belief sends a dangerous message to children, says Head. Telling victims they must protect themselves from bullies shows children that adults can't and won't protect them. And, he points out, it's an attitude adults would never tolerate themselves. "If you go to work and get slapped on the back of the head, you wouldn't expect your supervisor to say, 'It's your problem—you need to learn to deal with it yourself,'" says Head. "It's a human rights issue."

PAUSE: What do you think of the point made here about teachers' "secret admiration for the strong kids"?

12   Ignoring bullying is only part of the problem. Some teachers go further by blaming the victims for their abuse by letting their own dislike for the victimized child show. "There's a lot of secret admiration for the strong kids," says Eileen Faucette of Augusta, GA. Her daughter was teased so

2. **condoning:** approving

badly in the classroom that she was afraid to go to the blackboard or raise her hand to answer a question. The abuse happened in front of the teacher, who did nothing to stop it.

13   Head also encountered a blame-the-victim attitude toward his son. Brian would get into trouble for fighting at school, but when Head and his wife investigated what happened, they usually found that Brian had been attacked by other students. The school, Head said, wanted to punish Brian along with his attackers. "The school calls it fighting," Head says. "But it's actually assault and battery."

PAUSE: Think about a time when you witnessed bullying behavior. How did you feel?

14   And changes are coming. This past April, five months after Josh Belluardo's death, the Georgia State Legislature passed an anti-bullying law. The law defines bullying as "any willful attempt or threat to inflict injury on another person when accompanied by an apparent present ability to do so" or "any intentional display of force such as would give the victim reason to fear or expect immediate bodily harm." Schools are required to send students to an alternative school if they commit a third act of bullying in a school year. The law also requires school systems to adopt anti-bullying policies and to post the policies in middle and high schools.

15   Head was consulted by the state representatives who sponsored the bill, but he believes the measure won't go far enough. He urges schools to treat bullying behavior as a violation of the state criminal law against assault, stalking, and threatening and to call police when the law is broken.

16   He knows it's too late for Brian, too late for Josh, too late for the teens who died in Littleton. But he continues to work, to educate and lobby on the devastating effects of bullying so that his son's death will not have been in vain.

17   "We should come clean and say what we've done in the past is wrong," says Head. "Now we will guarantee we'll protect the rights of students."

. . . .

SUMMARIZE AND RESPOND

In your reading journal or elsewhere, summarize the main point of "Words That Wound." Then, go back and check off support for this main idea. Next, write a brief summary (three to five sentences) of the reading. Finally, jot down your initial response to the selection. How do your own experiences with teasing and bullying in school affect your response?

. . . .

CHECK YOUR COMPREHENSION

1. Which of the following would be the best alternative title for this essay?
    a. "Bullying in Elementary School"
    b. "The Tragic Story of a Bullied Teen"
    c. "The Causes of Adolescent Suicide"
    d. "Bullying: A Serious Problem"

2. The main idea of this essay is that

- **a.** educators and policymakers need to realize that bullying has serious negative consequences and take steps to reduce its occurrence.
- **b.** bullying should be made a criminal offense like assault, battery, stalking, and threatening.
- **c.** adults who tolerate bullying among schoolchildren would never tolerate the same kind of behavior if it were inflicted in the workplace.
- **d.** bullying is common in school settings because teachers, counselors, and administrators can do little about it.

3. According to Vail, teachers who ignore bullying

- **a.** are afraid to intervene.
- **b.** send the signal that they see nothing wrong with it.
- **c.** believe that parents have the responsibility for getting help for their children.
- **d.** were probably bullies themselves.

4. If you are unfamiliar with the following words, use a dictionary to check their meanings: endure (para. 2); import (4); crusader, taunted, coma (5); distractions, chronic, truancy, compromised (6); intimidate (8); prestige (10); devastating (16).

· ·

READ CRITICALLY

1. Evaluate Vail's opening. How effective do you find it as a way of introducing her main point?

2. Identify each of the examples that Vail presents. Do these examples convince you that the problem of bullying is serious and widespread? Why or why not?

3. Consider the statistics that Vail offers in paragraphs 3 and 7. What do they contribute to the essay? Which other kinds of statistics would you like to see?

4. In paragraph 12, Vail writes about "blaming the victims." What does she mean, and how does this idea contribute to the main point she is making?

5. In what ways does Vail tie her conclusion back to the opening part of her essay? What is the effect of this conclusion?

· ·

WRITE AN ESSAY

Write an essay developing your own ideas about what schools can do to reduce bullying among students. What policies might they adopt, and how could they enforce those policies? What could be done to stop the bullying that takes place in so-called transitional areas where students have no adult supervision? Use examples, either real or hypothetical, to help readers see that your plan would work.

· ·

Deborah L. Rhode

Why Looks Are the Last Bastion of Discrimination

Deborah L. Rhode, a distinguished professor at Stanford Law School, earned her B.A. from Yale University in 1974 and a J.D. from Yale Law School in 1977. She currently serves as the director of the Stanford Center on the Legal Profession and has been awarded a number of honors, including the American Bar Association's Pro Bono Publico Award. Author of over twenty books, her most recent is titled *The Beauty Bias: The Injustice of Appearance in Life and Law* (2010). This link between ethical and legal issues is echoed in the essay reprinted here, "Why Looks Are the Last Bastion of Discrimination," which originally appeared in the *Washington Post* in 2010.

GUIDING QUESTION
Does society have a strong bias toward physically attractive people?

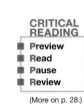

CRITICAL READING
- Preview
- Read
- Pause
- Review

(More on p. 28.)

1   In the nineteenth century, many American cities banned public appearances by "unsightly" individuals. A Chicago ordinance[1] was typical: "Any person who is diseased, maimed, mutilated, or in any way deformed, so as to be an unsightly or disgusting subject . . . shall not . . . expose himself to public view, under the penalty of a fine of $1 for each offense."

2   Although the government is no longer in the business of enforcing such discrimination, it still allows businesses, schools, and other organizations to indulge their own prejudices. Over the past half-century, the United States has expanded protections against discrimination to include race, religion, sex, age, disability, and, in a growing number of jurisdictions, sexual orientation. Yet bias based on appearance remains perfectly

1. ordinance: law

permissible in all but one state and six cities and counties. Across the rest of the country, looks are the last bastion of acceptable bigotry.[2]

3   We all know that appearance matters, but the price of prejudice can be steeper than we often assume. In Texas in 1994, an obese woman was rejected for a job as a bus driver when a company doctor assumed she was not up to the task after watching her, in his words, "waddling down the hall." He did not perform any agility tests to determine whether she was, as the company would later claim, unfit to evacuate the bus in the event of an accident.

4   In New Jersey in 2005, one of the Borgata Hotel Casino's "Borgata babe" cocktail waitresses went from a size 4 to a size 6 because of a thyroid condition. When the waitress, whose contract required her to keep an "an hourglass figure" that was "height and weight appropriate," requested a larger uniform, she was turned down. "Borgata babes don't go up in size," she was told. (Unless, the waitress noted, they have breast implants, which the casino happily accommodated with paid medical leave and a bigger bustier.)

5   And in California in 2001, Jennifer Portnick, a 240-pound aerobics instructor, was denied a franchise by Jazzercise, a national fitness chain. Jazzercise explained that its image demanded instructors who are "fit" and "toned." But Portnick was both: She worked out six days a week, taught back-to-back classes, and had no shortage of willing students.

6   Such cases are common. In a survey by the National Association to Advance Fat Acceptance, 62 percent of its overweight female members and 42 percent of its overweight male members said they had been turned down for a job because of their weight.

7   And it is not just weight that's at issue; it is appearance overall. According to a national poll by the Employment Law Alliance in 2005, 16 percent of workers reported being victims of appearance discrimination more generally—a figure comparable to the percentage who in other surveys say they have experienced sex or race discrimination.

8   Conventional wisdom[3] holds that beauty is in the eye of the beholder, but most beholders tend to agree on what is beautiful. A number of researchers have independently found that, when people are asked to rate an individual's attractiveness, their responses are quite consistent, even across race, sex, age, class, and cultural background. Facial symmetry and unblemished skin are universally admired. Men get a bump for height, women are favored if they have hourglass figures, and racial minorities get points for light skin color, European facial characteristics, and conventionally "white" hairstyles.

9   Yale's Kelly Brownell and Rebecca Puhl and Harvard's Nancy Etcoff have each reviewed hundreds of studies on the impact of appearance. Etcoff finds that unattractive people are less likely than their attractive peers to be viewed as intelligent, likable, and good. Brownell and Puhl

PAUSE: What is your reaction to these three examples of "bigotry"?

PAUSE: What point does Rhode make about the phrase "beauty is in the eye of the beholder"?

---

2. bigotry: prejudice   **3. conventional wisdom:** commonly accepted belief

have documented that overweight individuals consistently suffer disadvantages at school, at work, and beyond.

10   Among the key findings of a quarter-century's worth of research: Unattractive people are less likely to be hired and promoted, and they earn lower salaries, even in fields in which looks have no obvious relationship to professional duties. (In one study, economists Jeff Biddle and Daniel Hamermesh estimated that for lawyers, such prejudice can translate to a pay cut of as much as 12 percent.) When researchers ask people to evaluate written essays, the same material receives lower ratings for ideas, style, and creativity when an accompanying photograph shows a less attractive author. Good-looking professors get better course evaluations from students; teachers in turn rate good-looking students as more intelligent.

11   Not even justice is blind. In studies that simulate legal proceedings, unattractive plaintiffs receive lower damage awards. And in a study released this month, Stephen Ceci and Justin Gunnell, two researchers at Cornell University, gave students case studies involving real criminal defendants and asked them to come to a verdict and a punishment for each. The students gave unattractive defendants prison sentences that were, on average, twenty-two months longer than those they gave to attractive defendants.

12   Just like racial or gender discrimination, discrimination based on irrelevant physical characteristics reinforces invidious[4] stereotypes and undermines equal-opportunity principles based on merit and performance. And when grooming choices come into play, such bias can also restrict personal freedom.

13   Consider Nikki Youngblood, a lesbian who in 2001 was denied a photo in her Tampa high school yearbook because she would not pose in a scoop-necked dress. Youngblood was "not a rebellious kid," her lawyer explained. "She simply wanted to appear in her yearbook as herself, not as a fluffed-up stereotype of what school administrators thought she should look like." Furthermore, many grooming codes sexualize the workplace and jeopardize employees' health. The weight restrictions at the Borgata, for example, reportedly contributed to eating disorders among its waitresses.

14   Appearance-related bias also exacerbates[5] disadvantages based on gender, race, ethnicity, age, sexual orientation, and class. Prevailing beauty standards penalize people who lack the time and money to invest in their appearance. And weight discrimination, in particular, imposes special costs on people who live in communities with shortages of healthy food options and exercise facilities.

15   So why not simply ban discrimination based on appearance?

16   Employers often argue that attractiveness is job-related; their workers' appearance, they say, can affect the company's image and its profitability. In this way, the Borgata blamed its weight limits on market demands.

4. invidious: unflattering   **5. exacerbates:** makes worse

Customers, according to a spokesperson, like being served by an attractive waitress. The same assumption presumably motivated the L'Oreal executive who was sued for sex discrimination in 2003 after allegedly ordering a store manager to fire a salesperson who was not "hot" enough.

17   Such practices can violate the law if they disproportionately exclude groups protected by civil rights statutes — hence the sex discrimination suit. Abercrombie & Fitch's notorious efforts to project what it called a "classic American" look led to a race discrimination settlement on behalf of minority job-seekers who said they were turned down for positions on the sales floor. But unless the victims of appearance bias belong to groups already protected by civil rights laws, they have no legal remedy.

18   As the history of civil rights legislation suggests, customer preferences should not be a defense for prejudice. During the early civil rights era, employers in the South often argued that hiring African Americans would be financially ruinous; white customers, they said, would take their business elsewhere. In rejecting this logic, Congress and the courts recognized that customer preferences often reflect and reinforce precisely the attitudes that society is seeking to eliminate. Over the decades, we have seen that the most effective way of combating prejudice is to deprive people of the option to indulge it.

19   Similarly, during the 1960s and 1970s, major airlines argued that the male business travelers who dominated their customer ranks preferred attractive female flight attendants. According to the airlines, that made sex a bona fide[6] occupational qualification and exempted them from anti-discrimination requirements. But the courts reasoned that only if sexual allure were the "essence" of a job should employers be allowed to select workers on that basis. Since airplanes were not flying bordellos,[7] it was time to start hiring men.

20   Opponents of a ban on appearance-based discrimination also warn that it would trivialize[8] other, more serious forms of bias. After all, if the goal is a level playing field, why draw the line at looks? "By the time you've finished preventing discrimination against the ugly, the short, the skinny, the bald, the knobbly-kneed, the flat-chested, and the stupid," Andrew Sullivan wrote in the *London Sunday Times* in 1999, "you're living in a totalitarian state." Yet intelligence and civility are generally related to job performance in a way that appearance isn't.

21   We also have enough experience with prohibitions on appearance discrimination to challenge opponents' arguments. Already, one state (Michigan) and six local jurisdictions (the District of Columbia; Howard County, MD; San Francisco; Santa Cruz, CA; Madison, WI; and Urbana, IL) have

PAUSE: What logic did Congress and the courts reject during the civil rights era?

6. **bona fide:** real, genuine   7. **bordellos:** houses of prostitution
8. **trivialize:** devalue

banned such discrimination. Some of these laws date back to the 1970s and 1980s, while some are more recent; some cover height and weight only, while others cover looks broadly; but all make exceptions for reasonable business needs.

22   Such bans have not produced a barrage of loony litigation or an erosion of support for civil rights remedies generally. These cities and counties each receive between zero and nine complaints a year, while the entire state of Michigan totals about 30, with fewer than one a year ending up in court.

23   Although the laws are unevenly enforced, they have had a positive effect by publicizing and remedying the worst abuses. Because Portnick, the aerobics instructor turned away by Jazzercise, lived in San Francisco, she was able to bring a claim against the company. After a wave of sympathetic media coverage, Jazzercise changed its policy.

PAUSE: Summarize the positive effects of laws banning appearance-based discrimination.

24   This is not to overstate the power of legal remedies. Given the stigma[9] attached to unattractiveness, few will want to claim that status in public litigation. And in the vast majority of cases, the cost of filing suit and the difficulty of proving discrimination are likely to be prohibitive. But stricter anti-discrimination laws could play a modest role in advancing healthier and more inclusive ideals of attractiveness. At the very least, such laws could reflect our principles of equal opportunity and raise our collective consciousness when we fall short.

9. stigma: a mark of shame

• •

SUMMARIZE AND RESPOND

In your reading journal or elsewhere, summarize the main point of "Why Looks Are the Last Bastion of Discrimination." Then, go back and check off support for this main idea. Next, write a brief summary (three to five sentences) of the essay. Finally, jot down your initial response to the reading. Do you think looks-based prejudice is a serious issue? Do you think it can be eliminated by legislation? How has the essay changed your point of view on this issue?

• •

CHECK YOUR COMPREHENSION

1.   Which of the following would be the best alternative title for the essay?

   a. "Beauty Is in the Eye of the Beholder"

   b. "Appearance-Based Bigotry: A Real Problem with Real Solutions"

   c. "Anti-discrimination Laws Go Too Far"

   d. "The Worst Prejudice of All"

2. The main idea of this essay is that

   a. good-looking professors get better course evaluations from students.

   b. airlines are legally required to hire attractive female flight attendants because male passengers prefer them.

   c. bans on looks-based discrimination lead to pointless and expensive lawsuits.

   d. many states and cities still have laws that prohibit "unsightly" individuals from being seen in public.

3. If you are unfamiliar with the following words, use a dictionary to check their meanings: indulge, jurisdictions, bastion (2); agility (3); thyroid, accommodated (4); symmetry, unblemished (8); notorious (17); allure (19); totalitarian, civility (20).

• •

READ CRITICALLY

1. How effective is Rhode's opening? How does it support her main idea?

2. In discussing Jennifer Portnick in paragraph 5, the writer notes Portnick's workout and work schedule. Why do you think Rhode includes these details in her example?

3. What purpose do paragraphs 8 to 12 serve in the essay? How do they support Rhode's main idea?

4. Rhode compares contemporary looks-based discrimination to the issue of racial discrimination in the civil rights era. Does this seem like a valid comparison? Why or why not?

5. Andrew Sullivan claims, "By the time you've finished preventing discrimination against the ugly, the short, the skinny, the bald, the knobbly-kneed, the flat-chested, and the stupid, you're living in a totalitarian state" (para. 20). What is his point? Do you agree? Is this what Rhode wants?

• •

WRITE AN ESSAY

Rhode claims that in America, "looks are the last bastion of acceptable bigotry" (para. 2). How important are looks to one's social, educational, personal, and professional success? What value does our society and culture place on physical attractiveness? Using specific examples, write an essay that illustrates the significance and effects of personal appearance in American life.

• •

Illustration: Linked Readings

. . . .

THE PRESSURE TO CONFORM

Each of the following readings focuses on various aspects of the pressures people feel to conform.

> Kathleen Vail, "Words That Wound" (this chapter, p. 706)
>
> Langston Hughes, "Salvation" (Chapter 41, p. 691)
>
> Malcolm X, "My First Conk" (Chapter 44, p. 741)

Read the selections, and draw from at least one in addition to "Words That Wound" to write an essay titled "The Pressure to Conform in Our Society." You can refer to your own experience, but make sure to use material from the essays as well.

. . . .

CHASING BEAUTY

Though they have different tones, all of the following readings focus on the quest for female beauty and perfection.

> Deborah L. Rhode, "Why Looks Are the Last Bastion of Discrimination" (this chapter, p. 711)
>
> Dave Barry, "The Ugly Truth about Beauty" (Chapter 47, p. 787)
>
> Amy L. Beck, "Struggling for Perfection" (Chapter 48, p. 807)

Read the selections, and write an essay titled "The Dangers of Chasing Beauty and Perfection." You can refer to your own experience, but make sure to use material from the essays as well.

. . . .

THE COSTS OF WAR

Both of the following readings focus on the aftereffects and human costs of war.

> Tam Nguyen, "Reflection" (this chapter, p. 702)
>
> Michael Jernigan, "Living the Dream" (Chapter 48, p. 798)

Read the selections, and write an essay titled "The Costs of War." You can refer to your own experience, but make sure to use material from the essays as well.

. . . .

43

Description

IDEA JOURNAL
Describe a place
from your past (or
a family member's
past) that you
have visited.

Each essay in this chapter uses description to get its main point across. As you read these essays, consider how they achieve the four basics of good description that are listed below and discussed in Chapter 12 of this book.

Four Basics of Good Description

1. It creates a main impression — an overall effect, feeling, or image — about the topic.
2. It uses specific examples to support the main impression.
3. It supports those examples with details that appeal to the five senses.
4. It brings a person, place, or object to life for the reader.

718

Heaven Morrison

My Kingdom

As a student at the Technical College of the Lowcountry in Beaufort, South Carolina, Heaven Morrison plans to graduate in 2013 with a degree in wildlife biology. Morrison classifies "My Kingdom" as a descriptive essay, the style of writing she is most drawn to: "Telling someone how things looked, felt, smelled, and sounded makes me extremely motivated to write the piece and make it as descriptive as possible." She also believes in the importance of "vividness and good flow" in her essays and advises other student writers to "take your time writing and let things come to you. Don't force it."

CRITICAL READING
- ■ Preview
- ■ Read
- ■ Pause
- ■ Review

(More on p. 28.)

GUIDING QUESTION
Which image or sensory detail in this essay do you find most memorable?

1   Many things can be a source of inspiration. For me, inspiration came in the form of Mother Nature. In fact, nature inspired me enough to influence what I want to do in life and to understand where my heart lies. This inspiration was born during a family reunion in Maine at Baxter State Park.

PAUSE: What comes to mind when you think of the word *inspiration*?

2   The bumpy roads on the way to the park were slowly wearing on everyone's nerves. Every time someone asked, "How much longer?" we got the reply, "about fifteen more minutes." Giving up, I rested my head against the coolness of the car window and watched the pine trees fly by. Maine is a place of beauty, where northern wilderness welcomes people to its peaceful existence.

PAUSE: What do you think will happen to Morrison on this trip?

3   It was early spring, the frost still barely clinging to fresh new flower buds and blazing green patches of grass. The air stirred with the fresh, chilling scent of the remaining winter. We were driving from Lincoln, Maine, where we were staying, heading to Baxter State Park in Millinocket, Maine, near the Canadian border.

4   Finally, we went down an old gravel road and saw the state park sign, signaling our long-awaited arrival. What a relief. Passing the old brown booth with the park ranger, we parked and hurried to get out of the stuffy car. I felt a rush of anticipation accompanied by a rush of blood to my legs, stiff from sitting for so long. A quaint cabin was off to the left, probably filled with children, parents, and grandparents sipping hot chocolate. As nice as that sounded, I was eager to get out to the trails and stretch my legs.

COMBINING MODES: Notice that Morrison uses narration within her description essay.

PAUSE: How does the writer appeal to the senses in this paragraph?

5   I was so excited, even though ominous clouds hung large, grey, and imposing above. In my bones, I knew it would not rain. My two rowdy[1] younger brothers took the lead on the trails, likely scaring off any creature within miles. The fresh scent of wet dirt and soggy pine needles filled the air. Luckily, most of the trail was dry. Songs of the black-capped chickadees and orioles rang through the forest. With a slight breeze rustling leaves and twigs, it was an orchestra sending forth the melody of the forest.

6   The haughty red squirrels chattered angrily above, throwing a flat note into the music. They were yelling at us, as if annoyed about loud aliens thumping through their forest. I did not blame them because we were pretty awkward. I decided to pick up my pace[2] and trotted down a steep slope. Tree branches had been fashioned into stairs leading down the path. I lost my balance on one of them, almost falling, and the squirrels laughed.

7   The trail was filled with the sounds of laughter and cameras clicking. We were delighted. But the best was yet to come. At the end of the path, the trees parted, like a gateway to another place. When we walked through, it was not just to another place, but to what felt like a completely different world.

8   The water on the lake was paper smooth, clear, and clean. It sparkled whimsically,[3] even though the sun was not out to brighten it. In the background, Double-Top Mountain rose regally, presiding over the scene. Its snow-tipped peaks were shrouded in a veil of thick fog. The fog cascaded lazily down the side of the mountain like the gentle caress of a lover.

PAUSE: How can a boulder be "flattened by time"?

9   We sat by the lake, on top of a boulder flattened by time. There were no screeching tires, no noisy construction. It was merely a moment suspended in time. Mother Nature and Father Time wove their magic, revealing a natural world of splendor and beauty unfazed[4] by time.

10   Slowly, as we sat in quiet awe, the sun's brilliant rays poked through the quilt of clouds, scattering its light along the lake. There, in the near distance, something moved in the water, breaking the stillness. A large female moose waded into the water up to her knees. For a long moment, she looked over at us, until she finally deemed us safe. Then, she dipped her head under the cold water and munched on the plant life below.

11   The whole scene was majestic. In a natural world, we have become unnatural. Our instincts often go unused and rust with time. Have we become aliens to this world, when we were supposed to be part of it?

12   As we watched the moose, the clouds lazily drifted away, freeing the warmth of the sun that washed over our faces. It lit up the world, moving it from sober peacefulness to a miraculous kingdom. A loud squeak rang out.

---

1. **rowdy:** loud and noisy   2. **pick up my pace:** go faster
3. **whimsically:** lightly fanciful   4. **unfazed:** not affected

13   "What the heck was that?" I said, as we all looked at each other.

14   Had it come from the moose? It sounded again, and the moose turned and lumbered[5] over to the water's edge. Captivated, we all watched. From the thick veil of shrubs, a tiny calf emerged, complaining, as human children do. Mother and calf stood together for a long while. They looked like everything right in the world. The mother nudged her calf, who was trying to dunk its head under the water as the mother had done. Finally, like spirits, they vanished into the forest.

15   I realized then how much of the world I was missing out on. If I simply took the time, maybe I could see the more important elements of our world. There was so much peace in the natural setting.

16   The experience in Maine changed me and will forever linger in my mind. It showed me what was important in life by showing me what was important in my life. That kingdom showed me the past while it pointed the way to my future. Seeing the enchantment of the forest made me want to protect and preserve the peace and beauty in this world. The hand of God touched me and hatched the seed of my passion. That moment will always be my inspiration and will forever change my view of the world. The moose and her calf unknowingly gave me a new goal: to become a zoologist.[6] To them, I give thanks for a future they helped shape.

PAUSE: Summarize the dominant impression given by the moose and her calf in this scene.

---

5. lumbered: walked heavily and slowly mals and their environments

6. zoologist: one who studies animals and their environments

. . . .

SUMMARIZE AND RESPOND

In your reading journal or elsewhere, summarize the main point of "My Kingdom." Then, go back and check off support for this main idea. Next, write a brief summary (three to five sentences) of the reading. Finally, jot down your original response to the selection. What does Morrison's experience in Maine make her realize? How does it change her?

. . . .

CHECK YOUR COMPREHENSION

1.   Which of the following would be the best alternative title for this essay?

   a. "How Nature Inspired Me—and Changed Me Forever"

   b. "A Fun Family Reunion in the Wilds of Baxter State Park"

   c. "The Laughing Squirrels"

   d. "We Must Save the Wilderness"

2. The main idea of this essay is that
    a. we need to find more time to connect with our families.
    b. pollution, deforestation, and climate change threaten the natural beauty of the wilderness.
    c. human beings should avoid trespassing in the natural habitats of wild animals.
    (d.) the natural world can be inspiring and life-changing if we take the time to notice it.

3. The writer claims that
    a. more and more state parks are being sold off to private businesses.
    (b.) people have become too separated from the natural world.
    c. the moose and the calf show how fragile family relationships are.
    d. zoology is one of the fastest-growing professional fields.

4. If you are unfamiliar with the following words, use a dictionary to check their meanings: inspiration (para. 1); anticipation, quaint (4); ominous (5); haughty (6); regally, presiding, shrouded, cascaded, caress (8); awe (10); majestic (11); captivated, nudged (14).

. . . .

READ CRITICALLY

1. This essay is about an experience Morrison had during a family reunion. Yet she does not write much about her family members or her family relationships. Why does she leave out this material? Would the essay be stronger if she had included it? Why or why not?

2. Note Morrison's appeal to the senses throughout the essay. How effectively does she do this? Why would sensory detail be so important, given her main point? What feeling does Morrison illustrate in paragraph 6?

3. Morrison writes, "In a natural world, we have become unnatural" (para. 11). What does she mean? How does she support this statement?

4. The writer claims she has been changed forever by her experience. How would you summarize that change in your own words?

WRITE AN ESSAY

Can you identify with or relate to Morrison's experience? Write an essay about an event, experience, or encounter that inspired you or changed you in some way. What images and sensory details "forever linger" in your mind from the experience? How does the memory inspire you?

Alex Espinoza

An American in Mexico

Alex Espinoza was born in Tijuana, Mexico, in 1971 and spent his childhood in La Puenté, a community near Los Angeles. He attended San Bernardino Community College and transferred to the University of California at Riverside, where he earned a bachelor of arts degree in creative writing. He went on to receive his master of fine arts degree from the University of California at Irvine, where he was editor of the university's literary magazine, *Faultline*. Currently a member of the English faculty at California State University at Fresno, Espinoza published his first novel, *Still Water Saints*, in 2007. Espinoza is one of the Profiles of Success included in this book (see p. 190).

"An American in Mexico" originally appeared on February 25, 2007, in the *New York Times Magazine*. In it, Espinoza recounts a visit to Mexico that he made with his mother to connect to his roots in Mexico.

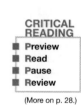

CRITICAL READING
- Preview
- Read
- Pause
- Review

(More on p. 28.)

GUIDING QUESTION

What expectations does Espinoza have for his visit to the house his mother built in Mexico? Are these expectations fulfilled or disappointed?

1   When my father came to the United States to work as a day laborer many years ago, he intended to move back to the village in Michoacán where my mother and seven of my siblings lived. He wired my mother money, some of which she used to build a house there in El Ojo de Agua on a parcel of land that has been in her family since before the Mexican revolution.[1] But at some point, my mother had enough of waiting for my father's return. She packed up what little she had and, with her children, traveled to Tijuana to be closer to him and to make visits easier. She stayed in Tijuana for several years—I was born there, the youngest of eleven children. Eventually, we moved to the three-bedroom house outside Los Angeles where I grew up.

TEACHING TIP
This essay is a good example of how narrative and description often function together. Have students identify places where narration is used as a framework for description.

---

1. Mexican revolution: a period of civil war lasting from 1910 to 1917

PAUSE: Summarize the main differences between Espinoza's childhood and his older siblings' childhoods.

2   My childhood was different from the childhood of most of my siblings. I rode my BMX bike through vacant lots, watched cable, and collected "Star Wars" action figures. They climbed mesquite trees, made handmade dolls from old rags, and stole chicken eggs from a neighbor's henhouse to sell for candy. They also shared hardships and misfortunes—hunger, long hours of working in the fields at young ages, the loss of two infant sisters.

3   Their connection to Mexico was close, deep, and also painful, something I simply could not grasp. Growing up, I felt no ties to El Ojo de Agua. I traveled into Mexico with my family as a child a few times, but I felt disconnected and uninterested during those trips—and was always eager to return to my American life. But as I grew older, I began to want to see the place most of my family called home, the place my siblings had talked about with such complicated feelings. Two years ago, at 33, I finally decided to go. I took my mother along; it had been more than 25 years since she had returned.

PAUSE: Why do you suppose that Espinoza finally decided to visit his family's former home?

4   We flew into Mexico City, where we stayed for one day—strolling through parks and museums and visiting the Basilica of Our Lady of Guadalupe; there we watched the steady flow of devotees making their pilgrimages to the altar on their knees, their hands clasped in prayer. The next day, we traveled by bus to the city of La Piedad, where my uncle picked us up at the depot.

5   After many years in the U.S., my uncle had recently returned home to sell agricultural equipment to local farmers. He employed a maid named Chavela, who lived in one of the nearby villages. Chavela told me that her boyfriend had left for the United States about a month before but that weeks had gone by without news of his whereabouts. She said she hoped to save enough money to be able to go and find him. It made me think of the trip my mother took more than three decades earlier, traveling by train to Tijuana with her children to be near my father.

PAUSE: What do you predict that Espinoza and his mother might find when they reach the house?

6   It was threatening to rain the afternoon my uncle drove us out over unpaved roads to the old house. Many of the houses along the main road of the village were empty and dark, with overgrown weeds and broken fences. Now and again, I'd spot one with dim lights illuminating the small windows. Tricycles and toys might be scattered around the front yard, and a column of white smoke threaded out through a hole in the corrugated-metal roof.

7   Gradually, the houses vanished, giving way to tall cornstalks, and we reached the wooden fence marking the entrance to my grandfather's property. We drove up a short distance before stopping and getting out. I spotted a reservoir behind some trees, and the water glistened when the clouds broke enough to allow a few beams of sunlight to touch the surface.

ESL Students from immigrant families may have stories of their own to share about visiting — or revisiting — a place that their families called home in their country of origin.

8   The house my mother built was nothing more than four walls made of orange bricks surrounded by thickets of wild shrubs and grass. The

windows had no glass, and the front door had been ripped from its hinges. My uncle said that the house was sometimes used as a stable for the live-stock that grazed in the hills not far away. There were broken bottles on the dirt floor, and it smelled of urine and manure.

9   "I lived here," my mother said to me, as if she couldn't believe it her-self. "Right here."

10   This was a place that had, over the years, become mythic[2] in my mind. But it was real. I touched the brick walls, and I saw the trees my siblings had climbed, the fields where they had worked. The soft mud gave way underneath my shoes. A clean set of my footprints remained.

11   I took pictures, and after the film was developed, I sat on the floor of my apartment back in California and took the photos out. I looked at each one and tried piecing them together, assembling a memory. I really wanted to connect to that land the way my brothers and sisters had — to get a bet-ter sense of our shared past. I thought I could understand things like sacrifice, the small traces of ourselves we are forced to leave behind. But all that the pictures showed were indistinguishable[3] sections of walls, win-dows, and dark doorways.

PAUSE: Why might the house have become "mythic" to Espinoza?

2. **mythic:** unreal but often with wondrous associations   3. **indistinguishable:** impossible to tell apart

. . . .

SUMMARIZE AND RESPOND

In your reading journal or elsewhere, summarize the main point of "An American in Mexico." Then, go back and check off support for this main idea. Next, write a brief summary (three to five sentences) of the reading. Finally, jot down your initial response to the selection. How does Espinoza make you feel about his visit to the house that his mother built in Mexico many years earlier?

. . . .

CHECK YOUR COMPREHENSION

1.   Which of the following would be the best alternative title for this essay?

   a. "Growing Up the Youngest of a Large Family"
   b. "A Journey to My Mexican Past"
   c. "Photographs and Memory"
   d. "A Connection to the Past"

2. The main idea of this essay is that

   a. immigrants have an obligation to visit the places where their families originally lived.

   b. the younger children in immigrant families generally have a more privileged life than do their elder siblings.

   (c.) the author's attempt to make a connection to his family's former life in Mexico was not successful.

   d. photographs can never do justice to one's memories of a place.

3. The author's mother's response to visiting the house she built in Mexico is one of

   a. disgust that the place is so filthy.

   (b.) amazement that she once lived there.

   c. sadness that no one lives there any longer.

   d. anger toward her brother for allowing it to become shabby.

4. If you are unfamiliar with the following words, use a dictionary to check their meanings: disconnected (para. 3); devotees, pilgrimages (4); illuminating, corrugated (6).

READ CRITICALLY

1. Espinoza begins his essay with a brief history of his immediate family. What purpose does this opening serve?

2. In paragraph 3, Espinoza refers to his siblings' feelings about their home in Mexico as "complicated." Why does he think that they might feel the way they do?

3. Note Espinoza's use of descriptive detail in paragraphs 6 to 8. To what senses does he appeal? What overall impression does he create?

4. Espinoza makes use of direct quotation only once in the essay, and he does so in a one-sentence paragraph (para. 9). Why do you suppose that he chose to do so? How would the effect be different if he had put what his mother said into his own words rather than quoting her directly?

5. Evaluate Espinoza's concluding paragraph. What impression does he seem to wish to create? What makes you think as you do?

WRITE AN ESSAY

Write an essay about a place that is special to you. Your associations with this place may be either positive or negative, or both. Include descriptive details to allow your readers to understand its significance.

Mary Brave Bird
The Sweat Bath Ritual

Mary Brave Bird (who also goes by her former name, Mary Crow Dog) was born in 1953 in South Dakota. She is the author of two memoirs: *Lakota Woman*, which won the 1991 American Book Award; and *Ohitika Woman* (1993). Both books chronicle her life on the reservation and her involvement in the American Indian Movement (AIM), a Native American activist organization begun in 1968 to address the many social problems afflicting Native Americans. At twenty, Mary Brave Bird participated in AIM's months-long occupation of Wounded Knee, South Dakota, on the Pine Ridge Reservation, during which her son Pedro was born. This essay is an excerpt from *Lakota Woman*.

CRITICAL READING
■ Preview
■ Read
■ Pause
■ Review

(More on p. 28.)

GUIDING QUESTION
What senses does the author appeal to in her essay?

1   Some of our medicine men always say that one must view the world through the eye in one's heart rather than just trust the eyes in one's head. "Look at the real reality beneath the sham realities of things and gadgets," Leonard always tells me. "Look through the eye in your heart. That's the meaning of Indian religion."

PAUSE: What do you think "the eye in one's heart" means?

2   The eye of my heart was still blind when I joined Leonard to become his wife. I knew little of traditional ways. I had been to a few peyote meetings[1] without really understanding them. I had watched one Sun Dance,[2] and later the Ghost Dance[3] held at Wounded Knee,[4] like a spectator — an emotional spectator, maybe, but no different from white friends watching these dances. They, too, felt emotion. Like myself, they did not penetrate

1. **peyote meetings:** ceremonies honoring the sacred peyote cactus   2. **Sun Dance:** ceremony usually performed at the summer solstice   3. **Ghost Dance:** ceremony of salvation and resurrection   4. **Wounded Knee:** site of an 1890 massacre in which hundreds of Lakota Sioux were killed by the U.S. Army

through symbolism to the real meaning. I had not yet participated in many ancient rituals of our tribe—the sweat bath, the vision quest, yuwipi, the making of relatives, the soul keeping. I did not even know that these ceremonies were still being performed. There were some rituals I did not know even existed.

3   I had to learn about the sweat bath, because it precedes all sacred ceremonies, and is at the same time a ceremony all by itself. It is probably the oldest of all our rituals because it is connected with the glowing stones, evoking thoughts of Tunka, the rock, our oldest god. Our family's sweat lodge, our oinikaga tipi, is near the river which flows through Crow Dog's land. That is good. Pure, flowing water plays a great part during a sweat. Always at the lodge we can hear the river's voice, the murmur of its waters. Along its banks grows washte wikcemna, a sweet-smelling aromatic herb— Indian perfume.

PAUSE: Why is the sweat bath important?

4   The lodge is made of sixteen willow sticks, tough but resilient and easy to bend. They are formed into a beehive-shaped dome. The sweat lodges vary in size. They can accommodate anywhere from eight to twenty-four people. The bent willow sticks are fastened together with strips of red trade cloth. Sometimes, offerings of Bull Durham tobacco are tied to the frame, which is then covered with blankets or a tarp. In the old days, buffalo skins were used for the covering, but these are hard to come by now. The floor of the little lodge is covered with sage. In the center is a circular pit to receive the heated rocks. In building a lodge, people should forget old quarrels and have only good thoughts.

5   Outside the lodge, wood is piled up in a certain manner to make the fire in which the rocks will be heated—peta owihankeshni—the "fire without end" which is passed on from generation to generation. After it has blazed for a while, white limestone rocks are placed in its center. These rocks do not crack apart in the heat. They come from the hills. Some of them are covered with a spidery network of green moss. This is supposed by some to represent secret spirit writing.

6   The scooped-out earth from the firepit inside the lodge is formed up into a little path leading from the lodge entrance and ending in a small mound. It represents Unci—Grandmother Earth. A prayer is said when this mound is made. A man is then chosen to take care of the fire, to bring the hot rocks to the lodge, often on a pitchfork, and to handle the entrance flap.

7   In some places, men and women sweat together. We do not do this. Among us, men and women do their sweat separately. Those taking part in a sweat strip, and wrapped in their towels, crawl into the little lodge, entering clockwise. In the darkness inside, they take their towels off and hunker down naked. I was astounded to see how many people could be swallowed up by this small, waist-high, igloo-shaped hut. The rocks are then passed into the lodge, one by one. Each stone is touched with the pipe bowl as, resting in the fork of a deer antler, it is put into the center

pit. The leader goes in first, sitting down near the entrance on the right side. Opposite him, at the other side of the entrance sits his helper. The leader has near him a pail full of cold, pure water and a ladle. Green cedar is sprinkled over the hot rocks, filling the air with its aromatic odor. Outside the entrance flap is a buffalo-skull altar. Tobacco ties are fastened to its horns. There is also a rack for the pipe to rest on.

8   Anywhere from twelve to sixty rocks can be used in this ceremony. The more rocks, the hotter it will be. Once the rocks have been passed into the lodge, the flap is closed. Inside it is dark except for the red glow of the rocks in the pit. Now the purification begins. As sage or cedar is sprinkled on the rocks, the men or women participating catch the sacred smoke with their hands, inhaling it, rubbing it all over their face and body. Then, cold water is poured on the rocks. The rising cloud of white steam, "grandfather's breath," fills the lodge. A sweat has four "doors," meaning that the flap is opened four times during the purification to let some cool outside air in, bringing relief to the participants.

9   Everybody has the privilege to pray or speak of sacred things during the ceremony. It is important that all take part in the ritual with their hearts, souls, and minds. When women have their sweats, a medicine man runs them—which is all right because it is so dark inside that he cannot see you.

10   The first time I was inside the oinikaga tipi, the sweat lodge, when water was poured over the rocks and the hot steam got to me, I thought that I could not endure it. The heat was beyond anything I had imagined. I thought I would not be able to breathe because it was like inhaling liquid fire. With my cupped hands, I created a slightly cooler space over my eyes and mouth. After a while, I noticed that the heat which had hurt me at first became soothing, penetrating to the center of my body, going into my bones, giving me a wonderful feeling. If the heat is more than a person can stand, he or she can call out "Mitakuye oyasin!"—All my relatives!—and the flap will be opened to let the inside cool off a bit. I was proud not to have cried out. After the sweat, I really felt newly born. More pores were opened and so was my mind. My body tingled. I felt as if I had never experienced pain. I was deliciously light-headed, elated, drunk with the spirit. Soon, I began looking forward to a good sweat.

· ·

SUMMARIZE AND RESPOND

In your reading journal or elsewhere, summarize the main point of "The Sweat Bath Ritual." Then, go back and check off descriptive details in the essay. Next, write a brief summary (three to five sentences) of the essay. Finally, jot down your initial response to the reading. What effect does the ritual have on the author? Have you ever experienced anything similar?

· ·

CHECK YOUR COMPREHENSION

1. Which of the following would be the best alternative title for the essay?

   a. "What I Did for Leonard"

   b. "Visiting My Family's Sweat Lodge"

   c. "Learning a Sacred Ritual"

   d. "Heat Is Restorative"

2. The main idea of this essay is that

   a. The author learned and appreciated an old Indian ritual that she had not participated in before.

   b. The author bonded with other people involved in the ritual.

   c. The author realized the significance of the medicine man in Indian culture.

   d. The author was proud that she could stand the heat in the sweat lodge.

3. According to the author,

   a. she had never had any experience with Indian rituals.

   b. sixty rocks were heated during her sweat bath.

   c. the sweat bath is supposed to have a purifying effect.

   d. her fiancé pressured her a bit to experience a sweat bath.

4. If you are unfamiliar with the following words, use a dictionary to check their meanings: sham (para. 1); penetrate (2); precedes, rituals, evoking (3); resilient, quarrels (4); purification (8); endure, elated (10).

READ CRITICALLY

1. What is the author's purpose in this essay? How would you describe her tone, particularly up until the last paragraph?

2. Do you think the author actively avoided Indian cultural rituals? Why or why not?

3. How is this essay both a description and a process analysis?

4. Can you as a reader visualize what happens during a sweat bath ritual? How does the author help you?

5. In your own words, describe how the author felt at the end of the sweat bath. How was it a positive experience for her?

. . . .

WRITE AN ESSAY

In some ways, Brave Bird's sweat bath helped her understand part of her cultural and family heritage that she had not paid much attention to. Write a description essay about a place or experience that made you feel a part of something larger: a family, a community, a team. Make sure to include details that help your readers experience what you felt.

. . . .

Description: Linked Readings

. . . .

FEELING FOREIGN

Each of the following readings focuses on various aspects of feeling foreign and the ways people can have divided identities.

> Alex Espinoza, "An American in Mexico" (this chapter, p. 723)

> Rui Dai, "A Whiff of Memory" (Chapter 47, p. 783)

Read the selections and write an essay entitled "Feeling Foreign." You can use the term *foreign* in the sense of being from another country or in the sense of being in a new situation, such as starting at a new job or a new school.

. . . .

EXPERIENCES THAT CHANGE US

Each of the following readings focuses on the ways a personal experience can change a person's life.

> Heaven Morrison, "My Kingdom" (this chapter, p. 719)

> Beth Trimmer, "Birdshot" (Chapter 41, p. 688)

> Michael Jernigan, "Living the Dream" (Chapter 48, p. 798)

Read the selections, and draw from at least one in addition to "My Kingdom" to write an essay titled "The Experiences That Change Us." You can refer to your own experience, but make sure to use material from the essays as well.

. . . .

··

FAMILY TIES

Each of the following readings discusses family relationships and the ways they affect and shape people's lives.

Alex Espinoza, "An American in Mexico" (this chapter, p. 723)

Daniel Flanagan, "The Choice to Do It Over Again" (Chapter 13, p. 206)

Beth Trimmer, "Birth Order" (Chapter 45, p. 747)

Nicholas Kristof, "Two Men and Two Paths" (Chapter 47, p. 791)

Read the selections, and draw from at least one in addition to "An American in Mexico" to write an essay entitled "How Family Ties Affect Our Lives." You may refer to your own experience, but make sure to use material from the essays as well.

··

44

Process Analysis

Each essay in this chapter uses process analysis to get its main point across. As you read these essays, consider how they achieve the four basics of good process analysis that are listed below and discussed in Chapter 13 of this book.

IDEA JOURNAL
Write about a time you felt pressured to do something that was not true to yourself.

Four Basics of Good Process Analysis

1. It helps readers either perform the steps themselves or understand how something works.

2. It presents the essential steps in the process.

3. It explains the steps in detail.

4. It arranges the steps in a logical order (usually in chronological order).

Katie Whitehead
How to Avoid Carpal Tunnel Syndrome

Katie Whitehead is a student at the University of Northern Colorado and is hoping to become a veterinarian. For as long as she can remember, she has loved all animals and wants to help them. She has enjoyed working in a vet's office as it gives her a real-world opportunity to apply what she is learning. Katie also plays the violin, performing with the university symphony, a campus Christian ministry, and with her musician friend. They have recently begun playing at weddings and are making a CD.

CRITICAL READING
■ Preview
■ Read
■ Pause
■ Review

(More on p. 28.)

GUIDING QUESTION
What causes carpal tunnel syndrome, and what steps can you take to avoid it?

1   In an office where I used to do data entry as a temp, one young woman was always knowledgeable, quick with her work, and successful. She was my "go-to" person if I had questions, and we became friends. Then she got carpal tunnel syndrome (CTS), an inflammation of the nerves where they travel through the narrow part of the wrist. It was obvious she was in a lot of pain, and her upbeat mood faded away. She became a different person. At first she started to have more absences, for medical appointments, cortisone injections, and operations. Then, she would return for short periods of time, wearing casts, braces that kept her wrists from bending, and hot packs. She got a special chair and keyboard and was limited in what work she could do and for how long. Finally, she had to quit and go on disability.[1] We had a going-away party for her and never heard from her again. Watching this experience made me want to know how to avoid getting carpal tunnel syndrome from typing at a computer.

2   To avoid getting CTS, first know about its dangers. It is important to know that CTS is caused by repetitive motion. In today's world, it mainly comes from typing, but it can also be caused by weightlifting, sports that use rackets, biking, operating machines in factories, and other activities that put repeated stress on the wrists. If you get CTS, you know you have it by the number one symptom, pain, which can be in your wrists, palms, fingers, and arms. Your hands may also become clumsy, and you may notice tingling, burning, and numbness. Workers of all ages can develop CTS, but there are some steps that can help prevent it.

PAUSE: In your own words, summarize the friend's symptoms.

PAUSE: What is the primary symptom of carpal tunnel syndrome?

1. **disability:** a leave of absence from work for medical reasons

3 How can a person keep CTS from developing into such a difficult problem? One way is to limit the repeated motion that is causing the nerve damage. If you have to continue the damaging motion, try to do it the right way, to protect yourself. In the case of typing at a computer, the right position to bend your elbows so they are horizontal with the floor, extend your hands up at about a 30-degree angle, and curl your fingers loosely down onto the keys.

4 There are a few other simple steps to help avoid this syndrome. First, get a keyboard that is arranged at an upward angle and that divides into two parts. Use a keyboard with a support that allows the hands to rest. Do not pound on the keys of your keyboard because that increases the risk of CTS. You can go to any pharmacy and get wrist braces that help your wrists from bending. These products can give your wrists a rest. Finally, if you feel any signs of CTS, go to the doctor right away. Do not put it off thinking that it will go away on its own. It could get much worse and have serious life consequences, as it did for my poor friend.

PAUSE: What will *you* do to avoid carpal tunnel syndrome?

. . . .

SUMMARIZE AND RESPOND

In your reading journal or elsewhere, summarize the main point of "How to Avoid Carpal Tunnel Syndrome." Then, go back and check off the steps in the process. Next, write a brief summary (three to five sentences) of the essay. Finally, jot down your initial response to the reading. Is it a good process analysis essay? Why or why not?

. . . .

CHECK YOUR COMPREHENSION

1. Which of the following would be the best alternative title for the essay?

  a. "How to Avoid a Painful Injury"

  b. "How to Survive at Work"

  c. "How to Stay Healthy at Work"

  d. "How to Type Properly"

2. The main idea of this essay is that

  a. the author lost a friend because of carpal tunnel syndrome.

  b. once carpal tunnel starts, it quickly causes great pain and limits ability.

  c. carpal tunnel syndrome is a very common workplace injury.

  d. there are some precautions people take against carpal tunnel syndrome.

3. According to Whitehead,

   a. her friend was somewhat secretive about her injury.

   b. her friend tried very hard to keep working but was unable to.

   c. the best way to avoid carpal tunnel is to wear wrist braces.

   d. many doctors are skeptical about carpal tunnel syndrome.

4. If you are unfamiliar with the following words, use a dictionary to check their meanings: knowledgeable, inflammation (para. 1); repetitive, tingling (2); horizontal (3); consequences (4).

READ CRITICALLY

1. What activities can cause people to develop carpal tunnel syndrome?

2. What steps can be taken to avoid carpal tunnel syndrome?

3. Does the essay have the Four Basics of Good Process Analysis?

4. How would you describe the author's tone in the essay?

WRITE AN ESSAY

Write about a process that you are familiar with but that, done incorrectly, is dangerous. Detail the correct process so readers could do this safely.

Farhad Manjoo

Fix Your Terrible, Insecure Passwords in Five Minutes

Farhad Manjoo is the technology columnist for *Slate* and is also a frequent contributor to the *New York Times*. After graduating from Cornell University in 2000, where he served as editor-in-chief of the *Cornell Daily Sun*, Manjoo wrote for both *Wired News* and *Salon.com* before his current position at *Slate* (where this essay appeared in 2009). He makes regular appearances on National Public Radio and is also the author of *True Enough: Learning to Live in a Post-fact Society* (2008).

GUIDING QUESTION
Why are most passwords at risk?

CRITICAL
READING
■ Preview
■ Read
■ Pause
■ Review

(More on p. 28.)

1   It is tempting to blame the victim. In May, a twenty-something French hacker broke into several Twitter employees' e-mail accounts and stole a trove[1] of meeting notes, strategy documents, and other confidential scribbles. The hacker eventually gave the stash to TechCrunch, which has since published notes from meetings in which Twitter execs discussed their very lofty goals. (The company wants to be the first Web service to reach 1 billion users.) How did the hacker get all this stuff? Like a lot of tech startups, Twitter runs without paper—much of the company's discussions take place in e-mail and over shared Google documents. All of these corporate secrets are kept secure with a very thin wall of protection: The employees' passwords, which the intruder managed to guess because some people at Twitter used the same passwords for many different sites. In other words, Twitter had it coming. The trouble is, so do the rest of us.

2   Your passwords are not very secure. Even if you think they are, they probably aren't. Do you use the same or similar passwords for several different important sites? If you don't, pat yourself on the back; if you do, you're not alone—one recent survey found that half of people online use the same password for all the sites they visit. Do you change your passwords often? Probably not; more than 90 percent don't. If one of your accounts falls to a hacker, will he find enough to get into your other accounts? For a scare, try this: Search your e-mail for some of your own passwords. You will probably find a lot of them, either because you've e-mailed them to yourself or because some Web sites send along your password when you register or when you tell them you have forgotten it. If an attacker manages to get into your e-mail, he'll have an easy time accessing your bank account, your social networking sites, and your fantasy baseball[2] roster. That's exactly what happened at Twitter. (Here's my detailed explanation of how Twitter got compromised.)

3   Everyone knows it's bad to use the same password for different sites. People do it anyway because remembering different passwords is annoying. Remembering different difficult passwords is even more annoying. Eric Thompson, the founder of AccessData, a technology forensics company that makes password-guessing software, says that most passwords follow a pattern. First, people choose a readable word as a base for the password—not necessarily something in *Webster's*[3] but something that is pronounceable in English. Then, when pressed to add a numeral or symbol to make the password more secure, most people add a 1 or ! to the end of that word. Thompson's software, which uses a "brute force" technique that tries thousands of passwords until it guesses yours correctly, can easily

PAUSE: Manjoo writes that it's "tempting to blame the victim" and that "Twitter had it coming." Do you agree?

1. **trove:** valuable collection   2. **fantasy baseball:** an online game where players manage players and compete against each other   3. **Webster's:** a well-known dictionary

PAUSE: After reading the opening paragraphs, what process do you think will be described in the essay?

suss out[4] such common passwords. When it incorporates your computer's Web history in its algorithm[5]—all your ramblings on Twitter, Facebook, and elsewhere—Thompson's software can come up with a list of passwords that is highly likely to include yours. (He doesn't use it for nefarious ends; AccessData usually guesses passwords under the direction of a court order, for military purposes, or when companies get locked out of their own systems—"systems administrator gets hit by a bus on the way to work," Thompson says by way of example.)

4   Security expert Bruce Schneier writes about passwords often, and he distills Thompson's findings into a few rules: Choose a password that doesn't contain a readable word. Mix upper and lower case. Use a number or symbol in the middle of the word, not on the end. Don't just use 1 or !, and don't use symbols as replacements for letters, such as @ for a lowercase A—password-guessing software can see through that trick. And of course, create unique passwords for your different sites.

5   That all sounds difficult and time-consuming. It doesn't have to be. In Schneier's comment section, I found a foolproof technique to create passwords that are near-impossible to crack yet easy to remember. Even better, it will take just five minutes of your time. Ready?

6   First, start with an original but memorable phrase. For this exercise, let's use these two sentences: *I like to eat bagels at the airport* and *My first Cadillac was a real lemon so I bought a Toyota.* The phrase can have something to do with your life or it can be a random collection of words—just make sure it's something you can remember. That's the key: Because a mnemonic[6] is easy to remember, you don't have to write it down anywhere. (If you can't remember it without writing it down, it's not a good mnemonic.) This reduces the chance that someone will guess it if he gets into your computer or your e-mail. What's more, a relatively simple mnemonic can be turned into a fanatically difficult password.

7   Which brings us to Step 2: Turn your phrase into an acronym. Be sure to use some numbers and symbols and capital letters, too. *I like to eat bagels at the airport* becomes *Ilteb@ta,* and *My first Cadillac was a real lemon so I bought a Toyota* is *M1stCwarlsIbaT.*

PAUSE: Do you find this method easy to understand?

8   That's it—you're done. These mnemonic passwords are hard to forget, but they contain no guessable English words. You can even create pass phrases for specific sites that are coded with a hint about their purpose. A sentence like *It's 20 degrees in February, so I use Gmail* lets you set a new Gmail password every month and still never forget it: *i90diSsIuG* for September, *i30diMsIuG* for March, etc. (These aren't realistic temperatures; they're the month-number multiplied by 10.)

---

4. suss out: investigate   **5. algorithm:** a step-by-step process for solving a problem   **6. mnemonic:** a way to assist memory

9   How many different such passwords do you need? Four or five at most. You don't have to keep unique passwords for every single site you visit—Thompson says it's perfectly OK to repeat passwords on sites that don't need to be kept very secure. For instance, I can use the same password for my accounts at the *New York Times*, the *New Republic*, *The New Yorker,* and other online magazines, because it won't hurt me too much if someone breaks into those. (My mnemonic is, *I like to read snooty publications quite often.*) You should probably use different passwords for each of your social networking accounts—someone can do real damage by breaking into your Facebook or Twitter, so you want to keep them distinct—but you can still come up with a single systematic mnemonic to protect them: *Twitter is my second favorite social networking site, MySpace is my third favorite social networking site,* etc. Reserve your strongest, most distinct passwords for the few very important services that, if cracked, could do the most damage—your bank account, your computer, and most of all your e-mail, which often contains the keys to everything else in your life.

PAUSE: What kind of "damage" is Manjoo referring to in this paragraph?

10   To be sure, this is more of a hassle than what you're doing now—but what you're doing now is going to come back to bite you. These days, we're all dishing personal information all the time; you may think that your password is totally unguessable, but your Facebook makes clear that you're a huge U2 fan and you graduated from college in 2000. *Achtung2000,* eh? Just go ahead and make some new passwords right now. Trust me, you'll feel better.

. . . .

SUMMARIZE AND RESPOND

In your reading journal or elsewhere, summarize the main point of "Fix Your Terrible, Insecure Passwords in Five Minutes." Then, go back and check off support for this main idea. Next, write a brief summary (three to five sentences) of the essay. Finally, jot down your initial response to the essay. Manjoo thinks this is an urgent problem: He urges his readers to change their passwords immediately. Do you see password security and online privacy protection as pressing issues? Does this essay change your view of them?

. . . .

CHECK YOUR COMPREHENSION

1. Which of the following would be the best alternative title for this essay?

   a. "How the Internet Is Changing Our Society"

   b. "Safeguarding Your Internet Passwords in Two Easy Steps"

   c. "We Need Stronger Laws to Punish Hackers"

   d. "Don't Put Personal Information on the Internet"

2. The main idea of this essay is that

   a. people are spending too much time online and neglecting direct human relationships.

   b. the government needs to do more to protect people's online security from hackers.

   c. people need to choose better online passwords and that it's easy for them to do so.

   d. popular sites such as Facebook and Twitter deserve to be hacked.

3. According to the author, most people should

   a. have only one password for all their Internet accounts, preferably a readable word that doesn't mix upper and lower case letters.

   b. have four or five different passwords at most.

   c. have a separate password for every online account and site.

   d. avoid shopping, networking, or banking online altogether because these activities are too risky.

4. If you are unfamiliar with the following words, use a dictionary to check their meanings: hacker (para. 1); roster (2); forensics, nefarious (3); distills (4); random (6); acronym (7).

READ CRITICALLY

1. Why does Manjoo begin with the story about Twitter? How does it support his overall purpose?

2. Where in the essay does the writer rely on experts? What do they contribute to Manjoo's main point?

3. How does Manjoo use examples to detail the steps of his process? Do you find them helpful?

4. In paragraph 9, the writer gives suggestions for how and when to use different online passwords. What order does he use to structure this advice?

5. After reading this essay, will you change your Internet passwords? Will you use Manjoo's method? Why or why not?

. . . .

WRITE AN ESSAY

According to Manjoo, people are sharing personal information online "all the time" (para. 10). Write an essay that provides rules, suggestions, and steps that people can use to protect themselves from problems like cyberbullying, identity theft, and other invasions of privacy. You may write from your own experience, but make sure that the essay offers a process that will be helpful to readers.

. . . .

Malcolm X

My First Conk[1]

Malcolm X was born Malcolm Little in Omaha, Nebraska, in 1925. When a teacher told Malcolm that he would never fulfill his dream of becoming a lawyer because he was black, Malcolm lost interest in school, dropped out, and spent several years committing drug-related crimes. Malcolm turned his life around, though, when he was sentenced to prison on burglary charges, using the time to further his education and to study the teachings of the Nation of Islam, the Black Muslim movement in America. He also changed his surname from Little to X, suggesting that he could never know his true name—the African name of his ancestors who were made slaves. Malcolm X became an important leader of the Nation of Islam soon after his release from prison, but he later left the group to form his own, less radical religious and civil rights group. In 1964, Malcolm X was assassinated while giving a speech.

"My First Conk" is an excerpt from *The Autobiography of Malcolm X,* which Malcolm cowrote with his friend Alex Haley. Using vivid details to bring the painful process to life, Malcolm takes readers step by step through his first "conk"—a process that straightens curly hair.

TEACHING TIP
Find a copy of Chapter 3 ("Homeboy") of *The Autobiography of Malcolm X*, from which this reading is excerpted. Assign this reading for homework, and ask students to comment on how the excerpt printed here fits in with the rest of the chapter.

GUIDING QUESTION

What main point does Malcolm X make about the process he analyzes?

1   Shorty soon decided that my hair was finally long enough to be conked.[2] He had promised to school me in how to beat the barbershop's three- and four-dollar price by making up congolene,[3] and then conking ourselves.

CRITICAL READING
■ Preview
■ Read
■ Pause
■ Review

(More on p. 28.)

1. **conk:** a method of straightening curly hair   2. **conked:** straightened
3. **congolene:** a product used to straighten hair

2   I took the little list of ingredients he had printed out for me, and went to a grocery store, where I got a can of Red Devil lye,[4] two eggs, and two medium-sized white potatoes. Then at a drugstore near the poolroom, I asked for a large jar of vaseline, a large bar of soap, a large-toothed comb and a fine-toothed comb, one of those rubber hoses with a metal spray-head, a rubber apron and a pair of gloves.

3   "Going to lay on that first conk?" the drugstore man asked me. I proudly told him, grinning, "Right!"

4   Shorty paid six dollars a week for a room in his cousin's shabby apartment. His cousin wasn't at home. "It's like the pad's mine, he spends so much time with his woman," Shorty said. "Now, you watch me—"

5   He peeled the potatoes and thin-sliced them into a quart-sized Mason fruit jar, then started stirring them with a wooden spoon as he gradually poured in a little over half the can of lye. "Never use a metal spoon; the lye will turn it black," he told me.

6   A jelly-like, starchy-looking glop resulted from the lye and potatoes, and Shorty broke in the two eggs, stirring real fast—his own conk and dark face bent down close. The congolene turned pale-yellowish. "Feel the jar," Shorty said. I cupped my hand against the outside, and snatched it away. "Damn right, it's hot, that's the lye," he said. "So you know it's going to burn when I comb it in—it burns *bad*. But the longer you can stand it, the straighter the hair."

7   He made me sit down, and he tied the string of the new rubber apron tightly around my neck, and combed up my bush of hair. Then, from the big vaseline jar, he took a handful and massaged it hard all through my hair and into the scalp. He also thickly vaselined my neck, ears, and forehead. "When I get to washing out your head, be sure to tell me anywhere you feel any little stinging," Shorty warned me, washing his hands, then pulling on the rubber gloves, and tying on his own rubber apron. "You always got to remember that any congolene left in burns a sore into your head."

8   The congolene just felt warm when Shorty started combing it in. But then my head caught fire.

PAUSE: What is the main point of paragraphs 8–15?

9   I gritted my teeth and tried to pull the sides of the kitchen table together. The comb felt as if it was raking my skin off.

10   My eyes watered, my nose was running. I couldn't stand it any longer; I bolted to the washbasin. I was cursing Shorty with every name I could think of when he got the spray going and started soap-lathering my head.

11   He lathered and spray-rinsed, lathered and spray-rinsed, maybe ten or twelve times, each time gradually closing the hot-water faucet, until the rinse was cold, and that helped some.

---

4. lye: a strong alkaline substance used in soaps and cleaners

12 "You feel any stinging spots?"

13 "No," I managed to say. My knees were trembling.

14 "Sit back down, then. I think we got it all out okay."

15 The flame came back as Shorty, with a thick towel, started drying my head, rubbing hard. "*Easy, man, easy,*" I kept shouting.

16 "The first time's always worst. You get used to it better before long. You took it real good, homeboy. You got a good conk."

17 When Shorty let me stand up and see in the mirror, my hair hung down in limp, damp strings. My scalp still flamed, but not as badly; I could bear it. He draped the towel around my shoulders, over my rubber apron, and began again vaselining my hair.

18 I could feel him combing, straight back, first the big comb, then the fine-tooth one.

19 Then, he was using a razor, very delicately, on the back of my neck. Then, finally, shaping the sideburns.

20 My first view in the mirror blotted out the hurting. I'd seen some pretty conks, but when it's the first time, on your *own* head, the transformation, after the lifetime of kinks, is staggering.

21 The mirror reflected Shorty behind me. We both were grinning and sweating. And on top of my head was this thick, smooth sheen of shining red hair—real red—as straight as any white man's.

> **PAUSE:** Why does Malcolm X refer to himself as "ridiculous" and "stupid" (para. 22) for being happy with his straightened hair?

22 How ridiculous I was! Stupid enough to stand there simply lost in admiration of my hair now looking "white," reflected in the mirror in Shorty's room. I vowed that I'd never again be without a conk, and I never was for many years.

23 This was my first really big step toward self-degradation:[5] When I endured all of that pain, literally burning my flesh to have it look like a white man's hair. I had joined that multitude of Negro men and women in America who are brainwashed into believing that the black people are "inferior"—and white people "superior"—that they will even violate and mutilate their God-created bodies to try to look "pretty" by white standards.

> **PAUSE:** Do you think Malcolm X's ideas in this essay are still relevant today?

5. **self-degradation:** loss of moral character or honor

. . . .

SUMMARIZE AND RESPOND

In your reading journal or elsewhere, summarize the main point of "My First Conk." Then, go back and check off support for this main idea. Next, write a brief summary (three to five sentences) of the essay. Finally, jot down your initial response to the essay. Did it surprise you that a well-known black activist leader once wanted to look more like a white man? What is something you have done to conform to a particular group?

. . . .

· ·

CHECK YOUR COMPREHENSION

1. Which of the following would be the best alternative title for this essay?
   - **a.** "The Pain of Conformity"
   - **b.** "Why I Hated My First Conk"
   - **c.** "Hairstyles of the Past"
   - **d.** "Does Anyone Remember Congolene?"

2. The main idea of this essay is that
   - **a.** most people regret something they have done to change their appearance.
   - **b.** making a homemade conking solution is a dangerous process.
   - **c.** when Malcolm X was younger, he wanted to straighten his hair.
   - **d.** conking is a painful and degrading process that Malcolm X later regretted having gone through.

3. According to the author,
   - **a.** he was very pleased when he first saw his straightened hair.
   - **b.** Shorty helped him conk his hair the first time because he didn't have his family's approval.
   - **c.** conking was such a painful experience that he never did it again.
   - **d.** the conk didn't change the way he saw himself.

4. If you are unfamiliar with the following words, use a dictionary to check their meanings: shabby (para. 4); bolted (10); blotted, staggering (20); sheen (21); endured, brainwashed, inferior, mutilate (23).

· ·

READ CRITICALLY

1. What do you think is Malcolm X's purpose in analyzing the process of conking?

2. Reread paragraphs 6 through 11, underlining the details that Malcolm X uses to appeal to readers' senses. How do these details support his main point?

3. Without going into too much detail, list the major steps in the conking process.

4. Describe the author's attitude toward conking when he was a teen-ager. How and why do you think this attitude changed as he grew older?

5. Are the essay's final two paragraphs a good example of an effective conclusion? Why or why not?

....

WRITE AN ESSAY

Write an essay about a process you have gone through to change your appearance (dieting, tattooing, body piercing, or bodybuilding, for example). In your essay, explain why you made the decision to change your appearance, and then explain the process. In your conclusion, examine how your percep-tion of the experience has changed over time.

....

Process Analysis: Linked Readings

....

THE PRESSURE TO CONFORM

Each of the following readings focuses on various aspects of the pressures people feel to conform.

Malcolm X, "My First Conk" (this chapter, p. 741)

Langston Hughes, "Salvation" (Chapter 41, p. 691)

Kathleen Vail, "Words That Wound" (Chapter 42, p. 706)

Read the selections, and draw from at least one in addition to "My First Conk" to write an essay titled "The Pressure to Conform in Our Society." You can refer to your own experience, but make sure to use material from the essays as well.

....

CHASING BEAUTY

Though they have different tones, each of the following readings focuses on the quest for an ideal of beauty or an attractive personal appearance.

Malcolm X, "My First Conk" (this chapter, p. 741)

Deborah L. Rhode, "Why Looks Are the Last Bastion of Discrimi-nation" (Chapter 42, p. 711)

Dave Barry, "The Ugly Truth about Beauty" (Chapter 47, p. 787)

Read the selections, and draw from at least one in addition to "My First Conk" to write an essay titled "The Dangers of Chasing Beauty and Perfection." You can refer to your own experience, but make sure to use material from the essays as well.

45

Classification

Each essay in this chapter uses classification to get its main point across. As you read these essays, consider how they achieve the four basics of good classification that are listed below and discussed in Chapter 14 of this book.

IDEA JOURNAL
Write about the different "languages" that you use in your life — with friends, with family, in college, and at work.

Four Basics of Good Classification

1. It makes sense of a group of people or items by organizing them into useful categories.

2. It has a purpose for sorting the people or items.

3. It uses a single organizing principle.

4. It gives detailed examples or explanations of the things that fit into each category.

Beth Trimmer

Birth Order

Beth Trimmer is currently pursuing a degree in general business from the Technical College of the Lowcountry in Beaufort, South Carolina. Her classification essay, "Birth Order," which explores the differences in characteristics and behavior between siblings based on the order in which they were born, was inspired by the author's own experiences with her older and younger sisters. Since receiving feedback on her essay, Trimmer remarks that "I have realized that I am a stronger writer than I thought," and she encourages other students to "never give up."

CRITICAL
READING
■ Preview
■ Read
■ Pause
■ Review

(More on p. 28.)

GUIDING QUESTION
Do you think birth order affects people's personalities?

1   Birth order is one way to gain an understanding of friends, family members, co-workers, and others. Birth order has an effect on personality, though it does not explain everything about human behavior and personality. A person's character is also affected by factors such as heritage, upbringing, family size, education, religion, and geographic location, among others. Birth order is not a precise or exact science, but it does give a fascinating possible explanation for why people are the way they are. A family with three children can illustrate some typical characteristics of the firstborn, middle, and youngest child.

PAUSE: What is Trimmer's organizing principle?

2   Firstborn children are the perfectionists. Firstborns may be more highly motivated to achieve than their younger siblings and may be drawn to professions that attract many high achievers, such as medicine, law, or science. The firstborn child is usually the one who has the most family attention given to him or her, if only because for a while there are no other children. Firstborns often exhibit precision, powerful concentration, and mental discipline. They are also typically reliable, well organized, cooperative, assertive, energetic, logical, and ambitious. They are natural leaders and people-pleasers. The firstborn child often feels more family pressure to behave well, and may experience more parental discipline. In school, firstborn children are more likely to participate in class and to achieve high grades. They are also more likely to attend college than their younger siblings.

PAUSE: What pressures do firstborn children experience?

3   Next are the middle-born children, the mysterious middle, whose general characteristics are the most diverse and contradictory of all birth orders. Some middle children are loners: quiet, shy, impatient, and tightly wound. Others, however, are outgoing, friendly, and gregarious. Most are attention-seeking, competitive, rebellious, and peacemaking. In families, middle children are the ones who can get lost and feel misunderstood or overlooked in favor of older or younger siblings. Middle children are competitive mainly with other siblings, especially the older ones, who seem to them to get more attention. Sometimes, middle children feel that life is unfair.

PAUSE: Why might a middle-born child be likely to think that life is unfair?

4   Finally comes the youngest child, the baby, who often gets lots of attention. They are often charming and a bit manipulative, as well as affectionate, uncomplicated, and sometimes a bit absent-minded. They are more carefree than their older siblings and, though charming, can also be critical, spoiled, and impatient. Youngest children may feel that they are not taken seriously, first by their families and then by the world at large. Some negative traits may be immaturity and secretiveness. More positive traits, in addition to those already cited, can make them risk-takers, idealists, humorous, and hardworking. Popular fields for youngest children are journalism, advertising, the arts, and sales.

PAUSE: How are the personalities of youngest children related to the careers they choose?

5   The types of birth orders and their characteristics are general personality traits and may not apply to all children. Certainly, families are different, and many factors influence how children grow and develop. Birth order may help explain why children are the way they are, and what they have to do to prove they are unique. Birth order offers one way to understand people and, if nothing else, it is interesting to consider and compare traits with other people.

....

SUMMARIZE AND RESPOND

In your reading journal or elsewhere, summarize the main point of "Birth Order." Then, go back and check off support for this main idea. Next, write a brief summary (three to five sentences) of the essay. Finally, jot down your initial response to the reading. Have you ever considered the effects of birth order? How much of an influence do you think it has?

....

CHECK YOUR COMPREHENSION

1. Which of the following would be the best alternative title for this essay?

  a. "Firstborn, Middle Child, or Baby? When You Were Born Affects Who You Are"

  b. "Many Factors Influence Character, Personality, and Career Choices"

  c. "Why Firstborn Children Are Perfectionists"

  d. "Sibling Rivalries and Unhappy Families: Why Life Isn't Fair"

2. The main idea of this essay is that

  a. parents have little or no control over the personalities or characters of their children.

  b. knowing whether someone is a firstborn, middle, or youngest child can be one useful way of understanding that person.

  c. we should choose careers that are suitable to our personalities, which are determined by birth order.

  d. people place too much emphasis on birth order when judging the personalities and behaviors of others.

3. According to Trimmer, youngest-born children are
   a. often perfectionists who choose careers in the sciences.
   b. sometimes misunderstood and out of place.
   c. always the most competitive of all siblings.
   d. usually the charmers and manipulators in the family.

4. If you are unfamiliar with the following words, use a dictionary to check their meanings: corresponding (para. 1); precision, assertive (2); gregarious (3); manipulative (4).

READ CRITICALLY

1. Where does Trimmer acknowledge that her classifications may only partly explain personality and character? Why do you think she does this? Does this choice strengthen her essay or weaken it? Explain.

2. What transitions does the writer use? Underline them. How do they help structure the essay?

3. Trimmer uses classification to generalize about personality traits based on birth order, but some of these generalizations are contradictory. Can you find specific examples? What effect do they have on her main point?

4. In the writer's view, birth order can explain "why children are the way they are, and what they have to do to prove they are unique" (para. 5). Which of the three kinds of sibling has the most difficult obstacles or pressures to "overcome"? Why do you think this is?

5. Does this essay have the Four Basics of Good Classification? Explain your answer.

WRITE AN ESSAY

Trimmer uses birth order to classify different personalities. But she notes other influences, including upbringing, family size, heritage, education, religion, and geographic location. Write an essay that uses one of these factors, or some other category of your choice, as an organizing principle to explain different personality types. Your essay should show how personalities or behaviors correspond to your different classifications and divisions, as "Birth Order" does.

Amy Tan

Mother Tongue

Amy Tan was born in Oakland, California, in 1952, several years after her mother and father emigrated from China. She studied at San Jose City College and later San Jose State University, receiving a B.A. with a double major in English and linguistics. In 1973, she earned an M.A. in linguistics from San Jose State. In 1989, Tan published her first novel, *The Joy Luck Club*, which was nominated for the National Book Award and the National Book Critics Circle Award. Tan's other books include *The Kitchen God's Wife* (1991), *The Hundred Secret Senses* (1995), *The Bonesetter's Daughter* (2001), and *Saving Fish from Drowning* (2005). Her short stories and essays have been published in the *Atlantic*, *Grand Street*, *Harper's*, the *New Yorker*, and other publications.

In the following essay, which was selected for *The Best American Essays 1991*, Tan discusses the different kinds of English she uses, from academic discourse to the simple language she speaks with her mother.

CRITICAL
READING

■ Preview
■ Read
■ Pause
■ Review

(More on p. 28.)

GUIDING QUESTION

In what ways did Tan's mother's "limited" ability to speak English affect Tan as she was growing up?

1   I am not a scholar of English or literature. I cannot give you much more than personal opinions on the English language and its variations in this country or others.

2   I am a writer. And by that definition, I am someone who has always loved language. I am fascinated by language in daily life. I spend a great deal of my time thinking about the power of language — the way it can evoke an emotion, a visual image, a complex idea, or a simple truth. Language is the tool of my trade. And I use them all — all the Englishes I grew up with.

3   Recently, I was made keenly aware of the different Englishes I do use. I was giving a talk to a large group of people, the same talk I had already given to half a dozen other groups. The nature of the talk was about my writing, my life, and my book, *The Joy Luck Club*. The talk was going along well enough, until I remembered one major difference that made the whole talk sound wrong. My mother was in the room. And it was perhaps the first time she had heard me give a lengthy speech, using the kind of English I have never used with her. I was saying things like "The intersection of memory upon imagination" and "There is an aspect of my fiction that relates to thus-and-thus" — a speech filled with carefully wrought grammatical phrases, burdened, it suddenly seemed to me, with

TEACHING TIP As Tan writes later (para. 21), she found her voice as a fiction writer by imagining her mother as the reader of her stories. Ask students to think how imagining a specific reader for their writing can help them find an appropriate voice.

nominalized forms, past perfect tenses, conditional phrases, all the forms of standard English that I had learned in school and through books, the forms of English I did not use at home with my mother.

4   Just last week, I was walking down the street with my mother, and I again found myself conscious of the English I was using, the English I do use with her. We were talking about the price of new and used furniture and I heard myself saying this: "Not waste money that way." My husband was with us as well, and he didn't notice any switch in my English. And then I realized why. It's because over the twenty years we've been together I've often used that same kind of English with him, and sometimes he even uses it with me. It has become our language of intimacy, a different sort of English that relates to family talk, the language I grew up with.

5   So you'll have some idea of what this family talk I heard sounds like, I'll quote what my mother said during a recent conversation which I videotaped and then transcribed. During this conversation, my mother was talking about a political gangster in Shanghai[1] who had the same last name as her family's, Du, and how the gangster in his early years wanted to be adopted by her family, which was rich by comparison. Later, the gangster became more powerful, far richer than my mother's family, and one day showed up at my mother's wedding to pay his respects. Here's what she said in part:

6   "Du Yusong having business like fruit stand. Like off the street kind. He is Du like Du Zong—but not Tsung-ming Island people. The local people call putong, the river east side, he belong to that side local people. That man want to ask Du Zong father take him in like become own family. Du Zong father wasn't look down on him, but didn't take seriously, until that man big like become a mafia. Now important person, very hard to inviting him. Chinese way, came only to show respect, don't stay for dinner. Respect for making big celebration, he shows up. Mean gives lots of respect. Chinese custom. Chinese social life that way. If too important won't have to stay too long. He come to my wedding. I didn't see, I heard it. I gone to boy's side, they have YMCA dinner. Chinese age I was nineteen."

7   You should know that my mother's expressive command of English belies how much she actually understands. She reads the *Forbes* report,[2] listens to *Wall Street Week*, converses daily with her stockbroker, reads all of Shirley MacLaine's[3] books with ease—all kinds of things I can't begin to understand. Yet some of my friends tell me they understand 50 percent of what my mother says. Some say they understand 80 to 90 percent.

---

1. Shanghai: a major city in eastern China   **2. *Forbes* report:** a financial publication geared toward investors   **3. Shirley MacLaine:** actress whose works of autobiography often referred to her past lives

Some say they understand none of it, as if she were speaking pure Chinese. But to me, my mother's English is perfectly clear, perfectly natural. It's my mother tongue. Her language, as I hear it, is vivid, direct, full of observation and imagery. That was the language that helped shape the way I saw things, expressed things, made sense of the world.

8   Lately, I've been giving more thought to the kind of English my mother speaks. Like others, I have described it to people as "broken" or "fractured" English. But I wince when I say that. It has always bothered me that I can think of no other way to describe it other than "broken," as if it were damaged and needed to be fixed, as if it lacked a certain wholeness and soundness. I've heard other terms used, "limited English," for example. But they seem just as bad, as if everything is limited, including people's perceptions of the limited English speaker.

9   I know this for a fact, because when I was growing up, my mother's "limited" English limited *my* perception of her. I was ashamed of her English. I believed that her English reflected the quality of what she had to say. That is, because she expressed them imperfectly her thoughts were imperfect. And I had plenty of empirical[4] evidence to support me: the fact that people in department stores, at banks, and at restaurants did not take her seriously, did not give her good service, pretended not to understand her, or even acted as if they did not hear her.

10   My mother has long realized the limitations of her English as well. When I was fifteen, she used to have me call people on the phone to pretend I was she. In this guise, I was forced to ask for information or even to complain and yell at people who had been rude to her. One time it was a call to her stockbroker in New York. She had cashed out her small portfolio and it just so happened we were going to go to New York the next week, our very first trip outside California. I had to get on the phone and say in an adolescent voice that was not very convincing, "This is Mrs. Tan."

11   And my mother was standing in the back whispering loudly, "Why he don't send me check, already two weeks late. So mad he lie to me, losing me money."

12   And then I said in perfect English, "Yes, I'm getting rather concerned. You had agreed to send the check two weeks ago, but it hasn't arrived."

13   Then she began to talk more loudly. "What he want, I come to New York tell him front of his boss, you cheating me?" And I was trying to calm her down, make her be quiet, while telling the stockbroker, "I can't tolerate any more excuses. If I don't receive the check immediately, I am going to have to speak to your manager when I'm in New York next week." And sure enough, the following week there we were in front of this astonished

PAUSE: In paragraphs 9–14, what evidence does Tan use to support her claim that others believed that her mother's English showed a lack of intelligence?

4. **empirical:** based on direct experience or observation

stockbroker, and I was sitting there red-faced and quiet, and my mother, the real Mrs. Tan, was shouting at his boss in her impeccable broken English.

PAUSE: Have you or anyone you know not been taken seriously because of language, age, race, or some other trait?

14   We used a similar routine just five days ago, for a situation that was far less humorous. My mother had gone to the hospital for an appointment, to find out about a benign brain tumor a CAT scan[5] had revealed a month ago. She said she had spoken very good English, her best English, no mistakes. Still, she said, the hospital did not apologize when they said they had lost the CAT scan and she had come for nothing. She said they did not seem to have any sympathy when she told them she was anxious to know the exact diagnosis, since her husband and son had both died of brain tumors. She said they would not give her any more information until the next time and she would have to make another appointment for that. So she said she would not leave until the doctor called her daughter. She wouldn't budge. And when the doctor finally called her daughter, me, who spoke in perfect English—lo and behold—we had assurances the CAT scan would be found, promises that a conference call on Monday would be held, and apologies for any suffering my mother had gone through for a most regrettable mistake.

15   I think my mother's English almost had an effect on limiting my possibilities in life as well. Sociologists and linguists probably will tell you that a person's developing language skills are more influenced by peers. But I do think that the language spoken in the family, especially in immigrant families which are more insular, plays a large role in shaping the language of the child. And I believe that it affected my results on achievement tests, IQ tests, and the SAT. While my English skills were never judged as poor, compared to math, English could not be considered my strong suit. In grade school I did moderately well, getting perhaps B's, sometimes B-pluses, in English and scoring perhaps in the sixtieth or seventieth percentile on achievement tests. But those scores were not good enough to override the opinion that my true abilities lay in math and science, because in those areas I achieved A's and scored in the ninetieth percentile or higher.

PAUSE: What has been your experience with the kinds of English tests that Tan writes about in paragraphs 16–17?

16   This was understandable. Math is precise; there is only one correct answer. Whereas, for me at least, the answers on English tests were always a judgment call, a matter of opinion and personal experience. Those tests were constructed around items like fill-in-the-blank sentence completion, such as "Even though Tom was ———, Mary thought he was ———." And the correct answer always seemed to be the most bland combinations of thoughts, for example, "Even though Tom was shy, Mary thought he was charming," with the grammatical structure "even though" limiting the correct answer to some sort of semantic[6] opposites, so you wouldn't get

5. **CAT scan:** a form of X-ray used to produce internal images of the body
6. **semantic:** related to the meaning of words

answers like, "Even though Tom was foolish, Mary thought he was ridiculous." Well, according to my mother, there were very few limitations as to what Tom could have been and what Mary might have thought of him. So I never did well on tests like that.

17   The same was true with word analogies, pairs of words in which you were supposed to find some sort of logical, semantic relationship—for example, "*Sunset* is to *nightfall* as _____ is to _____." And here you would be presented with a list of four possible pairs, one of which showed the same kind of relationship: *red* is to *stoplight, bus* is to *arrival, chills* is to *fever, yawn* is to *boring.* Well, I could never think that way. I knew what the tests were asking, but I could not block out of my mind the images already created by the first pair, "*sunset* is to *nightfall*"—and I would see a burst of colors against a darkening sky, the moon rising, the lowering of a curtain of stars. And all the other pairs of words—red, bus, stoplight, boring—just threw up a mass of confusing images, making it impossible for me to sort out something as logical as saying: "A sunset precedes nightfall" is the same as "a chill precedes a fever." The only way I would have gotten that answer right would have been to imagine an associative situation, for example, my being disobedient and staying out past sunset, catching a chill at night, which turns into feverish pneumonia as punishment, which indeed did happen to me.

18   I have been thinking about all this lately, about my mother's English, about achievement tests. Because lately I've been asked, as a writer, why there are not more Asian Americans represented in American literature. Why are there few Asian Americans enrolled in creative writing programs? Why do so many Chinese students go into engineering? Well, these are broad sociological questions I can't begin to answer. But I have noticed in surveys—in fact, just last week—that Asian students, as a whole, always do significantly better on math achievement tests than in English. And this makes me think that there are other Asian American students whose English spoken in the home might also be described as "broken" or "limited." And perhaps they also have teachers who are steering them away from writing and into math and science, which is what happened to me.

PAUSE: How do you think Tan might answer the questions she poses in paragraph 18?

19   Fortunately, I happen to be rebellious in nature and enjoy the challenge of disproving assumptions made about me. I became an English major my first year in college, after being enrolled as pre-med. I started writing nonfiction as a freelancer the week after I was told by my former boss that writing was my worst skill and I should hone my talents toward account management.

PAUSE: How do you respond when people make assumptions about you?

20   But it wasn't until 1985 that I finally began to write fiction. And at first I wrote using what I thought to be wittily crafted sentences, sentences that would finally prove I had mastery over the English language. Here's an

example from the first draft of a story that later made its way into *The Joy Luck Club*, but without this line: "That was my mental quandary[7] in its nascent[8] state." A terrible line, which I can barely pronounce.

21   Fortunately, for reasons I won't get into today, I later decided I should envision a reader for the stories I would write. And the reader I decided upon was my mother, because these were stories about mothers. So with this reader in mind—and in fact she did read my early drafts—I began to write stories using all the Englishes I grew up with: the English I spoke to my mother, which for lack of a better term might be described as "simple"; the English she used with me, which for lack of a better term might be described as "broken"; my translation of her Chinese, which could certainly be described as "watered down"; and what I imagined to be her translation of her Chinese if she could speak in perfect English, her internal language, and for that I sought to preserve the essence, but neither an English nor a Chinese structure. I wanted to capture what language ability tests can never reveal: her intent, her passion, her imagery, the rhythms of her speech, and the nature of her thoughts.

22   Apart from what any critic had to say about my writing, I knew I had succeeded where it counted when my mother finished reading my book and gave me her verdict: "So easy to read."

---

7. quandary: a state of uncertainty come into existence   **8. nascent:** developing; beginning to

....

SUMMARIZE AND RESPOND

In your reading journal or elsewhere, summarize the main point of "Mother Tongue." Then, go back and check off support for this main idea. Next, write a brief summary (three to five sentences) of the essay. Finally, jot down your initial response to the reading. What do you think of Tan's relationship with her mother? Do you think that Tan's mother's "limited" English has affected their relationship for the better, for the worse, or in some more complex way? What impression do you have of Tan herself?

....

CHECK YOUR COMPREHENSION

1. Which of the following would be the best alternative title for this essay?
    a. "The Englishes I Grew Up With"
    b. "My Mother's Difficulties Communicating in English"
    c. "How to Communicate with an Immigrant Parent"
    d. "A Writer's Fascination with the English Language"

2. The main idea of this essay is that

   a. children of immigrant parents have difficulties communicating in English because of their parents' "limited" command of the language.

   b. there is no single, proper way to speak English because different people communicate in different ways.

   c. teachers believe that Asian American students necessarily do better in math and science than they do in English and writing.

   d. the kind of English one uses may change in different contexts.

3. Tan concludes that

   a. to become a successful writer, she had to work harder than would someone who grew up in a home where English was the native language.

   b. her mother found her book easy to read because her mother grew up speaking Chinese.

   c. in finding her voice as a writer, she called on the memory of her mother and their communication with each other.

   d. to prove her mastery of the English language, she had to write in a way that her mother would find impossible to understand.

4. If you are unfamiliar with the following words, use a dictionary to check their meanings: evoke (para. 2); keenly, wrought, burdened (3); intimacy (4); belies (7); fractured (8); guise (10); impeccable (13); benign (14); linguists, insular (15); associative (17); freelancer, hone (19); wittily (20).

· ·

READ CRITICALLY

1. Why, when speaking with her husband, does Tan sometimes switch to the kind of English her mother speaks? What does this tell you of her feelings about her mother's way of speaking?

2. Why does Tan dislike using labels such as "broken" or "limited" in referring to the English her mother speaks?

3. In what ways does Tan say that the language spoken within immigrant families can limit the possibilities of the children in such families? Do you agree with her?

4. What, exactly, does Tan classify in this essay? What are the specific classifications she writes about?

5. Tan divides her essay into three sections, indicated by the spaces between paragraphs 7 and 8 and paragraphs 17 and 18. What is the focus of each of these sections? Why do you suppose she chose to organize her essay in this way?

WRITE AN ESSAY

Write an essay classifying your use of language in different situations—at home with family members, with friends outside of home, at school, in your workplace, and elsewhere that your language may change because of the circumstances. For each situation, give examples of the kind of language you use that differs from the language you use in other situations.

Martin Luther King Jr.
The Ways of Meeting Oppression

Martin Luther King Jr. was a leading figure in the African American civil rights movement, a Baptist minister known for his activist work throughout the country before being assassinated in 1968. The youngest person to be given the Nobel Peace Prize (in 1964), he was posthumously awarded the Presidential Medal of Freedom in 1977 and the Congressional Gold Medal in 2004. In "The Ways of Meeting Oppression," King discusses the failure of both acquiescence and physical violence as ways of responding to oppression and offers nonviolent resistance as the best means of fighting against racial injustice.

CRITICAL READING
■ Preview
■ Read
■ Pause
■ Review

(More on p. 28.)

GUIDING QUESTION
What is oppression? Where do you see oppression in the world today? How should people respond?

1   Oppressed people deal with their oppression in three characteristic ways. One way is acquiescence:[1] The oppressed resign themselves to doom. They tacitly adjust themselves to oppression, and thereby become conditioned to it. In every movement toward freedom, some of the oppressed

---

1. acquiescence: agreement by silence or lack of protest

prefer to remain oppressed. Almost 2800 years ago, Moses[2] set out to lead the children of Israel from the slavery of Egypt to the freedom of the promised land. He soon discovered that slaves do not always welcome their deliverers. They become accustomed to being slaves. They would rather bear those ills they have, as Shakespeare[3] pointed out, than flee to others that they know not of. They prefer the "fleshpots of Egypt"[4] to the ordeals of emancipation.

2   There is such a thing as the freedom of exhaustion. Some people are so worn down by the yoke[5] of oppression that they give up. A few years ago, in the slum areas of Atlanta, a Negro guitarist used to sing almost daily: "Been down so long that down don't bother me." This is the type of negative freedom and resignation that often engulfs the life of the oppressed.

PAUSE: What makes some people give up in the face of oppression?

3   But this is not the way out. To accept passively an unjust system is to cooperate with that system; thereby the oppressed become as evil as the oppressor. Noncooperation with evil is as much a moral obligation as is cooperation with good. The oppressed must never allow the conscience of the oppressor to slumber. Religion reminds every man that he is his brother's keeper. So acquiescence—while often the easier way—is not the moral way. It is the way of the coward. The Negro cannot win the respect of his oppressor by acquiescing; he merely increases the oppressor's arrogance and contempt. Acquiescence is interpreted as proof of the Negro's inferiority. The Negro cannot win the respect of the white people of the South or the peoples of the world if he is willing to sell the future of his children for his personal and immediate comfort and safety.

PAUSE: What do you think King means by saying, "The oppressed must never allow the conscience of the oppressor to slumber"?

4   A second way that oppressed people sometimes deal with oppression is to resort to physical violence and corroding hatred. Violence often brings about momentary results. Nations have frequently won their independence in battle. But in spite of temporary victories, violence never brings a permanent peace. It solves no social problem; it merely creates new and more complicated ones.

5   Violence as a way of achieving racial justice is both impractical and immoral. It is impractical because it is a descending spiral ending in destruction for all. The old law of an eye for an eye[6] leaves everybody blind. It is immoral because it seeks to humiliate the opponent rather

PAUSE: Why are violent responses to oppression both impractical and immoral? What examples do you know of that support King's position?

---

2. Moses: a Hebrew prophet   **3. Shakespeare:** a renowned British playwright who wrote in the late 1500s and early 1600s   **4. fleshpots of Egypt:** biblical reference to cooking vessels and luxurious living (Exodus 16: 3)   **5. yoke:** a harness that joins animals together as a team   **6. an eye for an eye:** from the Hebrew Bible, meaning that the victim can seek amends that duplicate the original crime

than win his understanding; it seeks to annihilate rather than to convert. Violence is immoral because it thrives on hatred rather than love. It destroys community and makes brotherhood impossible. It leaves society in monologue rather than dialogue. Violence ends by defeating itself. It creates bitterness in the survivors and brutality in the destroyers. A voice echoes through time saying to every potential Peter, "Put up your sword."[7] History is cluttered with the wreckage of nations that failed to follow this command.

6   If the American Negro and other victims of oppression succumb to the temptation of using violence in the struggle for freedom, future generations will be the recipients of a desolate night of bitterness, and our chief legacy to them will be an endless reign of meaningless chaos. Violence is not the way.

7   The third way open to oppressed people in their quest for freedom is the way of nonviolent resistance. Like the synthesis[8] in Hegelian[9] philosophy, the principle of nonviolent resistance seeks to reconcile the truths of two opposites—acquiescence and violence—while avoiding the extremes and immoralities of both. The nonviolent resister agrees with the person who acquiesces that one should not be physically aggressive toward his opponent; but he balances the equation by agreeing with the person of violence that evil must be resisted. He avoids the nonresistance of the former and the violent resistance of the latter. With nonviolent resistance, no individual or group need submit to any wrong, nor need anyone resort to violence in order to right a wrong.

PAUSE: How is nonviolence a "synthesis"?

8   It seems to me that this is the method that must guide the actions of the Negro in the present crisis in race relations. Through nonviolent resistance, the Negro will be able to rise to the noble height of opposing the unjust system while loving the perpetrators of the system. The Negro must work passionately and unrelentingly for full stature as a citizen, but he must not use inferior methods to gain it. He must never come to terms with falsehood, malice, hate, or destruction.

9   Nonviolent resistance makes it possible for the Negro to remain in the South and struggle for his rights. The Negro's problem will not be solved by running away. He cannot listen to the glib[10] suggestion of those who would urge him to migrate en masse to other sections of the country. By grasping his great opportunity in the South, he can make a lasting

7. **"Put up your sword":** order from Christ to Peter, who was trying to defend Christ from arrest (John 18:11)   8. **synthesis:** in philosophy, the combination of two contradictory ideas or propositions to attain a higher truth   9. **Georg Wilhelm Friedrich Hegel (1770–1831):** German philosopher   10. **glib:** easy, insincere, or superficial

contribution to the moral strength of the nation and set a sublime[11] example of courage for generations yet unborn.

10   By nonviolent resistance, the Negro can also enlist all men of good will in his struggle for equality. The problem is not a purely racial one, with Negroes set against whites. In the end, it is not a struggle between people at all, but a tension between justice and injustice. Nonviolent resistance is not aimed against oppressors but against oppression. Under its banner, conscience, not racial groups, are enlisted.

11. sublime: impressive; awe-inspiring

· ·

SUMMARIZE AND RESPOND

In your reading journal or elsewhere, summarize the main point of "The Ways of Meeting Oppression." Then, go back and check off support for this main idea. Next, write a brief summary (three to five sentences) of the selection. Finally, jot down your initial response to the reading. Do you agree with King about nonviolence? Do you think there are circumstances and injustices that justify a violent response?

· ·

CHECK YOUR COMPREHENSION

1. Which of the following would be the best alternative title for this essay?

   a. "Civil Rights Is a Racial Struggle"

   b. "Accepting Injustice Is Evil"

   c. "What the Bible Says about Oppression"

   (d.) "Nonviolent Resistance: The Moral and Practical Choice"

2. The main idea of this essay is that

   a. the struggle to achieve racial equality requires African Americans to take responsibility for their own actions.

   b. violence is justified when motivated by love, but immoral when motivated by hatred.

   (c.) nonviolent resistance is the best response to injustice, as it reconciles the truths of acquiescence and violence while avoiding their immorality.

   d. black people facing oppression in America should move to regions of the country that are more tolerant of racial diversity.

3. King argues that nonviolent resistance

  a. allows people to oppose an unjust system while still loving the perpetrators of that system.

  b. is dangerous and requires remarkable physical courage.

  c. may force white Americans to respond with violence, which would damage the cause of civil rights.

  d. is moral and idealistic, but ineffective at addressing real social problems.

4. If you are unfamiliar with the following words, check the dictionary for their meanings: tacitly, emancipation (para. 1); resignation, engulfs (2); conscience, inferiority (3); corroding (4); annihilate, monologue, dialogue (5); succumb, desolate, legacy (6); reconcile (7); perpetrators (8).

READ CRITICALLY

1. What is King's purpose in this essay? What effect do you think he wants his writing to have on his audience?

2. What different examples does King use to support his classifications? How effective are they? Explain.

3. Where in the essay does the writer use transitional words or phrases? Point to specific examples.

4. Why does King choose to present the different ways to meet oppression in this order? Would the essay be as effective if he had begun with nonviolent resistance? Why or why not?

5. According to King, the civil rights struggle is "not purely a racial one, with Negroes set against whites," but rather a "tension between justice and injustice." "Nonviolent resistance is not aimed against oppressors but against oppression" (para. 10). What do you think he means by these statements?

WRITE AN ESSAY

King's essay is "The Ways of Meeting Oppression." Write a classification essay entitled the "The Ways of Dealing with _____," filling in the blank with a particular problem or challenge—for example, bullying, stress, educational setbacks, family conflict, difficult bosses, or college pressures. Use specific examples, and make sure that the different ways of addressing the problem can be placed into at least three categories.

Classification: Linked Readings

OVERCOMING ADVERSITY AND TRAUMA

Each of the following readings show people overcoming challenges, adversity, or trauma in different ways.

> Amy Tan, "Mother Tongue" (this chapter, p. 751)
>
> Martin Luther King Jr., "The Ways of Meeting Oppression" (this chapter, p. 758)
>
> Beth Trimmer, "Birdshot" (Chapter 41, p. 688)
>
> Nicholas Kristof, "Two Men and Two Paths" (Chapter 47, p. 791)
>
> Michael Jernigan, "Living the Dream" (Chapter 48, p. 798)

Read the selections, and draw from at least one in addition to "The Ways of Meeting Oppression" to write an essay titled "Overcoming Adversity." You can refer to your own experience, but make sure to use material from the essays as well.

STEREOTYPES

Each of the following readings focuses on or uses stereotypes.

> Beth Trimmer, "Birth Order" (this chapter, p. 747)
>
> Nancy Mairs, "On Being a Cripple" (Chapter 46, p. 769)
>
> Dave Barry, "The Ugly Truth about Beauty" (Chapter 47, p. 787)
>
> Brent Staples, "Just Walk on By: Black Men and Public Space" (Chapter 48, p. 802)

Read the selections, and draw from at least one in addition to "Birth Order" to write an essay titled "Stereotypes: Are They Wrong?" You can refer to your own experience, but make sure to use material from the essays as well.

....

FAMILY TIES

Each of the following readings discusses family relationships and the ways they affect and shape people's lives.

Beth Trimmer, "Birth Order" (this chapter, p. 747)

Daniel Flanagan, "The Choice to Do It Over Again" (Chapter 13, p. 206)

Alex Espinoza, "An American in Mexico" (Chapter 43, p. 723)

Nicholas Kristof, "Two Men and Two Paths" (Chapter 47, p. 791)

Read the selections, and draw from at least one in addition to "Birth Order" to write an essay entitled "How Family Ties Affect Our Lives." You may refer to your own experience, but make sure to use material from the essays as well.

....

46

Definition

Each essay in this chapter uses definition to get its main point across. As you read these essays, consider how they achieve the four basics of good definition that are listed below and discussed in Chapter 15 of this book.

IDEA JOURNAL
What labels do people use to try to define you?

Four Basics of Good Definition

1 It tells readers what term is being defined.

2 It gives a clear definition.

3 It uses examples to show what the writer means.

4 It gives details about the examples that readers will understand.

Kevin Willey

The Optimistic Generation

Kevin Willey wrote this essay while he was a senior mechanical engineering major at the University of Maine. He graduated in May 2011 and, after looking for some time and contacting many companies, he landed a job in his field. In "The Optimistic Generation," Willey offers a defining trait of his generation that is perhaps different from what most people think of when they hear his age group called "the Millennials."

CRITICAL
READING
■ Preview
■ Read
■ Pause
■ Review

(More on p. 28.)

GUIDING QUESTION
How does the author define his generation, and what examples does he give?

1   The media are quick to name and define each generation of Americans, from the Baby Boomers to Generation X to Generation Y, also known as the Millennials. Already, there is Generation Z, to refer to children born after the early 1990s. My friends and I are Millennials, those people born between the mid-1970s to the early 1990s. When people try to sum up what we Millennials are like, they say that we are immature, impatient, restless, and distracted by constant technological interaction, and other negative descriptions. Instead, it is more accurate to say that we are optimistic. The *Merriam-Webster Dictionary Online* defines *optimism* as "an inclination to put the most favorable construction upon actions and events or to anticipate the best possible outcome" ("Optimism"). This optimism is a characteristic that will serve us and others well.

PAUSE: What is the definition of *optimism*?

2   One area we are optimistic about is our job prospects. As we enter young adulthood, the economy took a nosedive, and many of us are unable to find the jobs we thought would be there for us when we graduated. Many of us have large student loans to repay, and we need to find good work. Instead of jobs waiting for us, and companies ready to put us to work, we find too many people looking and not enough positions open: The older generation is not retiring fast enough, and many companies have cut thousands of jobs or sent jobs overseas, to be done by lower-paid workers. Many of us are settling for the kinds of jobs we had during high school. As a group, however, we are not bitter or angry. We believe that the future will be better. The Pew Research Center recently published a report about Millennials, describing us as "confident" and "upbeat and open to change" (Pew Res. Center 1). The report goes on to say: "Millennials have

PAUSE: Summarize what Willey says about optimism and job prospects.

not escaped the current economic downturn. But even though they're not happy with their current economic circumstances, they remain highly optimistic about their financial future" (20).

3   I am optimistic that our connectedness will help us, too. We do not have to make an effort to network because we already keep in frequent touch through all kinds of social and business groups online. We also like working in groups, and businesses operate to a large degree on good team-work. The Pew report also describes us as more open to technology and social media than previous generations (25), and that experience has helped us adapt to new things, since technology is always changing. This openness to change is part of our optimism. We believe that the world will always be changing and improving, and we are ready. We do not fight change; we welcome it. Bring it on.

PAUSE: How does Willey say his generation's connectedness will be helpful?

4   Our world has many other major threats, such as wars, global warming, and poverty. Here in the United States, we have not only a bad economy, but a Congress that cannot seem to work together and as a result is unproductive. The U.S. divorce rate is high, and the gap between the richest and the poorest just keeps growing. Prices are rising on necessities such as food, gasoline, and heating oil. And the cost of housing means that my friends and I, if we are lucky enough to get jobs, will need many roommates in our tiny apartments to help us keep up with the rent. Others will live with their parents, if they can. But our optimism here, too, helps us: We know it will get better.

PAUSE: What problems do Millenials face?

5   A 2011 report in *Time* magazine focused on optimism as a positive characteristic. Optimism allows us to get through bad times such as these because we believe in a better future (Sharot 39). We do not give up. This belief that the situation will improve gives us the initiative to try to solve the problems facing us. Author Tali Sharot says, "To make progress, we need to be able to imagine alternative realities—better ones—and we need to believe that we can achieve them. Such faith helps motivate us to pursue our goals" (42).

6   As I go out to find a job, I know I might not get exactly the position I want or the one that I thought a college degree would give me. My friends and I will not have it easy. But as a group, we have real and durable optimism. That characteristic will serve us well, and our generation, the Millennials, have a lot to contribute to the world.

Works Cited

"Optimism." *Merriam-Webster Dictionary Online*. Merriam-Webster Dictionary. Web. 10 Apr. 2011. <http://www.merriam-webster.com/dictionary/optimism>.

Pew Research Center. "Millennials: A Portrait of Generation Next." 24 Feb. 2010. Web. 4 Apr. 2011. <http://pewresearch.org/millennials/>.

Sharot, Tali. "The Optimism Bias." *Time* 28 May 2011: 39-46. Print.

SUMMARIZE AND RESPOND

In your reading journal or elsewhere, summarize the main point of "The Optimistic Generation." Then, go back and check off support for this main idea. Next, write a brief summary (three to five sentences) of the essay. Finally, jot down your initial responses to the essay. If you are a Millennial, do you agree with what Willey says?

CHECK YOUR COMPREHENSION

1. Which of the following would be the best alternative title for this essay?
   a. "What I Would Call My Generation"
   b. "Why Optimism Is Good"
   c. "The Future Looks Bright"
   d. "Getting a Job Will Not Be Easy"

2. The main idea of this essay is that
   a. every generation has its own strengths and weaknesses.
   b. the media categorizes every generation.
   c. Millennials have traits that will help them succeed.
   d. Millennials are not defined correctly by most people.

3. The author is aware that
   a. he will probably have to live with his parents.
   b. his generation faces many problems.
   c. life will be hard.
   d. people are retiring later in life.

4. If you are unfamiliar with the following words, use a dictionary to check their meanings: generation, interaction (para. 1); prospects, bitter (2); gap (4); characteristics, alternatives (5).

READ CRITICALLY

1. In the first paragraph, Willey lists some traits used to describe those of the Millennial generation. What are these traits, and does he agree or disagree with them being used to describe his generation?

2. What is his purpose for writing?

3. How does Willey show his generation to be optimistic, and why does he think optimism is a good quality to have?

4. Do you think the sources he uses help his purpose? Why or why not?

5. After reading Willey's essay, what do you think of his generation?

WRITE AN ESSAY

Willey writes about what he sees as one of his generation's major characteristics. If you are of the same generation, choose another word that you believe is one of its characteristics and define and give examples of it. If you are of another generation, choose a characteristic you think describes your own generation and define it.

Nancy Mairs
On Being a Cripple

In her essays, memoirs, and poetry, Nancy Mairs (b. 1943) often writes about multiple sclerosis and her experience, since 1993, of life in a wheelchair. Mairs attended Wheaton College and earned an M.F.A. and Ph.D. from the University of Arizona. Her essay collections include *Waist High in the World: A Life among the Nondisabled* (1996) and *A Troubled Guest* (2002).

This essay, from the collection *Plaintext* (1986), addresses the words we use to talk about people with disabilities. Mairs makes a case for honesty in language and explains what she means when she calls herself a cripple.

GUIDING QUESTION
How would you describe Mairs's attitude toward her disability?

CRITICAL
READING
■ Preview
■ Read
■ Pause
■ Review

(More on p. 28.)

> *To escape is nothing. Not to escape is nothing.* —LOUISE BOGAN

1   The other day I was thinking of writing an essay on being a cripple. I was thinking hard in one of the stalls of the women's room in my office building, as I was shoving my shirt into my jeans and tugging up my zipper. Preoccupied, I flushed, picked up my book bag, took my cane down from the hook, and unlatched the door. So many movements unbalanced me, and as I pulled the door open I fell over backward, landing fully

PAUSE: Why might this incident in the women's room have prompted Mairs to write her essay?

clothed on the toilet seat with my legs splayed in front of me: the old beetle-on-its-back routine. Saturday afternoon, the building deserted, I was free to laugh aloud as I wriggled back to my feet, my voice bouncing off the yellowish tiles from all directions. Had anyone been there with me, I'd have been still and faint and hot with chagrin. I decided that it was high time to write the essay.

2   First, the matter of semantics.[1] I am a cripple. I choose this word to name me. I choose from among several possibilities, the most common of which are "handicapped" and "disabled." I made the choice a number of years ago, without thinking, unaware of my motives for doing so. Even now, I'm not sure what those motives are, but I recognize that they are complex and not entirely flattering. People — crippled or not — wince at the word "cripple," as they do not at "handicapped" or "disabled." Perhaps I want them to wince. I want them to see me as a tough customer, one to whom the fates/gods/viruses have not been kind, but who can face the brutal truth of her existence squarely. As a cripple, I swagger.

TEACHING TIP
Discuss students' responses to Mairs's tone. Ask them what impression they have of her. What is it about the way she writes about herself that contributes to their impressions?

3   But, to be fair to myself, a certain amount of honesty underlies my choice. "Cripple" seems to me a clean word, straightforward and precise. It has an honorable history, having made its first appearance in the Lindisfarne Gospel in the tenth century. As a lover of words, I like the accuracy with which it describes my condition: I have lost the full use of my limbs. "Disabled," by contrast, suggests any incapacity, physical or mental. And I certainly don't like "handicapped," which implies that I have deliberately been put at a disadvantage, by whom I can't imagine (my God is not a Handicapper General), in order to equalize chances in the great race of life. These words seem to me to be moving away from my condition, to be widening the gap between word and reality. Most remote is the recently coined euphemism[2] "differently abled," which partakes of the same semantic hopefulness that transformed countries from "undeveloped" to "underdeveloped," then to "less developed," and finally to "developing" nations. People have continued to starve in those countries during the shift. Some realities do not obey the dictates of language.

PAUSE: Why does Mairs dislike the terms *disabled*, *handicapped*, and *differently abled*?

4   Mine is one of them. Whatever you call me, I remain crippled. But I don't care what you call me, so long as it isn't "differently abled," which strikes me as pure verbal garbage designed, by its ability to describe anyone, to describe no one. I subscribe to George Orwell's thesis that "the slovenliness[3] of our language makes it easier for us to have foolish thoughts." And I refuse to participate in the degeneration of the language to the extent that I deny that I have lost anything in the course of this calamitous disease; I refuse to pretend that the only differences between you and me are

1. semantics: in general, the study of words; here, the choice of particular words
2. euphemism: a word that puts a pleasant cover over an unpleasant condition
3. slovenliness: sloppiness

the various ordinary ones that distinguish any one person from another. But call me "disabled" or "handicapped" if you like. I have long since grown accustomed to them; and if they are vague, at least they hint at the truth. Moreover, I use them myself. Society is no readier to accept crippledness than to accept death, war, sex, sweat, or wrinkles. I would never refer to another person as a cripple. It is the word I use to name only myself.

5   I haven't always been crippled, a fact for which I am soundly grateful. To be whole of limb is, I know from experience, infinitely more pleasant and useful than to be crippled; and if that knowledge leaves one open to bitterness at my loss, the physical soundness I once enjoyed (though I did not enjoy it half enough) is well worth the occasional stab of regret. Though never any good at sports, I was a normally active child and young adult. I climbed trees, played hopscotch, jumped rope, skated, swam, rode my bicycle, sailed. I despised team sports, spending some of the wretchedest afternoons of my life, sweaty and humiliated, behind a field-hockey stick and under a basketball hoop. I tramped alone for miles along the bridle paths that webbed the woods behind the house I grew up in. I swayed through countless dim hours in the arms of one man or another under the scattered shot of light from mirrored balls, and gyrated through countless more as Tab Hunter and Johnny Mathis gave way to the Rolling Stones, Creedence Clearwater Revival, Cream. I walked down the aisle. I pushed baby carriages, changed tires in the rain, marched for peace.

6   When I was twenty-eight I started to trip and drop things. What at first seemed my natural clumsiness soon became too pronounced to shrug off. I consulted a neurologist, who told me that I had a brain tumor. A battery of tests, increasingly disagreeable, revealed no tumor. About a year and a half later I developed a blurred spot in one eye. I had, at last, the episodes "disseminated[4] in space and time" requisite for a diagnosis: multiple sclerosis. I have never been sorry for the doctor's initial misdiagnosis, however. For almost a week, until the negative results of the tests were in, I thought that I was going to die right away. Every day for the past nearly ten years, then, has been a kind of gift. I accept all gifts.

7   Multiple sclerosis is a chronic[5] degenerative[6] disease of the central nervous system, in which the myelin that sheathes the nerves is somehow eaten away and scar tissue forms in its place, interrupting the nerves' signals. During its course, which is unpredictable and uncontrollable, one may lose vision, hearing, speech, the ability to walk, control of bladder and/or bowels, strength in any or all extremities,[7] sensitivity to touch,

DISCUSSION
Mairs makes an important point about the use of the terms *crippled, handicapped, disabled,* and *differently abled.* Ask students which of these terms they are most comfortable with and whether they agree with Mairs that *crippled* is the most honest and accurate of the terms in her own case. Why do they think Mairs uses the term to refer to herself but not to others?

4. **disseminated:** spread over   5. **chronic:** marked by a long duration; always present   6. **degenerative:** having a worsening effect; causing deterioration
7. **extremities:** limbs of the body

vibration, and/or pain, potency, coordination of movements — the list of possibilities is lengthy and, yes, horrifying. One may also lose one's sense of humor. That's the easiest to lose and the hardest to survive without. . . .

8   Like many women I know, I have always had an uneasy relationship with my body. I was not a popular child, largely, I think now, because I was peculiar: intelligent, intense, moody, shy, given to unexpected actions and inexplicable notions and emotions. But as I entered adolescence, I believed myself unpopular because I was homely: my breasts too flat, my mouth too wide, my hips too narrow, my clothing never quite right in fit or style. I was not, in fact, particularly ugly, old photographs inform me, though I was well off the ideal; but I carried this sense of self-alienation with me into adulthood, where it regenerated in response to the depredations of MS. Even with my brace I walk with a limp so pronounced that, seeing myself on the videotape of a television program on the disabled, I couldn't believe that anything but an inchworm could make progress humping along like that. My shoulders droop and my pelvis thrusts forward as I try to balance myself upright, throwing my frame into a bony S. As a result of contractures, one shoulder is higher than the other and I carry one arm bent in front of me, the fingers curled into a claw. My left arm and leg have wasted into pipestems, and I try always to keep them covered. When I think about how my body must look to others, especially to men, to whom I have been trained to display myself, I feel ludicrous, even loathsome.

9   At my age, however, I don't spend much time thinking about my appearance. The burning egocentricity of adolescence, which assures one that all the world is looking all the time, has passed, thank God, and I'm generally too caught up in what I'm doing to step back, as I used to, and watch myself as though upon a stage. I'm also too old to believe in the accuracy of self-image. I know that I'm not a hideous crone, that in fact, when I'm rested, well dressed, and well made up, I look fine. The self-loathing I feel is neither physically nor intellectually substantial. What I hate is not me but a disease.

10   I am not a disease.

11   And a disease is not — at least not singlehandedly — going to determine who I am, though at first it seemed to be going to. Adjusting to a chronic incurable illness, I have moved through a process similar to that outlined by Elisabeth Kübler-Ross in *On Death and Dying*. The major difference — and it is far more significant than most people recognize — is that I can't be sure of the outcome, as the terminally ill cancer patient can. Research studies indicate that, with proper medical care, I may achieve a "normal" life span. And in our society, with its vision of death as the ultimate evil, worse even than decrepitude, the response to such news is, "Oh well, at least you're not going to *die*." Are there worse things than dying? I think that there may be.

PAUSE: Why might Mairs have chosen to write this one-sentence paragraph (para. 10)?

12   I think of two women I know, both with MS, both enough older than I to have served me as models. One took to her bed several years ago and has been there ever since. Although she can sit in a high-backed wheelchair, because she is incontinent she refuses to go out at all, even though incontinence pants, which are readily available at any pharmacy, could protect her from embarrassment. Instead, she stays at home and insists that her husband, a small quiet man, a retired civil servant, stay there with her except for a quick weekly foray[8] to the supermarket. The other woman, whose illness was diagnosed when she was eighteen, a nursing student engaged to a young doctor, finished her training, married her doctor, accompanied him to Germany when he was in the service, bore three sons and a daughter, now grown and gone. When she can, she travels with her husband; she plays bridge, embroiders, swims regularly; she works, like me, as a symptomatic-patient instructor of medical students in neurology. Guess which woman I hope to be.

8. **foray:** a trip, an outing

....

SUMMARIZE AND RESPOND

In your reading journal or elsewhere, summarize the main point of "On Being a Cripple." Then, go back and check off support for this main idea. Next, write a brief summary (three to five sentences) of the reading. Finally, jot down your initial response to the selection. What impression of Mairs do you come away with? What did you learn from her description of her disease? If you could write a note to Mairs, what would you say to her?

....

CHECK YOUR COMPREHENSION

1.   Which of the following would be the best alternative title for this essay?
   a.   "The Painfulness of a Disease"
   b.   "Surviving with Multiple Sclerosis"
   c.   "Learning to Laugh at My Disability"
   d.   "Coping with Others' Attitudes toward Disability"

2.   The main idea of this essay is that
   a.   multiple sclerosis is an incurable disease of the central nervous system that can affect movement, vision, hearing, and speech.
   b.   many labels are used to describe disabled people, but most such people prefer the term *crippled*.

    c. one needs a strong sense of humor and a circle of supportive friends to live with a disability.

    (d.) being disabled presents many difficulties and obstacles, but one can learn to cope with these challenges.

3. Mairs makes the point that

    (a.) she is grateful to have the memory of being able-bodied as a young woman.

    b. the greatest drawback to her disability is that it makes her feel unattractive.

    c. she feels doctors are not doing enough to discover a cure for multiple sclerosis.

    d. she believes everyone should use the word *crippled* rather than *disabled* or *handicapped*.

4. If you are unfamiliar with the following words, use a dictionary to check their meanings: splayed, chagrin (para. 1); wince, swagger (2); incapacity, partakes, dictates (3); degeneration, calamitous (4); gyrated (5); neurologist (6); inexplicable, regenerated, depredations, contractures, ludicrous, loathsome (8); crone (9); decrepitude (11); incontinent (12).

READ CRITICALLY

1. How effective do you find Mairs's opening paragraph as an introduction to the essay as a whole?

2. Why do you think Mairs devotes paragraphs 2–4 to discussing her use of the word *cripple* to describe herself? How do you respond to this section of the essay? Mairs also objects to terms like *differently abled*, which do not tell the full truth about a condition. Can you think of other such words? Why do you think such words come into the language?

3. How would you evaluate "On Being a Cripple" as a definition essay? What have you learned from the essay that you did not know before?

4. Mairs writes at the end of paragraph 11, "Are there worse things than dying? I think that there may be." What does she mean? How do this question and answer lead into the subject of paragraph 12?

5. What do you think of Mairs's closing sentence? What image of Mairs does it leave you with?

WRITE AN ESSAY

Write an essay defining an important aspect of yourself. This definition might relate to a challenge you face in life, or it might focus on another facet of your identity — your family heritage, your membership in a particular group, a personality or physical trait that you believe sets you apart from others. Think about titling your essay "On Being _____" and, as Mairs does, relating experiences that help communicate your definition to readers.

Juliet B. Schor

Age Compression

Juliet B. Schor (b. 1955) is a professor of sociology at Boston College. Her research and writings focus on work and leisure activities and their relation to family life. Her books include the best-selling *The Overworked American: The Unexpected Decline of Leisure* (1993) and *The Overspent American: Why We Want What We Don't Need* (1999) and *Sustainable Planet: Solutions for the Twenty-First Century* (2002).

In this essay, Schor describes a marketing trend in which products designed for adults or teenagers are pitched to younger kids. It is an excerpt from her most recent book, *Born to Buy* (2004), a study of the commercial pressures placed on today's children.

CRITICAL
READING
■ Preview
■ Read
■ Pause
■ Review

(More on p. 28.)

GUIDING QUESTION
What is Schor's attitude toward age compression as a marketing strategy?

1   One of the hottest trends in youth marketing is age compression — the practice of taking products and marketing messages originally designed for older kids and targeting them to younger ones. Age compression includes offering teen products and genres, pitching gratuitous violence to the twelve-and-under crowd, cultivating brand preferences for items that were previously unbranded among younger kids, and developing creative alcohol and tobacco advertising that is not officially targeted to them but is widely seen and greatly loved by children. "By eight or nine they want 'N Sync," explained one tweening expert to me, in the days before that band was eclipsed by Justin Timberlake, Pink, and others.

2   Age compression is a sprawling trend. It can be seen in the import of television programming specifically designed for one-year-olds, which occurred, ironically, with Public Broadcasting's *Teletubbies*. It includes the

DISCUSSION
Ask students to think about children under ten they know. Do these children seem more grown-up than students felt at the same age?

PAUSE: Underline each example of age compression in paragraph 2.

marketing of designer clothes to kindergartners and first graders. It's the deliberate targeting of R-rated movies to kids as young as age nine, a practice the major movie studios were called on the carpet for by the Clinton administration in 2000. It's being driven by the recognition that many children nationwide are watching MTV and other teen and adult programming. One of my favorite MTV anecdotes comes from a third-grade teacher in Weston, Massachusetts, who reported that she started her social studies unit on Mexico by asking the class what they knew about the country. Six or seven raised their hands and answered, "That's the place where MTV's Spring Break takes place!" For those who haven't seen it, the program glorifies heavy partying, what it calls "bootylicious girls," erotic dancing, wet T-shirt contests, and binge drinking.

3   A common argument within the marketing world is that age compression is being caused by social trends that make contemporary children far more sophisticated than their predecessors. These include the increased responsibilities of kids in single-parent or divorced families, higher levels of exposure to adult media, children's facility[1] with new technology, early puberty, and the fact that kids know more earlier. In the 1980s, Hasbro sold its GI Joe action figure to boys aged eleven to fourteen. Now, Joe is rejected by eight-year-olds as too babyish. Twenty years ago, *Seventeen* magazine targeted sixteen-year-olds; now it aims at eleven and twelves. In a telling gesture, the toy industry has officially lowered its upper age target from fourteen to ten.

PAUSE: Do you agree that the social trends described in paragraph 3 are leading to age compression? Can you think of other trends that are a factor?

4   Marketers have even coined an acronym to describe these developments. It's KAGOY, which stands for Kids Are Getting Older Younger. The social trends become part of the license for treating kids as if they were adults. Indeed, some advertisers are even arguing that current approaches are too protective of children. In a presentation at the 2001 annual Marketing to Kids Conference, executive Abigail Hirschhorn of DDB New York argued that it's time to stop talking down to kids and start "talking up" to them and that too much advertising denies kids what they really crave — the adult world. She argued for more "glamour, fashion, style, irony, and popular music."

PAUSE: What is tweening, and how has it changed?

5   Nowhere is age compression more evident than among the eight- to twelve-year-old target. Originally a strategy for selling to ten- to thirteen-year-olds, children as young as six are being targeted for tweening. And what is that exactly? Tweens are "in-between" teens and children, and tweening consists mainly of bringing teen products and entertainment to ever-younger audiences. If you're wondering why your daughter came home from kindergarten one day singing the words to a Britney Spears or Jennifer Lopez song, the answer is that she got tweened. Tween marketing has become a major focus of the industry, with its own conferences,

1. facility: ability to use easily

research tools, databases, books, and specialty firms. Part of why tweening is so lucrative is that it involves bringing new, more expensive products to this younger group. It's working because tweens have growing purchasing power and influence with parents. The more the tween consumer world comes to resemble the teen world, with its comprehensive branding strategies and intense levels of consumer immersion, the more money there is to be made.

6   In some cases, it's the advertisers pushing the trend with their clients. But clients are also initiating the process. Mark Lapham (pseudonym),[2] president of a company that has focused almost exclusively on the teen market, says, "We're being asked all the time about it" by makers of school supplies, apparel manufacturers, cosmetics companies. Lapham explains how his clients are thinking: "Hey, we can actually sell a cosmetic, not just bubble gum lip gloss . . . we can sell foundation possibly . . . nail polish."

7   Abigail Hirschhorn's plea for industry change is well behind the times. Children are being exposed to plenty of glamour, fashion, style, irony, and popular music, that is, sex. Even the family-friendly Disney Channel is full of sexually suggestive outfits and dancing. One Radio Disney employee explained to me that the company keeps a careful watch on lyrics but is hands-off with the other stuff. A stroll down the 6X–12 aisles of girls' clothing will produce plenty of skimpy and revealing styles. People in advertising are well aware of these developments. Emma Gilding of Ogilvy & Mather recounted an experience she had during an in-home videotaping. The little girl was doing a Britney Spears imitation, with flirting and sexual grinding. Asked by Gilding what she wanted to be when she grew up, the three-year-old answered: "A sexy shirt girl." As researcher Mary Prescott (pseudonym) explained to me in the summer of 2001, "We're coming out of a trend now. Girl power turned into sex power. A very sexy, dirty, dark thing. Parents were starting to panic." While Prescott felt that a reversal toward "puritanism" had already begun, other observers aren't so sure. Not long after Prescott's prediction, Abercrombie & Fitch came under fire for selling thong underwear with sexually suggestive phrases to seven- to fourteen-year-olds. And child development expert Diane Levin alerted parents to the introduction of World Wrestling Entertainment action figures recommended for age four and above, which include a male character with lipstick on his crotch, another male figure holding the severed head of a woman, and a female character with enormous breasts and a minimal simulated black leather outfit and whip. Four-year-olds are also targeted with toys tied to movies that carry PG-13 ratings.

8   Some industry insiders have begun to caution that tweening has gone too far. At the 2002 KidPower conference, Paul Kurnit spoke out publicly

PAUSE: Based on the second sentence, what do you predict paragraph 7 will be about?

ESL Ask students to discuss how one's cultural background might affect age compression. Ask them to compare children elsewhere to children in the United States. Do Schor's points apply to other parts of the world?

2. **pseudonym:** an assumed name, here to protect the identity of the speaker

PAUSE: Do you be-
lieve that these mem-
bers of the industry
really feel guilty? Why
or why not?

about companies "selling 'tude' to pre-teens and ushering in adolescence
a bit sooner than otherwise." Privately, even more critical views were
expressed to me. Mark Lapham revealed that he finds this "kind of an
amazing thing . . . this is where personally my guilt comes out, like gosh,
it's not really appropriate sometimes." But, he continues, "that's where
society's going, what do you do?" Prescott, who is more deeply immersed
in the world of tweening, confessed that "I am doing the most horrible
thing in the world. We are targeting kids too young with too many inappropriate things. . . . It's not worth the almighty buck."

SUMMARIZE AND RESPOND

In your reading journal or elsewhere, summarize the main point of "Age Compression." Then, go back and check off support for this main idea. Next, write
a brief summary (three to five sentences) of the reading. Finally, jot down your
initial response to the selection. Before reading this essay, had you already
noticed instances of age compression in advertising and the entertainment
media? Do you share Schor's concerns over such practices? Do you agree or
disagree that age compression is simply a reflection of the times we live in?
Why or why not?

CHECK YOUR COMPREHENSION

1. Which of the following would be the best alternative title for this
   essay?
   a. "Growing Up with the Media"
   b. "Sex and Violence for Kids"
   c. "Capturing the Tween Consumer"
   d. "Are Kids Getting Older Younger?"

2. The main idea of this essay is that
   a. today more and more children are being treated as if they were
      adults.
   b. many marketers today focus on attracting young children to
      increasingly mature products.
   c. age compression is the result of contemporary children having
      more responsibilities than did children in the past.
   d. some marketers are beginning to feel guilty about targeting
      inappropriate products to young children.

3. Schor suggests that one reason for age compression is

   a. children today have increased exposure to teenage and adult media.

   b. marketers now have more respect for children than they did in the past.

   c. parents take too little responsibility for monitoring the shopping habits of their children.

   d. contemporary children believe that most toys are just too baby-ish to play with.

4. If you are unfamiliar with the following words, use a dictionary to check their meanings: genres, gratuitous (para. 1); predecessors (3); irony (4); puritanism (7).

READ CRITICALLY

1. What would you describe as Schor's purpose in this essay? Who might her intended audience be?

2. On the basis of this essay, what would you say drives marketers to target younger children as they do?

3. Why do you suppose two of Schor's sources, Mark Lapham and Mary Prescott, agreed to be quoted only if their real names weren't used?

4. Evaluate Schor's use of examples in the essay. What do they tell us about age compression in marketing?

5. One researcher quoted in the essay suggests that "a reversal toward 'puritanism'" has begun (para. 7). In looking at marketing toward children today, do you see any evidence of such a reversal?

WRITE AN ESSAY

Write an essay in which you focus on the kinds of products and entertainment media that are targeted toward consumers ages thirteen to seventeen. You may wish to refer to television commercials, print ads in magazines, in-school advertising, advertising on Internet sites, film trailers, and the like, as well as to particular products. Do you find any evidence of age compression in marketing to this older group of consumers?

Definition: Linked Readings

....

STEREOTYPES

Each of the following readings focuses on or uses stereotypes.

Kevin Willey, "The Optimistic Generation" (this chapter, p. 766)

Nancy Mairs, "On Being a Cripple" (this chapter, p. 769)

Beth Trimmer, "Birth Order" (Chapter 45, p. 747)

Amy Tan, "Mother Tongue" (Chapter 45, p. 751)

Dave Barry, "The Ugly Truth about Beauty" (Chapter 47, p. 787)

Brent Staples, "Just Walk on By: Black Men and Public Space" (Chapter 48, p. 802)

Amy L. Beck, "Struggling for Perfection" (Chapter 48, p. 807)

Read the selections, and draw from at least one in addition to "On Being a Cripple" to write an essay titled "Stereotypes: Are They Wrong?" You can refer to your own experience, but make sure to use material from the essays as well.

....

OVERCOMING ADVERSITY AND TRAUMA

Each of the following readings show people overcoming adversity or trauma in different ways.

Nancy Mairs, "On Being a Cripple" (this chapter, p. 769)

Daniel Flanagan, "The Choice to Do It Over Again" (Chapter 13, p. 206)

Beth Trimmer, "Birdshot" (Chapter 41, p. 688)

Michael Jernigan, "Living the Dream" (Chapter 48, p. 798)

Read the selections, and draw from at least one in addition to "On Being a Cripple" to write an essay titled "Overcoming Adversity." You can refer to your own experience, but make sure to use material from the essays as well.

....

....

MEDIA IMAGES AND REALITIES

The following readings focus on the possible effects of media images on reality.

Kevin Willey, "The Optimistic Generation" (this chapter, p. 766)

Juliet Schor, "Age Compression" (this chapter, p. 775)

Deborah L. Rhode, "Why Looks Are the Last Bastion of Discrimination" (Chapter 42, p. 711)

Dave Barry, "The Ugly Truth about Beauty" (Chapter 47, p. 787)

Amy L. Beck, "Struggling for Perfection" (Chapter 48, p. 807)

Read the selections, and write an essay titled "Media Images and Reality" that examines how media images reflect or do not reflect real life. You can refer to your own experience, but make sure to use material from the essays as well.

....

47

Comparison and Contrast

IDEA JOURNAL
Compare your at-
titudes to those of
an older person in
your family.

Each essay in this chapter uses comparison and contrast to get its main point across. As you read these essays, consider how they achieve the four basics of good comparison and contrast that are listed below and discussed in Chapter 16 of this book.

Four Basics of Good Comparison and Contrast

1. It uses subjects that have enough in common to be usefully compared and contrasted.

2. It serves a purpose — either to help readers make a decision or to help them understand the subjects.

3. It presents several important, parallel points of comparison and/or contrast.

4. It is organized either point by point or whole to whole (see pp. 262–63).

Rui Dai

A Whiff of Memory

Rui Dai is currently studying neuroscience at Duke University, after earning a degree in fine arts and working as a research assistant. In high school, she served as co-editor-in-chief of the *Beachcomber* newspaper and, at Duke, has regularly contributed to the *Chronicle*, a student-run newspaper in which "A Whiff of Memory" first appeared in 2010. The piece describes the difference in smells between China and the United States, an observation that struck her while visiting China on a service project. Other of Dai's writings that have appeared in the *Chronicle* include "Engineered Happiness," a piece that looks at the satisfaction levels of engineering students versus those studying arts and sciences.

GUIDING QUESTION
What differences does Dai find between smells in the United States and in China?

CRITICAL READING
■ Preview
■ Read
■ Pause
■ Review

(More on p. 28.)

1   There are many things that distinguish China's street etiquette[1] from the U.S. equivalent: For example, China forbids honking except in the most extreme cases. In the United States, there are no car horns to habituate to,[2] nor are there so many people with so many voices. However, what is most distinctive about China is its smell.

2   Simply put, China smells different than America. It is a weird and completely overwhelming phenomenon that seems wholly inexplicable in scientific terms. How can one country smell different from another? China and the United States are both vast countries with obviously different, idiosyncratic[3] odors in separate regions of each. The American Northeast smells of the sea, and the Midwest, dry cornfields. What is so distinctive between the two that, without opening my eyes, I can tell which country is which? Let me explain. The smell of China carries a distinctive musk[4] that is the combination of age and non-ammonia cleaning supplies. America, on the other hand, smells clean—literally, and not necessarily in a good way. Cleaning detergents are used almost ubiquitously in America, while relatively rare in China. In the States, the

1. **etiquette:** rules about how to behave   2. **habituate to:** to get used to
3. **idiosyncratic:** peculiar or unique to one place, individual, or thing   4. **musk:** a strong scent

complex chemical combinations in cleaning agents destroy almost any endogenous[5] smell of the environment, leaving only a hint of pine or lavender, or whatever oil extract the manufacturer had dropped into the mixture.

3   In every grocery store in America there is always an entire row of cleaning supplies, each with bottles of 409 or Scrubbing Bubbles lined neatly on steel shelves. In China, there are no comparable brands; there is classic soap and there is liquid soap: no ammonia in sight. Such a difference in cleaning protocol[6] has a dramatic effect on the resulting odor of each country.

PAUSE: According to Dai, why is smell distinctive?

4   The reason why the difference in odor between the two countries is so distinctive and apparent is because olfaction[7] evokes strong emotional memories. Biologically, the olfactory system is one of the few senses in the human body that has a direct connection to the part of the brain that is in charge of emotional memories, the amygdala. The olfactory system's mitral cells and olfactory receptor neurons help send information about scents to the amygdala. This is the reason why the smell of cinnamon evokes more memories and emotions than just the sight of cinnamon. It also elicits memories of Christmas morning or the cinnamon rolls after a Thanksgiving dinner. In comparison, few other sensory faculties call to mind a similar distinctive memory. Hearing, for example, does not evoke as powerful memories as olfaction, or else, every single time we heard something we would be reliving the past.

COMBINING MODES: Notice that in this contrast essay, the author also uses description.

5   To me, America smells like driving alone down a road really fast with the wind in your hair; it is freedom. China smells like getting breakfast with my grandmother at dawn in the street market just as it is beginning to bustle; it is nostalgia. As a Chinese American, it is always difficult to distinguish between which part of my heritage is which. I have always wondered what I would have been like if I stayed with my grandmother and had gotten breakfast with her everyday at the street market. Would I still be as argumentative as I am today? Or would I be more pliable?

PAUSE: What do the smells of America and China mean to Dai?

6   The distinction between my identity as both Chinese and American is even harder now that I am on a service project in China. I alternate sporadically[8] as needed between my personalities as a Duke student and another Chinese pedestrian on the street. I converse normally with the rest of my service group as I would on Duke's campus, but the moment I turn to speak to a native or to translate something from English to Chinese, I become one of the more than 1.3 billion people who populate China.

---

5. endogenous: coming from within   **6. protocol:** a specific system for how to proceed   **7. olfaction:** the act of smelling or the sense of smell
8. sporadically: appearing or happening irregularly or occasionally

7   Right now, the unique scent of China is correlated[9] with a set of childhood memories. Once in a while, under the influence of a particular familiar waft of odor, memories of my childhood will rush me back in time. But memory is malleable.[10] And soon, new memories will become associated with the scents of old, for better or for worse. I hope it will be for the better.

9. correlated: closely connected   **10. malleable:** flexible, easily changed

....

SUMMARIZE AND RESPOND

In your reading journal or elsewhere, summarize the main point of "A Whiff of Memory." Then, go back and check off support for this main idea. Next, write a brief summary (three to five sentences) of the reading. Finally, jot down your initial response to the selection. What smells evoke childhood memories for you? Do you agree with Dai that olfaction can evoke strong emotions from the past?

....

CHECK YOUR COMPREHENSION

1.   Which of the following would be the best alternative title for this essay?
   - **a.** "The Smell of Freedom, the Smell of Nostalgia"
   - **b.** "Memories of My Chinese Grandmother"
   - **c.** "America: Clean, But Not Necessarily in a Good Way"
   - **d.** "My Chinese Heritage Is Important to Me"

2.   The main idea of this essay is that
   - **a.** Americans use too many artificial and dangerous cleaning products, while Chinese people use natural and environmentally friendly cleaners.
   - **b.** the smells of China and America not only distinguish the two countries, but also show different aspects of Dai's Chinese American identity.
   - **c.** America's smell evokes childhood memories for the writer, while she associates the smell of China with freedom and independence.
   - **d.** becoming more American has made Dai more argumentative and stubborn.

3. According to the essay,

    a. the olfactory system has a direct connection to emotional memory.

    b. hearing and seeing are the two most important senses.

    c. Chinese Americans may be shy about their Chinese heritage.

    d. the driving habits of Chinese people and Americans are similar.

4. If you are unfamiliar with the following words, use a dictionary to check their meanings: distinctive (para. 1); phenomenon, inexplicable, ubiquitously (2); evokes, elicits (4); bustle, nostalgia, pliable (5); converse (6); waft (7).

··

READ CRITICALLY

1. Where in the essay does the author use point-by-point organization?

2. What impression does Dai create for you in this essay? What leads you to that impression?

3. Why does smell evoke such strong memories for people generally and for Dai in particular?

4. Does Dai prefer the smell of China or America? Why? How can you tell?

5. How are the contrasting smells of China and America related to the author's identity as a Chinese American?

··

WRITE AN ESSAY

Write an essay comparing and contrasting two different places that are important to you based on the way each one smells. How are they different? Why? What memories and emotions do the smells evoke for you? What do the two places mean to you?

··

Dave Barry
The Ugly Truth about Beauty

According to the *New York Times*, humorist Dave Barry is "the funniest man in America." Born in 1947 in Armonk, New York, Barry earned a B.A. from Haverford College. He then worked for several years as a newspaper reporter and a lecturer on business writing before discovering his talent as a humor columnist. The columns he wrote for the *Miami Herald* from 1983 to 2004 have been collected in numerous books. Barry's hilarious observations on American life won him the Pulitzer Prize for Commentary in 1988.

In "The Ugly Truth about Beauty," first published in the *Philadelphia Inquirer Magazine* in 1998, Barry compares and contrasts men's and women's beauty routines. The essay humorously highlights differences in the ways that men and women view themselves.

GUIDING QUESTION
Why do men and women think of their looks differently?

1   If you're a man, at some point a woman will ask you how she looks.

2   "How do I look?" she'll ask.

3   You must be careful how you answer this question. The best technique is to form an honest yet sensitive opinion, then collapse on the floor with some kind of fatal seizure. Trust me, this is the easiest way out. Because you will never come up with the right answer.

4   The problem is that women generally do not think of their looks in the same way that men do. Most men form an opinion of how they look in seventh grade, and they stick to it for the rest of their lives. Some men form the opinion that they are irresistible stud muffins, and they do not change this opinion even when their faces sag and their noses bloat to the size of eggplants and their eyebrows grow together to form what appears to be a giant forehead-dwelling tropical caterpillar.

5   Most men, I believe, think of themselves as average-looking. Men will think this even if their faces cause heart failure in cattle at a range of three hundred yards. Being average does not bother them; average is fine, for men. This is why men never ask anybody how they look. Their primary form of beauty care is to shave themselves, which is essentially the same form of beauty care that they give to their lawns. If, at the end of his four-minute daily beauty regimen,[1] a man has managed to wipe most of the shaving cream out of his hair and is not bleeding too badly, he feels that

CRITICAL READING
■ Preview
■ Read
■ Pause
■ Review

(More on p. 28.)

PAUSE: Based on the first sentence of paragraph 4, how do you think Barry will go on to develop this essay?

---

1. regimen: routine

he has done all he can, so he stops thinking about his appearance and devotes his mind to more critical issues, such as the Super Bowl.

6   Women do not look at themselves this way. If I had to express, in three words, what I believe most women think about their appearance, those words would be: "not good enough." No matter how attractive a woman may appear to be to others, when she looks at herself in the mirror, she thinks: woof. She thinks that at any moment a municipal animal-control officer is going to throw a net over her and haul her off to the shelter.

PAUSE: What two subjects does Barry contrast in paragraph 7?

7   Why do women have such low self-esteem? There are many complex psychological and societal reasons, by which I mean Barbie. Girls grow up playing with a doll proportioned such that, if it were a human, it would be seven feet tall and weigh eighty-one pounds, of which fifty-three pounds would be bosoms. This is a difficult appearance standard to live up to, especially when you contrast it with the standard set for little boys by their dolls . . . excuse me, by their action figures. Most of the action figures that my son played with when he was little were hideous-looking. For example, he was very fond of an action figure (part of the He-Man series) called "Buzz-Off," who was part human, part flying insect. Buzz-Off was not a looker. But he was extremely self-confident. You could not imagine Buzz-Off saying to the other action figures: "Do you think these wings make my hips look big?"

PAUSE: What is Barry's main point in paragraph 8?

8   But women grow up thinking they need to look like Barbie, which for most women is impossible, although there is a multibillion-dollar beauty industry devoted to convincing women that they must try. I once saw an *Oprah* show wherein supermodel Cindy Crawford dispensed makeup tips to the studio audience. Cindy had all these middle-aged women applying beauty products to their faces; she stressed how important it was to apply them in a certain way, using the tips of their fingers. All the women dutifully did this, even though it was obvious to any sane observer that, no matter how carefully they applied these products, they would never look remotely like Cindy Crawford, who is some kind of genetic mutation.

9   I'm not saying that men are superior. I'm just saying that you're not going to get a group of middle-aged men to sit in a room and apply cosmetics to themselves under the instruction of Brad Pitt, in hopes of looking more like him. Men would realize that this task was pointless and demeaning.[2] They would find some way to bolster their self-esteem that did not require looking like Brad Pitt. They would say to Brad: "Oh YEAH? Well what do you know about LAWN CARE, pretty boy?"

10   Of course many women will argue that the reason they become obsessed with trying to look like Cindy Crawford is that men, being as

2. **demeaning:** degrading, lowering one's character

shallow as a drop of spit, WANT women to look that way. To which I have two responses:

11   1. Hey, just because WE'RE idiots, that does not mean YOU have to be; and

12   2. Men don't even notice 97 percent of the beauty efforts you make anyway. Take fingernails. The average woman spends 5,000 hours per year worrying about her fingernails; I have never once, in more than forty years of listening to men talk about women, heard a man say, "She has a nice set of fingernails!" Many men would not notice if a woman had upward of four hands.

13   Anyway, to get back to my original point: If you're a man, and a woman asks you how she looks, you're in big trouble. Obviously, you can't say she looks bad. But you also can't say that she looks great, because she'll think you're lying, because she has spent countless hours, with the help of the multibillion-dollar beauty industry, obsessing about the differences between herself and Cindy Crawford. Also, she suspects that you're not qualified to judge anybody's appearance. This is because you have shaving cream in your hair.

ESL Ask ESL students to compare and contrast cultural differences in definitions of beauty, including various words for *beauty* in their native languages.

· ·

SUMMARIZE AND RESPOND

In your reading journal or elsewhere, summarize the main point of "The Ugly Truth about Beauty." Then, go back and check off support for this main idea. Next, write a brief summary (three to five sentences) of the essay. Finally, jot down your initial response to the essay. Do you agree with Barry's assessment of why there are differences in the ways men and women view themselves? What examples from your experience do or do not support his points?

· ·

CHECK YOUR COMPREHENSION

1. Which of the following would be the best alternative title for this essay?

   a. "Barbie versus He-Man"

   b. "Men and Women: What They See in the Mirror"

   c. "It's Kinder to Lie"

   d. "The Beauty Industry's Dark Secret"

2. The main idea of this essay is that

   a. men don't know how to respond when women ask about their appearance.

   b. men don't care how much effort women put into their looks.

   (c.) because of society and the media, men and women view their physical appearances differently.

   d. childhood toys influence the way men and women think about their looks.

3. According to Barry,

   a. most men are concerned with how women view their appearance.

   b. women want men to be honest about their looks.

   (c.) most women are dissatisfied with their appearance.

   d. a woman's perception of her appearance is influenced by her moods and her female friends.

4. If you are unfamiliar with the following words, use a dictionary to check their meanings: societal, proportioned (para. 7); mutation (8); bolster (9).

READ CRITICALLY

1. Who is Barry's intended audience, and what do you think is his purpose in writing this essay?

2. In paragraphs 7 and 8, Barry discusses children's toys. Why did he choose these particular toys, and how do they help him explain his points of contrast?

3. What is Barry's attitude toward Cindy Crawford and Brad Pitt? Explain how he uses these examples to support his main point.

4. Explain the significance of the title. What do you think Barry would say is the ugly truth about beauty?

5. Why do you think the beauty industry is so successful? Support your answer with examples from this essay.

WRITE AN ESSAY

Look through your family photographs, or use the Internet or magazines to view men's and women's fashions over the last fifty years. Think about how fashions have changed, and write an essay that compares and contrasts fashion trends from two different decades. Use concrete examples to show differences and similarities in the two time periods' styles.

Nicholas Kristof

Two Men and Two Paths

Nicholas Kristof is a leading American journalist and author known best for his commitment to human rights, bringing attention to global issues such as human trafficking, genocide, and poverty. He has worked extensively for the *New York Times* as a correspondent, columnist, and editor. Among his many honors, Kristof has been awarded two Pulitzer Prizes: in 1990 for International Reporting, which he won with his wife Sheryl WuDunn; and in 2006 for Commentary. "Two Men and Two Paths" was originally published in his *New York Times* op-ed column in 2010.

GUIDING QUESTION

What factors affect whether people rise out of poverty?

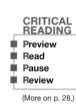

CRITICAL READING
■ Preview
■ Read
■ Pause
■ Review

(More on p. 28.)

1   When Wes Moore won a Rhodes scholarship[1] in 2000, the *Baltimore Sun* published an article about his triumph. He was the first student at Johns Hopkins to win a Rhodes in thirteen years, and the first black student there ever to win the award.

2   At about the same time, the *Sun* published articles about another young African American man, also named Wes Moore. This one was facing charges of first-degree murder for the killing of an off-duty police officer named Bruce Prothero, a father of five.

3   Both Wes Moores had troubled youths in blighted neighborhoods, difficulties in school, clashes with authority, and unpleasant encounters with police handcuffs. But one ended up graduating Phi Beta Kappa[2] and serving as a White House fellow, and today is a banker with many volunteer activities. The other is serving a life prison sentence without the possibility of parole.

4   "One of us is free and has experienced things that he never even knew to dream about as a kid," the successful Wes Moore writes in a new book, *The Other Wes Moore*. "The other will spend every day until his death behind bars. . . . The chilling truth is that his story could have been mine. The tragedy is that my story could have been his."

5   For me, the book is a reminder of two basic truths about poverty and race in America.

---

1. Rhodes scholarship: prestigious scholarship given to college graduates that allows them to study at the University of Oxford in England   **2. Phi Beta Kappa:** national academic honor society of outstanding college and university students

6   The first is that American antipoverty efforts have been disgracefully inadequate. It should be a scandal that California spends $216,000 on each child in the juvenile justice system, and only $8,000 on each child in the Oakland public schools.

7   Far too many Americans are caught in a whirlpool of poverty, broken families, failed schools, and self-destructive behavior that is replicated generation after generation. The imprisoned Wes Moore became a grandfather last year at thirty-three.

PAUSE: What does Kristof imply about the reason for Moore's father's diagnosis?

8   The writer Wes Moore offers clues from his own experience about how boys get sucked into that whirlpool. His father, a radio and television journalist, died of a virus after a hospital emergency room—seeing only a disoriented, disheveled black man—misdiagnosed him and sent him home to get "more sleep," Mr. Moore writes. The writer Wes grew up in a poor, drug-ravaged neighborhood of the Bronx.

9   His mother worked multiple jobs and scrounged[3] to send him to Riverdale Country School, an elite[4] prep school, but Wes felt out of place among wealthy, white students—and his black friends at home teased him for going to "that white school." Wes skipped classes, let his grades slip, hung out with a friend who was dealing drugs, and collided with the police. Despairing, Wes's mother dispatched him to a military school. There he finally began to soar.

PAUSE: What important influence did the two Wes Moores share? Why did one work out and the other not?

10   In the case of the other Wes, there were some moments when he almost escaped. His mother was earning a college degree at Johns Hopkins—which probably would have provided the family a ladder to the middle class—when Reagan-era budget cuts terminated her financial aid and forced her to drop out.

11   Then, the criminal Wes almost found his footing with the Job Corps.[5] There he earned his G.E.D.,[6] testing near the top of his class, and began reading at a college level. He learned carpentry skills—but afterward never found a good job and tumbled back into his old life.

12   The second basic truth underscored by this story is that kids can escape the whirlpool—but they need help.

13   The author Wes Moore escaped partly because of family support and partly because he was helped by mentors[7] at his military school. Not surprisingly, Mr. Moore believes passionately in mentoring, partly because so many boys in poor families have no father at home and lack male role models. He mentors boys and girls in Baltimore and New York and is

---

3. scrounged: to get by digging around, borrowing, and other methods   **4. elite:** one of the best   **5. Job Corps:** U.S. Department of Labor program that offers free educational and vocational training   **6. G.E.D.:** General Educational Development tests; passing grades a substitute for a high school diploma   **7. mentors:** counselors or guides

directing some of the profits from his book to two organizations that provide mentoring.

14   One is City Year, which supports young people taking a year of public service to work in impoverished neighborhoods. Another is the U.S. Dream Academy, which supports children whose parents are in prison (and who are consequently at great risk themselves of tumbling into trouble).

15   There are no quick fixes to solve poverty. But carefully conducted experiments show that some strategies work: intensive early childhood education modeled after the Abecedarian Project,[8] rigorous schools like those in the KIPP[9] network, volunteer reader tutoring like that done by Start Making a Reader Today, and subsidized[10] jobs programs like Canada's Self-Sufficiency Project that build the employment habit. These approaches have a much better record than juvenile detention and are far cheaper.

16   Mr. Moore ends his book with a call to action, arguing that each of us can play a role through volunteer work or donations. His own trajectory[11] underscores that lives are at stake, and they can be turned around.

> **PAUSE:** Summarize the factors that can help people that Kristof suggests in this part of his essay.

> **PAUSE:** Why did the author Wes Moore escape his background? Why didn't the other Wes Moore?

8. Abecedarian Project: a scientific study and educational program demonstrating that high-quality early education had enormous benefits for children from disadvantaged backgrounds   **9. KIPP:** Knowledge Is Power Program, a national network of free, open-enrollment college-preparatory public schools   **10. subsidized:** helped paying the costs of   **11. trajectory:** a path of development or movement

. . . .

SUMMARIZE AND RESPOND

In your reading journal or elsewhere, summarize the main point of "Two Men and Two Paths." Then, go back and check off support for the main idea. Next, write a brief summary (three to five sentences) of the reading. Finally, jot down your initial response to the selection. How is poverty related to "broken families, failed schools, and self-destructive behavior"? Do you agree with Kristof that "American antipoverty efforts have been disgracefully inadequate" (para. 6)?

. . . .

CHECK YOUR COMPREHENSION

1.   Which of the following is the best alternative title for this essay?

   a.   "Wes Moore Escapes Poverty and Finds Success"

   b.   "Two Wes Moores Teach Two Lessons about Poverty and Race in America"

   c.   "Two Men Prove That Good Family Values Are the Key to Happiness"

   d.   "America Remains a Land of Opportunity, Regardless of Your Race or Class"

2. The main idea of this essay is that

   a. too many young people in America are trapped in poverty, but they can escape if they have help.

   b. people must show personal responsibility instead of relying on others for help.

   c. social programs like welfare have created a generation of people who expect to be taken care of.

   d. the two Wes Moores had little in common, except their names and their race.

3. According to the essay, the author Wes Moore

   a. had hoped to be a carpenter, but had to drop out of school to support his mother after his father died.

   b. came from a middle-class background, but lost many opportunities because of his drug use and bad behavior at school.

   c. mentors young people in Baltimore and New York because many of them have no male role models.

   d. shows that a determined person can succeed without the help of a supportive family or positive role models.

4. If you are unfamiliar with the following words, use a dictionary to check their meanings: blighted (para. 3); whirlpool, replicated (7); disheveled, ravaged (8); collided, dispatched, soar (9); terminated (10).

· ·

READ CRITICALLY

1. What is Kristof's purpose in writing this column?

2. According to Kristof, the story of the two Wes Moores should remind us of "two basic truths about poverty and race in America" (para. 5). What are they? How do the examples of these two men illustrate Kristof's point?

3. Does Kristof use point-by-point or whole-to-whole organization?

4. What role do you think the government should play in helping people out of poverty? What is the author's view on this question? Do you agree?

5. How effective are Kristof's two concluding paragraphs? Do they provide more than just a summary of the essay? Explain.

WRITE AN ESSAY

Write an essay comparing and contrasting the opportunities and prospects for a poor child in America with those of a middle-class or an affluent child. Make sure you establish a basis for comparison (e.g., similarities and differences in education). In what ways are they different? How are they similar? What role does environment play? The family? Generally, can individuals succeed, regardless of circumstances? Do you come to conclusions similar to those of Kristoff, or do you have a different view?

Comparison and Contrast: Linked Readings

CONCEPTIONS OF GENDER

Each of the following readings focuses on various aspects of the effects of gender on people's behavior and lives.

Dave Barry, "The Ugly Truth about Beauty" (this chapter, p. 787)

M. Catherine Maternowska, "Truck-Stop Girls" (Chapter 41, p. 694)

Deborah L. Rhode, "Why Looks Are the Last Bastion of Discrimination" (Chapter 42, p. 711)

Amy L. Beck, "Struggling for Perfection" (Chapter 48, p. 807)

Read the selections, and draw from at least one in addition to "The Ugly Truth about Beauty" to write an essay titled "How Gender Affects Behavior." You can refer to your own experience, but make sure to use material from the essays as well.

CHASING BEAUTY

Though they have different tones, each of the following readings focuses on the quest for beauty, perfection, or an ideal of physical appearance.

Dave Barry, "The Ugly Truth about Beauty" (this chapter, p. 787)

Malcolm X, "My First Conk" (Chapter 44, p. 741)

Amy L. Beck, "Struggling for Perfection" (Chapter 48, p. 807)

Read the selections, and draw from at least one in addition to "The Ugly Truth about Beauty" to write an essay titled "The Dangers of Chasing Beauty and Perfection." You can refer to your own experience, but make sure to use material from the essays as well.

FEELING FOREIGN

Both of the following readings focus on various aspects of feeling foreign and the ways people can have divided identities.

Rui Dai, "A Whiff of Memory" (this chapter, p. 783)

Alex Espinoza, "An American in Mexico" (Chapter 43, p. 723)

Read the selections and write an essay entitled "Feeling Foreign." You can use the term *foreign* in the sense of being from another country or in the sense of being in a new situation, such as starting at a new job or a new school.

48

Cause and Effect

Each essay in this chapter uses cause and effect to get its main point across. As you read these essays, consider how they achieve the four basics of good cause and effect that are listed below and discussed in Chapter 17 of this book.

IDEA JOURNAL
What event or situation has influenced who you are?

Four Basics of Good Cause and Effect

1. The main point reflects the writer's purpose — to explain causes, effects, or both.

2. If the purpose is to explain causes, it presents real causes.

3. If the purpose is to explain effects, it presents real effects.

4. It gives clear and detailed examples or explanations of the causes and/or effects.

Michael Jernigan

Living the Dream

Michael Jernigan served with the Second Marine Regiment of the U.S. Marine Corps in Iraq but was medically retired in 2005 after a roadside bomb left him blind and wounded. After returning from Iraq, Jernigan was accepted at Georgetown University, finished his studies at the University of South Florida, and now serves on the board of the Blinded American Veterans Foundation. This essay was posted in 2009 as part of the Home Fires series on the *New York Times* Opinionator blog.

CRITICAL READING
■ Preview
■ Read
■ Pause
■ Review

(More on p. 28.)

PAUSE: Based on the first paragraph, what cause-and-effect relationship do you think this essay will describe?

GUIDING QUESTION
How does post-traumatic stress disorder affect Jernigan's life?

1   I would like to bring some awareness to an issue facing many of us returning war veterans. Post-traumatic stress disorder (PTSD)[1] is a monster that war veterans have been facing since the beginning of armed conflict. Basically, it is the stress brought on by a traumatic event. I understand that it is more complicated than that, but I would like to keep it as simple as possible for our purposes here. Post-traumatic stress can manifest itself in many different ways. It is usually brought on by a trigger mechanism, or what some might call a catalyst.[2] It can be something very minor that can be easily controlled or it can be so large that it has life-altering circumstances. I am living with PTSD, and I am thriving in some respects and having problems in others. In this and future posts, I plan to use myself and my experiences as examples.

2   What do I mean when I say I am both thriving and having problems at the same time? Well, I can tell you that in school I am thriving. I have been back for a couple of years now and continue to pull a 3-plus grade point average every semester. It is in other parts of my life that I am struggling.

PAUSE: Summarize the ways in which Jernigan's relationship with his wife is strained.

3   My relationship with my wife has been strained because of the way I react to certain things; my relationship with my stepson has suffered as well. I have quick reactions full of emotion that are not checked before they come out. In many cases, they are very aggressive and quite

1. **post-traumatic stress disorder (PTSD):** a range of effects caused by the experience of trauma   2. **catalyst:** something that provokes action or change

counterproductive. I am impatient in numerous situations and become frustrated easily. To top it all off, I often have to overcome bouts of anxiety, especially when I am outside my house. I do well in social situations, but I find them physically taxing. I have been receiving help with all of these problems and I am improving at a good rate. My wife and I have worked hard to help me overcome a lot of these symptoms.

4   One of the most common problems facing our war veterans when we return home is drug and alcohol abuse. We turn to these to escape from emotions. I drank heavily when I returned home. I would drink to the point that I would pass out at night. I would do this because I could not sleep. I could not sleep because there was a healthy wave of emotions that I refused to face. What made sleep hard was the PTSD in conjunction with a traumatic brain injury. When I would finally sleep, I had to deal with some strange and horrific dreams.

PAUSE: According to Jernigan, why do many veterans abuse drugs and alcohol?

5   I would have dreams that most people would be scared by. I was scared, too, especially when I would have the same dream more than once. One of the strangest dreams took place in Iraq. We would be returning from a foot patrol at night. It was as if I were looking through a set of night-vision goggles. There were two gates that we would have to come through at our forward operating base (FOB). I can remember gaining access through the first gate but then not being able to enter the inner part of the base until daybreak. Since we could not get back to our hooches³ we would decide to sleep under the gun line (155-millimeter howitzers),⁴ something that would not be done for safety purposes. Just when I would be drifting off to sleep the gun line would open up. It was at that point that I would awake for real. I was never able to go back to sleep after that.

6   There were dreams that were both strange and violent. In one of them, I was in the spare bedroom of a condominium that I had rented before I enlisted. When I lived there, the only thing in this room was my gun cabinet with all of my rifles and shotguns in it. During my dream, I was in this room waist deep in stuffed animals. Someone would enter the room (I could never identify the person) and attack me. We would be fighting in this room. At a certain point in the fight, I would gain the advantage. I would bend over this individual and bite his throat out. It was always bloody. Just then I would wake up.

7   One of the hardest dreams to deal with came back many times. It was one of the scariest in my mind. It took place in Iraq as well. I can remember being on patrol in Mahmudiya,⁵ the town that I was wounded in. I was always on patrol with a group of Marines. At some point in the dream I would become separated from my patrol. Iraq can be a scary place to find yourself alone in. It got worse. I cannot remember how, but I would lose

---

3. **hooches:** living quarters or barracks   4. **howitzers:** cannons
5. **Mahmudiya:** Iraqi city just south of Baghdad

my rifle (a good Marine does not lose his weapon). I would see a small kid scampering off with my rifle and follow him. I was terrified of returning back to base without my rifle. The kid would enter a building, and I knew that I would have to follow him into the building. Keep in mind that I am defenseless. When I would enter the building, I always encountered hand-to-hand combat with a few different individuals at one time. I would always defeat those attacking me. I can remember that I also would find a number of weapons that had once belonged to Marines—pistols, rifles, and shotguns. To my dismay, I would never find my rifle.

8   I would see the kid again and chase him one more time. I always wound up chasing him into another building and encountering more and more hand-to-hand combat situations. I would always find more weapons but never mine. I always picked up the weapons that I would find and bring them with me before I gave pursuit to that kid again. This cycle would never end. I would thrash around in my bed until I would wake up hot and sweating. I could never get back to sleep and was quite disturbed by this dream.

9   While I was in Washington, D.C., I started to make significant progress on many different fronts. I found a counselor there named Carey Smith, a disabled veteran from the Vietnam War. He has been through what I have. He began to teach me how to interpret my dreams in a positive way. I know that this can be hard to do. When he first told me I was very hesitant. As he explained it to me, I started to understand what he was talking about.

10   We came to the conclusion that the dreams were my mind's way of reconciling[6] problems I had. They usually dealt with some guilt I had over one thing or another. In many of these situations, I would have no way of making things better, so my brain would do it for me in my sleep. Once I grasped this concept the dreams became much easier to deal with. I would then wake up in the middle of the night and be able to tell myself that there was nothing wrong and return to sleep. It is great. Currently, I am not dealing with any harsh dreams. I use the term "harsh" because I no longer see these dreams as bad but as healthy and productive.

11   One of the things that I am learning as I am living with PTSD is that these feelings can be dealt with positively, that these different symptoms do not have to control my life. I am doing my best to live my life and be happy. There is no magic pill that will make things better. By facing the difficult emotions and learning how to positively react to them my life becomes easier. The emotions are still there—they will probably never go away. But when I face them sober and head on, I can live my good dreams and not be controlled by the difficult ones.

Semper Fidelis,[7]
Michael Jernigan

PAUSE: What overall impression do you get from Jernigan's descriptions of his dreams? Note also that within his cause-and-effect essay, he uses both description and narration.

PAUSE: Summarize what Jernigan has learned about his dreams.

PAUSE: What effect has counseling by a peer had on the author?

6. reconciling: bringing together   **7. Semper Fidelis:** Latin for "always faithful," the motto of the U.S. Marine Corps

....

SUMMARIZE AND RESPOND

In your reading journal or elsewhere, summarize the main point of "Living the Dream." Then, go back and check off support for this main idea. Next, write a brief summary (three to five sentences) of the essay. Finally, jot down your initial responses to the essay. What are the lasting emotional and psychological effects of combat on veterans? How does Jernigan learn to deal with his post-traumatic stress disorder?

....

CHECK YOUR COMPREHENSION

1. Which of the following would be the best alternative title for this essay?

    a. "The Immorality of War"

    b. "My Struggles with Alcohol and Drug Abuse"

    c. "Facing my PTSD Nightmares"

    d. "Civilian Life Is a Challenge for Veterans"

2. The main idea of this essay is that

    a. returning war veterans sometimes have a hard time adjusting to life on a college campus.

    b. psychologists can learn much about human nature by interpreting dreams.

    c. children are often the innocent victims in times of war.

    d. PTSD is a difficult challenge for many war veterans, but they can get help and take control of their lives.

3. The author tells us that he is

    a. doing well in school, but struggling with his relationships at home.

    b. having difficulties in school, but maintaining a good relationship with his parents.

    c. frustrated by the failures of counseling.

    d. planning on reenlisting in the Marine Corps after he finishes college.

4. If you are unfamiliar with the following words, use a dictionary to check their meanings: traumatic, manifest (para. 1); counterproductive, bouts (3); conjunction (4); scampering, dismay (7); thrash (8).

READ CRITICALLY

1. In the first paragraph, Jernigan acknowledges that PTSD is "more complicated" than his brief definition, but writes that he "would like to keep it as simple as possible for our purposes here." What is his purpose in writing this essay? Why might he simplify his definition to suit this purpose?

2. Who is the audience for this essay? What effect do you think the writer wants to have on his readers?

3. What is the causal relationship between combat experience and drug and alcohol abuse, according to the essay?

4. How could Jernigan's "harsh dreams" become both "healthy and productive" (para. 10)?

5. Do you find the essay's conclusion effective? Explain.

WRITE AN ESSAY

Jernigan writes about how combat experience and PTSD have affected his life. Write an essay about an experience you have had that affects your life. Can a negative experience have positive effects, or vice versa? Have you learned to manage the consequences, or learn from them, as Jernigan does?

Brent Staples

Just Walk on By: Black Men and Public Space

Brent Staples was born in 1951 in Chester, Pennsylvania. After graduating from Widener University, he earned a Ph.D. in psychology from the University of Chicago. He is a member of the editorial board of the *New York Times,* writing commentary on politics and culture. He has published a memoir, *Parallel Time: Growing Up in Black and White* (1994).

In "Just Walk on By," Staples observes how people, particularly women, react to him when he goes out for a walk. This essay was first published in *Ms.* magazine.

GUIDING QUESTION
How does Staples affect people, and why?

CRITICAL
READING
■ Preview
■ Read
■ Pause
■ Review

(More on p. 28.)

1   My first victim was a woman—white, well dressed, probably in her early twenties. I came upon her late one evening on a deserted street in Hyde Park, a relatively affluent neighborhood in an otherwise mean, impoverished section of Chicago. As I swung onto the avenue behind her, there seemed to be a discreet, uninflammatory[1] distance between us. Not so. She cast back a worried glance. To her, the youngish black man—a broad six feet two inches with a beard and billowing hair, both hands shoved into the pockets of a bulky military jacket—seemed menacingly close. After a few more quick glimpses, she picked up her pace and was soon running in earnest. Within seconds she disappeared into a cross street.

PAUSE: After reading the title and the first paragraph, what do you predict Staples will write about in the rest of the essay?

2   That was more than a decade ago, I was twenty-two years old, a graduate student newly arrived at the University of Chicago. It was in the echo of that terrified woman's footfalls that I first began to know the unwieldy inheritance I'd come into—the ability to alter public space in ugly ways. It was clear that she thought herself the quarry[2] of a mugger, a rapist, or worse. Suffering a bout of insomnia, however, I was stalking sleep, not defenseless wayfarers. As a softy who is scarcely able to take a knife to a raw chicken—let alone hold one to a person's throat—I was surprised, embarrassed, and dismayed all at once. Her flight made me feel like an accomplice in tyranny.[3] It also made it clear that I was indistinguishable from the muggers who occasionally seeped into the area from the surrounding ghetto. That first encounter, and those that followed, signified that a vast, unnerving[4] gulf lay between nighttime pedestrians—particularly women—and me. And I soon gathered that being perceived as dangerous is a hazard in itself. I only needed to turn a corner into a dicey situation, or crowd some frightened, armed person in a foyer somewhere, or make an errant[5] move after being pulled over by a policeman. Where fear and weapons meet—and they often do in urban America—there is always the possibility of death.

3   In that first year, my first away from my hometown, I was to become thoroughly familiar with the language of fear. At dark, shadowy intersections, I could cross in front of a car stopped at a traffic light and elicit the *thunk, thunk, thunk, thunk* of the driver—black, white, male, or female—hammering down the door locks. On less traveled streets after dark, I grew accustomed to but never comfortable with people crossing to the other side of the street rather than pass me. Then there were the

1. **uninflammatory:** unlikely to cause fear in a hunt   3. **tyranny:** the abuse of power   2. **quarry:** one that is chased, as   4. **unnerving:** upsetting
5. **errant:** stray, unintended

PAUSE: In paragraph 3, what does Staples mean by "standard unpleasantries"?

standard unpleasantries with policemen, doormen, bouncers, cabdrivers, and others whose business it is to screen out troublesome individuals *before* there is any nastiness.

4   I moved to New York nearly two years ago and I have remained an avid night walker. In central Manhattan, the near-constant crowd cover minimizes tense one-on-one street encounters. Elsewhere—in SoHo, for example, where sidewalks are narrow and tightly spaced buildings shut out the sky—things can get very taut indeed.

DISCUSSION
Staples alludes to the idea of racial profiling, the alleged practice by law enforcement officials of targeting nonwhites for special scrutiny. Have members of your class do some research on the Internet using the key phrase "racial profiling" and report on the debate surrounding this issue.

5   After dark, on the warrenlike[6] streets of Brooklyn where I live, I often see women who fear the worst from me. They seem to have set their faces on neutral, and with their purse straps strung across their chests bandolier-style, they forge ahead as though bracing themselves against being tackled. I understand, of course, that the danger they perceive is not a hallucination. Women are particularly vulnerable to street violence, and young black males are drastically overrepresented among the perpetrators of that violence. Yet these truths are no solace against the kind of alienation that comes of being ever the suspect, a fearsome entity with whom pedestrians avoid making eye contact.

6   It is not altogether clear to me how I reached the ripe old age of twenty-two without being conscious of the lethality nighttime pedestrians attributed to me. Perhaps it was because in Chester, Pennsylvania, the small, angry industrial town where I came of age in the 1960s, I was scarcely noticeable against a backdrop of gang warfare, street knifings, and murders. I grew up one of the good boys, had perhaps a half-dozen fistfights. In retrospect, my shyness of combat has clear sources.

PAUSE: Summarize the point that Staples makes about himself in paragraphs 6 and 7.

7   As a boy, I saw countless tough guys locked away; I have since buried several, too. They were babies, really—a teenage cousin, a brother of twenty-two, a childhood friend in his mid-twenties—all gone down in episodes of bravado played out in the streets. I came to doubt the virtues of intimidation early on. I chose, perhaps unconsciously, to remain a shadow—timid, but a survivor.

TEACHING TIP
Ask students to identify places in the essay where Staples uses narration to relate a brief story (paras. 1, 8, 9, and 10). What do these stories add to the essay that Staples could not achieve by including only more general discussions of his experiences?

8   The fearsomeness mistakenly attributed to me in public places often has a perilous flavor. The most frightening of these confusions occurred in the late 1970s and early 1980s, when I worked as a journalist in Chicago. One day, rushing into the office of a magazine I was writing for with a deadline story in hand, I was mistaken for a burglar. The office manager called security and, with an ad hoc[7] posse, pursued me through the labyrinthine halls, nearly to my editor's door. I had no way of proving who I was. I could only move briskly toward the company of someone who knew me.

9   Another time I was on assignment for a local paper and killing time before an interview. I entered a jewelry store on the city's affluent Near North

6. **warrenlike:** narrow and having many blind spots   7. **ad hoc:** made up of whatever is available (Latin, *for this purpose*)

Side. The proprietor excused herself and returned with an enormous red Doberman pinscher straining at the end of a leash. She stood, the dog extended toward me, silent to my questions, her eyes bulging nearly out of her head. I took a cursory look around, nodded, and bade her good night.

10   Relatively speaking, however, I never fared as badly as another black male journalist. He went to nearby Waukegan, Illinois, a couple of summers ago to work on a story about a murderer who was born there. Mistaking the reporter for the killer, police officers hauled him from his car at gunpoint and but for his press credentials would probably have tried to book him. Such episodes are not uncommon. Black men trade tales like this all the time.

11   Over the years, I learned to smother the rage I felt at so often being taken for a criminal. Not to do so would surely have led to madness. I now take precautions to make myself less threatening. I move about with care, particularly late in the evening. I give a wide berth to nervous people on subway platforms during the wee hours, particularly when I have exchanged business clothes for jeans. If I happen to be entering a building behind some people who appear skittish,[8] I may walk by, letting them clear the lobby before I return, so as not to seem to be following them. I have been calm and extremely congenial[9] on those rare occasions when I've been pulled over by the police.

> **PAUSE:** In paragraph 11, underline each of the precautions Staples says he takes to appear less threatening.

12   And on late-evening constitutionals[10] I employ what has proved to be an excellent tension-reducing measure: I whistle melodies from Beethoven and Vivaldi and the more popular classical composers. Even steely New Yorkers hunching toward nighttime destinations seem to relax, and occasionally they even join in the tune. Virtually everybody seems to sense that a mugger wouldn't be warbling bright, sunny selections from Vivaldi's *Four Seasons*. It is my equivalent of the cowbell that hikers wear when they know they are in bear country.

> **PAUSE:** How do you respond to the image, in paragraph 12, of Staples whistling classical music as he walks at night?

8. skittish: nervous, jumpy   **9. congenial:** pleasant, agreeable
10. constitutionals: walks taken for one's health

SUMMARIZE AND RESPOND

In your reading journal or elsewhere, summarize the main point of "Just Walk on By: Black Men and Public Space." Then, go back and check off support for this main idea. Next, write a brief summary (three to five sentences) of the reading. Finally, jot down your initial response to the selection. Did you find any of what Staples relates surprising, or do his observations match your own experience? Did reading about Staples's experiences change your attitudes in any way? What impression do you have of the writer himself?

··

CHECK YOUR COMPREHENSION

1. Which of the following would be the best alternative title for this essay?
   a. "Walking the Streets after Dark"
   b. "The Burdens of Racial Identity"
   c. "Being Mistaken for a Criminal Because of One's Skin"
   d. "How to Avoid Muggers and Other Street Criminals"

2. The main idea of this essay is that
   a. the author had to learn how to make himself appear less threatening to others.
   b. the author recognizes that strangers may be unjustifiably afraid of him because he is a black man.
   c. the author believes that people should try to see black men as individuals and not stereotype them as muggers.
   d. the author knew criminals as he was growing up but wants readers to understand that he himself is not one.

3. An important point that Staples makes in this essay is that
   a. the police and other authorities often stop black men for questioning for no good reason.
   b. he felt angry because of strangers' behavior toward him but found ways to suppress his anger.
   c. people in large cities like Chicago and New York are more likely than others to fear black men.
   d. he was once almost arrested because he was mistaken for a murderer he was writing a story about.

4. If you are unfamiliar with the following words, use a dictionary to check their meanings: menacingly (para. 1); unwieldy, insomnia, wayfarers, dismayed, indistinguishable, dicey (2); hallucination, perpetrators, solace, alienation, entity (5); lethality, retrospect (6); bravado (7); perilous, posse, labyrinthine (8); affluent, cursory (9); credentials (10); warbling (12).

··

READ CRITICALLY

1. What, specifically, is the cause-and-effect relationship that Staples is describing in the essay? How well do you think he shows this relationship? What is the effect of the situation on Staples himself?

2. Why do you suppose Staples opens his essay by referring to "my first victim"? What is the effect of this language?

3. Who would you say Staples imagined as his audience for this essay? What vision of himself does he seem to want his readers to come away with?

4. Why do you think Staples refers to the experience of another black man in paragraph 10, when all of his other examples are drawn from his own experience?

5. What is your response to Staples's final two paragraphs? To his final sentence? How would you evaluate this conclusion?

WRITE AN ESSAY

Write an essay, based on your own experiences, about the causes and effects of stereotypes and mistaken perceptions. You might focus on mistaken perceptions others have had of you or on mistaken perceptions you have had of others — or on both kinds of mistaken perceptions. You might also focus on instances of mistaken perceptions and stereotyping that you have witnessed. Be sure to establish clear cause-and-effect relationships.

Amy L. Beck

Struggling for Perfection

Amy L. Beck was born in 1979 in Greenwich, Connecticut. After graduating from Harvard University in 2000, Beck joined Teach for America, a program that places recent college graduates in inner-city or rural schools, and she taught first graders in Long Beach, California, for two years. She has also worked in France as a researcher for the travel guide *Let's Go* and as an intern with the French Public Health Administration. Dr. Beck is currently a pediatrician at the University of California, San Francisco Medical Center.

In "Struggling for Perfection," which she wrote for the *Harvard Crimson* in 1998, Beck explores eating disorders and domestic abuse. How are these two problems linked? According to Beck, they are both partly caused by media images.

CRITICAL READING
- Preview
- Read
- Pause
- Review

(More on p. 28.)

GUIDING QUESTION
What is the cause-and-effect relationship that Beck writes about?

PAUSE: After reading her second paragraph, what do you predict that Beck will do in her essay?

1   Sex sells. This truth is a boon[1] for marketing gurus and the pornography industry but a rather unfortunate situation for women. Every issue of *Playboy*, every lewd poster, and even the Victoria's Secret catalog transform real women into ornaments, valued exclusively for their outward appearance. These publications are responsible for defining what is sexy and reinforce the belief that aesthetic[2] appeal is a woman's highest virtue.

2   Some argue that the proliferation[3] of pornography and other sexually explicit images of women is both harmless for society and inevitable. Just this point was made in a recent *Crimson* column titled "In Defense of Hooters and the St. Pauli Girl." In the tone of an expert, the author boldly claims that the objectification[4] of women in the media does not affect the way men treat the real women in their lives, nor does it give those with pathological[5] tendencies "the decisive nudge into misogyny."[6] Furthermore, the author says, those women who feel pressure to conform to beauty standards set by the media are suffering from a classic psychosis in which they "confuse fiction with reality."

3   My first reaction was to ask how anyone could possibly believe that the pervasiveness[7] of pornography and sexually explicit depictions of women could fail to have any sort of effect on society. Having spent twelve weeks working in a psychiatric hospital last summer, I am writing from a starkly different perspective.

4   During my first eight weeks at the hospital, I worked on an eating disorder unit in constant contact with anorexics and bulimics. Many patients on the unit were so emaciated[8] that I could never accustom myself to their appearance; every time I saw them I experienced the same shock. Most had been in and out of countless other hospitals and treatment programs, improving slightly each time but always sliding back into eating-disordered behavior when released.

PAUSE: Underline the sentence that best expresses the main point of paragraph 5.

5   These people were truly at rock bottom, considered by many to be incurable. Their eating disorders had consumed them entirely, leaving no trace of the vibrant, intelligent people that once inhabited their now skeletal bodies. Certainly, these people also had family problems, alcoholic parents, histories of abuse and clinical depression, to name a few, all of which contribute to feelings of worthlessness and extremely low self-esteem—cited by experts as a major cause of eating disorders. What I find significant, however, is not the root of their problems but that these women (there were a few men, but never more than five percent of the patient population) turned to their bodies as a means of expression and self-healing. Profoundly

---

1. boon: a welcome benefit   **2. aesthetic:** having to do with beauty
3. proliferation: rapid growth   **4. objectification:** the treatment of a person as an object   **5. pathological:** abnormal, diseased   **6. misogyny:** hatred of women   **7. pervasiveness:** the extension or spread of one thing throughout something else   **8. emaciated:** extremely thin

influenced by the depiction of women by the fashion industry, they had been convinced that the only way to attain love, respect, and personal fulfillment was through a relentless pursuit of physical perfection. Most were perfectly aware that they would never look like a supermodel, but it was inconceivable not to try to do so. They found that they were good at dieting and that they were praised and rewarded for their success. And by the time things had gone too far, they had lost all sense of perspective.

6   Convinced by the media and popular culture to believe that, as women, they should look a certain way and that only if they looked that way would they be loved and respected, they turned to dieting as a means of personal fulfillment and self-definition. While cases as extreme as those I saw at the hospital are rare, many women experience milder but still debilitating[9] forms of eating disorders. They may never get sick enough to require hospitalization, but they nonetheless devote excessive mental and physical energy to diet and exercise, often jeopardizing their health in the process.

7   For my last four weeks at the hospital I transferred from eating disorders to a general psychology unit. The diagnoses varied, but the number of patients with histories of abuse was astounding. After listening to and reading countless case histories, I began to recognize the patterns. In many cases, domestic battering was chronic, occurring weekly or daily whenever the victim broke some sort of household rule, such as serving dinner late or dressing "too sexy." The majority of the sexual abuse victims had been raped by people close to them: relatives, ex-boyfriends, or family friends. In one particularly striking case, a patient's boyfriend made her have sex with five of his friends on a frequent basis.

PAUSE: Summarize the main point of paragraph 7.

8   The men who committed these heinous crimes were rarely pathological rapists or batterers. Few would even be deemed mentally ill or classically misogynistic. Rather, they are men who view the real women in their lives in the same manner that they would view a *Playboy* model, a waitress at Hooters, or a prostitute—as objects that exist solely for their pleasure and convenience. These men are not genetically predisposed[10] to disrespect and abuse women. Their attitudes towards women were societally conditioned.

9   Some would argue that pornography did not contribute to these men's behavior towards women. I disagree. Rape and battery are not new problems, and objectification of women by the media reinforces historically entrenched beliefs that a woman's main reason for existence is procreation and the sexual pleasure of her mate. Pornographic magazines and lewd posters reduce women to a commodity[11] that can be purchased and owned, divorcing the physical manifestation[12] from the person within. The power

---

9. debilitating: weakening   **10. predisposed:** inclined to something in advance   **11. commodity:** a thing of use, value, or advantage
12. manifestation: a visible presence, an outward show

of popular culture to affect how we eat, how we dress, and how we behave is enormous. Conceptions of gender are in no way immune to this phenomenon.

PAUSE: How are you and others you know affected by media images?

10   Certainly some of us are more affected by the media than others. Not all teenage girls develop anorexia, nor do all men who read *Playboy* abuse their wives. Nonetheless, the prevalence of both eating disorders and various forms of domestic and sexual abuse indicate major societal trends. The American Anorexia/Bulimia Association reports that 5 percent of women will develop a full-fledged eating disorder, while 15 percent have "substantially disordered eating." The Family Violence Prevention Program documents that 4 million American women were battered last year. And, yes, I am absolutely convinced that the objectification of women by the media is an integral part of both of these problems, presenting women with unrealistic role models while encouraging men to think of women solely in terms of their sexuality.

11   Women are up against a long history of devaluation and oppression, and, unfortunately, the feminist movements have been only partially successful in purging[13] those legacies. Sexually charged images of women in the media are not the only cause of this continuing problem, but they certainly play a central role.

13. **purging:** removing something unwanted

. . . .

SUMMARIZE AND RESPOND

In your reading journal or elsewhere, summarize the main point of "Struggling for Perfection." Then, go back and check off support for this main idea. Next, write a brief summary (three to five sentences) of the essay. Finally, jot down your initial response to the essay. Do you agree or disagree with Beck's points? What else do you think causes eating disorders and domestic abuse?

. . . .

CHECK YOUR COMPREHENSION

1. Which of the following would be the best alternative title for this essay?
    a. "The Alarming Growth of Eating Disorders"
    b. "The Causes and Effects of Eating Disorders"
    c. "The Media's Influence on Eating Disorders and Domestic Abuse"
    d. "Pressure to Conform"

2. The main idea of this essay is that
   a. media images of women are not the only cause of eating disorders.
   b. publications such as *Playboy* and the Victoria's Secret catalog transform women into sexual objects.
   c. low self-esteem is a major cause of eating disorders.
   (d.) media images of women contribute to eating disorders and violence against females.

3. According to the author,
   a. women who try to look like supermodels are unable to tell the difference between fiction and reality.
   (b.) many of the women she met while working in the hospital had backgrounds that included abuse, family problems, and depression.
   c. patients with eating disorders are often incurable.
   d. feminist movements have been very successful in their attempts to lessen the prevalence of eating disorders and abuse against women.

4. If you are unfamiliar with the following words, use a dictionary to check their meanings: gurus, lewd (para. 1); inevitable, psychosis (2); anorexics, bulimics (4); depiction (5); chronic (7); heinous, genetically (8); entrenched, procreation (9); integral (10); devaluation, legacies (11).

. . . .

READ CRITICALLY

1. Why do you think Beck begins her essay by discussing the column "In Defense of Hooters and the St. Pauli Girl" (para. 2)?

2. Media images of women lead to what two major problems, according to Beck? How are these problems linked?

3. Describe Beck's attitude toward men who commit domestic abuse. What examples from the essay support your response?

4. Does Beck provide clear links between media images of women and the effects of those images? Discuss some of the supporting details she uses to show these links.

5. Beck presents some statistics about eating disorders and domestic abuse. How does she use these statistics to make a further observation about her main point?

. . . .

WRITE AN ESSAY

Beck acknowledges the fact that sexually charged media images of women are not the only cause of eating disorders and abuse. Write an essay about a different possible cause of one of these problems. You could also choose to write about a similar problem (what causes some men to take steroids, for example). If you addressed other causes of eating disorders and abuse for the Summarize and Respond section above, feel free to use those ideas.

. . . .

Cause and Effect: Linked Readings

. . . .

CONCEPTIONS OF GENDER

Each of the following readings focuses on various aspects of the effects of gender on people's behaviors and lives.

> Amy L. Beck, "Struggling for Perfection" (this chapter, p. 807)

> M. Catherine Maternowska, "Truck-Stop Girls" (Chapter 41, p. 694)

> Dave Barry, "The Ugly Truth about Beauty" (Chapter 47, p. 787)

Read the selections, and draw from at least one in addition to "Struggling for Perfection" to write an essay titled "How Gender Affects Behavior." You can refer to your own experience, but make sure to use material from the essays as well.

. . . .

CHASING BEAUTY

Though they have different tones, each of the following readings focuses on the quest for beauty, perfection, or an ideal of physical appearance.

> Amy L. Beck, "Struggling for Perfection" (this chapter, p. 807)

> Malcolm X, "My First Conk" (Chapter 44, p. 741)

> Dave Barry, "The Ugly Truth about Beauty" (Chapter 47, p. 787)

Read the selections, and draw from at least one in addition to "Struggling for Perfection" to write an essay titled "The Dangers of Chasing Beauty and Perfection." You can refer to your own experience, but make sure to use material from the essays as well.

. . . .

· ·

STEREOTYPES

Each of the following readings focuses on or uses stereotypes.

> Brent Staples, "Just Walk on By: Black Men and Public Space" (this chapter, p. 802)
>
> Beth Trimmer, "Birth Order" (Chapter 45, p. 747)
>
> Amy Tan, "Mother Tongue" (Chapter 45, p. 751)
>
> Nancy Mairs, "On Being a Cripple" (Chapter 46, p. 769)
>
> Kevin Willey, "The Optimistic Generation" (Chapter 46, p. 766)
>
> Dave Barry, "The Ugly Truth about Beauty" (Chapter 47, p. 787)

Read the selections, and draw from at least one in addition to "Just Walk on By" to write an essay titled "Stereotypes: Are They Wrong?" You can refer to your own experience, but make sure to use material from the essays as well.

· ·

49

Argument Casebook

Assisted Suicide

TEACHING TIP
Each essay has a discrete writing assignment that directly follows it. At the end of the three "In Favor" essays is a writing assignment that asks students to use the essays to write an argument in favor of legal assisted suicide. At the end of the two "Opposed" essays is an assignment to write an argument against the issue, drawing from the opposed essays. Following that is a third assignment that asks students to draw from both sets of essays to argue their position.

This chapter includes five essays on the issue of legalized assisted suicide. The first three, in favor of it, are written by a nurse, a doctor, and an individual with terminal cancer. Their essays argue that legal physician-assisted suicide is a humane choice and, in some cases, is the only way for people to maintain their dignity and humanity in the face of acute suffering. The last two essays, written by doctors, are against legalization of physician-assisted suicide. These essays reveal another side of what legal physician-assisted suicide could bring—not a humane end but rather the triumph of cost-effectiveness over compassionate end-of-life care.

As you will see when you read these five essays, physician-assisted suicide is not an easy issue. It is, however, an issue that has significance for all of us. Physical trauma can dramatically affect an individual's quality of life at any time. Any of us could be seriously injured in a traffic accident or suddenly afflicted with an untreatable disease.

Some of you may already have an opinion on physician-assisted suicide. As you read the essays, however, consider carefully the arguments that they present. Try to imagine that someone you love is the patient, and evaluate the arguments as though you were going to have to make a decision about the end of that person's life.

Four Basics of Good Argument

1 It takes a strong, definite position on an issue or advises a particular action.

2 It gives good supporting evidence to defend the position or recommended action.

3 It considers opposing views.

4 It has enthusiasm and energy from start to finish.

LEGALIZED ASSISTED SUICIDE: IN FAVOR

Barbara Huttmann

A Crime of Compassion

Barbara Huttmann was middle-aged when she returned to school to study nursing, receiving her degree in 1976. She went on to earn a master's degree in nursing administration and later worked as an administrator for a health-care consulting firm. She is also the author of two books, *The Patient's Advocate* (1981) and *Code Blue: A Nurse's True Story* (1982), which recount her years in nursing school and her later years as a practicing nurse.

The following essay, adapted from *Code Blue* for *Newsweek* magazine in 1983, focuses on her decision to honor a patient's wishes to be allowed to die.

GUIDING QUESTION
What motivates Huttmann to act as she does?

CRITICAL READING
■ Preview
■ Read
■ Pause
■ Review

(More on p. 28.)

1   "Murderer," a man shouted. "God help patients who get *you* for a nurse."

2   "What gives you the right to play God?" another one asked.

3   It was the *Phil Donahue Show*[1] where the guest is a fatted calf[2] and the audience a two-hundred-strong flock of vultures hungering to pick at the bones. I had told them about Mac, one of my favorite cancer patients. "We resuscitated[3] him fifty-two times in just one month. I refused to resuscitate him again. I simply sat there and held his hand while he died."

1. *Phil Donahue Show* (1970–1996): one of the earliest audience-participation television talk shows   **2. fatted calf:** from the biblical parable of the prodigal son, in which a father kills a specially fed calf to celebrate the return of his son who had left home years earlier   **3. resuscitated:** brought back to life

4   There wasn't time to explain that Mac was a young, witty, macho cop who walked into the hospital with thirty-two pounds of attack equipment, looking as if he could single-handedly protect the whole city, if not the entire state. "Can't get rid of this cough," he said. Otherwise, he felt great.

5   Before the day was over, tests confirmed that he had lung cancer. And before the year was over, I loved him, his wife, Maura, and their three kids as if they were my own. All the nurses loved him. And we all battled his disease for six months without ever giving death a thought. Six months isn't such a long time in the whole scheme of things, but it was long enough to see him lose his youth, his wit, his macho, his hair, his bowel and bladder control, his sense of taste and smell, and his ability to do the slightest thing for himself. It was also long enough to watch Maura's transformation from a young woman into a haggard, beaten old lady.

6   When Mac had wasted away to a sixty-pound skeleton kept alive by liquid food we poured down a tube, IV solutions we dripped into his veins, and oxygen we piped to a mask on his face, he begged us: "Mercy . . . for God's sake, please just let me go."

7   The first time he stopped breathing, the nurse pushed the button that calls a "code blue"[4] throughout the hospital and sends a team rushing to resuscitate the patient. Each time he stopped breathing, sometimes two or three times in one day, the code team came again. The doctors and technicians worked their miracles and walked away. The nurses stayed to wipe the saliva that drooled from his mouth, irrigate the big craters of bedsores that covered his hips, suction the lung fluids that threatened to drown him, clean the feces that burned his skin like lye, pour the liquid food down the tube attached to his stomach, put pillows between his knees to ease the bone-on-bone pain, turn him every hour to keep the bedsores from getting worse, and change his gown and linen every two hours to keep him from being soaked in perspiration.

8   At night I went home and tried to scrub away the smell of decaying flesh that seemed woven into the fabric of my uniform. It was in my hair, the upholstery of my car—there was no washing it away. And every night I prayed that Mac would die, that his agonized eyes would never again plead with me to let him die.

9   Every morning I asked his doctor for a "no-code" order. Without that order, we had to resuscitate every patient who stopped breathing. His doctor was one of several who believe we must extend life as long as we have the means and knowledge to do it. To not do it is to be liable for negligence, at least in the eyes of many people, including some nurses. I thought about what it would be like to stand before a judge, accused of murder, if Mac stopped breathing and I didn't call a code.

4. code blue: a signal that is used in hospitals to announce a patient's life-
threatening emergency (usually cardiac arrest)

10   And after the fifty-second code, when Mac was still lucid enough to beg for death again, and Maura was crumbled in my arms again, and when no amount of pain medication stilled his moaning and agony, I wondered about a spiritual judge. Was all this misery and suffering supposed to be building character or infusing us all with the sense of humility that comes from impotence?

11   Had we, the whole medical community, become so arrogant that we believed in the illusion of salvation through science? Had we become so self-righteous that we thought meddling in God's work was our duty, our moral imperative, and our legal obligation? Did we really believe that we had the right to force "life" on a suffering man who had begged for the right to die?

12   Such questions haunted me more than ever early one morning when Maura went home to change her clothes and I was bathing Mac. He had been still for so long, I thought he at last had the blessed relief of coma. Then he opened his eyes and moaned, "Pain . . . no more . . . Barbara . . . do something . . . God, let me go."

PAUSE: What do you predict that Huttmann will do in the next few paragraphs?

13   The desperation in his eyes and voice riddled me with guilt. "I'll stop," I told him as I injected the pain medication.

14   I sat on the bed and held Mac's hand in mine. He pressed his bony fingers against my hand and muttered, "Thanks." Then there was one soft sigh, and I felt his hands go cold in mine. "Mac?" I whispered, as I waited for his chest to rise and fall again.

DISCUSSION
Ask students whether they believe that what Huttmann describes doing is something they would call *murder*.

15   A clutch of panic banded my chest, drew my finger to the code button, urged me to do something, anything . . . but sit alone with death. I kept one finger on the button, without pressing it, as a waxen pallor slowly transformed his face from person to empty shell. Nothing I've ever done in my forty-seven years has taken so much effort as it took *not* to press that code button.

16   Eventually, when I was as sure as I could be that the code team would fail to bring him back, I entered the legal twilight zone and pushed the button. The team tried. And while they were trying, Maura walked into the room and shrieked, "No . . . don't let them do this to him . . . for God's sake . . . please, no more!"

17   Cradling her in my arms was like cradling myself, Mac, and all those patients and nurses who had been in this place before, who do the best they can in a death-defying society.

18   So a TV audience accused me of murder. Perhaps I am guilty. If a doctor had written a no-code order, which is the only *legal* alternative, would he have felt less guilty? Until there is legislation making it a criminal act to code a patient who has requested the right to die, we will all of us risk the same fate as Mac. For whatever reason, we developed the means to prolong life, and now we are forced to use it. We do not have the right to die.

PAUSE: What are your reactions to Huttmann's story?

· ·

SUMMARIZE AND RESPOND

In your reading journal or elsewhere, summarize the main point of "A Crime of Compassion." Then, go back and check off support for this main idea. Next, write a brief summary (three to five sentences) of the selection. Finally, jot down your initial response to the reading. Do you think that Huttmann's action makes her a "murderer"? Or do you sympathize with her decision? What makes you think as you do?

· ·

CHECK YOUR COMPREHENSION

1. Which of the following would be the best alternative title for this essay?

   a. "A Defense for Murder"

   b. "The Difficult Job of Being a Nurse"

   c. "The Right to Die"

   d. "Prolonging Life: The Responsibility of Medical Professionals"

2. The main idea of this essay is that

   a. the author believes that suffering patients who have no chance of recovery should not be kept alive artificially against their wishes.

   b. the author believes that television talk shows do not provide an adequate forum for discussing complex issues such as the right to die.

   c. the author believes that most readers do not understand all the tasks that are required of a nurse.

   d. the author believes that advances in medical science make it possible to prolong life and that doing so is the responsibility of medical professionals.

3. According to Huttmann, several medical professionals that she worked with when Mac was a patient felt that all patients must be resuscitated because

   a. it was the ethical thing to do.

   b. they had the medical expertise to do so.

   c. most patients wanted to be resuscitated.

   d. not to do so might have led to legal liability for negligence.

4. If you are unfamiliar with the following words, use a dictionary to check their meanings: vultures (para. 3); macho (4); haggard (5); feces (7); negligence (9); lucid, infusing, impotence (10); pallor (15).

READ CRITICALLY

1. Evaluate Huttmann's three opening paragraphs. What do they contribute to her essay? How and why does she refer back to them in her conclusion?

2. How well do you think Huttmann presents her patient Mac and his wife, Maura? How does she attempt to make their situation seem real to the reader?

3. What is the purpose of paragraph 9 in this essay? Why do you think that Huttmann waits until this point in the essay to offer this information?

4. What is the effect of the questions that Huttmann poses in paragraphs 10 and 11? Why do you think she presents these thoughts as questions here?

5. What is your overall evaluation of Huttmann's argument? How effectively do you think she presents her case? How is her argument shaped by her role as a nurse? How do you explain your evaluation?

WRITE AN ESSAY

Write an essay about a belief that you have come to hold through personal experience but that many other people might disagree with or find controversial. Like Huttmann, show readers what happened to make you think as you do, and take a clear stand on the issue.

Marc Siegel
Treating the Pain by Ending a Life

Dr. Marc Siegel, a 1985 graduate of the School of Medicine and Biomedical Sciences at the State University of New York, Buffalo, is an associate professor at the New York University School of Medicine as well as a practicing internist. A prolific writer for general audiences, he writes a regular column, "The Unreal World," for the *Los Angeles Times* in which he explains the facts behind widely held but mistaken beliefs about medicine. His essays have appeared in the *Washington Post*, *USA Today*, and *Slate*, and he is a frequent guest on television news programs and National Public Radio. His books include *False Alarm: The Truth about the Epidemic of Fear* (2005), named one of the top twenty books of the year by *Discover* magazine, and *The Inner Pulse: Unlocking the Secret Code of Sickness and Health* (2011).

"Treating the Pain by Ending a Life" first appeared in the *Boston Globe* in January 2006, shortly after the U.S. Supreme Court upheld an Oregon state law permitting physician-assisted suicide.

CRITICAL READING
■ Preview
■ Read
■ Pause
■ Review

(More on p. 28.)

TEACHING TIP
Have students do some research about the Oregon law. The Oregon Department of Human Services Web site at **oregon.gov/ DHS/** is a good place to start.

DISCUSSION
In paragraph 2, Siegel says that he did not use morphine as a murder weapon. How do students respond to his language here?

GUIDING QUESTION
What does Siegel say are the two primary roles for a physician, and how do these two roles shape his argument?

1   The U.S. Supreme Court ruled this week that doctors in Oregon should not be charged with a crime for overdosing patients in the name of treating pain and hastening death. This decision should be applauded and must not be circumvented[1] by new laws.

2   Ten years ago, I assumed the care of a woman with advanced pancreatic cancer that had spread to her spine. She was a well-known writer, and we quickly became friends. I would travel to her apartment and visit her for hours there, something I'd rarely done before and haven't done since. She had a close group of friends who visited her constantly, and an Irish nursing agency that cared for her impeccably around the clock. At first, her cancer wasn't causing her pain, though it paralyzed her below the waist and bound her to her bed and wheelchair. Still, she enjoyed the visits, mine and everyone else's, until the fateful day when the cancer spread to her bones and began what was clearly an escalating pain. I dialed up the morphine[2] to compensate, until the day came when the amount of morphine necessary clearly hastened her death. I was able to predict roughly the time she would die, and her friends said their goodbyes. I used

1. **circumvented:** bypassed; gotten around   2. **morphine:** a powerful pain-relieving medication

morphine in the name of relieving suffering, not as a murder weapon. No one who knew her seemed upset by the trade-off, a tortured life for a peaceful death, and all thanked me for my care at the end.

3   Morphine and other narcotics suppress breathing and lower blood pressure. It is not unusual for physicians to use these drugs to relieve suffering and thereby accelerate death in terminal cases. What is unusual is for doctors to be prosecuted for overdosing their patients deliberately in the name of this cause. Oregon has been the focus of the Bush administration's attempts to criminalize the activity, but this use of medications to knowingly end a tortured life is not confined to Oregon. It has been part of a physician's end-of-life role for many years, whether it is formalized in the law or not.

4   Any effective physician has two fundamental roles. The first is to prolong life. The second is to ease suffering. In most situations, easing suffering is part of prolonging life, as when we guide a patient through an accident or a surgery and treat pain as part of ensuring survival. Sometimes, though, our two roles collide, and a decision must be made as to which to prioritize.[3] This decision is made, in part, by considering long-term outcome as well as the wishes of the patient. It is never a perfect situation, but we physicians have been making this determination for eons, and we cannot be penalized or prosecuted and still be expected to function.

5   In the Netherlands, active euthanasia[4] is legal, which means that a cancer patient who is still ambulatory and thinking clearly can ask a doctor for a lethal injection. I am not in favor of this policy, not because I believe that a person doesn't have a right to end his or her life when given a terminal diagnosis, but because I question the role of a physician in facilitating[5] this outcome. Such a role should not be assumed, because it is not strictly a part of relieving suffering.

6   But this is not the same thing as the Oregon law, which allows a physician to participate when pain predominates, when the patient is in agony, when reducing morphine cannot bring back quality of life. When the only choice is pain or death, doctors routinely—with their patients' advance approval—help them choose death. The U.S. Supreme Court is wise to acknowledge one of our fundamental roles. We are not "Kevorkian-izing"[6] our doomed patients when we help ease their path from this world.

PAUSE: How do you respond to the "trade-off" of "a tortured life for a peaceful death"?

PAUSE: Summarize the central point of this paragraph.

PAUSE: Under what conditions, according to Siegel, should doctors be allowed to prescribe potentially lethal doses of narcotics to patients?

---

3. prioritize: give greater importance to   **4. active euthanasia:** the assistance in or hastening of death by using drugs or other means. In passive euthanasia, death is a side-effect of the treatment of pain or the withholding of other forms of treatment.   **5. facilitating:** making easier   **6. "Kevorkian-izing":** actively helping people commit suicide. Dr. Jack Kevorkian created several devices that allowed individuals to self-administer lethal dosages of drugs. Kevorkian, a trained physician whose medical license was revoked in 1991, claimed to have participated in the suicide of some 130 people and was convicted of second-degree murder in 1999. He served eight years in prison, and died in 2011 after a brief illness.

SUMMARIZE AND RESPOND

In your reading journal or elsewhere, summarize the main point of "Treating the Pain by Ending a Life." Then, go back and check off support for this main idea. Next, write a brief summary (three to five sentences) of the essay. Finally, jot down your initial response to the reading. How sympathetic are you toward Siegel's beliefs about doctors' "end-of-life role"?

CHECK YOUR COMPREHENSION

1. Which of the following would be the best alternative title for this essay?
   a. "A Doctor's Competing Roles: The Need to Prioritize"
   (b.) "The Right to Relieve a Patient's Suffering"
   c. "The Use of Morphine to Treat Pain"
   d. "Active Euthanasia"

2. The main idea of this essay is that
   (a.) doctors should not be barred from using narcotics to relieve the suffering of patients who are in incurable, unbearable pain—even if the narcotics prove to be lethal.
   b. a doctor's primary roles are to prolong life and to ease suffering.
   c. doctors should do everything in their power to save a patient's life.
   d. the patient's wishes are irrelevant when a doctor decides to administer a potentially lethal dosage of pain medication.

3. Siegel makes the point in the essay that he is opposed to
   a. the use of morphine and other narcotics.
   b. Oregon's law permitting doctors to administer narcotics to hasten a patient's death.
   (c.) active euthanasia.
   d. predicting when a patient will die.

4. If you are unfamiliar with the following words, use a dictionary to check their meanings: impeccably, compensate (para. 2); collide (4); predominates (6).

READ CRITICALLY

1. What is the point of the example that Siegel writes about in paragraph 2? Why do you suppose that he decided to develop it in detail and include it early in the essay?

2. What is the purpose of paragraph 3? Does the information that Siegel offers here surprise you in any way?

3. What distinction does Siegel make between using drugs in potentially lethal doses to relieve pain and practicing active euthanasia, which is legal in the Netherlands? Why do you think that he feels the need to make this distinction?

4. Evaluate Siegel's final paragraph. How effectively do you think he makes his case here?

5. How would you define Siegel's intended audience? How does his perspective as a physician shape his argument?

WRITE AN ESSAY

Write an essay in which you argue your views regarding another controversy in the practice of medicine—for example, the medical use of marijuana, animal testing and experimentation, condom distribution in schools to stem the spread of disease, human cloning, the effectiveness of alternative medical practices, or the mandatory treatment of the dying children of parents whose religion forbids it. You may wish to do some research so that you have a good grasp of differing opinions on the issue.

Jerry Fensterman

I See Why Others Choose to Die

Jerry Fensterman was a devoted father, husband, and golfer, among other things. He graduated from University of California, Santa Cruz, and received a graduate degree from the University of California at Berkeley. His last and perhaps most satisfying job was as director of development at the Fenway Institute. After he was diagnosed with cancer, Fensterman found solace in writing. During his illness, his writing energized him, and he said that if his health improved, he would write seriously about topics that he thought were important. After Fensterman's death in 2007, his wife, Lisa Bevilaqua, sorted through his belongings and discovered journals that began in his years in college and continued beyond graduation. In these journals, Fensterman confronted a range of life issues and worked through problems of all sorts. He also left many letters for family and friends to read after his death. Fensterman discovered himself in the act of writing, and his writings during his terminal illness inspired others.

In the essay that follows, Fensterman offers a unique position on the issue of physician-assisted suicide, showing that complex questions rarely have simple black-and-white, one-size-fits-all answers.

GUIDING QUESTION

What kinds of changes, both physical and psychological, does Fensterman describe undergoing in the years following April 2004?

CRITICAL
READING
■ Preview
■ Read
■ Pause
■ Review

(More on p. 28.)

PAUSE: What do you predict will be Fensterman's position on physician-assisted suicide?

TEACHING TIP
You may want to assign this essay in conjunction with other essays in this chapter, all of which focus on some aspect of assisted suicide.

1   The U.S. Supreme Court's decision to let stand Oregon's law permitting physician-assisted suicide[1] is sure to fuel an ongoing national debate. Issues of life and death are deeply felt and inspire great passions. It would be wonderful, and unusual, if all those joining the fray would do so with the humility and gravity[2] the matter deserves.

2   I am approaching fifty, recently remarried, and the father of a terrific thirteen-year-old young man. By every measure, I enjoy a wonderful life. Or at least I did until April 2004, when I was diagnosed with kidney cancer. Surgery was my only hope to prevent its spread and save my life. The discovery of a new lump in December 2004 after two surgeries signaled that metastasis[3] was under way. My death sentence had been pronounced.

3   Life may be the most intense addiction on earth. From the moment I first heard the words "you have cancer," and again when I was told that it was spreading out of control, I recognized my addiction to life almost at the cellular level. I have tried since then, as I did before, to live life to the fullest. I also committed myself to doing everything within my power to extend my life.

4   Toward that end, I am participating in my third clinical trial in a year. I have gained some small benefit from it. I am, however, one of the first people with my cancer to try this drug. Its median benefit seems to be only on the order of three months. So my expectations are modest. The side effects of these drugs are significant, as are the symptoms of the cancer's gallop through my body. All things considered, I believe I have earned my merit badge for "doing all one can in the face of death to stay alive."

1. Oregon's law permitting physician-assisted suicide: the Death with Dignity Act, the 1997 Oregon law that allowed terminally ill Oregonians to end their lives through the voluntary self-administration of lethal medications expressly prescribed by a physician for that purpose. In 2006, the U.S. Supreme Court struck down the Bush administration's legal challenge to the law.   **2. gravity:** seriousness
3. metastasis: the process by which cancer spreads throughout the body

5   That the experience has changed me is obvious. I have a few scars, have lost 50 pounds, and my hair is thinner. I rely on oxygen nearly all the time, can no longer perform the job I loved, and have difficulty eating. More profoundly, my universe has contracted. Simply leaving home has become an enormous task, and travel is essentially out of the question. I can no longer run, swim, golf, ski, and play with my son. I haven't yet learned how to set goals or make plans for a future that probably consists of weeks or months, not years. I am also nearing a point where I will not be able to take care of my most basic needs.

PAUSE: Underline the changes that Fensterman describes going through.

6   Mine has been a long, difficult, and certain march to death. Thus, I have had ample time to reflect on my life, get my affairs in order, say everything I want to the people I love, and seek rapprochement with friends I have hurt or lost touch with. The bad news is that my pain and suffering have been drawn out, the rewarding aspects of life have inexorably shrunk, and I have watched my condition place an increasingly great physical and emotional burden on the people closest to me. While they have cared for me with great love and selflessness, I cannot abide how my illness has caused them hardship, in some cases dominating their lives and delaying their healing.

PAUSE: Summarize Fensterman's main point in this paragraph.

7   Perhaps the biggest and most profound change I have undergone is that my addiction to life has been "cured." I've kicked the habit! I now know how a feeling, loving, rational person could choose death over life, could choose to relieve his suffering as well as that of his loved ones a few months earlier than would happen naturally. I am not a religious person, but I consider myself and believe I have proved throughout my life to be a deeply moral person. Personally, I would not now choose physician-assisted suicide if it were available. I do not know if I ever would. Yet now, I understand in a manner that I never could have before why an enlightened society should, with thoughtful safeguards, allow the incurably ill to choose a merciful death.

PAUSE: Underline Fensterman's thesis statement.

TEACHING TIP
Students should identify Fensterman's thesis, which he does not state directly until paragraph 7. When does it make sense to introduce the thesis late in an essay?

8   The Supreme Court's ruling will inflame the debate over physician-assisted suicide. Besides adding my voice to this debate, I ask you to carefully search your soul before locking into any position. If you oppose physician-assisted suicide, first try to walk a mile in the shoes of those to whom you would deny this choice. For as surely as I'm now wearing them, they could one day just as easily be on your feet or those of someone you care deeply about.

PAUSE: How do you respond to Fensterman's argument?

SUMMARIZE AND RESPOND

In your reading journal or elsewhere, summarize the main point of "I See Why Others Choose to Die." Then, go back and check off support for this main idea. Next, write a brief summary (three to five sentences) of the essay. Finally, jot down your initial response to the essay. What impression of Fensterman does the essay create for you? How do you react to his basic argument?

· ·

CHECK YOUR COMPREHENSION

1. Which of the following is the best alternative title for this essay?
   a. "Physician-Assisted Suicide: The Perspective of an Incurably Ill Patient"
   b. "Physician-Assisted Suicide: An Issue That Inspires Great Passions"
   c. "Life: The Most Intense Addiction on Earth"
   d. "How Illness Changed My Life"

2. The main idea of this essay is that
   a. the debate over physician-assisted suicide should be approached with great seriousness.
   b. people with incurable illnesses suffer physically, psychologically, and emotionally, but they are also able to escape their addiction to life.
   c. physician-assisted suicide should be legal, and people opposed to the practice should consider the wishes of those suffering incurable illnesses.
   d. the U.S. Supreme Court's ruling in favor of Oregon's law has fueled the debate over the practice.

3. Fensterman implies that some people who oppose physician-assisted suicide are
   a. humble.
   b. acting reasonably.
   c. overly passionate.
   d. no longer addicted to life.

4. If you are unfamiliar with the following words, use a dictionary to check their meanings: median (para. 4); rapprochement, inexorably (6); enlightened (7).

· ·

READ CRITICALLY

1. What do you think of Fensterman's suggestion in paragraph 3 that "[l]ife may be the most intense addiction on earth"? How do you react to the idea that he has "kicked the habit" (para. 7)? How well do you think this language serves his argument?

2. Fensterman waits until late in the essay to state his thesis. Why do you think that he might have chosen to position the thesis as he does? Do you find his choice appropriate given his purpose and audience?

3. In paragraphs 5 and 6, Fensterman describes the changes that suffering from an incurable illness have brought about in his life. What effect do these details have on his overall argument?

4. In paragraph 7, Fensterman writes that he is "not a religious person" but considers himself to be "a deeply moral person." Why do you think he reveals this about himself? How does this information affect your reading of his argument?

5. Evaluate Fensterman's concluding paragraph. Do you think that it will have its intended effect on those who oppose physician-assisted suicide? Why or why not?

WRITE AN ESSAY

Write an essay arguing for or against a controversial legal decision that you feel strongly about or that affects your life directly. Alternatively, you may choose to write about a particular law that you agree or disagree with and about which opinions differ. The issue can be one on the local, state, or federal level, but be sure to define it clearly for your readers. Feel free, as Fensterman does, to base your argument in part on personal experience. Keep in mind that, like Fensterman, you are writing to an audience that doesn't necessarily share your views.

WRITE AN ESSAY IN FAVOR OF LEGALIZED PHYSICIAN-ASSISTED SUICIDE

Read the three essays that support physician-assisted suicide. Each of the authors has a different perspective on the subject. Drawing from at least two of the three essays, write your own argument supporting physician-assisted suicide. You may use your own experiences in your argument as well as outside sources. When you use material from the essays here or from another source, be sure to cite the source. (For information on citing sources, see Chapter 21.)

Your introduction should include a statement of your position on the issue. In the body of your essay, develop reasons for your opinion, using the essays and other sources. In your conclusion, summarize your reasons, and restate your opinion based on the evidence you have presented.

LEGALIZED ASSISTED SUICIDE: OPPOSED

Marilyn Golden

Why Progressives Should Oppose the Legalization of Assisted Suicide

Marilyn Golden has been an advocate for the rights of the disabled since shortly after her graduation from Brandeis University, when she herself acquired a disability. She was closely involved with development of the Americans with Disabilities Act, which Congress passed in 1990. She also served for nine years as director of Access California, a clearinghouse for information on architectural accessibility for people with disabilities, and in 1996 was appointed by President Bill Clinton to the U.S. Architectural and Transportation Barriers and Compliance Board, a position she still holds. On the international front, she has served as codirector of the Disabled International Support Effort. The author of numerous articles and policy papers, Golden is currently a policy analyst with the Disability Rights Education and Defense Fund, the country's foremost advocacy group for disability civil rights, based in Berkeley, California.

The following essay originally appeared in *BeyondChron,* San Francisco's alternative online daily newspaper. In it, Golden takes a stand against the legalization of assisted suicide in California.

CRITICAL
READING
■ Preview
■ Read
■ Pause
■ Review

(More on p. 28.)

GUIDING QUESTION
What kinds of evidence and outside authorities does Golden cite to support her argument?

PAUSE: Do you think that legalizing assisted suicide is supported mostly by liberals?

1   There is a widespread public perception that those opposed to legalization of assisted suicide in California are religious conservatives, and that the logical position for a liberal is in support.

2   But Californians Against Assisted Suicide shows a diversity of political opinion that may be surprising to those who have not looked closely at the issue. In opposition are numerous disability rights organizations generally seen as liberal-leaning: the Southern California Cancer Pain Initiative, a group associated with the American Cancer Society; the American Medical Association and the California Medical Association; and the Coalition of Concerned Medical Professionals, which does anti-poverty work in poor communities. Catholic organizations are in the mix, but no one could consider this a coalition of religious conservatives. They represent many groups coming together across the political spectrum. Why?

Managed Care and Assisted Suicide: A Deadly Mix

3   Perhaps the most significant reason is the deadly mix between assisted suicide and profit-driven managed health care. Again and again, health maintenance organizations (HMOs) and managed care bureaucracies[1] have overruled physicians' treatment decisions, sometimes hastening patients' deaths. The cost of the lethal medication generally used for assisted suicide is about $35 to $50, far cheaper than the cost of treatment for most long-term medical conditions. The incentive to save money by denying treatment already poses a significant danger. This danger would be far greater if assisted suicide were legal.

4   Though the bill would prohibit insurance companies from coercing[2] patients, direct coercion is not necessary. If patients with limited finances are denied other treatment options, they are, in effect, being steered toward assisted death. It is no coincidence that the author of Oregon's assisted suicide law, Barbara Coombs Lee, was an HMO executive when she drafted it.

5   A 1998 study from Georgetown University's Center for Clinical Bioethics underscores the link between profit-driven managed health care and assisted suicide. The research found a strong link between cost-cutting pressure on physicians and their willingness to prescribe lethal drugs to patients, were it legal to do so. The study warns that there must be a "sobering degree of caution in legalizing [assisted suicide] in a medical care environment that is characterized by increasing pressure on physicians to control the cost of care."

Oregon Is a Deeply Flawed Model

6   The California bill is modeled after a nearly identical law that went into effect in Oregon in 1997. Assisted suicide advocates laud Oregon's example. But Oregon shines only if you don't look too closely. Californians concerned with good government have reason to be highly skeptical.

7   Each year, Oregon publishes a statistical report that leaves out more than it states. Several of these reports have included language such as "We cannot determine whether assisted suicide is being practiced outside the framework of the law." (In fact, the statute provides no resources or even authority to detect such violations.) All of the information in the report comes from doctors who prescribed the drugs, not from family members or friends who probably have additional information about the patients. The state doesn't even talk to doctors who refused to assist the very same patients, though these doctors may have viewed the patients as not

1. health maintenance organizations (HMOs) and managed care bureaucracies: group health insurance plans that entitle members to the services of participating physicians, hospitals, and clinics for a flat fee, usually paid monthly. HMOs often are criticized for making treatment decisions based on considerations of profit.
2. coercing: forcing

PAUSE: Underline the two sentences that best express Golden's argument in paragraph 3.

PAUSE: How might Lee's position have influenced her action?

ESL Ask students how their own opinions on assisted suicide are shaped by their culture and religion.

PAUSE: What, according to Golden, is troubling about Oregon's reporting system?

TEACHING TIP Have students identify the political perspective from which Golden builds her argument and the likely political perspective of her audience. How do these perspectives affect the way she argues?

meeting legal requirements. Autopsies are not required, so there's no way to know if the deceased was actually terminally ill, opening the door to another Dr. Kevorkian.[3] The state's research has never reported on several prominent cases inconsistent with the law—these cases came to light only via the media. Last month, an editorial in *The Oregonian* complained that the law's reporting system "seems rigged to avoid finding" the answers.

8   Also disturbing, end-of-life care in Oregon has been touted as improving because of this law, but when the full situation is taken into account, the claim lacks data, or the improvement has been explainable by other factors. For example, assisted-suicide advocates have lauded the increased use of hospice[4] care in Oregon—but hospice referrals increased dramatically across the U.S. during the same period. In July 2004, a study in the *Journal of Palliative Medicine* showed that dying patients in Oregon are nearly twice as likely to experience moderate or severe pain during the last week of life as similar Oregon patients around the time the Oregon law came into effect, suggesting a significant *decline* in care.

PAUSE: Why is Golden critical of the "good faith" standard?

9   Most troubling, the California bill and Oregon's law legalize negligence by means of the "good faith" standard, which says that no practitioners of assisted suicide will be subject to any legal liability if they act in good faith, something nearly impossible to disprove, making all other rules unenforceable. For everything else doctors do, they are liable if they are negligent. But on assisted suicide, even if negligent, health care practitioners cannot be found to be violating the law, as long as they practice in good faith.

10   There are many more reasons progressives[5] should oppose the legalization of assisted suicide. We must focus not on what we hope to have available for ourselves someday but, rather, on the significant dangers of legalizing assisted suicide in this society as it operates today. This column is sure to bring howls from those already ideologically supportive of legalization, but those who want to look deeper, beyond the simplistic mantras of choice and "right to die," are encouraged to read other articles and testimony that can be found in these locations:

DISCUSSION Ask students what they think about the arguments in favor of assisted suicide that Golden mentions in her final paragraph (freedom of "choice" and the "right to die"). To what extent should a terminally ill person in significant pain have the "right to die"?

- a longer article by this author at **http://dredf.org/assisted_suicide/ assistedsuicide.html**

3. Dr. Kevorkian: Dr. Jack Kevorkian, a controversial figure in the debate over physician-assisted suicide. He created several devices that allowed individuals to self-administer lethal dosages of drugs. Kevorkian, a trained physician whose license was revoked in 1991, claimed to have participated in the suicide of some 130 people and was convicted of second-degree murder in 1999. He served eight years in prison, and died in 2011 after a brief illness.   **4. hospice:** a program or facility that provides special care for people who are near the end of life   **5. progressives:** people whose political philosophy leads them to advocate for social justice and the rights of workers and the lower classes

- commentary by Dr. Herbert Hendin, Medical Director of the American Foundation for Suicide Prevention, at **http://www .psychiatrictimes.com/p040201b.html**

- testimony by Dr. Gregg Hamilton, Physicians for Compassionate Care, at **http://www.pccef.org/articles/art32HouseOfLords.htm**

- analysis of the first six years of Oregon's assisted suicide law by the International Task Force on Euthanasia and Assisted Suicide at **http://www.patientsrightscouncil.org/site/oregon**

. . . .

SUMMARIZE AND RESPOND

In your reading journal or elsewhere, summarize the main point of "Why Progressives Should Oppose the Legalization of Assisted Suicide." Then, go back and check off support for this main idea. Next, write a brief summary (three to five sentences) of the selection. Finally, jot down your initial response to the reading. What do you think of the arguments that Golden makes here? Does anything in the essay tempt you to rethink your position on physician-assisted suicide? What might you say to Golden about her stand on this issue?

. . . .

CHECK YOUR COMPREHENSION

1. Which of the following would be the best alternative title for this essay?

   a. "Conservative Opposition to Legalizing Physician-Assisted Suicide"

   b. "Physician-Assisted Suicide and Managed Care"

   c. "The Oregon Model of Physician-Assisted Suicide"

   (d.) "Liberals Should Rethink Their Position on the 'Right to Die'"

2. The main idea of this essay is that

   a. the California Assembly Judiciary Committee has begun conducting hearings on whether the state should legalize physician-assisted suicide.

   (b.) liberals in favor of assisted suicide should rethink their position based on its potential misuse under managed-care programs and problems that arise under governmental oversight.

   c. the Oregon model of physician-assisted suicide is deeply flawed because it does nothing to detect violations, it allows the only information about patients to come from the prescribing doctors, and it protects doctors from charges of negligence by a "good-faith" clause.

   d. although insurers could not force clients to seek assisted suicide, poor patients whose managed-care program denies them other treatment options are being pushed in that direction.

3. Golden makes the point that when physicians are pressured to cut costs,

   a. state governments should step in to make sure that patient treatment does not suffer.

   b. they are more likely to refer their patients to hospices.

   c. their practice may come under scrutiny for medical negligence.

   d. their willingness to participate in assisted suicide increases.

4. If you are unfamiliar with the following words, use a dictionary to check their meanings: coalition (para. 2); bureaucracies (3); skeptical (6); autopsies (7); lauded, palliative (8); negligence (9); ideologically, mantras (10).

. . . .

READ CRITICALLY

1. In paragraph 2, why does Golden list the groups that have come together to oppose an assisted-suicide bill in California? What does this suggest to you about her intended audience?

2. Golden ends her second paragraph with a question. Why? What is the effect of this strategy?

3. In paragraph 4, Golden notes that the author of Oregon's assisted-suicide law is a former HMO executive. Why does she do so? What does this information make you think of the Oregon law? Is this a fair conclusion?

4. Why do you suppose that Golden focuses on the Oregon assisted-suicide law in paragraphs 6–9? How does she expect readers to respond?

5. Golden ends her argument with a list of "other articles and testimony" that oppose assisted suicide. What is her reason for doing so? Do you feel that you should seek out these other sources? Why or why not?

....

WRITE AN ESSAY

Write an essay in which you assume that your audience is made up of readers who share your general political views but disagree with you regarding the specific issue that you are writing about. For example, if your politics are conservative, you still might support amnesty for illegal immigrants, marriage for same-sex partners, or more money for prisoner rehabilitation. Try to convince an audience of conservatives to consider your position even if they don't embrace it. If your politics are liberal, you still might oppose the previously mentioned issues or another issue that liberals tend to support. Try to convince an audience of liberals that your differing views have merit. In either case, try to establish some common ground with your readers.

....

Herbert Hendin

The Case against Physician-Assisted Suicide: For the Right to End-of-Life Care

Born in New York City in 1926, psychiatrist Herbert Hendin received his bachelor's degree from Columbia University and his medical degree from New York University. A clinical professor of psychiatry at New York Medical College in Valhalla, New York, he was also a founding director of the American Foundation for Suicide Prevention in 1987, serving as its first president, its executive director, and its medical director. He founded Suicide Prevention International in 2006. Hendin's research has focused on suicide, post-traumatic stress disorder, substance abuse, and euthanasia, and his books include *Black Suicide* (1967), *Wounds of War: The Psychological Aftermath of Combat in Vietnam* (1984), *Living High: Daily Marijuana Use among Adults* (1987), *Suicide in America* (1996), and *Seduced by Death: Doctors, Patients, and the Dutch Cure* (1997).

In the following essay, originally published in *Psychiatric Times,* Hendin uses his access to studies of physician-assisted suicide in the Netherlands, where it has been practiced in some form since 1984, to make a case against its legalization elsewhere.

CRITICAL READING

■ Preview
■ Read
■ Pause
■ Review

(More on p. 28.)

PAUSE: Summarize the contrast that Hendin establishes in his opening paragraph.

PAUSE: Underline the sentence in this paragraph that best summarizes Hendin's main idea.

PAUSE: Based on this paragraph, what do you predict Hendin will discuss in the paragraphs that follow?

GUIDING QUESTION

Why does Hendin use information obtained from the Netherlands regarding physician-assisted suicide? What does this information contribute to his argument?

1   *Euthanasia* is a word coined from Greek in the seventeenth century to refer to an easy, painless, happy death. In modern times, however, it has come to mean a physician's causing a patient's death by injection of a lethal dose of medication. In physician-assisted suicide, the physician prescribes the lethal dose, knowing the patient intends to end his or her life.

2   Compassion for suffering patients and respect for patient autonomy[1] serve as the basis for the strongest arguments in favor of legalizing physician-assisted suicide. Compassion, however, is no guarantee against doing harm. A physician who does not know how to relieve a patient's suffering may compassionately, but inappropriately, agree to end the patient's life.

3   Patient autonomy is an illusion when physicians are not trained to assess and treat patient suffering. The choice for patients then becomes continued agony or a hastened death. Most physicians do not have such training. We have only recently recognized the need to train general physicians in palliative[2] care, training that teaches them how to relieve the suffering of patients with serious, life-threatening illnesses. Studies show that the less physicians know about palliative care, the more they favor assisted suicide or euthanasia; the more they know, the less they favor it.

4   What happens to autonomy and compassion when assisted suicide and euthanasia are legally practiced? The Netherlands, the only country in which assisted suicide and euthanasia have had legal sanction for two decades, provides the best laboratory to help us evaluate what they mean in actuality. The Dutch experience served as a stimulus for an assisted-suicide law in Oregon—the one U.S. state to sanction it.

5   I was one of a few foreign researchers who had the opportunity to extensively study the situation in the Netherlands, discuss specific cases with leading Dutch practitioners, and interview Dutch government-sponsored euthanasia researchers about their work. We all independently concluded that guidelines established by the Dutch for the practice of assisted suicide and euthanasia were consistently violated and could not be enforced. In the guidelines, a competent patient who has unrelievable suffering makes a voluntary request to a physician. The physician, before going forward, must consult with another physician and must report the case to the authorities.

1. **autonomy:** freedom to act independently and to carry out one's own wishes
2. **palliative:** concerned with easing pain

6   Concern over charges of abuse led the Dutch government to undertake studies of the practice in 1990, 1995, and in 2001 in which physicians' anonymity[3] was protected, and they were given immunity for anything they revealed. Violations of the guidelines then became evident. Half of Dutch doctors feel free to suggest euthanasia to their patients, which compromises the voluntariness of the process. Fifty percent of cases were not reported, which made regulation impossible. The most alarming concern has been the documentation of several thousand cases a year in which patients who have not given their consent have their lives ended by physicians. A quarter of physicians stated that they "terminated the lives of patients without an explicit request" from the patient. Another third of the physicians could conceive of doing so.

7   An illustration of a case presented to me as requiring euthanasia without consent involved a Dutch nun who was dying painfully of cancer. Her physician felt her religion prevented her from agreeing to euthanasia so he felt both justified and compassionate in ending her life without telling her he was doing so. Practicing assisted suicide and euthanasia appears to encourage physicians to think they know best who should live and who should die, an attitude that leads them to make such decisions without consulting patients—a practice that has no legal sanction in the Netherlands or anywhere else.

8   Compassion is not always involved. In one documented case, a patient with disseminated[4] breast cancer who had rejected the possibility of euthanasia had her life ended because, in the physician's words: "It could have taken another week before she died. I just needed this bed."

9   The government-sanctioned studies suggest an erosion of medical standards in the care of terminally ill patients in the Netherlands when 50% of Dutch cases of assisted suicide and euthanasia are not reported, more than 50% of Dutch doctors feel free to suggest euthanasia to their patients, and 25% admit to ending patients' lives without their consent.

10   Euthanasia, intended originally for the exceptional case, became an accepted way of dealing with serious or terminal illness in the Netherlands. In the process, palliative care became one of the casualties, while hospice[5] care has lagged behind that of other countries. In testimony given before the British House of Lords, Zbigniew Zylicz, one of the few palliative care experts in the Netherlands, attributed Dutch deficiencies in palliative care to the easier alternative of euthanasia.

11   The World Health Organization has recommended that governments not consider assisted suicide and euthanasia until they have demonstrated

DISCUSSION In paragraph 7, Hendin writes that practicing assisted suicide "appears to encourage physicians to think they know best who should live and who should die." Have students discuss why physicians have such authority in most circumstances and whether this is a good thing.

PAUSE: How do you respond to the behavior of the physician that Hendin describes in paragraph 7?

PAUSE: Summarize Hendin's point about palliative care in this paragraph.

---

3. anonymity: a state of not being identified by name   **4. disseminated:** spread widely   **5. hospice:** a program or facility that provides special care for people who are near the end of life

the availability and practice of palliative care for their citizens. All states and all countries have a long way to go to achieve this goal.

12   People are only beginning to learn that, with well-trained doctors and nurses and good end-of-life care, it is possible to avoid the pain of the past experiences of many of their loved ones and to achieve a good death. The right to such care is the right that patients should demand and the challenge that every country needs to meet.

PAUSE: What would you say a "good death" (para. 12) means to Hendin?

TEAMWORK In small groups, have students come up with at least five qualities that they associate with a "good death." When individual groups share their lists with the rest of the class, list all of the qualities on the board, and have the class rank them from most to least important.

SUMMARIZE AND RESPOND

In your reading journal or elsewhere, summarize the main point of "The Case against Physician-Assisted Suicide: For the Right to End-of-Life Care." Then, go back and check off support for this main idea. Next, write a brief summary (three to five sentences) of the essay. Finally, jot down your initial response to the selection. Were you surprised by the information given on assisted-suicide practices in the Netherlands? Do you agree with Hendin that these studies make a strong case against legalizing assisted suicide? Why or why not?

CHECK YOUR COMPREHENSION

1. Which of the following would be the best alternative title for this essay?
    a. "Physician-Assisted Suicide: A Lack of Compassion"
    b. "Guidelines to Be Followed in Cases of Physician-Assisted Suicide: An Overview"
    c. "Physician-Assisted Suicide for Exceptional Cases Only"
    (d.) "The Potential for Abuse in Physician-Assisted Suicide and the Need for Greater Palliative Care"

2. The main idea of this essay is that
    a. physician-assisted suicide is acceptable only when a patient's suffering cannot be eased and the patient requests the prescription voluntarily.
    (b.) rather than legalizing assisted suicide, the United States should work toward better end-of-life care for all patients.
    c. most physicians lack compassion for their patients when it comes to assisted suicide.
    d. the Dutch government's concern over potential abuses of that country's assisted-suicide laws led it to commission studies that allowed physicians to respond anonymously and without threat of punishment.

3. The Dutch government studied physician abuse of assisted-suicide laws and did *not* find that

   a. many physicians performed assisted suicide only when they could remain anonymous.

   b. physicians suggested assisted suicide to patients who had not brought the subject up themselves.

   c. a large number of physicians did not report cases of assisted suicide to authorities.

   d. some physicians felt that they could decide when patients should end their lives, whether out of compassion or because it was convenient.

4. If you are unfamiliar with the following words, use a dictionary to check their meanings: sanction (para. 4); immunity (6); erosion (9); casualties, deficiencies (10).

READ CRITICALLY

1. In his opening paragraph, why does Hendin contrast the original definition of *euthanasia* with how the word is currently used? How does this original definition tie into the larger point Hendin is making?

2. What is Hendin's strategy in paragraph 3? Do you find it is effective in terms of his overall argument?

3. How does Hendin establish his authority to make his particular case against physician-assisted suicide? Do you find his authority believable?

4. In paragraph 8, Hendin refers to a case in which a physician performed assisted suicide without a patient's consent and primarily for the doctor's convenience, not to relieve the patient's suffering. Do you find this example sufficient for the point Hendin is trying to make? Why or why not?

5. In his next-to-last paragraph, Hendin summarizes recommendations that were made by the World Health Organization. Why does he do so? Do you think that this passage serves its intended purpose?

· ·

WRITE AN ESSAY

Write an essay that argues for a position on one side of a debatable issue to which you can bring personal expertise and authority. Like Hendin, you should have knowledge of the topic that most of your audience will not have, either because you have learned things through research that others are not familiar with or because you have had life experiences that relatively few other people have shared. In your essay, be sure to establish your authority on the subject.

· ·

WRITE AN ESSAY AGAINST LEGALIZED PHYSICIAN-ASSISTED SUICIDE

Read the essays by Golden and Hendin that argue against legalized physician-assisted suicide. Drawing from both essays, write your own argument against physician-assisted suicide. You may use your own experiences in your argument as well as outside sources. When you use material from the essays here or from another source, be sure to cite the source. (For information on citing sources, see Chapter 21.)

Your introduction should include a statement of your position on the issue. In the body of your essay, develop reasons for your opinion, using the essays and other sources. In your conclusion, summarize your reasons, and restate your opinion based on the evidence you have presented.

· ·

Write an Essay: What Do You Think?

Using material from at least four of the five essays in this chapter, write an essay either for or against legalized physician-assisted suicide.

In your introduction, state your position on the issue. In the body of your essay, acknowledge the opposite side of the issue—either pro (Huttmann, Siegel, and Fensterman) or con (Golden and Hendin). Use the appropriate selections to support your position, along with any relevant experiences you have had and outside sources you use. Cite all sources. (For information on citing sources, see Chapter 21.) In your conclusion, restate your position, review the reasons you have given, and make a last pitch for your side of the argument. As you write your argument, imagine that someone you love will be directly affected by the issue.

Appendix

Problem Solving in Writing

Some writing assignments, both in English and in other subjects, will require you to use problem-solving skills. Such assignments will ask you to read and analyze a problem in order to develop possible solutions, often by synthesizing information from various sources.

Problem-solving skills are necessary not only in college but also—and even more so—in the work world. Often, managers assign a team to work on and pose possible solutions to a problem that the organization faces. Also, problem-solving skills will help you in your everyday life when you run into a situation that you want to change.

Each of the chapters in Part 2 includes problem-based writing assignments ("Writing to Solve a Problem"). These assignments offer you the opportunity to solve real-world problems by working alone or as part of a team. Use the following section to complete those assignments or to address any problem you may face in college, at work, or in your everyday life.

Problem Solving

Problem solving is the process of identifying a problem and figuring out a reasonable solution.

Problems range from minor inconveniences like finding a rip in the last clean shirt you have when you're running late to more serious problems such as being laid off from your job. While such problems disrupt our lives, they also give us opportunities to tackle difficult situations with confidence.

Too often, people are paralyzed by problems because they don't have strategies for attacking them. However, backing away from a problem rarely helps solve it. When you know how to approach a challenging situation, you are better able to take charge of your life.

Problem solving consists of five basic steps, which can be used effectively by both individuals and groups of people.

The Problem-Solving Process

Understand the problem.

You should be able to say or write it in a brief statement or question.

EXAMPLE:

Your ten-year-old car needs a new transmission, which will cost at least $1500. Do you keep the car or buy a new one?

Identify people or information that can help you solve the problem (resources).

EXAMPLES:

- Your mechanic
- Friends who have had similar car problems
- Car advice from print or Web sources

List the possible solutions.

EXAMPLES:

- Pay for the transmission repair.
- Buy a new car.

Evaluate the possible solutions.

1. Identify the steps each solution would require.
2. List possible obstacles for each solution (like money or time constraints).
3. List the advantages and disadvantages of the solutions.

EXAMPLES (considering only advantages and disadvantages):

- Pay for the transmission repair.

ADVANTAGE: This would be cheaper than buying a new car.

DISADVANTAGE: The car may not last much longer, even with the new transmission.

- Buy a new car.

ADVANTAGE: You will have a reliable car.

DISADVANTAGE: This option is much more expensive.

↓

Choose the most reasonable solution.

Choose the solution that is realistic—the simpler the better. Be able to give reasons for your choice.

SOLUTION: Pay for the transmission repair.

REASONS: You do not have money for a new car, and you do not want to assume more debt. Opinions from two mechanics indicate that your car should run for three to five more years with the new transmission. At that point, you will be in a better position to buy a new car.

Acknowledgments

Mary Brave Bird. "The Sweat Bath Ritual." Excerpt from "Cante Isha—The Eye of the Heart" from *Lakota Woman*, copyright © 1990 by Mary Crow Dog and Richard Erdoes. Used by permission of Grove/Atlantic, Inc.

Rui Dai. "A Whiff of Memory." *The Chronicle*, May 20, 2010. Reprinted by permission of *The Chronicle*, independent student daily of *Duke* University in Durham.

Alex Espinoza. Excerpt from *Still Water Saints*, copyright © 2007 by Alex Espinoza. Used by permission of Random House, Inc. "An American in Mexico." From the *New York Times*, February 25, 2007. © 2007 The New York Times. All rights reserved. Used by permission and protected by the Copyright Laws of the United States. The printing, copying, redistribution, or retransmission of this Content without express written permission is prohibited. http://www.nytimes.com

Jerry Fensterman. "I See Why Others Choose to Die." First published in the *Boston Globe*, January 31, 2006. Copyright © 2006 Jerry Fensterman. Used by permission of Lisa Bevilaqua.

Daniel Flanagan. "The Choice to Do It Over Again." Copyright © 2008 by Daniel Flanagan. From the book *This I Believe: On Fatherhood*, edited by Dan Gediman. Copyright ©2011 by This I Believe, Inc. Reprinted with permission of John Wiley & Sons, Inc.

Michael Gates Gill. "How I Learned to Be a Barista." Originally titled "On the Front Lines—Ready or Not." From *How Starbucks Saved My Life* by Michael Gates Gill, copyright © 2007 by Michael Gates Gill. Used by permission of Gotham Books, an imprint of Penguin Group (USA) Inc.

Marilyn Golden. "Why Progressives Should Oppose the Legalization of Assisted Suicide." Originally published at *BeyondChron: San Francisco's Alternative Online Daily News*, April 12, 2005. www.beyondchron.org. Copyright © 2005. Reprinted with permission.

Herbert Hendin. "The Case against Physician-Assisted Suicide: For the Right to End-of-Life Care." Originally published in *Psychiatric Times*, titled, "Commentary: Assisted Suicide and Euthanasia: Oregon Tries the Dutch Way," by Herbert Hendin, MD, April 1995, Vol. XII, Issue 4. Reprinted with permission from Hendin, H. Copyright 1995. *Psychiatric Times*. UBM Medica. All rights reserved.

Don H. and Sandra E. Hockenbury. "When the Regulation of Eating Behavior Fails: Anorexia and Bulimia," an excerpt from *Discovering Psychology*, Fifth Edition, by Don H. Hockenbury and Sandra Hockenbury. Copyright © 2010. Reprinted by permission of Worth Publishers.

Baxter Holmes. "My Date with Fifteen Women," as appeared in *The Boston Globe*, Jan. 11, 2009. Reprinted by permission of the author.

Barbara Huttmann. "A Crime of Compassion." Adapted from "Code Blue" for *Newsweek* magazine. Reprinted by permission of the author.

Langston Hughes. "Salvation." From *The Big Sea* by Langston Hughes. Copyright © 1940 by Langston Hughes. Copyright renewed 1968 by Arna Bontemps and George Houston Bass. Reprinted by permission of Hill and Wang, a division of Farrar, Straus and Giroux, LLC and by permission of Harold Ober Associates Incorporated.

Michael Jernigan. "Living the Dream." From *The New York Times*, October 11, 2009. © 2009 The New York Times. All rights reserved. Used by permission and protected by the Copyright Laws of the United States. The printing, copying, redistribution, or retransmission of this Content without express written permission is prohibited. http://www.nytimes.com

Martin Luther King Jr. "The Ways of Meeting Oppression." From *Stride toward Freedom: The Montgomery Story*. Reprinted by arrangement with the Heirs to the Estate of Martin Luther King Jr., c/o Writer's House as agent for the proprietor, New York, NY. Copyright © 1958 by Dr. Martin Luther King Jr. Copyright renewed © 1987 by Coretta Scott King.

Nicholas D. Kristof. "Two Men and Two Paths." From the *New York Times*, June 13, 2010. Copyright © 2010 The New York Times. All rights reserved. Used by permission and protected by the Copyright Laws of the United States. The printing, copying, redistribution, or retransmission of this Content without express written permission is prohibited. http://www.nytimes.com

Stephanie Lindsley. "Autism and Education: Who Should We Focus on—My Disabled Son or My Gifted Girl?" From *Newsweek*, February 28, 2009. Copyright © 2009 Harman Newsweek LLC, Inc. All rights reserved. Used by permission and protected by the Copyright Laws of the United States. The printing, copying, or retransmission of this Content without express written permission is prohibited. http://www.newsweek.com

Farhad Manjoo. "Fix Your Terrible, Insecure Passwords in Five Minutes." From *Slate*. Copyright © July 24, 2009 The Slate Group. All rights reserved. Used by permission and protected by the Copyright Laws of the United States. The printing, copying, redistribution, or retransmission of the Material without express written permission is prohibited. http://www.slate.com

M. Catherine Maternowska. "Truck Stop Girls." From *The New York Times*, August 23, 2009. © 2009 The New York Times. All rights reserved. Used by permission and protected by the Copyright Laws of the United States. The printing, copying, redistribution, or retransmission of this Content without express written permission is prohibited. http://www.nytimes.com

Nancy Mairs. "On Being a Cripple." From *Plaintext* by Nancy Mairs. © 1986 by The Arizona Board of Regents. Reprinted by permission of the University of Arizona Press.

Deborah Rhode. "Why Looks Are the Last Bastion of Discrimination," as appeared in *The Washington Post*, May 23, 2010. Reprinted by permission of Deborah Rhode.

Monique Rizer. "When Students Are Parents" as appeared in *The Chronicle of Higher Education*, December 16, 2005. Reprinted by permission of the author.

Juliet B. Schor. "Age Compression." Reprinted with permission of Scribner, an imprint of Simon & Schuster, Inc., from *Born to Buy* by Juliet Schor. Copyright © 2004 by Juliet B. Schor. All rights reserved.

Christopher Shea. "In Praise of Peer Pressure." Originally published in the *Boston Globe*, April 29, 2007. Copyright © 2007 by Christopher Shea. Reprinted by permission of Christopher Shea.

Marc Siegel. "Treating the Pain by Ending a Life." First published in *The Boston Globe*, January 19, 2006. Copyright © 2006 by Marc Siegel. Used by permission of the author.

Brent Staples. "Just Walk on By: Black Men and Public Space." Originally published in *Ms.* Magazine. Used by permission of the author.

Amy Tan. "Mother Tongue." Copyright © 1989 by Amy Tan. First appeared in *The Threepenny Review*. Reprinted by permission of the author and the Sandra Dijkstra Literary Agency.

Deborah Tannen. *You Just Don't Understand.* Excerpt from pages 43–44 ("It Begins at the Beginning") from *You Just Don't Understand* by Deborah Tannen. Copyright © 1990 by Deborah Tannen. Reprinted with permission of HarperCollins Publishers and International Creative Management, Inc.

Kathleen Vail. "Words That Wound." Originally published in *American School Board Journal*, September 1999. Copyright © 1999 National School Boards Association. Reprinted by permission of the American School Board Journal. All rights reserved.

Malcolm X. "My First Conk." Originally titled "Hair" from *The Autobiography of Malcolm X* by Malcolm X and Alex Haley. Copyright © 1964 by Alex Haley and Malcolm X. Copyright © 1965 by Alex Haley and Betty Shabazz. Used by permission of Random House, Inc.

Rob Walker. "Stuck on You." From *The New York Times*, June 6, 2010. © 2010 The New York Times. All rights reserved. Used by permission and protected by the Copyright Laws of the United States. The printing, copying, redistribution, or retransmission of this Content without express written permission is prohibited. http://www.nytimes.com

Howard White. "The Power of Hello," Copyright ©2008 by Howard White. From the book *This I Believe: Life Lessons*, edited by Dan Gediman. Copyright © 2011 by This I Believe, Inc. Reprinted with permission of John Wiley & Sons, Inc.

Photo Credits

Pages 1, 143, 381, 493, 601, 623, and 685: Patricia Lee
Page 14: Bergen Community College Office of Public Relations
Page 38: America Corporation
Page 46: Romain Laurent/Bransch New York
Page 62: Markku Lahdesmaki
Page 85: Both photos © Andrew Dillon Bustin
Page 86: Universal/The Kobal Collection
Page 87: Reinhard Hunger/Bransch New York
Pages 101–02: © Jason Baker
Page 117: © Andrew Dillon Bustin
Page 120: © Andy Goldsworthy. Courtesy Galerie Lelong, New York.
Page 129: Cultura Creative/Alamy
Page 133: AP Photo/Bebeto Matthews
Page 139: Cory Petty
Page 146: Ibrahim Siddo: Photo by Jacob Rosenzweig. Used with permission. / Tea kettle © Andrew Dillon Bustin
Page 147: Alex Wong/Getty Images
Page 160: © Scott Roper
Page 161: Matthew Porter/CXA Inc.
Page 162: Eric Eggly/Point Seven Studios
Page 166: © Susan A. Barnett
Page 179: Justin Sullivan/Getty Images
Page 184: REUTERS/Mihal Barbu/Landov
Pages 185, 190: Courtesy Alex Espinoza
Page 196: Amy Eckert
Page 198: Flyer Courtesy of Western Nevada College
Page 202: Robin Beck/Getty Images
Page 215: REUTERS/Carlos Barria/Landov
Page 222: Brooks Jensen/LensWork Publishing
Page 234–36: © Diane Meyer
Page 241: Cheryl K. Kretzler
Page 253: Andrew J. Scott

Page 260: Tom Hussey

Page 275: MATTEL, BARBIE and associated trademarks and trade dress are owned by, and used under permission from, Mattel, Inc. ©2011 Mattel, Inc. All Rights Reserved.

Page 281: Left: ©Kate & Camilla/Corbis / Right: Lauri Rotko/Getty Images

Page 294: © Erin Hanson

Page 301: REUTERS/China Photo/Landov

Page 323: © Andrew Dillon Bustin

Page 341: Santa Monica College Library

Page 350: U.S. Environmental Protection Agency

Page 351: Courtesy of http://www.thegoodhuman.com

Page 691: Library of Congress

Page 711: Photographer: David Weintraub

Page 723: Courtesy of Alex Espinoza

Page 727: Ulf Andersen/Getty Images

Page 736: Courtesy of Farhad Manjoo

Page 741: Library of Congress

Page 751: Alberto E. Rodriguez/Getty Images

Page 758: Reg Lancaster/Getty Images

Page 769: fotosmith

Page 775: Courtesy of Juliet Schor

Page 787: Paul Rubiera/Miami Herald staff

Page 791: © James Leynse/Corbis

Page 798: s70/ZUMA Press/Newscom

Page 802: Fred Conrad/The New York Times/Redux

Page 820: Courtesy of Marc Siegel

Page 828: Courtesy of Marilyn Golden

Page 833: Courtesy of Herbert Hendin

Index

Useful Editing and Proofreading Marks

The marks and abbreviations below are those typically used by instructors when marking papers (add any alternate marks used by your instructor in the left-hand column), but you can also mark your own work or that of your peers with these helpful symbols.

ALTERNATE SYMBOL	STANDARD SYMBOL	HOW TO REVISE OR EDIT (numbers in boldface are chapters where you can find help)
	adj	Use correct adjective form **Ch. 28**
	adv	Use correct adverb form **Ch. 28**
	agr	Correct subject-verb agreement or pronoun agreement **Chs. 25 and 27**
	awk	Awkward expression: edit for clarity **Ch. 9**
	cap or triple underline [example]	Use capital letter correctly **Ch. 40**
	case	Use correct pronoun case **Ch. 27**
	cliché	Replace overused phrase with fresh words **Ch. 34**
	coh	Revise paragraph or essay for coherence **Ch. 9**
	coord	Use coordination correctly **Ch. 30**
	cs	Comma splice: join the sentences correctly **Ch. 24**
	dev	Develop your paragraph or essay more completely **Chs. 4 and 6**
	dm	Revise to avoid a dangling modifier **Ch. 29**
	frag	Attach the fragment to a sentence or make it a sentence **Ch. 23**
	fs	Fused sentence: join the two sentences correctly **Ch. 24**
	ital	Use italics **Ch. 38**
	lc or diagonal slash [Éxample]	Use lowercase **Ch. 40**
	mm	Revise to avoid a misplaced modifier **Ch. 29**
	pl	Use the correct plural form of the verb **Ch. 26**
	ref	Make pronoun reference clear **Ch. 27**
	ro	Run-on sentence; join the two sentences correctly **Ch. 24**
	sp	Correct the spelling error **Ch. 35**
	sub	Use subordination correctly **Ch. 30**
	sup	Support your point with details, examples, or facts **Ch. 6**
	tense	Correct the problem with verb tense **Ch. 26**
	trans	Add a transition **Ch. 9**
	w	Delete unnecessary words **Ch. 34**
	wc	Reconsider your word choice **Chs. 34 and 35**
	?	Make your meaning clearer **Ch. 9**
	⌄ ,	Use comma correctly **Ch. 36**
	; : ( ) - —	Use semicolon/colon/parentheses/hyphen/dash correctly **Ch. 39**
	" " ⌄ ⌄	Use quotation marks correctly **Ch. 38**
	∧	Insert something
	⟋ [exaⱥmple]	Delete something
	∪ [words example]	Change the order of letters or words
	¶	Start a new paragraph
	# [example#words]	Add a space
	⌢ [ex⌢ample]	Close up a space

Real Take-Away Points

Four Basics of Good Writing

1 It considers what the audience knows and needs.

2 It fulfills the writer's purpose.

3 It includes a clear, definite point.

4 It provides support that explains or proves the main point.

2PR   The Critical Reading Process

Preview the reading. Establish a guiding question.

Read the piece, locating the thesis, support, and transitions, and considering the quality of the support.

Pause to think during reading. Take notes and ask questions about what you are reading: Talk to the author.

Review the reading, your guiding question, and your marginal notes and questions.

Critical Thinking

Summarize   When you are reading, consider the author's purpose, main point, and the evidence given in support of the main point.

Analyze   Consider whether the support is logical or if it leaves you with questions; what assumptions the author might be making about the subject or reader; and what assumptions you as the reader may be making.

Synthesize   Consider how the reading relates and connects to your own experience and knowledge, and what new ideas it has given you.

Evaluate   Consider whether the author seems biased, whether you are reading with a biased point of view, and whether or not the piece achieves the author's intended purpose.